THE NEW CATERING REPERTOIRE

Volume I   Aide-Mémoire du Chef

The New Catering Repertoire

Volume I
Aide-Mémoire du Chef

H. L. CRACKNELL, FHCIMA, ACF
and
G. NOBIS, BA (Hons), MSc., MHCIMA

 VAN NOSTRAND REINHOLD
New York

Library of Congress Catalog Card Number 89–009203
ISBN 0–442–23962–9

Published in the United States of America by
Van Nostrand Reinhold
115 Fifth Avenue
New York, New York 10003

Distributed in Canada by
Nelson Canada
1120 Birchmount Road
Scarborough, Ontario, M1K 5G4, Canada

Printed in Hong Kong

16 15 14 13 12 11 10 9 8 7 6 5 4 3 2 1

Library of Congress Cataloging-in-Publication Data
Cracknell, H. L. (Harry Louis). 1916–
The new catering repertoire / H. L. Cracknell, G. Nobis.
p. cm.
"Published by Macmillan Education Ltd., Houndmills, Basingstoke.
Hampshire"—T.p. verso.
Contents: v. 1. Aide-Memoire du chef.
ISBN 0–442–23962–9
1. Caterers and catering. 2. Quantity cookery. I. Nobis. G.
II. Title.
TX911.2.C72   1989
642'.4–dc20
                                                    89–9203
                                                       CIP

CONTENTS

ix

FOREWORD

While one can have a great deal of fun writing a cookery book and receive a lot of publicity from marketing and selling it, to write a manual of practice for educational purposes is not always so glamorous. Nevertheless, it is a very necessary tool, not only for young people who will enter the profession, but also for established chefs. To produce a manual like the *New Catering Repertoire* demands a certain quality which is very rarely found in our profession.

The thorough checking of all recipes and terminologies requires experience, broad knowledge and a lot of hard work from the authors. I have known Harry Cracknell and Gianfranco Nobis for several years and I am proud to have been associated with them in a small way through the Dorset Institute of Higher Education. I am sure that this splendid work will be referred to by those who love cookery and it will be regarded as a masterpiece in the field of education.

ALBERT H. ROUX
Chevalier du Mèrite Agricole
Meilleur Ouvrier de France
DSc (Honoris Causa)

INTRODUCTION

This book is the source of the body of present-day culinary knowledge and has been compiled with the aim of assisting all who are engaged on the food production side of the hotel and catering industry.

By listing and outlining the contents of the composition of all the major classic dishes and by cataloguing the details of daily kitchen operation it is hoped this book will be of great value to all chefs, chefs de partie, commises and commis in carrying out their daily duties in an efficient manner. The book should also be of value to head chefs and catering managers charged with the production of meals, to make every dish a masterpiece. It will be an *aide-mémoire* in the compilation of menus. The directory of dishes embraces every course of the menu and has been compiled with a view of codifying the extensive inventory of dishes, so as to make it acceptable to all chefs. The authors hope this will help to achieve uniformity of dish composition and description. The pleasant practice of giving names to dishes has been carried on for more than 200 years and many great chefs of the past were inspired to create new presentations in honour of a person or an occasion, or to introduce new ideas of food combinations. In effect, a dictionary of culinary titles acts as a link in the chain of human history by recording personalities and events of the past, thus keeping them alive in the minds of those who consume these delectable dishes. In many cases the dish is more famous than the person or event it was dedicated to.

Various aspects of kitchen operation are included, purchasing, equipment, hygiene and nutrition, all given in concise form for ease of assimilation. This book is written for the professional chef which means that recognised culinary terms are used wherever necessary to contain the thousands of formulas within the shortest possible descriptions. The user of this book will not expect to be given precise weights and measures in all cases, neither will he be in need of information on portion yield or cooking times and temperatures. No indication is given of how and when to season with salt and pepper. Accompaniments to dishes as against actual garnishes will be found in Volume II.

In his introduction to the first edition of the *Guide Culinaire*, Escoffier wrote that 'the more one learns the more one sees the need to learn more and that study, as well as broadening the mind of the craftsman, provides an easy way of perfecting himself in the practice of our art'. The present authors cannot do more than echo his sentiments in the sincere hope that this book will be of much benefit to their fellow craftsmen and craftswomen.

H. L. CRACKNELL
G. NOBIS

1   HORS-D'ŒUVRE

Hors-d'œuvre Variés

These are items that form the selection for a trolley of mixed hors-d'œuvre.

Artichokes, globe

à la Crecque Cook small ones in water, lemon juice and oil with fennel, bayleaf, thyme and coriander; serve with some of the cooking liquid.

Lyonnaise Cook in thin espagnole sauce with chopped onion and wine.

Portugaise Blanch, cut up then cook in a sauce made with chopped onion and garlic, diced tomato, white wine and herbs.

Avocados

Antillaise Garnish with dressed crab and segments of grapefruit and orange.

Soubrette Fill with chopped pimento and walnuts and garnish with hard boiled egg and shrimps.

Other suitable garnishes include caviar, lobster, prawns, anchovy fillet or essence, flaked cooked fish, mussels, apple, olives, salami, ham, tomato, etc.

(When expensive, avocados are served only as a single hors-d'œuvre.)

Beetroot

Creamed	Cut into bâtons and mix with cream containing made English mustard and lemon juice.
Normande	Cut into bâtons, mix with French dressing and garnish with bâtons of apple.
Réforme	Cut into bâtons, add bâtons of gherkin, ham and hard boiled egg white and mix with French dressing.
Suzanne	Cut into bâtons, add gherkins and chopped onion and dress with vinaigrette.
Yvette	Add bâtons of hard boiled egg white and tomato and mix with French dressing.

Cabbage, green

Paupiette	Wrap blanched outer leaves around the chopped cooked centre mixed with chopped ham and gherkin.
Stuffed	Wrap sausage meat in blanched cabbage leaves and braise; serve cold with the cooking liquid flavoured with tomato ketchup.
Cabbage, red Pickled	Blanch finely shredded cabbage, cover with spiced cold vinegar and use as required.

Cabbage, white

Coleslaw	This is finely shredded white cabbage and carrot mixed with mayonnaise. Optional additions include gherkin, nuts, onion, pimento, sultanas, etc.

Carrots

Creamed	Mix cooked bâtons of carrot with double cream flavoured with lemon juice and English mustard.
à l'Indienne	Mix cooked bâtons in a thin curry sauce, finished with cream.
Jardinière	Marinate cooked bâtons in French dressing.
à la Russe	Mix with mayonnaise and grated horseradish.

Cauliflower

Andalouse Coat cooked florets with cream flavoured with English mustard and tomato puree.

à la Grecque Cook in water, oil, lemon juice, coriander and thyme.

Mayonnaise Coat cooked florets with mayonnaise and sprinkle with paprika.

Portugaise Cook in a mixture of chopped onion and diced tomato in oil with thyme and bayleaf.

Celeriac

Cut into fine julienne and mix with mayonnaise.

Celery

Bonne Femme Mix bâtons of apple and celery with mustard-flavoured acidulated cream.

Espagnole Mix julienne of celery, tomato, green pimento and cooked potato with French dressing.

à la Grecque Cook in water, lemon juice and oil with cor-ianders and peppercorns and serve in some of the cooking liquid.

Portugaise Cook with oil, onion, diced tomato, garlic, herbs and water.

Provençale Cook in oil with chopped shallot, garlic and tomato, and white wine.

à la Russe Mix bâtons of celery with grated horseradish, cream and mustard.

Yolande Mix bâtons of celery, carrot, apple and beetroot with thin mayonnaise.

Chicory (Belgian endive)

Archiduc Cut bâtons of chicory, apple and beetroot and mix with French dressing.

Aurelius Cut julienne of chicory, celery, apple and green pimento and mix with dressing.

Aurore	Chop the chicory and mix with cream flavoured with sieved tomato pulp and lemon juice.
Turquoise	Mix julienne of chicory, apple and green pimento with dressing and serve surrounded with small half slices of beetroot.

Cucumber

Américaine	Arrange alternate slices of tomato and peeled cucumber in a ravier; coat with dressing.
Danoise	Blanch barquettes of cucumber and fill with puree of smoked salmon and herring; garnish with hard boiled egg cut into quarters.
Norvégienne	Fill blanched cases with puree of salmon by means of a piping bag and star tube.
Suédoise	Mix diced apple, potato and smoked herring with cucumber and mayonnaise and fill into 3 cm. blanched cases of cucumber.

Fennel

May be prepared as for Celery.

Leeks

May be prepared as for Celery.

Mushrooms

Marinated	Cook in a mixture of vinegar, oil, garlic, thyme, bayleaf, fennel and coriander and serve with some of the liquid.

(Mushrooms may also be used sliced raw in many hors-dœuvre salads.)

Onions

Curried	Cook in thin curry sauce and finish with cream.
aux Tomate	Cook button onions in thin tomato sauce.

Soused Cook as for à la Grecque with the addition of some tomato ketchup.

Pimentos

Espagnole Cut into julienne and mix with dressing; garnish with onion rings on top.

Farcis Braise pimentos stuffed with sausage meat or rice pilaff; cut into rounds and sprinkle with dressing.

Salad Finely shred green, yellow and white pimentos and mixed with bâtons of tomato flesh and vinaigrette dressing.

Potatoes

Lorraine Mix diced potato, anchovy, lobster and ham and bind with mayonnaise.

Deux Pommes Mix with diced apple and bind with vinaigrette or mayonnaise.

au Lard Mix crisply fried lardons of streaky bacon with diced potato and a little lemon juice.

Berrichonne Add diced ham, chopped onion and tomato ketchup-flavoured dressing to ordinary potato salad.

Forestière Mix sliced potato with sliced raw mushroom, chopped shallot, oil and lemon juice.

Ordinary Cut hot potatoes into dice, season with a little vinaigrette then bind loosely with mayonnaise; serve sprinkled with parsley or paprika.

Radishes

Creamed Peel, slice and mix with cream flavoured with English mustard and lemon juice.

Nature Remove the roots and leaves and place into ice water to get crisp; serve with butter curls.

Salad Slice the radishes and mix with sliced cucumber; dress with vinaigrette.

5

Sweetcorn

Creamed	Mix cooked grains of corn with cream.
Curried	Mix cooked grains of corn with cream flavoured with curry paste.
Paprika	Mix cooked grains of corn with cream flavoured with paprika.

Tomatoes

Antiboise	Fill small or half tomatoes with flaked fish and diced pimento and dress with vinaigrette.
Genoise	Arrange slices of tomato and yellow pimento overlapping; coat with anchovy-flavoured dressing.
Hongroise	Fill small tomatoes with paprika-flavoured chicken mousse containing chopped pimento.
Mexicaine	Mix diced chicken, cucumber and tomato flesh with chutney sauce.
Madras	Fill small tomatoes with curry-flavoured chicken mousse containing chopped chutney.
Monégasque	Fill half tomatoes with puree of tunny fish.
Moscovite	Fill small emptied tomatoes with Russian salad containing a little chopped fennel.
Paris-Plage	Fill half tomatoes with Russian salad mixed with diced truffle.
Salad	Peel and cut into slices, keeping them in shape; dress with vinaigrette and small rings of onion.

Turnips

May be prepared as for carrots.

MIXED VEGETABLE SALADS
— SERVED AS HORS-D'ŒUVRE —

Vegetables only

Jardinière   Mix equal quantities of bâtons of carrot and turnip, peas and diamonds of French beans and flavour with vinaigrette.

Macédoine   Mix equal quantities of 0.75 cm dice of carrot and turnip, peas and diced French beans and dress with mayonnaise.

Russian   Take equal quantities of 8 mm dice of carrot and turnip, peas and diced French beans and mix with mayonnaise.

Coleslaw   Mix a fine julienne of white cabbage and grated carrot with mayonnaise.

Mixtures including vegetables

Fécampoise   Mix diced potato, apple, red pimento, hard boiled egg and shrimps with mayonnaise.

Italienne   This is Russian salad with the addition of diced salami and anchovy.

Niçoise   Mix sliced French beans, diced tomato and stoned black olives with chopped onion and dressing.

Parisienne   This is Russian salad with the addition of diced lobster.

Espagnole   Mix diced chicken, pimento, tomato and onion with chopped garlic and vinaigrette.

Westminster   Mix bâtons of cooked potato, raw cucumber and tomato flesh with French dressing.

Rice

These hors-dœuvre may be made with plain boiled or pilaff rice, preferably using it as soon as it is cooked.

Bergerette   Mix the rice with chopped hard boiled egg and

7

	chives and dress with cream and mustard or horseradish.
Brésilienne	Mix the rice with diced pineapple and acidulated cream.
Carmen	Add diced chicken, red pimento and peas to the rice and vinaigrette dressing.
Castelnau	Add diced crayfish, red pimento and truffle to the rice and mix with mayonnaise flavoured with marjoram.
Créole	Add diced tomato and cooked mushrooms to the rice and bind with French dressing.
Dorzia	Add diced chicken and cucumber to the rice and mix with vinaigrette made with mustard.
Hollandaise	Add diced apple and smoked herring fillet to the rice and mix with vinaigrette made with mustard.
Midinette	Mix the rice with peas and dress with vinaigrette containing chopped tarragon and chervil.
Monte Carlo	Add diced prawns, celery and truffle to the rice and mix with mayonnaise seasoned with paprika.
Nantaise	Mix the rice with flaked tunny fish and diced tomato and flavour with fines herbes vinaigrette dressing.
Normande	Mix with apple and acidulated cream dressing.
Orientale	Mix with diced tomato, green and red pimento, French beans and anchovy; season with vinaigrette salad dressing.
Pêcheurs	Mix with chopped baked Spanish onion and anchovy, and season with mustard vinaigrette.
Spanish	Add chopped onion, diced red pimento and peas to the rice and mix with vinaigrette dressing.
Valencienne	Add diced ham and tomatoes and peas; to the rice and dress with French dressing.

FISH

Many of these items may be served as they come from the tin, with little or no embellishment.

Anchovies

Moderne	Arrange trellis fashion with a border of sieved yolk and white of egg and chopped parsley.
Niçoise	Arrange trellis fashion and coat with essence of tomato flavoured with tarragon.
Paupiettes	Flatten the fillets, spread with butter and roll up, or place a stuffed olive with a slice of cucumber at one end and roll up; moisten with a little of the oil.
Provençale	Arrange trellis fashion and cover with tomato essence cooked with onion and garlic.
des Tamarins	Place an anchovy paupiette with a black olive in the centre, on a layer of grated cooked warm potato.

Brisling and Sild

These small fish can be served in any of the ways as for tinned sardines.

Cooked Fish

Place any kind of flaked fish on shredded lettuce, coat with mayonnaise and place a trellis work of anchovy fillets on top; finish with capers, quarters of tomatoes, fans of gherkin and stuffed olives.

Goujons en Cascamêche

Deep fry goujons of fish, or gudgeons and place to pickle for 3 days in wine vinegar with onion, garlic, thyme and bayleaf.

Herrings

Bismarck	These are soused boned herrings usually purchased ready for use.
Dieppoise	Cook the pieces of fish in white wine and vinegar with sliced carrot and onion, shallot, bayleaf and thyme; serve with slices of lemon.

Hors-d'œuvre

Livonienne	Mix diced smoked fillet of herring, potato and apple with oil and vinegar and reshape in the form of the fish.
Lucas	Soak smoked herring fillets, cut into strips and cover with mayonnaise made with hard boiled yolks and flavoured with chopped shallot, tarragon and gherkin.
Roll Mops	Roll fillets into paupiettes, pack in jars, cover with vinegar and white wine, flavour with onion rings, bayleaf and keep refrigerated for 3 to 4 days before serving.
à la Russe	Cut smoked fillets of herring into thin slices, arranged on sliced cooked potato and sprinkle with chopped chervil, shallot, fennel, oil and vinegar.

Kilkis

These are Norwegian anchovies that are served as purchased, in some of the brine.

Kippers

Cook kipper fillets in water, cut into small sections, and serve cold as for Sardines.

Mussels

Plain	Mix small cooked mussels with chopped onion and parsley and flavour with salad dressing or mayonnaise.
à la Crème	Cook in white wine, remove the beard and serve cold in a creamy sauce made from the cooking liquid and velouté.

Sardines

à la Crème	Coat with mustard-flavoured acidulated cream.
au Currie	Coat with thin mayonnaise flavoured with curry paste.
à l'Oeuf	Cover with sieved hard boiled egg mixed with chopped parsley.
au Paprika	Coat with thin paprika sauce.

Remoulade   Coat with remoulade sauce.

Soft Roes

Cook in court-bouillon and serve coated with any compatible cold sauce; or dip in flour, shallow fry and serve with a suitable cold sauce.

Smoked Cod Roe

Taramasalata   Mash smoked cod roe with cream, bread-crumbs, onion and lemon juice and add oil as for mayonnaise; serve garnished with black olives.

Salmon roe and the roe of the lumpfish may be served as part of an hors-d'œuvre selection either on its own or as a filling for shaped cucumber pieces, in hard-boiled eggs or in tartlet and barquette cases.

Smoked Sprats

Remove the head and skin and marinate with chopped onion, parsley, oil and vinegar, or serve plainly as purchased.

Tunny Fish

Salade   Flake the fish, arrange in a ravier on shredded lettuce and sprinkle with oil.

Marinette   Arrange alternate slices of tunny fish, tomato and onion within a border of sliced potato and sprinkle with French dressing.

EGGS

Aurore   Fill halves of hard-boiled eggs with the yolks made into a puree with béchamel; coat with cocktail sauce.

Mayonnaise   Arrange sliced, halved or quartered eggs on shredded lettuce and mask with mayonnaise; garnish to choice.

Stuffed   Fill halves with a suitable stuffing such as anchovy, cooked fish, tunny fish puree, the yolk creamed with butter, salmon paste etc, piped back in the whites.

Sliced   Mask with mayonnaise, tartare, remoulade or other cold sauce.

———— PASTAS ————

Any kind of cooked small pasta may be used.

Humbert   Mix with batons of tomato and red and green pimento and flavour with French dressing.

Lucullus   Mix with julienne of chicken, ham and mushroom and flavour with French dressing.

Milanaise   Mix with julienne of tongue, mushroom and truffle and bind with mayonnaise.

HARICOT OR BUTTER
———— BEANS ————

Américaine   Mix cooked beans with lardons of bacon and tomato sauce.

Bourguignonne   Cook some chopped onions and mushrooms in red wine, add the cooked beans and simmer for 20 minutes; finish with a little anchovy essence.

Bretonne   Cook chopped onion and garlic and diced tomato in oil; add the cooked beans and a little of the cooking liquid and simmer for 20 minutes.

———— MEAT ————

Beef

Salad
(1) Mix diced cooked beef with diced potato and tomato, chopped onion and French dressing.

(2) Mix together diced beef, potato, gherkin, tomato and French dressing.

(3) Mix diced beef, tomato, anchovy and olives with chopped garlic and French dressing.

Pork

Brawn
This is made from the pickled head and feet; serve cut into small slices (potted head is a type of brawn).

Trotters
Cut into julienne and mix with mustard-flavoured French dressing; julienne of gherkin, potato, pimento etc may be added.

Ham

Cornets
Roll thinly cut triangular shape slices into cones and fill with ham puree.

Salad
Cut the ham into bâtons, add bâtons of gherkin and olives and cooked short macaroni; mix with French dressing flavoured with tomato ketchup.

Veal

Calf's Feet
Cut into bâtons, add chopped shallot and garlic, French mustard and vinaigrette dressing.

Ears
Cut into julienne and mix with julienne of gherkin and pimento; mix with French dressing.

Sausages

Garlic
Liver
Mortadella
Salami, etc.
Remove the skin, cut the sausage into very thin round slices and arrange overlapping in a ravier with thin elongated slices of gherkin between each slice, or form the slices into cornets.

——— MISCELLANEOUS ———

Agoursis
These are pickled small cucumbers; serve very small ones whole or cut larger ones into thick slices.

Carolines
Fill small chou buns with any kind of savoury puree and coat with chaudfroid or aspic jelly.

Cocktail Onions
These are available in several colours already

	pickled; serve as they are.
Gherkins	Serve plain or cut fan-shape.
Olives	These are available as green and black, whole queen olives, or stuffed with pimento, anchovy or almonds; serve as they are.
Pickled Walnuts	Serve as bought or home made, whole or in halves.

Single Hors-d'œuvre, Cold

This course consists of one single item served at the beginning of a meal, at a stated price. The dishes are usually listed on the à la carte menu and a good selection from the following is offered, possibly with some from the section on Hot Hors-d'œuvre.

Asparagus

Arrange a portion of from six to twelve sticks, according to size, on a folded table napkin or plate; serve with French dressing or mayonnaise.

Artichoke

Pull the choke from a large plain boiled globe artichoke, scrape the inside clean and replace the centre leaves upside down; place in a folded table napkin and serve with French dressing or thin mayonnaise.

Avocado Pear

Cut in half through the length and remove the stone; place in a pear-shape dish or on a leaf of lettuce on a plate and serve one or two halves per portion, according to size, accompanied with mayonnaise or French dressing. Because of its smooth texture and neutral taste, an avocado is one of the most versatile of cold hors-d'œuvre and it can be garnished with all kinds of shellfish, cottage cheese, various kinds of fruit, tomato, mayonnaise, cocktail sauce or French dressing.

The menu name should indicate the garnish, such as Avocat aux Crevettes, Avocat Pasadena (filled with crab meat, tomato and olives, with seafood cocktail sauce).

Caviar

This is served by the spoonful from the tin or jar it was imported in, or a porcelain container, set in a timbale of crushed ice or on an ice socle. It is served accompanied by a half of lemon, finely chopped onion, sieved yolk and white of hard boiled egg, and hot toast or blinis which are yeast pancakes made with buckwheat.

Cocktails or Coupes

Fruit   *Florida* Segments of grapefruit and orange with a cocktail cherry in the centre.
Hawaïenne Segments of grapefruit, orange, pineapple and melon.
Grapefruit Segments of grapefruit with sugar and a cocktail cherry.
Miami Segments of grapefruit and orange and small wedges of pineapple; a cocktail cherry in the centre.

Seafood Place shredded lettuce into a goblet or special glass container that fits into an outer container filled with crushed ice; add the main ingredients and cover with cocktail sauce. Decorate with a slice of lemon, quarter of tomato, mustard and cress, lobster coral, chopped parsley, etc.
Cocktail sauce is made by mixing 2 dl of any brand of tomato ketchup or fresh tomato pulp and 1 dl lightly whipped cream with 7 dl of mayonnaise; it may be flavoured with tabasco, Worcester sauce, lemon juice, celery salt, onion juice, etc.

Ingredients for a seafood cocktail can include one or more of the following – crabmeat, prawns, shrimps, crayfish, mussels, flaked cooked white fish, flaked salmon, diced lobster etc and diced

15

asparagus, avocado, anchovy, pineapple, chicken, cucumber etc. may be added.

Charcuterie

Arrange overlapping thin slices of one or more of the following items on a plate and garnish with mustard and cress or picked parsley, a fan of gherkin, leaf of lettuce or radicchio, bunch of sprue, etc. The most popular items are bierwurst, coppa, garlic sausage, liver sausage, Bath chap, mortadella, salami, etc.

Confit d'Oie

Cut up a goose and cure with salt, spices and herbs for 24 hours, then cook very slowly in its own, rendered fat for $2\frac{1}{2}$ hours. Place into earthenware pots, cover with the fat and serve cold.

Cornets of Ham

Mould thin triangular slices of york ham into cornet shapes and fill with any of the following – puree of chicken, egg or foie gras, potted shrimps, cottage cheese, Russian salad etc; they may be brushed with almost setting aspic jelly.

Corn on the Cob

Serve a cold, whole boiled sweetcorn with mayonnaise, or a flavoured mayonnaise-based sauce.

Crab

Serve some of the flaked claw meat and some of the creamy flesh in a small crab shell and decorate with sieved yolk and white of hard boiled egg, paprika, chopped parsley, lobster coral etc.; add lettuce and tomato and serve with mayonnaise.

Crudités

Serve an assortment of very crisp pieces of raw vegetables with several kinds of dips; it is usual to put a large bowlful on the table for guests to help themselves from the following items – carrots, celery, cauliflower, cucumber, Belgian endive, fennel, radishes, pimento, spring onions, mooli, etc.

Délice de Grison

Serve several very thinly cut slices of air dried smoked beef, with grated horseradish.

Egg Mayonnaise

Cut hard-boiled eggs into halves, quarters or slices, cover with mayonnaise and decorate trellis fashion with strips of anchovy and capers. The eggs may be arranged on a leaf of or some shredded lettuce, decorated with tomato, olives, gherkin, mustard and cress, etc., and the mayonnaise may be coloured and flavoured with curry, tomato, spinach, cream, etc. A cornet of smoked salmon filled with shrimps may be added.

Escabèche

Marinate small pieces of fish that have been deep fried in oil, in a cooked marinade of oil and vinegar flavoured with garlic, onion, pimento and herbs.

Fennel

Cook small whole or halved large fennel in a court-bouillon of water, oil, lemon juice, herbs and spices and serve in the cooled liquid.

Foie gras

1. Serve shell shape spoonfuls scooped from a whole foie gras with chopped aspic or port-flavoured jelly and watercress; hot toast and butter is the normal accompaniment.
2. Cut into slices, decorate with a slice of truffle and coat with aspic or port wine jelly; serve on a leaf of lettuce or radicchio.
3. Shallow fry slices of raw foie gras in butter, place on some leaves of salad and finish with the butter mixed with a little hot vinegar.

17

4. Scoop out spoonfuls of foie gras en croûte and serve with hot toast; garnish with a sprig of watercress.

Grapefruit

May be served–
1. As segments in a coupe.
2. In prepared halves with a cocktail cherry in the middle.
3. Sprinkled with brown sugar and sherry and grilled gently until the sugar caramelises

Segments may be served as an accompaniment with crabmeat, prawns, etc.

Gravlax

This is a side of fresh salmon marinated with seasonings especially dill, sugar and vinegar for several days.
To serve, cut into thin slices and garnish with a quarter of lemon and a sprig of dill

Guacamole

Make a puree of avocado pear, tomato, onion and lime juice and serve on its own or as a dip

Gulls' Eggs

Hard boil for 7–8 minutes and serve cold in the shell in a nest of mustard and cress, with brown bread and butter; various flavoured salts and peppers may be offered.

Quails' Eggs

Hard boil for 3 minutes and serve three or four per portion in the shell, set in a nest of mustard and cress; offer various seasonings and brown or white bread and butter.

Ham, Raw

Cut wafer thin slices of smoked raw ham and dress on a few leaves of lettuce. The hams in general use include: Parma, Bayonne, Westphalia and Serrano. It may be served with slices of avocado, melon, pear, etc.

Herrings

Serve a pickled or smoked herring with rings of raw onion and sliced rye bread and butter or pumpernickel.

Juices

Serve a reasonable amount of freshly pressed and chilled juice in a goblet on an underplate and doily. Offer Worcester sauce, salt and pepper when serving tomato juice.
The following are the most popular: orange, grapefruit, mango, pineapple and tomato; mixed juices include tropical, exotic and vegetable.

Kiwi d'Oeufs

Fill an emptied kiwi fruit with scrambled egg and serve in an eggcup with hot toast.

Mango

Cut in half to reveal the stone and serve as it is, or scoop out the flesh with a spoon. Diced mango may be served as a cocktail with diced avocado, lobster, prawns, etc, covered with spiced cocktail sauce.

Mayonnaise of Chicken, etc

Arrange the sliced or flaked main item on leaves of or shredded lettuce, coat with mayonnaise and decorate with strips of anchovy, capers, fans of gherkin, olives, cucumber, tomato, etc. Suitable items include chicken, cod, mussels, salmon, egg, mixed shellfish etc. It can be finished by sprinkling with parsley, paprika, lobster coral, shredded almonds, etc.

Melon

May be served
1. Cut in half and remove the seeds then cut into wedges and serve on crushed ice; it may be decorated with slices of kiwi fruit, orange, peach, strawberry etc, and served with ground ginger and caster sugar.
2. Scoop out with a parisienne cutter and place into a coupe with a cocktail cherry on top.
3. Fill whole or halved small melons with port, madeira or sherry, or a liqueur, and allow to stand for 1 hour before serving.
4. Add de-pipped grapes, maraschino cherries, diced cucumber, pear, prawns etc. to small balls of any kind of melon.

Mousses and Mousselines

A cold mousse can be made with cooked finely minced chicken, ham, liver, lobster etc mixed with the appropriate flavour of velouté and aspic jelly and lightened with slightly whipped cream; it can be decorated and covered with aspic jelly. The same mixture can be moulded with spoons or in dariole moulds, and served as mousselines.

Mushrooms

Stuffed, crumbed and deep fried mushrooms may be served hot or cold. The very white ones can be cooked in oil, lemon juice, herbs and spices and served cold in some of the cooking liquid.

Mussels

Very fresh and clean, large size mussels may be opened and served raw on a bed of crushed ice with lemon and brown bread and butter.

Oysters

Open, turn over in the shell and serve a portion of six or twelve in a soup plate on crushed ice with a half of lemon, brown bread and butter and shallot sauce.

Potted Shrimps

These are usually purchased ready prepared for serving on a leaf of lettuce with brown bread and butter; or they can be made by adding peeled brown shrimps to melted butter with seasonings, including ground mace, and set in moulds. They may be garnished with grapefruit segments, slices of kiwi fruit, etc.

Poutargue

Cut slices of the salted pressed roes of the mullet or tunny fish and serve with quarters of lemon and oil and vinegar dressing.

Proscuitto

This is the Italian name for smoked ham, served raw in very thin slices with avocado pear, melon, fresh pear, etc.

Salads

A fairly substantial salad that contains fish or meat can be served as an hors-d'œuvre on its own, neatly arranged on a plate or in a dish in the same way as for Mayonnaise of Chicken.

Smoked Foods

Fish items include smoked eel, mackerel, salmon, sturgeon and trout. Meat items include smoked chicken, goose, grouse and turkey.

Eel	Cut an 8cm length, remove all skin and bone and serve with lemon, horseradish sauce and brown bread and butter.
Mackerel and Trout	Serve as for smoked eel, skinning the trout.
Salmon and Sturgeon	Cut into thin slices on the slant, arrange flat on the plate or roll into cornets and serve with lemon, brown bread and butter and mustard and cress. Cornets may be filled with caviar, shrimps, diced avocado, etc.

21

Smoked meats are cut into thin slices and garnished with salad vegetables.

Seafood Platter

This is an assortment of various kinds of shellfish arranged in a neat pattern on a bed of crushed ice or salad stuff with a garnish of tomato, cucumber, etc., and mayonnaise.

Snails' Eggs

This rare commodity is imported from Tibet and is like an amber coloured caviar with an aroma of almond; it is served on toast.

Steak Tartare

Mould finely chopped fillet of beef into approximately 5 cm flat round cake, place a raw yolk of egg in an indent in the centre and garnish with chopped onion and parsley, capers, fan of gherkin etc. The steak is eaten raw.

Terrine Maison or Pâté Maison

Indicates a home-made liver or meat pie without pastry, cooked in an earthenware container from which it is served, cut into slices or scooped out with a spoon. It can be made as a coarse or fine textured pâté, flavoured with various herbs and spices and brandy or other spirit. The main item can be chicken, ox or pig's liver, hare, venison or rabbit, mixed with fresh or salt belly of pork, streaky bacon, onion, garlic, eggs and cream. When cooked it should be covered with melted butter or lard to exclude air and kept refrigerated. Serve on a leaf of lettuce with a fan of gherkin or sprig of watercress accompanied with hot thick slices of toast and butter.

Hot Hors-d'œuvre

This kind of hors-d'œuvre is equally as varied and interesting as the more widely used selection of cold hors-d'œuvre. It is certainly a substantial course as many of the recipes contain pastry and could constitute a meal in itself, specially lunch.

Many of the following are also suitable for serving as an after-dinner savoury; some of the traditional English savouries can be used as part of a hot hors-d'œuvre selection.

It is essential that these items be served hot but not dried out.

Eggs

Egg Cutlets	Bind finely chopped hard-boiled eggs with hot béchamel and yolks and when cool, mould cutlet shape; egg and crumb and deep fry. A small piece of blanched macaroni can be inserted to represent the bone.
Egg Croquettes	Bind finely chopped cooked mushroom and hard-boiled egg with hot béchamel and egg yolks and when cool mould cork-shape, round- or pear-shape; egg and crumb and deep fry.
Egg Fondants	Mix finely chopped hard-boiled egg and chopped truffle with hot béchamel and egg yolks and when cool, mould pear-shape; egg and crumb and deep fry.
Pannequets	Spread creamed hard-boiled or scrambled egg-mix onto small pancakes; roll up and cut into diamond-shaped pieces, reheat and serve.
Quails' Eggs Christiana	Place a hot hard-boiled egg into a glazed pommes duchesse nest; coat it with foie gras-flavoured demi-glace and sprinkle with finely chopped truffle.

Fish

Allumettes d'Anchois	Coat strips of puff pastry (6cm × 1cm) with anchovy-flavoured fish forcemeat, cover with anchovy fillets and bake for 10–12 minutes.
Allumettes Caprice	Coat strips of puff pastry (6cm × 1cm) with sole or whiting forcemeat containing diced ox tongue and truffle and bake for 10–12 minutes. Allumettes can be made with all kinds of fish and shellfish.

Attereaux d'Huîtres Villeroy	Spear small poached oysters and slices of cooked mushroom on cocktail sticks, dip into hot sauce Villeroy and when cool, egg and crumb and deep fry; serve garnished with fried parsley.
Barquettes de Crevettes	Fill pastry barquettes with diced prawns mixed with shrimp sauce; cover with some of the sauce and decorate with a whole prawn.
Barquettes d' Ecrevisses	Fill pastry barquettes with diced crayfish mixed with crayfish sauce, cover with some of the same sauce and finish with a crayfish tail.
Barquettes de Homard	Fill pastry barquettes with diced lobster, mushroom and truffle mixed with lobster sauce and place a small thin slice of lobster and truffle on top.
Barquettes d'Huîtres	Fill pastry barquettes with poached, bearded oysters mixed with béchamel and sprinkle with chopped truffle.
Barquettes de Laitances Florentine	Half fill pastry barquettes with buttered leaf spinach, place a poached soft roe on top and coat with mornay sauce; sprinkle with cheese and glaze.
Beignets d'Anchois	Cover small round slices of tunny fish with thin strips of anchovy, dip into batter and deep fry.
Beignets Bénédictine	Mould puree of salt cod and potato into walnut size pieces; dip into batter and deep fry.
Beignets Cardinal	Coat poached soft roes with thick lobster sauce and when cold, dip into batter and deep fry.
Beignets de Laitances	Marinate poached herring roes in oil and lemon juice, dip into batter and deep fry.
Beignets à la Mathurine	Add diced smoked herring and diced sardine to chou paste and deep fry spoonfuls of it.
Bouchées Joinville	Fill oval bouchées with diced shrimps, mushroom and truffle mixed with sauce joinville, and cover each with a diamond shape of truffle.
Bouchées Marie-Rose	Fill diamond shape bouchées with buttered shrimps mixed with julienne of truffle and cover with a diamond shape of pink coloured fish forcemeat.
Bouchées Monseigneur	Fill oval bouchées with puree of poached soft roe and finely chopped truffle and cover each with a

diamond shape piece of truffle.

Bouchées Nantua	Fill oval shape bouchées with diced crayfish and truffle mixed with sauce nantua and decorate with a stuffed crayfish head.
Coquilles de Crevettes, d'Ecrevisses, etc.	Pipe small scallop shells with a border of duchesse potato; fill the centre with the shellfish mixed with béchamel sauce, coat with mornay sauce, sprinkle with cheese and glaze.
Côtelettes de Poisson	Bind chopped cooked fish with hot béchamel and egg yolks, mould into small cutlet shapes, egg and crumb and shallow or deep fry; a small length of blanched macaroni may be inserted to represent the bone.
Croquettes de Poisson	Bind chopped cooked fish such as salmon, crab, cod and optional, diced cooked mushroom or truffle, with hot béchamel and egg yolks; when cool, mould into balls, corks or cakes, egg and crumb and deep fry.
Croquettes de Morue	Mix finely flaked salt cod with duchesse potato and reduced béchamel; mould into balls, egg and crumb and deep fry. Serve with tomato sauce.
Croquettes à la Dominicaine	Mix poached oysters with diced mushroom into onion-flavoured béchamel containing also some lobster butter; mould into elongated oval shapes, egg and crumb and deep fry. Serve with Sauce Vin blanc.
Croquettes de Homard	Mix diced lobster, mushroom and truffle with béchamel coloured with red butter; mould into elongated egg shapes, egg and crumb and deep fry. Serve with lobster sauce.
Croquettes à l'Indienne	Mix cooked rice and diced lobster with curry and coconut milk-flavoured reduced béchamel; mould cork shape, egg and crumb and deep fry. Serve with curry sauce.
Croquettes Jean-Bart	Mould a poached oyster inside a mixture of finely chopped lobster and reduced béchamel coloured with red butter; egg and crumb, mould

25

	into balls and deep fry. Serve with béchamel sauce flavoured with lobster butter.
Croquettes Nantaise	Mix together finely flaked fish, chopped mushroom, and well reduced fish sauce; mould into small squares, egg and crumb and deep fry. Serve with tomato sauce.
Croustades	These small containers can be made as
	(1) round or oval pastry cases.
	(2) emptied deep fried breadcrumbed mould of duchesse potato, or
	(3) semolina boiled in white stock, thickened with egg yolks and flavoured with cheese and spread 3 cm thick to cool. Stamp out with a 5 cm round cutter, egg and crumb and deep fry then cut out the lid and empty the inside in preparation for filling with flaked cooked fish and shellfish mixed with an appropriate sauce and garnish.
Croûtes	Shallow fry round or square pieces of bread approximately 5 cm wide and $1\frac{1}{2}$ cm thick having marked a line for the lid; remove the lid, empty the inside and refill with flaked cooked fish or shellfish in a suitable sauce.
Dartois aux Anchois	Roll out puff pastry 9 cm wide and spread with fish forcemeat flavoured with anchovy essence; lay anchovy fillets on top leaving the two edges clear, dampen these and cover with a second length of pastry sealing it well at the edge. Egg-wash, mark in 3cm divisions, bake in a hot oven and cut into slices immediately.
Dartois aux Sardines	Make in the same way as Dartois aux Anchois, using plain fish forcemeat and skinned tinned sardines.
Fish Balls and Fish Cakes	Mix finely flaked cooked fish with duchesse potato and a little reduced béchamel; mould into small balls or flat cakes, egg and crumb and deep fry.
Fondants	Mix flaked cooked fish with hot béchamel and egg yolks, allow to cool and mould into small pear shapes; egg and crumb and deep fry.

Fritots	Marinate small pieces of cooked fish in oil and lemon juice, coat with frying batter, deep fry and serve with tomato sauce.
Harengs à l'Esthonienne	Mix a puree of salt herrings, breadcrumbs lightly tossed in butter, cream and eggs to form a batter and cook in the form of small pancakes.
Huîtres Baltimore	Arrange several oysters in a deep oyster shell, sprinkle with breadcrumbs, cheese, chopped parsley and melted butter and bake in the oven.
Huîtres Delmonico	Coat poached oysters with cream sauce flavoured with a little lemon juice.
Huîtres Favorite	Place a poached oyster on a layer of béchamel, coat with sauce béchamel, sprinkle with cheese and butter and glaze under a salamander; decorate with a slice of truffle.
Huîtres Florentine	Place chopped buttered spinach in a deep oyster shell, a poached oyster on top, coat with mornay sauce and glaze.
Huîtres Manhattan	Sprinkle oysters in the half shell with fried small lardons, chopped cooked green and red pimento, sliced mushroom and chopped cooked onion; cook in the oven.
Huîtres Maréchal	Dip poached oysters in batter and deep fry.
Huîtres Polonaise	Sprinkle oysters with fried breadcrumbs and cook in the oven.
Huîtres Villeroy	Dip poached oysters in hot sauce villeroy, when set coat with egg-wash and breadcrumbs and deep fry.
Jalousie de Mousseline de Sole	Spread puff pastry rolled 9cm wide with sole forcemeat; cover with a second length of pastry that has been slashed across at 5mm intervals and bake. Cut into 3cm pieces.
Moules Farcies Frites	Stuff large cooked mussels with garlic butter; egg and crumb and deep fry.
Piroguis à la Moscovite	Fill the centre of 8cm rounds of unsweetened brioche paste with a mixture of chopped cooked fish, hard boiled eggs and vésiga; fold the two sides to the centre, allow to prove then bake in a hot oven. Finish by pouring a little Sauce Colbert in each.

Piroguis de Poisson	Garnish 8cm rounds of puff pastry with minced cooked fish mixed with plain boiled rice; cover with another round of pastry, egg-wash and bake.
Piroguis au Vésiga	Garnish one side of 8cm rounds of puff pastry with a filling of chopped cooked vésiga and celery, parsley roots and hard boiled egg mixed with béchamel; fold over the pastry, seal well, brush with egg-wash and bake in a hot oven.
Pommes Georgette	Cut an incision in a medium sized baked potato and fill with diced crayfish mixed with Sauce Nantua.
Rastegaïs	Fill 8cm rounds of unsweetened brioche paste with a mixture of diced raw salmon and chopped cooked hard-boiled eggs and vésiga; fold the two sides to the centre, allow to prove then bake in a hot oven.
Rissoles de Crevettes à la Dauphine	Fill the centre of 8cm rounds of unsweetened brioche paste with chopped prawns mixed with béchamel finished with lobster butter; fold over the pastry, seal well and deep fry.
Rissoles à l'Indienne	Fill one side of 8cm rounds of rough puff pastry with chopped lobster in curry-flavoured béchamel; add an oyster cooked à la Villeroy and fold over the paste and seal well, coat with breadcrumbs and deep fry.
Rissoles Joinville	Fill one side of 8cm rounds of puff pastry with a mixture of diced crayfish, julienne of mushroom and truffle mixed with reduced Sauce Normande; fold over the pastry, seal well and deep fry.
Rissoles Nantua	Make small puff pastry turnovers filled with diced crayfish and truffle mixed with béchamel finished with crayfish butter; deep fry and serve garnished with fried parsley.
Rissoles Normande	Make small puff pastry turnovers filled with diced mussels, oysters and shrimps mixed with thick Sauce Normande; deep fry at 180°C and serve with fried parsley.
Rissoles Victoria	Make small fancy oval, puff pastry turnovers filled with diced lobster and truffle mixed with

	reduced lobster sauce and deep fry in the usual manner.
Sausselis aux Anchois	This is another name for Dartois aux Anchois.
Soufflés aux Crustacés	Add a puree of cooked fish or shellfish to ordinary soufflé mixture, fill into small soufflé dishes and bake at 175°C for 12 minutes.
Tartelettes Écossaise	Fill warm tartlets with creamed puree of smoked haddock.
Tartelettes Tiffin	Fill warm tartlets with flaked smoked haddock mixed with curry sauce.
Tartelettes Tosca	Fill warm puff pastry tartlets with diced crayfish in lobster sauce, cover with cheese soufflé mixture and bake in the oven.
Timbales Dessoliers	Coat small buttered moulds lined with chopped truffle, with a layer of crayfish and whiting forcemeat, fill up with diced crayfish and lobster mixed with Sauce Normande, cover with more forcemeat and poach au bain-marie; turn out and serve with crayfish-flavoured velouté.
Timbales Régine	Line dariole moulds with fish and duxelles forcemeat, fill with poached soft roes mixed with velouté containing crayfish butter; cover with more forcemeat, cook au bain-marie and serve with crayfish-flavoured velouté.
Visnisckis	Place a little flaked cooked fish mixed with chopped cooked fennel and fish velouté in the centre of 5cm rounds of brioche paste; cover with another round of paste, allow to prove then deep fry for 6 minutes.
Whitebait	Deep fry floured whitebait for 1 minute; drain, season with cayenne and serve garnished with fried parsley.

The cocktails of fish and shellfish may be served hot using hot lobster or other fish sauce to cover the normal ingredients. Potted shrimps may be heated in an oven and served as an hors-dœuvre.

Meat

Attereaux à la Genevoise	Thread small pieces of cooked artichoke bottoms, calf's brain, chicken liver, mushroom, lamb's sweetbread and truffle on small skewers; dip into stiff sauce duxelles, then coat smoothly with chicken forcemeat; egg and crumb and deep fry.
Attereaux Villeroy	Thread several items from brain, foie gras, ham, cockscombs, mushroom, sweetbread, tongue, truffle etc. on small skewers; dip into Sauce Villeroy, allow to cool then egg and crumb and deep fry.
Barquettes	Fill short pastry barquettes with hot salpicon of various meats e.g. ham, sweetbread, tongue, with mushroom or truffle, mixed with an appropriate sauce.
Beignets de Cervelle	Marinate slices of cold poached calf's brain in oil and lemon juice, dip in batter and deep fry
Bouchées Isabelle	Fill oval bouchées with creamed puree of chicken mixed with diced ox-tongue and truffle and cover with a small round of tongue.
Bouchées Megador	Fill diamond-shape bouchées with diced ox-tongue and chicken mixed with foie gras-flavoured béchamel sauce; cover with diamonds of truffle.
Brochettes	Coat small cooked pieces of liver, ham, mushrooms, sweetbreads etc. with thick duxelles; impale on small skewers, sprinkle with breadcrumbs and grill. The menu title will stem from the main ingredient used.
Cassolettes	Fill small fireproof dishes with diced mixture of cooked meat bound with an appropriate sauce; sprinkle with breadcrumbs and gratinate in the oven.
Cannelons Mogador	Fill cooked puff pastry horns with diced ox-tongue and chicken mixed with foie gras-flavoured béchamel sauce.
Cannelons à l'Ancienne	Spread thin oblongs of puff pastry 9cm × 4cm

	with forcemeat; roll up, seal well and bake for 10–12 minutes.
Colombines	Line buttered tartlet moulds with semolina gnocchi mixture, fill with finely chopped cooked meat mixed with an appropriate sauce, turn out, cover with egg-wash and breadcrumbs and deep fry. The menu term is decided by the main ingredient of the filling.
Cromesquis	Bind finely chopped cooked meat and mushrooms with a well reduced sauce, allow to cool and mould oblong or cork shape; dip into batter and deep fry. The menu term is decided by the main ingredient e.g. Cromesquis de Boeuf.
Cromesquis Polonaise	Envelop the moulded mixture in a very thin pancake, dip into batter and deep fry.
Cromesquis à la Russe	Envelop the moulded mixture in a piece of pig's caul, dip into batter and deep fry.
Croquettes	Bind finely chopped cooked meat and mushrooms, ham, ox-tongue or truffle with well reduced béchamel or demi-glace; allow to cool, mould, egg and crumb and deep fry.
Croquettes à la Bergère	Bind chopped cooked lamb, ham and mushroom with reduced béchamel; mould into small balls, egg and crumb and deep fry.
Croquettes à la Hongroise	Bind finely chopped calf's feet, ham and mushroom with reduced velouté flavoured with paprika; mould oval shape, egg and crumb and deep fry. Serve accompanied with paprika-flavoured sauce demi-glace.
Croquettes Savigny	Bind finely chopped ham, artichoke bottoms and morels with reduced béchamel and thicken with yolks of egg; mould into small flat cakes, egg and crumb and deep fry.
Croustades de Ris de Veau Financière	Fill deep short paste tartlets with a mixture of small slices of braised calf's sweetbread, cockscombs, mushroom and quenelles, mixed with Sauce Madère.
Croûtes à la Champenoise	Shallow fry 5cm × 1½cm rounds of bread, cut an incision around the top and remove the inside; fill with small dice of brain flavoured with onion and garlic.

Croûtes à la Moelle Shallow fry 4cm × 1½cm squares of bread, cut an incision on top and remove the inside; fill with poached dice of bone marrow and a slice of it on top then coat with melted meat glaze and decorate with a slice of truffle.

Fritots These are similar to fritters being slices of calf's head, brain or trotter, marinated in oil and lemon juice, then dipped into batter and deep fried; serve with tomato sauce.

Mazagrans Line a buttered tartlet mould with duchesse potato, fill with any kind of finely diced meat in reduced sauce and cover with a top cut out of duchesse potato; bake in a hot oven until golden brown.

Pannequets Spread small pancakes with any kind of finely chopped meat mixture, roll up and cut in diamond shape pieces.

Pâtés à la Bourgeoise Fill 5cm rounds of puff pastry with a finely chopped meat and mushroom mixture; cover with a second round of pastry, seal well, egg-wash and bake in a hot oven for 10–15 minutes

Pâtés Dauphine Cut out 5cm rounds of brioche paste and fill with a finely chopped meat mixture in reduced sauce; cover with a second round of paste, allow to prove, egg-wash and bake in a hot oven.

Pâtés Manon Fill 5cm rounds of puff pastry with veal forcemeat containing diced ox-tongue; cover with a second round of pastry, seal well, brush with egg-wash and bake in a hot oven.

Pâtés Mazaran Fill baked deep tartlets with a salpicon of mushroom, quenelles and lamb's sweetbread mixed with demi-glace, and cover with a lid cut from puff pastry and cooked separately.

Pâtés Nimoise Fill 6cm rounds of puff pastry with a stuffing of diced fillet of lamb, chicken liver and fat pork all sauted in butter, made into a puree and flavoured with chopped fines herbes and truffle; cover with a second round of pastry, seal well, egg-wash and bake in a hot oven.

Pâtés à la Parisienne
Fill 5cm rounds of puff pastry with a chopped meat, mushroom and truffle mixture; cover with a second round of pastry, seal well, egg-wash and bake in a hot oven.

Pâtés au Verjus
Enclose two small unripe depipped grapes in veal and chive forcemeat and place in the centre of 5cm rounds of puff pastry; cover with a second round of pastry, seal well, egg-wash and bake in a hot oven.

Petits Pains Victoria
Cut the tops off small bridge rolls, hollow out then fill with hot ham, tongue, foie gras, chicken etc; replace the tops and serve warm.

Petits Pâtés
Fill 3cm rounds of puff pastry with finely minced sauted fillet of beef, onion and sieved hard boiled egg; cover with a second round of pastry, seal well, egg-wash and bake in a hot oven.
These patties are also part of the garnish served with Bortsch soup.

Piroguis Polonaise
Cut oval pieces of puff pastry 10cm long and place in a little sauted diced veal and calf's udder flavoured with onion, in the centre; fold over to seal well, brush with egg-wash and bake in a hot oven.

Petits Pains de Windsor
Cut small bridge rolls in half lengthways remove some of the crumb and fill with fine puree of ham, tongue, foie gras etc. replace the top and serve warm.

Pommes à l'Ardennaise
Cut small baked potatoes in half, empty out then refill with a fine mixture made of the scooped out potato, butter, egg yolks, chopped mushroom, parmesan and chopped parsley; smooth the surface, sprinkle with cheese and gratinate in the oven.

Pomponettes
Place a little cooked meat mixture in the centre of rounds of puff pastry; bring up the edges to form a purse, seal well and deep fry.

Quichelettes au Jambon
Place small rounds of ham in small tartlet cases, fill with raw egg and cream custard and bake in a moderate oven until set.

Rissoles à la Bergère	Place a small amount of salpicon of braised lamb's sweetbread and mushroom mixed with onion-flavoured béchamel in the centre of 6cm round of puff pastry; fold over, seal well and deep fry.
Rissoles Pompadour	Place a small amount of salpicon of ox-tongue, mushroom, foie gras and truffle mixed with sauce périgueux in a round of puff pastry; add a slice of poached bone marrow, fold over and deep fry
Saucisson en Brioche	Envelop a small poached sausage in brioche paste, allow to prove and bake.
Soufflés au Jambon	Add puree of ham to béchamel together with yolks and paprika then the stiffly beaten whites; fill into small moulds and bake in a moderate oven for approximately 12 minutes.
Subrics à l'Italienne	Flavour a batter with grated parmesan and mix in diced cooked calf's brain; shallow fry small spoonfuls and serve with quarters of lemon
Tartelettes	Line lightly baked short-paste tartlets with forcemeat, cook in the oven then fill with any kind of hot meat mixture in sauce.
Varenikis Lithuanien	Fill 6cm squares of noodle pastry with cooked chopped onion, fillet of beef and suet mixed with a little reduced béchamel; cover with another piece of pastry so making square raviolis, poach for 15 minutes, drain well and sprinkle with melted butter.

Poultry and Game

Allumettes Caprice	Coat 6cm × 1cm strips of puff pastry with chicken forcemeat containing diced ox-tongue and truffle and bake for 10 minutes.
Attereaux à la Genevoise	Thread small pieces of sauted chicken livers, poached calf's brain and artichoke bottom, mushroom, braised lamb sweetbread and truffle, all previously dipped into reduced Sauce Duxel-

les – onto small skewers; coat smoothly with forcemeat, egg and crumb and deep fry.

Barquettes Chevreuse
Line buttered barquette moulds with semolina gnocchi mixture and fill with puree of chicken etc. cover with more semolina and demould; egg and crumb and deep fry.

Beignets à l'Italienne
Mould small balls of paste made of fresh parmesan cheese, cooked calf's brain, diced chicken and ham; dip into frying batter and deep fry.

Bouchées à la Bohémienne
Fill hollowed out small brioches with a salpicon of foie gras and truffle mixed with melted meat glaze and madeira; replace the tops of the brioche as lids.

Bouchées à la Diane
Fill round puff pastry bouchées with diced game bird and truffle mixed with salmis sauce and cover with a glazed round slice of truffle.

Bouchées Mogador
Fill diamond-shape bouchées with diced chicken and ox-tongue mixed with béchamel and a little foie gras puree; cover with a glazed diamond shape slice of truffle.

Bouchées à la Périgourdine
Fill tall bouchées with foie gras mixed with madeira sauce and chopped truffle.

Bouchées Petite-Princesse
Fill tall square bouchées with puree of cooked chicken mixed with velouté and diced truffle and cover with square slices of truffle.

Bouchées à la Reine
Fill bouchées with diced chicken, mushroom and truffle, mixed with sauce allemande.

Bouchées Saint-Hubert
Fill bouchées with diced game meat mixed with espagnole and cover with a cooked turned mushroom.

Brochettes
Dip small pieces of chicken liver, mushroom, bacon, ham, etc. in thick sauce duxelles; impale on short skewers, sprinkle with breadcrumbs and grill gently.

Cannelons
Fill puff pastry horns baked on cream horn tins with diced chicken, mushroom, tongue etc. mixed with stiff béchamel sauce.

Cassolettes Aiglon
Line the rims of individual fireproof dishes with puff pastry and half fill with diced foie gras and

truffle mixed with demi-glace; fill dome shape with foie gras soufflé mixture and bake in a moderate oven for 15 minutes.

Cassolettes Alice
Line individual fireproof dishes with a thin layer of duchesse potato and fill with sliced chicken mixed with velouté; cover with a fancy round of duchesse potato, brush with egg-wash and bake for 15 minutes.

Cassolettes Suzanne
Fill individual dishes full with diced asparagus in velouté; add a small slice each of chicken and ox-tongue and decorate with a slice of truffle

Chaussons de Foies de Volaille
Make turnovers with puree of chicken liver and bake or deep fry.

Colombines
Line tartlet moulds with semolina cheese gnocchi paste, fill with salpicon of chicken, ham, mushroom etc. mixed with sauce and cover with a round of semolina paste; turn out, egg and crumb and deep fry.

Cornets à la Reine
Fill small puff pastry cornets with puree of chicken and seal with a round of chicken.

Côtelettes de Volaille
Add finely diced cooked chicken with mushroom or truffle to reduced boiling béchamel, thicken with egg yolks and spread out to cool; mould into small cutlet shapes, egg and crumb and deep fry.

Cromesquis
Add finely diced cooked chicken with mushroom or truffle to reduced boiling béchamel; mould into shape, wrap in pig's caul, bacon or thin pancakes then dip into batter and deep fry.

Croquettes de Volaille
Add finely chopped cooked chicken with ham, mushroom or truffle to reduced boiling béchamel and spread out to cool; mould cork shape, pass through flour, egg-wash and bread-crumbs and deep fry. Serve with sauce périgueux or demi-glace.

Croquettes Chasseur
Mix finely chopped cooked game, mushroom and truffle with reduced boiling demi-glace;

mould into rectangles, egg and crumb and deep fry.

Croquettes à la Gastronome Mix finely diced game and truffle into reduced boiling sauce suprême; mould cork shape, egg and crumb and deep fry.

Croquettes à la Milanaise Mix cooked short cut macaroni and short julienne of chicken, ox-tongue and truffle with tomato and cheese flavoured-reduced béchamel; when cold, cut into small squares, egg and crumb and deep fry. Serve with tomato sauce.

Croquettes Sully Mould small balls of foie gras-flavoured chicken forcemeat inside a coating of chicken croquette mixture made with velouté; egg and crumb and deep fry.

Croustades de Volaille Régence Fill dariole moulds with duchesse potato, turn out, egg and crumb and deep fry; cut out a lid, empty the inside and refill with very small slices of chicken, cockscombs and kidneys, quenelles and truffle mixed with sauce allemande.

Croûtes d'Oie Fumée Shallow fry 4cm × 1½cm rounds of rye bread; hollow out, fill with braised sauerkraut and place a slice of smoked goose on top; glaze with espagnole.

Fondants de Bécasse Castellane Mix puree of cooked woodcock, chicken liver and chestnuts with sauce salmis; spread to cool, mould pear shape, egg and crumb and deep fry

Fondants de Faisan Marly Mix puree of cooked pheasant with puree of sauted chicken liver with reduced sauce salmis; spread to cool, mould pear shape, egg and crumb and deep fry.

Fondants de Volaille Louisette Mix together puree of cooked chicken, foie gras and ox-tongue with reduced sauce allemande; allow to cool, mould pear shape, egg and crumb and deep fry.

Mazagrans Line tartlet moulds with duchesse potato, fill with small dice of chicken, ham, tongue etc. mixed with sauce and cover with a round piece of duchesse potato; bake until golden brown and firm.

Pannequets Spread pancakes with small dice of chicken, ham, tongue etc. mixed with sauce; roll up and cut into diamond shapes.

Pellmènes Sibérien Pipe small pieces of stuffing made of hazelhen, ham and demi-glace onto 3cm rounds of noodle pastry; cover with more pastry, seal well and poach for 15 minutes. Drain and serve sprinkled with melted butter, lemon juice and meat glaze

Piroguis de Gibier Fill 6cm rounds of puff pastry with finely chopped cooked game mixed with sieved hard-boiled egg and rice; cover with a second round of pastry, egg-wash and bake in a hot oven.

Pomponettes Place a little cooked chicken mixture in the centre of small rounds of puff pastry, bring up the edges to form a purse, seal well and deep fry

Rissoles à la Bohémienne Place a little diced foie gras and truffle mixed with reduced demi-glace in the centre of small rounds of brioche paste; fold over, seal well, allow to prove and deep fry.

Rissoles à la Bressane Place a little diced sauted chicken liver and mushroom mixed with reduced sauce duxelles in the centre of small rounds of short pastry, fold over, seal well and deep fry.

Rissoles de Volaille à la Dauphine Place a little cooked chicken mixture in the centre of rounds of brioche paste; fold over to seal well, allow to prove then deep fry.

Rissoles Marly Fill small oblongs of puff pastry with diced cooked pheasant and truffle mixed with reduced demi-glace; cover with another piece of pastry and deep fry.

Rissoles à la Reine Fill small rounds of puff pastry with finely chopped chicken mixed with reduced béchamel; fold over, seal well and deep fry.

Soufflés de Gibier Mix puree of cooked game with béchamel, add yolks and stiffly beaten whites and bake in small soufflé moulds for 12 minutes.

Subrics de Foie Gras Add diced foie gras to a batter made of flour, eggs and cream and shallow fry small spoonfuls.

Tartelettes Châtillon	Fill partly cooked tartlets with sliced cooked mushrooms mixed with béchamel; spread with a cover of chicken forcemeat and bake in the oven.
Tartelettes Diane	Line tartlet moulds with game forcemeat and cook in the oven; fill with sliced partridge, truffle and demi-glace and cover dome shape with more forcemeat; pipe with a crescent of forcemeat and bake in the oven.
Tartelettes Gauloise	Line tartlet moulds with chicken forcemeat and cook in the oven; fill with small cooked cockscombs and kidneys mixed with meat glaze and cover dome shape with forcemeat made with chicken and ham; bake in the oven.
Tartelettes Marly	Spread partly baked short-paste tartlets with game forcemeat; fill with slices of pheasant and truffle and sauce salmis, cover with more forcemeat and bake in the oven.
Tartelettes Olga	Cook small tartlet moulds filled with hazelhen forcemeat au bain-marie; turn out, place into baked tartlets, coat with sauce salmis and decorate with a small cooked mushroom.
Tartelettes à la Reine	Spread baked tartlets with chicken forcemeat and cook in the oven; fill with small slices of chicken, mushroom and truffle and sauce suprême, cover dome shape with more forcemeat and bake in the oven.
Timbales Agnes Sorel	Place a round each of truffle and ox-tongue in the bottom of buttered dariole moulds and coat the inside with chicken forcemeat; fill with diced chicken, ox-tongue and truffle mixed with velouté, cover with forcemeat and cook au bain-marie for 15 minutes. Serve with demi-glace.
Timbales Maréchal	Place a slice of truffle in the bottom of buttered dariole moulds and coat with chicken forcemeat containing finely chopped ox-tongue; fill with puree of chicken mixed with sauce soubise and cover with more forcemeat, cook au bain-marie and serve with sauce périgueux.

Timbales Médicis	Empty babas made without sugar and fill with diced foie gras, ox-tongue and truffle mixed with sauce allemande flavoured with tomato; cover with a round slice of truffle.
Timbales Païva	Line dariole moulds with pancakes, spread with chicken forcemeat and fill up with puree of chicken containing diced ox-tongue; cover with forcemeat and cook au bain-marie for 12 minutes. Serve with sauce albuféra.
Timbales Reynière	Place a slice of truffle at the bottom of buttered dariole moulds, sprinkle with chopped ox-tongue and spread with pheasant forcemeat; fill with diced foie gras and truffle mixed with demi-glace and cover with forcemeat, cook au bain-marie for 20 minutes and serve with demi-glace.

Miscellaneous

Attereaux au Gruyère	Cut 2cm × 5mm thick rounds of semolina gnocchi mixture and impale on small skewers alternating with small round slices of Gruyère cheese; coat with egg and breadcrumbs and deep fry.
Barquettes	Baked pastry barquettes may be filled with asparagus tips, macédoine of vegetable etc. in cream sauce.
Beignets d'Artichauts	Dip marinated artichoke bottoms in batter and deep fry.
Beignets Pignatelli	Add toasted slivered almonds or pine nuts and diced ham to chou paste and pipe small bulbs onto sheets of oiled paper; deep fry until golden brown.
Beignets Soufflés au Fromage	Add diced Gruyère and grated parmesan to chou paste and pipe or mould small bulbs onto oiled greaseproof paper; deep fry until golden brown.
Beurrecks à la Turque	Add diced Gruyère to cold reduced béchamel, mould cigar shape and wrap in very thin strips of

noodle pastry; coat with egg and crumbs and deep fry.

Blinis Make a yeast pancake batter using half ordinary and half buckwheat flour, aerate with whisked whites and cook as pancakes; serve with sour cream, caviar, chopped hard boiled egg etc.

Blintzes Spread small pancakes with a mixture of cottage cheese, sauted sliced mushrooms and sour cream; roll up and trim the ends.

Bouchées Bouquetière Fill bouchées with brunoise of carrot, celery, leek and turnip mixed with velouté and cover with a fancy slice of cooked carrot.

Bouchées Grand-Duc Fill bouchées with asparagus tips and thick julienne of truffle mixed with cream sauce, and cover with a slice of truffle.

Bouchées Printanière Fill bouchées with small dice of carrot and turnip, peas, flageolet beans and diamonds of French beans mixed with velouté.

Champignons Frits Dip marinated whole mushrooms in batter and deep fry.

Champignons Farcis Fill sauted open mushrooms with duxelles; sprinkle with breadcrumbs and butter and gratinate.

Chausson aux Noix Make nutmeat turnovers with puff pastry and bake or deep fry.

Ciernikis Mould 4cm cakes of cottage cheese, flour, butter and eggs; poach in salted water and serve sprinkled with melted butter.

Galettes Mould 4cm rounds of grated cheese and duchesse potato mixture; flour and shallow fry.

Galettes Briarde Mould puree of brie cheese and eggs into 4cm rounds; coat with flour and shallow fry.

Gorgonzola Frit Wrap small cubes of gorgonzola in thin rashers of bacon, dip in batter and deep fry; Roquefort and other kinds of cheese can also be prepared in this way.

Gougère Bourgui Fill small chou buns with finely grated Gruyère cheese mixed with cream.

Mazagrans Line buttered tartlet moulds with duchesse po-

41

	tato; fill with grated cheese mixed with cream, cover with a round of duchesse potato and bake in the oven.
Millefeuilles	Sandwich 3 pieces of baked puff pastry with any kind of savoury fillings and decorate the top
Nalesnikis	Wrap 60g pieces of mixed cottage cheese, butter and egg in thin pancakes, dip into batter and deep fry.
Oeufs à la Christiana	Place a cooked quails' egg in a glazed nest of duchesse potato, coat with demi-glace flavoured with foie gras and sprinkle with chopped truffle.
Perles Suisse	Pipe small balls of chou paste containing finely diced Gruyère cheese and bake until crisp and golden brown.
Petits Choux au fromage	Bake small balls of chou paste until nearly cooked; cut open, fill with cheese soufflé mixture and return to the oven until cooked.
Piroguis Caucasien	Spread cheese-flavoured chou paste thinly into 2 baking trays; bake, then spread with cooked sliced mushroom mixed with reduced béchamel and grated cheese; cover with the other piece of pastry, cut into small oblongs, coat with egg-wash and breadcrumbs and deep fry.
Piroguis en Croissants	Mix rye breadcrumbs with melted butter and veal gravy to a stiff paste, spread 6mm thick and cut into crescents; sandwich two of these together with cream cheese mixed with butter and egg, and shallow fry.
Piroguis au Fromage	Line dariole moulds with brioche paste, fill with a mixture of cream cheese, butter and egg and cover with a round of brioche paste; allow to prove then bake for 20 minutes in a hot oven.
Piroguis aux Légumes	Fill 5cm rounds of puff pastry with a mixture of finely diced cooked vegetables, hardboiled egg and rice, bound with béchamel; cover with a second round of pastry, egg-wash and bake in a hot oven.
Piroguis Livoniens	Mix rye breadcrumbs with melted butter and veal gravy to a stiff paste, spread 6mm thick and

cut into 4cm rounds; shallow fry and sprinkle with parmesan and buckwheat breadcrumbs.

Piroguis de Smolensk Fill 5cm squares of puff pastry with a mixture of semolina puree, sieved hard boiled egg and sauted onion, heated in butter; cover with a second square of pastry, seal well, egg-wash and bake in a hot oven.

Pommes à l'Ardennaise Fill halves of emptied baked potatoes with a mixture of potato pulp, butter, diced ham, chopped mushroom, egg yolks and parmesan; smooth the surface, sprinkle with cheese and gratinate.

Pommes Dietrich Fill whole emptied baked potatoes with small cheese-flavoured potato gnocchi mixed with grated white truffle and cream sauce; cover with the tops of the potato and reheat in the oven.

Quichelettes Lorraine Line small flat tartlet cases with short-pastry, add fried lardons of bacon, small pieces of Gruyère and fill with raw egg and cream custard; bake in a moderate oven until set.

Ramequins Pipe small bulbs of chou paste containing finely grated and diced Gruyère cheese; egg-wash, sprinkle with chopped Gruyère and bake.

Ramequins can also be made with soaked breadcrumbs, butter, eggs, cheshire or parmesan cheese, moulded into small balls and baked.

Rissoles Bouquetière Fill 7cm rounds of puff pastry with small dice of cooked asparagus, carrot, turnip, French beans, and peas; fold over to seal and deep fry.

Sausselis au Chou Spread 6cm × 1cm strips of puff pastry with stewed finely shredded white cabbage mixed with sieved hard-boiled egg; cover with a second piece of pastry, egg-wash and bake in a moderate oven.

Soufflés Florentine Add finely chopped cooked spinach to reduced béchamel together with yolks and stiffly beaten whites; fill into buttered soufflé dishes and bake for 12 minutes.

Soufflés au Parmesan Soufflé mixture made with parmesan cheese, cooked in small soufflé dishes which have been buttered and coated with grated cheese.

Soufflés à la Suissesse	Fill buttered tartlet moulds with cheese-flavoured soufflé mixture and cook au bain-marie; when cooked, turn out into small dishes, sprinkle with parmesan, moisten half way up with cream and bake in the oven.
Subrics Piémontaise	Add some risotto to a batter of flour, eggs and cream and shallow fry spoonfuls in oil.
Talmouses	Pipe bulbs of chou paste containing grated and diced Gruyère cheese into tartlet moulds lined with short pastry; egg-wash, sprinkle with chopped Gruyère and bake.
Talmouses à l'Ancienne	Pipe bulbs of chou paste containing grated and diced Gruyère cheese in the centre of 10cm of short pastry, bring the corners to the centre in the shape of a tricorne hat, egg-wash and seal well then bake in a moderate oven; finish by filling the chou bun with cheese-flavoured pastry cream. These are also called Talmouses Bagration.
Tartelettes aux Gnocchi	Fill parcooked tartlets with small cheese-flavoured chou paste gnocchi mixed with béchamel; sprinkle with cheese and melted butter and bake in the oven.
Tartelettes Polonaise	Fill short pastry tartlets with cooked sauerkraut mixed with sieved hard boiled egg and rye breadcrumbs; cover with another round of pastry, seal well and make a small hole in the centre; bake for 20 minutes and finish by filling with demi-glace.
Timbales Talleyrand	Line buttered dariole moulds with bands of finely chopped chicken, ox-tongue and truffle; spread with forcemeat and fill with truffle puree; cover with more forcemeat and cook au bain-marie.
Varenikis Polonaise	Fill the centre of 5cm rounds of noodle pastry with cream cheese mixed with softened butter and egg; cover with a second round of pastry, seal well and poach in salted water for 15

minutes; drain and sprinkle with melted butter and serve with sour cream.

Vatrouskis au Fromage   Fill the centre of rounds of brioche paste with cream cheese mixed with butter and egg; fold over as a turnover, egg-wash, allow to prove, and bake in a moderate oven.

2   *SOUPS*

The wide range of soups is dealt with in the accepted professional categories which are

1. consommés
2. bouillons
3. broths
4. purée soups
5. potages
6. cream soups
7. veloutés

8. brown roux soups
9. tomato-based soups
10. thick game soups
11. bisques
12. foreign soups
13. cold soups

A definition of each category of soups is given before each recipe section.

It is usual to make stock for soups slightly different from those used to make sauces, by using less flavouring materials and more water for soup stock but cooking it more slowly and for a longer time so that it does not take on too much character. Old recipes sometimes use the word consommé when they mean very clear but unclarified soup stock. Today it is accepted that consommé is a finished soup in its own right. Bouillon is the name given both to the basic stock and to a finished soup.

———— CONSOMMES ————

Consommé is made by clarifying soup stock, either beef, chicken or game and occasionally fish, duck or mutton, at the same time adding further flavour from the clarifying agent, vegetables and herbs.

To make 5 litres of basic beef consommé, mix 1kg minced beef with 2 egg whites, 250g chopped carrot, celery, leek and onion, seasoning and 6 litres cold stock; after bringing slowly to a boil it is left to simmer very gently for $1\frac{1}{2}$ hours. It is usual to strain the consommé through a double muslin and remove all traces of fat. Other flavours of consommé are made in the same way, using the appropriate stock and whenever possible, a clarifying agent in keeping with the finished soup.

Consommé Double is the same crystal clear soup as ordinary consommé but made with a richer stock and additional clarifying materials so that the soup acquires extra flavour and becomes slightly sticky on the lips even before any arrowroot is added.

The finishing, garnishing and serving of consommé entails the following.

1. Many consommés are served slightly thickened by adding 50g seed tapioca or diluted arrowroot per 5 litres when finishing the consommé; it is then re-strained.
2. It is advisable to keep the garnish separate until adding it to the soup at the time of service.
3. Sprigs of chervil (pluches de cerfeuil) can be added to all ordinary consommés, in addition to the garnishes as listed.
4. Royale is a popular garnish for consommé; it is savoury egg custard cooked in moulds au bain-marie until set, then cooled, turned out and cut into shapes. The flavoured royales are made with 100g cooked puree and 3 yolks plus a little stock or sauce as appropriate.
5. Where quenelles are part of a garnish, they are made by piping or moulding chicken forcemeat into very small shapes, using a 4mm tube or coffee spoons, and poaching in salted water.
6. Small Italian pastas are cooked whole, long ones like spaghetti should be broken into approximately 2cm lengths and cooked separately.
7. All garnishes should be small enough to go onto a soup spoon and be cooked, but still firm enough to be recognisable.
8. Profiteroles are often served separately as an accompaniment; they are made by piping unsweetened chou paste in 5mm balls. and baking until crisp. They are sometimes filled with a puree but are more often served as they are.

9. Cheese straws – long, round, circular, etc., can be served with most consommés, particularly the turtle consommés.
10. Madeira, port or sherry is often added to enhance the flavour of consommé, adding it just before serving; it is advisable to use the dry types of these wines.
11. Diablotins are very small rounds of toasted cheese on bread, well seasoned with cayenne pepper and served as an accompaniment.
12. It is customary to serve consommé in the traditional shallow two-handled consommé cups.

In the following, consommés are listed according to their flavour i.e. beef, chicken, game, mutton, fish.

Beef Consommés

Africaine	Garnish with rice and dice of artichoke bottoms; serve with any flavoured profiteroles.
d'Aremburg or d'Arenburg	Garnish with small balls of carrot, turnip and truffle, and with peas.
Arlequin	Garnish with three different kinds of royale – ordinary, spinach and tomato and with short pieces of vermicelli.
Arlequin	Garnish with julienne of very green cabbage, and garden peas.
Baron Brisse	Garnish with small dice of three kinds of royale – ordinary, spinach and truffle, and with rice.
Belle Fermière	Garnish with julienne of cabbage, diced French beans, and small lengths of pasta.
Berny	Thicken with tapioca and accompany with small dauphine potatoes containing almond and truffle, served in a dish separately.
Bismarck	Thicken with arrowroot, garnish with diced hard cheese and mushroom and flavour with port.
Bonne Femme	Garnish with julienne of carrot and leek and with diced potato.
Bouchère	Garnish with slices of bone marrow and accompany with very small braised stuffed cabbages.
Bouquetière	Thicken the consommé with tapioca; garnish

	with very small spring carrots and turnips, diamonds of French beans, peas, and florets of cauliflower.
Braganza	Garnish with small dice of four kinds of royale – ordinary or carrot, spinach, tomato and truffle, also with small balls of cucumber and seed tapioca.
Brésilienne	Garnish with julienne of carrot, celery, leek, red pimento and turnip, and with boiled rice
Breton	Garnish with julienne of celeriac, leek and mushroom.
Carlton	Garnish with dice of ordinary royale, and quenelles; serve with cheese-flavoured profiteroles.
Carmen	Make the consommé with the flavour of tomato and pimento; garnish with diced tomato, julienne of pimento, rice and sprigs of chervil
Catalane	Garnish with diced tomato and green pepper, and boiled rice.
Cauchoise	Garnish with dice of bacon and mutton, and small slices of carrot, celery, leek and turnip, cooked glacé.
Célestine	Garnish with julienne of very thin pancakes made with fines herbes in the mixture.
Cendrillon	Garnish with julienne of truffle and with rice.
Chancelière	Garnish with rounds of pea-flavoured royale and julienne of chicken, mushroom and truffle.
Charivari	Garnish with julienne of cabbage, carrot, celeriac, onion and turnip, cooked glacé.
Chartreuse	Thicken with tapioca and garnish each portion with three small ravioli – one filled with foie gras, one with spinach and the other with duxelles.
Cherbourgeoise	Garnish with ham-flavoured quenelles, julienne of mushroom and truffle, and a small poached egg per portion.
Choiseul	Garnish with fancy shapes of ordinary royale and asparagus tips.
Claremont	Garnish with rounds of ordinary royale.
Clothilde	Garnish with very tiny button onions.

Colbert	Garnish with paysanne of vegetables and one small poached egg per portion.
Czarina	Flavour the consommé with fennel and garnish with diced vésiga.
Daumont	Thicken with tapioca; garnish with julienne of beef and mushrooms, and boiled rice.
Deslignac	Thicken with tapioca and garnish with diced royale and small rounds of lettuce stuffed with chicken puree.
Don Carlos	Garnish with ordinary royale and tomato flesh cut into dice, and boiled rice.
Dubarry	Thicken with tapioca, garnish with round pieces of royale and small sprigs of cauliflower.
Dumesnil	Garnish with julienne of vegetables and slices of bone marrow.
Dumont	Garnish with julienne of cabbage, mushroom and ox-tongue.
Edouard VII	Flavour the consommé with curry; garnish with pearl barley, diced mutton and diced carrot, celery, leek and turnip.
Elizabeth	Garnish with julienne of leek, short pieces of vermicelli, and diced artichoke bottoms; serve parmesan cheese separately.
Fermière	Garnish with julienne of carrot and turnip and with diced potato.
Flamande	Garnish with dice of sprout-flavoured royale and peas.
Franklin	Garnish with small balls of carrot and turnip, and dice of ordinary royale; serve with profiteroles.
Garibaldi	Thicken with tapioca and garnish with small pieces of spaghetti.
Germinal	Flavour the consommé with tarragon; garnish with asparagus tips, diced French beans, peas and quenelles containing fines herbes.
Girondine	Garnish with round pieces of royale, diced ham and julienne of carrot.
Grenade	Flavour the consommé with tomato; garnish with tomato-flavoured royale, diced carrot, turnip and tomato.

Grimaldi	Flavour the consommé with tomato, garnish with diced royale and julienne of celery.
Gutenberg	Garnish with asparagus tips, diced mushroom, peas, small rounds of carrot and turnip, and thin slices of Frankfurter sausage.
Henriette	Flavour the consommé with curry; garnish with dice of ordinary royale and a small poached egg per person; serve with parmesan cheese.
Irma	Garnish with julienne of mushroom and with curry-flavoured quenelles.
Italienne	Garnish with tomato-flavoured royale and spinach-flavoured royale cut into dice, and small pieces of spaghetti; serve with parmesan cheese
Jacobine	Garnish with diced carrot, French beans, turnip and truffle, and peas.
Julienne	Garnish with julienne of carrot, celery, leek and turnip, and shredded sorrel.
Kléber	Garnish with small balls of carrot and potato, peas and dice of salt brisket of beef.
Leo XIII	Garnish with ordinary royale cut into crowns and crosses.
de Lesseps	Garnish with dice of royale made with calf's brain.
Lilloise	Flavour the consommé with tarragon and chervil; garnish with julienne of mushroom and truffle and serve with salted almonds.
Londonderry	Thicken the consommé with tapioca and garnish with diced calf's head and quenelles; flavour with dry Madeira before serving.
Londres	Flavour the consommé with turtle herbs and garnish with diced calf's head and with rice.
Longchamp	Garnish with julienne of sorrel and vermicelli.
Lord Chesterfield	Flavour with turtle herbs; garnish with three kinds of quenelles – chicken, crayfish and truffle, and finish with sherry.
Lucette	Garnish with small Italian pastes and serve with a small poached egg per person.
Lucullus	Flavour with quail; garnish with breasts of quails, julienne of truffle, and quenelles; serve with small foie gras patties.

Macdonald	Garnish with royale made with calf's brain, with diced cucumber and very small ravioli.
Macédoine	Garnish with small dice of carrot, French beans and turnip, and with peas.
Madrilène	Flavour the consommé with pimento, celery, and tomato; garnish with dice of tomato and red pimento and with rice.
Marquise	Garnish with tomato-flavoured quenelles, shredded lettuce and julienne of truffle.
Marie-Stuart	Thicken with tapioca and garnish with quenelles decorated with truffle.
Médicis	Thicken with tapioca; garnish with tomato-flavoured royale cut into dice, and shredded sorrel.
Meissonier	Garnish with dice of artichoke bottom and of tomato, and with peas.
Mercédès	Flavour with dry sherry; garnish with small rings of red pimento and cockscombs.
Mirette	Garnish with quenelles and julienne of lettuce.
Molière	Garnish with quenelles made with the addition of breadcrumbs, eggs, shallot and parsley; serve accompanied with small portions of bone marrow on toast.
Mona Lisa	Garnish with quenelles and peas.
Monselet	Garnish with julienne of ox-tongue, with peas and slices of bone marrow.
Montesquieu	Garnish with julienne of chicken, ham and mushroom, and with florets of cauliflower.
Nansen	Add a little vodka to the consommé and serve it with small canapés of caviar.
Napolitaine	Flavour the consommé with tomato; garnish with julienne of celeriac and ham and short lengths of macaroi; serve with parmesan cheese
New York	Garnish with dice of onion-flavoured royale and tomato royale, and with quenelles made of game flesh.
Nivernaise	Garnish with small balls of carrot and turnip, and with dice of onion-flavoured royale.
Olga	Flavour the consommé with port and garnish with julienne of carrot, celeriac, gherkin and leek.

Orléanaise	Garnish with dice of Belgian endive-flavoured royale, dice of French beans, and with flageolet beans.
Otéro	Garnish Consommé Madrilène with frogs' legs and peas; serve with paprika-flavoured puff-pastry straws.
de Queue de Boeuf	Garnish with small balls of carrot and turnip and with small pieces of oxtail; flavour with dry Madeira.
Palestine	Garnish with small balls of carrot and turnip, diced French beans, and peas.
Palestro	Garnish with julienne of carrot, celery, leek, lettuce and turnip, and with dice of tomato-flavoured royale.
La Perouse	Thicken the consommé with tapioca; garnish with peas, and a small poached egg per person
Pierre le Grand	Garnish with julienne of celery, lettuce and turnip.
Petrarque	Garnish with julienne of leek and serve with toasted pistachio nuts and with diablotins.
Picard	Garnish with julienne of leek.
Piémontaise	Flavour and colour the consommé with saffron; garnish with rice and diced ham, tomato and white truffle.
Polignac	Garnish with small rounds of forcemeat containing ox-tongue and truffle.
Portalis	Flavour the consommé with saffron and tomato; garnish with spaghetti and serve with parmesan cheese.
Portugaise	Flavour the consommé with tomato; garnish with rice and tomato flesh cut into dice.
Raphaël	Garnish with diced celeriac.
Raspail	Garnish with asparagus tips and quenelles.
Remusat	Garnish with three kinds of quenelles – carrot, spinach and tomato.
Richelieu	Garnish with quenelles, small rounds of lettuce filled with chicken puree, and julienne of carrot and turnip.
Robespierre	Flavour the consommé with tomato and serve it without any garnish.

Soups

Royale Add a garnish of ordinary egg royale, cut into various shapes.

St-Germain Garnish with julienne of lettuce and with peas and quenelles.

Sévillaise Flavour the consommé with tomato and thicken with tapioca; garnish with diced tomato-flavoured royale.

Solange Garnish with pearl barley, squares of lettuce and julienne of chicken.

Solferino Garnish with small balls of carrot, potato and turnip.

Toscane Garnish with dice of eggplant, mushroom and tomato and with small pieces of macaroni.

Vaudoise Garnish with dice of beef, carrot and turnip and serve accompanied with grated Gruyère cheese and sliced French bread.

Vénitienne Flavour the consommé with herbs; garnish with rice and serve with a dish of gratinated gnocchi italienne.

Verdi Garnish with short lengths of macaroni and three kinds of quenelles – ordinary, spinach and tomato.

Véron Flavour with truffle liquor and port; garnish with julienne of pimento and diced flageolet bean royale.

Vert-Pré Thicken with tapioca; garnish with asparagus tips, diamonds of French beans, and julienne of lettuce and sorrel.

VGE (Valéry Giscard d'Estaign) Garnish with plenty of sliced truffle, place in cups, cover with puff pastry and bake in the oven.

Victor Emmanuel Garnish with diced tomato and very short pieces of macaroni, and serve with parmesan cheese.

Viennoise Make the consommé with paprika; garnish with julienne of cheese-flavoured pancakes and serve accompanied by a dish of small gnocchi romaine.

Windsor Use calf's feet in making the consommé and flavour it with turtle herbs; garnish with julienne of calf's feet, chicken quenelles and sieved hard-boiled egg yolk.

Xavier	Thicken the consommé with arrowroot; garnish with julienne of pancake and flavour with Madeira.

Chicken Consommés

Adèle	Garnish with peas, small balls of carrot and quenelles.
Adelina Patti	Garnish with diced chestnut-flavoured royale, with peas and small balls of carrot.
Albion	Garnish with asparagus tips, quenelles, cock-scombs and julienne of truffle.
Alexandre	Thicken with tapioca; garnish with quenelles and julienne of chicken and lettuce.
Ambassadeur	Garnish with round pieces of truffle-flavoured royale, dice of mushroom and diced chicken.
Ambassadrice	Garnish with dice of three different royales – pea, tomato, and truffle, also diced chicken and mushroom.
Aurore	Flavour with tomato and thicken the consommé with tapioca; garnish with julienne of chicken.
Behague	Serve the consommé with a small poached egg in each cup.
Bellini	Serve accompanied with a dish of gratinated small gnocchis made of semolina.
Boïeldieu	Garnish with three different kinds of quenelles – chicken, foie gras and truffle.
Bonaparte	Garnish with ordinary chicken quenelles.
Bourbon	Thicken with tapioca; garnish with quenelles decorated with lilies cut from truffle.
Bourdaloue	Garnish with dice of four different royales – asparagus, carrot, chicken and tomato.
Briande	Garnish with dice of chicken, ham and veal.
Brieux	Thicken with sago; garnish with rounds of pistachio royale and truffle royale, and small balls of truffle.
Brillat-Savarin	Flavour the consommé with celery and thicken with arrowroot; garnish with julienne of carrot, mushroom and truffle.

Britannia	Garnish with triangular shapes of tomato royale, asparagus tips, julienne of truffle, and quenelles made of foie gras.
des Capucines	Garnish with julienne of lettuce and spinach; serve with chicken-filled profiteroles.
Carême	Garnish with asparagus tips, rounds of carrot and turnip, and julienne of lettuce.
Caroline	Garnish with almond-flavoured royale cut into dice, and plain boiled rice.
Cavour	Garnish with short lengths of macaroni and with peas and serve with a dish of deep-fried strands of pancake batter.
Cendrillon	Garnish with boiled rice and julienne of truffle
Châtelaine	Thicken with tapioca; garnish with dice of onion and artichoke royale, and quenelles.
Cheveux d'Anges	Add very fine vermicelli just before sering, it will cook in the heat of the consommé.
Chevreuse	Garnish with rounds of two kinds of royale – chicken and semolina, and julienne of chicken and truffle.
Christoph Colomb	Flavour the consommé with tomato and thicken it with tapioca; garnish with dice of tomato royale and quenelles.
Cincinnati	Garnish with small balls of carrot, turnip and potato; serve with profiteroles filled with chicken puree.
Cléopâtre	Garnish with dice of tomato flesh.
Colombine	Garnish with small balls of carrot and turnip, julienne of pigeon flesh and a small poached egg per person.
Comtesse	Thicken with tapioca; garnish with asparagus tips, decorated quenelles and julienne of lettuce.
Dame Blanche	Thicken with tapioca; garnish with dice of almond royale and with white of chicken cut star shape.
Dante	Garnish with julienne of ox-tongue and truffle and with saffron-coloured quenelles.
Daudet	Garnish with lobster quenelles, julienne of celeriac, and with dice of two royales – chicken and ham.

Delavergne	Garnish with asparagus tips, dice of ordinary royale and a small soft boiled egg per portion.
Delriche	Garnish with vermicelli and with slices of bone marrow.
Demidoff	Garnish with small balls of carrot, truffle and turnip, and with quenelles containing fines herbes.
Dijonnaise	Thicken with tapioca; garnish with quenelles made of game and with juliénne of ox-tongue.
Diplomat	Thicken with tapioca; garnish with rounds of chicken forcemeat flavoured with crayfish, and julienne of truffle.
Diva	Garnish with dice of lobster-flavoured royale, and with a fairly large quenelle previously decorated with truffle.
Divette	Garnish with rounds of crayfish-flavoured royale, quenelles made of fish and with small dice of truffle.
Dolores	Garnish with rice flavoured and coloured with saffron and with julienne of chicken.
Dominicaine	Garnish with julienne of chicken and small shapes of pasta; serve accompanied with parmesan cheese.
Doria	Garnish with paysanne of carrot, cucumber, leek and turnip and small pieces of macaroni filled with quenelle mixture; serve with profiteroles.
Douglas	Garnish with small round pieces of veal sweetbread and artichoke bottom, and with asparagus tips.
Dubourg	Garnish with dice of chicken-flavoured royale, and boiled rice.
Duchesse	Garnish with tapioca, plain egg royale and julienne of lettuce.
Dupré	Garnish with small balls of carrot and turnip, and with quenelles.
Duse	Garnish with tomato-flavoured quenelles and with two or more small fancy shapes of soup pasta.
Edouard VII	Flavour the consommé with curry; garnish with rice and serve with small chicken patties

57

Emmanuel	Garnish with dice of tomato-flavoured royale, julienne of chicken, and small pieces of spaghetti; serve with parmesan cheese.
des Epicuriens	Garnish with shredded almonds.
Favorite	Thicken with tapioca; garnish with small balls of potato, and julienne of artichoke bottom and mushroom.
Fédéral	Garnish with small rounds of ordinary royale and with small slices of truffle.
Flavigny	Garnish with rice, julienne of chicken, and small morels.
Fleury	Garnish with peas and small flat quenelles.
Florial	Garnish with pistachio-flavoured quenelles, asparagus tips, small balls of carrot and turnip, and peas.
Florentine	Garnish with three kinds of quenelles – chicken, spinach and ox-tongue.
Florian	Garnish with bâtons of carrot and turnip, diamonds of beans, peas, and a small poached egg per portion.
Francatelli	Garnish with quenelles made of foie gras, dice of chicken royale, and cockscombs and kidneys.
Frou-Frou	Garnish with small balls of carrot and serve with profiteroles.
Gabrielle	Garnish with dice of chicken royale, diced crayfish and a soft boiled egg yolk per portion.
Gauloise	Garnish with dice of ham-flavoured royale and with cockscombs and kidneys.
Germaine	Garnish with dice of carrot and turnip, rounds of pea-flavoured royale and quenelles.
Gouffé	Thicken with tapioca; garnish with julienne of chicken, ox-tongue and truffle and pour in beaten egg yolk to cook in the consommé.
Gourmet	Garnish with small rounds of forcemeat, dice of game flesh, foie gras and ox-tongue, and chopped pistachio nuts.
Grande Duchesse	Garnish with asparagus tips, julienne of chicken and tongue and with quenelles.
Hélène	Flavour the consommé with tomato; garnish with small rounds of ordinary royale and serve with cheese-flavoured profiteroles.

Impériale	Garnish with round pieces of royale, asparagus tips and small cockscombs.
Indienne	Make the consommé with curry; garnish with coconut milk royale and rice.
Infante	Thicken with tapioca; garnish with rice and julienne of red pimento.
Isabelle de France	Garnish with julienne of truffle, quenelles and peas.
Isoline	Garnish with quenelles flavoured with asparagus, and julienne of chicken, mushroom and truffle.
Ivan	Make the consommé with the addition of beet-root juice; garnish with rice and serve with small duck patties.
Jacqueline	Garnish with asparagus tips, peas, slices of grooved carrot cooked glacé, and with dice of ordinary royale.
Jean Granier	Garnish with small crayfish tails and rice.
Jockey Club	Garnish with dice of royales of three flavours – carrot, chicken and pea.
Johore	Flavour the consommé with curry; garnish with dice of curry-flavoured royale, rice and julienne of chicken.
Juanita	Garnish with diced tomato royale and sieved hard boiled egg yolk.
Judic	Garnish with small rounds of lettuce stuffed with chicken, julienne of mushroom, and quenelles.
Julia	Thicken the consommé with tapioca; garnish with diced royale and serve with profiteroles.
Juliette	Garnish with julienne of hard boiled egg white, small dice of spinach-flavoured royale and quenelles.
Lafite	Garnish with julienne of mushroom and truffle, small balls of cucumber, cockscombs and kidneys, and small stoned and blanched green olives.
Lorette	Flavour the consommé with pimento; garnish with asparagus tips, julienne of truffle and serve a dish of small Pommes Lorette separately.
Madeleine	Garnish with dice of celery, julienne of lettuce and oval quenelles. Serve with profiteroles.

Magenta	Thicken with tapioca; garnish with quenelles containing chopped truffle, dice of tomato and julienne of mushroom and truffle.
Maria	Thicken with tapioca; garnish with rounds of royale made with French beans and small squares of carrot, celery, leek and turnip.
Marie-Louise	Garnish with peas and dice of ordinary royale
Margot	Garnish with some chicken quenelles and some spinach quenelles.
Marigny	Garnish with julienne of cucumber, peas and quenelles.
Marly	Garnish with julienne of celery, chicken, leek and lettuce and serve with toasted croûtons sprinkled with cheese.
Messaline	Flavour the consommé with tomato; garnish with julienne of pimento, small cockscombs and rice.
Midinette	Thicken the consommé with tapioca; garnish with one small poached egg per person.
Mikado	Flavour the consommé with tomato; garnish with diced chicken and tomato flesh.
Milanaise	Flavour with tomato; garnish with small pieces of spaghetti and julienne of ham, mushroom and truffle and serve parmesan cheese separately.
Mimosa	Garnish with dice of three kinds of royale – ordinary, carrot and pea.
Mireille	Garnish with tomato-flavoured forcemeat cut into oval shapes, and saffron-flavoured rice.
Mogador	Thicken with tapioca; garnish with foie gras-flavoured royale and small rounds of chicken, ox-tongue and truffle.
Monaco	Garnish with small balls of carrot, turnip and truffle and serve with profiteroles.
Monsigny	Garnish with cockscombs, rice and squares of lettuce.
Monte-Carlo	Garnish with paysanne of carrot, turnip and truffle and julienne of savoury pancake made with fines herbes.
Montespan	Garnish with julienne of truffle and one moulded crayfish mousseline per person; serve with patties each containing a stuffed bunting or quail.

Murillo	Garnish with flat vermicelli and diced tomato flesh.
Nana	Arrange sliced French bread and grated cheese in the soup bowls, pour the very hot consommé over and add one poached egg to each.
Nantaise	Garnish with peas, pearl barley and julienne of chicken.
Nantua	Garnish with asparagus tips, cockscombs and kidneys; serve with rounds of forcemeat, each with a crayfish on it, coated with Sauce Nantua and cheese and gratinated.
Napoleon	Garnish with small triangular ravioli filled with foie gras.
Nemours	Thicken with tapioca; garnish with diced carrot and truffle, and dice of carrot-flavoured royale.
Niçoise	Flavour the consommé with tomato; garnish with dice of French beans, potato and tomato.
Nilson	Thicken with tapioca; garnish with quenelles made with ham, peas, dice of truffle, and chopped chives.
Ninon	Garnish with small balls of carrot, turnip and truffle; serve with a small tartlet made of forcemeat, filled with chicken puree and decorated with a star cut from truffle.
Noailles	Garnish with dice of artichoke royale, and julienne of chicken and tongue.
d'Orléans	Thicken with tapioca; garnish with three different kinds of quenelles – chicken, spinach and tomato.
d'Orsay	Garnish with asparagus tips, pigeon quenelles, julienne of pigeon and a poached yolk of egg per portion.
Othello	Flavour the consommé with tomato; serve accompanied with a dish of risotto à la piémontaise with the addition of grated white truffle.
Palermo	Garnish with dice of tomato royale, dice of chicken, and spaghetti; serve with parmesan cheese.
Parisienne	Garnish with carrot royale and turnip royale cut into dice, and diced carrot and turnip.

Pascale	Garnish with dice of carrot and turnip royale, peas and chopped green fennel leaves.
Polaire	Thicken with tapioca; place a raw egg yolk in each cup as the soup is served.
Pompadour	Garnish with quenelles, crayfish, and julienne of celery and truffle.
Prince de Galles	Garnish with quenelles containing chopped truffle, and asparagus tips.
Princesse	Garnish with dice of pea-flavoured royale, pearl barley, and julienne of chicken.
Princesse Alice	Thicken with tapioca; garnish with julienne of artichoke bottom, chicken and lettuce.
Printanière	Garnish with small bâtons of carrot and turnip, with peas, and diced asparagus tips.
Rachel	Garnish with small rounds of asparagus royale and chicken royale and serve with cheese-flavoured profiteroles.
Récamier	Garnish with asparagus tips, julienne of truffle and birds' nests; serve with crayfish patties.
Réjane	Garnish with dice of carrot royale and hazelnut royale and just before serving, pour well-beaten eggs through a strainer into the very hot consommé.
Rembrandt	Garnish with pea-flavoured royale, and dice of chicken.
Reine	Thicken with tapioca; garnish with diced chicken royale and julienne of chicken.
Renaissance	Garnish with pieces of ordinary royale, and small balls of carrot and turnip.
Riche	Garnish with quenelles containing chopped truffle.
Richepin	Garnish with julienne of carrot and turnip, small rounds of stuffed lettuce and quenelles.
Rossini	Flavour the consommé with truffle liquor and thicken with tapioca; serve with profiteroles filled with truffled foie gras.
Royale	Garnish with ordinary royale cut into any shapes
Rubens	Flavour the consommé with tomato and garnish with small pieces of hop shoots.

Saint-Saëns	Garnish with small balls of potato and pearl barley.
San Remo	Garnish with small rounds of carrot, plain boiled rice, and serve accompanied with parmesan.
Sans-Gène	Garnish with cockscombs and kidneys and julienne of truffle.
Santa-Maria	Flavour the consommé with tarragon; garnish with vermicelli and quenelles and serve with profiteroles filled with duxelles.
Sarah Bernhardt	Flavour with turtle herbs and thicken with tapioca; garnish with tomato-flavoured quenelles and slices of bone marrow.
Ségurd	Garnish with julienne of chicken and ox-tongue.
Séverine	Garnish with small balls of cucumber and potato, peas and rice.
Sévigné	Garnish with asparagus tips, quenelles and julienne of lettuce.
Soubrette	Flavour with tomato; garnish with shrimps and quenelles decorated with a ring of truffle.
Souveraine	Garnish with quenelles and small dice of carrot, celery, leek and turnip.
Staël	Garnish with peas and a small poached pigeon's egg per person; serve accompanied with cheese-flavoured profiteroles.
Stanley	Garnish with curry-flavoured quenelles, rice, and julienne of mushroom and truffle.
Surprise	Flavour the consommé with beetroot; garnish with small quenelles with a small piece of very red chicken jelly in the centre.
Talleyrand	Garnish with dice of truffle, cockscombs and squares of partridge flesh.
Talma	Garnish with dice of almond royale and boiled rice.
Tchèque	Garnish with peas, diced chicken and tomato, and julienne of pancake.
Théodore	Garnish with asparagus tips, flageolet beans, and diced chicken.
Toreador	Garnish with peas, rice, diced tomato flesh and very small chipolata sausages.

63

Tosca	Flavour the consommé with turtle herbs, garnish with julienne of leeks and serve with profiteroles filled with chicken; add Madeira wine before serving.
Trévise	Garnish with julienne of chicken, ox-tongue and truffle.
Trianon	Thicken with tapioca and garnish with small rounds of three kinds of royale – carrot, chicken and spinach.
Turbigo	Garnish with short lengths of vermicelli, julienne of carrot and of chicken.
Valencienne	Garnish with quenelles and julienne of lettuce
Valentino	Garnish with heart-shape quenelles, julienne of chicken and truffle.
Valromey	Garnish with cockscombs, julienne of truffle, and dice of crayfish royale
Vermandoise	Thicken with seed tapioca, garnish with asparagus tips, diamonds of French beans, peas, and small rounds of lettuce and sorrel.
Villeneuve	Garnish with dice of ordinary royale, small square pieces of lettuce sandwiched with puree of chicken and tongue, and triangles of pancake sandwiched with puree of ham.
Vivian	Garnish with small rounds of chicken and truffle
des Viveurs	Flavour the consommé with duck, beetroot and celery; garnish with julienne of celery and serve with diablotins.
Voltaire	Garnish with quenelles, and diced chicken and diced tomato flesh.
Wladimir	Serve accompanied with a dish of gratinated cheese quenelles made from cream cheese, butter, yolks, flour and cream and the whisked whites of egg.
Yvette	Flavour with turtle herbs and garnish with spinach-coloured quenelles.
Zingara	Garnish with pieces of three different kinds of royale – ordinary, carrot and pea.
Zorilla	Flavour the consommé with tomato and garnish with rice and chick peas.

Game and Duck Consommés

Anjou   Garnish with asparagus tips, rice and with quenelles made of any game.

d'Artagnan   Garnish with julienne of game and peas.

Castellane   Flavour with woodcock; garnish with dice of green pimento and tomato and with rice.

Chasseur   Flavour with port; garnish with julienne of mushrooms and serve with profiteroles filled with puree of game.

Cussy   Garnish with diced chestnut and game royale, julienne of truffle and game quenelles; flavour with brandy.

Cyrano   Duck flavoured consommé; serve with a dish of gratinated small duck quenelles.

Czarevitch   Garnish with julienne of truffle and quenelles of hazelhen; flavour with sherry.

Danoise   Wild duck-flavoured consommé; garnish with diced mushroom and game quenelles and serve with the addition of Marsala.

Diane   Pheasant-flavoured consommé; garnish with pearl barley, julienne of celery and pheasant quenelles.

Georges V   Pheasant-flavoured consommé; garnish with julienne of celery, pearl barley, and pheasant quenelles containing truffle.

Jenny Lind   Flavour with quails; garnish with julienne of quail and mushroom.

Laguipierre   Garnish with game quenelles and serve with a poached pigeon's egg per person.

Maintenon   Flavour with partridge; garnish with partridge quenelles containing truffle, rice and cockscombs

Mancelle   Garnish with dice of game royale and pieces of chestnut.

Metternich   Flavour with pheasant; garnish with dice of artichoke royale and julienne of pheasant

Nesselrode   Flavour with hazel-hen; garnish with julienne of dried mushroom and hazel-hen and rounds of chestnut royale.

Soups

Rabelais Flavour with partridge; garnish with partridge quenelles and julienne of truffle; serve with cheese-flavoured profiteroles.

Rohan Garnish with julienne of lettuce and add a small poached game egg per person; serve with toast spread with puree of game.

Rothschild Flavour with pheasant; garnish with pheasant and chestnut royale cut into dice, and julienne of bunting or other small bird and truffle; finish with sauternes wine.

St-Georges Flavour with hare; garnish with game quenelles and julienne of truffle; finish with port wine.

St-Hubert Garnish with dice of game and lentil royale, and diced game flesh.

Sappho Flavour with partridge; garnish with partridge quenelles, a short julienne of truffle and of cucumber.

Tyrolienne Flavour with partridge and tomato; garnish with julienne of partridge and very thin noodles; serve with parmesan cheese.

d'Uze Flavour with hare; garnish with hare quenelles, pearl barley, and diced carrot.

Mutton Consommés

Ecossaise Garnish with brunoise of vegetables, diced mutton and pearl barley.

Egyptienne Flavour with saffron; garnish with dice of egg-plant and okra and with rice.

Orientale Flavour with saffron and tomato; garnish with crescent shapes of brain royale, rice and sieved yolk of hard-boiled egg.

Pondicherry Flavour with curry; garnish with rice and julienne of pancake.

Tewki Pasha Flavour with pimento and tomato; garnish with julienne of green and red pimento and with rice.

Tunisienne Flavour with saffron; garnish with dice of green pimento and tomato, and with chick peas and rice.

Fish Consommés

Amiral	Garnish with dice of lobster and mushroom, quenelles and rice.
Cancalaise	Thicken with tapioca; garnish with oysters, quenelles and small strips of fish.
Cardinale	Flavour with lobster; garnish with quenelles of lobster.
Carmelite	Thicken with arrowroot; garnish with rice and quenelles.
Dufferin	Flavour with curry; garnish with curry-flavoured quenelles, rice and with small strips of fish.
George Sand	Garnish with diced morels and crayfish quenelles; serve with croûtons spread with carp roe.
Lady Morgan	Garnish with julienne of mushroom and truffle, crayfish quenelles, oysters and small strips of fish.
Mignon	Garnish with quenelles, shrimps, and small balls of truffle.
Moldave	Flavour with pickled cucumber brine; garnish with dice of sturgeon and vésiga, and julienne of mushroom; flavour with Madeira.
Murillo	Flavour with tomato; garnish with thin noodles and diced tomato.
Nelson	Thicken with arrowroot; garnish with rice and serve with profiteroles filled with lobster puree.
Ostendaise	Garnish with oysters.
Pêcheurs	Garnish with mussels, peas, and diced tomato flesh.
Polignac	Garnish with diced mushroom and lobster quenelles.
Potemkin	Garnish with julienne of carrot and celery and with asparagus tips.
Rivoli	Garnish with short lengths of spaghetti and quenelles.
Russe	Garnish with small balls of cucumber and with quenelles.
Vatel	Garnish with dice of fish and of lobster royale.
Victoria Regina	Flavour with lobster; garnish with asparagus tips

and small balls of truffle; serve with lobster patties.

Miscellaneous Consommés

In addition to all the classical garnishes there are many special consommés which take their name from a particular flavouring agent. It can be meat or a vegetable added to the clarifying materials, or a wine added after the consommé has been strained.

The following are the main ones:

Consommés à l'Essence de –	Caille
	Céleri
	Estragon
	Perdreau
	Piment
	Tomate
	Truffe
Consommés au Vin de –	Madère
	Marsala
	Porto
	Xérès

and any of the well known wines such as –

          Chablis
          Chambolle-Musigny
          Château Latour
          Clos de Vougeot
          Muscadet
          Musigny, etc.

Consommés au Liqueur de –	Bénédictine
	Calvados
	Chartreuse
	Danziger Goldwasser, etc.

Turtle Soup – Tortue Clair

Turtle soup is nowadays made in the same way as beef consommé, thickened to give an oily consistency by using arrowroot, and flavoured with garlic and turtle herbs to suggest an exotic provenance. Real turtle meat is added as garnish, in either canned or dried form. There are several variations on basic turtle soups as follows:

Potage aux Terrapines	Garnish with turtle meat and serve with slices of lemon and hard-boiled egg.
Green Turtle or *Tortue Vert*	This is ordinary turtle soup finished with sherry.
Lady Curzon	Serve the soup in cups, cover completely with a layer of curry-flavoured whipped cream and glaze under the salamander.
Sir James	Finish with Madeira and brandy.
Tortue Clair	Finish with Madeira; garnish with diced turtle meat and serve with milk punch.
Tortue Lié	Make it slightly thicker than usual and garnish with diced turtle.

Mock Turtle Soup – Fausse Tortue Claire
This soup is usually regarded as being a thick soup, indeed the recipe is included in the section on Roux Soups, but it can also be made as a consommé from stock derived from calf's head, flavoured with turtle herbs and thickened with arrowroot.

Balmoral	Garnish with quenelles and dice of calf's foot.
Dounou	Garnish with diced artichoke bottom and truffle, and with quenelles.
Fausse Tortue Claire	Garnish with diced calf's head and quenelles
Londinienne	Garnish with diced calf's head and rice.
Windsor	Garnish with julienne of calf's foot.

———— BOUILLONS ————

Bouillon is a clear soup that is garnished with meat and vegetables. It originates from the housewife's stockpot in which she cooked joints of meat and fowls with vegetables, serving the liquid as a nourishing soup followed by the meat and vegetables as a main dish. Bouillon differs from consommé in that it is not clarified but it must be kept crystal clear by slow cooking and constant skimming. It should have a pronounced flavour of meat and vegetables and be free from fat. The bread for use with bouillons should be the long thin bread called flûtes.

It is usual to serve bouillon in earthenware soup bowls or marmites. The full menu names are as listed.

Petite Marmite	Garnish with small turned carrot and turnip, bâtons of cabbage, celery and leek, and slices of bone marrow; serve accompanied with toasted slices of French bread.
Petite Marmite Albigeoise	Garnish with diced beef, calf's foot, ham and saucisson; diced cabbage, carrot, leek, lettuce and celery, also broad beans.
Petite Marmite Beaucaire	Garnish with squares of cabbage, celery and leek, pearl barley, julienne of chicken gizzard and small pieces of chicken liver.
Petite Marmite Béarnaise	Add potatoes and rice to an ordinary Petite Marmite soup.
Petite Marmite Bouchère	Garnish with small squares of cabbage and slices of bone marrow.
Petite Marmite Bourguignonne	Garnish with dice of salt pork and ham, slices of smoked sausage, small pieces of carrot, cabbage, celery, leek and turnip; serve with toasted slices of French bread.
Petite Marmite Henri IV	Garnish with vegetables and pieces of chicken and serve with cheese and croûtons.
Bouillabaisse	This is both a soup and a main dish so a full explanation is included in the Fish Section.
Bouillon à l'Ancienne	Serve with diablotins made with puree of vegetables.
Bouillon à l'Aveyronnaise	Garnish with small pieces of cabbage, carrot, potato and turnip, haricot beans, dice of ham, salt belly of pork and Confit d'Oie (see Hors-d'œuvre).
Bouillon Laboureur	Garnish with diced salt pork and small pieces of carrot, celery, leek and with button onions.
Bouillon du Marriage	Flavour with saffron; garnish with dice of beef, chicken and mutton, small pieces of carrot, celery, leek and turnip, button onions and rice.
Bouillon aux Oeufs	Pour beaten egg into the very hot bouillon so that it sets in shreds.

Bouillon Viennoise	Dice of salt silverside and salt pork, diced beef, carrot and onion; haricot beans, rice and pearl barley.
Bouillon de Volaille	Garnish clear chicken stock with short pieces of vermicelli.
Croûte-au-Pot	This is the same bouillon as for ordinary Petite Marmite, garnished with diced carrot, celery, leek and turnip; serve accompanied with toasted slices of French bread.
(Potage) Queue de Boeuf Claire	Garnish with small pieces of the end of the tail and with small dice of carrot, celery and turnip.
Queue de Boeuf Charollaise	Serve ordinary clear oxtail soup with small stuffed cabbages.
Queue de Kangourou	Prepare as for ordinary clear oxtail soup but add small pieces of canned kangaroo tail instead of oxtail (this soup can also be made as a thick soup).
Pot-au-Feu	Garnish with small squares of carrot, celery, leek and turnip, dice of beef and boned chicken winglets; serve with toasted slices of French bread and with grated cheese.
Pot-au-Feu de la Mer	Cook pieces of fish and shellfish with paysanne of vegetable in fish fumet.
Potée Bourguignonne	This is another name for Petite Marmite Bourguignonne.
Poule-au-Pot	This is the same as ordinary Petite Marmite with the addition of plenty of diced chicken.

BROTHS

Broth soups are made by cooking cut vegetables in clear white stock, either beef, chicken, game or mutton, adding cereals or pulses and often, some of the meat cut into dice. The vegetables etc. should not be overcooked nor should the stock be allowed to go milky excepting for those made with milk. The word Potage or Soupe can be used in front of the named broths given below, except those names given in English.
Dried sippets can be served with most broths.

Aïgo à la Ménagère	Paysanne of leek, onion and potato; flavour with fennel, garlic, dried orange peel and saffron and add diced tomato; serve with a poached egg per person and toasted cheese croûtons.
Aïgo Saou	Diced tomato, onion and potato cooked with pieces of fish in water, poured over slices of bread sprinkled with oil and pepper; serve with Rouille mixture (garlic and red pimento pounded with oil to make a mayonnaise).
Ardennaise	Cook shredded Belgian endive and leek in butter, add diced potato and milk; finish with butter and serve with French bread.
Auvergnate	Cook a salted pig's head in water, add diced carrot, leek, potato and turnip and lentils; garnish with dice of the head.
Beaucaire	Cook julienne of cabbage, celery and leek in butter, moisten with stock and add pearl barley; garnish with julienne of chicken gizzard and pieces of chicken liver; serve with grated cheese
Bennett	Diced beef and pearl barley cooked in water with haricot beans and diced cabbage, carrot, celery and turnip.
Bili-bil or Billy-By	Cook mussels with mixed vegetables in fish fumet and finish with cream.
Bonne Femme	Cook white of leek in butter; add chicken stock and squares of potato and finish with cream, butter and chopped parsley.
Bortsch	Cook julienne of raw beetroot, cabbage and leek with shredded onion in butter; add white stock, a piece of beef and duck and colour with beetroot juice. Garnish with dice of the beef, and julienne of duck and serve with sour cream, beetroot juice and small pâtés of duck separately.
Brabançonne	Cook squares of carrot, leek, onion and turnip in butter, moisten with stock and add shredded Belgian endive; serve with rusks.
Brésilienne	Cook paysanne of carrot, celery, leek, onion and turnip in butter, add stock, black beans and rice; finish with dice of tomato.
Bûcheronne	Cook squares of kohlrabi, potato, turnip and fat

pork in butter, add stock and small haricot beans; serve with sliced wholemeal bread.

Camaro Cook a small boiling fowl in water with rice, carve the bird and replace it in the soup.

Chicken Broth Small dice of vegetables, diced chicken and rice, cooked in chicken stock; finish with chopped parsley.

Clam Chowder Cook sliced onion and diced salt pork in butter; add diced celery, clams, leek, potato and tomato; finish with cream and crumbled water biscuits.

Cockie Leekie Cook julienne of white of leek in butter, add chicken stock and serve garnished with julienne of chicken and strips of prunes.

Cultivateur Cook dice of salt belly of pork, carrot, celery, leek, onion and turnip in butter; add chicken stock and diced potato, finish with chopped parsley.

Dauphinoise Cook squares of vegetable marrow, potato and turnip in butter; moisten with milk, add shredded chard and vermicelli.

Esterel Cook shredded onion in butter, add stock, pumpkin and haricot beans, make into a puree and add a garnish of vermicelli.

Fermière Cook squares of carrot, leek, onion and turnip in butter, add stock and shredded white cabbage; serve with slices of French bread.

Flamande Cook cut Brussels sprouts and potatoes in stock.

Franc-Comtoise Cook squares of potato and turnip and shredded lettuce and sorrel in butter; add milk and garnish with vermicelli.

Garbure Béarnaise Cook dice of salt belly of pork, cabbage, potato and turnip in water with haricot beans and some Confit d'Oie. Serve with vegetables and pork of the soup with slices of goose, gratinated with slices of French bread and cheese.

Garbure Crécy Spread fried bread croûtons with stiff puree of carrot, gratinate them and arrange in soup bowls with fatty stock. Serve these as garnish with a good plain stock.

Garbure à l'Oignon	Cook sliced onion in butter, add flour then stock and serve this liquid with gratinated croûtons covered with the pureed onion on top.
Garbure Paysanne	Cook chopped vegetables in butter, add stock then puree the vegetables and spread on fried bread croûtons; gratinate with cheese and serve with the broth.
Grand'mère	Cook diced cabbage, celery, leek, onion and potatoes in water, add shredded lettuce, sorrel and spinach and Italian pasta; finish with milk and butter.
Gratinée Lyonnaise	This is the same as Soupe à l'Oignon; it may be made with the addition of red wine or port.
Gumbo	Cook pieces of chicken and sliced onion in stock; cut the flesh into dice and return to the soup with oysters and sliced okras.
Hochepot	Pigs' trotters, salt belly of pork, beef and vegetables cooked in water, sausages added and the broth served with croûtons as the soup, and the meat and vegetables as main course.
Jeannette	Cut leek, potato and turnip into squares, cook in butter, add stock, peas, diamonds of French beans, shredded sorrel and leaves of watercress; finish with milk and butter and serve with French bread.
Maraîchère	Cook squares of leek in butter, add stock and squares of potato, then shredded lettuce and spinach and vermicelli; finish with cream and butter.
Mille-fante	Mix breadcrumbs, parmesan cheese and eggs to a paste and add slowly to boiling stock, whisking well; allow to cook and stir again before serving.
Minestrone	Cook squares of cabbage, carrot, celery, leek, onion and turnip in butter; add stock, tomato puree, peas, diced potato, spaghetti and diced tomato; finish with a paste of chopped fat of bacon, garlic and parsley. Serve with dried croûtons and grated cheese.
Miss Betsy	Pearl barley cooked in water, finished with fresh

concentrated tomato; garnish with dice of dessert apple.

Mutton Broth   Brunoise of carrot, celery, leek, onion and turnip cooked in mutton stock with pearl barley; add diced mutton and chopped parsley.

Nevers   Cook sliced carrot and small Brussels sprouts separately in butter, place both into white stock, add vermicelli and cook together.

Normande   Cook squares of carrot, leek and potato in butter, moisten with stock and add haricot beans; finish with milk, cream and butter.

Soupe à l'Oignon   Cook shredded onion in butter, add flour and brown stock; portion into soup marmites, cover with toasted rounds of French bread, sprinkle with cheese and gratinate.

Soupe au Pistou   Cook lima beans, chopped onion and potato and dice of courgette and French beans in chicken stock; garnish with vermicelli and serve accompanied with a paste made of comté and parmesan cheeses, basil and oil.

Olla Podrida   Pigs trotters, knuckle of ham, chicken, beef, vegetables and chick peas cooked in water with garlic sausage; serve the broth with bread croûtons and the meats and vegetables as the main course, or cut up and use as the garnish.

Okra   Cook chopped onion, diced bacon and dice of raw chicken in butter, moisten with chicken stock, add sliced okras and diced tomato; garnish with rice.

Paysanne   Cook squares of carrot, celery, leek, onion, and turnip in butter, add stock, peas and diamonds of French beans; finish with chopped parsley.

Philadelphia Pepper Pot   Dice of potato, tripe and veal cooked in a slightly peppery stock; garnish with small suet dumplings.

Poireaux et Pommes   Cook squares of leek in butter, add chicken stock and squares of potatoes; finish with chopped parsley.

Potage Réjane   Julienne of chicken, leek and potato in chicken stock.

75

Pouchero	Ham, beef and chick peas cooked in water; add garlic sausage, cut the meats into pieces and serve the soup with small balls of forcemeat made of bacon, breadcrumbs, garlic and egg – fried in oil.
Rabbit Broth	Cook a jointed rabbit in water, add squares of vegetables and some of the flesh cut into small dice.
Scotch Broth	Cook pearl barley in white stock, add brunoise of carrot, celery, leek, onion and turnip; finish with chopped parsley.
Selianka	Add braised sauerkraut to ham-flavoured bouillon and garnish with small sprigs of parsley.
Villageoise	Cook julienne of cabbage and leek in butter, add white stock and vermicelli; finish with pluches of chervil.

PUREES

This kind of soup is usually made of a particular kind of vegetable, either fresh or dried, often with potatoes or rice if the vegetable used is not a starchy one. Fresh vegetables are first cooked in butter before adding stock or water; dried pulses are cooked in water. The consistency should be smooth and the colour and flavour very delicate.

Albert	Cook leek in butter, add stock and potato, make into a puree and finish with cream; garnish with julienne of carrot, celery and leek.
Alice	Cook leek in butter, add stock, potatoes and turnips, make into a puree and finish with cream; serve with fried croûtons.
Argenteuil	Stew sliced onion and trimmings of asparagus in butter, cook in stock and make into a puree; finish with cream and garnish with asparagus tips.
Avocado	Make a puree of cooked avocado and garnish with diced avocado.

Balvais	Puree of green split pea soup; garnish with small balls of carrot and turnip.
Balzac	Puree of celeriac soup; thicken with barley flour and garnish with julienne of celery and leek
Bressane	Puree of pumpkin; finish with butter and cream and garnish with small pastas.
Bretonne	Puree of haricot beans; finish with butter and garnish with julienne of leek and mushroom.
Briarde	Cook sliced onion in butter, add carrots and potatoes and make into a puree; serve with fried croûtons.
Bruxelloise	Puree of Brussels sprouts, finish with cream and garnish with small balls of carrot.
Campagnarde	Cook carrot, celery, leek and turnip in with haricot beans; make into a puree and garnish with peas and diced carrot and turnip.
Céleri	Puree of celery; finish with butter and cream and garnish with diced celery.
Champenoise	Puree of celery and potato soup; garnish with diced carrot and celery.
Champignons	Puree of mushroom stalks; finish with butter and milk and garnish with diced mushroom.
Chantilly	Puree of lentil soup; finish with lightly whipped cream and garnish with quenelles.
Charlotte	Cook leeks in butter, add stock, potato and watercress; make into a puree and finish with butter and pluches of chervil.
Clamart	Cook green split peas in water or stock with ham bone, carrot and onion; make into a puree and garnish with peas.
Clermont	Cook celery and onion in butter, add shelled chestnuts and milk; make into a puree, garnish with small pasta and serve with fried onion rings.
Cormeilles	Puree of French beans thickened with potato; finish with milk and garnish with dice of French beans.
Compiègne	Puree of haricot beans; finish with butter and milk and garnish with shredded sorrel.
Comté	Cook carrot, celery, leek, onion and turnip with

	lentils; make into a puree and serve garnished with julienne of vegetables.
Condé	Puree of red beans with red wine; finish with butter.
Conti	Puree of lentils and salt belly of pork; finish with butter and garnish with pluches of chervil.
Coquelin	Puree of green pea soup; garnish with julienne of chicken and leek.
Crécy	Slice carrots and onion and cook in butter, moisten with stock, make into a puree and finish with butter. May be thickened with potatoes, rice or fried croûtons.
Cressonière	Stew watercress in butter then cook in stock with potatoes, make into a puree and finish with milk; serve garnished with leaves of watercress
Darblay	Garnish Puree Parmentier with julienne of carrot, celery, leek and turnip.
Doria	Cook sliced onion in butter, add stock and cucumber; make into a puree, finish with butter and garnish with small balls of cucumber.
Dubarry	Cook cauliflower and potatoes in milk, make into a fine puree and finish with butter; garnish with pluches of chervil and fried croûtons.
Egyptienne	Puree of yellow split peas; serve with fried croûtons.
Esaü	This is puree of lentil soup with a garnish of boiled rice.
Estoril	Mix puree of pumpkin with puree of haricot beans; finish with butter and garnish with short pieces of vermicelli.
de Fèves	Cook broad beans in water with some savory, make into a puree and thicken with arrowroot and butter; garnish with small broad beans.
Flamande	Cook shredded onion in butter, add Brussels sprouts, potato and stock; make into a puree and finish with butter.
Florentine	Cook shredded onion in butter, add spinach and stock; make into a puree and finish with cream.
Freneuse	Cook sliced turnips in butter, add potatoes and

stock and make into a puree soup; finish with butter.

Garbure   Cook carrot, celery, leek, onion and turnip in butter, add stock and potatoes, make into a puree and serve with fried croûtons.

Georgette   Cook the white parts of globe artichokes in butter, moisten with stock and thicken with fried croûtons; make into a puree and garnish with seed tapioca.

Gibier   Cook a tough game bird in stock with lentils, make it into a puree and serve garnished with dice of the game.

de Herbes   Cook chervil, pimpernel, sorrel and watercress in butter, add potatoes and moisten with stock; make into a puree and finish with herb butter.

Hôtelière   Add potatoes and French beans to lentil soup, make into a puree and finish with butter; garnish with pluches of chervil.

Josephine   Cook some seed tapioca in green pea soup and finish with julienne of carrot, celery and turnip.

Julienne d'Arblay   This is another name for Puree Darblay.

Kempinski   Add sliced carrot whilst cooking green split peas, make into a puree and garnish with rice.

Lamballe   Puree of green split pea soup; garnish with seed tapioca.

Longchamps   Puree of green split pea soup with a garnish of vermicelli and shredded sorrel.

Maraîchère   Make puree of green split pea soup flavoured with onion; garnish with button onions and noodles.

Maria   Puree of haricot beans; finish with milk and garnish with small balls of carrot and turnip.

Marianne   Cook shredded onion in butter, add potato, pumpkin and stock, make into a puree and garnish with shredded lettuce and sorrel.

Médicis   Cook carrots with green split peas; make into a puree and garnish with shredded sorrel.

Montpensier   Thicken puree of cauliflower with cream of rice powder; serve with fried croûtons.

Musart	Cook flageolet beans in stock, make into a puree and finish with butter; garnish with flageolet beans.
Nemours	Make a puree soup of mushroom and potato and garnish with seed tapioca and julienne of mushroom.
Normande	Add leek, potato and turnip to haricot beans, make into a puree and finish with cream.
Palestine	Make a puree of Jerusalem artichoke, finish with milk and serve with fried croûtons.
Paquita	Add a garnish of sago and diced tomato to puree of green pea soup.
Parmentier	Cook sliced leek in butter, add stock and potatoes, make into a puree and finish with cream and butter; serve with fried croûtons.
Pastorelle	Cook sliced leek, mushroom and onion in butter, add potatoes and stock, make into a puree and finish with milk and butter; garnish with diced mushroom and diced sauté potato.
de Perdreau	Cook an old partridge in with puree of lentils and make into a puree soup; finish with butter.
de Pois	May be made with green split, marrowfat or fresh peas, make into a puree and finish with butter; garnish with peas and pluches of chervil.
Potiron	Puree of pumpkin and potato; finish with milk and serve with fried croûtons.
Portugaise	Fry a mirepoix of vegetables and bacon, add tomatoes and stock, make into a puree, finish with tomato butter and garnish with diced tomato and with rice.
Québec	Puree of haricot beans; finish with milk and garnish with small balls of carrot and turnip.
Royan	Make a puree of cauliflower soup and garnish it with seed tapioca.
St-Cloud	Cook sliced onion in butter, add peas and lettuce and make into a puree soup; garnish with shredded lettuce.
St-Cyr	Cook cauliflower and potatoes and make into a puree soup; serve garnished with diamonds of French beans and florets of cauliflower.

St-Germain	Puree of green split peas; serve with fried croûtons.
St-Marceau	Cook shredded leeks in butter, add peas and stock and make into a puree soup; garnish with julienne of leek and lettuce.
St-Martin	Thicken puree of lentil soup with potato and serve with fried croûtons.
Sigurd	Cook shredded leek in butter, add potatoes, tomatoes and stock and make into a puree soup; garnish with dice of green pimento and quenelles
Tomate	Cook a mirepoix in butter, add squashed tomatoes and stock and make into a puree.
Tourangelle	Cook shredded leek in butter, add French beans, flageolet beans and stock and make into a puree soup; garnish with diamonds of French beans and flageolet beans.
Washington	Puree of sweetcorn; finish with butter and cream and garnish with grains of corn.

—————— POTAGES ——————

There is a wide range of different kinds of soup in this category and there is no single identity to cover them all except that they are thick and all bear the name **Potage**. Some are a mixture of two or more soups, others are slightly more refined puree soups but not so refined or rich as the Cream and Velouté soups.

Ambassadeur	Add shredded lettuce and sorrel and boiled rice to puree of green split pea soup and finish with butter.
Bagration	Cook pieces of veal and chicken in thin velouté; make into a puree, enrich with yolks and butter and garnish with macaroni.
Balvet	Thin a thick puree of green split peas with stock and add a garnish of bâtons of carrot and turnip.
Beaulieu	Mix equal quantities of Puree Garbure and ordinary consommé thickened with tapioca; garnish with diced carrot, celery and turnip.
Bohémienne	Mix six parts of Chicken Velouté soup with one

	part of chicken consommé; garnish with rice and julienne of truffle.
Bonvalet	Make a puree soup of leek, potato and turnip, mix with velouté and garnish with diamonds of French beans and of carrot-flavoured royale.
Boula-Boula	Mix together equal quantities of thick mock turtle soup and puree of green split peas; finish with cream and glaze each portion under a salamander.
Bressane	Puree of pumpkin with added stock and bechamel; garnish with any kind of small pasta.
Chabrillon	Mix three parts of consommé with one part Cream of Tomato soup and garnish with vermicelli.
Champenoise	Mix six parts of Puree Parmentier soup with one part Cream of Celeriac soup and garnish with small dice of carrot and celery.
Chantilly	Finish puree of lentil soup with cream and garnish with quenelles.
Connaught	Garnish puree of lentil soup with diced chicken and finish with cream.
Conti Brunoise	Garnish Purée Conti soup with brunoise of carrot, celery, leek and turnip and finish with butter.
Courlandaise	Make a puree soup of cabbage, carrot, celeriac, onion, potato and turnip, using duck stock; finish with butter and garnish with julienne of duck.
Derby	Cook a mirepoix in butter, add tomatoes and make into a puree soup; finish with butter and garnish with dice of oxtail meat.
Emilienne d'Alençon	Mix equal amounts of Consommé Eduoard VII and Velouté de Volaille; finish with cream.
Fanchette	Flavour Velouté de Volaille soup with puree of asparagus and garnish with peas and small rolls of lettuce spread with forcemeat.
Faubonne	Garnish Purée Soissonaise soup with julienne of carrot, celery, leek and turnip.
Fémina	Thicken good chicken stock with a liaison of yolks and cream; garnish with bâtons of carrot, turnip and truffle, peas and asparagus tips.

Fontages	Thin three parts of thick fresh pea soup with one part of stock and garnish with shredded sorrel.
Garbure	Cook carrot, celery, leek, onion and turnip in butter, add potato and stock and make into a puree soup.
Gentilhomme	Make a puree of partridge soup, finish it with brandy and garnish with quenelles and small balls of truffle.
Germiny	Stew shredded sorrel in butter, moisten with chicken stock and velouté and thicken with yolks and cream; finish with butter.
Girondon	Finish puree of red bean soup with red wine by adding cream; garnish with diced carrot, celery and turnip.
Grand'mère	Garnish Purée Parmentier with julienne of cabbage, leek and lettuce and with short lengths of macaroni.
Jack	Thicken ordinary consommé with a liaison of yolks and cream and garnish with julienne of cabbage, carrot, celery, leek, onion and turnip.
Jubilée	Thin out a thick puree of green split peas with stock and garnish with bâtons of carrot and turnip. This is also called Potage Balvet.
Julienne Darblay	Finish Purée Darblay with a liaison of yolks, cream and butter.
Lamballe	Add a garnish of seed tapioca to a puree of green split pea soup.
Languedoci-enne	Finish puree of green split pea soup with butter and add a garnish of small rounds of carrot and turnip.
Longchamps	Garnish puree of fresh pea soup with shredded sorrel and vermicelli.
Madelon	Mix three parts puree of green split pea soup with one part of tomato soup; garnish with peas.
Marcilly	Mix equal quantities of puree of fresh green pea soup and Cream of Chicken soup; garnish with seed tapioca.
Marigny	Thin three parts of thick fresh pea soup with one part of stock and garnish with peas, diamonds of French beans and shredded sorrel.

83

Mistinguette	Thin out puree of green pea soup with chicken stock and garnish with tapioca.
Narbonnaise	Thin out a fairly thick puree of haricot beans with stock and garnish with rice and shredded sorrel.
Nicolini	Mix three parts of puree of vegetable soup with one part of puree of fresh tomato; pour onto rounds of toast and serve with slices of Gruyère cheese.
d'Oseille	Cook sorrel in butter, add stock and either vermicelli or tapioca; make into a puree then thin with milk and thicken with a liaison of yolks and cream.
Polignac	Thin out thick puree of carrot soup with stock, garnish with tapioca and thicken with a liaison of yolks and cream.
Pompadour	Finish puree of tomato soup with cream and garnish with sago and julienne of lettuce.
Portugaise	Garnish puree of tomato soup with rice.
Rabagas	Dilute thick green split pea soup with chicken stock and garnish with julienne of chicken, leek and potato.
St-Julien	Mix together equal quantities of puree of pumpkin soup and Purée Parmentier; serve with toasted French bread and grated cheese.
St-Marceau	Thin out thick fresh green pea sop with chicken stock and garnish with pluches of chervil and julienne of leek.
Santé	Garnish Purée Parmentier with shredded sorrel and thicken with a liaison of yolks and cream; serve with toasted French bread.
Simone	Mix equal quantities of cream of carrot soup and puree of potato soup with two parts of beef stock; garnish with small squares of lettuce, julienne of chicken and pearl barley.
Solferino	Add puree of tomato when making Purée Parmentier; finish with butter and garnish with small balls of carrot and potato.
Sport	Garnish puree of potato soup with shredded sorrel and vermicelli.

Thourins	Prepare puree of vegetable soup, well flavoured with onion and thicken with a liaison of yolks, cream and butter; serve with toasted French bread
Tyrolienne	Add cucumber, lettuce and sorrel when making puree of green pea soup; serve with fried croûtons.
Ursuline	Cook rice in milk, flavour with almond milk and finish with cream.
Valaison	Mix equal quantities of puree of potato soup and puree of vegetable soup and finish with cream; serve with toasted cheese on rounds of French bread.
Velours	Dilute two parts of thick puree of carrot soup with one part chicken stock and garnish with tapioca.
Verneuil	Mix equal quantities of fresh pea soup and cream of barley soup; garnish with oval shapes of carrot, mushroom and ordinary royale.
Waldéze	Flavour and colour ordinary consommé with tomato and thicken with tapioca; serve accompanied with mixed grated Gruyère and parmesan.
Windham	Garnish Purée Washington soup with tapioca and rice.
Windsor	Prepare calf's foot stock and infuse with turtle herbs; add to Cream of Rice soup and finish with a liaison of yolks, cream and butter; garnish with julienne of calf's foot and quenelles made from forcemeat and hard-boiled egg yolk.

CREAM SOUPS

This type of soup is usually made simply by finishing a purée soup with cream. It can also be made by adding velouté sauce to a puree of vegetables or meat and finishing with cream. It always used to be made by mixing together equal quantities of the basic puree, béchamel and stock. Any of the puree and potage soups can be creamed and included under this heading. The resultant soup should be very smooth and creamy.

Agnes Sorel	Cream of chicken soup cooked with mushroom puree; garnish with julienne of chicken, mushroom and ox-tongue.
Amazone	Mix together equal quantities of Cream of Chicken soup and Cream of Rice soup; serve with fried croûtons.
Antonelli	Add very red cooked tomato to béchamel and thin with stock; finish with cream and serve with braised stuffed chicken winglets.
Argenteuil	Add asparagus puree to béchamel; garnish with asparagus tips.
Armenonville	Finish puree of green pea soup with cream and garnish with sago and diced carrot and turnip.
Avocat	Cook peeled avocados in chicken velouté; blend and serve garnished with diced avocado.
Balmoral	Cook calf's feet in velouté, flavour with turtle herbs and serve with a garnish of julienne of calf's foot and quenelles.
Barley Cream	Cook barley flour in milk, finish with cream and add some cooked pearl barley.
Beaucaire	Garnish Cream of Barley soup with julienne of celeriac, chicken and leek.
Bristol	Finish Purée St. Germain with cream and garnish with julienne of carrot, celery, leek and turnip.
Caroline	Garnish a puree of sweetcorn with nibs of corn and rice.
de Céleri	Finish puree of celery with cream and garnish with julienne of celery.
Cérès	Puree of unripe wheat added to béchamel; garnish with pluches of chervil.
Chevalière	Add julienne of ox-tongue and truffle to Cream of Chicken soup.
Célestine	Cook artichoke bottoms in with Cream of Chicken soup; pass and serve with croûtons.
Chabrillan	Garnish Cream of Tomato soup with vermicelli and quenelles.
Châtelaine	Mix together equal quantities of Cream of Chicken soup and puree of green pea soup; garnish with quenelles.

86

Châtillon	Garnish Cream of Tomato Soup with shredded sorrel and vermicelli.
Chesterfield	Finish veal velouté with cream and garnish with dice of veal.
Chevreuse	Mix equal quantities of Cream of Chicken soup and semolina cooked in milk; garnish with julienne of chicken and truffle.
Choisy	Add purée of lettuce to béchamel; finish with cream and serve with fried croûtons.
Comtesse	Mix together equal quantities of velouté sauce and Crème Argenteuil; garnish with asparagus tips and shredded sorrel.
Concombres	Make a puree with cucumber, peas and mint and finish with cream.
Cormeilles	Add French beans whilst making Purée Parmentier, strain, finish with cream and garnish with diamonds of French beans.
Corneille	Garnish Crème Choisy with sago.
Crécy	Finish puree of carrot soup with cream and butter.
Dubarry	Cook pieces of cauliflower in chicken velouté, pass and finish with cream; garnish with florets of cauliflower.
Durham	Add three kinds of quenelles to Cream of Chicken soup – chicken, lobster and spinach.
Esmeralda	Flavour Cream of Chicken soup with some puree of mushrooms and of celery; serve with profiteroles filled with foie gras.
Favorite	Cook French beans in chicken velouté; pass, finish with cream and garnish with diamonds of French beans.
Gastronome	Mix puree of chestnuts with Cream of Chicken soup and garnish with cockscombs, morels and julienne of truffle.
Genin	Make a puree soup of vegetables including tomatoes and mushrooms; finish with cream and garnish with shredded sorrel.
Gervais	Mix together equal quantities of Barley Cream soup and Cream of Chicken soup; garnish with cockscombs and diced lamb.

Gounod	Add a garnish of diced chicken to Crème St-Germain and serve with fried croûtons.
Grenada	Add julienne of chicken and diced tomato to Cream of Chicken soup.
Hamilton	Flavour Barley Cream soup with curry, finish with cream and garnish with small dice of vegetables.
Jackson	Make a Purée Parmentier with the addition of flageolet beans; pass, add seed tapioca and garnish with julienne of leek.
Jenny Lind	Add sago to Cream of Chicken soup.
Judic	Mix equal quantities of Crème Choisy and Cream of Chicken soup; garnish with small cockscombs and small rounds of lettuce with forcemeat piped on them with a small slice of truffle on top.
Lafite	Mix together béchamel, puree of partridge and stock; finish with marsala and cream and garnish with cockscombs.
Lavallière	Mix equal quantities of Cream of Chicken and Cream of Celery soup; garnish with diced celery royale and serve with profiteroles.
Lejeune	Add tapioca to Cream of Chicken soup.
Lison	Mix together two thirds Cream of Rice soup and one third Cream of Celery; finish with cream and seed tapioca.
Longueville	Finish Purée St-Germain with cream and garnish with shredded sorrel.
Louisette	Finish puree of celery soup with cream and garnish with peas and julienne of chicken and truffle.
de Maïs	Cook the corn in boiling water, make into a puree and add to béchamel; finish with cream and garnish with grains of maize.
Malakoff	Mix equal quantities of Cream of Tomato soup and Purée Parmentier; garnish with shredded spinach.
Maréchal	Add a garnish of asparagus tips and diced chicken and truffle to Cream of Chicken soup.
Memphis	Finish puree of globe artichoke soup with cream

	and garnish with diced artichoke royale and artichoke bottoms cut into dice.
Milanaise	Add very red tomato puree to Cream of Chicken soup and garnish with julienne of ham, ox-tongue and truffle.
Molière	Finish puree of green split pea soup with cream and garnish with asparagus tips, cockscombs and dice of sweetbread.
Monte Cristo	Add nettle shoots when making Cream of Chicken soup and garnish with julienne of mushroom and truffle.
Montesquieu	Cook cucumber and mushroom in chicken velouté; strain, finish with cream and garnish with dice of cucumber.
Montmorency	Add a garnish of stuffed chicken winglets, shredded lettuce and vermicelli to Cream of Chicken soup; serve with grated parmesan.
Nanette	Add very red tomato puree while making Cream of Chicken soup; garnish with diamonds of French beans, peas and julienne of truffle.
Nivernaise	Add puree of carrot to béchamel; finish with cream and garnish with diced carrot.
d'Orge	Cook pearl barley in white stock, make into a puree and finish with cream; garnish with pearl barley.
Perette	Add cullis of lobster to Crème de Riz soup, finish with cream and garnish with small pieces of frogs' legs.
Princesse	Mix equal quantities of Crème de Riz and Crème de Volaille soups and garnish with asparagus tips and small rounds of chicken.
Régence	Add crayfish butter and cream to cream of barley soup and garnish with cockscombs, pearl barley and quenelles made with crayfish.
Reine	Garnish Cream of Chicken soup with diced chicken.
Riche	Add truffle juice to Cream of Chicken soup and garnish with julienne of chicken and small balls of truffle.
Riz, Crème de	Dilute ground rice or cream of rice powder with

	milk, add to chicken stock and finish with cream.
Rubens	Cook sliced onion in butter and add when making Cream of Rice soup; strain and garnish with diced mushroom.
St-Germain	Prepare puree of green split pea soup, finish with cream and garnish with peas.
St-Louis	Finish Cream of Tomato soup with tapioca and garnish with quenelles.
Sévigné	Add puree of lettuce while making Cream of Chicken soup; garnish with julienne of lettuce and quenelles.
Simone	Finish puree of haricot bean soup with cream and add diced carrot and turnip.
Sultane	Add puree of chicken to béchamel, flavour with hazelnut milk and pistachio butter and garnish with dice of truffle.
Suzanne	Cook pinhead oats in milk for 1 hour and strain; finish with cream and garnish with peas.
Suzon	Garnish Crème St-Germain with a small poached egg per portion.
de Tomate	Cook diced vegetables and bacon in butter, add flour, tomato puree and white stock; strain and finish with cream. Serve with fried croûtons.
Turbigo	Mix one part very red stewed tomato puree with two parts béchamel and thin with stock; garnish with soup pasta and serve with parmesan cheese.
Vefour	Add very red stewed tomato to Cream of Chicken soup and garnish with quenelles and tapioca.
Vénitienne	Garnish Cream of Chicken soup with small ravioli made with spinach filling.
de Volaille	Cook chicken flesh or bones in chicken velouté, finish with cream and garnish with julienne of chicken.
Vuillemot	Finish puree of haricot bean soup with cream and garnish with rice and shredded sorrel.
Wilhelmina	Add ground rice whilst making Cream of Chicken soup; garnish with julienne of ox-tongue and truffle and with asparagus tips.

VELOUTES

This category of soup is made by cooking cut meat or vegetables in velouté sauce made with chicken or veal stock; after being pureed the soup is thickened and enriched with a liaison of yolks of egg and cream, after which it must not be allowed to boil. The velvety smoothness and fine flavour is further enhanced by the addition of butter, either plain or a flavoured and coloured one.

Albuféra Finish Velouté d'Écrevisses soup with a liaison of egg yolks, cream and butter and garnish with a poached pigeon's egg per portion.

d'Artichauts Cook globe artichokes in veal velouté, puree it, add a liaison and garnish with diced artichoke bottoms.

Andalouse Mix together five parts of velouté with one and a half parts of puree of tomato and one part of onion Soubise; finish with a liaison and garnish with rice, diced tomato and julienne of pimento.

Belle Otéro Add puree of sweet potato to chicken velouté, enrich with a liaison and garnish with slices of bone marrow.

Boïeldieu Finish chicken velouté with a liaison and garnish with quenelles of chicken, diced foie gras and truffle.

Bordaloue Add some cream of rice when making a Velouté de Volaille soup; finish with a liaison and garnish with four kinds of royale cut in dice – ordinary, green, red and orange colours.

Brillat-Savarin Cook pieces of chicken and rabbit in chicken velouté; puree it, finish with a liaison and Madeira and garnish with julienne of carrot, mushroom and truffle.

Camelia Add puree of green split peas made with tapioca to chicken velouté, enrich with a liaison and garnish with julienne of leek and chicken.

Carême Cook puree of artichoke bottoms and puree of white mushrooms in chicken velouté; strain, finish with cream and garnish with julienne of truffle.

Carmen	Flavour chicken velouté with puree of red pimento; thicken with a liaison and garnish with rice.
Champenoise	Add puree of celeriac to chicken velouté, enrich with a liaison and garnish with diced carrot and celery.
Chartreuse	Garnish Velouté de Volaille soup with tapioca and garnish with small ravioli stuffed with foie gras and spinach.
Chevrière	Cook shredded leek, lettuce and sorrel in butter, add to chicken velouté and make into a puree; enrich with a liaison and garnish with diced fried potato.
Choiseuil	Mix puree of lentils into chicken velouté, add the liaison and a garnish of rice and sorrel.
Choisy	Cook shredded lettuce in butter, add to chicken velouté and puree it; finish with a liaison of yolks of egg, cream and butter.
Claremont	Garnish Velouté de Volaille soup with asparagus tips, quenelles and julienne of chicken.
Colombine	Cook pigeons in chicken velouté flavoured with aniseed, make into a puree and finish with yolks, cream and butter; garnish with julienne of pigeon.
Créole	Cook some okras in chicken velouté; puree it, then finish with a liaison and garnish with diced tomato and julienne of red pimento.
Dame Blanche	Flavour chicken velouté with almond milk; thicken with yolks of egg, cream and butter and garnish with quenelles and dice of chicken.
Dartois	Mix puree of haricot beans into chicken velouté soup and garnish with julienne of carrot, celery, leek and turnip.
Diane	Cook a partridge in game velouté, puree it, then add the liaison and garnish with julienne of partridge and truffle.
Doria	Cook cut cucumber in butter and finish cooking in velouté; pass, thicken with a liaison and garnish with small balls of cucumber, and rice.

Doyenne	Add puree of green split peas to chicken velouté soup and garnish with peas and quenelles.
Eliza	Add stewed sorrel to Velouté de Volaille soup and serve accompanied with fried croûtons.
Elizabeth	Cook some ground rice in chicken velouté, finish with a liaison and garnish with dice of chicken and truffle.
Erica	Add red pimento to chicken velouté and finish with a liaison.
Evaline	When serving Velouté de Volaille soup, decorate it in the soup plate with a circle of thick tomato soup.
Excelsior	Add puree of asparagus to Cream of Barley soup, thicken with a liaison and garnish with pearl barley.
Fanchette	Cook some asparagus in chicken velouté; pass, add a liaison and garnish with asparagus tips, peas and small squares of stuffed cabbage.
Fédora	Colour and flavour chicken velouté with very red cooked tomato pulp; add a liaison and garnish with vermicelli.
Fleury	Add some barley flour to chicken velouté, add a liaison and garnish with florets of cauliflower and dice of carrot and turnip.
Gasconne	Add very red tomato pulp to chicken velouté; finish with the liaison and garnish with dice of Confit d'Oie (preserved goose).
Gauloise	Cook celeriac and chestnuts in chicken velouté; puree it, add a liaison and garnish with diced tomato flesh.
Germinal	Add tarragon when making Velouté de Volaille soup; garnish with asparagus tips.
Gosford	Cook asparagus in with chicken velouté; puree it and finish with tapioca and a liaison.
Impérial	Cook ground rice in chicken velouté, add the liaison and garnish with dice of almond-flavoured royale.
Indienne	Flavour chicken velouté with curry paste and coconut milk; add a liaison and a garnish of rice.

Irma Garnish Velouté de Volaille soup with curry-flavoured quenelles and rice.

Isoline Cook chicken flesh in chicken velouté; puree the result, thicken with a liaison and finish with crayfish butter. Garnish with tapioca.

Japonnaise Cook Japanese artichokes (stachys) in chicken velouté; puree it, add the liaison and serve with fried croûtons.

Jeannette Cook salsify in veal velouté, puree it, add the liaison and garnish with rice and dice of chicken.

Juanita Cook ground rice in velouté; add the liaison and garnish with dice of tomato and quenelles made with the addition of sieved hard-boiled egg.

Jussieu Garnish Velouté de Volaille soup with quenelles and julienne of chicken.

de Laitue Cook shredded lettuce in butter, add to chicken velouté and pass through a strainer.

Lady Morgan Cook ground rice in chicken velouté, add a liaison and garnish with cockscombs and dice of chicken.

Ledoyen Cook flageolet beans in with velouté; puree it, add a liaison and serve with fried croûtons.

Londonderry Cook ground rice in with veal velouté made with the addition of white wine and mushroom trimmings; strain, add the liaison and garnish with diced turtle.

Lucullus Garnish Velouté de Volaille soup with cockscombs and kidneys and with quenelles containing chopped truffle.

Lyonnaise Garnish Velouté de Volaille soup with dice of chestnut royale.

Macdonald Cook puree of calf's brain in chicken velouté; add the liaison, some sherry and a garnish of diced cucumber.

MacMahon Cook puree of calf's brain in veal velouté; add the liaison and a garnish of dice of brain and of cucumber.

Madeleine Mix equal quantities of velouté of artichokes and puree of haricot beans and garnish with sago.

Mancelle Cook celery, chestnuts and a game bird in

chicken velouté; make into a puree, enrich with a liaison and garnish with julienne of game.

Marcilly   Add puree of green peas to velouté of chicken soup and garnish with quenelles and tapioca.

Marie-Antoinette   Cook asparagus in with chicken velouté; pass and finish with liaison of yolks, cream and butter and garnish with asparagus tips.

Marie-Louise   Thicken chicken stock with barley flour; add a liaison of yolks, cream and butter and a garnish of short lengths of macaroni.

Marie-Stuart   Cook barley flour in with velouté of chicken; garnish with pearl barley and small balls of carrot and turnip.

Marquise   Cook ground rice in with chicken velouté, add a liaison and garnish with peas and julienne of lettuce.

Martha   Cook sauted onions in chicken velouté; pass, thicken with a liaison and garnish with quenelles containing dice of vegetables.

Mathilde   Cook chopped cucumber and ground rice with velouté; pass, thicken with a liaison and garnish with small balls of cucumber.

Mercédès   Cook artichoke bottoms in chicken velouté; pass, add a liaison and garnish with diced artichoke bottoms.

Mikado   Cook Japanese artichokes (stachys) in veal velouté; pass, add a liaison and garnish with tapioca.

Nelusko   Cook chicken flesh in chicken velouté; puree it, flavour with crushed toasted hazelnuts and finish with the liaison; garnish with quenelles flavoured with hazelnuts.

d'Orléans   Cook some chicken in chicken velouté, puree it and finish with a liaison; garnish with three kinds of quenelles – ordinary, spinach and crayfish.

Orloff   Cook chopped cucumber and onion in chicken velouté; pass through a sieve, add a liaison and garnish with julienne of truffle. Serve with diablotins.

Parisienne	Cook sliced leek and potato in veal velouté, pass, enrich with cream and serve with fried croûtons.
Pavillon	Cook Japanese artichokes (stachys) and watercress in chicken velouté; puree, add a liaison and garnish with dice of carrot and celery.
Rachel	Add puree of green peas cooked with sorrel to Velouté of Chicken soup made with the addition of ground rice; garnish with rice and serve with fried croûtons.
Régence	Cook barley flour in with chicken velouté; finish with yolks, cream and crayfish butter and garnish with cockscombs, pearl barley and crayfish quenelles.
Rosamonde	Cook white mushrooms in chicken velouté; puree it, add a liaison and finish with crayfish butter and julienne of truffle.
Rossini	Finish Velouté de Volaille soup with yolks, cream and foie gras butter and garnish with quenelles made with foie gras.
Volaille	Cook pieces of chicken or raw chicken bones in velouté made with chicken stock; strain, finish with yolks of eggs and cream and garnish with julienne of chicken.
Xavier	Cook cream of rice in with chicken velouté; add a liaison and garnish with diced chicken.
Yvonne	Mix equal quantities of Velouté de Volaille and Velouté Choisy; add a liaison and garnish with seed tapioca.

Fish Velouté Soups

Bagration Maigre	Cook mushroom puree in fish velouté, add a liaison and garnish with strips of sole, crayfish tails and crayfish quenelles.
Bâtalière	Flavour fish velouté with puree of shrimps and garnish with mussels and shrimps.
Beauharnais	Cook cream of barley in fish velouté, finish with yolks, cream and crayfish butter; garnish with quenelles and crayfish tails.

Billy-By Make a velouté with mussel liquid; finish with cream and garnish with small mussels.

Borely Cook pieces of whiting fillet in fish velouté, make into a puree, add a liaison and garnish with quenelles and small mussels.

Cambacérès Mix equal quantities of Velouté d'Ecrevisses soup and velouté made with pigeon stock and garnish with pigeon quenelles and crayfish quenelles.

Campbell Flavour fish velouté with curry paste; add a liaison and garnish with strips of Dover sole.

Cardinale Make a fish velouté with trimmings of mushrooms; pass, thicken with a liaison, colour and flavour with lobster butter and garnish with diced lobster.

Carmelite Cook pieces of whiting in fish velouté; make into a puree, add a liaison and garnish with strips of sole and quenelles.

Catherine Garnish velouté soup with peas and shrimps.

Chanoinesse Finish fish velouté with yolks of egg, cream and crayfish butter and garnish with dice of soft roe.

de Crevettes Sauté raw shrimps with a mirepoix in butter, add fish velouté, cook and strain; finish with yolks, cream and shrimp butter and garnish with shrimps.

Dieppoise Cook leek and mushroom trimmings in butter, add to fish velouté with mussel liquor; enrich with a liaison and garnish with mussels and shrimps.

Divette Finish Velouté d'Éperlan Soup with crayfish butter and garnish with crayfish quenelles and small balls of truffle.

Doris Make a velouté with whiting stock, add a liaison and garnish with oysters.

d'Ecrevisses Cook crayfish with a mirepoix in butter, add fish velouté, cook and pass; finish with a liaison and garnish with some of the crayfish and julienne of mushroom and truffle.

d'Eperlan Cook smelt and whiting fillet with onion in butter; add fish velouté, pass and finish with a liaison of yolks, cream and butter.

97

d'Estaing   Add puree of crabmeat to fish velouté and garnish with quenelles made of crab, and with julienne of fish.

Eugenie   Add a liaison to Velouté de Crevettes soup and garnish with prawns.

George Sand   Garnish fish velouté soup with julienne of lettuce and crayfish.

de Grenouilles   Cook frogs' legs in with fish velouté; make into a puree, add a liaison of yolks and cream and garnish with dice of frogs' legs.

de Homard   Cook pounded lobster shells in fish velouté; pass, thicken with a liaison and add a garnish of diced lobster.

de Homard à la Cleveland   Cut up a raw lobster and cook as for lobster Américaine then finish cooking in fish velouté; remove the flesh, pound the shells and cook further, strain, add a liaison and garnish with dice of lobster.

aux Huîtres   Thicken a velouté made with fillets of fish with a liaison and add a garnish of bearded oysters

Jacqueline   Garnish fish velouté soup with asparagus tips, balls of carrot, peas and rice.

Jean-Bart   Garnish fish velouté soup with julienne of leek, macaroni, quenelles and diced tomato.

Joinville   Cook crayfish in butter with a mirepoix; add to fish velouté, pass, enrich with yolks, cream and crayfish butter and garnish with diced mushroom and truffle.

Josselin   Use fish and mussel stocks to make a velouté; add a liaison of yolks and cream and garnish with vermicelli.

Jouvence   Cook frogs' legs and rice in chicken velouté; puree it, add a liaison of yolks, cream and shrimp butter and a garnish of shrimps.

Malmsbury   Garnish fish velouté soup with dice of pike and lobster and with small mussels.

Maturin   Garnish fish velouté soup with small salmon quenelles.

Mignon   Add purée of shrimps to fish velouté soup and

	garnish with shrimps, quenelles and small balls of truffle.
Nelson	Finish Velouté d'Éperlan soup with lobster butter and garnish with rice and dice of lobster.
Nîmoise	Cook fish velouté with tomato paste, finish with a liaison and serve with fried croûtons.
St-Jean	Garnish fish velouté soup with small quenelles which have been poached, then egg-and-crumbled and deep fried.
St-Malo	Garnish fish velouté soup with quenelles and shrimps.
Thermidor	Garnish Velouté de Homard Cleveland with quenelles containing puree of red pimento.
Trouvillaise	Finish fish velouté soup with shrimp butter and garnish with shrimps.
Victoria	Cook ground rice and puree of tomato in fish velouté, add a liaison of yolks and cream and finish with lobster butter.
Yvette	Finish fish velouté soup with lobster butter and garnish with quenelles, diced lobster and truffle.

——— BROWN ROUX SOUPS ———

This kind of soup is usually made by adding the appropriate brown stock to brown roux and cooking the particular ingredient in the soup together with a fried mirepoix of vegetables and tomato puree to give additional flavour. When strained, some of the main ingredient may be added as a garnish.

Brown Windsor	Garnish the finished soup with cooked dice of carrot and turnip, peas and diamonds of green beans (This soup is sometimes made as a cream soup with calfs' feet, ground rice and a liaison of egg yolks).
Hare	Cook pieces of marinated hare in the soup, remove and flavour with Madeira.
Kangaroo Tail	Garnish the finished soup with small pieces of kangaroo tail.

Liver Cook pieces of ox-liver in the soup then cut the liver into dice and place back in as the garnish.

Mock Turtle Make the soup with a brown roux, ordinary brown stock and a calf's head; flavour the finished soup with turtle herbs and sherry. It may be garnished with the calf's head cut into small dice.

Mulligatawny Sauté onion and garlic, add curry powder and cook and make into a soup with tomato puree and brown stock; flavour with coconut milk and serve garnished with rice.

Oxtail Cook pieces of oxtail in the soup, strain and garnish with small pieces of the tail and small balls of carrot and turnip; flavour with sherry.

aux Rognons Cook the soup with minced ox kidney, strain and garnish with dice of ox kidney.

Sharks' Fin (Nageoire de requin) Cut and cook the fin in the soup, strain and garnish with some of the diced flesh (This soup can also be made as a broth type of soup with chicken soup and soy sauce, or as a velouté finished with cream and butter).

—— TOMATO-BASED SOUPS ——

Américaine Add one third lobster bisque to two parts of tomato soup and garnish with crayfish and rice.

Andalouse Cook tomato soup with rice and additional onion, pass, then finish with cream; garnish with julienne of green pimento and dice of tomato.

Aurore Blend Cream of Tomato soup and cream of chicken soup and garnish with quenelles.

Bolivia Garnish tomato soup with julienne of ham, dice of lamb and diced tomato.

Carmen Garnish Cream of Tomato soup with rice.

Chabrillon Garnish Cream of Tomato soup with tarragon-flavoured quenelles and vermicelli.

Chicago Blend Cream of Tomato soup and Bisque of Lobster and garnish with tapioca seeds and dice of lobster.

Clementine	Garnish Cream of Tomato soup with dice of ordinary royale.
Cleveland	Add lobster bisque to tomato soup and garnish with dice of lobster and julienne of tomato.
Espagnole	Serve tomato soup garnished with rice and sprinkled with chopped parsley.
Gasconne	Mix tomato soup and chicken velouté, add cream and garnish with julienne of ham and mushroom
Grenada	Garnish Cream of Tomato soup with julienne of chicken and dice of tomato.
Holstein	Garnish tomato soup with asparagus tips, small buds of cauliflower and quenelles of lobster.
Juanita	Garnish tomato soup with quenelles.
Julie	Flavour tomato soup with mushrooms, finish with cream and garnish with julienne of ham and mushroom.
Madelon	Garnish cream of tomato soup with vermicelli.
Mongole	Blend tomato soup and green pea soup together in the soup plate.
Pompadour	Garnish cream of tomato soup with shredded lettuce and sago.
Portugaise	Garnish tomato soup with rice.
Sicilienne	Garnish tomato soup with seed tapioca.
Sigurd	Blend tomato soup and potato soup and garnish with diced green pimento and quenelles.
Solferino	Flavour potato soup with tomato and garnish with small balls of carrot and potato.
Stamboul	Blend Cream of Tomato soup and Cream of Rice soup and serve with crescent shape croûtons.
Waldéze	Garnish Cream of Tomato soup with tapioca seeds and serve with grated parmesan.

——— THICK GAME SOUPS ———

This kind of soup is usually a derivative of the brown roux soup formula but can also be made by cooking a pulse such as lentils in game stock.

Beaufort	Garnish hare soup with julienne of hare and sliced chipolata sausages.

Berchoux	Cook lentils in game stock, make into a puree and serve with croûtons.
Capri	Use quail stock to make the soup and serve garnished with julienne of quail breast.
Castillane	Use woodcock to flavour the soup and serve garnished with dice of woodcock and lentil royale, and julienne of woodcock breast.
Chasseur	Flavour the finished soup with sherry and serve with croûtons.
Choiseul	Cook lentils in game stock, make into a puree and garnish with rice and a chiffonade of sorrel.
Condorcet	Use any kind of game to make a puree soup; garnish with julienne of game and with game quenelles.
Cussy	Add julienne of partridge breast and truffle to thick game soup, and a garnish of dice of chestnut royale.
Gentilhomme	Cook lentils in game stock, pass and flavour with Madeira; serve garnished with quenelles and small balls of truffle.
des Gourmets	Flavour thick pheasant-flavoured soup with puree of foie gras and port and garnish with julienne of pheasant breast and quenelles of pheasant.
Grand-Duc	Garnish thick partridge-flavoured soup with diced mushroom and quenelles.
Grand-Veneur	Flavour pheasant soup with sherry and garnish with diced breast of pheasant and truffle.
Imperatore	Garnish thick pheasant and morel-flavoured soup with dice of foie gras, quenelles of pheasant, dice of ordinary royale and julienne of truffle.
Jacobine	Flavour thick game soup with Madeira and garnish with dice of game royale and quenelles.
Julius César	Garnish thick hazel-hen-flavoured soup with julienne of hazel-hen, mushroom and truffle.
Lucullus	Flavour thick pheasant soup with puree of foie gras and port and garnish with quenelles and small balls of truffle; serve accompanied with small bouchées of pheasant puree.

Magellan	Flavour partridge soup with Madeira and serve with croûtons.
Maître d'Hôtel	Cook lentils, ham and partridge in game stock, make into a puree and garnish with quenelles of partridge.
Mancelle	Cook celery and chestnuts in game soup, strain and serve garnished with julienne of partridge.
Masséna	Garnish pheasant-flavoured thick soup with dice of chestnut royale.
Médicis	Flavour thick game soup with tomato puree and garnish with macaroni and quenelles.
Metternich	Garnish pheasant-flavoured thick soup with julienne of breast of pheasant and dice of artichoke royale.
Nesselrode	Cook chestnuts in woodcock soup, pass and garnish with quenelles of woodcock.
Nimrod	Flavour thick game soup with sherry and serve with profiteroles filled with puree of game.
Petit-Duc	Finish thick woodcock-flavoured soup with puree of foie gras, cream and brandy and garnish with julienne of woodcock and diced woodcock royale.
Quirinal	Flavour thick pheasant soup with sherry and garnish with julienne of pheasant and truffle.
Rohan	Garnish thick plover-flavoured soup with a poached egg and serve with croûtons.
St-Georges	Thick game soup with hare and mushrooms; flavour with red wine and garnish with julienne of hare, mushroom and truffle.
St-Hubert	Use venison, lentils and chestnuts to make a thick game soup; strain, add cream and redcurrant jelly and garnish with julienne of truffle.
Tzar	Finish hazel-hen soup with goose liver puree and truffle essence and garnish with julienne of truffle.
Tzarina	Garnish hazel-hen and celery soup with julienne of celeriac.
Valois	Garnish pheasant soup with garden peas and quenelles of pheasant.

——————— BISQUES ———————

It is generally accepted that this category of soups is made only with crustacea but there is no reason why other shellfish and fish such as salmon should not be used. The old English word 'cullis' meant the concentrated puree of cooked fish or meat that had been pounded and sieved; it is still used as an alternative name for a bisque soup.

The shellfish is cooked raw in butter with a mirepoix, flamed with brandy then cooked in white wine and stock with rice as the thickening agent. The shells are crushed and replaced in the soup which is then passed and finished with cream and butter.

Shellfish soups may also be made as a velouté but these should not be named bisque.

Calmar	Cut squid into rings and cook as for bisque of lobster.
Chicago	Mix bisque of lobster with tomato soup and garnish with seed tapioca and dice of lobster.
de Crabe	This is best made by cooking prepared white and dark crab meat in fish velouté.
de Crevettes	Finish the soup with shrimp butter and garnish with small prawns.
de Crevettes Roses	Finish the soup with shrimp butter and garnish with prawns.
d'Ecrevisses	Make the bisque with crayfish and serve garnished with diced crayfish.
de Homard	Cut a raw lobster, cook in hot butter with a mirepoix until it turns red; flambé, add white wine, fish stock and tomato puree and cook; thicken the liquid with diluted ground rice and finish with butter, cream and brandy.
de Langouste	Use a whole raw crawfish or cooked crawfish shells to make the cullis, finish with cream and garnish with dice of crawfish.
de Langoustines	Cook Dublin Bay prawns as for bisque of lobster and serve with some of the diced flesh.
Potage Américaine	Blend bisque of crayfish with Cream of Tomato soup and garnish with tapioca seeds.

Spider Crab (Araignée de Mer)	Use raw spider crabs to make the cullis, as for bisque of lobster.
Vintimille	Garnish lobster bisque with seed tapioca and dice of crayfish.

Bisques of fowl and game birds, including pigeon, are made by cooking the main ingredient in the soup and using the flesh to flavour and thicken it.

——— FOREIGN SOUPS ———

Albigeoise (France)	This is a well-garnished broth made of beef, ham, dried sausage, and veal with paysanne of cabbage, carrot, leek, lettuce and turnips and a good amount of small broad beans. Serve with French bread and Confit d'Oie.
Barszcz (Poland)	Thicken the juices expressed from pickled beetroots and cucumber with semolina and add a liaison of yolks and sour cream.
Biersuppe (Germany)	Add light ale to a brown roux, flavour with cinnamon, salt, sugar and lemon rind; cook, strain and serve with diced fried croûtons.
Boronia (Spain)	Sauté diced aubergine, pumpkin and tomato in oil, add water, saffron, garlic and caraway seeds; cook, pass through a sieve and thicken with breadcrumbs.
Borschtschock (Russia)	Stew julienne of cabbage, carrot, leek and beetroot in butter, add stock and cook; colour deep red with raw beetroot juice and serve accompanied with sour cream.
Chowder (USA)	Stew diced leek, onion and pickled belly of pork in butter, add potatoes, moisten with stock and simmer; finish with cream and crushed cream crackers.
Cherry (Scandinavia)	Cook cherries in red wine and water with cinnamon and sugar; sieve, thicken with diluted cornflour and garnish with cooked stoned cherries.

Clam Chowder (USA)	Stew diced leek, onion, salt belly of pork, potatoes and cooked clams in butter; add fish stock, finish with cream and crushed cream crackers.
Garbanzo (Spain)	Puree of chick peas flavoured with saffron and caraway seeds.
Goulash Soup (Hungary)	Make a goulash stew with beef and garnish with julienne of red pimento, diced potato and tomato, and noodles or gnocchi.
Lithuanienne (Russia)	Add julienne of celery to thin Purée Parmentier soup and finish with sour cream and chiffonade of sorrel; garnish with rectangles of bacon, sliced sausage and a small fried egg per portion.
Livornien (Russia)	Stew chopped onion and sorrel in butter, add blanched spinach and béchamel, cook and strain; thin out with stock, finish with cream and butter and garnish with kloskis which are poached chou paste dumplings made with chopped ham and shallot, and diced fried croûtons.
Olla Podrida (Spain)	Make a well-garnished broth soup with beef, mutton, belly of pork, trotters and ears, bacon, partridge and chicken with diced cabbage, carrot, leek, onion and potato together with chick peas and chorizo sausages. Serve the broth, the sliced meats and the vegetables in separate dishes.
Ouka (Russia)	Clarify good fish stock, garnish with julienne of celery, leek and parsley root and very small paupiettes of fish; serve with buckwheat kaches and a dish of rastegaïs (Kache is the crumb of an unleavened buckwheat loaf mixed to a paste with butter, cut into rounds and shallow fried. Rastegaïs are small pasties of brioche dough filled with a mixture of salmon, hard-boiled egg and vésiga).
Philadelphia Pepperpot (USA)	Cook tripe, knuckle of veal and salt belly of pork in stock with onion, leek, celeriac, pimento and potato; season well with pepper and lightly thicken the broth with beurre manié.

Puchero **(Spain)**	Make a fairly well-garnished broth with beef, mutton, pork, ham, diced mixed vegetables, chick peas and chorizo sausages and serve the liquid, the sliced meats and the vegetables in separate dishes.
Rabagas **(Brazil)**	Make a broth containing julienne of leek, potato and chicken and mix with an equal quantity of cream of green pea soup.
Rossolnick **(Russia)**	Cook blanched shaped pieces of parsley root and celeriac and diamonds of large gherkins in fairly thin chicken velouté mixed with juice expressed from a cucumber; finish with a liaison of yolks, cream and cucumber juice and garnish with quenelles.
Selianka **(Russia)**	Add braised sauerkraut to ham-flavoured stock and garnish with small blanched sprigs of parsley.
Shchi **(Russia)**	Cook chopped blanched sauerkraut and diced beef in thin velouté for several hours then finish the soup with sour cream and chopped parsley.
Zuppa Pavese **(Italy)**	Break an egg onto a slice of toast in a fireproof bowl, cover with boiling beef broth, sprinkle with parmesan and place in the oven to cook the egg.

———————— COLD SOUPS ————————

Ajo Blanco	Emulsify almonds and garlic with olive oil, moisten with water and serve poured over dried slices of bread.
Avocado	Stew chopped onion in butter, add chopped avocado, lemon juice and chicken stock, cook then liquidise; add cream and serve cold decorated with cream and chopped chives.
Apple	Cook apples in a little water with sugar; sieve, dilute with white wine and garnish with diced raw apple and plumped sultanas.
Batwinia	Stew shredded beet leaves, sorrel and spinach in butter, add very dry white wine, shallot,

	tarragon and diced pickled gherkin; cook and serve with ice in it.
Chicken	Add cream to cold chicken velouté. (Variations can include finishing it with crayfish butter, tomato, pimento, etc.)
Chotodriece	Fermented pickled gherkin juice garnished with chives, crayfish, dill, diced beetroot and sliced hard-boiled egg.
Cucumber	Stew pieces of cucumber in butter and make into a puree soup with velouté; strain, add a liaison and garnish with diced cucumber and shredded sorrel.
Gazpacho	Blend raw cucumber, pimento and tomato to a liquid with vinegar, add crushed garlic and bread emulsified with oil; season with cumin and serve accompanied with chopped onion, diced cucumber, tomato, pimento and fried bread croûtons.
Lilly	Garnish cream of chicken soup with chopped stewed sorrel and julienne of chicken.
Madrilène	Make a consommé with celery, pimento and tomato and set with very little gelatine.
Mulligatawny	Stew onion and garlic in butter, add curry powder and cook; moisten with brown stock and flavour with tomato puree, chutney, chopped apple and coconut; strain, add cream and plain boiled rice.
Okroshko	Mix hard-boiled egg-yolks with mustard, cooked mashed potato and sour cream and moisten with kvas; add diced cooked white of egg, cooked beetroot, carrot and pickled gherkin and flavour with dill. (Kvas is dried rye rusks fermented in water with yeast, raisins and sugar).
Princesse Royale	Mix equal quantities of cold cream of chicken soup and Cream of Asparagus soup; garnish with julienne of chicken, ham and ox-tongue.
Ritz	Add concentrated tomato juice to Vichyssoise and finish with chopped chives and diced tomato.

St-Cloud	Add chopped fresh mint to cream of green pea soup and garnish with dice of green pea royale.
Strawberry	Macerate strawberries with stock syrup, pass through a sieve then add white wine and lemon juice.
Vichyssoise	Stew leek and onion in butter, add chicken stock, milk and potato, pass and finish with cream and chopped chives.

Other cold soups include cucumber, watercress, carrot and orange, smoked salmon; they may be finished with plain yoghurt or fromage frais.

3　EGG DISHES

Egg dishes are grouped under the six basic methods of cooking them. These are grouped as:

1. soft boiled, poached, moulded
2. hard boiled, stuffed
3. en cocotte, sur le plat
4. deep and shallow fried
5. scrambled
6. omelettes

In general the method of serving each of these groups is the same and the same garnishes are suitable.

Size 2 chicken eggs are normally used; duck eggs must be thoroughly cooked.

SOFT BOILED,
──POACHED, MOULDED──

(a) Soft boiled – Oeuf Mollet

Place into boiling water, reboil and cook steadily for 6 minutes for a size 2 egg, slightly less for smaller ones. Cool, remove the shell and reheat in hot salted water when required, ensuring that the yolk is still runny.

(b) Poached – Oeuf Poché

Break the egg into steadily boiling water containing very little salt and some vinegar; the vinegar will prevent the white from spread-

110

ing; cook for 3 minutes until the white is hard but the yolk still soft. Remove, trim and keep in cold water until required then reheat in hot salted water, or wash in hot water and serve immediately.

(c) Moulded – Oeuf moulé

Break into buttered dariole moulds and cook au bain-marie, almost covered with a lid, for approximately 10 minutes; the yolk should still be soft. Turn out and serve

Africaine	Serve on a slice of ham placed on a round of buttered toast and garnish with one spoonful of pilaff rice and one of tomato concassée.
Alsacienne	Serve on a tartlet filled with cooked sauerkraut and garnish with a slice of ham.
Archiduc	Fill a tartlet with sauted chicken livers and truffle in brandy; place an egg on top and cover with Sauce Hongroise.
Argenteuil	Fill a tartlet with diced asparagus and arrange small sticks of asparagus on it; place the egg on top and coat with asparagus-flavoured cream sauce.
Armenonville	Serve the egg on a toasted slice of brioche, cover with sherry-flavoured velouté and garnish with some sprue and a spoonful of carrot puree.
Auber	Place the egg in a tartlet filled with stewed finely chopped beef and mushrooms then coat with Sauce Madère.
Aurore	Place the egg in an oval or round bouchée and coat with Sauce Suprême coloured and flavoured with tomato.
Beauregard	Serve the egg in a tartlet filled with puree of aubergine; cover with demi-glace and garnish with a slice of truffle.
Bénédictine	Cover a toasted crumpet with a round of ox-tongue, place the egg on top and coat it with Sauce Hollandaise.
en Berceau	Fill the skin of a baked potato with creamed minced chicken, pipe the edge with duchesse potato, place an egg inside and cover with Sauce Aurore.

111

Egg dishes

Berlioz Place some creamed minced venison and mush-room in the dish, put the egg on it and coat with Sauce Poivrade.

Bignon Place the egg in a ring of poached chicken forcemeat, coat with tarragon-flavoured Sauce Suprême and decorate with leaves of tarragon.

Bohémienne Spread a slice of toast with Sauce Mornay and cover half with chopped ham and half with truffle; place on top an egg that has been coated with Sauce Mornay and gratinated.

Boïeldieu Place the egg in a tartlet filled with creamed chicken, foie gras and truffle and coat with Sauce Suprême.

Bonvalet Place an egg on a round of buttered toast, coat with Sauce Suprême and pipe a border of Sauce Choron; garnish with a slice of truffle.

Bourguignonne Place an egg on a toasted slice of French bread and coat with red wine sauce.

Bragance Place an egg in an emptied half of cooked tomato, coat with Sauce Béarnaise, place on a dish and pour demi-glace around.

Bretonne Fill a tartlet with puree of haricot beans, place an egg on top and cover with jus lié.

Bruxelloise Place an egg in a dish on some puree of Belgian endive, cover with Sauce Crème and sprinkle with browned breadcrumbs.

Cambridge Cut an oval shape of pumpkin, hollow out and cook; fill with chicken puree, place an egg on top and cover with Sauce Vénitienne.

Cardinal Place the egg in a tartlet filled with diced lobster mixed with Sauce Crème, coat with Sauce Homard and sprinkle with lobster coral.

Carignan Line a dariole mould with chicken forcemeat containing lobster butter, break in the egg and cook; serve on toast, coated with Sauce Chateaubriand.

Cecilia Fill a hollowed out fried bread croûton with asparagus puree, place an egg on top, coat with Sauce Mornay and glaze.

Cendrillon Place an egg in an emptied baked potato skin;

112

pipe with a border of duchesse potato, cover
with Sauce Mornay and glaze.

Chambéry   Place an egg on a fried bread croûton spread
with chestnut puree, and coat with Sauce
Madère.

Chantilly   Fill a bouchée with creamed green pea puree,
place an egg on top and cover with Sauce
Mousseline.

Chartres   Coat an egg with tarragon-flavoured jus lié, place
on a round of buttered toast and garnish with
blanched leaves of tarragon.

Chasseur   Fill a tartlet with sauted chicken's livers and
mushrooms; place an egg on top, coat with
Sauce Chasseur and sprinkle with parsley.

Châtelaine   Fill a tartlet with chopped chestnuts mixed with
buttered meat glaze, place the egg on top and
coat with Sauce Soubise.

Chivry   Fill a tartlet with puree of sorrel, spinach and
watercress mixed with béchamel; place an egg
on top and cover with Sauce Chivry.

Cingalaise   Place an egg on a bed of plain boiled rice and
cover with curry sauce.

Clamart   Place an egg in a tartlet filled with puree of
green peas and cover with Sauce Suprême.

Clementine   Arrange asparagus tips and French beans in a
dish, place an egg on top and cover half with
Sauce Crème and half with demi-glace.

Colbert   Fill a tartlet with small macédoine of vegetables,
place an egg on top and coat with Beurre
Colbert (melted meat glaze mixed with maître
d'hôtel butter and chopped tarragon); serve at
once.

Comtesse   Fill a tartlet with asparagus puree, place an egg
on top, coat with Sauce Supréme and decorate
with a slice of truffle.

Condé   Place a mound of puree of red beans in a dish
and an egg coated with jus lié on top.

Continentale   Spread a round of toast with foie gras, place an
egg on top and cover with tomato-flavoured
Sauce Madère.

113

Crécy   Spread a toasted slice of brioche with carrot puree; place an egg on it, coat with Sauce Crème and decorate with fluted slices of carrot.

Danoise   Place an egg in a shallow bouchée filled with puree of smoked salmon.

Daumont   Fill a large cooked mushroom with diced crayfish in Sauce Nantua; place an egg on it, coat with some of the same sauce and decorate with a slice of truffle.

Dauphinoise   Pass a poached egg through flour, egg and breadcrumbs, deep fry quickly and serve with Sauce Tomate.

Diane   Fill a tartlet with puree of game and mushroom; place the egg on top, cover with Sauce Madère and decorate with a slice of truffle.

Dino   Coat an egg with curry sauce, sprinkle with julienne of chicken and place on a round of toast.

Doriac   Place a slice of ox-tongue on a round of toast, the egg on top, Sauce Suprême and chopped truffle to decorate.

Dubois   Fill a scallop shell with diced lobster and truffle mixed with curry-flavoured Sauce Crème; place an egg in it, coat with Sauce Homard, sprinkle with cheese and glaze.

Duchesse Colour a small round piece of duchesse potato in the oven, place an egg on it and coat with buttered jus lié.

Escoffier Fill a toasted slice of brioche with mixed diced artichoke and mushroom puree; coat with Sauce Suprême, sprinkle with lobster coral and decorate with a slice of truffle.

Fédora   Fill a tartlet with diced foie gras and truffle mixed with Sauce Suprême, place the egg on top and coat with the same sauce.

Flamande Fill a tartlet with puree of Brussels sprouts, place the egg on top and cover with Sauce Crème.

Flaubert Egg and crumb a poached egg and deep fry it; place it on a bouchée filled with diced lobster, mushrooms and mussels and coat with Sauce Hollandaise containing some lobster butter.

Flora
Coat one half of an egg with chicken velouté and the other with tomato sauce; sprinkle the white part with chopped truffle and the red with chopped parsley then place in an empty bouchée.

Floréal
Coat an egg with velouté containing chopped chervil; place on a puff-pastry base, pipe around with a scroll of green pea puree and decorate with pluches of chervil.

Florentine
Fill a tartlet with buttered chopped spinach; coat an egg with Sauce Mornay, glaze it and place on the tartlet.

Forestière
Place an egg in a nest made of duchesse potato filled with sauted slice morels mixed with jus lié.

Française
Hollow out a round flat potato cake; fill it with tomato concassée, place the egg on this and surround with demi-glace.

Gabriel
Add diced foie gras and sauted veal kidney to pilaff of rice, place it in a dish, the egg on top and Sauce Madère over.

Gambetta
Fill a hollowed out bread croûton with truffled soubise and place one ordinary poached and one deep fried poached egg on it.

Gastronome
Place an egg in a tartlet filled with duxelles, cover with Sauce Madère and sprinkle with chopped truffle.

Georgette
Place an egg in an emptied baked potato case that has been filled with diced lobster in Sauce Nantua; pipe a border of potato, coat with Sauce Mornay and glaze.

Grand Duc
Place the egg on a fried bread croûton and garnish it with a crayfish and a slice of truffle; coat with Sauce Mornay, glaze then add a bunch of sprue.

au Gratin
Place an egg on a fried bread croûton, coat with Sauce Mornay, sprinkle with breadcrumbs and cheese and glaze.

Halévy
Fill a tartlet half with creamed chicken and half with stewed tomato; coat an egg half with Sauce Suprême and half with Sauce Tomate; place on the tartlet and pipe a line of meat glaze along the centre.

115

Héloise   Place an egg on a fried croûton of bread, coat with Sauce Allemande containing finely diced chicken, tongue and truffle and surround it with a circle of tomato sauce.

Henri IV   Coat the egg with Sauce Béarnaise and place it in a bouchée.

Hollandaise   Fill a bouchée with puree of smoked salmon, and place an egg coated with Sauce Hollandaise on top.

Hussarde   Fill an emptied half tomato with sauted chopped onion and ham mixed with Sauce Demi-glace; coat an egg with Sauce Suprême and place it on the tomato.

Indienne   Place a poached egg on a bed of plain boiled rice and cover it with curry sauce.

Infante   Fill a tartlet with duxelles containing truffle; place the egg on top; coat with Sauce Mornay, glaze and decorate with a slice of truffle.

Italienne   Place an egg on a bed of Spaghetti Italienne and coat it with tomato sauce.

Lapérouse   Fill a shallow bouchée with artichoke puree, place an egg on top, cover with Sauce Suprême and decorate with truffle.

La Vallière   Fill a shallow bouchée with creamed puree of sorrel, place an egg on top, cover with Sauce Suprême and garnish with sprue.

Lithuanienne   Place the egg in a bouchée filled with duxelles and coat it with Sauce Périgueux.

Lorette   Deep fry a round of dauphine potato mixture, arrange asparagus tips on top then the egg and a slice of truffle; serve with jus lié.

Madras   Place a poached egg on a bed of plain boiled rice and coat it with curry sauce.

Maintenon   Fill a tartlet with soubise, place the egg on top, cover with Sauce Mornay and glaze; finish with a thread of meat glaze.

Malmaison   Fill a tartlet with peas, diamonds of French beans and diced sprue, mixed with cream; place the egg on top, pipe around with Sauce

Béarnaise and sprinkle over with chopped chervil and tarragon.

Masséna   Fill an artichoke bottom with Sauce Béarnaise; put an egg on top, coat with tomato sauce and garnish with a poached slice of bone marrow and chopped parsley.

Mazarin   Fill a shallow bouchée with diced mushroom, place an egg on top and coat it with tomato sauce.

Médicis   Fill a shallow bouchée with a little puree of sorrel and a few slices of carrot; add the egg and coat it with Sauce Crème flavoured with puree of green peas.

Mentonnaise   Place the egg on a bed of stewed leek, cover with Sauce Mornay, sprinkle with cheese and glaze.

Metternich   Fill an artichoke bottom with julienne of ox-tongue bound with Sauce Suprême; place an egg coated with Sauce Mornay on top and glaze.

Mignon   Fill an artichoke bottom half with peas and half with shrimps; coat an egg with shrimp sauce, decorate with truffle and place on the artichoke.

Milanaise   Fill a tartlet with Spaghetti Milanaise, place an egg on top, coat with Sauce Mornay and glaze.

Mireille   Coat the egg with saffron-coloured Sauce Crème and place it on a bed of saffron rice; garnish with a fried round bread croûton and a spoonful of cooked tomato concassée.

Mogador   Pipe out a rosette of tomato-flavoured duchesse potato, glaze in the oven then place an egg on top coated with Sauce Crème flavoured with foie. gras; add a garnish of ox-tongue and truffle.

Molière   Fill a cooked half tomato with chicken puree, place an egg on top and coat with Sauce Régence.

Moncelet   Fill a shallow bouchée with julienne of artichoke bottom and truffle mixed with Sauce Demi-glace; place an egg on top and cover with tomato-flavoured Sauce Madère.

Montglas   Fill a tartlet with diced foie gras, mushroom, tongue and truffle mixed with Sauce Madère;

place an egg on top and coat it with some of the same sauce.

Monseigneur Fill a tartlet with cooked sorrel, place an egg on it and mask with Sauce Colbert.

Montmorency Arrange asparagus tips on a large artichoke bottom, place the egg on top and coat it with tomato-flavoured Sauce Suprême.

Montpensier Place an egg on a tartlet filled with scrambled egg containing diced shrimps, and coat with shrimp sauce.

Montrouge Coat the egg with Sauce Suprême containing mushroom puree and place it in a large grilled mushroom.

Mornay Place the egg on a croûton of fried bread, coat with Sauce Mornay, sprinkle with grated cheese and breadcrumbs and glaze.

Mozart Coat the egg with Sauce Crème. decorate it with a lyre cut from truffle and serve on a croûton spread with foie gras.

Nantua Fill a tartlet with diced crayfish mixed with Sauce Nantua, coat it with Sauce Nantua and put two crayfish tails in the form of a cross.

Nicolas Fill a tartlet with puree of salmon, place the egg on top and coat with Sauce Hollandaise containing some caviar; garnish with a small fried cèpe.

Ninon Place the egg on a croûton of fried bread and garnish it with a bouquet of sprue, a slice of truffle and some diced creamed asparagus.

Normande Place three poached oysters mixed with Sauce Normande in a tartlet, place an egg on top and cover with Sauce Normande.

Orléans Mix diced chicken with tomato sauce and fill into a tartlet; coat an egg with pistachio-coloured Sauce Crème and place it on top.

Orsay Serve the egg on a fried bread croûton coated with Sauce Chateaubriand.

Ostendaise Fill a bouchée with diced mushroom, shrimps and truffle mixed with Sauce Nantua; coat an egg with Sauce Nantua and place it on top.

Otéro	Fill an emptied baked potato skin with diced mushroom, shrimps and truffle mixed with Sauce Nantua; pipe around with duchesse potato, place an egg on top and coat with the same sauce.
Pasha	Form flat rounds of saffron-flavoured pilaff of rice mixed with diced tomato; coat an egg with Sauce Crème, sprinkle it with cheese then place it on the rice; glaze under the salamander.
Parisienne	Coat half the egg with Sauce Crème and the other half with Sauce Nantua, sprinkle with chopped truffle and place in a dish.
Patti	Place an egg on a tartlet filled with puree of artichoke; coat with Sauce Madère, decorate with a slice of truffle and garnish the dish with asparagus.
Persane	Coat an egg with tomato sauce, sprinkle it with chopped chives and ham and place on a round of buttered toast.
Petit-Duc	Place an egg on a large grilled mushroom and coat it with Sauce Chateaubriand.
Piémontaise	Place an egg on a bed of risotto containing julienne of mushroom, pimento, tomato and truffle; coat with Sauce Crème and shave some white truffle over.
Polonaise	Place an egg on a layer of minced cooked mutton and mushroom and cover it with Sauce Poivrade.
Portugaise	Place the egg in an emptied half of cooked tomato and coat it with Sauce Portugaise.
Princesse	Fill a tartlet with diced asparagus on one side and creamed chicken on the other; coat an egg with Sauce Crème, decorate with a slice of truffle and place it in the tart.
Rachel	Place an egg in an artichoke bottom, coat it with red wine sauce and decorate with a slice of bone marrow and chopped parsley.
Regina	Fill a tartlet with a salpicon of mushroom, prawn and sole; coat an egg with Sauce Normande, sprinkle with julienne of truffle and place on top.
Reine	Fill a tartlet with puree of chicken, place an egg on top and cover with Sauce Suprême.

119

Ritz Fill a shallow bouchée with diced cooked green pimento and shrimps mixed with shrimp sauce; coat the egg with the same sauce and place on top.

Roland Fill a hollowed-out fried bread croûton with creamed chicken; place an egg on top, cover with velouté containing chopped chicken and truffle and finish with chopped parsley.

Rossini Place a slice of foie gras in a tartlet, the egg on it and Sauce Madère over; finish with a slice of truffle.

Rougemont Place Risotto Milanaise in a dish, an egg on top then Sauce Mornay; glaze and surround with tomato sauce.

Royale Mix diced cockscombs, mushroom and truffle with Sauce Suprême, fill into a tartlet and place an egg coated with the same sauce on top.

Saint-Hubert Mix diced game with sauce from a civet, place in a dish with the egg on top and pour Sauce Poivrade over.

Sans-Gène Place an egg on an artichoke bottom, coat it with red wine sauce and place a slice of bone marrow and chopped parsley on top.

Savoyarde Place an egg on a round of Pommes Savoyarde, coat it with Sauce Mornay, sprinkle with bread-crumbs and cheese and gratinate.

Sévigné Spread puree of braised lettuce on a fried croûton; coat the egg with Sauce Suprême, decorate with a slice of truffle and place on the croûton.

Soubise Fill a tartlet with soubise, coat an egg with jus lié and place on top.

Souveraine Coat an egg with Sauce Suprême, decorate it with a slice of truffle and place in a bouchée filled with puree of asparagus.

Stanley Fill a tartlet with curry-flavoured rice soubise, coat the egg with curry-flavoured Sauce Suprême and place on top.

Sultane Place scrambled egg finished with diced truffle in a tartlet, add a poached egg, coat with Sauce

Madère and decorate with a crescent-shaped slice of truffle.

Suzette   Pour some Sauce Mornay into an emptied baked potato, place in the egg, coat with the same sauce, sprinkle with cheese and glaze.

Toupinel   Place some of the mashed puree back inside an emptied baked potato, then buttered spinach and the egg; coat with Sauce Mornay, sprinkle with cheese and gratinate.

Tourangelle   Fill a tartlet with puree of flageolet beans, coat an egg with Sauce Crème containing puree of French beans and place on top.

Toussenel   Cover an egg with Cullis of game mixed with chestnut puree and place it on a deep fried flat croquette of game.

Ursuline   Hollow out a cooked oval of salmon forcemeat, fill with creamed mushrooms, place an egg on top, coat with Sauce Mornay and glaze.

Verdi   Mix chopped ham and fines herbes into Sauce Crème; fill into a tartlet and place an egg coated with truffle-flavoured demi-glace on top.

Victoria   Fill a tartlet with diced lobster and truffle mixed with lobster sauce; coat an egg with Sauce Mornay mixed with crayfish butter, place on top and glaze.

Vieville   Place an egg in a border of risotto, garnish with a half of grilled lamb kidney and coat with Sauce Madère.

Villaret   Fill a dish with sliced sauted artichoke bottoms mixed with soubise; place an egg on top, coat with Sauce Mornay and glaze.

Villeroy   Pass a cooked egg through flour, egg and breadcrumbs and deep fry quickly; serve with tomato sauce and fried parsley.

Viroflay   Fry a slice of brioche in butter, hollow out and fill with buttered spinach; coat an egg with Sauce Allemande and place on top.

Wyvern   Place an egg in a puff-pastry case, coat with Sauce Vin blanc and sprinkle with crushed cooked Bombay Duck.

—HARD-BOILED – OEUF DUR—

Place eggs into boiling water, reboil and cook at boiling point for 8–10 minutes according to size; cool immediately under running water and roll on a board to crack the shell before peeling. Keep in a basin of cold water.

Stuffed – Oeufs farcis

Cut hard-boiled eggs in half, remove the yolks and refill with various fillings, usually including the sieved yolk

Antiboise	Refill with a stuffing made with the yolks, dice of lobster and tomato and some stiffly beaten egg white; sprinkle with cheese and cook in the oven.
Belloy	Fill with a stuffing of egg yolk, diced lobster, mushroom and truffle; coat with Sauce Mornay and glaze.
Bretonne	Sauté sliced leek, mushroom and onion, place some in a dish, put the halved eggs on it and cover with the remaining mixture.
Carême	Arrange sliced egg, artichoke bottom and truffle in a dish, cover with Sauce Nantua and decorate with more truffle.
Chimay	Mix the yolks with duxelles, refill the whites, cover with Sauce Mornay and glaze.
Commerce	Place halved eggs on a layer of creamy mashed potato; cover with rice soubise, sprinkle with breadcrumbs, Gruyère and butter and gratinate.
Côtelettes	Mix diced egg with reduced béchamel, add raw yolks to bind and when cold, mould cutlet shape; egg and crumb, deep fry and serve with Sauce Tomate (a small length of blanched macaroni may be inserted to represent the cutlet bone).
Croquette	Make the mixture as for Côtelettes; mould cork-shape, egg and crumb and deep fry quickly.
des Gourmets	Mix the yolks with diced crayfish, salmon and truffle and Sauce Mornay; refill the whites, coat with the same sauce and glaze.

Hongroise	Lay sliced egg in a dish and coat with paprika sauce containing diced cooked onion and tomato.
Indienne	Mix the yolks with puree of chicken, curry powder and cream sauce, use this to reform the eggs, egg and crumb and deep fry; serve with curry sauce.
Percheronne	Arrange layers of sliced egg, béchamel and slices of cooked potato in a dish, dot with butter and reheat.
Portugaise	Place a hard boiled egg in an emptied half of cooked tomato and coat with Sauce Portugaise.
Rissoles	Cut out ovals of puff pastry, add puree of hard boiled egg, fold over to seal and deep fry.
Scotch Egg	Dip a hard boiled egg into flour, cover completely with a thin coating of sausage meat, egg and crumb and deep fry; serve cold or hot.
à la Tripe	Place halved or sliced egg in a dish and cover with onion sauce.
Vol-au-Vent	Place layers of sliced egg, sliced truffle, quarters of mushrooms and Sauce Crème into a vol-au-vent case; finish it with sauce and a slice of truffle.

—EN COCOTTE; SUR LE PLAT—

(a) In cocotte – Oeuf en cocotte

Break an egg into a buttered egg cocotte dish, cook in the oven in a bain-marie of hot water for approximately 6 minutes, covered with a lid. The yolk should still be soft.

(b) Shirred egg – Oeuf sur le plat

Heat butter in the egg dish, break in the egg and cook on the side of the stove or in the oven just until the yolk becomes glazed over.

123

Eggs in cocotte

Bergère Line the cocotte with puree of lamb and mushroom, add the egg and cook; surround with jus lié or meat glaze.

Bordelaise Place a poached slice of bone marrow in the cocotte; when cooked finish with red wine sauce.

Buckingham Line a cocotte with ham puree, add the egg, sprinkle with parmesan and cook; garnish with diced fried bread croûtons.

Café Anglais Line the cocotte with chicken forcemeat, add the egg, cook and finish with lobster sauce.

Chambertin Pour red Chambertin wine sauce into a cocotte, add the egg and cook.

Colbert Line a cocotte with chicken and fines herbes forcemeat, add the egg, cook and finish with Beurre Colbert.

Commodore Cook an egg plainly and cover with Sauce Béarnaise when serving.

à la Crème Pour boiling cream into a cocotte, add the egg, season and cook.

Diane Line a cocotte with game forcemeat, add the egg, cook and finish with game sauce.

Diplomate Place a slice of foie gras in the cocotte, add the egg, cook and surround with a cordon of tomato sauce.

Florentine Place buttered spinach mixed with diced anchovy in the cocotte, add the egg, cover with cream and grated cheese and cook and glaze.

Forestière Place fried lardons and sliced morels in the cocotte, add the egg, cook and finish with game sauce.

Jeannette Line a cocotte with chicken and foie gras forcemeat, add the egg, cook and finish with a cordon of chicken velouté.

Josephine Place duxelles in the cocotte, add the egg and cook then cover with tomato-flavoured Sauce Mornay.

au Jus When the egg is cooked, cover it with jus lié.

Leontine Line a cocotte with fish forcemeat containing diced crayfish and truffle; add the egg, cook and finish with tomato sauce.

Lucullus Place a slice each of foie gras and truffle in the cocotte, break an egg on top, cook and finish with Sauce Madère.

Marigny Place a round of ham and two cooked oysters in the cocotte; add an egg, cook, coat with Sauce Mornay and grated cheese and glaze.

Marly Place cooked minced veal and mushrooms in the cocotte; add an egg, cook and finish with Demi-glace.

Nancy Line a cocotte with puree of foie gras-truffé, add the egg, cook and finish with demi-glace.

Parisienne Line a cocotte with chicken forcemeat made with diced mushroom, ox-tongue and mushroom; add the egg, cook and finish with demi-glace.

Portugaise Place cooked concassée tomato in a cocotte; break in the egg, cook and surround with tomato sauce.

Princesse Place diced asparagus in the cocotte, add the egg, cook and surround with Sauce Crème.

Reine Fill creamed chicken in the cocotte, add an egg, cook and finish with Sauce Suprême.

Rossini Place a slice of foie gras in the cocotte, then the egg; cook and finish with Sauce Périgueux.

St-Hubert Line a cocotte with puree of game, add an egg and cook; garnish with a slice of truffle and surround with Sauce Poivrade.

Voltaire Cover the bottom of a cocotte with creamed diced chicken, add an egg, cook then coat with Sauce Mornay, sprinkle with cheese and glaze.

Oeufs sur le plat

Alsacienne Place cooked sauerkraut in the dish, break the egg on top and cook; serve with a slice of hot garlic sausage.

Américaine   Place a slice of grilled ham in the dish, add the egg and cook; finish with a cordon of tomato sauce.

aux Anchois   Place strips of anchovy in the dish, add the egg and cook; place a circular fillet of anchovy around the yolk.

Bercy   Cook in the usual way then garnish with a pair of small chipolatas and a cordon of tomato sauce.

au Beurre Noir   Mask the cooked egg with butter cooked until it is brown then flavoured with a few drops of vinegar.

Bruxelloise   Mix chopped braised Belgian endive with béchamel, place in a dish, add the egg, sprinkle with crushed dry biscuits and cook.

Caruso   Garnish the cooked egg with sauted chicken livers, mushrooms and diced tomato and surround with basil-flavoured jus lié.

Chasseur   Garnish the cooked egg with sauted chicken livers mixed with Sauce Chasseur.

Cluny   Garnish the cooked egg with a small round chicken croquette and a cordon of tomato sauce.

Crécy   Place some Carottes Vichy in the dish, add the egg and cook; finish with a cordon of Sauce Crème.

Doria   Garnish the cooked egg with diamonds of sauted cucumber mixed with cream.

Duchesse   Pipe the dish with duchesse potato, break in the egg, add some cream and cook in the usual way; finish with a slice of truffle.

Florentine   Place buttered chopped spinach in the dish, sprinkle with cheese, add the egg and coat with Mornay Sauce; cook and gratinate at the same time.

Forestière   Place some sauted dice of morels, bacon and chopped shallot in the dish, add the egg and when cooked garnish with sauted morels and chopped parsley.

Jean Granier   Place creamed asparagus tips and slices of truffle in the dish, add the egg and when cooked garnish it with asparagus and truffle.

Gounod	When the egg is cooked add some sliced sauted mushrooms and surround with a line of tomato sauce.
Huguenote	Heat some lamb stock in the dish, add the egg and cook as usual; garnish with sauted diced lamb kidney and onion mixed with demi-glace.
Isoline	Garnish the cooked eggs with small tomatoes cooked à la provençale with sauted chicken livers mixed with madeira sauce in each one.
au Jus	When the egg is cooked surround with a little jus lié and sprinkle with chopped parsley.
Lorraine	Place small pieces of grilled bacon and slices of Gruyère in the dish, break in the egg, add a little cream and cook in the usual way.
Lully	Place a round of toast with a slice of sauted ham in the dish, break in the egg and cook, then garnish with tomatoed macaroni.
Lyonnaise	Place some fried shredded onion in the dish, break in the egg and cook in the usual way.
Maraîchère	Place stewed shredded lettuce, sorrel and chervil in the dish, add the egg and cook as usual; serve garnished with two rashers of streaky bacon.
Mascot	When the egg is cooked add some sauted diced artichoke bottom, potato and truffle and a line of Madeira sauce.
Matelote	Pour some Sauce Matelote into the dish, break in the egg and cook; serve surrounded with some of the same sauce with added butter.
Maximilienne	Cook emptied halves of large tomatoes, add chopped garlic and parsley and the egg, sprinkle with mixed grated cheese, chopped parsley and fried breadcrumbs and cook and gratinate in the oven.
Meyerbeer	Garnish the cooked egg with a grilled lamb's kidney and a cordon of Sauce Périgueux.
Mirabeau	Spread the dish with anchovy butter, add the egg and cook; surround the yolk with fillets of anchovy, decorate with blanched tarragon leaves and a large olive filled with tarragon butter.

127

Monégasque Place some diced cooked tomato with tarragon in the dish, add the egg and cook; serve garnished with anchovy fillets and a line of tomato sauce.

Montmorency Cook the egg on asparagus tips, then garnish with asparagus tips and sauted artichoke bottoms.

Nantua Place diced crayfish in Nantua sauce in the dish, break in the egg and cook; garnish with a crayfish and a slice of truffle and finish with a cordon of Nantua sauce.

Niçoise Break the egg into the dish on some diced cooked tomato and tarragon, cook and garnish with anchovy fillets and a thread of demi-glace.

Normande Place six oysters, some cream and fish essence in the dish, add the egg and cook; finish with a little Sauce Normande.

Omar Pasha Place sauted sliced onion in the dish, add the egg, sprinkle with cheese and cook; finish with a cordon of tomato sauce.

Opéra Add sauted diced chicken livers in madeira sauce and a bunch of buttered asparagus tips to the cooked egg.

Parmentier Half fill emptied baked potatoes with the mashed flesh, break in the egg, coat with cream and cook in the oven; replace the top when serving.

Parmesan Break the egg into the dish, sprinkle with parmesan and melted butter, cook and glaze at the same time.

Périgourdine Pour some truffle essence in the buttered dish and cook the egg as usual, garnish with small piles of diced truffle and a cordon of truffle-flavoured demi-glace.

Piémontaise Sprinkle the buttered dishes with cheese, add the egg, sprinkle with cheese and cook; garnish with cheese-flavoured risotto and grated white truffle.

Richemont Cook the egg in the usual way then garnish with diced morels and truffle and surround with a cordon of Madeira sauce.

Rossini	Garnish the cooked egg with a small slice of foie gras and truffle and surround with Sauce Périgueux.
Rothomago	Garnish the cooked egg with a slice of grilled ham and a chipolata sausage; surround with tomato sauce.
Soubise	Put some soubise in the dish, break the egg on top and cook in the usual manner; serve surrounded with demi-glace.
Turandot	Garnish the cooked egg with a cooked half of tomato filled with sauted sliced chicken livers mixed with Madeira sauce.
Turque	Add a garnish of sauted diced chicken liver mixed with tomato-flavoured demi-glace; surround with some of the same sauce.
Vaucourt	Pipe the dish with a border of duchesse potato, place some scrambled egg mixed with diced asparagus in the dish and break the egg on top; cook in a tray of cold water in the oven and garnish with a slice of truffle.
Victoria	Garnish the egg when cooked with diced lobster and truffle mixed with lobster sauce.
Vladimir	When the egg is cooked add a small bunch of asparagus tips and a slice of truffle; coat with cream, sprinkle with cheese and glaze quickly.

——FRIED EGG – OEUF FRIT——

(a) **French fried –**
Oeuf frit à la Française Break the egg into a small pan of deep oil and mould the white evenly around the yolk, using a well dried wooden spoon; fry until golden brown and remove with a perforated spoon.
(b) **English fried –**
Oeuf à la Poêle Break the egg into fairly hot shallow fat in a frying pan and cook until the white is set, basting occasionally.

French fried eggs

Andalouse   Serve the egg on a slice of fried egg-plant with a cordon of tomato sauce.

Bayonnaise   Serve on a grilled half of tomato on a grilled round slice of ham, with Madeira sauce separately.

Benoîton   Place some brandade of salt cod on a dish, sprinkle with breadcrumbs and butter and gratinate; place the fried egg on top.

Bergère   Gratinate some minced lamb and mushrooms mixed with cream sauce and place the fried egg on top.

Bordelaise   Cook halves of emptied tomatoes with some chopped shallot inside then fill with cèpes cooked bordelaise style; place the egg on top and garnish with fried parsley.

Bûcheronne   Remove the flesh from baked potatoes, mash and fry in butter, place on a dish and put the egg containing a pinch of chives, on top.

Cavour   Cook halves of emptied tomatoes in oil, fill with piedmontaise risotto, place the egg on top and serve with jus lié.

Louisienne   Garnish the egg with a sweet potato fritter, a fried banana, a spoonful of creamed sweetcorn and a mould of risotto.

Mexicaine   Empty halves of large tomatoes and cook in oil, fill with Créole rice and place an egg in each; serve with tomato sauce.

des Moissonneurs   Arrange the cooked egg and grilled streaky bacon on a dish and fill the centre with peas cooked with shredded lettuce and sliced potato.

Palmerstone   Place the fried egg on a slice of fried ham on a round of buttered toast; serve with Sauce Poivrade.

Pastourelle   Serve the egg with grilled rashers of bacon and lamb kidneys and sliced sauted mushrooms flavoured with shallot; sprinkle with parsley.

Provençale   Fry the egg, place in a cooked emptied half tomato and place on a slice of fried eggplant; garnish with parsley.

Romaine Make subrics of spinach and anchovy and serve an egg on each.

St-Amand Add finely chopped ham whilst cooking the egg and serve with grilled rashers of bacon

Serbe Mix sauted dice eggplant into pilaff rice and mould on a dish, place the fried egg on top with a slice of grilled ham.

English fried eggs

à l'Américaine Serve the fried egg with grilled streaky rashers and grilled tomatoes.

à l'Anglaise Place the fried egg on a round of fried bread and surround with jus lié.

au Beurre noir Pour some hot nut-brown butter mixed with a little vinegar, over the fried egg.

à la Bouchère Place on a sauted thin fillet steak, with a little demi-glace.

Diable Fry the egg on both sides, place on a dish and add hot nut-brown butter mixed with a little vinegar.

Espagnole Place the fried egg on a grilled half of tomato and garnish with fried onion rings.

Lorraine Serve with grilled bacon rashers and slices of Gruyère cheese and mask with a little hot cream.

Mikado Place the egg on a grilled half tomato and garnish with fillets of anchovy and capers; serve with a little demi-glace.

Mirabeau Decorate the fried egg with fillets of anchovy, stuffed olives and blanched tarragon leaves.

Montargis Mix sautéd strips of chicken livers, ox-tongue and mushroom with béchamel, fill in tartlets, coat with Mornay sauce and glaze; place a trimmed fried egg on top and decorate with a round of ox-tongue.

Nero Trim the egg round and serve on a flat chicken croquette with some tomato sauce.

Princesse Alice	Cut out a round from the centre of a square slice of bread, fry in butter with an egg in the middle; serve with a grilled rasher of bacon, sauted sliced mushrooms and asparagus tips. Coat the egg and bread with Hollandaise Sauce.
Rachel	Place the trimmed egg on a round of toast and decorate with a poached slice of bone marrow and of truffle; surround with demi-glace.
Rothomago	Serve the fried egg with a fried slice of ham, a grilled chipolata sausage and a little tomato sauce
Vaucourt	Pipe a ring of duchesse potato and glaze; fill with scrambled egg mixed with diced asparagus and truffle, fry the egg and place on top; decorate with truffle and surround with demi-glace.

SCRAMBLED EGG –
———OEUF BROUILLÉ———

Whisk the egg with salt and pepper; melt butter in a pan, add the egg and cook over a low heat, stirring continuously until lightly coagulated. Mix in a little butter and cream and serve as follows.

Amiral	Add diced lobster and serve with a cordon of Sauce Homard.
Archiduchesse	Flavour with paprika and add diced ham and mushroom; serve on a glazed hollow round cake of duchesse potato and garnish with asparagus tips.
Arlesienne	Add diced sauted aubergine and tomato.
Argenteuil	Serve with asparagus tips on top of the egg.
d'Aumale	Add diced tomato to the cooked egg and garnish with sauted diced kidney in Sauce Madère.
Balzac	Add diced ox-tongue and truffle and serve on fried bread croûtons coated with soubise; add a cordon of tomato-flavoured demi-glace.
Batelière	Add chopped chives and serve in tartlets lined with fish puree.
Bordelaise	Add diced mushroom, garnish with triangular croûtons and surround with Sauce Bordelaise.

Brésilienne	Add julienne of cooked red pimento and serve in a flat pastry case; surround with tomato sauce containing chopped ham.
Bressane	Garnish with sauted chicken liver, a slice of truffle and finish with a border of demi-glace.
Carême	Add diced chicken, foie gras and truffle and serve on a flat pastry case; decorate with a slice of truffle and surround with demi-glace.
Chalonnaise	Serve with a garnish of cockscombs and kidneys and a border of Sauce Crème.
aux Champignons	Garnish with sauted sliced mushrooms.
Chambord	Serve on a fried round of aubergine and surround with demi-glace.
Chasseur	Serve with a garnish of chicken liver sauted with mushroom and tomato; surround with Sauce Chasseur and sprinkle with tarragon and parsley.
Châtillon	Serve garnished with sauted sliced mushrooms, a thread of meat glaze and small pale baked fleurons.
Clamart	Add peas cooked à la Française and surround with Sauce Crème.
Comtesse	Add shrimps, garnish with asparagus tips and surround with demi-glace.
Divette	Add diced asparagus and crayfish and garnish with crayfish; finish with a border of Sauce Homard.
Don Juan	Add diced cooked green pimento; decorate with a trellis work of anchovy and pour a cordon of Sauce Madère around.
Epicurienne	Add diced foie gras, mushrooms and truffle and serve with demi-glace.
Espagnole	Serve in cooked emptied halves of tomato and garnish with French-fried onion rings and chopped red pimento.
Figaro	Garnish with thinly sliced chipolata sausages and surround with Sauce Béarnaise mixed with tomato sauce.
aux Fines Herbes	Add chopped chervil, chives, parsley and tarragon to the eggs.

aux Foies de Volaille	Place a garnish of sauted chicken liver mixed with Sauce Madère in the centre of the eggs.
Forestière	Add sauted quartered morels and lardons and garnish with a large sauted morel.
Georgette	Garnish with crayfish, finish with crayfish butter and serve in emptied baked potato skins.
Grand'Mère	Add small diced fried bread croûtons and chopped parsley.
Héloise	Add julienne of chicken, mushroom and ox-tongue and serve with a cordon of tomato sauce.
Huysmann	Add diced artichoke bottom and mushroom, place in a round flat puff-pastry case and garnish with sauted kidney mixed with Sauce Madère.
Italienne	Serve inside a border of risotto made with diced tomato and surround with tomato sauce.
Joinville	Add diced mushroom, shrimps and truffle to the eggs; serve in a bouchée with some shrimps, a mushroom and a slice of truffle on top.
Lucullus	Add diced truffle, garnish with a slice of truffle and serve with a cordon of demi-glace.
Magda	Add chopped fines herbes, made mustard and grated Gruyère cheese and serve surrounded with small rectangular fried bread croûtons
Manon	Add chopped mushrooms and truffle; serve on a flat chicken croquette and surround with velouté finished with chopped truffle.
Marinette	Add chopped chervil and serve garnished with rounds of ox-tongue and a salpicon of asparagus, chicken and truffle.
Marivaux	Add finely chopped truffle and garnish with a large turned mushroom and a circle of sliced mushrooms; finish with a line of meat glaze.
Mary Garden	Add chopped truffle and red pimento to the scrambled egg and serve in a vol-au-vent case.
Mercédès	Mix chopped chives with the egg and serve in an emptied brioche filled with tomato concassée.
Méxicaine	Add diced green pimento and surround with tomato sauce.
Monégasque	Garnish with a slice of lobster and surround with Sauce Homard.

Nantua	Add diced crayfish and truffle and serve decorated with a slice of truffle and a cordon of sauce Nantua.
Normande	Garnish with poached oysters and surround with Sauce Normande.
Norvégienne	Serve on a slice of toast spread with anchovy butter and decorate with a trellis work of anchovy fillets.
Opéra	Mix with sauted diced chicken liver and garnish with a bouquet of asparagus tips.
Orientale	Add tomato concassée and diced green pimento; garnish with toasted croûtons spread with soubise and pipe with a thread of meat glaze.
Orloff	Add diced crayfish to the eggs and serve decorated with a slice of truffle.
Portugaise	Add diced tomato to the egg, serve with some on top and a cordon of tomato sauce around.
Princesse	Add diced asparagus to the egg and serve garnished with asparagus tips and a slice of truffle; surround with Sauce Crème.
Princesse-Marie	Flavour the egg with parmesan and truffle-flavoured velouté finished with diced truffle and serve in bouchées covered with the pale baked lids.
Provençale	Garnish with diced tomato cooked in oil with garlic and serve sprinkled with parsley.
Rachel	Add diced asparagus and truffle; garnish with a bouquet of asparagus tips and a slice of truffle.
Ranhofer	Serve the scrambled egg on an artichoke bottom containing a poached slice of bone marrow, and surround with red wine sauce.
Reine-Margot	Finish with almond butter, fill into tartlets and pipe a circle of béchamel finished with pistachio butter.
Romaine	Add chopped anchovy, chopped buttered spinach and garlic to the egg and serve surrounded with demi-glace-tomatée.
Rothschild	Add creamed puree of crayfish to the eggs then scramble them; serve garnished with asparagus tips, crayfish and slices of truffle.

Sans Gène	Fill the scrambled egg into a large artichoke bottom and add a slice of poached bone marrow coated with red wine sauce, and sprinkle with parsley.
Sarah Bernhardt	Serve with a garnish of cockscombs and kidneys; decorate with a slice of truffle and a cordon of Sauce Crème.
Suisse	Add diced emmenthal cheese, place in a tartlet, sprinkle with cheese and gratinate.
Sultane	Served scrambled egg finished with pistachio butter in an emptied deep fried brioche shape made with duchesse potato.
Sylvette	Place the egg on top of some crayfish puree in a vol-au-vent and garnish with a slice of truffle.
aux Tomates	Place some tomato concassée in the centre of the cooked egg and add a pinch of chopped parsley.
Turque	Serve the egg on a baked stuffed aubergine.
Vaucourt	Add diced asparagus and truffle and serve in a glazed border of duchesse potato; surround with demi-glace.
Waldorf	Serve in a large mushroom with a slice of foie gras and a slice of truffle on top and Sauce Périgueux around.
Walewska	Add diced lobster and truffle and serve with a cordon of Sauce Homard.
Yvette	Add diced asparagus and crayfish to the scrambled egg, mix in some Sauce Nantua and serve in a tartlet; decorate with a slice of truffle.

OMELETTES

There are two main kinds – the oval and the round flat. To make an ordinary omelette beat the eggs with salt and pepper until thoroughly mixed. Heat an omelette pan, add a little butter and allow to get hot and coat the pan. Add the egg and stir it around over a brisk heat so as to coagulate. When slightly set, remove from the heat and fold one side to the centre, knock the pan so as to bring the other side to the centre to form an oval shape. Allow to colour slightly then turn over onto a warm dish. Brush with butter and serve immediately. The filling can be added to the raw egg, put in the centre before folding, or placed on the omelette after it is cooked.

A flat omelette is made by allowing the egg to coagulate to the shape of the pan then tossed over or placed under the salamander to finish cooking.

A soufflé omelette is made by separating the eggs and folding the stiffly whisked whites into the beaten yolks then cooking on top of the stove and when shaped, finishing to cook in the oven. This kind is known as Omelette Viennoise or Mousseline and is usually a sweet one.

Agnes Sorel	Fold over with sauted sliced mushrooms mixed with a little chicken velouté and serve decorated with round slices of ox-tongue and a cordon of jus lié.
Algérienne	Add diced cooked onion, pimento and tomato to the beaten eggs and make the omelette in the usual manner.
Américaine	Make the omelette, cut a slit in the top and fill with tomato concassée; serve with grilled rashers of streaky bacon.
Andalouse	Add diced cooked mushroom, pimento and tomato to the beaten eggs; make the omelette and serve garnished with French fried onion rings.
Archiduc	Slit the top of the omelette and fill with sauted diced chicken liver in demi-glace; serve decorated with a slice of truffle and surround with demi-glace.
Arnold Bennett	Fold with creamed smoked haddock inside, place on a dish and coat with Sauce Mornay; sprinkle with cheese and gratinate quickly. This may also be made flat.
d'Aumale	Fill the inside with sauted dice of kidney mixed with Sauce Madère; make the omelette and place tomato concassée on top.
Bénédictine	Fill the inside with creamed puree of salt cod

137

	mixed with chopped truffle, and surround with Sauce Normande.
Berwick	Roll a poached soft roe in a slice of smoked salmon and place inside a herb omelette.
Bonne Femme	Add fried lardons, sliced mushroom and onion to the beaten eggs and make the omelette flat.
Bouchère	Cut a slit in the top of the omelette and fill with poached dice of bone marrow mixed with meat glaze and serve with a slice of bone marrow on top, brushed with melted meat glaze.
Bretonne	Add stewed shredded leek and onion and sliced mushroom to the beaten eggs and make the omelette in the usual way.
Brillat-Savarin	Cut open the top and fill with dice of truffle and woodcock mixed with Sauce Salmis; decorate with a slice of truffle and surround with game glaze mixed with truffle essence.
aux Champignons	Add sauted sliced mushrooms to the egg mixture and garnish the omelette with a sauted button mushroom or a line of sliced mushrooms.
Chartres	Add chopped tarragon to the eggs and decorate the omelette with blanched tarragon leaves.
Chasseur	Slit the omelette and fill with sauted diced chicken liver and mushroom in Sauce Madère; finish with chopped parsley and a cordon of Sauce Madère.
Châtelaine	Fold the omelette with chopped braised chestnuts mixed with meat glaze and serve with a border of velouté flavoured with soubise.
Chevreuse	Add diced artichoke bottom, asparagus and truffle to the beaten egg, make the omelette and decorate with round slices of artichoke and truffle.
Choisy	Cut a slit in the omelette and fill with shredded cooked lettuce mixed with Sauce Crème; surround with a border of the same sauce.
Clamart	Cut a slit in the omelette and fill with peas cooked à la française.
Continentale	Add chopped chives to the eggs and fill the omelette with fried diced mushroom and potato; serve surrounded with demi-glace.

138

Crécy	Fold with carrot puree inside, decorate with slices of cooked carrot and surround with Sauce Crème.
aux Crevettes	Stuff the omelette with diced shrimps in shrimp sauce and decorate with prawns; surround with Sauce Crème.
Demidoff	Fill the inside with diced artichoke bottom, decorate with poached bone marrow and surround with a border of demi-glace.
Dieppoise	Fill the inside with diced mussels and shrimps mixed with Sauce Vin blanc and serve with a border of the same sauce.
Diplomate	Fill the inside with diced artichoke bottom and truffle mixed with Sauce Périgueux.
Doria	Fill the inside with cooked diced cucumber mixed with velouté and surround with a border of the same sauce.
Durand	Add sauted artichoke bottom and mushroom to the eggs and fill inside with diced asparagus and julienne of truffle mixed with velouté; surround with demi-glace-tomatée.
Duse	Fill the inside with diced cooked calf's brain and crayfish mixed with Sauce Madère.
Espagnole	Add cooked julienne of pimento, sauted sliced onion and diced cooked tomato to the beaten eggs and make the omelette flat.
Favorite	Fill the inside with diced asparagus and ham mixed with Sauce Crème, decorate with a slice of truffle and surround with more of the same sauce.
Fermière	Add diced ham and chopped parsley to the eggs and make the omelette flat.
aux Fines Herbes	Add chopped chervil, chives, parsley and tarragon to the beaten eggs and make the omelette in the usual manner.
Florentine	Fill the inside with buttered spinach, fold and serve with a cordon of Sauce Crème.
Forestière	Add sliced morels and fried lardons to the egg mixture and fill the omelette with sauted sliced morels; decorate with a line of morels and surround with jus lié.

139

au Fromage   Add grated cheddar and parmesan to the beaten eggs and make the omelette in the usual manner; if desired it may be sprinkled with cheese and glazed.

Gargamelle   Fill with duxelles, coat with double cream, cover with thinly sliced Gruyère then more cream; sprinkle with parmesan and glaze under a salmander.

Gounod   Fill the inside with diced braised sweetbread and truffle and serve with a cordon of Sauce Périgueux.

Grand'mère   Add freshly fried diced bread croûtons and chopped parsley to the eggs and make the omelette in the usual manner.

Grandval   Fill the inside with garlic-flavoured cooked puree of tomato, coat the made omelette with tomato sauce and decorate with slices of hard-boiled egg.

Grenobloise   Add cooked shredded onion and sorrel to the beaten eggs and make the omelette in the usual manner.

Grimaldi   Fill the inside with diced crayfish mixed with fish velouté and garnish with a whole crayfish.

Havanaise   Cut a slit in the top, open out and fill with sauted diced chicken liver, green pimento and tomato; surround with tomato sauce.

Hollandaise   Add a short julienne of smoked salmon to the beaten eggs, make the omelette and serve with a border of Sauce Hollandaise.

Hongroise   Add sauted shredded onion, tomato concassée and paprika to the beaten eggs; make the omelette and serve surrounded with Sauce Hongroise.

Impériale   Cut a slit in the top of the omelette, open out and fill with dice of foie gras and truffle mixed with Sauce Madère.

Ivanhoe   Fill the inside with creamed flaked smoked haddock and serve the omelette surrounded with Sauce Crème.

au Jambon   Add diced ham to the beaten eggs, make the

	omelette and decorate with diamond shapes of ham.
Joinville	Fill the inside with diced mushroom, shrimps and truffle mixed with Sauce Joinville and serve surrounded with more of the same sauce.
Jurassienne	Add fried lardons and chopped chervil to the beaten eggs; make the omelette, filling it with chiffonade of sorrel and surround with a border of Sauce Creme.
Limousine	Àdd sauted diced potato and diced ham to the eggs and make the omelette in the usual manner
Lorraine	Add chopped chives, sauted lardons of bacon, small dice of Gruyère cheese and some cream to the beaten eggs and make the omelette in the usual way.
Loti	Cut a slit in the top of the omelette, fill with puree of truffle and serve surrounded with Sauce Madère.
Louis XIV	Fill the inside with creamed chicken and truffle and serve surrounded with Sauce Crème.
Lucernoise	Add fried diced rye bread sippets to the egg mixture and make into a flat omelette.
Lyonnaise	Add sauted sliced onions to the beaten eggs and proceed in the usual manner.
Marie-Jeanne	Add cooked lardons of bacon and small dice of potato, chopped chervil, cooked shredded sorrel and spinach and some cream to the beaten eggs; make the omelette and serve sprinkled with chopped parsley.
Marseillaise	Fill the inside with puree of salt cod mixed with diced tomato and serve the omelette with a cordon of tomato sauce.
Mascotte	Add diced artichoke bottom, fried diced potato and diced truffle to the eggs; make into an omelette and surround with Sauce Madère.
Masséna	Fill the inside with sliced artichoke bottoms mixed with tomato sauce and serve with poached slices of bone marrow brushed with meat glaze on top and a cordon of Sauce Béarnaise around.

141

Maxim   Garnish the omelette with crayfish and a slice of truffle and shallow fried frogs' legs.

Maugham   Stuff with a mixture of diced sweetbread, chicken liver and spaghetti mixed with stewed onion, garlic and tomato; coat with cream, sprinkle with parmesan and gratinate quickly.

Mexicaine   Add sauted sliced mushroom and chopped red pimento to the eggs and fill the inside with stiff cooked puree of tomato.

Mireille   Fold the omelette with garlic-flavoured stewed tomato and serve it with a cordon of saffron-flavoured Sauce Crème.

Monégasque   Add chopped tarragon and diced tomato to the beaten eggs; make the omelette and decorate it with trellis work of anchovy and a thread of anchovy essence.

Monselet   Fill the omelette with foie gras puree containing diced asparagus and julienne of mushroom and truffle; fold over and pour demi-glace around.

Nantua   Fill the inside with diced crayfish mixed with Sauce Nantua and serve garnished with a crayfish and slice of truffle and a cordon of Sauce Nantua.

Nature   This is a plain omelette without a garnish.

Newburg   Fill the inside with dice of lobster mixed with Sauce Newburg and surround with more of the same sauce.

Niçoise   Add cooked diamonds of French beans and diced tomato to the eggs, make the omelette and serve with a cordon of jus lié.

Ninon   Fill the inside with puree of asparagus, coat with Sauce Crème and decorate with slices of truffle

Noailles   Fill the inside with sauted diced chicken liver and serve surrounded with a cordon of Sauce Crème.

Normande   Fill the inside with poached oysters mixed with Sauce Normande and surround it with the same sauce.

Olympia   Fill with crabmeat mixed with diced cooked pimento and cream sauce.

Omar Pasha	Add sauted chopped onion to the beaten eggs; make the omelette, sprinkle with cheese, glaze under the salamander and surround with tomato sauce.
Opéra	Fill the inside with sauted diced chicken liver in Sauce Madère; garnish with a bouquet of asparagus and surround with Sauce Madère.
Parisienne	Add julienne of mushroom, tongue and truffle to the beaten eggs and fill the centre with puree of chicken.
Parmentier	Add cooked small dice of potato and chopped parsley to the beaten eggs and make the omelette flat.
Parmesan	Add grated parmesan to the eggs and sprinkle the omelette with grated parmesan cheese before serving.
Patti	Add diced asparagus, artichoke bottoms and truffle to the beaten eggs, make the omelette, decorate with slices of artichoke and truffle and surround with demi-glace.
Paysanne	Add cooked small dice of potato, fried lardons, chopped fines herbes and chiffonade of sorrel to the eggs and make the omelette flat.
Périgord	Make a truffled omelette and surround with Sauce Périgueux.
Persane	Mix the eggs with chopped chives, parsley, spring onion, dill, saffron and fresh coriander leaves; pour into a buttered dish, cover with the lid and bake in the oven until set.
aux Pointes d'Asperges	Add diced asparagus to the beaten egg and garnish the omelette with a bouquet of asparagus tips.
Portugaise	Slit the top of the omelette and insert tomate concassée, add a pinch of chopped parsley and surround with tomato sauce.
Princesse	Add diced truffle to the eggs, fill the inside with asparagus and garnish with a bouquet of asparagus tips; surround with Sauce Suprême.
Provençale	Cut a slit in the top, open out and fill with tomato concassée flavoured with garlic.

Raspail　　　Fill the inside with a salpicon of beef and ham in demi-glace and serve surrounded with some of the same sauce.

Réforme　　　Fill the omelette with julienne of cooked white of egg, ham, gherkin, tongue and truffle mixed with Sauce Poivrade and serve surrounded with the same sauce.

Régence　　　Fill the omelette with a salpicon of cockscombs and kidneys, ham, mushroom, tongue and truffle mixed with Sauce Régence.

Richemont　　Fill the inside with creamed mushrooms, coat the omelette with Sauce Mornay and glaze under a salamander.

aux Rognons　Cut a slit in the omelette and fill with sauted diced kidney in Sauce Madère; sprinkle with parsley and surround with Sauce Madère.

Rossini　　　Add diced foie gras and truffle to the beaten eggs; make the omelette, garnish with a slice of foie gras and truffle and surround it with truffle-flavoured demi-glace.

Rouennaise　Stuff with puree of sauted duck liver and serve surrounded with Sauce Vin rouge.

Royale　　　Stuff with creamed puree of chicken with chopped truffle; decorate with a slice of truffle and surround with Sauce Crème.

Russe　　　Stuff the omelette with caviar.

Saint-Hubert　Stuff with puree of game, place a turned mushroom on top and serve surrounded with demi-glace.

Salvator　　Fill the inside with julienne of ham and truffle mixed with Sauce Madère.

San-Simeon　Add diced avocado, white of chicken and chopped chives to the eggs before making the omelette.

Sarah Bernhardt　Fill the omelette with diced cockscombs and truffle mixed with Sauce Crème.

Savoyarde　　Add cream, grated Gruyère cheese and sauted small slices of potato to the beaten eggs and make into a flat omelette.

Sévillaise	Fill the omelette with cooked diced tomato and green olives, flavoured with garlic and serve with a border of velouté flavoured and coloured with tomato.
Suissesse	Add diced Gruyère cheese to the eggs, make the omelette flat, sprinkle with grated Gruyère and gratinate quickly.
Tapas	This is an Omelette Espagnole served cold cut into slices.
aux Tomates	Cut a slit in the top of the omelette and fill with hot tomato concassée; sprinkled with chopped parsley and surround with tomato sauce.
Trouvillaise	Fill the inside with a salpicon of mushroom, mussel and shrimps mixed with Sauce Vin blanc, and serve surrounded with Sauce Crevettes.
Turque	Fill the inside with sauted chicken liver and serve surrounded with demi-glace-tomatée.
Vanderbilt	Add diced green pimento, diced tomato and shrimps to the omelette mixture and make as usual.
Valencienne	Fill the inside with risotto and coat the omelette with Sauce Crème containing diced red pimento.
Victoria	Fill the inside with diced crayfish and truffle mixed with Sauce Homard and serve surrounded with more of the same sauce.
Villageoise	Add chopped parsley and sauted sliced mushroom to the beaten egg and make the omelette in the usual manner.
Vosgienne	Add lardons of bacon and diced fried bread croûtons to the eggs and make the omelette in the usual manner.
Walewska	Fill the inside with a salpicon of lobster and truffle mixed with Sauce Crème and serve surrounded with the same sauce finished with lobster butter.
Yorkaise	Add diced ham to the beaten egg, make the omelette and decorate with diamonds of ham.

4 FARINACEOUS DISHES – PASTAS

There are more than a hundred different shapes and sizes of these farinaceous products which are such a splendid feature of Italian cookery. They are served as a first course, as a main course, or as a garnish with a few fish and many meat dishes, mainly for lunch. Some pastas are used as a garnish in soups, some in sweet milk puddings, and several interesting salads are based on a pasta item.

Pasta dough is made in several qualities, mainly according to the type of flour and the number of eggs per kilogram of flour. The flour is hard durum wheat, either white or wholemeal. Factory-made pasta is thoroughly dried and keeps almost indefinitely while freshly made pasta as produced by many local firms or on the restaurant premises, is a perishable item.

To cook, boil $4\frac{1}{2}$ litres water with 50g of salt and 2 tbspns of oil, add 500g pasta, stir, and cook until almost soft; add 3dl cold water to arrest the cooking, drain, wash under hot water and toss in hot butter.

Allow 30g raw weight for a first course and as a garnish and 50g for a main course; cook to the 'al dente' stage which means that there is still need to bite and chew it before swallowing.

The main types of pasta in general use are:

1. *Long round and long flat* buccatini   very thin macaroni
                              fettucine   strips, similar to nood-
                                            les
                              fusilli   long hollow spirals
                              lasagne   wide flat straps (made
                                            also in green and red
                                            colours)
                              linguini   even thin flat ribbons
                              macaroni   long or short tubes

	maccheroncini	long thin macaroni
	noodles	long flat strips
	spaghetti	long thin rods
	tagliatelli	fairly broad strips
	vermicelli	very thin long rods
2. *Short and small*	biavettini	like grains of rice
	cappelleti	small hats
	conchiglie	small shells
	genovese	elbow macaroni
	farfalle	bows or butterflies
	penine	angled tubes
	ruote	cog wheels
	semi de mela	melon seeds
	stellini	stars
3. *For filling and*	agnelotti	semi-circles
ready-filled	cannelloni	large tubes
	manecotti	smooth tubes
	ravioli	stuffed rounds or squares
	rigatoni	ribbed tubes
	tortelloni	stuffed folded and twisted rounds
	ziti	large tubes

The most popular ways of serving and garnishing farinaceous dishes are as follows. It is usual to offer grated parmesan cheese with each of them.

Agrodolce Sauce made of pineapple juice, soya sauce, vinegar and cornflour, add julienne of carrot, pimento and pineapple and pour over the pasta; garnish with deep fried balls of sausage meat.

al Burro Add raw butter, seasonings and cheese and toss together.

Amatriciana Add lardons of bacon, chopped onion and red pimento, garlic and diced tomato – all sautéd together.

Anglaise Add jus lié and gratinate with breadcrumbs and cheese.

Bayonnaise Mix with diced ham and demi-glace.

147

Bolognaise   Sauté chopped onion and minced beef until brown, add sliced mushroom and red wine, reduce, add brown sauce and garlic and cook; pile in centre of buttered pasta.

Bressane   Add sautéd chicken liver and mix with Madeira sauce.

Calabrese   Sauté diced artichoke in oil, add chopped or grated pecorino cheese and the cooked pasta-sciutta.

Carbonara   Sauté chopped garlic and ham, add whisked raw egg and cream and cook lightly before mixing with pasta.

Casalinga   Add brown mushroom sauce.

Cussy   Garnish with cockscombs and diced truffle.

Dominicaine   Mix with chopped anchovy and duxelles.

Fegatini   Sauté chopped onion and garlic, lardons of bacon and small pieces of chicken liver and mix into the pasta.

al Forno   Arrange layers of cooked pasta, white sauce, sliced mozzarella and minced beef with onion, garlic, tomato and red wine, finishing with sauce; sprinkle with parmesan and bake.

Genoise   Add sliced sauté mushrooms and hot cream.

Giardiniera   Sauté chopped bacon and onion, add diced carrot and tomato and cook; add small florets of cooked broccoli, batons of egg-plant and sliced mushroom, mix and pour on top of the pasta.

au Gratin   Mix cooked pasta with mornay sauce, place in a dish and sprinkle with mixed breadcrumbs and cheese; colour under a salamander.

Hussarde   Add diced ham and mix with sauce hussarde (mirepoix, white wine, demi-glace, garlic and tomato purée, finished with grated horseradish).

Imperiale   Add dice of foie gras, mushroom and truffle and mix with Madeira sauce.

Italienne   Toss the drained pasta in hot butter, season with salt, pepper and grated nutmeg and finish by adding Parmesan cheese (this is the basic method of preparing pasta in the Italian style).

Levantine	Add diced ham and tomato-flavoured cream sauce.
Macaroni Cheese	Mix cooked short-cut macaroni into cream sauce, place in a dish, sprinkle with cheese and melted butter and gratinate.
Marinière	Add poached mussels, oysters and prawns and mix with fish velouté flavoured with liquid from cooking the mussels.
Mediterraneo	Add reduced cooked and sieved tomato and garlic to the pasta and toss to mix.
Ménagère	Add grated Emmenthal cheese and cream.
Milanaise	Add julienne of ham, tongue and mushroom, diced cooked tomato and tomato sauce, and toss over to mix.
Montglas	Add julienne of chicken, mushroom, tongue and truffle to buttered pasta.
Mornay	Add mornay sauce, sprinkle with Parmesan and melted butter and gratinate.
Nantua	Mix with cream and crayfish butter and garnish with crayfish tails and julienne of truffle.
Napolitaine	Add diced cooked tomato and tomato sauce.
Nationale	Add diced cooked tomato and tomato sauce.
Niçoise	Sauté chopped onion and garlic in oil with diced tomato and add to the pasta.
Paglia e Fieno	Sauté chopped onion, lardons and sliced mushroom; add cream and mix into the pasta. (The pasta is usually sold as a mixture of green and white thin ribbons.)
Palermitaine	Mix with tomato sauce and sprinkle with fines herbes.
Pasticcia di Pasta	Arrange layers of cooked pasta, brown or white sauce, cooked minced meat in sauce, and grated cheese in a buttered pie dish and bake; serve cut into portions.
Quattro Formaggi	Offer grated Parmesan, gruyère, pecorino, Cheddar, etc. to choice.
Ragu	Serve two or three different sauces with the buttered pasta, such as Bolognaise, tomato, cream, or egg-plant sauce.

Rossini	Add diced foie gras and truffle and mix with Madeira sauce.
Royale	Add sliced mushroom and truffle to buttered pasta.
Sicilienne	Make a fine purée of lightly sautéd chicken liver, mix with a little chicken velouté and stir into the pasta.
al Sugo	Toss in hot butter with seasoning and cheese and mix with jus lié.
al Tartufo Bianco (Truffes) Blanches)	Toss the pasta in hot butter with cheese and seasonings and garnish with grated shavings of white truffle.
Veneziana	Add julienne of chicken, ham, mushroom and truffle and mix with veal velouté.
al Vongole	Add pasta to velouté flavoured with mussel or clam juice and garnish with poached mussels.

5 FISH DISHES

The large number of fish dishes in the repertoire are categorised here by methods of cooking instead of by species of fish. Each method is dealt with separately and it can be taken that all the fish in general use, either whole or in fillets, are suitable for that particular method.

The accepted methods of cooking fish are:

Methods of dealing with frogs' legs, snails and shellfish are given separately, as are recipes for paupiettes, timbales, bordures, turbans, pojarskis and fish pies.

The kinds of fish envisaged are:

White Fish: Brill, Carp, Cod, Coley, Gurnard, Haddock, Hake, Halibut, John Dory, Pike, Plaice, Lemon Sole, Dover Sole, Skate, Turbot, Whiting.

Oily Fish: Eel, Herring, Mackerel, Red Mullet, Salmon, Salmon Trout, Sardine, Sprats, Trout, Whitebait.

The cuts of fish in general use are:

Darne   A slice cut on the bone from a round fish such as cod.

151

Délice	Menu term denoting a folded fillet.
Fillet	Whole side cut off the bone of a round fish, or in two pieces from one side of a flat fish.
Goujon	Strips, approximately 6cm × 1cm cut from a fillet. A gougonette is cut 5cm × ½cm.
Paupiette	A fillet spread with fish farce and rolled up.
Suprême	Portion cut on the slant from a large fillet such as salmon.
Tronçon	Section cut on the bone from a large flat fish such as turbot.
Whole	A small fish for one portion of 200–250g cleaned weight.
Zéphyr	Menu term for a folded fillet.

Braised Fish

Whole fish and cuts of large fish can be braised in either red or white wine and fish stock, on a layer of sliced carrot and onion with parsley stalks, bay-leaf and peppercorns. The fish can be larded with strips of salt pork fat, carrot or truffle before being braised. The cooking liquid is reduced and thickened with arrowroot or sabayon to form the accompanying sauce and a suitable fish garnish is added. Brill and turbot are the kinds that are most suitable for this method of cooking.

Ambassade	Coat with sauce vin blanc flavoured with crayfish butter and garnish with slices of lobster and truffle.
Américaine	Coat with sauce américaine and garnish with slices of lobster.
Amiral	Finish the sauce with crayfish butter; garnish with bouchées of crayfish tails, turned mushrooms, slices of truffle, mussels dipped in sauce Villeroy and fried and oysters done in the same way; serve with plain boiled potatoes.
Bordelaise	Thicken the cooking liquid with beurre manié and cream, mask the fish and garnish with plain-boiled olive-shaped potatoes.

Cambacérès   Braise in white wine and truffle essence; garnish with croquettes of crayfish, and breadcrumbed-and-deep-fried mussels and mushrooms.

Chambord   Braise in red wine, coat with sauce vin rouge and garnish with mushrooms, quenelles, braised button onions, sautéd soft roes, and slices of truffle.

Champs-Elysées   Braise, serve on a bed of duxelles and garnish with prawns; cover with sauce vin blanc and marble with a little lobster cullis.

Chartreuse   Braise in white wine and stock, garnish with bouquets of glazed carrots, turnips, French beans and peas.

Daumont   Garnish of mushrooms filled with crayfish tails mixed with sauce Nantua, round quenelles and breadcrumbed-and-deep-fried soft roes; serve with plain boiled potatoes.

Fricandeau   Cut the fillets into thick suprêmes and lard each with back fat, carrot or truffle; braise and serve with any appropriate fish garnish.

Française   Coat the fish, half with ordinary sauce vin blanc and half with tarragon-coloured sauce vin blanc; garnish with crayfish and bouchées of mussels à la poulette.

Impériale   Braise in champagne, coat with sauce vin blanc, sprinkle with julienne of truffle and garnish with prawns and poached herring roes.

Jeannette   Coat with sauce mornay finished with crayfish butter and garnish with bouchées of crayfish; the fish may be stuffed with purée of spinach.

Kléber   Braise, sprinkle with diced mushroom, prawns and truffle and coat with sauce bercy finished with fish glaze.

Lucullus   Garnish with bouchées of crayfish, tartlets containing soft roes, quenelles containing a poached oyster, and coat with sauce made from the braising liquid.

Masséna   Braise and finish the sauce with demi-glace and anchovy butter; garnish with a salpicon of lobster, mushroom and mussels.

Mirabeau   Braise in red wine and make the cooking liquid into sauce genevoise; coat the outside with sauce vin blanc, the centre with the red sauce and decorate with a trellis of anchovies and tarragon.

Montebello   Braise in white wine; garnish with barquettes filled with soft roes, trussed crayfish, small round flat prawn croquettes and serve with the cooking liquid made into sauce velouté flavoured with anchovy essence and containing poached oysters.

Normande   Braise in white wine, coat with sauce Normande and surround with poached oysters, button mushrooms, trussed crayfish, large prawns, slices of truffle, fried goujons and croûtons cut N-shape.

Parisienne   Arrange slices of lobster on top of the braised fish; garnish with quenelles and soft roes and serve with plain boiled potatoes and sauce Normande containing sliced mushroom and truffle and flavoured with crayfish butter.

Prince Albert   Braise in white wine, reduce the cooking liquid, add to sauce vin blanc and flavour with crayfish butter; garnish with tartlets filled with crayfish in sauce Nantua, truffled quenelles, and deep-fried breadcrumbed mussels.

Prince de Galles   Coat with curry-flavoured sauce vin blanc and garnish with croquettes of rice, and mussels and oysters both coated with sauce Villeroy and deep fried.

Prince Henri   Braise in white wine, Madeira and fish stock; serve garnished with crayfish, mushroom, mussels and quenelles.

Provençale   Lard with anchovies, braise in white wine and fish stock; thicken the cooking liquid with Espagnole, coat the fish and sprinkle with capers.

Régence   Braise in white wine court-bouillon and reduce it to add to a sauce Normande; pipe the dish with pommes marquise mixture, glaze it and garnish the fish with crayfish quenelles, mushrooms, oysters, soft roes and truffles.

Royale	Braise in white wine; garnish with tartlets of crayfish, quenelles, mushrooms, truffle and plain boiled potatoes and coat with the sauce made from the braising liquid.
Suzette	When nearly braised, pipe a border of fish forcemeat to decorate the fish; finish to cook then sprinkle with a salpicon of mushroom, prawns and truffle and coat with sauce homard. Decorate with turned mushrooms with a prawn piercing each.

Deep Fried Fish

There are three methods of coating fish for deep frying:

1. With flour, egg-wash and breadcrumbs, which can be done beforehand
2. With flour, then into frying batter and directly into the hot fat. For some recipes the fish should be marinated in oil and lemon juice prior to frying
3. Dip in milk, drain the surplus, coat with flour only and deep-fry

Amphytrion	Spread the fish with anchovy-flavoured farce containing diced oysters; fold in two, egg and crumb, and deep fry. Serve garnished with quarters of lemon and fried parsley.
Antiboise	Egg and crumb, and deep fry; serve with stuffed tomatoes à la Provençale.
Armenonville	Fold in half, pass through flour, egg-wash and breadcrumbs and deep fry; serve garnished with creamed diamonds of cucumber, a crayfish tail for each portion, and sauce Nantua.
Bamboche	Dip into flour, twist into a spiral and deep fry; serve on a bed of buttered macédoine of vegetables.
Benoiton	Cut into 10cm pieces, dip into flour and deep fry; serve accompanied with a sauce made by reducing red wine with shallots and parsley stalks and thickened with butter.

155

en Buisson	Cut into strips 6cm × 1cm, flour, egg and crumb, and deep fry; serve in a pile, garnished with quarters of lemon and fried parsley.
Charlemagne	Spread the raw fillet of fish with truffled salmon forcemeat, coat with egg and crumbs and deep fry; serve in a barquette filled with duxelles, accompanied with lobster sauce containing julienne of truffle.
Colbert	Lay back the top fillets and break the backbone; egg and crumb, and deep fry; remove the centre bone, replace the coating and serve with slices of maître d'hôtel butter in the cavity.
en Colère	Use a small fish and secure the tail through the mouth, egg and crumb, and deep fry; serve with fried parsley and quarters of lemon.
Colinette	Cover with forcemeat containing chopped fines herbes; coat with egg-wash and breadcrumbs, deep fry and serve with tomato sauce.
Comtesse	Spread with forcemeat, fold over and egg and crumb; deep fry and serve each on a cooked half-tomato filled with buttered shrimps.
Crawford	Prepare and deep fry as for colbert; fill the centre with sauce béarnaise and sprinkle with chopped truffle.
Dauphine	Spread with fish farce, fold over and dip in Sauce Villeroy; coat with egg and breadcrumbs, deep fry and serve with sauce tartare made with the addition of diced tomato.
Friture	Egg and crumb and deep fry small pieces of mixed fish and shellfish.
Frit	Flour, egg and crumb, and deep fry at 180°C; serve on a dish paper with quarters of lemon and fried parsley accompanied with a sauceboat of sauce tartare.
Fritto Misto and Fritot	This is a variety of small pieces of fish and shellfish, deep fried and served with lemon, parsley and a sauce.
Frit à la Française	Dip into milk then coat with flour; deep fry immediately and serve with fried parsley and quarters of lemon.

Gougonettes	Cut into strips 5cm × ½cm, egg and bread-crumb, and deep fry; serve with quarters of lemon, fried parsley and a sauceboat of sauce tartare.
Goujons	Cut into strips 8cm × 1cm, coat with flour, egg-wash and breadcrumbs and deep fry; serve with quarters of lemon and fried parsley, accompanied with sauce tartare.
à la Juive	Marinate in oil and lemon juice, dip into batter and deep fry; serve lukewarm with sauce tartare.
Julienne	Cut into thin strips, dip in milk and coat with flour and deep fry; serve with quarters of lemon and fried parsley.
Jutland	Marinate in oil and lemon juice, dip into batter and deep fry; serve accompanied with sauce Joinville.
Lorgnette	Use small whole fish, remove the backbone and roll up each fillet towards the head; secure, egg and crumb, and deep fry; serve with fried parsley and lemon.
Madeleine	Coat poached stuffed fish with egg and crumbs, deep fry and serve with tomato-flavoured sauce hollandaise.
Maître d'Hôtel	Egg and crumb, deep fry and serve with slices of maître d'hôtel butter on each piece of fish.
Marinette	Sandwich two poached fillets with thick cheese-flavoured béchamel, dip into sauce Villeroy and when set, egg and crumb and deep fry.
Mignonettes	Cut into strips, 6cm × ½cm, egg and crumb, and deep fry; serve with lemon and sauce tartare.
Mireille	Serve as for colbert replacing the butter with sauce béarnaise; surround with cooked tomato concassée made with garlic.
Orly	Marinate in lemon juice, oil and chopped parsley, coat with flour, dip into frying batter and deep fry; drain and serve garnished with fried parsley and a sauceboat of tomato sauce.
Richelieu	Prepare and deep fry as for colbert and garnish the centre with slices of truffle.

Sayadia   Egg and crumb, and deep fry; place in a casserole, cover with a sauce made of sautéd chopped onion, tomato and garlic with tomato sauce and cumin and cook in the oven for 15 minutes.

Sicilienne   Prepare as for colbert; deep fry and serve with nut-brown butter containing capers, chopped anchovy and sieved hard-boiled egg.

Sully   Deep fry and serve with a sauceboat of sauce béarnaise and slices of anchovy butter on the fish.

Tolstoi   Cut into goujons, egg and crumb, and deep fry; serve accompanied with sauce vin blanc.

Tressé   Divide a fillet into three strips leaving attached at one end; plait, coat with egg and crumbs and deep fry.

Villeroy   Spread with fish farce, fold in half, poach then dip into sauce Villeroy; coat with egg-wash and breadcrumbs and deep fry; serve with tomato sauce.

Whitebait   These are rolled in flour and deep fried until crisp; season with salt and cayenne and serve with fried parsley and quarters of lemon.

Shallow Fried

The basic method is known as cooking à la meunière (q.v.).

Alphonse   Shallow fry in butter and dress on a fried half aubergine cut lengthways; serve with tomato sauce garnished with julienne of green pimento.

Amandine   Dip in flour, shallow fry then sprinkle with sautéd shredded almonds; add a squeeze of lemon juice and coat with nut-brown butter.

Anglaise   Coat with flour, egg-wash and breadcrumbs, mark the best side trellis fashion and shallow fry on both sides; serve garnished with picked parsley and slices of maître d'hôtel butter.

Antiboise	Shallow fry, garnish with bouquets of cooked diced tomato, julienne of leek and julienne of celery; sprinkle with lemon juice and coat with beurre noisette.
aux Aubergines	Dip in flour and shallow fry; arrange several sautéd $\frac{1}{2}$cm rounds of aubergine on top instead of lemon, sprinkle with lemon juice and chopped parsley and coat with nut-brown butter.
Baloise	Shallow fry and cover with sliced shallow-fried onion; coat with nut-brown butter and sprinkle with parsley.
Belle Meunière	Dip in flour, shallow fry in butter, basting from time to time; garnish with half a skinned tomato, a mushroom, a sautéd soft roe and sprinkle with lemon juice and parsley and coat with nut-brown butter.
Benjamin	Fold in half, egg and crumb and shallow fry; place in an emptied baked potato filled with creamed mushroom and serve with sauce américaine.
Benvenuto Cellini	Shallow fry and serve on a bed of tomato concassée flavoured with garlic; garnish with sliced white truffle and cèpes, coat with beurre noisette and sprinkle with chopped tarragon.
au Beurre Noisette	Shallow fry in butter, basting with the butter; place on the dish and cover with nut-brown butter.
Bonnefoy	Dip in flour, shallow fry and serve accompanied with sauce bordelaise made with white wine; it is usual to serve with a dish of plain boiled potatoes.
Bretonne	Dip in flour, shallow fry and garnish with sautéd sliced mushrooms, prawns and slices of lemon; sprinkle with lemon juice and chopped parsley and coat with nut-brown butter.
aux Câpres	Shallow fry and serve garnished with capers, slices of lemon, nut-brown butter and chopped parsley.
Capri	Serve garnished with a sautéd banana and a spoonful of chutney.

159

Carmen   Shallow fry in butter, decorate with strips of red pimento and blanched leaves of tarragon and serve with slices of pimento butter.

Carlier   Cut into strips, dip in flour and shallow fry; place on a bed of creamed macaroni, coat with sauce bercy and glaze under the salamander.

Cecilia   Shallow fry, garnish with asparagus tips and coat with nut-brown butter.

Chanoine   Pipe a figure of eight of fish farce on the fried fish, set in the oven and fill the holes with shrimps in shrimp sauce.

Chesterfield   Shallow fry in butter, dress on a bed of shrimps covered with shrimp sauce and serve surrounded with shrimp sauce.

Chevigné   Cover raw fish with salmon forcemeat, coat with egg and crumbs and shallow fry; serve garnished with creamed quarters of mushrooms and a sauceboat of sauce béarnaise.

Clara Ward   Cut into strips, dip in flour and shallow fry; separately, shallow fry diced artichoke bottoms and celeriac, toss together with the fish in butter with lemon juice and chopped parsley.

Cléopâtre   Shallow fry then garnish with prawns, soft roes and capers; sprinkle with lemon, coat with nut-brown butter and finish with chopped parsley.

Cooch Behar   Shallow fry, place each fillet in a stuffed half of aubergine, sprinkle with breadcrumbs and butter and gratinate.

Cubane   Shallow fry and serve garnished with plain boiled rice and sauce créole.

David   Shallow fry, sprinkle with fried breadcrumbs, lemon juice and chopped parsley.

Dejarzet   Dip in flour, egg-wash and breadcrumbs and shallow fry; serve on slices of tarragon butter and decorate with blanched leaves of tarragon.

Dorée   Shallow fry in butter and garnish with peeled slices of lemon.

Doria	Shallow fry, arrange on a dish and sprinkle with 2cm diamonds of cooked cucumber; coat with nut-brown butter and sprinkle with parsley.
Dubois	Cut into strips 8cm × 1cm, egg and crumb and shallow fry; drain and roll in very little sauce chateaubriand.
Edouard	Marinate in brandy, dip in flour and shallow fry; serve with sauce bercy finished with anchovy butter.
Egyptienne	Shallow fry in oil and serve sprinkled with cooked tomato concassée and French fried onion rings.
Emmanuel II	Shallow fry and serve garnished with an artichoke bottom filled with small balls of truffle, creamed mushrooms and sauce vin blanc flavoured with sherry.
Epicurienne	Serve sprinkled with diced tomato cooked in shallot butter and surround with a little jus lié.
Espagnole	Shallow fry in oil and dress on a layer of cooked tomato concassée; garnish with bouquets of strips of red pimento and French fried onions.
des Gourmets	Cut into strips 8cm × 1cm, dip in flour and shallow fry; mix with sautéd strips of mushroom and of artichoke bottoms; sprinkle with lemon juice, coat with nut-brown butter and finish with chopped parsley.
Grand Hôtel	Shallow fry, garnish with bouquets of sautéd diced potato and of artichoke bottoms; cover with nut-brown butter with a little meat glaze and sprinkle with parsley.
Gourmande	Egg and crumb and shallow fry; serve with sauce béarnaise.
Grenobloise	Pass through flour and shallow fry in hot butter; garnish with segments of lemon and capers, sprinkle with lemon juice, coat with nut-brown butter and finish with chopped parsley.
Grecque	Shallow fry in oil, serve on a bed of riz pilaff and surround with tomato sauce mixed with diced pimento.

Jeanne d'Arc   Arrange the fried fish on a bed of rice coated with sauce Nantua and garnish with crayfish, oysters, mushrooms and quenelles.

Kotschoubey   Fold in half, coat with egg and crumbs and shallow fry; serve on a bed of riz pilaff with a sauce made of half sauce hollandaise and half sauce vin blanc, flavoured with Worcestershire sauce.

Levantine   Cut into pieces and shallow fry; mix with some sautéd dice of aubergine; place in a border of riz pilaff containing diced red pimento and coat with curry sauce.

Louisiane   Place a sautéd half banana on each cooked fillet.

Lutèce   Shallow fry, dress on a layer of sautéd leaf spinach and arrange sautéd onion rings and sliced artichoke bottoms on top; surround with sautéd sliced potato.

Lyonnaise   Flour and fry, cover with sliced sautéd onions and sprinkle with a few drops of vinegar, nut-brown butter and parsley.

Magny   Cook in hot butter, place in a dish and coat with melted butter.

Maréchal   Dip into melted butter then into breadcrumbs mixed with chopped truffle; shallow fry and serve with a cordon of jus lié and nut-brown butter.

Marigny   Dip in flour and shallow fry; serve on a layer of cooked tomato concassée and garnish with bouchées of diced bone marrow mixed with sauce bercy.

Mascotte   Fold in half, dip in flour and shallow fry; serve garnished with sautéd quarters of artichoke bottom, pommes olivettes and turned truffle and mask with butter mixed with chopped herbs and meat glaze.

Meunière   Dip in flour and shallow fry in hot butter, basting occasionally; place on a dish with a peeled slice of lemon on each and sprinkle with lemon juice; pour nut-brown butter all over at the last moment and sprinkle with parsley.

Mignonette	Shallow fry and garnish with pommes noisettes and sliced truffle; coat with melted butter mixed with meat glaze.
Minute	Dip in flour and shallow fry in oil; serve coated with melted butter.
Mirabeau	Shallow fry in anchovy butter and serve decorated trellis fashion with strips of anchovy and blanched tarragon leaves.
Miramar	Cut into large diamonds and shallow fry in butter; serve on a bed of riz pilaff and surround with fried slices of aubergine.
Montalbon	Shallow fry and serve on a layer of purée of artichoke bottoms; mask with nut-brown butter.
Monte Carlo	Shallow fry, sprinkle with capers and a little anchovy essence and coat with nut-brown butter.
Montesquieu	Dip in melted butter then in chopped onion and parsley and flour, shallow fry and serve with lemon.
Murat	Cut into 8cm × 1cm strips, flour and shallow fry in butter; mix with shallow-fried batons of potato and artichoke bottoms cut 3cm × 1cm, toss all together with butter, lemon juice and chopped parsley and serve.
à l'Orange	Shallow fry and arrange peeled slices or segments of orange on top; sprinkle with orange juice, coat with nut-brown butter and sprinkle with parsley.
Polonaise	Shallow fry, sprinkle with sieved hard-boiled egg, fried breadcrumbs and chopped parsley and mask with nut-brown butter.
Portière	Spread with made English mustard and coat with breadcrumbs; shallow fry and cover with nut-brown butter and a few drops of vinegar.
Provençale	Dip into flour, shallow fry in oil and garnish with cooked slices of tomato, stoned olives and trellis work of anchovy fillets; coat with nut-brown butter and sprinkle with parsley.
aux Raisins	Cook as for Meunière and serve garnished with chilled peeled and depipped grapes.

Remoi Serve on a bed of truffled duxelles, coat with beurre noisette and decorate with a slice of truffle.

Richelieu Lay back the two top fillets and break the backbone; egg and crumb keeping the fillets rolled back; shallow fry, remove the backbone and fill the cavity with maître d'hôtel butter and a slice of truffle.

Riviera Shallow fry, garnish with quartered artichoke bottoms, mushrooms and truffle; sprinkle with lemon juice, coat with nut-brown butter and finish with chopped parsley.

Rosalie Shallow fry and serve sprinkled with sautéd chopped shallot, sliced mushroom and crushed garlic; finish with chopped parsley.

Talma Shallow fry and cover with sautéd diced artichoke bottom, mushroom and potato; sprinkle with capers, parsley and fish glaze.

Traviata Shallow fry and serve garnished with cooked tomatoes filled with diced crayfish in lobster sauce.

Vaucluse Shallow fry in oil, sprinkle with lemon juice, coat with hot olive oil and sprinkle with parsley.

Vauclusienne Shallow fry in olive oil and finish in the usual Meunière manner.

Véron Coat with melted butter and breadcrumbs and shallow fry; serve accompanied with sauce véron.

Viennoise Marinate with oil, lemon juice, chopped onion and parsley then coat with egg and breadcrumbs and shallow fry; serve garnished with quarters of lemon and fried parsley.

Washington Shallow fry, garnish with a slice of lobster coated with sauce américaine and sprinkle with julienne of truffle.

Grilled Fish

Arménienne	Grill and serve garnished with bouquets of crab-meat and poached oysters; sprinkle with chopped chives and serve sauce vin blanc separately.
Baron Brisse	Grill and serve with slices of maître d'hôtel butter on top and pommes parisienne at the side; serve with sauce Madère.
Bedfort	Place the grilled fish on a layer of beurre maître d'hôtel mixed with fish glaze and garnish with hollowed-out bread croûtons, one filled with sliced mushroom and truffle mixed with demi-glace and one filled with chopped spinach, coated with sauce mornay and glazed.
Brochette	Impale pieces of firm fish, shellfish, mushroom, pimento, tomato, bacon, etc., on skewers and grill; serve on a bed of pilaff of rice.
Clermont	Grill and serve with deep-fried soft roes and oysters au gratin, accompanied with maître d'hôtel butter.
Diablé	Grill in the usual manner and serve accompanied with sauce diable.
Francillon	Place the grilled fish on a fried bread croûton spread with anchovy butter, and garnish with pommes pailles; serve with sauce tomate.
Grillé	Pat the fish dry, season and flour lightly; brush with oil and grill gently on both sides; brush with butter and garnish with picked parsley and slices of lemon.
Kebab	Impale pieces of firm fish, shellfish, mushroom, pimento, tomato, etc., on skewers and grill; serve on a bed of pilaff of rice.
Maître d'Hôtel	Serve grilled fish with slices of soft maître d'hôtel butter.
Niçoise	Cover the grilled fish with stewed tomato and garlic and decorate with olives and a trellis of anchovy.

St-Henri	Serve with purée of cooked sea urchins at the side.
St-Malo	Decorate the grilled fish with a border of shallow fried slices of small potatoes and serve accompanied with Sauce St-Malo.
Martinière	Marinate the fish in oil and white wine then grill and serve with a sauceboat of mayonnaise containing chopped walnut.
Ménage	Serve the grilled fish with pickled gherkins and mustard-flavoured maître d'hôtel butter.

—GRILLED IN BREADCRUMBS—

Pass the fish through flour, melted butter and white breadcrumbs, flatten and mark trellis fashion; place on a buttered tray, sprinkle with butter and grill gently under a salamander

Bannaro	Serve the fish surrounded with fried slices of banana and coat it with beurre noisette in which have been cooked some splintered almonds and a few drops of lemon juice.
Caprice	Serve the fish with a grilled half of banana and a sauceboat of sauce Robert; garnish with picked parsley.
Diablé	Spread with made mustard, coat with crumbs and grill; serve with sauce ravigote.
Epigramme	Coat with fish forcemeat, poach and press until cold; cut into diamonds pass through melted butter and breadcrumbs and grill gently.
Médicis	Garnish with small tomatoes, emptied and cooked then filled with sauce béarnaise.
Montesquieu	Dip in melted butter and coat with breadcrumbs mixed with finely chopped onion and parsley; grill and serve with peeled slices of lemon.
Oseille	Serve accompanied with chiffonade of sorrel cooked in butter until soft.
Pompadour	Arrange the cooked fish on a dish, pipe with sauce béarnaise and decorate with a slice of truffle; surround with pommes noisettes and garnish with slices of truffle.

St-Germain	Arrange the cooked fish on a dish, pipe with sauce béarnaise and surround with pommes noisettes.
Ste-Menehould	Poach in white wine, drain then coat with butter and breadcrumbs; grill gently and serve with sauce hachée and a garnish of fans of gherkin and trellis work of anchovy.
Soleil	Cut into three and plait; coat with crumbs, grill and serve with tomato sauce.
Véron	Grill the fish and serve with a sauceboat of sauce Véron.

Shallow-poached Fish

Method for shallow poaching

Butter a shallow tray, lay the prepared fish in it and season with salt and a little white pepper. Barely cover with 2 parts fish fumet and 1 part white wine; cover with a buttered greaseproof paper. Cook in the oven at 175°C for 10–20 minutes according to the thickness of the fish. Drain off the cooking liquid and keep the fish warm and moist. Use the liquid to make the accompanying sauce.

To serve, drain the fish well on a clean cloth, place in the serving dish and coat with the sauce; many recipes call for finely chopped shallot and a garnish to be cooked with the fish and this should be put back on the fish after straining the cooking liquid. Other garnishes are usually added at the last minute. If available, mushroom cooking liquid can also be used in the poaching of fish.

Sauces used for shallow poached fish

Sauce Vin Blanc	Add 2 parts fish velouté to 1 part fish cooking liquid, reduce to coating consistency and add 1 part cream to 6 parts sauce and 75g unsalted butter per 1 litre. The butter is shaken in small pieces; a small pinch of cayenne and a squeeze of lemon juice helps to bring out the flavour.

Sauce Vin Blanc glacée	If the formula requires that the fish is to be glazed for service, add either some sauce hollandaise or sabayon of egg yolks to ordinary sauce vin blanc, after the cream has been added.

For **à la carte work** the cooking liquid is reduced to a syrupy consistency and knobs of butter whisked or shaken in to form an emulsion and if desired, a little lightly whipped cream; this sauce will glaze.

For **table d'hôte work** the sauce is made as in (1) or (2) according to whether the fish is to be glazed, and is then kept in a warm but not hot place.

Other sauces used for shallow-poached fish are:

Sauce Bercy	Sauté chopped shallot in butter, add 2 parts fish fumet to 1 part white wine and reduce by two thirds; add twice the amount of fish velouté, bring to the correct consistency and finish with cream, butter and chopped parsley.
Sauce Cardinal	Finish sauce homard with cream, butter and a little brandy.
Sauce Crème	Add cream and butter to béchamel; season and strain.
Sauce Crevettes	Thin out béchamel with fish fumet and cream, finish with shrimp butter and shelled shrimps.
Sauce Diplomat	Prepare sauce Normande with lobster butter and add a garnish of diced lobster and truffle.
Sauce Homard	Cook a mirepoix of vegetables and herbs in oil with crushed cooked lobster shells; add squashed tomatoes and purée and fish stock and cook for 1 hour. Strain, add fish velouté and finish with butter, brandy and cream.
Sauce Joinville	Finish sauce Normande with shrimp butter and crayfish butter.
Sauce Mornay	When used with fish, add reduced fish cooking liquid to ordinary sauce mornay.
Sauce Nantua	Add cream to béchamel and finish with crayfish butter and diced crayfish.

Sauce Newburg	Fry a raw cut lobster or cooked lobster shells in butter; flame with brandy and cook in fish stock, pass with pressure, thicken with cream and finish with butter mixed with the raw coral and liver of the lobster.
Sauce Normande	Reduce fish velouté with mushroom, mussel and fish cooking liquids, yolks, cream and lemon juice to the correct consistency and finish with cream and butter.
Sauce Riche	Add some truffle essence and diced truffle only to sauce diplomate.
Sauce Genevoise	Cook fish bones and mirepoix in butter, add 2 parts fish stock to 1 part each demi-glace and red wine and cook to the required consistency. Strain, add a little anchovy essence and finish with butter.
Sauce Vin Rouge	Reduce chopped shallot and red wine by two thirds; add demi-glace, strain and finish with anchovy essence.
Sauce Victoria	This is sauce homard with chopped truffle.
Sauce Américaine	This is sauce homard with diced lobster.
Sauce Régence	Reduce fish stock and German wine with raw mushroom and truffle trimmings; strain, add to sauce Normande and flavour with truffle essence.
Sauce Vénitienne	Flavour sauce vin Blanc with a reduction of tarragon vinegar, shallot and chervil; finish with green butter and chopped tarragon and chervil.
Sauce St-Malo	Flavour sauce vin Blanc with anchovy essence and made English mustard.
Sauce Thermidor	Sauté chopped shallot in butter, add 2 parts fish fumet and 1 part white wine and reduce by two thirds; add fish velouté, a little béchamel, made English mustard and cream.

RECIPES FOR SHALLOW-POACHING

Adrienne   Cook the fish with sliced button mushrooms and julienne of truffle; coat with sauce vin Blanc and garnish with a poached soft roe and a tartlet of crayfish.

Aïda   Serve on a bed of leaf spinach; coat with sauce mornay, sprinkle with breadcrumbs and cheese and gratinate.

Aiglon   Place the cooked fish on a bed of duxelles, coat with sauce made by adding some soubise to the reduced cooking liquid and velouté; decorate with a marbled pattern of fish glaze.

Alexandre   Place a slice of lobster and truffle on the fish, coat with sauce made by adding the cooking liquid to béchamel and cream, reducing and finishing with crayfish butter and sabayon; glaze and garnish with fleurons.

Alexandrine   Arrange the fish on a layer of cooked diced tomato and sliced mushroom, add a slice of lobster and coat with sauce vin blanc finished with chopped parsley; glaze under a salamander.

Alice   Cook with chopped shallot and oysters and a pinch of powdered thyme; reduce the cooking liquid, thicken it with crushed cream crackers and butter and coat the fish. This dish is suitable for preparation by the waiter in front of the customer.

Alsacienne   Arrange cooked fish on a bed of braised sauerkraut; coat with sauce mornay, sprinkle with Parmesan and glaze.

Ambassade   Garnish with a slice of lobster and of truffle and coat with sauce made with the reduced liquid, velouté, cream, sabayon and lobster butter; glaze under a salamander.

Ambassadeur   Arranged cooked fish on a bed of duxelles, coat with sauce vin Blanc glacée and glaze under a salamander; decorate with a slice of truffle and surround with fleurons.

170

Ambassadrice
Coat the cooked fish with sauce made by reducing the cooking liquid, mushroom and mussel cooking liquids with velouté, cream and egg yolks; garnish with a crayfish carapace stuffed with fish farce and poached.

Amélia
Place a border of sliced cooked potato and truffle around the serving dish, arrange the cooked fish in the centre and coat with sauce Nantua containing diced crayfish.

Américaine
Garnish the fish with slices of lobster and coat with lobster sauce.

Amoricaine
Garnish with a poached oyster, a soft roe and a slice of lobster and coat with lobster sauce.

Amiral
Cook with chopped shallot then add the reduced cooking liquid to sauce vin blanc flavoured with crayfish butter; garnish with crayfish, mushrooms, mussels and oysters and coat with sauce.

Archiduc
Cook with blanched diced carrot, celery, leek, truffle and turnip in fish stock flavoured with port and whisky; reduce the liquid, thicken with cream and butter and pour over the fish.

Argenteuil
Coat the cooked fish with sauce vin blanc and garnish with asparagus tips.

Arlésienne
Cook with chopped garlic and onion and diced tomato; coat with the reduced cooking liquid thickened with butter and garnish with turned cooked pieces of courgette and French fried onion rings.

Bagration
Coat the poached fish with sauce mornay, sprinkle with cheese and glaze under a salamander; serve sprinkled with julienne of truffle.

Bâtelière
Place the cooked fish on a barquette filled with diced mussels and shrimps; coat with sauce vin blanc finished with chopped parsley and garnish with goujons of fish.

Beaufort
Coat the poached fish with sauce homard containing diced lobster and mushroom and poached oysters.

171

Fish dishes

Beaumanoir   Coat one half of the fish with sauce vin blanc and the other half with sauce homard; place a slice of truffle on top and garnish with oysters fried à la Villeroy.

Belle Hélène   Poach in red wine and fish stock and coat with sauce vin rouge; garnish with bouchées of soft roes coated with paprika sauce and decorate with a slice of truffle.

Belle de Nuit   Spread with forcemeat flavoured with crayfish butter and fold with an oyster inside; poach, coat with crawfish-flavoured sauce Normande and garnish with pommes noisettes.

Bénédictine   Serve coated with sauce crème and garnish with some brandade of salt cod finished with chopped truffle.

Bercy   Cook in white wine and fish stock with chopped shallot and parsley; add the cooking liquid to some fish velouté and reduce, finish with sabayon, butter and lemon juice, coat the fish and glaze under the salamander.

Biron   Coat with sauce genevoise finished with chopped truffle and garnish with fleurons.

Boistelle (Boitelle)   Cook with sliced button mushrooms and coat with the reduced cooking liquid finished with butter.

Bolivar   Spread with fish farce made with the addition of soubise and purée of tomato; shallow poach and coat with sauce vin blanc flavoured with soubise.

Bonaparte   Make the sauce with the reduced cooking liquid emulsified with butter; garnish with small plain boiled potatoes and coat with the sauce.

Bonne Femme   Cook in white wine and fish stock with chopped shallot and parsley and sliced button mushrooms; reduce the cooking liquid, finish with butter and cream, coat the fish and glaze. A border of sliced cooked potato is authentic.

Bordelaise   Cook in fish stock and red wine with chopped shallot and serve coated with sauce vin rouge.

Bosniaque   Poach with julienne of carrot, mushroom and truffle and coat with sauce vin blanc flavoured and coloured with paprika.

172

Bourguignonne Cook with blanched button onions and mush-rooms in red wine and serve coated with sauce vin rouge.

Bréval Cook with shallot, sliced button mushrooms, diced tomato and chopped parsley; add the cooking liquid to some fish velouté, reduce and finish with cream, sabayon and butter; coat the fish and glaze.

Brillat-Savarin Cook with a brunoise of carrot, celery, leek and onion; coat with the reduced cooking liquid finished with cream and butter and garnish with stuffed crayfish, mushrooms and small trimmed truffles.

Byron Shallow poach in red wine, coat with sauce vin rouge and sprinkle with julienne of truffle.

Café de Paris Shallow poach with julienne of truffle; garnish with asparagus tips, button mushrooms with a prawn stuck in each and poached oysters; pour sauce Victoria around the dish.

Café Riche Serve garnished with diced crayfish and truffle and coated with sauce Victoria.

Cancalaise Shallow poach in fish stock, white wine and oyster liquid; serve garnished with oysters and prawns and coated with sauce Normande.

Cap Martin Garnish with a poached oyster and crayfish, coat with sauce vin blanc and decorate with fish glaze.

Cardinal Spread with lobster forcemeat, fold and shallow poach; serve with a slice of lobster and truffle, coat with sauce cardinal and sprinkle with lobster coral.

Carême Serve with a garnish of button mushrooms, oysters and soft roes; coat with sauce vin blanc flavoured with celery and decorate with fleurons.

Carmelite Spread with crayfish farce, fold and poach; coat with sauce vin blanc flavoured with crayfish butter and garnish with bouchées of crayfish mixed with some of the same sauce.

Carmencita Serve on a bed of garlic-flavoured tomato con-cassée and coat with sauce vin blanc containing

173

julienne of green pimento; garnish with a bouchée of brandade of salt cod.

Caroline   Serve with asparagus tips, mushrooms and shrimps and garnish with fried scampi.

Carvalho   Serve coated with sauce béarnaise with the reduction of the cooking liquid added; decorate with blanched tarragon and garnish with cooked tomato concassée.

Caruso   Spread with lobster forcemeat, fold and poach; decorate with a slice of lobster and of truffle, coat with sauce vin blanc glacée and glaze; garnish with a bouchée of caviar.

Casanova   Coat with sauce vin blanc, garnish with mussels, oysters and a slice of truffle and decorate with fleurons.

Casino   Cut into pieces and poach, mix with mussels, oysters and shrimps and sauce crème; place into a deep dish, sprinkle with cheese and gratinate.

Castellane   Shallow poach and garnish with slices of lobster, button mushrooms and small balls of potato; coat with sauce vin blanc glacée and glaze.

Castiglione   Place in a border of sliced boiled potato, garnish with a slice of lobster and a turned mushroom, coat with sauce vin blanc glacée and glaze.

Caylus   Serve with cooked halves of tomato filled with stewed julienne of carrot, celery and leek; coat with sauce mornay and glaze.

Cecil Rhodes   Garnish with asparagus tips, oysters and pieces of truffle; cover with sauce vin blanc glacée and glaze under the salamander.

au Chambertin   Cook in red wine; reduce the cooking liquid, thicken with beurre manié and butter and pour over the fish and glaze; garnish with goujons of fish which have been shallow fried.

au Champagne   Shallow poach in dry champagne; reduce the cooking liquid, add a little velouté and butter, pour over the fish and glaze; garnish with shallow-fried goujons.

aux Champignons	Shallow poach in mushroom cooking liquid; garnish with very white button mushrooms and coat with white sauce champignons made with fish velouté.
Chauchat	Place the poached fish on a layer of sauce mornay and surround with slices of boiled potato; coat with sauce mornay and glaze.
Cherubim	Place the cooked fish in a puff-pastry case together with some creamed mushrooms; coat half with sauce vin blanc and half with the same sauce flavoured and coloured with purée of smoked salmon and decorate with a trellis work of strips of smoked salmon.
Chivry	Coat with sauce chivry made by flavouring fish velouté with infusion of herbs and white wine; garnish with heart-shaped fried bread croûtons.
Choiseul	Poach with julienne of white truffle and coat with sauce vin blanc.
Choisy	Poach with julienne of lettuce and truffle and coat with sauce vin blanc.
Cingalaise	Arrange the poached fish in a border of riz pilaff containing julienne of red and green pimento and coat with sauce vin blanc flavoured with curry.
Claremont	Serve coated with sauce vin blanc containing diced tomato and chopped parsley and garnish with fleurons.
Clarence	Arrange the poached fish in a glazed border of duchesse potato, garnish with soft roes and shrimps and coat with sauce américaine flavoured with curry.
Claudine	Shallow poach with finely chopped carrot, celery, leek and turnip, diced tomato and chopped parsley; add the reduced cooking liquid to sauce vin blanc flavoured with lobster, coat the fish and garnish with prawns.
Commodore	Coat the poached fish with sauce Normande flavoured with anchovy essence and garnish with crayfish, lobster croquette, an oyster deep-fried à la Villeroy, a quenelle and some pommes noisettes.

175

Condé	Coat the poached fish with sauce vin blanc glacée and pipe a cross and border of stiff purée of fresh tomato; glaze under the salamander.
Condorcet	Shallow poach with a round of blanched cucumber and a round piece of tomato; coat with sauce vin blanc.
Coqueline	Dress in a border of sliced potatoes, mask with a sauce made from the cooking liquid and glaze.
Crécy	Spread with fish farce containing purée of cooked carrot, fold and poach; serve coated with sauce vin blanc and garnished with artichoke bottoms filled with small balls of carrot.
aux Crevettes	Serve garnished with prawns and coated with sauce crevettes made from either béchamel or fish velouté.
Crillon	Garnish with a slice of lobster, coat with sauce américaine flavoured with brandy and cream and decorate with a slice of truffle.
Cubat	Place the cooked fish on a bed of duxelles; coat with sauce mornay made with the reduced cooking liquid, sprinkle with parmesan and glaze and garnish with a slice of truffle.
Czarine	Serve coated with sauce vin blanc flavoured with horseradish and garnish with tartlets of caviar.
Daumont	Spread with crayfish forcemeat, poach and serve with crayfish tails, mushrooms and quenelles decorated with truffle; coat with sauce Nantua and garnish with deep-fried crumbed soft roes.
Deauvillaise	Shallow poach with stewed sliced onion in cream and butter; make this into a sauce, finish with butter and coat the fish; decorate with puff-pastry diamonds.
Demi-Deuil	Coat with sauce vin blanc and decorate with crescent-shapes of truffle.
Demidoff	Poach in white wine with chopped celeriac and fennel; add the cooking liquid to jus lié and reduce; coat the fish and garnish with crayfish, mushrooms, olives and truffle.

Desmoulins	Poach with chopped shallot, sliced mushrooms, diced tomato and chopped parsley; reduce the cooking liquid, add butter and pour over the fish.
Dieppoise	Garnish the cooked fish with button mushrooms, mussels and prawns; coat with sauce vin blanc glacée and glaze under the salamander.
Diplomat	Poach in the usual way, coat with sauce diplomate and decorate with a slice of truffle.
Donia	Spread with fish farce, fold over and poach; serve in a border of riz pilaff, garnish with crayfish, mushrooms and truffle and coat with sauce vin blanc.
Dragomiroff	Coat with sauce mornay, glaze and garnish with mussels in the half shells.
Dubarry	Garnish with soft roes and slices of truffle; coat with sauce mornay, glaze and pour a border of lobster-flavoured demi-glace around.
Dugléré	Cook in white wine and fish stock with chopped shallot and parsley and diced tomato; reduce the cooking liquid, add cream and finish with butter; pour over the fish and garnish and sprinkle with chopped parsley.
Duguesclin	Coat with sauce crevettes and garnish with artichoke bottoms filled with buttered shrimps.
Dumas	Coat with sauce vin blanc containing diced tomato and chopped fines herbes.
Duse	Spread with farce, fold and poach; place on a bed of riz pilaff, coat with sauce mornay and glaze; garnish with prawns bound with sauce vin blanc and sprinkle with chopped truffle.
Egyptienne	Cut into goujons and poach in butter and lemon juice, mix with button mushrooms, quenelles and slices of truffle and bind with sauce vin rouge flavoured with lobster butter; serve in individual cocottes.
Eléonore	Serve on a layer of stewed julienne of lettuce and coat with sauce vin blanc that has been flavoured and coloured with paprika.
Elizabeth	Spread with forcemeat, fold and shallow poach; serve on an artichoke bottom, decorate with a

177

	mushroom and slice of truffle, coat with sauce mornay and glaze.
Epicurienne	Shallow poach in white wine and Madeira; flavour the reduced cooking liquid with anchovy essence and lemon juice, finish with butter and coat the fish.
Favorite	Line buttered dariole moulds with strips of fillet of fish, fill with farce and poach; serve coated with sauce vin blanc with a slice of truffle on top and a cordon of Sauce Nantua around.
Fécampoise	Garnish the poached fish with mussels and shrimps, coat with sauce crevettes and garnish with fleurons.
Fermière	Cook with blanched slices of carrot, celery and onion, and thyme and bay-leaf, in red wine; garnish with sautèd sliced mushrooms and coat with the cooking liquid reduced and thickened with beurre manié.
aux Fines Herbes	Shallow poach and coat with sauce vin blanc containing chopped chervil, parsley and tarragon.
Flaubert	Poach with paysanne of carrot, celery, leek and turnip, sliced mushrooms and shrimps; coat with sauce vin blanc glacée and glaze.
Florentine	Arrange the cooked fish on a bed of buttered leaf spinach, coat with sauce mornay, sprinkle with cheese and glaze under the salamander.
Fontainebleau	Coat the poached fish with sauce crevettes and garnish with asparagus tips and prawns.
Foyot	Cook in fish stock and white wine with chopped shallot and parsley; reduce the cooking liquid with velouté, finish with sabayon, fish glaze and butter, pour over the fish and glaze.
Francois Ier	Cook with chopped shallot and parsley, sliced mushroom and diced tomato; reduce the cooking liquid, thicken with cream and butter, coat the fish and sprinkle with parsley.
Gallia	Poach the fish with julienne of lettuce and truffle; reduce the cooking liquid, add cream and fish glaze and coat the fish; decorate with fleurons.

Galliera   Cook with julienne of lettuce, mushroom and truffle; reduce the cooking liquid and thicken with cream and butter, pour over the fish and sprinkle with parsley.

Gastronome   Garnish the cooked fish with a mushroom, shrimps and truffle; coat with sauce riche and add a bouquet of prawns.

Geisha   Arrange the poached fish on a galette of potato, coat with curry sauce and garnish with a bouquet of diced tomato sprinkled with chopped parsley.

George Sand   Serve garnished with crayfish and quenelles; coat with sauce Normande flavoured and coloured with crayfish butter.

Georgette   Place a portion of poached fish on a salpicon of crayfish and mushroom in an emptied baked potato; coat with sauce Nantua and decorate with truffle.

Gillet   Serve the poached fish in a glazed border of pomme duchesse; coat with sauce vin blanc, sprinkle with cheese and glaze.

Giselle   Garnish with prawns, coat with sauce crevettes and add a bouquet of asparagus tips.

Gismonde   Shallow poach in fish stock and port wine; reduce the cooking liquid, thicken with sabayon and cream and pour over the fish; serve garnished with small turned, boiled potatoes.

Godard   Serve in a border of glazed duchesse potato, garnish with mushrooms, shrimps and truffle and coat with sauce vin blanc finished with lobster butter.

Gondolier   Fill a glazed boat-shape of duchesse potato with shrimps bound with sauce crevettes, place the poached fish on top and coat with sauce vin blanc coloured and flavoured with green herbs and spinach.

Gounod   Spread with farce and fold; shallow poach and garnish with a slice of lobster and an oyster and coat with sauce homard.

Gourmet   Shallow poach in fish stock, mushroom cooking liquid and port wine; reduce the liquid, thicken

179

	with butter and pour over the fish; garnish with a crayfish tail.
Grammont	Arrange on a bed of duxelles, spread with more duxelles and garnish with a poached oyster and a slice of truffle; sprinkle with cheese and butter, gratinate and serve accompanied with sauce hollandaise.
Grand-Duc	Poach in fish stock, mushroom cooking liquid and white wine; serve garnished with a crayfish and a slice of truffle, coat with sauce mornay, glaze and add a bouquet of asparagus tips.
Grande-Duchesse	Arrange on a dish with a bouquet of asparagus tips and a slice of truffle; coat with sauce mornay and glaze.
Granville	Garnish the poached fish with mushrooms, shrimps and a slice of truffle and coat with sauce vin blanc.
Gringoire	Serve with a soft roe and a slice of lobster and coat with sauce américaine.
Halévy	Place the poached fish in a glazed border of duchesse potato; coat half with truffled sauce vin blanc, the other half with sauce Nantua and sprinkle with sieved yolk of hard-boiled egg.
Havraise	Coat the poached fish with sauce bercy and garnish it with deep-fried breadcrumbed mussels.
Heliopolis	Arrange the poached fish in a lobster carapace filled with salpicon of lobster, mushroom and truffle bound with sauce vin blanc; decorate with a slice of truffle and coat with sauce Normande containing julienne of mushroom and truffle; glaze.
Héloïse	Shallow poach with chopped mushroom and serve coated with sauce bercy.
Henriette	Cut into goujons, poach and bind with paprika-flavoured sauce vin blanc; fill into an emptied baked potato, pipe potato around the edge, coat with sauce mornay, glaze then sprinkle with chopped walnuts.

Hongroise   Shallow poach with chopped onion and diced tomato; coat with paprika-coloured and flavoured sauce vin blanc glacée and glaze.

aux Huîtres   Garnish the poached fish with oysters and coat with sauce Normande.

Ile de France   Cook with julienne of mushroom and truffle; coat with sauce bercy, glaze and garnish with a bouquet each of asparagus tips and tomato concassée.

Impératrice   Arrange the poached fish on a fried bread croûton, coat with sauce vin blanc containing julienne of truffle and decorate with a poached oyster.

Impériale   Garnish with crayfish and soft roes, coat with sauce vin blanc containing julienne of truffle and garnish with fleurons.

Indienne   Shallow poach in fish stock, coat with curry sauce and serve accompanied with plain boiled rice.

Infante   Place the poached fish on a bed of duxelles, coat with sauce mornay, sprinkle with cheese and glaze.

Ismailia   Place a border of riz pilaff containing peas and diced pimento on a dish, arrange the fish in the centre and coat with the reduced cooking liquid thickened with butter.

Jackson   Place the cooked fish on a bed of soubise flavoured with chopped tarragon, coat with the reduced and buttered cooking liquid and glaze.

Jean Bart   Place a dome-shaped salpicon of mushrooms, mussels and prawns bound with béchamel on a dish, arrange the fish on the side and coat with sauce Normande containing chopped truffle; garnish with mussels in the half shell coated with sauce mornay and glazed.

Jehovah   Serve on a salpicon of asparagus and shrimps bound with sauce vin blanc; coat with sauce mornay and glaze.

Joinville   Garnish the fish with a crayfish, coat with sauce Joinville and decorate with a slice of truffle; add

181

	a salpicon of mushrooms, prawns and truffle bound with sauce Joinville.
Josette	Poach with thinly sliced new carrots and shredded lettuce, coat with sauce crème finished with sabayon, and glaze.
Jouffroy	Cook with sliced mushrooms, coat with sauce vin blanc glacée and glaze under a salamander; garnish with bouchées of asparagus tips and a slice of truffle.
Judic	Garnish the fish with a braised lettuce and quenelles; coat with sauce mornay and glaze.
Jules Janin	Shallow poach with a fine mirepoix previously cooked in butter; serve on duxelles containing chopped truffle, garnish with crayfish, mussels and slice of truffle, and coat with sauce tortue made with the reduced cooking liquid and mirepoix, finished with butter.
Lacam	Sprinkle the poached fish with diced truffle, coat with sauce vin blanc and garnish with heart-shaped fried-bread croûtons.
Lacharme	Decorate the poached fish with slices of truffle and coat with sauce bercy from which the chopped parsley has been omitted.
Lady Egmont	Shallow poach the fish and cook sliced mushrooms in butter, lemon juice and water; reduce the fish and mushroom liquids and make into a sauce with butter and cream; add the mushrooms and some diced asparagus and coat the fish.
Laguipierre	Coat the poached fish with sauce vin blanc and sprinkle with a small dice of truffle.
Laperouse	Garnish with mussels and shrimps coated with Sauce Crevettes and coat the fish with sauce vin blanc.
Lavallière	Spread with truffled farce, fold and poach, place a poached mould of farce on the dish, fill with a mixture of mushrooms, oysters, quenelles and soft roe and sauce Normande; place the fish on top, coat with the sauce and decorate with a slice of truffle.

Léopold Poach the fish and coat one half with sauce homard and sprinkle with chopped truffle, the other half with sauce genevoise and sprinkle with lobster coral; garnish with shrimps mixed with sauce vin blanc.

Livornaise Poach with chopped shallot, diced tomato and julienne of truffle; coat with the reduced cooking liquid finished with butter and glaze under a salamander.

Londonderry Spread with crayfish farce, fold and poach; garnish with mushrooms and mussels and coat with sauce vin blanc flavoured with anchovy essence.

Louis XIV Cook the fish with brunoise of carrot, celery, leek and turnip; sprinkle with shrimps and coat with sauce nantua.

Louis XV Coat the poached fish with sauce vin blanc, sprinkle with lobster coral and decorate with crescents of truffle.

Lydia Garnish the poached fish with shrimps and asparagus tips, coat with sauce vin blanc glacée, glaze and decorate with fleurons.

Marcel Prévost Place the poached fish on a bed of duxelles, coat with sauce mornay, sprinkle with cheese and glaze.

Marcelle Spread with truffled forcemeat, fold and poach in lemon juice and butter; serve on a barquette filled with purée of soft roe and decorate with truffle; coat with a little sauce vin blanc.

Marchand de Vins Cook with chopped shallot and red wine then reduce the cooking liquid, thicken with butter and flavour with fish glaze, lemon juice and chopped parsley; pour over the fish.

Marguerite Poach in fish stock and white wine, coat with sauce vin blanc and decorate with slices of truffle.

Marguéry Garnish the fish with mussels and prawns, reduce the cooking liquid with fish velouté and cream and finish with sabayon and butter; coat the fish, glaze and garnish with fleurons; winkles may be added to the garnish.

Marie-Louise   Cover with mushroom, truffle and fish forcemeat and poach; coat one half with sauce vin blanc and the other half with sauce italienne.

Marie-Stuart   Garnish the fish with a quenelle decorated with truffle and coat with sauce Newburg.

Maurice   Serve with a garnish of mussels and shrimps, coat with sauce crevettes finished with a sabayon and glaze under a salamander.

Marinière   Garnish the poached fish with mussels and prawns and coat with sauce bercy made with mussel cooking liquid and finished with egg yolks.

Marquise   Place the poached fish in a glazed border of pommes Marquise; garnish with prawns, salmon quenelles and truffle and coat with sauce crevettes.

Marseillaise   Poach with chopped garlic and onion and diced tomato in white wine and a little oil; coat with saffron-coloured and flavoured sauce vin blanc and sprinkle with chopped parsley.

Mathilde   Coat the poached fish with sauce vin blanc flavoured with soubise and garnish with small pieces of cucumber cooked in butter.

Ménagère   Poach in red wine with sliced carrot, celery and onion and coat with the reduced cooking liquid thickened with beurre manié.

Messaline   Poach in champagne, reduce the cooking liquid, add tomato purée and butter and pour over the fish; garnish with quarters of fonds d'artichauts.

Metternich   Coat the poached fish with paprika-flavoured sauce vin blanc and decorate with slices of truffle.

Minerva   Poach with chopped shallot and diced tomato; coat with sauce vin blanc and garnish with a trellis work of strips of anchovy and small slices of potato between.

Miromesnil   Poach with shredded lettuce, diced tomato and julienne of truffle and coat with sauce made from the reduced cooking liquid thickened with butter.

Mogador Spread with farce, fold and poach; arrange on a bed of crayfish bound with sauce Nantua in a poached circle of fish farce; decorate with a slice of truffle and a crayfish carapace filled with prawns and farce and poached, and serve with sauce Nantua.

Monaco Garnish the poached fish with poached oysters and coat with tomato-flavoured sauce vin blanc; decorate with fried heart-shaped croûtons.

Monseigneur Garnish with a small poached egg, a quenelle and a slice of truffle and coat with the reduced cooking liquid finished with butter.

Montespan Shallow poach with sliced mushrooms and chopped parsley and coat with the reduced cooking liquid enriched with butter.

Montgolfier Shallow poach with julienne of crayfish, mushroom and truffle; coat with sauce vin blanc and garnish with fleurons.

Mon Rêve Spread with farce, fold and poach; serve on a bed of riz pilaff containing diced green pimento and tomato, decorate with a crayfish and coat with sauce mousseline containing the reduced cooking liquid.

Montreuil Shallow poach in fish stock and white wine and garnish with small balls of plain boiled potato; coat the fish with sauce vin blanc and the garnish with sauce crevettes.

Montreux Place the poached fish in a border of alternate slices of boiled potato and truffle, coat with sauce mornay and glaze.

Montrouge Poach in fish stock and mushroom cooking liquid; coat with sauce mornay made with the addition of mushroom purée and garnish with creamed sliced mushrooms.

Mornay Poach the fish in fumet de poisson, reduce the cooking liquid, add to béchamel with cream and reduce; add sabayon, butter and Parmesan, coat the fish, sprinkle with cheese, and glaze.

Nantua   Poach in fish stock and mushroom cooking liquid; garnish with crayfish, coat with sauce Nantua and decorate with truffle.

Nelson   Add the cooking liquid from the fish to velouté and cream and reduce; finish with sabayon and butter, coat the fish and garnish with pommes noisettes and poached soft roes.

Nemours   Spread with farce, fold and poach; place on a dish, coat with sauce crevettes and decorate with truffle; garnish with mushrooms, soft roes and quenelles bound with sauce Normande, and a shrimp croquette coated with chopped truffle.

Newburg   Coat the poached fish with sauce Newburg and decorate with a slice of lobster and a slice of truffle.

Noilly Prat   Cook in fish stock and dry vermouth, garnish with button mushrooms and coat with the reduced cooking liquid thickened with butter.

Normande   Poach in fish stock and mushroom cooking liquid, garnish with mushrooms, mussels, oysters and prawns and coat with sauce Normande; decorate with a slice of truffle, a diamond- or N-shaped fried-bread croûton, a trussed crayfish, and some deep-fried goujons; finish with piped fish glaze.

Offremont   Poach with chopped shallots and white wine; coat with sauce vin blanc and garnish with creamed morels and a few turned pieces of truffle.

Olga   Place the poached fish on a salpicon of prawns and sauce vin blanc in an emptied baked potato; coat with Sauce Mornay, sprinkle with cheese and glaze.

Opéra   Coat the poached fish with sauce vin blanc and garnish with asparagus tips and small rounds of truffle.

Orientale   Coat the poached fish with curry-flavoured sauce Newburg and serve accompanied with a dish of plain boiled rice.

Ostendaise Spread with farce, fold and poach; garnish with poached oysters, coat with sauce Normande and decorate with a slice of truffle; finish with a small fish croquette.

Otéro Place some sauce mornay in an emptied baked potato skin, the cooked fish on it and pipe the edge with duchesse potato; coat with sauce mornay, sprinkle with cheese and glaze.

Paillard Garnish the poached fish with sautéd morels and crayfish, coat with sauce bercy and decorate with heart-shaped croûtons.

Palace Cook the fish with chopped shallot, sliced mushroom, diced tomato and chopped tarragon; make the sauce in the usual way finishing it with a little brandy; mask the fish and glaze under the salamander.

Palestrina Serve the poached fish on a bed of creamed spaghetti containing julienne of mushroom and truffle; coat with sauce vin blanc containing julienne of lettuce, sprinkle with cheese, glaze and decorate with fleurons.

Parisienne Garnish the poached fish with slices of mushroom and truffle and a trussed crayfish; coat with sauce vin blanc with the addition of the reduced cooking liquid.

Paysanne Shallow poach the fish with a cooked paysanne of carrot, celery, leek and onion with beans and peas; reduce the cooking liquid, thicken with butter and pour over the fish.

Perroquet Coat the poached fish with sauce mornay, glaze and garnish with a bouchée of salpicon of mussels, oysters, quenelles and shrimps bound with sauce vin blanc.

Persane Poach the fish, coat with sauce Newburg flavoured with paprika and serve in a border of riz pilaff.

Petit-Duc Cook with sliced mushrooms, coat with sauce vin blanc glacée, garnish with asparagus tips and a slice of truffle and glaze.

Pierre-le-Grand	Coat the poached fish with sauce vin blanc and sprinkle one end with chopped ham and the other with chopped truffle.
Picardy	Garnish the poached fish with mussels, oysters, prawns and truffle and coat with sauce vin blanc glacée; glaze under a salamander.
Piccadilly	Shallow poach with chopped shallot and tarragon; reduce the cooking liquid, flavour with brandy and Worcester sauce, thicken with butter and pour over the fish.
Polignac	Cook the fish with julienne of mushroom and truffle; make the sauce in the usual way, mask over the fish and garnish with fleurons.
Portugaise	Coat with sauce vin blanc glacée, surround with stewed mushroom, onion and tomato, glaze and sprinkle chopped parsley on the tomato.
Princesse	Coat the poached fish with sauce vin blanc containing purée of asparagus; decorate with truffle and garnish with nests of duchesse potato filled with asparagus tips.
Princière	Coat with sauce Nantua containing diced truffle, glaze and decorate with a slice of truffle.
Provençale	Shallow poach in fish stock and oil with chopped garlic; coat with sauce provençale containing the reduced cooking liquid and garnish with a half tomato stuffed à la provençale.
Prunier	Cook in white wine and mushroom cooking liquid, garnish with whole button mushrooms, oysters and a slice of truffle, and coat with sauce vin blanc.
Quo Vadis	Coat the poached fish with sauce vin blanc finished with tarragon butter; decorate with a slice of truffle and garnish with a trussed crayfish.
Rachel	Spread with farce, add a slice of truffle, fold and poach; coat with sauce vin blanc with the addition of diced asparagus and truffle.
Régence	Spread with truffled farce, fold and poach in Chablis; garnish the poached fish with a salpicon of mushrooms, oysters, crayfish quenelles,

soft roes and truffle mixed with sauce Normande, and coat with sauce régence.

Reine Garnish with quenelles, coat with sauce vin blanc and decorate with a slice of truffle.

Réjane Coat the poached fish with sauce vin blanc finished with crayfish butter, and garnish with prepared pommes duchesse.

Renaissance Coat the poached fish with sauce vin blanc and garnish with small bouquets of asparagus tips, carrots, cauliflower, peas, turnips and pommes noisettes.

Reynière Stuff with forcemeat, poach and serve coated with onion-flavoured sauce vin blanc and garnished with a trellis work of anchovy fillets; add mushrooms and sautéd soft roes.

Riche Garnish the poached fish with a crayfish, sprinkle with chopped truffle and coat with sauce Nantua.

Richembourg Coat the poached fish with sauce américaine, decorate with a slice of truffle and garnish with oysters cooked à la Villeroy.

Rochelaise Poach in fish stock and red wine and chopped onion; garnish with mussels, oysters and soft roes and coat with the reduced cooking liquid added to demi-glace.

Romaine Place a layer of macaroni mixed with chopped anchovy, shredded spinach, cheese and butter in a dish, lay the poached fish on top, coat with sauce crème, sprinkle with cheese and butter and gratinate.

Rosine Coat with sauce vin blanc flavoured and coloured with tomato and garnish with small cooked tomatoes filled with a poached quenelle and coated with sauce vin blanc.

Rouennaise Poach in red wine with chopped shallot; garnish with mushrooms, mussels, oysters and prawns and coat with the reduced cooking liquid added to demi-glace; finish by adding a shallow fried smelt.

Royal Monceau	Serve the fish in a puff-pastry case on quenelles and lobster covered with sauce Amoricaine, and decorate with a slice of truffle.
Royale	Garnish the poached fish with crayfish, mushrooms, quenelles and truffle and coat with sauce Normande.
Russe	Cook with parcooked slices of grooved carrot and button onion; make the sauce as usual and finish it with chopped parsley; coat the fish and garnish.
Saint-Cloud	Coat the poached fish with sauce vin blanc, pipe diagonal lines of purée of tomato and garnish with deep-fried breadcrumbed mussels.
Saint-Georges	Spread with lobster farce, fold and poach; place in an emptied baked potato on a bed of diced lobster in sauce and coat with sauce bercy.
Saint-Valéry	Poach with diced mushroom and shrimps; coat with sauce vin blanc glacée and glaze quickly under a salamander.
Sappho	Poach with julienne of mushroom and truffle; coat with sauce vin blanc and garnish with a trussed crayfish, a croquette of lobster, and a bouchée filled with salpicon of mushroom, prawn and truffle.
Sarah Bernhardt	Poach with julienne of carrot and truffle and coat with sauce vénitienne.
Savoy	Shallow poach in fish stock, mushroom cooking liquid, truffle essence and white wine; garnish with bouquets of asparagus tips and tomato concassée, coat with sauce vin blanc glacée and glaze under the salamander.
Suchet	Cook the fish with julienne of carrot, celery, leek and truffle, make the sauce in the usual way and coat the fish.
Sullivan	Spread with fish farce, fold and poach; coat with sauce mornay, glaze and garnish with a bunch of asparagus tips and a slice of truffle.
Sultane	Coat the poached fish with sauce vin blanc flavoured and coloured with pistachio butter; decorate with a crescent of truffle and garnish

with a bouchée of shrimps mixed with sauce crevettes.

Suzanne   Cook the poached fish with julienne of mushroom and truffle; garnish with a crayfish and soft roe, coat with sauce vin blanc and decorate with fleurons.

Sylvette   Cook with small dice of carrot, celery, leek, mushroom, truffle and turnip; coat with the reduced cooking liquid thickened with butter and garnish with tomatoes filled with creamed fish purée, sprinkled with cheese and gratinated.

Taillevent   Place the poached fish on creamed purée of mushrooms, coat with sauce mornay and glaze; garnish with a tartlet of brandade of salt cod flavoured with garlic.

Talleyrand   Arrange the poached fish on a mound of creamed spaghetti mixed with julienne of truffle; decorate with truffle slices, coat with sauce vin blanc glacée and glaze under a salamander.

Théodore   Coat one half of the poached fish with sauce vin blanc containing chopped truffle and the other half with sauce vénitienne.

Thermidor   Coat the poached fish with sauce bercy flavoured with English mustard and decorate with a thread of fish glaze.

Tivoli   Garnish the poached fish with a mushroom, oyster and soft roe; coat with sauce genevoise made with Chianti and sprinkle with shallow-fried raw noodles.

Tosca   Place a poached soft roe on the cooked fish; coat with crayfish-flavoured sauce vin blanc and garnish with a quenelle with a crayfish and slice of truffle on top, previously coated with crayfish-flavoured sauce mornay and glazed.

Tout-Paris   Coat one half of the fish with sauce vin blanc and the other half with sauce Nantua; decorate with truffle and garnish with crayfish.

Trois Frères   Coat one half of the poached fish with ordinary sauce vin blanc and the other with the same sauce containing chopped parsley and truffle.

Trophy Shallow poach, then sandwich two pieces with cooked tomato pulp; coat with sauce thermidor and glaze under the salamander.

Trouvillaise Garnish with mussels and prawns and coat with sauce crevettes.

Tzarine Garnish the poached fish with small pieces of cucumber cooked in butter and coat with paprika-flavoured and coloured sauce mornay.

Urbain-Dubois Coat the cooked fish with sauce mornay containing diced crayfish and truffle; cover with crayfish soufflé mixture and bake in the oven.

d'Urville Spread with farce, insert a slice of truffle, fold, and poach; place in a glazed barquette of duchesse potato filled with shrimps mixed with sauce crevettes.

Valentine Coat with sauce mornay, glaze and serve garnished with deep-fried boat shapes of duchesse potato, filled with risotto containing diced white truffle.

Valois Garnish the poached fish with a crayfish, soft roe and small plain boiled potatoes; coat with sauce béarnaise finished with meat glaze.

Vatel Coat the poached fish with sauce chambord and garnish with cassolettes of cucumber filled with fish forcemeat and cooked in butter; add a few deep-fried goujons.

Vénitienne Coat the poached fish with sauce vénitienne and garnish with heart-shaped fried-bread croûtons.

Verdi Place a bed of creamed macaroni with cheese, diced lobster and truffle on a dish; place the poached fish on top, coat with sauce mornay and glaze.

Véronique Cook the fish and place on a dish with a garnish of blanched peeled and depipped grapes; coat with sauce and glaze. If preferred the grapes may be kept chilled and placed on the dish at the last moment.

Victor Hugo Coat the fish with tomato-flavoured sauce vin blanc containing diced mushroom and truffle and chopped tarragon.

Victoria	Garnish with dice of crawfish and truffle and coat the fish and garnish with béchamel flavoured with crayfish butter.
Vierville	Serve on a bed of tomato concassée, coat with sauce vin blanc mixed with the same amount of sauce hollandaise and glaze under a salamander.
Vin Blanc	Cook the fish with chopped shallots in white wine and fish stock; make the sauce in the usual way, coat the fish and garnish with fleurons.
Vin Blanc Glacée	Add a sabayon to the sauce, coat the cooked fish, glaze and garnish with fleurons.
au Vin Rouge	Cook the fish with chopped shallot in red wine, reduce the cooking liquid, add demi-glace and finish with anchovy essence and butter; coat the fish and garnish with fleurons.
Virginie	Half fill an emptied baked potato with a salpicon of crayfish, place the poached fish on top, coat with sauce mornay and glaze.
Viveur	Cook with julienne of celery, mushroom, pimento and truffle; coat with sauce américaine and decorate with a slice of truffle.
Walewska	Cook in fish stock, reduce the cooking liquid and add to béchamel and cream, finish the sauce with Parmesan and butter; place a slice of lobster on each portion of fish, mask with sauce, glaze, and decorate with a slice of truffle.
Wilhelmine	Half-fill emptied baked potatoes with creamed pieces of cucumber; place the fish on top then add a poached oyster and coat with sauce mornay and glaze.
Windsor	Poach with brunoise of carrot, celery, leek and turnip in fish stock and lemon juice and coat with sauce vin blanc containing poached oysters and finished with purée of pocher soft roe.
Yvette	Coat the poached fish with sauce vénitienne and garnish with small tomatoes filled with fish forcemeat and cooked in butter.

────── PAUPIETTES OF FISH ──────

These are made by lightly flattening a fillet of fish and spreading the skinned side with fish farce. Roll up starting at the thin end and keep in the rolled shaped by packing closely together in the cooking pan, by tying, or by cooking in a buttered dariole mould. They are shallow poached and may be served in most of the ways given for shallow poached fish. The following are specific formulas for paupiettes.

Andalouse	Use a farce containing diced cooked pimento and place each paupiette in half of a cooked tomato filled with risotto, standing on a round of fried aubergine; serve coated with beurre noisette.
Baron Brisse	Arrange in a border of cooked fish farce filled with crayfish mixed with Sauce Américaine; coat the paupiette with sauce vin blanc and decorate with a slice of truffle.
Beatrice	Serve on a cooked mushroom with a garnish of soft roes and prawns; coat with sauce vin blanc flavoured with shrimp butter and decorate with a turned mushroom and slice of truffle.
Boïeldieu	Add diced crayfish, shrimps and truffle to the farce; serve on a round flat lobster croquette, coat with sauce Nantua and decorate with truffle.
Bristol	Serve on a fond d'artichaut, coat with sauce vin blanc, garnish with pommes parisienne and decorate with a slice of truffle.
Catalane	Arrange the paupiette in half a cooked tomato filled with sautéd sliced onion; coat with sauce vin blanc glacée and glaze.
Cazenove	Arrange in a hollowed-out cooked half of apple, coat with the reduced cooking liquid added to sauce hollandaise and sprinkle with julienne of red pimento.
Cherbourg	Serve with a garnish of mussels, oysters and shrimps mixed with sauce crevettes and coat with the same sauce.

Chevalière
Spread with crayfish forcemeat and serve coated with sauce vin blanc and a garnish of crawfish, mushrooms and truffle mixed with sauce homard.

Coquelin
Roll with an oyster and tomato-flavoured fish farce; serve on half a cooked tomato, coat with sauce vin blanc glacée, glaze and decorate with a slice of each lobster and of truffle.

Daumont
Spread with crayfish forcemeat and serve on a mushroom filled with diced crayfish mixed with sauce Normande; coat with the sauce and garnish with a stuffed crayfish and a shallow-fried soft roe.

Excelsior
Garnish with lobster cooked à la Newburg, coat the paupiette with sauce Normande containing julienne of mushroom and decorate with a slice of truffle.

Floréal
Serve on creamed pieces of asparagus, coat with sauce vin blanc coloured and flavoured with beurre printanière and decorate with a slice of cooked carrot and sprig of chervil.

Grimaldi
Serve on a layer of creamed spaghetti, coat with sauce Nantua and decorate with a slice each of lobster and truffle.

Hélèna
Place on a bed of creamed noodles, coat with sauce mornay, sprinkle with cheese and glaze.

Ivanhoe
Spread with smoked haddock forcemeat and roll up, cook with a little lemon juice and whisky with artichoke bottoms and garnish with a grilled mushroom; make the sauce from the cooking liquid.

Killarney
Serve with a salpicon of lobster, mushroom and truffle and coat with sauce Normande.

Manon
Arrange the cooked paupiette on a glazed border of duchesse potato; sprinkle with julienne of mushroom and truffle, coat with sauce vin blanc and garnish with asparagus tips.

Mascotte	Serve in a glazed border of duchesse potato filled with a salpicon of lobster and truffle; coat with sauce mornay, glaze and decorate with a slice of truffle.
Mexicaine	Serve on a grilled mushroom filled with tomato concassée and coat with sauce vin blanc flavoured and coloured with tomato and diced red pimento.
Montmorency	Serve with a salpicon of mushroom, shrimps and truffle in sauce crevettes; coat with sauce vin blanc and decorate with large-size pommes noisettes.
Niçoise	Spread with duxelles, roll up and enclose in the flowers of vegetable marrows; poach in fish stock and serve coated with the cooking liquid thickened with beurre manié and flavoured with anchovy essence.
Palestine	Roll with a crayfish inside, poach then coat with sauce vin blanc containing diced crayfish; decorate with fried-bread croûtons.
Paulette	Serve in a tartlet filled with creamed morels and truffle and coat with sauce vin blanc.
Pisane	Place the poached paupiette in a border of leaf spinach, garnish with quarters of hard-boiled egg and coat with the cooking liquid added to a tomato-flavoured béchamel.
Renoir	Arrange in a hollowed-out cooked apple filled with duxelles; coat with sauce hollandaise and sprinkle with chopped truffle.
Rhodésia	Serve on a slice of lobster and coat with sauce américaine.
Rossini	Spread with foie gras-flavoured fish farce, roll up and poach; serve coated with sauce vin blanc, sprinkle with chopped truffle and garnish with a tartlet of cooked forcemeat with a slice of truffle on top.
Sylvia	Stuff with forcemeat containing purée of globe artichoke and serve on an artichoke bottom; coat with the reduced cooking liquid made into

a sauce with velouté, cream and butter and decorate with a slice of truffle.

Tabellion Serve with a garnish of quenelles, cover with sauce Normande and sprinkle with julienne of truffle.

Thérèse Serve coated with sauce vin blanc flavoured with truffle essence, decorate with a slice of truffle and surround with small balls of plain-boiled potato.

Timbales of Fish

A timbale may be a silver dish with a lining so that boiling water or crushed ice can be poured in to keep food hot or cold, or it may be a container made of bread, pastry, cooked paste, etc. It is used to serve what are known as composite entrées of fish, poultry, etc., with appropriate garnishes bound with a sauce. The following may be served in a pastry case baked blind in a charlotte mould, in a flan ring, or in a silver timbale dish;

Argentie Fill the pastry case with paupiettes made with salmon forcemeat, boned cooked frogs' legs and prawns; coat with sauce américaine and finish by decorating with prawns.

Bottin Fill the case with poached strips of fish, mussels, slices of lobster and prawns mixed with the reduced and thickened cooking liquid from the fish.

Carême Line a shallow mould with fillets of fish and keep in place with a layer of farce; fill with mushrooms, mussels, oysters and prawns bound with béchamel and cover with more fillets of fish; cook au bain-marie, turn out, garnish with paupiettes of salmon with a crayfish inside and carapaces of crayfish filled with farce and cooked. Serve with sauce Nantua.

Cardinal Fill with paupiettes made with crayfish farce, slices of lobster, button mushrooms, truffle and sauce cardinal; finish with a circle of sliced truffle and a large grooved mushroom and cover with the lid.

Carmelite   Fill with paupiettes made with lobster farce and slices of lobster cooked à la Newburg, mixed with sauce homard; decorate with slices of truffle and cover with the lid.

Escoffier   Fill with sautéd slices of the white part of scallops flamed with brandy, slices of crawfish, quenelles, mushrooms and short lengths of cooked macaroni filled with forcemeat and poached.

Grimaldi   Fill with paupiettes made with truffled farce, macaroni cooked then finished with cream and truffle bound with béchamel, and Dublin Bay prawns in a cullis made from the shells; cover with the lid and serve.

Marivaux   Fill with sliced lobster cooked in sherry, crayfish, quenelles of salmon and morilles, mixed with lobster sauce finished with sauce hollandaise and cream.

Marquise   Fill a fluted timbale with fish paupiettes, and a garnish of oysters, quenelles of salmon and truffle, bound with paprika-flavoured sauce vin blanc; cover with the lid and serve.

Prunier   Fill with paupiettes of fish, sliced mushroom, oysters and slices of truffle, mixed with sauce vin blanc.

Richepin   Fill a timbale with paupiettes made with truffled farce, spinach raviolis and crayfish; cover with sauce crème finished with crayfish butter and decorate with slices of truffle.

Tourte   This is a variation of a timbale in which several items of fish, shellfish, mushroom, quenelles, etc., are mixed with a sauce and filled into a pastry flan, covered with a round of pastry and baked as for example, in Valencay.

Valencay   Fill with pieces of fish, crayfish, sliced white mushrooms, oyster, prawns and truffle; bake then fill up with crayfish butter.

Deep-poached

This is cooking in a depth of liquid sufficient to cover the fish; the liquids used include:

1(a) salted water
 (b) water and lemon juice
2(a) milk
 (b) milk and water
3   water and vinegar
4   any of the following court-bouillons:
      (a) vinegar
      (b) red wine
      (c) white wine

The fish is cooked at just below boiling-point then drained and served with one or two plain-boiled turned potatoes, a slice of lemon, sprig of parsley and an accompanying sauce. Smoked fish is usually served plain.

Anglaise	Poach in salted water slightly flavoured with fennel and serve with plain boiled potatoes.
au Beurre Noir	Poach in vinegar court-bouillon, place in a dish and cover with plenty of beurre noisette flavoured with vinegar and capers; sprinkle with chopped parsley.
au Bleu	Quickly stun and clean a live fish, place in a little vinegar to produce a blue colour then slide into boiling vinegar court-bouillon; poach and serve in the liquid accompanied with potatoes, sauce hollandaise and melted butter.
Bouilli	Plain boil in salted water and serve garnished with small boiled potatoes, picked parsley and either anchovy, egg, or shrimp sauce.
Boulonnaise	Poach in vinegar court-bouillon and serve with a bouquet of mussels and butter sauce.
Breteuil	Plain boil, garnish with a poached soft roe and small boiled potatoes, accompanied with melted butter.

Commodore	Cook in salted water and serve garnished with crayfish, lobster croquettes, oysters Villeroy, large pommes noisettes and small quenelles, accompanied with sauce Normande finished with anchovy butter.
Crimped	Cut several incisions in a freshly caught fish, soak in very cold water for 1 hour then plain boil for the minimum possible time to cook it; serve with potatoes and a suitable English sauce.
Danoise	Poach in vinegar court-bouillon and serve with boiled potatoes and anchovy sauce.
Eau de Sel	Poach in salt water and serve with a dish each of capers and chopped fennel, and a sauceboat of butter sauce.
Flamande	Poach in salted water and serve accompanied with mustard-flavoured fish velouté.
Hollandaise	Poach in salted water and serve with a slice of lemon, plain-boiled potatoes and melted butter.
à la Nage	Cook freshly caught fish in white wine court-bouillon and serve plainly with potatoes and melted butter.
Saint-Nazaire	Serve plainly poached fish with garnish of poached oysters and slices of lobster and a sauceboat of sauce vin blanc.
au Vin Rouge	Poach in red wine court-bouillon; thicken the reduced cooking liquid with beurre manié and pour over the fish.

Baked or Roasted – au Four

Whole fish may be larded with backfat, anchovy, truffle, etc., and stuffed with an English stuffing or forcemeat; fillets and other small cuts can also be used. The fish used include bass, bream, carp, cod, haddock, mackerel, perch, pike, trout and whiting.

Andalouse	Bake with sautéd onion rings, sliced mushroom, diced tomato and julienne of red pimento in white wine; sprinkle the fish with breadcrumbs.

Angevine	Remove backbone and fill with duxelles and sorrel stuffing then bake with a little white wine; add a little vinegar to the cooking liquid, then add a liaison of cream, yolks and butter and pour over.
Béarnaise	Stuff with forcemeat and bake in a buttered dish with a little white wine; serve covered with sauce béarnaise.
Boulangère	Cover with sliced potato and onion, add a few button onions, moisten with fish stock and bake.
Café de Paris	Sprinkle with chopped shallot and cook in fish stock and white wine.
Calaisienne	Stuff with the mashed roes mixed with butter, lemon juice, chopped mushroom and shallot; wrap in greased paper and bake.
Dinardaise	Egg and crumb the fish and bake in the oven on a bed of shredded sorrel and spinach cooked in butter; cover with sauce mornay and gratinate.
Farci	Fill with fish forcemeat, duxelles or breadcrumb and herb stuffing, wrap in buttered paper and bake in the oven; serve with Sauce Bercy.
au Four	Lard the fish, wrap in buttered paper and bake with sliced carrot and onion, white wine and mushroom cooking liquid; remove the paper when half cooked and baste well; serve with the reduced and buttered cooking liquid.
Gavarni	Place the fish on a layer of maître d'hôtel butter on an oiled sheet of paper, fold over to seal, bake in the oven and serve with plain boiled potatoes.
Genevoise	Bake with butter, sliced carrot and onion and white wine; reduce the cooking liquid, add cream and Sauce Hollandaise and pour over the fish.
Jean-Bart	Roast in butter and serve with French-fried onions and mustard-flavoured Sauce Bercy.
Jetée-Promenade	Bake with a little fish stock and white wine with previously braised celery, whole mushrooms and slices of truffle.
Lerina	Bake with chopped shallot, sliced mushroom and diced tomato, in white wine and fish stock.

Madrilène Bake on a layer of onion rings, shredded fennel, quarters of red pimento and halves of tomato, with white wine, basting frequently.

Nantaise Place the fish in a buttered dish on a layer of chopped shallot and chives and sliced mushrooms; moisten with white wine, sprinkle with breadcrumbs and bake.

Niçoise Bake on a bed of cooked diced tomato and garlic and serve garnished with black olives, a trellis work of anchovy fillets and slices of lemon.

Oseille Place the fish in a buttered dish on a bed of stewed shredded sorrel, dot with butter and bake in the oven.

Pélerin Bake in a buttered dish and serve coated with sour-cream sauce (smitaine) containing julienne of gherkin.

au Plat Bake with chopped shallot and white wine and serve with the buttered cooking liquid.

Poitevin Lay the fish in a buttered dish on a layer of small dice of potato and chopped onion, flame with brandy and bake with white wine; thicken the cooking liquid with yolks and cream and pour over.

Provençale Cover with sliced tomato and chopped garlic, add fish stock, anchovy essence, lemon juice and bake in the oven.

Touraine Bake with chopped shallot, chives and chervil, sliced mushroom and cream; when cooked sprinkle with fines herbes.

Valvins Lard with strips of anchovy, wrap in oiled paper and bake; serve with mustard-flavoured maître d'hôtel butter.

en Papillote This is a method of baking small whole fish (and items of meat) in a tightly-sealed piece of greaseproof paper, serving it in the paper. Grill the fish, place on some duxelles on an oiled heart-shaped piece of greaseproof paper; add more duxelles and fold over the paper and seal the edge tightly. Bake on an oiled dish at 175°C for 5 minutes until swollen up and coloured brown.

Paramé Seal the fish in hot butter, place on a layer of duxelles on an oiled piece of greaseproof paper, fold over to seal and bake in the oven.

Stewed Fish

These stews originated in the fishing ports of Europe as a means of using undersized or damaged parts of the catch to make a cheap and nourishing meal, the liquid from the stew being served with bread as a soup to accompany the mixture of fish as main dish. Many countries and regions have their own versions, some being made with fresh water fish, others include several kinds of sea fish and shellfish with the larger fish being cut up and the small ones left whole.

Blanquette Cook dice of conger eel and scampi in white wine and water, make the cooking liquid into a sauce with a roux and simmer with julienne of carrot and some button mushrooms for 10 minutes. Finish with a liaison, replace the fish and garnish with white glazed button onions. Buttered noodles may be served separately.

Bouillabaisse à la Marseillaise Barely cover pieces of bass, conger eel, gurnard, John Dory, rascasse, red mullet, rock-fish, whiting and Dublin Bay prawns with water, add chopped onion, leek and tomato, oil, garlic, parsley, saffron, bay-leaf, savory and fennel leaves and boil rapidly until all is cooked. Pour the liquid onto thick slices of French bread in a soup plate and arrange the fish in a serving dish. (If necessary the fish may be added to the pan at intervals according to texture and size; use approximately 3kg fish and 2kg shellfish per 12 persons.)

Bouillabaisse à la Parisienne	Cook chopped onion and leek in oil, add water, white wine, garlic, saffron and tomato to make the cooking liquid; place pieces of conger eel, crawfish, gurnard, red mullet, mussels, sole, weever and whiting into the strained liquid, add oil and boil rapidly for approximately 15 minutes. Thicken the liquid with beurre manié and serve with garlic-flavoured toasted slices of French bread for dipping in the sauce.
Bouillabaisse de Morue	Cook chopped onion, leek and garlic in oil, add water, saffron, sliced potato, square pieces of soaked salt cod and oil; finish with chopped parsley and serve with the liquid poured over slices of garlic toast.
Bouillabaisse de Cornouailles	Cook chopped celery, leek, potato and tomato in water then add pieces of gurnard, mackerel, red mullet, rock salmon, tunny, turbot and whiting; finish with a liaison of yolks and cream and serve sprinkled with diced fried croûtons.
Bouilliture	Sauté pieces of fish in hot oil with chopped onion and garlic, dust with flour, singe, moisten with red wine and cook.
Bourride	Cook the fish in water with onion, garlic, oil and saffron and very little dried bitter orange peel; thicken with a liaison of yolks of egg, flavour with some sauce Aioli and serve poured over fried slices of French bread.
Chaudrée (also spelt Caudrée and Caudière)	Cook pieces of conger eel, gurnard, John Dory, mackerel, rock-fish, sole and turbot in some very thin fish velouté; serve sprinkled with chopped chervil and parsley, accompanied with toasted slices of bread.
Cotriade	Arange layers of sliced onion and potato and diced tomato in a buttered dish with pieces of filleted fish in between; moisten with well-flavoured fish stock, dot with butter and cook in the oven.
Daube	Marinate pieces of fish with red wine and brandy; drain, seal in hot fat, place in a pan with

	the marinade, cover with a lid, seal and cook for 1 hour.
Fricassée	Seal the pieces of fish with some button mushrooms and onions in hot butter; cook in thin cream then thicken with yolks of egg, flavour with a little lemon juice and serve with heart-shaped croûtons.
Hochepot	Cook pieces of fish in water with small turned carrots and turnips and button onions, until tender.
Marmite de poisson	This is a soup-cum-stew of several kinds of fish, plainly boiled with various vegetables and potatoes.
Matelote Marinière	Cook pieces of any suitable kind of fish with sliced onion and chopped garlic in white wine; reduce the cooking liquid, thicken it with fish velouté and add a garnish of crayfish, button mushrooms and glazed button onions; decorate with heart-shaped croûtons.
Matelote Meunière	Cook pieces of fish with sliced onion and chopped garlic in red wine, thicken the cooking liquid with beurre manié and add cooked crayfish to the other fish in the sauce; decorate with heart-shaped croûtons.

Other matelotes are made with particular species of fish and moistened with other liquids; brandy may be included.

Matelote Batelière	Cook the pieces of fish in red wine with chopped onion then thicken the liquid with beurre manié; garnish with glazed button onions and serve with heart-shaped croûtons.
Matelote Canotière	Cook pieces of carp and eel with sliced onion and garlic in white wine; thicken the cooking liquid with beurre manié and garnish with crayfish and glazed button onions and serve with gudgeons that have been crumbed and deep-fried to make them look like a muff.

Matelote Mâconnaise	Cook the pieces of fish in red wine, thicken the liquid and garnish with glazed button onions, crayfish, mushrooms and heart-shaped croûtons.
Matelote Normande	Cook pieces of conger eel, gurnard, and sole in cider and flame with calvados liqueur; thicken the liquid with velouté and garnish with crayfish, mussels and oysters.
Meurette	Marinate pieces of fresh-water fish including eel, perch, pike and tench or trout with brandy; cook some chopped leek and onion in butter, add red wine and diced potato, cook then pour over the pieces of fish and cook until tender; serve on slices of toasted bread previously rubbed with garlic.
Niçoise	Sauté chopped onion and garlic and diced tomato in oil; add the pieces of fish, cover with water, add sliced potato and stoned black olives and simmer gently until cooked.
Pouchouse	Sauté slices of fresh water fish such as carp, eel, pike and tench in hot butter, flame with brandy then cook in red wine; thicken the cooking liquid with beurre manié and garnish with fried lardons, glazed button onions and mushrooms and serve with toasted croûtons of French bread previously rubbed with garlic.
Potée	This is a fish soup-cum-stew that can be made from fresh- or salt-water fish.
Poulette	Stiffen the pieces of fish in hot butter then cover with fish stock and cook; make the cooking liquid into a velouté, add a liaison of cream and yolks and strain over the fish; garnish with cooked mushrooms.
Romaine	Stiffen the pieces of fish in hot butter then moisten with white wine; add peas and shredded lettuce, cook and thicken with beurre manié.
Waterzoi	Cook sections of fresh-water fish rapidly in water, with some celery, in order that the liquid is thickened at the same time as the fish is cooked; if necessary add finely crushed water

biscuits to thicken. Serve with buttered slices of brown or white bread.

The following are suitable: barbel, carp, chub, eel, perch, pike and tench.

Gratinated – au Gratin

To gratinate fish, place it in a buttered dish on some finely chopped shallot and a layer of sauce gratin; garnish with turned button mushrooms, add a little white wine then cover completely with more of the sauce. Sprinkle with breadcrumbs and melted butter and bake until crisp and brown; finish with a little lemon juice and chopped parsley.

Sauce Gratin	Cook chopped shallot and mushroom in butter, add demi-glace and finish with chopped parsley.
Canotière	Add a garnish of whole crayfish, fried goujons of fish and puff pastry fleurons to fish cooked au gratin.
aux Courgettes	Add slices of baby marrow and dice of tomato to the fish before coating with sauce gratin and cooking.
aux Fines Herbes	When the fish is finished sprinkle with chopped chervil, chives, parsley and tarragon.
Italienne	Add sliced mushrooms to the fish and cook as for au gratin; add a garnish of small peeled and cooked tomatoes.
Livournaise	Cover the fish with cooked diced tomato, add white wine and breadcrumbs and gratinate; finish by sprinkling with lemon juice and capers.
Moulin d'Or	Spread the fish with purée of foie gras, add sliced cèpes, slices of foie gras and truffle then sauce gratin, and cook as usual.

——BORDURES AND TURBANS——

These are made by lining buttered savarin moulds with flattened fillets of fish, filling with fish forcemeat, folding over the overhanging ends and cooking au bain-marie. Various kinds of garnishes and sauces may be added as shown in the following example:

Turban de Sole et Saumon Villaret   Line a mould with flattened fillets of sole and fill with salmon forcemeat; poach au bain-marie, turn out and soak up any moisture then fill the centre with button mushrooms, prawns, pieces of soft roe and slices of truffle, all mixed with béchamel and lobster sauce.

Pojarski

These can be made of pike, salmon etc. by chopping or by making a purée of the raw flesh in a food processor, adding soaked and squeezed breadcrumbs, butter and double cream. Mould cutlet shape in flour, insert a piece of blanched macaroni, shallow fry and serve with sauce vin blanc or lobster sauce and a garnish.

Quenelles and Mousselines

Quenelles are made by blending pieces of skinned fillet of fish, especially pike, sole and whiting to a purée in a liquidiser; add panada or soaked and squeezed bread then white of egg, blending well after each addition. Refrigerate for 1 hour then blend in double cream. Mould this forcemeat with two spoons onto a butter tray, fill with hot fish stock or salted water and poach gently until firm.

Mousselines are made as for quenelles but without the panada so giving a lighter result; fill the mixture into buttered moulds, cook au bain-marie and turn out.

All the garnishes for shallow poached fish are suitable for these items.

Quenelles of pike are made with the fish, beef suet, bone marrow and panada, blended in a liquidiser or processor; this mixture may also be placed in a large buttered mould and cooked au bain-marie; it is then known as Pain de Brochet.

Shellfish can be used with whiting to produce quenelles and mousselines of shellfish using the tomalley to give a red colour.

Fish Pies

Coulibiac de Saumon
Roll out puff pastry or brioche paste 45cm × 25cm, spread with a layer of cooked rice then a layer of sliced pieces of salmon set in hot butter, chopped hard-boiled egg, chopped cooked mushroom and cooked chopped vésiga; add another layer of rice then enclose all with the pastry; turn over, egg-wash and bake for approximately 50 minutes. When cooked pour melted butter in through a hole in the top.

This kind of pie may be made with eel, sardines, sole, trout, etc., instead of salmon.

Pâté Chaud de Poisson
Line a pie-mould with short pastry, coat the inside with pike forcemeat and fill with layers of small slices of fish set in hot butter, and forcemeat; cover with pastry, decorate, egg-wash and bake in a moderate oven for approximately 50 minutes.

Pâté Chaud de Saumon
Line a pie-mould with short pastry, coat the inside with pike forcemeat containing chopped truffle and fill with alternate layers of fresh salmon and forcemeat; cover with pastry, decorate, egg-wash and bake.

Pâté de Sole
Line a pie-mould with short pastry, coat the inside with lobster forcemeat and fill with fillets

of sole wrapped as a long sausage around a length of truffle; add a layer of forcemeat, more fillets, then forcemeat and cover with pastry. Brush with egg-wash, decorate and bake.

Rastegaï This is an individual pie made with the same ingredients as Coulibiac, using a 10cm round of pastry and baking for 25 minutes.

Piroguis Fill 10cm rounds of brioche or puff pastry with a
Moscovite mixture of chopped cooked white fish, chopped hard-boiled egg and vésiga; bring the outside to the centre, seal, egg-wash and bake in a hot oven for 20 minutes. If using brioche paste allow to prove before baking.

Vol-au-Vent of Fish

Vol-au-Vent de Fill the vol-au-vent with flaked salt cod, truffle
Morue and sautéd shredded onion, mixed with sauce crème.

Vol-au-Vent de Fill the vol-au-vent with brandade of salt cod
Morue mixed with cream, and sprinkle with chopped
Bénédictine truffle.

Vol-au-Vent de Fill the vol-au-vent with small quenelles made of
Quenelles de whiting forcemeat, sliced crawfish, button mush-
Merlan rooms and slices of truffle mixed with béchamel
Cardinal flavoured with lobster butter; decorate with a circle of slices of truffle and a turned mushroom on top.

Vol-au-Vent de Fill the vol-au-vent with very small paupiettes of
Sole sole, quenelles, mussels, oysters and prawns
Marinière mixed with sauce marinière; serve garnished with a trussed crayfish.

Vol-au-Vent de Fill the vol-au-vent with small pieces of fillet of
Sole sole fried in butter, quenelles, grated truffle, and
Présidence crayfish, mixed with béchamel.

Bouchées

Bouchées may be served as a fish course, allowing two or more per portion; barquettes with the same fillings can also be served.

Bouchées Hollandaise	Fill with dice of smoked salmon mixed with sauce hollandaise and place a poached oyster on top.
Bouchées Joinville	Fill with diced crayfish, mushroom and truffle mixed with sauce joinville and place a slice of truffle on top.
Bouchées Montglas	Fill with crayfish, mushrooms, mussels, oysters and truffle mixed with sauce vin blanc.
Bouchées Victoria	Fill with diced lobster and truffle mixed with lobster sauce mixed with mayonnaise.

Made-up Fish Dishes

Coquilles de Poisson Mornay	Pipe scallop shells with duchesse potato and fill the centre with flaked fish tossed in butter; coat with sauce mornay, sprinkle with cheese and gratinate.
Côtelettes de Poisson	Add chopped cooked fish to reduced béchamel, thicken with egg yolks and spread on a tray to cool; mould to cutlet-shape, egg and crumb and fry.
Cromesquis de Poisson	Add chopped cooked fish to reduced béchamel or velouté, thicken with egg yolks and spread on a tray to cool; mould into cork shapes or cubes, wrap in a thin pancake or a rasher of streaky bacon, dip into frying batter and deep fry.
Croquettes de Poisson	Add chopped cooked fish to reduced béchamel, thicken with egg yolks and spread on a tray to cool; mould into cork shapes, egg and crumb and deep fry. Côtelettes and croquettes may be served with tomato sauce.

211

Fish Cakes   Mix minced cooked fish and dry mashed potato, egg yolks and chopped parsley; mould into flat rounds, 6cm in diameter, egg and crumb and deep fry. Serve with tomato sauce.

Fish Rolls   Mould mixed flaked cooked fish and duxelles into small ovals, press a few rounds of hard-boiled egg into each, then envelop in brioche pastry; egg-wash, allow to prove and bake in a hot oven.

Fish Pie   Place flaked cooked fish mixed with Sauce Crème into a pie-dish, cover with slices of hard-boiled egg then with duchesse potato; brush with egg-wash and bake.

Fish Pudding   Line a greased basin with brown breadcrumbs, fill with mixed cooked fish, then with mashed potato and cream sauce; cover and steam.

Kedgeree   Toss flaked cooked smoked cod or haddock in butter, add cooked rice, chopped hard-boiled egg, and toss to reheat; place in a dish and serve with curry sauce.

Omelette au Poisson   Fill the centre of the omelette with flaked cooked fish mixed with cream sauce, fold over and finish in the usual way.

Omelette Arnold Bennett   Fill the centre of the omelette with flaked cooked smoked haddock mixed with cream, fold over and finish to cook. Place on a dish, coat with sauce mornay and gratinate very quickly under a salamander. If desired it may be made as a flat omelette.

Pancakes   Roll some purée of cooked fish in small pancakes, trim the edges, lay in a buttered dish, coat with sauce mornay and gratinate.

Rissoles de Poisson   Fill rounds of puff or brioche pastry with a salpicon of cooked fish, shellfish, mushroom, truffle, etc., fold over to seal, then deep fry.

Roes   Cut poached cod roe into 1½cm slices, egg and crumb or dip into batter, and deep fry.

Brandade of Salt Cod   Soak dry salt cod in running cold water for 12 hours, cut into dice and poach, leaving it slightly undercooked; drain, flake and cook in hot oil with a little chopped garlic, mixing well to a smooth paste. Remove from the heat and work in sufficient olive oil to produce a smooth white result, adjusting the consistency with boiling milk. Serve scrolled, garnished with triangular bread crôutons.

Brandade may also be made with the addition of dry mashed potatoes and cream instead of oil.

Other dishes made from cooked fish are in the section on Hot Hors-d'Oeuvre.

Frogs' Legs –
Cuisses de Grenouille

au Beurre	Dust with flour, shallow fry in hot butter and serve sprinkled with lemon juice and nut-brown butter.
Bordelaise	Marinate in brandy and sauté in butter with the addition of sliced mushrooms and short julienne of red pimento; finish with a squeeze of lemon juice.
Fricassée	Cook in white wine and fish fumet; make the cooking liquid into velouté, finish it with cream and then pour over the legs, adding button mushrooms.
Frites	Pass through flour, egg-wash and breadcrumbs and deep fry.
au Gratin	Cook in white wine and fish stock, place in a piped border of duchesse potato, coat with sauce mornay, sprinkle with cheese and bread crumbs and gratinate.
Italienne	Cook in butter and lemon juice, drain and coat with sauce italienne.
Lyonnaise	Sauté in hot butter together with sliced onion; finish with lemon juice and nut-brown butter.

Nimoise Sauté in butter, place in a dish and cover with sautéd chopped onion and garlic with diced tomato, pimento and egg-plant.

Orley Marinate in oil and lemon juice for 1 hour then dip into batter and deep fry; serve with tomato sauce.

Parmentier Coat with flour, fry in hot butter then mix in diced sautéd potato.

Princesse Cook in butter and lemon juice, coat with cream sauce and garnish with a bouquet of asparagus tips.

Provençale Dip in flour, sauté in oil and add tomato concassée, chopped garlic and shallot, fines herbes and tomato sauce.

Snails – Escargots

Freshly caught live snails need to be washed in cold water then left in vinegar and salt for 2 hours. Wash, cook for 5 minutes, remove from the shells which should be boiled in soda and water to sterilise them, and discard the cloaca. Cook in white wine courtbouillon for 3 hours. Snails are mainly served (six per person) as a hot hors-d'œuvre in a special snail dish.

à l'Abbaye Sauté chopped onion in butter, add the cooked snails and a little flour, moisten with cream then thicken with a liaison of butter, cream and yolks.

Bourguignonne Half-fill shells with snail butter, push the snail in and fill with more snail butter; place in the dish containing a little water and heat in a hot oven for 7–8 minutes.

Brochettes Thread on skewers with cubes of bacon, coat with egg and breadcrumbs and deep fry or grill.

Chablaisienne Half-fill shells with reduced white wine with chopped shallot and meat-glaze, add the snail and fill with snail butter; place in the snail dish with a little water and heat in a hot oven for 7–8 minutes.

Dijonaise Half-fill shells with reduced white wine with chopped shallot and meat glaze; add the snail and fill with mixed butter, bone marrow, shallot, garlic and truffle; heat in a hot oven.

Grenobloise Half-fill shells with snail butter containing ground hazelnuts, push the snail in and fill with more of the same butter; place on a snail dish with a little water and heat in a hot oven.

Vigneronne Shallow fry with chopped shallot and garlic, allow to cool then dip each in batter containing chopped chives and deep fry.

Vin Rouge Cover prepared snails with red wine, add blanched lardons, garlic and button onions and cook in a closed dish in the oven; thicken the cooking liquid with beurre manié and flavour with brandy.

Snail Butter is made by adding finely chopped shallot, garlic and parsley, salt and pepper to softened butter.

6 SHELLFISH DISHES

There are two types of shellfish – *crustaceans* of which there are seven and *molluscs* of which there are three in general use. All are highly perishable and require careful storage and handling. Apart from prawns and shrimps and sometimes crabs, shellfish are purchased raw.

Crab – Crabe

The cock crab has more meat content and a better texture and taste than a hen crab; it is distinguishable by a narrow triangular belly apron on the underside, the female having a much broader and more triangular shape. The edible portion is approximately one third of the purchased weight; the yield is 60 per cent white to 40 per cent brown meat; flaked white meat is used in the following formulas.

It is necessary to kill a crab before boiling by inserting an ice pick into the centre of the body under the apron flap and stabbing several times at different angles. Place in boiling salted water and simmer a 2kg crab for 30 to 40 minutes.

A spider crab has little flesh in the legs and needs only 20 minutes cooking time.

A soft-shell crab is one that has shed its hard outer shell, a portion being two or three whole ones of approximately 10cm length each. They can be deep or shallow fried, baked or grilled. The apron and gills must be removed.

Baltimore   Reheat in butter with chopped shallot and flavour with mustard and Worcestershire sauce; place in a shell, coat with sauce mornay and glaze.

Bordelaise	Sauté sliced mushrooms in butter, add the crab-meat and reheat; mix with sauce bordelaise and serve on a round of toast.
Créole	Mix with tomato sauce, add a liaison of yolks of egg and serve with boiled rice.
Dewey	Sauté chopped shallot and sliced mushrooms, add the crab-meat and chopped truffle, add white wine and reduce and mix with cream; place on toast and glaze.
Diablé	Reheat in butter with chopped onion, add cayenne, mustard and Worcester sauce and mix with sauce crème; place in a shell, sprinkle with breadcrumbs and gratinate.
Grecque	Cook chopped leek and onion in butter, add diced tomato, flaked crab and a few cooked mussels; moisten with a little saffron-flavoured fish stock and serve with rice pilaff.
Indienne	Mix the crabmeat with curry sauce and serve with boiled rice.
Italienne	Cook chopped onion and garlic in butter, add the crabmeat and tomato sauce; put into a shell, sprinkle with breadcrumbs and cheese and gratinate.
à la King	Cook chopped shallot, sliced mushroom and diced green and red pimento in butter, add crab-meat, flavour with sherry and cover with cream; thicken with a liaison of yolks and lemon juice, place on a slice of toast and glaze.
Maryland	Reheat in butter, flavour with brandy and mix with cream.
Mexicaine	Sauté chopped onion and garlic and diced pimento in butter, add the crabmeat, mustard and Worcester sauce; mask with sauce mornay and glaze.
Nelson	Mix with cream sauce, fill into shells with poached oysters, cover with more sauce, sprinkle with cheese and gratinate.
Newburg	Reheat in butter, flavour with sherry, mix with cream and thicken with a liaison of yolks and serve with rice pilaff.

Portugaise   Sauté chopped onion, add sliced mushrooms and diced tomato, mix in the crabmeat, add tomato sauce, place in a shell and sprinkle with breadcrumbs; gratinate in a hot oven.

Valencienne   Sauté chopped onion and garlic, sliced mushrooms and diced green and red pimento, add the crab, flavour with mustard and Worcester sauce and fill into a shell; sprinkle with cheese and gratinate.

Crabmeat may also be served in pancakes, vols-au-vent, in scallop shells and as crab croquettes; it can be mixed with velouté, replaced in the cleaned shell and gratinated with cheese and breadcrumbs.

Crawfish – Langouste

Large whole crawfish are mostly served cold as a buffet item; the canned or frozen small tails can be prepared in any of the ways shown for lobster and prawns.

Crayfish – Écrevisses

These are small fresh-water shellfish weighing up to 120g and 7cm long in the shell. The grit must be removed before the fish is cooked by pulling it out from halfway along the tail end. Cook in boiling salted water for 3 minutes and serve five or six per portion, according to size but they are used mainly as a garnish to other fish.

Américaine   Sauté live crayfish in oil, flame with brandy, add shallot, white wine, fish stock and diced tomato and cook for 5 minutes; remove the fish, reduce the cooking liquid, thicken with butter and pour over the shelled tails.

Bordelaise   Sauté with shallot and garlic, flame with brandy and cook in white wine, fish stock, tomato sauce and espagnole; remove the fish, correct the sauce, add lemon juice and tarragon and pour over.

en Buisson	Serve boiled crayfish hanging head down over the side of a dish, or in a pile and garnish with parsley.
Cardinal	Place shelled tails on a layer of sauce cardinal, cover with more sauce and garnish with a slice of truffle. They may be served in a glazed border of duchesse potato on a scallop shell.
Georgette	Fill an emptied baked potato with shelled crayfish, coat with sauce Nantua, sprinkle with cheese and gratinate.
Lafayette	Sauté shelled crayfish in butter, add brandy and sherry and cook in cream; finish with a liaison of yolks of egg.
Liègeoise	Boil in white-wine court-bouillon, reduce the cooking liquid, thicken with butter and pour over the fish.
Magenta	Sauté in oil with diced tomato and a mirepoix; add white wine and cook; thicken the cooking liquid with butter and strain over the fish.
Marinière	Sauté in butter with shallot, add white wine and cook; thicken the reduced liquid with velouté, enrich with butter and pour over.
Nage	Boil in white-wine court-bouillon and serve in some of the cooking liquid in a deep dish.
Parisienne	Pipe scallop shells with duchesse potato and glaze; fill with small crayfish, coat with sauce vin blanc glacée and glaze under a salamander.

Dublin Bay Prawns – Langoustine (Scampi)

This orange-and-white-coloured crustacean of up to 12cm in length may be boiled and served whole but is more usually available shelled raw in frozen form under the name scampi.

à l'Absinthe	Sauté in oil, add finely chopped carrot, onion and garlic and diced tomato, flame with brandy and cook in white wine and fish stock; reduce the strained cooking liquid, thicken with butter and flavour with Pernod, pour over the fish and serve with pilaff of rice.

Barcelonaise	Sauté in oil, add chopped onion and diced tomato and cook in white wine; serve in the liquid.
Bordelaise	Sauté in butter, moisten with red wine and reduce; mix with sauce bordelaise and serve.
Frit (i)	Pass through flour, egg-wash and breadcrumbs, roll into shape and deep fry; serve with quarters of lemon and sauce tartare or other piquant sauce.
(ii)	Marinate in oil and lemon juice, dip into batter and deep fry.
Istrienne	Sauté in butter, flame with brandy, add diced tomato and cook in white wine; serve in the liquid.
Italienne	Sauté in oil, add chopped garlic and diced tomato and toss over until cooked.
Lacroix	Sauté in butter, add sliced mushroom, chopped shallot and diced red pimento, flame with brandy and cook in cream together with a pinch of curry powder; thicken with yolks and serve with pilaff of rice.
Meunière	Toss in flour and shallow fry in hot butter, basting occasionally, place on a dish, sprinkle with lemon juice and parsley and mask with nut-brown butter; decorate with a slice of lemon.
Pizzaiola	Sauté floured scampi in butter and oil and add a sauce made with chopped garlic, onion, green and red pimento, diced anchovy and tomato, oregano and sliced olives in tomato-flavoured jus lié.
Provençale	Dip in flour and shallow fry in oil until brown, place in a dish and coat with sauce provençale (which is made of diced tomato and garlic tossed in oil, a little white wine and tomato sauce).
Quarnero	Sauté in butter, add chopped shallot, diced tomato and lemon juice and toss over to cook.

220

Prawns – Bouquets or Crevettes Roses

Ordinary prawns are available whole in the shell or as peeled tails, the former coming mainly from Scandinavia and the cooked shelled ones from the cold waters of the North Atlantic, and taste better than those imported from the Pacific and Indian Ocean regions. Mediterranean prawns are big and are sold whole and cooked. King prawns or gambas are the largest and come frozen, uncooked, without the head, from the Far East. All the recipes for prawns can be applied to shrimps (crevettes) which are available as grey or pink, the former being the tastier.

Coquille de	Reheat in butter, place in a scallop shell piped with a border of duchesse potato, coat with sauce mornay, sprinkle with cheese and gratinate; asparagus tips, sliced mushroom, etc., may be added.
Créole	Toss in butter and mix with sauce créole (sautéd chopped onion and garlic in oil, reduce with white wine, add tomato sauce and julienne of red pimento); serve with pilaff of rice.
Curry	Reheat in butter, mix with curry sauce and serve with boiled rice.
Danoise	Reheat in butter, add diced asparagus tips and mix with shrimp sauce.

Lobster – Homard

Dark blue when live, lobsters change colour to red when cooked by being placed in boiling water, reboiled and simmered for 20 minutes for the average size lobster of 450–650g. The yield of edible flesh is approximately 25 per cent of the whole fish. Most recipes call for a whole boiled lobster cut along the length and served in the half shell. The tomally is the liver of the lobster and imparts colour to lobster dishes.

Américaine	Kill a raw lobster by inserting a knife through the centre line of the head, cut into sections,

discard the sac and keep the coral and tomally then sauté in oil until red; flame with brandy, add shallot, garlic, diced tomato, white wine and fish stock and cook for 20 minutes; take the meat from the shell, thicken the reduced liquid with the tomally mashed with butter and strain over the lobster. Serve with pilaff of rice.

This is also known as Homard Amoricaine.

Biarritz Par-grill, cover with cream, dot with anchovy butter and finish to cook; serve coated with a mixture of melted butter, tomato purée, sherry, mustard, lemon and horseradish.

Bohémienne Arrange slices of cooked lobster, foie gras and truffle in the half shell and coat with sauce bohémienne (béchamel flavoured with brandy and port); sprinkle with cheese, decorate with truffle and gratinate.

Bordelaise Colour a cut lobster in butter, flame with brandy and cook with shallot and garlic in white wine, fish stock and espagnole; remove the meat from the shell and coat with the reduced liquid thickened with the tomally mixed with butter and flavoured with lemon juice.

Brillat-Savarin Arrange slices of lobster and sautéd slices of baby marrow in a circle, coat with sauce Américaine and fill the centre with diced mushroom, lobster and truffle mixed with the same sauce.

Cardinal Fill the bottom of the half shell with sautéd diced mushroom mixed with lobster sauce, arrange sautéd slices of lobster on top, add the claw and cover with lobster sauce enriched with a sabayon, butter and cream; sprinkle with cheese, gratinate and decorate with a slice of truffle.

Clarence Fill the half-shell with plain boiled rice, arrange slices of lobster and truffle on top and coat with sauce béchamel flavoured with curry and lobster butter.

Crème Reheat slices of lobster in butter with slices of truffle; add a little brandy, cream, lemon juice and meat glaze and serve.

Delmonico Reheat slices of lobster in butter, add sherry and reduce then cover with cream mixed with egg yolks; shake and allow to thicken and serve accompanied with pilaff of rice.

Dumas Reheat slices of lobster in butter, add white wine and tomato-flavoured demi-glace and serve decorated with fleurons.

Française Sauté a cut-up raw lobster in butter, flame with brandy, add white wine and julienne of carrot, celery, leek and turnip; cook, remove the flesh from the shell and cover with sauce made from the cooking liquid mixed with velouté and butter.

Grillé Cut a raw lobster in half through the length, dot with butter and grill gently; serve with sauce diable. It is advisable to grill halves of boiled lobster.

Hollandaise Cut a freshly boiled lobster in half and serve with small boiled potatoes and melted butter.

Hongroise Sauté a cut-up raw lobster in butter, flame with brandy, sprinkle with paprika and cook in fish stock, cream and Marsala; remove the flesh from the shell and coat with the cooking liquid thickened with the tomally mixed with butter.

Monégasque Reheat slices of lobster in butter; arrange in the half-shell, coat with lobster sauce containing diced tomato and tarragon, sprinkle with cheese and gratinate.

Mornay Arrange reheated slices of lobster on a bed of sauce mornay in the half-shell; coat with the same sauce, sprinkle with cheese and gratinate.

Newburg Reheat slices of lobster in butter, add Madeira and reduce; add cream mixed with egg yolks, cook to thicken and serve with pilaff of rice.

Palestine Sauté a cut-up raw lobster in butter with a mirepoix, flame with brandy and cook in white wine and fish stock; remove the flesh from the

	shell and cover with sauce made from the reduced liquid, fish velouté and the tomally mixed with butter; add a pinch of curry powder.
Phocéene	Sauté a cut-up raw lobster in oil, flame with brandy, add shallot, garlic, tomato, saffron, white wine and fish stock and cook; remove from the shell and coat with the reduced cooking liquid thickened with the tomally mashed with butter and garnished with julienne of red pimento; serve with pilaff of saffron rice.
St-Moritz	Mix sauted lobster with curry sauce and serve in a circle of rice pilaff.
Thermidor	Add a sabayon and some made English mustard to sauce bercy, place a little in the bottom of half shells, arrange reheated slices of lobster on top, coat with more sauce and glaze under a salamander.
Tourville	Reheat slices of lobster in butter with sliced mushroom, poached mussels and oysters and slices of truffle; mix with fish velouté and serve in a border of risotto.
Turque	Cook a raw lobster as for Américaine and serve accompanied with saffron-flavoured pilaff of rice.
Vanderbilt	Half-fill the shell with diced crayfish, mushroom and truffle mixed with lobster sauce; arrange sliced lobster on top, coat with lobster sauce finished with cream, sprinkle with cheese and gratinate.
Victoria	Half-fill the shell with diced lobster, mushroom and truffle mixed with lobster sauce; arrange sliced lobster on top, coat with the same sauce, sprinkle with cheese and gratinate.
Xavier	Fill half-shells with sliced lobster and mushroom mixed with béchamel flavoured with crayfish butter; sprinkle with cheese and gratinate.

Mussels – Moules

These are purchased alive allowing approximately 20 per person in the shell, or in shelled frozen form, the former need to be washed, scraped and any protruding tufts of weed removed before being cooked. The usual way of cooking mussels is with shallot and white wine in a covered pan for approximately 5 minutes. Remove from the shells, pull off the beards and replace in the half shell; use the cooking liquid for the sauce to serve with them.

Pickled mussels are unsuitable for dishes other than hors-d'œuvre; fresh raw mussels can be eaten in the same way as oysters for an hors-d'œuvre.

Bonne Femme	Cook as described above, beard and replace in the half shells; decant the cooking liquid, reduce, thicken with cream and yolks, add a garnish of cooked julienne of celery and mushrooms and pour over.
Bordelaise	Add poached mussels to sauce bordelaise (sautéd chopped shallot and red wine reduced with demi-glace).
Bourguignonne	Cover mussels in the half-shell with red wine sauce finished with the mussel cooking liquid.
Californienne	Sprinkle cooked mussels with cooked dice of celeriac and mushroom, add mussel cooking liquid and butter and reheat in the oven.
Catalane	Replace cooked mussels in the half shells, coat with the thickened and buttered cooking liquid and glaze under a salamander.
Chasseur	Sprinkle mussels in the half shells with cooked chopped shallot and mushroom, fried lardons and breadcrumbs, and gratinate.
Commodore	Dot mussels in the half shells with beurre maître d'hôtel, sprinkle with fried lardons and cook in the oven.
Frites	Marinate cooked mussels in oil and lemon juice, dip into batter and deep fry.
Mariniére	Cook in white wine for approximately 5 minutes, remove shell and beard and replace mussels in the half shell; decant the cooking liquid, thicken with beurre manié and cream, add parsley and pour over.

Mornay	Replace large mussels in the half shells, coat with sauce mornay, sprinkle with cheese and gratinate.
Newburg	Mix cooked mussels with sauce newburg and serve accompanied with pilaff of rice.
Poulette	Place cooked mussels in a dish and cover with a sauce made from the reduced decanted cooking liquid mixed with sauce allemande.
Pompadour	Mix cooked mussels with sauce crème flavoured with lobster butter.
Provençale	Mix cooked mussels with sauce provençale made by cooking shallot and diced tomato in oil, adding white wine, the reduced mussel liquid and tomato sauce.
Rochelaise	Stuff large cooked mussels with maître d'hôtel butter and reheat gently.
Toulonnaise	Serve cooked mussels in a circle of risotto and cover with the cooking liquid thickened with yolks and butter.
Villeroy	Dip large cooked mussels into sauce Villeroy; allow to set then coat with egg-wash and bread-crumbs and deep fry.

Oysters – Huîtres

Although oysters are usually thought of as an hors-d'œuvre for eating raw, they lend themselves to cooking and as a garnish with fish and meat dishes. Native oysters are graded in sizes from the largest, No 1, to the smallest, No 4, known as buttons.

To cook oysters, open them and cook in their own juice for a few seconds only.

Américaine	Mix poached oysters with sauce Américaine (fish velouté finished with lobster butter) and serve in the deep shells.
Anglaise	Wrap raw oysters in thin rashers of streaky bacon, place on skewers and grill gently, sprinkling with breadcrumbs.

226

Baltimore	Sprinkle raw oysters in the deep shell with breadcrumbs, cheese, parsley and melted butter and bake.
Beignets (i)	Dip poached oysters into frying batter and deep fry.
(ii)	Coat poached oysters with egg-wash and breadcrumbs and deep fry; serve with quarters of lemon and tartare sauce.
Bénédict	Place a sautéd slice of ham on a toasted crumpet, add four or five sautéd oysters and coat with sauce hollandaise.
Boston	Sauté oysters and scallops in butter, add a little fish velouté, thicken with yolks and serve sprinkled with fried breadcrumbs and chopped parsley.
Brochette	Wrap raw oysters in thin rashers of streaky bacon and impale on skewers with mushrooms; dip in melted butter and breadcrumbs and grill gently.
Casino	Sprinkle raw oysters in the half shell with chopped pimento; cover with a square of bacon and grill, turning the bacon when done on one side.
Dubarry	Fill an emptied baked potato with eight poached oysters, coat with sauce mornay, sprinkle with cheese and gratinate.
Favorite	Pour a layer of sauce mornay in the deep shells, place a poached oyster in each, coat with sauce mornay, sprinkle with cheese and gratinate.
Florentine	Pour a layer of sauce mornay in the deep shells, cover with buttered leaf spinach and a poached oyster; coat with sauce mornay, sprinkle with cheese and gratinate.
Frites (i)	Coat poached oysters with egg-wash and breadcrumbs and deep fry.
(ii)	Coat dried raw oysters with coarse cornmeal and shallow fry.
(iii)	Dip poached oysters in batter and deep fry.

227

Gratin	Replace poached oysters in the half-shells, sprinkle with lemon juice, fried breadcrumbs and butter and gratinate.
Louis	Replace poached oysters in the half-shells, sprinkle with a mixture of breadcrumbs, paprika and chopped shallot and gratinate in the oven.
Louise	Add sautéd sliced cèpes to poached oysters, coat with béchamel flavoured with lobster butter and reheat.
Manhattan	Sprinkle poached oysters in the half-shell with a mixture of cooked chopped bacon, green and red pimento and onion and sliced mushroom and reheat in the oven.
Maréchal	Dip poached oysters in batter, deep fry and serve three on a rinded slice of lemon.
Mornay	Place a poached oyster on a layer of sauce mornay in the deep shells; cover with more of the same sauce, sprinkle with cheese and gratinate.
Pilote	Half-fill deep shells with a mixture of chopped anchovy, mushroom and shallot cooked in butter; add a poached oyster, coat with sauce mornay, sprinkle with cheese and paprika and gratinate.
Polonaise	Cover raw oysters in the half-shells with fried breadcrumbs and bake for 2 minutes.
Pompadour	Coat poached oysters with sauce hollandaise containing finely chopped truffle.
Rockefeller	Place poached oysters on a bed of buttered leaf spinach, flavour with Pernod and cook in the oven.
Victor Hugo	Sprinkle raw oysters in the half-shells with a mixture of breadcrumbs, finely grated horse-radish, Parmesan and melted butter and cook quickly in the oven.
Villeroy	Dip poached oysters into hot sauce Villeroy and allow to set; coat with egg-wash and bread-crumbs and deep fry.
Virginia	Wrap raw oysters in thin rashers of streaky

bacon, coat with egg-wash and breadcrumbs
and deep fry.

Wladimir   Cover poached oysters in the half-shells with
sauce suprême, sprinkle with fried breadcrumbs
mixed with Parmesan and a little butter and
gratinate.

Scallops   – Coquilles St Jacques

Soak fresh scallops in cold water for a a few hours so as to tenderise
and make them swell, then place on the side of a solid top stove to
get the heat to cause them to open. Wash, cover with milk, add
sliced onion and poach for approximately 5 minutes. The roe
should be bright red.

Bercy   Place on a bed of sauce bercy in a coquille shell
piped with duchesse potato and glazed; coat with
sauce bercy containing egg yolks and glaze under
a salamander.

Brochettes   Cut into slices, coat with egg-wash and breadcrumbs and impale on skewers with cubes of
bacon; grill gently.

Créole   Cut poached scallops into slices, sauté in butter
and mix with sauce créole (tomato sauce fla--
voured with sautéd chopped onion and garlic and
julienne of red pimento); serve in a circle of
boiled rice.

Frite   Dip whole poached scallops into egg-wash and
breadcrumbs, deep fry and serve with sauce
tartare.

Gratin   Half-fill shells with duxelles, add sliced poached
scallops and mushrooms, cover with sauce dux-
elles, sprinkle with butter and breadcrumbs and
gratinate.

au Lard   Dip whole poached scallops into egg-wash and
coat with breadcrumbs, deep fry and serve with
grilled rashers of bacon.

Mornay   Place poached sliced scallops on a bed of sauce
mornay in deep shells piped with duchesse

	potato, coat with the same sauce, sprinkle with cheese and gratinate.
Nantaise	Half-fill the deep shells with sauce vin blanc, add sliced poached scallops and mussels and button mushrooms; coat with more of the same sauce and glaze under a salamander.
Parisienne	Half-fill the deep shells with sauce vin blanc glacée, add sliced poached scallops, coat with more sauce and glaze.

Clams, Cockles and *Whelks* are sometimes available, usually in cooked, fresh, or frozen form and can be prepared as for mussels and oysters.

Squid (Calmar or *Calamare), Cuttlefish (Seiche)* and *Octopus (Poulpe)* are classified as molluscs and are obtainable throughout the year. Cut squid into rings, dip in batter and deep fry, or fill with duxelles stuffing or fish farce and bake with butter.

Sea Urchin (Oursin) The reddish part is usually eaten raw as an hors-d'œuvre by dipping fingers of bread into it; the raw or cooked edible part may also be used to colour and flavour fish sauces.

Seafood Fishsticks are made in various shellfish flavours to resemble King prawns, crabs' legs, etc; these are made of white fish, starch and perhaps a small percentage of the actual shellfish it is meant to resemble. They can be made into cold or hot dishes but care is necessary in wording the menu term.

| **Fish Kebabs** | These can be made with mussels, scallops, squid and pieces of white fish together with bay-leaves, tomato, pimento, bacon, grilled mush-rooms, etc., impaled on a skewer and grilled. |

Mixtures of several different kinds of shellfish can be prepared in any of the ways given in this section and are usually called Assiettes de Fruits de Mer, or Plateau de Fruits de Mer. The selection can be a cold one, dressed on crushed ice, seaweed etc., or a hot one.

7 GARNISHES FOR MAIN MEAT DISHES

This list shows the names of most of the well-known classical garnishes for main dishes of meat, currently in use in the international repertoire. It should be remembered that new dishes are constantly being invented, some only for a particular occasion, but which merit widespread acceptance and are then handed down through generations and eventually become classical additions to the international repertoire.

Africaine	Quarters of cèpes and tomatoes, sautéd in oil, fried slices of egg-plant and château potatoes.
Agnes Sorel	Tartlets filled with chicken and mushroom forcemeat and cooked with slices of salt ox-tongue on top.
Albuféra	Tartlets filled with salpicon of cockscombs, mushrooms, quenelles and truffle with sauce Albuféra; moulds of risotto containing diced foie gras and truffle.
Alexandra	Asparagus tips or peas; glaze the joint with sauce mornay and decorate it with truffle.
Algérienne	Whole small tomatoes, croquettes of sweet potato and tomato sauce containing julienne of red pimento.
Alhambra	Quarters of artichoke bottoms and tomatoes sautéd in oil with squares of skinned and cooked green pimentos.
Alliance	Quarters of artichoke bottoms, glazed button onions and turned carrots.
Alsacienne	Tartlets filled with braised sauerkraut with a round piece of ham on top of each.

Ambassadeur Artichoke bottoms filled with duxelles and duchesse potato nests; serve with grated horseradish.

Ambassadrice Salpicon of cockscombs, cocks' kidneys, mushrooms and chicken livers and bouquets of pommes Parisienne.

Américaine Grilled rashers of streaky bacon, mushrooms and tomatoes, pommes pailles and watercress.

Ancienne White glazed button onions and button mushrooms; decorate with heart-shaped croûtons.

Andalouse Pimentos filled with pilaff of rice and shallow fried slices of egg-plant; serve with demi-glace flavoured with pimento butter.

Anversoise Tartlets filled with creamed hop shoots, and plain boiled potatoes.

Arenburg (or d'Arenburg) A tartlet each of buttered spinach and glazed small carrots; slices of truffle.

Argenteuil Asparagus tips, and sauce hollandaise served separately.

Arlequin One tartlet each of cauliflower, balls of carrots and turnip, purée of spinach, pommes noisettes, and tomato concassée.

Arlésienne French-fried onion rings, shallow-fried slices of egg-plant and diced cooked tomato.

Armenonville Quarters of artichoke bottoms, French beans, diced tomato and pommes cocotte.

Artois Hollow rounds of duchesse potato filled with buttered peas.

Athénienne Hollow rounds of fried egg-plant filled with duxelles.

Auber Artichoke bottoms filled with purée of cooked chicken.

Auvergnate Button onions, chestnuts and lardons.

Badoise Braised red cabbage, sliced cooked streaky bacon and mashed potato.

Baltimore Tartlets of creamed sweetcorn, a round of tomato with a smaller round of green pimento on top.

Balzac Chicken quenelles, and olives stuffed with game forcemeat and poached.

Banquière	Chicken quenelles, slices of truffle and one boned stuffed lark per portion.
Baron Brisse	Artichoke bottoms filled with small balls of truffle, diced tomato and pommes soufflées.
Bayarde	Hollow fried-bread croûtons filled with salpicon of artichoke bottoms, slices of foie gras and sliced mushrooms and truffle, mixed with sauce Madère.
Bayonnaise	Macaroni à la crème with julienne of Bayonne ham mixed into it.
Beatrice	Quarters of artichoke bottoms, glazed carrots, whole morels, and small pommes fondantes.
Beaucaire	Braised lettuces and pommes croquettes.
Beaugency	Artichoke bottoms filled with diced tomato with a slice of bone marrow on top.
Beauharnais	Mushrooms filled with duxelles, and quarters of artichoke bottoms.
Belle-Alliance	Slices of foie gras and truffle.
Belle-Hélène	Glazed carrots, peas, mushrooms filled with diced tomato, and pommes croquettes.
Belmont	Green pimentos filled with rice and stuffed tomatoes with duxelles.
Benjamin	Large mushrooms filled with duxelles and small round pommes Dauphine containing chopped truffle.
Bérnoise	Noodles à la crème and large-size chip potatoes.
Berny	Tartlets of chestnut purée with a slice of truffle on top, potato croquettes containing diced truffle.
Berrichonne	Small braised cabbage, slices of cooked streaky bacon, glazed button onions and chestnuts.
Bizontine or **Byzantine**	Hollow rounds of duchesse potato filled with cauliflower purée, braised stuffed lettuces.
Bohémienne	French-fried onions rings, pilaff of rice and diced tomato.
Bouquetière	Glazed carrots, glazed turnips, bouquets of French beans, peas in artichoke bottoms, cauliflower florets, small-size pommes château.

233

Bourgeoise   Glazed carrots, glazed button onions, lardons of bacon, and pommes cocottes.

Bourguignonne   Lardons of bacon, brown-glazed button onions, quarters of mushrooms.

Brabançonne   Tartlets filled with purée of Brussels sprouts and glazed with sauce mornay; pommes galettes.

Bragance   Stuffed tomatoes and pommes croquettes; sauce béarnaise served separately.

Bréhan   Tartlets of broad bean purée, florets of cauliflower mornay and pommes persillées.

Breton   Haricot beans in demi-glace sauce flavoured with tomato, onion and white wine.

Briarde   Carrots in cream sauce and braised stuffed lettuces.

Brillat-Savarin   Tartlets filled with woodcock and truffle soufflé mixture and cooked; thick slices of truffle as decoration.

Bristol   Small round croquettes of rice, flageolot beans in velouté sauce, large size pommes noisettes.

Bruxelloise   Braised Belgian endives, buttered Brussels sprouts and château potatoes.

Bulow   Nests of duchesse potato, one filled with purée of spinach and one with turnip purée.

Café Anglaise   One artichoke bottom filled with duxelles and one with purée of truffle, per person.

Camargo   A slice of foie gras with a slice of truffle on top and tartlets of creamed noodles.

Capucine   Small stuffed cabbages and stuffed mushrooms.

Carême   Olives filled with ham purée and poached, and pommes croquettes.

Carnegie   Asparagus tips arranged in artichoke bottoms, and slices of truffle.

Castillane   Flat nests of duchesse potato filled with tomato concassée, and French fried onion rings.

Catalane   Pilaff of rice, quarters of artichoke bottoms and diced egg-plant, arranged in separate bouquets around the dish.

Cavour   Semolina and cheese croquettes, and mushrooms stuffed with purée of chicken liver.

Cecilia   Mushrooms filled with asparagus tips, and pommes soufflées.

Cendrillon   Artichoke bottoms filled with soubise containing diced truffle.

Centenaire   Braised stuffed lettuces and pommes croquettes.

Cévenole   Sautéd whole mushrooms and braised chestnuts.

Champenoise   Small braised stuffed cabbages, small braised stuffed onions and small moulds of pommes anna.

Chancelière   Brown glazed button onions and pommes parisienne.

Charles V   Salpicon of cockcombs, mushrooms, quenelles and truffle, bound with sauce madère.

Charolaise   Tartlets filled with purée of turnip, glazed carrots, and cooked florets of cauliflower dipped in sauce Villeroy, egg and crumbed and deep fried.

Chartres   Small pommes fondantes; the meat decorated with blanched leaves of tarragon.

Chatham   Buttered noodles on rounds of ham, sauce soubise with sliced mushroom.

Châtelaine   Artichoke bottoms filled with soubise, braised chestnuts and pommes noisettes.

Chevreuse   Artichoke bottoms filled with duxelles and a slice of truffle on top; pommes parisienne.

Chinonnaise   Small braised stuffed cabbages and pommes persillées.

Chipolata   Brown glazed button onions, chipolata sausages, braised chestnuts and large fried lardons of bacon.

Choiseul   Artichoke bottoms filled with foie gras purée.

Choisy   Braised lettuces and château potatoes.

Choron   Artichoke bottoms filled with asparagus tips or peas; pommes parisienne.

Clamart   Tartlets or artichoke bottoms filled with petits pois à la française; small pommes château.

Clermont   Dariole moulds of chestnut royale and French fried onions.

Colbert   Small croquettes of chicken, French fried eggs and sliced truffle.

Garnishes for main meat dishes

Comtesse	Braised lettuces and veal quenelles.
Concorde	Glazed carrots, French beans and purée of potato.
Condé	Purée of red beans, squares of cooked streaky bacon.
Conti	Purée of lentils, squares of cooked streaky bacon.
Continentale	Quarters of artichoke bottoms and sautéd halves of lamb kidneys.
Cordon Bleu	Escalopes sandwiched with ham and gruyère cheese, egg-and-breadcrumbed.
Cussy	Mushrooms filled with purée of chestnut, large cockscombs, small whole truffles.
Cyrano	Artichoke bottoms filled with duxelles.
Danichef	Spoonfuls of caviar, peas, and pommes croquettes.
Dartois	Glazed carrots and turnips, braised celery and pommes rissolées.
Dauphine	Dauphine potato mixture shaped in the form of croquettes or galettes.
Denise	Chou paste fritters, mushroom croquettes, and haricot beans in sauce hollandaise.
Descartes	Artichoke bottoms filled with salpicon of chicken, and pommes croquettes.
Dijonnaise	Quenelles containing diced tongue, and pommes parmentier.
Diplomate	Salpicon of cockscombs and kidneys, sweetbread and mushroom.
Dorsay	Poached stuffed olives filled with forcemeat, and pommes château.
Dreux	Cockscombs and kidneys, quenelles, mushrooms and truffle.
Dubarry	Florets of cauliflower Mornay and pommes château.
Dubley	Nests of duchesse potato filled with duxelles, and whole sautéd mushrooms.
Duchesse	Pommes galette or pommes brioche.
Dugléré	Belgian endives, mushrooms and tomatoes.
Dumas	Small braised cabbages, glazed carrots and lardons.

236

Durand	Braised lettuces, poached stuffed olives, quenelles and truffle.
Duroc	Pommes nouvelles rissolées.
Duse	French beans, small tomatoes and parmentier potatoes.
Elizabeth Deuxième	Asparagus tips, julienne of ham, chicken forcemeat.
Egyptienne	Stuffed pimentoes and croquettes of saffron-flavoured rice pilaff.
Elysée	Small slices of sweetbread, crumbed and shallow-fried mushrooms.
Esplanade	Asparagus tips, artichoke bottom with diced tomato, fried banana, pineapple ring, pilaff of rice.
Empereur	Tomato-halves with a poached slice of bone marrow on top, asparagus tips and pommes parmentier.
Excelsior	Braised lettuces and pommes fondantes.
Favart	Creamed noodles with julienne of truffle.
Favorite	Sautéd slices of foie gras with a slice of truffle on each.
Fédora	Tartlets of asparagus tips, glazed balls of carrot and turnip, braised chestnuts and orange segments.
Fermière	Paysanne of carrot, celery, onion and turnip.
Ferval	Quarters of artichoke bottoms and pommes brioche containing finely chopped ham.
Figaro	Nests of duchesse potato coated with broken vermicelli and deep-fried, then filled with small balls of carrot.
Financière	Salpicon of cockscombs and kidneys, olives, mushrooms, quenelles and truffle.
Flamande	Small braised cabbages, small boiled potatoes, carrots and turnips, slices of cooked garlic sausage and squares of cooked streaky bacon.
Fleuriste	Tomatoes filled with buttered peas, artichoke bottoms filled with balls of carrot and turnip, bundles of French beans, florets of cauliflower hollandaise.

Florentine	Cheese-flavoured semolina croquettes and subrics of spinach.
Florian	Braised lettuces, brown glazed button onions, glazed carrots and pommes fondantes.
Fontainebleau	Nests of duchesse potato filled with creamed macédoine of vegetables.
Forestière	Lardons of bacon, whole morels, and pommes parmentier.
Française	Florets of cauliflower, bouquets of asparagus tips, braised lettuce and tartlets filled with small dice of mixed vegetables.
Frascati	Slices of foie gras, turned mushrooms, asparagus tips, small truffles and surround with glazed crescents of duchesse potato.
Gastronome	Cocks' kidneys, glazed chestnuts, small truffles and halves of large morels.
Gauloise	Tartlets of cocks' kidneys, cockcombs cooked à la Villeroy, mushrooms and slices of truffle.
Godard	Quenelles made with the addition of chopped mushroom and truffle, cockscombs, mushrooms, lamb-sweetbreads, and oval pieces of truffle.
Gouffé	Moulds of risotto, mushrooms, quenelles and oval pieces of truffle.
Gourmet	Quarters of artichoke bottoms, mushrooms and slices of truffle.
Grand-Duc	Asparagus tips and slices of truffle.
Grand'Mère	Brown glazed button onions, button mushrooms and baton shaped bread croûtons.
Grand-Hotel	Braised celery, artichoke bottoms filled with Sauce Béarnaise, and soufflé potatoes.
Grecque	Pilaff of rice.
Helder	An artichoke bottom each of (1) pommes parisienne, (2) asparagus tips, (3) tomate concassée.
Helvetia	Two small stuffed tomatoes – one filled with purée of spinach, the other with onion purée.
Henri IV	Artichoke bottoms filled with pommes parisienne.
Holstein	Fried egg garnished with fillets of anchovy.
Hongroise	Florets of cauliflowers glazed with sauce mornay flavoured with paprika and chopped ham.

Hussarde	Hollowed-out potatoes filled with onion purée, and stuffed halves of egg-plant.
Impériale	Cockscombs, mushrooms, slices of foie gras, sweetbread and truffle.
Indienne	Plain boiled rice.
Infante	Macaroni with julienne of truffle, whole mushrooms, stuffed tomatoes and pommes pailles.
Imam-Bayaldi	Fried sliced egg-plant, pilaff of rice and tomate concassée.
Italienne	Round flat macaroni croquettes, quarters of artichoke braised in white wine and mixed with sauce italienne.
Japonnaise	Pastry cases filled with creamed Japanese artichokes, and rice croquettes.
Jardinière	Glazed turned carrots and turnips, peas, flageolet beans, diamonds of French beans and florets of cauliflower with sauce hollandaise – arranged in bunches around the meat.
Jockey Club	Stuffed tomatoes, quenelles containing crayfish butter and chopped mushroom, and pommes croquettes.
Judic	Whole cockscombs, braised lettuces, and slices of truffle.
Jules Verne	Potatoes and turnips hollowed-out and filled with forcemeat, and quarters of mushrooms.
Jussieu	Braised stuffed lettuces, braised stuffed onions, pommes château.
Jetée-Promenade	Cooked tomato filled with sauce béarnaise, and pommes soufflées.
Kléber	Artichoke bottoms filled with foie gras purée.
Kotschoubey	Brussels sprouts sautéd with lardons, and sliced truffle.
Laguipierre	A round of ox-tongue with a slice of foie gras on top.
Lakmi	Tartlets filled with purée of broad beans, grilled mushrooms.
Langtry	A small tomato on an artichoke bottom with a stoned olive inside and blanched tarragon around.

239

Langue-docienne	Fried slices of egg-plant, sliced cèpes and tomate concassée.
Lavallière	Artichoke bottoms filled with asparagus tips, and pommes château.
Léopold	Tartlets filled with creamed sliced mushrooms.
Ligurienne	Moulds of saffron-flavoured risotto, stuffed tomatoes, and pommes duchesse.
Lili	Tartlets containing a slice of foie gras and truffle, and small moulds of pommes Anna.
Limousine	Brown-glazed button onions and braised chestnuts.
Lithuanienne	Button mushrooms in sour cream sauce.
Lombarde	Tomatoes filled with cheese-flavoured risotto containing chopped Italian truffle.
Lorette	Asparagus tips, and small croquettes of chicken.
Lorraine	Small braised red cabbages, braised sauerkraut and potato gnocchi.
Louis XIV	Artichoke bottoms filled with duxelles, flat moulds of pommes Anna, and slices of truffle.
Louisiane	Small moulds of risotto, fried banana, and creamed sweetcorn.
Lucullus	Cockscombs, quenelles containing purée of truffle, small hollowed-out truffles filled with cockscombs mixed with meat glaze and the lids replaced.
Lyonnaise	Braised small onions, and pommes fondantes.
Macédoine	$\frac{3}{4}$cm dice of carrot and turnip, peas, flageolet beans, diamonds of French beans, all mixed together.
MacMahon	Flageolet beans, pommes parmentier, and slices of truffle.
Madeleine	Artichoke bottoms filled with onion puree, and tartlets filled with purée of haricot beans.
Maillot	Glazed carrots and turnips, brown glazed button onions, peas, French beans, and braised lettuces.
Maintenon	Artichoke bottoms, mushrooms, quenelles and slices of truffle.
Majestic	Potato croquettes containing diced mushroom, whole okras and mushrooms.

Maraîchère	Buttered Brussels sprouts, pieces of salsify mixed with velouté, and pommes château.
Maréchale	Cockscombs, quenelles containing chopped truffle, and slices of truffle.
Marie-Louise	Artichoke bottoms filled with a mixture of duxelles and onion purée.
Marie-Stuart	Tartlets of turnip purée with a slice of bone marrow on top.
Marie-Jeanne	Tartlets filled with duxelles and a slice of truffle on top; pommes noisettes.
Marigny	One tartlet of peas and one of diamonds of French beans; pommes fondantes.
Marion-Delorne	Artichoke bottoms filled with a mixture of two thirds duxelles, one third purée of onion.
Marivaux	Glazed nests of duchesse potato filled with mixed vegetables.
Marquise	Pommes marquise, tartlets filled with salpicon of asparagus tips, spinal marrow and truffle bound with sauce allemande finished with crayfish butter.
Marseillaise	Emptied halves of small tomatoes filled with a large stuffed olive surrounded by an anchovy fillet, and spiral-cut deep-fried potatoes (pommes copeaux).
Maryland	Rashers of streaky bacon, fried bananas, galettes of sweetcorn, and tomatoes; cold horseradish sauce served separately.
Mascagni	Tartlets of chestnut purée with a slice of fried calf's brain on top; pommes pailles.
Mascotte	Quarters of artichoke bottoms, pommes olivettes and small balls of truffle.
Masséna	Artichoke bottoms filled with sauce béarnaise, and poached slices of bone marrow.
Masseult	Artichoke bottoms containing a poached slice of bone marrow, French beans, and scone-shape pommes Anna.
Mazarin	Artichoke bottoms filled with macédoine of vegetables; mushrooms, quenelles and rice croquettes.

Médicis   Tartlet cases filled with diced macaroni and truffle mixed with foie gras purée, and buttered peas.

Melba   Braised lettuces, stuffed tomatoes, mushrooms and slices of truffle.

Mentonnaise Artichoke bottoms filled with pommes parisienne, and stuffed chard.

Mercédès   Braised lettuces, tomatoes, mushrooms, and pommes croquettes.

Metternich   Asparagus tips and slices of foie gras and truffle.

Mexicaine   Mushrooms filled with tomate concassée, and cooked halves of pimentos.

Meyerbeer   Grilled halves of lambs' kidneys.

Mignon   Artichoke bottoms filled with peas, and quenelles decorated with a slice of truffle.

Mikado   Sautéd Japanese artichokes, and halves of tomato.

Milanaise   Spaghetti mixed with julienne of ham, mushrooms, tongue and truffle, flavoured with Parmesan cheese and mixed with tomato sauce.

Mirabeau   Decorate the meat trellis fashion with strips of anchovy, stoned olives filled with anchovy butter and a border of blanched tarragon leaves.

Mireille   Sautéd sliced potatoes with sliced artichoke bottoms and truffle.

Mirette   Very small dice of potatoes cooked in butter with truffle and meat glaze, moulded in dariole moulds.

Moderne   Braised lettuces, quenelles decorated with ox-tongue and braised cabbages moulded hexagonally.

Moissonneuse Peas à la française with the addition of sliced potatoes and lardons.

Monaco   Sautéd slices of calf's brain, slices of ham and whole mushrooms.

Monselet   Stuffed egg-plant, and pommes parisienne.

Montagné   Artichoke bottoms filled with mushrooms, stuffed tomatoes.

Montbazon   Studded lamb's sweetbreads, quenelles decorated with truffle, mushrooms and sliced truffle.

Monte Carlo	One tartlet of French beans and one of peas, stuffed cassoulets of cucumber, pommes croquettes.
Montglas	Salpicon of mushroom, tongue and truffle in sauce madère.
Montmorency	Artichoke bottoms filled with macédoine of vegetable and bouquets of asparagus tips.
Montpensier	Bouquets of asparagus tips and slice of truffle.
Montreuil	Artichoke bottoms filled half with peas and half with small balls of carrot.
Mozart	Artichoke bottoms filled with purée of celeriac, and pommes soufflées.
Nantaise	Peas, pommes purée, and glazed turnips.
Napolitaine	Spaghetti in tomato sauce with diced tomato.
Nemours	Glazed carrots, peas and pommes duchesse.
Nesselrode	Braised whole chestnuts.
Niçoise	Bouquets of French beans, tomatoes, and pommes château.
Nemrod	Tartlets filled with cooked cranberries, mushrooms filled with chestnut purée, French beans, rissoles of beef marrow, and pommes croquettes.
Ninon	Bouchées of asparagus tips and truffle, dariole moulds of pommes Anna made with sliced artichoke bottoms, and sliced truffle.
Nivernaise	Braised lettuces, glazed button onions, and turned glazed carrots and turnips.
Opéra	Tartlets of chicken livers in Madeira sauce, and emptied round potato croquettes filled with asparagus tips.
Orientale	Tomatoes filled with moulded rice, and croquettes of sweet potato.
Orléanaise	Chopped braised chicory mixed with egg yolks, and a dish of pommes maître d'hôtel.
Orloff	Braised stuffed lettuces, braised celery, and small whole tomatoes.
Palermitaine	Croquettes of macaroni, stuffed egg-plant, and small whole tomatoes.

Palestine	Quarters of artichoke bottoms, brown-glazed button onions, and semolina gnocchi.
Palois	New carrots, onions and turnips, and florets of cauliflower.
Parisienne	Artichoke bottoms filled with salpicon of mushroom, tongue and truffle mixed with velouté and glazed; pommes parisienne.
Parmentier	Fried 1cm dice of potato arranged in piles around the meat.
Paysanne	Paysanne of carrot, celery, onion and turnip, pommes olivettes, lardons.
Pergamon	Croquette potatoes, sauce béarnaise, and slices of truffle.
Persane	Fried banana, tomatoes, and small green pimentos stuffed with rice.
Péruvienne	Hollowed-out roots of wood sorrel (oxalis) filled with the chopped pulp mixed with chicken and ham and braised.
Petit-Duc	Tartlets of purée of chicken, bundles of asparagus tips and a slice of truffle.
Piémontaise	Moulded risotto containing grated white truffle.
Polignac	Julienne of mushroom and truffle.
Pompadour	Artichoke bottoms filled with purée of lentils and a slice of truffle on top, and small round pommes croquettes.
Porte-Maillot	Bouquets of glazed carrots and turnips, flageolot beans, peas, French beans and florets of cauliflower coated with sauce hollandaise.
Portugaise	Stuffed tomatoes and pommes château.
Primeurs	Glazed new carrots and turnips, French beans, peas in artichoke bottoms, florets of cauliflower and small pommes château – all arranged in bouquets.
Princesse	Artichoke bottoms filled with asparagus tips, truffle cut in slices.
Printanière	Glazed new carrots and turnips, button onions, and bundles of asparagus tips.
Provençale	Stuffed mushrooms and stuffed tomatoes both with duxelles made with garlic.

Quirinal	Mushrooms filled with poached diced bone marrow, pommes pailles and watercress.
Rachel	Artichoke bottoms containing a slice of poached bone marrow.
Raphaël	One artichoke bottom filled with creamed purée of carrot and one with sauce béarnaise.
Réforme	Julienne of cooked egg white, gherkin, ham, mushroom, ox-tongue and truffle in sauce poivrade; serve with sauce réforme.
Régence	Cockscombs, slices of foie gras, mushrooms, quenelles and slices of truffle.
Réjane	Tartlets of foie gras purée and of asparagus tips.
Renaissance	Bouquets of new carrots and turnips, French beans, peas, asparagus tips, new potatoes, and cauliflower coated with sauce hollandaise.
Richelieu	Stuffed mushrooms, stuffed tomatoes, braised lettuces and pommes château.
Rita	Artichoke bottoms filled with tomate concassée, mushrooms and pommes olivettes.
Rochambeau	Shallow nests of duchesse potato filled with carottes Vichy, cauliflower à la polonaise, braised stuffed lettuces, pommes Anna.
Rohan	Tartlets filled with creamed cock's kidneys and cockscombs, artichoke bottoms brushed with meat glaze and filled with a slice of foie gras and of truffle.
Romane	Gratinated tartlets of small gnocchi romaine and subrics of spinach.
Romanoff	Nests of duchesse potato filled with creamed mushrooms mixed with celeriac, and glazed turned cucumber.
Rosebery	French beans, stuffed tomatoes, turned and glazed cucumber, and hollowed-out semolina gnocchi filled with sautéd morels.
Rossini	A slice of foie gras with a slice of truffle on top.
Rostand	Quarters of artichoke bottoms, and creamed quarters of mushrooms.
Roumanille	Grilled tomatoes coated and glazed à la mornay, fried slices of aubergine, and stoned olives with an anchovy fillet wound round them.

245

Royale	Cockscombs, slices of foie gras, mushrooms, quenelles and slices of truffle.
Sagan	Mushrooms filled with purée of calf's brain and chopped truffle, and dariole moulds of risotto.
Saint-Florentin	Cèpes cooked à la bordelaise, and pommes St-Florentin.
Saint-Germain	Glazed carrots, moulds of pea purée set with egg-yolks, and pommes fondantes.
Saint-Lambert	Glazed carrots, French beans, peas, florets of cauliflower, and brown-glazed button onions.
Saint-Mandé	French beans, peas, and small round pommes macaire.
Saint-Saëns	Bundles of asparagus tips, cockscombs, slices of foie gras and truffle croquettes.
Samaritaine	Braised lettuces, pommes dauphine, and dariole moulds of risotto.
Sarah Bernhardt	(1) Braised lettuces and tomatoes *or* (2) Mixed sliced fried potato and quarters of globe artichokes.
Sarde	Stuffed tomatoes, stuffed cucumber, and rice croquettes.
Sarladaise	Boulangère potatoes cooked with the addition of sliced truffle.
Savoyarde	Pommes savoyarde (sliced potatoes mixed with beaten egg, stock and gruyère cheese, cooked in the oven and gratinated with cheese).
Schubert	Tartlets of asparagus tips, cassolettes of celeriac filled with mashed potato and cassolettes of potato filled with peas. (A cassolette is a small fireproof dish.)
Sévigné	Braised stuffed lettuces, whole mushrooms, and pommes château.
Sévillaise	A tartlet each of tomato concassée and diced red pimento; pommes Parmentier.
Sicilienne	Lasagnes prepared à la Sicilienne (with cheese, purée of sautéd chicken liver and velouté).
Siguid	Ham croquettes, and stuffed tomatoes.
Soissonnaise	Butter beans in tomato sauce.
Staël	One mushroom filled with peas and one with

	purée of chicken, and small round chicken croquettes.
Strasbourgeoise	Braised sauerkraut, pieces of streaky bacon and slices of foie gras.
Sully	Cock's kidneys, braised lettuce, pommes parisienne and slices of truffle.
Sultane	Braised small green pimentos stuffed with rice, fried banana and small whole tomatoes.
Suzanne	Artichoke bottoms and braised stuffed lettuces; decoration of blanched tarragon leaves.
Suzeraine	Stuffed cucumber and stuffed tomatoes.
Talleyrand	Short lengths of macaroni tossed in butter and cheese with dice of foie gras and julienne of truffle.
Tivoli	Asparagus tips, and mushrooms filled with creamed cockscombs and kidneys.
Tortue	Mushrooms, olives, gherkins, quenelles, truffle and heart-shaped bread croûtons.
Toscane	Macaroni mixed into foie gras and velouté.
Toulousaine	Cockscombs and kidneys, mushrooms, quenelles, lamb's sweetbreads and slice of truffle.
Tourangelle	Flageolet and French beans mixed with béchamel sauce.
Trévisaine	Beignets of artichoke, hollowed-out bread croûtons filled with duxelles, and pommes noisettes.
Tyrolienne	Piles of tomate concassée and French-fried onion rings.
Tzarine	Cucumber cooked in cream sauce.
Valencay	Flat croquettes of noodles and ham, and the garnish financière (cockscombs, mushrooms, olives, quenelles and truffle).
Valenciennes	Pilaff rice containing diced ham and red pimento, peas and chipolatas.
Valentine	Piles of cooked diced tomato and pommes noisettes.
Vénitienne	Cockscombs, calf's brain and mushrooms.
Vatel	Belgian endives, cèpes, small pommes Anna, and purée of green peas.

Garnishes for main meat dishes

Vendôme	Tomato filled with sauce béarnaise, pommes soufflées, and French-fried onion rings.
Verdi	Slice of foie gras, nests of duchesse potato filled with small balls of carrot, and braised lettuces.
Vert-Pré	Pommes pailles, watercress and parsley butter.
Vichy	Carrots à la Vichy.
Victor	Pilaff of rice containing peas and diced red pimento; serve with curry-flavoured cream sauce.
Victoria	Sautéd artichoke bottoms and stuffed tomatoes.
Viennoise	Sieved yolk and white of hard-boiled egg, chopped parsley, slices of lemon, stoned olives, anchovy fillets.
Villaret	Purée of flageolet beans, mushrooms and sauce chateaubriand.
Viroflay	Sautéd artichoke bottoms, pommes château, and small balls of spinach Viroflay.
Westmoreland	Stuffed tomatoes, peas and glazed turned cucumber.
Wladimir	Glazed cucumber and sautéd slices of vegetable marrow; serve with grated horseradish.
Zingara	Julienne of ham, mushrooms, ox-tongue and truffle.

Garnishes can also be described on the menu with one of the following words, in conjunction with others that give an outline of the contents of the dish or actually name the main ingredients. The following can be used to describe a dish in which several different foods are either cooked together or are brought together to form a dish as in Rendezvous de Fruits de Mer à la Roscoff, or Assemblage de Coquilles St-Jacques et Homard, the first being made of a variety of ordinary fish with perhaps mushrooms, in a fish sauce, the second being scallops and lobster with mushrooms and sauce. Other words that may be used to describe various combinations are:-

Alliance	Intégration
Amalgame	Jumelé
Assemblage	Mélange
Collocation	Méli-mélo
Combinaison	Rassemblement

Convergence	Rendezvous
Fondre	Réunion
Fusion	Totalité
Galaxie	Unanimité
Harmonie	Union
Incorporation	Unification

There are many classical garnish names that apply to more than one course of the menu although obviously the contents of each differ. This indicates that it is perfectly possible to compose a menu with every dish bearing the same name yet each course being entirely different. Such a menu is unlikely to be acceptable because it is confusing and goes against the precepts of good menu composition.

Such a menu could be:

> Crème Ambassadrice
> Filet de Sole Ambassadrice
> Suprème de Volaille Ambassadrice
> Sorbet au Champagne
> Noix de Veau Poêlé à l'Ambassadrice
> Pommes Ambassadrice
> Charlotte de Fraises Ambassadrice
> Café

There can also be some discrepancy between the garnish name for an entrée and the same name for a relevé and a poultry dish may have an entirely different garnish from a piece of meat, although the name is the same. The following are examples of classical names that apply to three or more courses of the menu, e.g. eggs, fish, meat and sweets:

Alexandria	Maréchale
Alsacienne	Melba
Armenonville	Nelson
Balzac	Niçoise
Belle Hélène	Opéra
Bohémienne	Parisienne
Brillat-Savarin	Pompadour
Carême	Printanière

Main courses of meat, poultry & game

Carlton	Régence
Condé	Richelieu
Elizabeth	Royale
Favorite	Savoyarde
Fédora	Trianon
Gastronome	Tzarina
Grand-Duc	Urbain-Dubois
Henri IV	Valois
Jacques	Victoria
Lorraine	Viennoise
Lucullus	Windsor

8 MAIN COURSES OF MEAT, POULTRY AND GAME

When selecting main dishes for the menu it is necessary to know the distinction that exists between entrée and a relevé. The word entrée is now used loosely to describe all kinds of main dishes though actually it should only be used in connection with a meal in which there are two main meat courses – first the entrée which consists of a small meat item without a garnish or any accompanying vegetables and second, the relevé which is a joint of any kind of meat, served with a garnish and some accompanying vegetables.

There are actually three different kinds of main meat courses, the third being the roast, but the distinction betwen these three has become blurred because meals with so many main courses are seldom served nowadays. Most menus include only one main meat course and this can be drawn from amongst the long lists of entrées, relevés and roasts in this chapter, and served with a vegetable and potatoes.

The French word relevé is translated into English as 'remove' and is accepted as indicating a more substantial course than the preceeding entrée.

A roast joint can constitute a course in its own right, often accompanied with only a salad; however requests for twelve-course meals in which all these main courses are included, are few and far between, mainly because of the changing demands of customers and the high price involved.

Whilst it makes good sense to keep the strict division between these courses, in order to avoid duplication in this section all the main meat dishes are dealt with in Sections by cooking methods, the only exception being offals which are grouped into one section covering all cooking methods.

The distinction between entrée and relevé is left to the user as is the appropriateness of certain dishes for lunch as against dinner as there are no written rules that decide what dishes are permissible for lunch yet are completely unsuitable for a good dinner menu.

251

The very large number of main meat dishes are dealt with in the following order:

1. Baked, including pies, terrines and pâtés, timbales and tourtes;
2. Boiled, poached and steamed, including meat puddings;
3. Braised, including pot roasted;
4. Deep-fried;
5. Grilled, including gratinated and barbecued dishes;
6. Poêléd, including dishes en casserole;
7. Roasted;
8. Shallow-fried (sautéd), including stir-fried;
9. Stewed, including sautés;
10. Made-up main dishes using raw meat;
11. Made-up main dishes using cooked meat;
12. Offals;
13. Game and wild birds;
14. Game animals.

Baked Dishes

This section includes all the dishes that are cooked by baking, including pies, joints and cuts, terrines and pâtés, tourtes and timbales. Meat dishes cooked in pastry are also discussed.

Pies

An *ordinary British pie* is made in a pie-dish and has a top crust only, which may be of either puff or short pastry; it is decorated with pastry leaves, crescents, etc., egg-washed and baked. A raised pie is made in a special mould or around a jam jar, using hot-water paste, with a puff-pastry lid or decorations. Both kinds of pie are suitable for serving cold by the addition of a few leaves of soaked gelatine or pouring aspic jelly in when cool; it is necessary to season pies made for cold more highly than for hot as cold food seldom tastes as sapid as hot. The pie-dish should be surrounded by a pie frill.

Blackbird   Soak the breasts only in milk for 2 hours, then lay in a pie-dish with thin streaky rashers, chopped onion and parsley; moisten with stock, cover with pastry, decorate, egg-wash and bake for approximately $1\frac{1}{2}$ hours at 150°C. If using puff pastry start to bake at 200°C for the first 10 minutes.

Chicken

Wrap pieces of chicken cut for sauté, in thin streaky rashers; place in a pie-dish, add chopped onion and parsley, a few drops of Worcester sauce and cold chicken stock. Cover with puff pastry, allow to stand then bake at 200°C for 10 minutes then at 150°C for approximately $1\frac{1}{2}$ hours.

Chicken and Bacon

Arrange layers of skinned and boned chicken and lean raw ham in a pie-dish, flavour with onion and parsley; add Worcester sauce and chicken stock and cover with puff pastry, egg-wash, decorate and bake as for chicken pie.

Chicken and Leek

Add layers of pieces of blanched leek to chicken pie and finish as stated.

Chicken and Liver Patties

Fill the centre of 12cm squares of short pastry with raw chicken, veal and chicken liver forcemeat; cut in from each corner, fold over the filling, seal and turn over onto a tray, egg-wash and bake at 175°C for 40 minutes.

Cornish Pasty

Cut chuck steak and ox kidney into $\frac{1}{2}$cm dice, add chopped carrot, onion and swede, season well and place some in 10–12cm rounds of short pastry; fold over or to the centre, crimp the edge, egg-wash and bake for approximately 1 hour. Some recipes suggest the use of left-over cooked meat but they are not authentic.

Cottage Pie

Sauté chopped onion in butter, add finely chopped cooked beef and demi-glace, bring to a boil and cook for 10 minutes; half fill a pie-dish, pipe with duchesse or mashed potato, brush with melted butter or egg-wash and bake until brown.

Duck

Line a charlotte mould with short pastry then with an inner lining of gratin forcemeat; fill with layers of parcooked slices of duck, sliced cooked mushroom, truffle, and the forcemeat; cover with a lid of pastry, decorate, egg-wash and bake for 1 hour. Remove the lid, decorate the top with slices of truffle and coat with Madeira sauce.

Fidget   Fill a pie-dish with alternate layers of large dice of bacon, sliced cooking apples, and slices of potato; add chopped onion, a little white stock, cover with short pastry and bake.

Foie gras (1)   Stud a raw whole goose liver with truffle, wrap in thin slices of back fat and put into a tall round mould lined with brioche paste; cover with pastry, allow to prove then bake in a moderately hot oven; turn out to serve hot or cold.

Foie gras (2)   Line a raised pie-mould with hot-water paste, line with pork forcemeat and fill with a whole raw goose-liver; cover with more forcemeat, then a lid of puff pastry, decorate, egg-wash and bake.

Game   Line a raised pie-mould with short pastry, fill with skinned and boned game-birds; cover with pastry, decorate, egg-wash and bake.

Grouse   Use the breast only of an old grouse together with slices of rump steak, rashers of streaky bacon, game forcemeat, sliced mushroom, etc., to fill the pie-dish; cover with puff pastry and bake in the usual way.

Ham   Line a raised pie-mould with short pastry then with thin slices of back fat; fill with pork forcemeat containing 2½cm dice of cooked ham, add a bay-leaf, cover with a pastry lid, decorate, egg-wash and bake.

Hare   Line a charlotte mould with short pastry then with a layer of hare forcemeat; fill with thick slices of saddle of hare stiffened in hot butter, add a little salmis sauce and close with a pastry top; bake for 1¼ hours.

Hunter's   This is a raised pie containing mixed diced beef, raw ham, venison and swede moistened with a little game stock. It may be served hot or cold.

Kournick
Arrange sliced cooked chicken, sliced hard-boiled egg, sliced mushroom and velouté in layers on a sheet of brioche pastry; fold so as to form a bell shape, egg-wash, decorate, allow to prove then bake in a hot oven. Pour hot cream in through a hole.

Melton Mowbray
This is a raised pork pie filled with minced lean and fat pork lightly flavoured with anchovy essence.

Mutton
Line individual moulds with hot-water pastry, fill with minced neck of mutton cooked with chopped mushroom, onion and parsley; cover with a pastry lid, bake, then turn out to serve.

Partridge
May be made in a pie-dish or as a raised pie, with alternate layers of boned and marinated partridge and game forcemeat.

Pâté de Poulet Challonaise
Line a charlotte mould with short pastry then cover the bottom with a layer of chicken forcemeat containing chopped raw mushroom; fill with cooked cold fricassée of chicken with the addition of cockscombs and kidneys, cover with a layer of forcemeat and seal with a pastry top. Bake at 180°C for approximately 1 hour, turn out and serve with velouté sauce.

Pâté Financière
Line a raised pie-mould with short pastry, cover the bottom with veal forcemeat and fill up with a stiff mixture of cooked cockscombs and kidneys, mushrooms, stoned olives, quenelles and truffle in Madeira sauce; cover with a layer of the forcemeat, then the pastry lid; decorate, egg-wash and bake for 50 minutes.

Pâté de Poulet Vallauris
Line a pie-dish with thin slices of veal, fill with a partly cooked sauté of chicken garnished with stoned black olives, cover with slices of veal then a lid of short pastry; decorate, egg-wash and bake for 1 hour.

Pheasant
Line a charlotte mould with short pastry, add a layer of buttered noodles and fill with chopped cooked pheasant, mushroom and truffle mixed with salmis sauce; add a layer of noodles then the lid of pastry and bake for 50 minutes.

255

Pigeon, Wood Colour wood pigeons in hot fat, cook in stock then cut in half and bone out; arrange in a pie-dish with thin slices of rump steak, sliced mushroom and chopped onion; moisten with brown stock, cover with pastry, decorate, egg-wash and bake.

Pigeon, ham and egg Line a pie-dish with streaky rashers, sprinkle with chopped shallot then fill with skinned and boned pigeon breasts, hard-boiled eggs and a little stock; cover with puff pastry, decorate, egg-wash and bake for $1\frac{1}{2}$ hours.

Pigeon Line a charlotte mould with short pastry and fill with alternate layers of gratin forcemeat and skinned and boned pieces of cooked young pigeon, sliced mushroom and truffle; season with powdered bay-leaf and thyme, cover with pastry and bake. To serve, cut off the lid, and cut it into triangles and cover the meat with demi-glace.

Pork Line a raised pie-mould with hot-water paste and fill with a mixture of minced lean and fat pork and streaky bacon; cover with a pastry lid, make a hole in the centre, decorate with leaves, egg-wash and bake. Pour some cool melted jelly through the hole as soon as the pie comes from the oven. The filling for this pie may be varied by the addition of slices of apple, stoned cooked prunes, etc.

Pork Patties Fill the centre of 12cm squares of short pastry with pork, veal and chicken liver forcemeat containing diced bacon, veal and ham; cut 3cm squares from each of the four corners of the pastry and envelop the meat, turn over, egg-wash and bake at 175°C for 45 minutes.

Priddy Oggy This is made in the same shape as a Cornish pasty using cheese-flavoured flaky pastry and a filling of cheese paste wrapped in a small pork escalope then in a rasher of bacon; egg-wash, par-bake then deep fry.

Rabbit Cook cut rabbit and salt belly of pork in water, remove the bones and place layers of these meats and sliced hard-boiled egg in a pie-dish;

moisten with the stock, cover with short pastry, decorate and bake at 200°C.

Rabbit and Pigeon
Arrange layers of boned rabbit and boned breast of pigeon in a pie-dish with chopped onion; moisten with stock, cover with short pastry, decorate, egg-wash and bake for $1\frac{1}{2}$ hours.

Raised
Line an oval, round or oblong raised pie-mould, or the outside of a jam jar, with hot-water paste, fill with the minced meat such as pork, veal, game; cover with a pastry lid, decorate, egg-wash and bake; when cooked fill with jelly.

Rook
Soak the skinned breasts in milk for 2 hours then place in a pie-dish with streaky rashers, chopped onion and parsley; moisten with cream, cover with short pastry, decorate and bake for $1\frac{1}{2}$ hours at 150°C.

Sea Pie
Bake pieces of cheap cut of beef or lamb with diced potato, carrot, onion and turnip under a covering of suet pastry.

Shepherd's Pie
Sauté chopped onion in butter, add finely chopped cooked lamb and demi-glace, bring to a boil and cook for 10 minutes; half fill pie-dishes, pipe with pommes duchesse or mashed potato, brush with melted butter, or egg-wash and bake until brown.

Steak and Kidney
Mix together two parts of diced raw beef to one part of diced ox kidney, chopped onion and parsley, Worcester sauce and cold brown stock; place in a pie-dish, cover with puff pastry rolled out 3mm thick, decorate with leaves of pastry, egg-wash, allow to stand for 30 minutes then bake at 210°C for 15 minutes then at 150°C for a total of 2 hours. If desired the kidney may be cut into finger shapes and rolled in thin slices of beef.

Steak, Kidney and Mushroom (cooked filling)
Sauté chopped onion, diced raw beef and kidney in hot dripping until brown; dust with flour, add a little tomato purée, sliced mushrooms, brown stock and Worcester sauce and cook for $1\frac{1}{2}$ hours; place in a pie-dish, allow to cool then

	cover with puff-pastry and bake for approximately 30 minutes.
Steak, Kidney and Oyster	Add raw oysters to the beef and kidney mixture (canned or frozen ones may be used as a cheaper alternative to fresh oysters) and proceed as for Steak and kidney pie.
Sweetbread	Line a mould with short pastry, spread the inside with pork and bacon forcemeat and fill with blanched and trimmed sweetbreads; cover with a layer of forcemeat and a round of pastry and bake.
Turkey	Arrange layers of boned turkey meat, streaky bacon and chopped onion in a pie-dish; moisten with white stock, cover with puff pastry, egg-wash, decorate and bake at 210°C for 15 minutes then at 150°C for a total of 1½ hours.
Veal, Ham and Egg	Line a pie-dish with rashers of streaky bacon, fill with layers of thin escalopes of veal, sliced raw gammon, finely chopped onion and whole hard-boiled eggs; cover with puff pastry, egg-wash and decorate, then bake at 220°C for 15 minutes then at 150°C for a total of 1¾ hours.
Vermont Chicken Pie	Cover creamed dice of chicken with 5cm overlapping rounds of plain scone mixture, brush with melted butter and bake for 25 minutes.

Joints Baked in Pastry

In some of the following formulas it is possible to use a pastry other than the one stated; brioche, croissant, hot-water, puff and rich short pastry and pâte brisée are all equally suitable.

| **Beef Wellington** | Seal and colour a piece of fillet of beef in hot fat for 10 minutes, allow to get cold, then place on a bed of duxelles spread along the centre of an oblong of puff pastry; cover approximately 1cm thick with duxelles, envelop in the pastry, turn over onto a tray, decorate, egg-wash and allow to rest for 30 minutes. Bake at 200°C for 10 minutes then at 150°C until cooked through but |

keeping the meat underdone. Serve accompanied with Madeira sauce.

Cailles Frères Provençaux
Coat stuffed boned quails with duxelles and enclose each one in puff pastry; egg-wash and bake at 200°C for 30 minutes.

Cailles George Sand
Stuff quails with foie gras and colour in hot butter; wrap in puff pastry, egg-wash and bake.

Cailles Normande
Brown in hot butter, place each in a peeled scooped-out apple; replace the top, enclose in short pastry, egg-wash and bake.

Cailles sous la Cendre
Stuff boned quails with truffled game forcemeat, wrap in a slice of salt pork fat and enclose in short pastry as for a turnover; egg-wash and bake for 30 minutes.

Coq en Pâté
Stuff a boned chicken with veal, pork and liver forcemeat; place on a 45cm square of short pastry and enclose completely; egg-wash, decorate then bake for approximately 2 hours. (The head used to be left on and threaded through a hole in the pastry, covering it with paper during the cooking but this is not now considered hygienic.)

Coq en Pâté
Colour a trussed chicken, previously stuffed with foie gras or forcemeat; place in a suitably sized terrine, cover with short pastry, egg-wash and bake so that the chicken and pastry are cooked and coloured at the same time.

Côtelette d'Agneau en Croûte
Colour the cutlet quickly in hot fat, allow to cool then wrap in pastry; decorate, egg-wash and bake. If desired the cutlet may be spread with duxelles.

Entrecôte Georgienne
Set a sirloin steak in hot butter, allow to cool then spread with anchovy butter; enfold in puff pastry, egg-wash and bake in a hot oven.

Filet de Boeuf Nemrod
Lard a fillet of beef with small strips of back fat, ham and truffle and marinate for several hours; roast rapidly for 10 minutes, allow to get cold then spread all over with foie gras; wrap in puff pastry and cook as for Beef Wellington. Serve with brown sauce made from the marinade and

259

	garnished with short julienne of carrot, ham and truffle.
Fillet Steak en Croûte	Seal and colour a fillet steak in hot fat, allow to cool then wrap in pastry; decorate, egg-wash and bake until coloured and cooked underdone.
Gigot d'Agneau en Croûte	Bone out the leg, fill with stuffing and roast until three parts cooked; envelop in pastry, decorate, egg-wash and finish cooking.
Jambon sous Croûte au Madère	Parboil a ham until about half cooked, cool, remove the skin then cover with cooked matignon and envelop in hot-water paste; decorate, egg-wash and bake for 1½ hours then pour Madeira in through a hole in the top, close and cook for a further 30 minutes. Serve with Madeira sauce.
Jambon sous Croûte au Xérès	Cook a ham by boiling, remove the skin, allow to cool then envelop in short pastry; decorate, egg-wash and bake. When cooked pour in a little sweet sherry.
Jambon Metternich	Serve slices of ham baked in a pastry case with a garnish of a slice of foie gras with a slice of truffle on top.
Jambon Norfolk	Serve slices of ham baked in a pastry case with a garnish of a slice of braised sweetbread, petits pois paysanne and port wine sauce.
Jambon braisé Port-Maillot	Boil a ham, remove the skin, allow to cool and envelop in short pastry; decorate, egg-wash and bake and serve with a garnish of glazed carrots, onions and turnips, braised lettuce, buttered peas and French beans.
Longe d'Agneau sous la Cendre	Roast a boned and rolled loin for 10 minutes, remove the string and allow to cool; cover with a mixture of duxelles and purée of foie gras, add slices of foie gras and envelop in puff pastry; decorate, egg-wash and bake in the oven.
Pheasant Prince Nicolai	Stiffen the suprêmes of a pheasant in hot butter, coat with liver forcemeat and enclose in puff pastry; egg-wash, decorate and bake in a hot oven.

Poularde Louis d'Orléans	Stuff a chicken with a cooked foie gras studded with truffle, roast it for 20 minutes then cover with slices of truffle and thin slices of back fat; envelop in hot-water pastry, decorate, egg-wash and bake in a moderate oven for $1\frac{1}{2}$ hours.
Suprême de Volaille en Croûte	Place a suprême of chicken, stuffed with duxelles on a square of puff pastry and fold over to seal, brush with egg-wash and bake at 210°C to colour then reduce the temperature to 150°C until cooked. Foie gras, ham, garlic butter, etc., may be used in place of duxelles.
Suprême de Volaille en Enveloppe	Wrap a strip of puff pastry 30cm long by $1\frac{1}{2}$cm wide around a suprême of chicken starting from the tip and proceeding to the bone; decorate, egg-wash, allow to rest for 30 minutes then bake at 200°C until coloured then at 150°C until cooked.
	Foie gras, Gruyère cheese, duxelles, bacon, etc., may be wrapped around the suprême before covering with pastry.
Toad-in-the-Hole	Colour sausages quickly in hot fat, arrange neatly in hot fat in a baking dish and pour Yorkshire pudding batter all over; bake at 220°C for approximately 35 minutes and serve with thickened gravy.
	Other items of meat such as pieces of rump steak, lamb chops with the kidney inside, etc., may be used instead of sausages.
Tournedos Zola	Sauté the tournedos to seal the outside, wrap with anchovy fillets and enclose in brioche pastry; allow to prove then bake in a hot oven. Serve with Madeira sauce.
Venison in Pastry Case	Enclose a whole marinated haunch of venison in any kind of pastry and bake. It is usual to make this pastry with flour and water only and use it to prevent the meat from drying out during the long baking process, rather than for serving with the meat.

261

Baked Meat Dishes

Chump Chop Champvallon	Colour chops in hot fat and sauté some sliced onions until coloured; arrange layers of sliced potato and onions with the chops at the centre until the dish is full, arranging the top layer of potato neatly. Add white stock, brush with butter and bake at 180°C for 1½ hours. a layer of sliced tomato is sometimes added.
Lobscouse (also known as **Scouse**)	Arrange layers of neck and breast of lamb, sliced potato and sliced carrot, onion and turnip in a dish, moisten, cover with ship's biscuits and bake in the oven.
Lancashire Hotpot	Colour chops or pieces of middle neck of lamb in hot fat, arrange in a dish with layers of sliced onion and potato finishing with a neat layer of potato; moisten with white stock, brush with butter and bake covered with a lid at 180°C for 1 hour; remove the lid to colour the potato and serve with pickled red cabbage.
Meat Loaf	Finely mince any kind of raw meat, chicken, ham, etc., mix with chopped onion, soaked and squeezed bread and raw eggs; bake in an oblong loaf tin until firm and serve cut into slices with thickened gravy or brown sauce.
Pain de Veau en Feuilletage	Stiffen diced lean and fat pork and veal in hot butter and make into a forcemeat with soaked bread, and raw eggs; spread on a sheet of puff pastry, cover with a second piece, decorate, egg-wash and bake.
Pasticcia di Lasagne	Arrange layers of cooked lasagne, minced beef cooked as for spaghetti bolognaise, and grated mozzarella cheese, in a buttered pie-dish; sprinkle withh Parmesan and mozzarella and bake for 20 minutes at 350°C.

Terrines and Pâtés

A *terrine* is a pie made without a pastry crust, the filling being covered with bacon or back fat. The name comes from the earthenware dish in which it is cooked. A *pâté* was originally a raised pie, e.g., pâté de foie gras, in which a whole fattened goose liver is baked in a pastry case. These two terms – terrine and pâté – are now interchangeable and there is no real difference between them. Any kind of meat, but particularly liver, can be used but the name given should identify the major constituent. A pâté or terrine of a coarse texture is referred to as a 'country' one, i.e., pâté de campagne, as against one with a smooth texture containing additional cream.

de Canard	Line a dish with thin streaky bacon or back fat, fill with finely minced duck, together with a small proportion of pork and veal with strips of marinated duck and back fat in between; cover and bake at 170°C for 2 hours; decorate with slices of orange.
de Faisan	Mince the flesh of a pheasant with some belly of pork and chicken liver, mix with brandy and red wine, place in a dish and bake uncovered for $1\frac{3}{4}$ hours at 170°C.
de Foie aux Pruneaux	Mince pig's liver, streaky bacon and soaked prunes, add brandy and put into a lined dish; bake at 170°C for $1\frac{3}{4}$ hours.
Pâté Maison (de foie de ...)	Sautéd diced bacon and chopped onion in hot lard, remove and quickly fry chicken or other livers to seal; pass through a mincer or blender with brandy, cream, garlic and spices, pour into a dish lined with streaky bacon rashers, fold over the top, cover and cook au bain-marie at 150°C for 2 hours. When cold cover with melted lard or butter to exclude the air.
Terrine de Gibier	Marinate pieces of venison or game bird in brandy and spices for 12 hours; reserve some strips, mince the remainder with chicken livers and belly of pork, mix with brandy and eggs and pour into a dish lined with back fat, arranging the strips of meat and of back fat in the middle. Cover with back fat and a lid and cook au bain-marie at 150°C for 2 hours.

Tourtes

A tourte is a French version of a pie or tart, made in a medium-size deep round mould or flan ring with a pastry top and bottom enclosing the filling. In some recipes the pie is filled with crumpled paper and baked blind the lid being cut off after, in others the tourte is baked whole from raw. The base can be of short pastry and the top of puff pastry; it can be covered with a lattice work top.

Tourte Bourguignonne	Fill with small balls of veal and pork forcemeat, cover with a lid of the same pastry, score, egg-wash and bake at 180°C for 45 minutes.
Tourte de Foie Gras à l'Ancienne	Spread a lined mould with sausage-meat mixed with foie gras, arrange slices of foie gras and truffle on top and cover with more of the sausage-meat; cover with a pastry lid, egg-wash and bake at 180°C for 45 minutes.
Tourte de Lard et Poireaux	Fill a lined mould with layers of sliced potato, blanched sliced leek and diced streaky bacon; cover with a lid of puff-pastry, egg-wash and bake in a hot oven.
Tourte de Poulet	Fill a lined mould with marinated pieces of boned chicken, chicken livers, button onions, sautéd lardons and a little marinade; cover with a lid of pastry, decorate, egg-wash and bake at 175°C for approximately $1\frac{1}{4}$ hours.

Timbales

The word timbale means a round container and there are many kinds of them ranging from a silver dish with an inner lining to a deep case made of bread, pastry or polenta and for sweet dishes, a sponge cake. In some recipes all the ingredients are cooked from raw while others are a mixture of cooked ingredients reheated in the timbale. Timbales are classified as an entrée.

Ambassadrice	Line a charlotte mould with rounds of ox tongue having a smaller round of truffle in the middle; coat with chicken forcemeat, fill with layers of a

mixture of chicken liver, sliced mushrooms, lambs' sweetbreads and truffle tossed in butter and bound with tomato-flavoured Madeira sauce, and noodles bound with jus lié; cover with more forcemeat and cook au bain-marie. Turn out and serve with Madeira sauce.

d'Amourettes à l'Ecossaise Line a hexagonal shape mould with slices of ox tongue and coat with veal forcemeat; fill with a mixture of ox tongue and spinal marrow bound with sauce allemande; cover with a layer of forcemeat and cook au bain-marie. Serve with sauce écossaise (sauce crème with small dice of carrot, celery, French beans and onion).

d'Amourettes Napolitaine Line dariole moulds with lengths of cooked macaroni, coat with forcemeat and fill with diced spinal marrow and mushroom bound with tomato-flavoured demi-glace; cover with more forcemeat, cook au bain-marie and serve with tomato-flavoured demi-glace.

de Bécasse Nesselrode Line a charlotte mould with short pastry and coat with woodcock and foie-gras forcemeat; press sliced breasts of woodcock into the farce, fill the mould with truffles in espagnole, cover with forcemeat then with a pastry lid; bake in a moderate oven for 45 minutes.

de Bécasse Saint-Martin Fill a cooked timbale case with layers of breasts of roast woodcock, sautéd slices of foie gras and cooked julienne of mushroom and truffle; coat with sauce made from the bones.

Bontoux Decorate a short-pastry timbale with shapes of noodle paste, bake, then fill with layers of cheese and tomato-flavoured macaroni and slices of chicken and truffle sausage, cockscombs and kidneys and slices of truffle, all bound with tomato-flavoured demi-glace.

Bourbonnaise Line a charlotte mould with chicken forcemeat containing chopped ox tongue and set in the oven; fill with sliced white of chicken, cock-scombs and kidneys, mushroom and truffle all bound with thick sauce allemande; cover with forcemeat, cook au bain-marie and serve with mushroom-flavoured velouté.

de Cailles Alexandra Line a mould with short pastry then with slices of back fat; fill with boned quails stuffed with foie gras coloured in butter, truffles and Madeira-flavoured stock; cover with pastry and bake for 1¼ hours.

de Caneton Mirabeau Line a charlotte mould with poached olives stuffed with duck forcemeat, coat with a lining of the same forcemeat and fill with thin slices of roast duck, mushroom and truffle bound with thick sauce salmis; close with a layer of forcemeat and cook au bain-marie.

This recipe can also be used for game birds, sweetbreads, etc.

de Chevreuil Napolitaine Half-fill a short-pastry timbale with cheese and tomato-flavoured macaroni, arrange braised slices of larded venison on top and coat with the cooking sauce.

de Foie gras à l'Alsacienne Line a baked timbale case with gratin forcemeat mixed with foie gras, cook and fill with small slices of foie gras, mushroom and truffle bound with thick Madeira sauce, decorate the top with a large turned mushroom and slices of truffle.

de Foie gras Cambacérés Line a dome-shaped mould with small lengths of cooked macaroni filled with chicken and truffle forcemeat, coat with the same forcemeat and fill with slices of foie gras, truffle and a layer of creamed macaroni mixed with truffle and foie gras; cover with a layer of forcemeat and cook au bain-marie for 45 minutes. Serve with sauce périgueux.

de Foie gras Cussy Coat the inside of a pastry timbale with chicken forcemeat, cook then fill with a circle of sliced foie gras and ox tongue and fill the centre with cocks' kidneys, mushrooms and truffle bound with sauce Madère; garnish with cockscombs and serve with sauce Madère.

de Foie gras et Line a mould with short pastry then with thin

de Cailles Tzarine	slices of back fat, a whole, raw, goose liver, quails filled with truffle, and some whole truffles to fill the mould; cover with back fat then with pastry and bake for $1\frac{1}{4}$ hours.
Maréchal Foch	Place a layer of buttered macaroni finished with tomato-flavoured demi-glace in a silver timbale, sprinkle with cheese and add a layer of sliced truffle cooked in Marsala; arrange fairly thick slices of cooked breast of capon on top, then more sliced truffle, grated cheese, more macaroni and finally another layer of truffle in Marsala; cover with the lid and reheat in an oven.
Milanaise	Bake a short-pastry timbale decorated with shapes of noodle pastry, line with buttered spaghetti flavoured with cheese and tomato, then fill with a mixture of cockscombs and kidneys, mushrooms, stoned olives, quenelles and truffle bound with meat-glaze and tomato; cover with more spaghetti and decorate with slices of truffle.
Milanaise à l'Ancienne	Decorate a charlotte mould with shapes of noodle-paste and line it with short pastry, then with spaghetti mixed with cheese and tomato; fill with a mixture of cockscombs and kidneys, mushrooms, stoned olives, quenelles and truffle bound with meat-glaze and tomato; cover with more spaghetti, then with a round of pastry and bake in a hot oven for 45 minutes. Cut off the top to serve, coat with tomato sauce and decorate with cockscombs, mushrooms and truffle.
de Ris de Veau à la Baloise	Fill a cooked pastry timbale two-thirds full with noodles garnished with julienne of ham; cover with slices of braised sweetbread and finish with some financière garnish in the middle.
de Ris de Veau Condé	Cover the bottom of a baked pastry timbale with sliced mushrooms, add slices of braised sweetbread which have been coated in a dome shape with chicken, mushroom and truffle forcemeat and cooked, and finish with slices of truffle glazed with Madeira sauce.

Boiled, Poached and Steamed Dishes

Although the title boiled beef, boiled chicken, etc., often appears on menus, the method of cooking used is in fact simmering or poaching since to boil meat rapidly causes excessive shrinkage, and can render it tough. It is much more economical to cook protein foods slowly wherever possible, using the cooking liquid to make well-flavoured accompanying sauce, soup or gravy.

Fresh meat is immersed in water at boiling point, brought back to a boil then simmered gently with barely discernible movement of the water. Salted or cured meat is put to cook in cold water as this draws out excess salt from the joint.

Meats

The joints used for boiling include, brisket, gammon, hock, leg of lamb, leg of pork, plate, silverside, thick flank.

Boeuf bouilli à l'Anglaise	Place a piece of salt silverside to poach in cold water, add carrots, button onions and turnips and serve with the cooking liquid; dumplings may also be served and they may be flavoured with mustard, onion, parsley.
à la Berlinoise	Served with boiled carrots, potatoes and turnips accompanied with pickled beetroots, cranberries, gherkins and horseradish.
Boeuf à l'Ecarlate	Poach a joint of salt silverside with a variety of vegetables such as carrots, onions, swede, turnips.
Boeuf bouilli à la Française	Boil a joint of fresh brisket or thin flank with carrots, short lengths of celery, quarters of cabbage, bundles of leeks, button onions and turnips; serve with some of the cooking liquid accompanied by gherkins, French mustard and rock salt.

à la Russe	Coat the poached joint with sour-cream sauce flavoured with horseradish, sprinkle with bread-crumbs and melted butter, and gratinate.
Boiled Gammon	Place in cold water, bring to a boil then simmer gently until cooked; remove the skin, trim the fat and serve with the cooking liquid, parsley or Madeira sauce and if required, pease pudding or purée of spinach. Glazed apricots, peaches or pineapple are often served with boiled gammon and ham.
Boiled Leg of Mutton	Boil in salt water with a flavouring of carrot and studded onion; serve in slices moistened with the cooking liquid and caper sauce made from the stock. Purée of turnip or mixed root vegetables may be served.
Boiled Leg of Pork	Place into hot water and simmer gently until cooked; serve with pease pudding.
Boiled Salt Belly of Pork	Cook with cabbage, carrots, parsnips and turnips and serve cut into slices with purée of yellow split peas and some of the vegetables.
Boiled Salt Silverside and Dumplings	Place in cold water, bring to a boil then simmer gently with carrots, button onions and turnips; serve medium-thick slices with some of the vegetables and boiled dumplings.
Bollito Misto	Serve slices of boiled beef, chicken, smoked sausage, ox tongue and veal knuckle with some of the cooking liquid and sauces gribiche and one made of shallot, carrot, red pimento and tomato.
Collared Beef	Roll a piece of topside or thick flank into a tight round joint, boil, allow to cool and glaze with dark brown jelly.
Derby Round	Cut the middle part of a leg of beef into one large joint, remove the centre bone, tie up and cure in a brine; boil, allow to cool and glaze with dark brown jelly.
Manzo Lesso	Serve slices of boiled beef and cotecchino (smoked sausage) accompanied with sauce gribiche flavoured with garlic.

New England Boiled Dinner	Cook salt brisket of beef with small beetroots, cabbage, carrots, potatoes, swedes and haricot beans and serve with grated horseradish and mustard.
Petite Marmite	Cook a piece of fresh brisket in stock with various turned vegetables as for the clear soup of the same name; serve the meat as a main course.
Pot-au-Feu and Poule-au-Pot	Although these two dishes are known as soups each was originally a substantial meal of various meats and boiling fowl, cooked and served with garden vegetables, but they are now served mainly as soups.
Potée Bretonne	Colour a duck in hot fat then poach in water with belly of pork and boned shoulder of lamb, together with cabbage, leeks, potatoes, turnips, tomatoes and thyme; serve portions of the meats with the vegetables and cooking liquid.
Pot-Royale	Plain boil a fattened chicken, a piece of topside and a piece of gammon with cabbage, carrots, celery, leeks, onions, potatoes and turnips; serve with horseradish cream and some of the cooking liquid.
Sauerbraten	Colour a joint of beef in hot fat, cover with one part vinegar to three parts water, add brown sugar, pickling spices and garlic and keep in the refrigerator for seven days; boil in the pickle and serve in slices with the thickened cooking liquid, finished with sour cream.
Yankee Pot Roast	Colour a joint of fresh beef in hot fat, cover with equal quantities of water and white wine, add tomato purée, onion and garlic and simmer until tender; serve cut into slices covered with the thickened cooking liquid.

For boiled calf's brain, ox tongue, tripe etc. see the Section on Offals.

Poultry

Boiled Chicken Place an old boiling fowl into boiling water,

reboil, skim and add carrot, onion, peppercorns, pot-herbs and salt and simmer gently for
2–3 hours according to size and age of bird. The
flesh is used mainly in made-up dishes such as
vol-au-vent, Chicken à la King, croquettes, etc.

Poularde A very young bird that weighs 2–2½kg prepared
weight, is used in the following formulas; it is
trussed by entering the legs inside the body, or
by removing the bone from the drumstick and
entering the lower leg and trimmed claw into
the cavity, securing it by trussing with string.
The breast may be rubbed with lemon and
protected with thin slices of salt-pork fat, but
this is not always necessary. It is poached in
slightly salted chicken stock.

The following recipes are for Poulardes:

Adelina Patti Stuff with pilaff of rice containing diced foie
gras and truffle and poach in chicken stock;
place on a fried-bread socle, coat with paprika-
flavoured sauce suprême and garnish with small
artichoke bottoms filled with a small truffle.

Albuféra Stuff with pilaff of rice containing diced foie
gras and truffle, poach and serve coated with
sauce albuféra made by flavouring sauce suprême
with meat-glaze and pimento butter; decorate
with slices of truffle, quenelles, mushrooms and
crescents of ox tongue.

Alexandra Poach, then cut off the two breasts and re-form
the bird with chicken forcemeat, coat with sauce
mornay and colour and cook the forcemeat;
serve the bird surrounded with tartlets of asparagus tips with slices of the breast on top and a
thread of meat-glaze over.

Andalouse Coat a poached chicken with sauce suprême
flavoured with pimento butter and garnish with
fried slices of aubergine and braised stuffed
pimentos.

Anglaise Coat a poached chicken with sauce béchamel
flavoured with chicken stock and garnish with

271

	bouquets of small balls of carrot and turnip, round slices of ox tongue, peas and diced celery.
Argenteuil	Coat a poached chicken with sauce suprême finished with purée of asparagus and garnish with bouquets of asparagus tips.
Aurore	Stuff with tomato-flavoured chicken forcemeat, poach and serve coated with velouté flavoured and coloured with tomato purée and butter.
Bouquetière	Coat with mushroom-flavoured sauce suprême and surround with bouquets of small turned carrots and turnips, cauliflower, French beans, asparagus tips, peas and new potatoes.
Cardinalisée	Cut the breasts of a poached chicken into thin slices and replace dome shape in position with layers of truffle and of forcemeat containing foie gras; decorate with egg white, ox tongue and truffle and place in an oven to cook the forcemeat; garnish with bouchées of crayfish, croûtons with a slice of the chicken and truffle on top and serve with sauce suprême flavoured with crayfish butter.
aux Champignons	Coat a poached chicken with mushroom-flavoured sauce allemande and decorate with very white turned mushrooms.
Chancelière	Stud with back fat and truffle, poach, then coat with sauce suprême; decorate with slices of truffle and garnish with truffled forcemeat quenelles.
Chivry	Coat a poached chicken with sauce chivry (reduce white wine with herbs, add velouté and finish with mixed herbs and shallot butter) and serve accompanied with macédoine of vegetables.
Demi-deuil	Arrange slices of truffle beneath the skin over the breast, fill the cavity with forcemeat and poach; coat with sauce suprême and garnish with the stuffing cut into large dice.
Devonshire	Stuff a boned chicken with chicken and pork forcemeat with a cooked calf's tongue in the centre; poach then cut into portions, reform and

	coat with sauce suprême containing diced tongue; garnish with artichoke bottoms filled with purée of peas.
Diva	Stuff a chicken with pilaff of rice containing diced foie gras and truffle; poach, then coat with sauce hongroise and surround with cèpes à la crème.
Dreux	Stud a chicken with ox tongue and truffle, poach then coat with sauce allemande; decorate with slices of truffle and garnish with quenelles, cockscombs and kidneys.
Ecossaise	Stuff a chicken with forcemeat containing diced cooked vegetables and pearl barley; poach, coat with sauce écossaise (cream sauce with brunoise of vegetables) and serve accompanied with buttered French beans.
Edouard VII	Stuff with pilaff of rice containing diced foie gras and truffle; poach, then coat with curry-flavoured sauce suprême containing diced red pimento and serve accompanied with cucumber à la crème.
Elysée Palace	Stud with truffle and fill with forcemeat containing dice of foie gras and truffle; poach and garnish with bouquets of mixed cockscombs, kidneys, mushrooms and quenelles, add some whole truffles and serve with sauce suprême.
English Style	Poach a chicken with a piece of salt belly of pork and serve portions of chicken and slices of pork with parsley sauce and cooking liquid.
Escoffier	Coat a poached chicken with sauce suprême and garnish with morels, button mushrooms, quenelles and slices of truffle.
Estragon	Poach in stock with tarragon stalks; decorate with blanched tarragon leaves and serve with sauce made from the thickened cooking liquid finished with chopped tarragon.
Favorite	Stuff with forcemeat containing diced foie gras and truffle; poach and serve coated with sauce suprême and surrounded with truffles, cockscombs and kidneys.

Fédora	Coat a poached chicken with crayfish-flavoured sauce suprême and garnish with bouquets of asparagus tips.
Grammont	Cut off the breasts of a poached chicken and re-form the bird with a salpicon of cockscombs and kidneys, lark breasts and mushrooms mixed with truffle-flavoured béchamel; cover with the sliced breasts, coat with sauce suprême, sprinkle with cheese and gratinate.
Grimod de la Reynière	Stuff with a mixture of chopped chicken liver, mushroom, bone marrow and truffle, truss and cover with 5mm slices of bread and ham. Wrap and tie in greaseproof paper, poach and serve with slices of the stuffing, ham, and a sauce made from the cooking liquid.
Gros Sel	Poach a chicken with turned carrots and turnips and serve surrounded with the vegetables and accompanied with some of the cooking liquid; serve a dish of coarse freezing salt separately.
Héloïse	Cut off the breasts of a poached chicken and re-form with truffled forcemeat and slices of the breast; decorate with cooked egg white and cook gently in the oven; serve coated with sauce allemande.
Hindle Wakes	Stuff a chicken with chopped soaked prunes mixed with breadcrumbs and chopped onion; poach and serve coated with some of the stock thickened with a roux and flavoured with lemon juice, and some of the stuffing.
Impératrice	Serve a poached chicken surrounded with white braised sweetbread, bouquets of button onions and diced calf brain, coated with sauce suprême.
Indienne	Coat a poached chicken with curry sauce and serve with boiled rice.
Infante	Coat a poached chicken with mushroom-flavoured sauce suprême and garnish with grilled tomatoes.
Isabelle de France	Stuff with risotto containing crayfish and truffle and poach in stock and white wine; serve coated

with sauce suprême and garnish with whole truffles placed on small round bread croûtons.

Ivoire Serve a poached chicken with a sauceboat each of the cooking liquid and sauce ivoire (sauce suprême finished with meat-glaze) and a garnish of buttered pasta.

Lady Curzon Stuff a chicken with pilaff of rice containing diced foie gras and truffle, poach, then coat with curry-flavoured sauce suprême and garnish with cucumbers à la crème.

Mancini Remove the breasts from a poached chicken and fill the carcase with creamed macaroni mixed with diced foie gras and julienne of truffle; cover with the sliced breast and slices of truffle and coat with creamed tomato sauce.

Maréchal Stuff with mushrooms, calf's brain and sweetbreads bound with velouté; poach, then coat with sauce suprême and garnish with bouquets of cockscombs and kidneys, quenelles and truffle.

Marie-Louise Stuff with pilaff of rice containing mushroom and truffle mixed with sauce soubise; poach, coat with sauce allemande and garnish with artichoke bottoms filled with duxelles and with braised lettuces.

Ménagère Serve in a casserole with sliced carrot, onion and potato cooked in some of the cooking liquid from the chicken.

Metropole Coat with sauce suprême and garnish with button onions, mushrooms, artichoke bottoms cut into pieces, and heart-shaped croûtons.

Montbazon Stud with truffle, poach, then coat with sauce suprême and garnish with bouquets of lamb's sweetbreads, mushrooms and quenelles.

Monte Carlo Coat one side of a poached chicken with sauce suprême and the other with sauce aurore and garnish with pink quenelles and white quenelles.

Nantua Coat with crayfish-flavoured sauce suprême, decorate with truffle and garnish with crayfish and quenelles of crayfish.

Normande   Coat with sauce suprême and garnish with bouquets of carrot, leek, potato and turnip.

aux Nouilles Stuff with cheese-flavoured creamed noodles, dice of truffle and foie gras and poach; coat with sauce mornay and glaze.

Orientale   Stuff with saffroned rice, poach, then slice and remove the breasts, coat the carcase with tomato and saffron-flavoured béchamel and replace the sliced breasts; garnish with buttered pieces of chayote (member of the marrow family, also called chow chow).

Orloff   Coat with sauce soubise, decorate with slices of truffle and garnish with braised lettuce.

Parisienne   Coat the poached chicken with sauce allemande, decorate with crescents of ox tongue and truffle and garnish with quenelles containing chopped ham and others containing truffle.

Parsifal   Stuff with truffled forcemeat and poach; coat with sauce suprême flavoured with purée of chicken liver and garnish with artichoke bottoms filled with purée of green peas and moulds of risotto containing diced mushroom and tomato.

Paysanne   Coat the poached chicken with sauce suprême containing cooked paysanne of carrot, celery and onion, diamonds of French beans and peas.

Petite-Mariée Poach with small carrots, button onions, new potatoes and peas and serve in a casserole covered with some of the reduced cooking liquid thickened with velouté.

Polignac   Remove the breasts of a poached chicken and fill the carcase with forcemeat containing julienne of mushroom and truffle; cover with the slices of breast and slices of truffle and cook in the oven; coat with sauce suprême finished with mushroom purée and containing julienne of mushroom and truffle.

Princesse   Coat with asparagus-flavoured sauce allemande and garnish with duchesse potato nests filled with asparagus tips and a slice of truffle on top, quenelles and bouquets of asparagus tips.

Princesse Hélène	Stuff with pilaff of rice mixed with diced foie gras and truffle; poach, coat with sauce suprême, garnish with subrics of spinach and serve accompanied with a dish of warmed, grated white truffle.
Régence	Stuff with crayfish-flavoured chicken forcemeat, poach and coat with truffle-flavoured sauce suprême; garnish with bouquets of cockscombs, sliced foie gras, mushrooms, truffled quenelles and truffles.
Reine	Coat the poached chicken with sauce suprême and garnish with poached darioles of purée of chicken with a slice of truffle on top.
Reine-Blanche	Stuff with chicken forcemeat containing dice of ox tongue and truffle, coat with sauce allemande and garnish with cockscombs and kidneys, mushrooms and sliced truffle.
Reine-Marguerite	Cut the breasts of a poached chicken into small thin slices and add to cheese soufflé mixture together with slices of truffle; re-form the chicken with the soufflé mixture, cover with slices of gruyère cheese and cook as a soufflé; serve with sauce suprême containing sliced white truffle.
Renaissance	Coat the chicken with mushroom-flavoured sauce allemande and garnish with bouquets of carrots, French beans, cauliflower, new potatoes, peas and asparagus.
au Riz	Serve coated with sauce allemande and surrounded with darioles of riz pilaff.
Saxonne	Coat the poached chicken with crayfish-flavoured sauce suprême and garnish with crayfish and small balls of cauliflower gratinated with sauce mornay.
Sicilienne	Cut the breasts off a poached chicken and re-form with mixed macaroni, cockscombs and kidneys, dice of foie gras and truffle, all mixed with jus lié; cover with a piece of caul, sprinkle with breadcrumbs and butter and colour in the oven; serve garnished with tartlets of slices of the chicken breast and of foie gras and truffle; brush the chicken with buttered meat-glaze.

Soufflée   Cut the breasts off a poached chicken and re-form with layers of forcemeat, the sliced breasts and truffle; decorate with shapes of cooked egg-white, ox tongue and truffle and cook in the oven; serve with truffle-flavoured sauce allemande.

Stanley   Stuff with pilaff of rice containing julienne of mushroom and truffle, poach in white stock flavoured with onion and curry powder then sieve the onion and make it and the cooking liquid into a sauce, finishing it with cream; pour over the chicken.

Toscane   Stuff with cooked noodles mixed with dice of foie gras and truffle, poach, then coat with sauce hongroise (velouté flavoured with sautéd onion and paprika) and serve with buttered cèpes.

Toulousaine   Coat a poached chicken with sauce allemande and garnish with slices of sweetbread, cockscombs and kidneys, mushrooms, quenelles and slices of truffle; serve mushroom-flavoured sauce allemande separately.

Vénitienne   Coat a poached chicken with sauce suprême flavoured with herb butter, and garnish with slices of calf's brain; cockscombs and mushrooms.

Vert-Pré   Coat a poached chicken with sauce suprême flavoured with vegetable butter and garnish with bouquets of asparagus tips, French beans and peas.

en Vessie   Insert the prepared poularde in a pig's bladder and seal the end; poach in boiling chicken stock and serve in the bladder accompanied with plain boiled vegetables and some of the cooking liquid.

Vichy   Coat with sauce suprême coloured and flavoured with carrot purée and garnish with tartlets filled with carrots Vichy.

Vierge   Coat with chicken-flavoured béchamel and garnish with slices of calf's brain and sweetbreads and cockscombs.

278

Villars	Coat with mushroom-flavoured sauce allemande and garnish with cockscombs, mushrooms and sweetbreads and decorate with cockscomb-shaped slices of ox tongue.
Wladimir	Coat with a sauce made of sauces suprême and béarnaise with julienne of carrot, celery and truffle in it.

Turkey

Turkey is sometimes cooked by poaching, often with a piece of salt belly of pork which is sliced and served with the turkey; slices of ham or salt ox tongue, plain-boiled vegetables and parsley or plain white sauce are the usual accompaniments.

Daubes

A *daube* is actually a stew cooked by poaching but is done in a closed earthenware container (daubière) in an oven.

Lard slices of beef, marinate in red wine with chopped shallot then colour in hot fat; place in the container, add the marinade, seal and cook gently for several hours. Serve as it is.

Daube Avignonnaise	Marinate larded cubes of mutton in red wine and oil, place in a daubière with layers of bacon and sliced onion, moisten with the marinade and brown stock, seal well and cook in a moderate oven for 5 hours.
Daube à la Provençale	Marinate larded cubes of beef in white wine, oil and brandy for 12 hours, place in a daubière with small squares of salt-pork rind, blanched cubes of salt belly of pork, sliced carrot, mushroom and onions, chopped tomato, garlic, black olives, dried orange peel and the marinade. Seal well and cook in a moderate oven for 6 hours.

── STEAMED MEAT DISHES ──

Steaming is the alternative to boiling and poaching and most items normally cooked by immersing in water can be cooked by steaming under pressure. What is missed is the cooking liquid for making the accompanying sauce or gravy.

Suet pastry is used for making savoury steamed puddings and dumplings.

Steak and Kidney Pudding	Mix two parts diced chuck of beef with one part diced ox kidney, chopped onion and parsley, brown stock and a few drops of Worcester sauce; place in a pudding basin lined with suet pastry, cover with a lid of the same paste, tie with a cloth and steam for several hours.
Steak, Kidney and Mushroom Pudding	Add quartered or sliced mushrooms to the meat, and cook as for steak and kidney pudding.
Steak, Kidney and Oyster Pudding	Add fresh or canned oysters to the meat, and cook as for steak and kidney pudding.
Norfolk Dumpling or Roll	Roll out suet pastry, sprinkle with minced streaky bacon and mixed herbs, roll up and steam; it may be made round and boiled tied in a floured pudding-cloth. Variations include minced beef or pork.

Braised Meats

This method of cookery is used to make tougher cuts of meat, poultry and game tender by long slow cooking, half-submerged in a liquid in a tightly enclosed utensil. The cooking liquid is made into the accompanying sauce.

If the meat is very lean it is usual to insert strips of salt-pork fat into the joint and to marinate it in red wine with herbs and vegetables for 12 hours before cooking. If the joint is to be on display it should be glazed by frequent basting during the last part of the cooking period so that it takes on a high gloss.

The practice of inserting small thin strips of salt-pork fat, truffle, carrot, etc., known as larding, is time-consuming yet does not contribute much to the looks or taste of the finished dish when sliced. It is therefore an optional procedure.

Beef

Pièce de Boeuf Braisé	Colour a joint cut from the chuck or thick flank, in hot fat, place in a braising pan on a layer of fried sliced carrot and onion, moisten with espagnole and brown stock to come two-thirds of the way up and cook at 180°C until tender. Serve cut into 3mm slices and coat with the strained and thickened cooking liquid. Suitable garnishes include pasta, pilaff of rice, and turned vegetables, or it can be served in the following ways:
Boeuf Braisé Bourguignonne	Braise a larded and marinated joint and serve with a garnish of glazed button onions, fried lardons and button mushrooms added to the sauce made from the cooking liquid.
Bordelaise	Braise in brown stock and red wine, coat with the thickened cooking liquid and garnish with sauted cèpes.
Brillat-Savarin	Lard the joint with strips of truffle, braise and serve with braised small onions stuffed with sausage-meat and braised lamb sweetbreads.
Bulow	Serve with a garnish of nests of pommes duchesse filled with spinach purée and with turnip purée, allowing one of each per portion.
Flamande	Serve garnished with small braised cabbages, turned carrots and turnips, new potatoes and the thickened cooking liquid.
Grecque	Braise with added tomato purée and serve garnished with moulds of pilaff of rice containing shredded lettuce, peas, dice of red pimento and

very small balls of sausage-meat; coat with the thickened gravy.

Italienne   Lard the joint with strips of back fat and fillets of anchovy, braise with red wine and tomato purée and serve with buttered macaroni; coat with the reduced thickened cooking liquid.

Limousine   Braise with added madeira and tomato and serve coated with the thickened cooking liquid.

London House Open a whole fillet, fill with slices of foie gras and truffle, close and stud with truffle; braise with Madeira and jus lié and serve garnished with mushrooms and truffle and the reduced cooking liquid.

Lorraine   Braise with added white wine and serve garnished with small stuffed cabbages, triangles of bacon and glazed turnips.

Lyonnaise   Braise with sliced onions, white wine and vinegar and serve with bouquets of sauté sliced onion and the strained reduced gravy.

à la Mode   Braise a previously larded and marinated joint in red wine and stock with the addition of calfs' feet; serve garnished with glazed carrots, button onions, and the calfs' feet boned and cut into dice. This may also be served as a cold dish.

Nivernaise   Serve cut into fairly thick slices, coat with the reduced cooking liquid and garnish with glazed carrots and button onions.

Noailles   Braise a larded and marinated joint adding sliced onion and rice, making these into a soubise; spread over the joint, sprinkle with fried breadcrumbs and gratinate.

Parisienne   Lard with strips of ox tongue and truffle, braise and serve garnished with artichoke bottoms filled with salpicon of mushroom, tongue and truffle mixed with velouté, and with pommes Parisienne (sauté small balls of potato rolled in meat-glaze).

Provençale   Braise with added garlic and tomato and serve coated with the sauce and garnished with mushrooms stuffed with duxelles, and cooked small tomatoes.

282

Providence   Serve fairly thick slices coated with the resultant sauce with a garnish of glazed carrots, bouquets of cauliflower covered with sauce hollandaise, and French beans.

Primeurs   Serve fairly thick slices coated with the thickened cooking liquid; garnish with bouquets of spring vegetables including carrots, turnips, peas and French beans.

Braised steak   Shallow fry 120g slices cut from the chuck or thick flank until brown, add a fried mirepoix, dust with flour and singe; add tomato purée and brown stock and braise at 180°C for 1 hour – do not overcook. Strain the cooking liquid and serve with noodles, pilaff of rice, mixed vegetables, etc. This dish is often termed Stewed Steaks.

Lamb and Mutton

The leg, shoulder and saddle can be braised and served as in the following formulas:

Australienne   Stuff a boned leg with pork sausage-meat mixed with cooked chopped onion and gherkin; braise and serve with the thickened cooking liquid.

Bonne Femme   Stuff a boned leg with pork sausage-meat; braise and serve garnished with haricot beans, carrots and sauté onion.

Bordelaise   Lard with ham, braise in red wine and serve with lardons of bacon, turned carrots and turnips and the thickened cooking liquid.

Dubouzet   Lard with back fat and ox tongue; braise and serve with small potato gnocchis filled with a little sausage-meat.

Espagnole   Braise with added tomato and garlic and serve garnished with French-fried onions, pimentos filled with pilaff of rice and cooked tomatoes.

Fermière   Braise and serve with sliced carrot and turnip, button onions and new potatoes.

Polonaise	Serve fairly thick slices of the braised lamb coated with the reduced cooking liquid and a garnish of round pieces of cucumber stuffed with sausage-meat and braised.
Windsor	Stuff a boned leg with forcemeat containing duxelles; braise and serve with slices of braised ox tongue and coat with the reduced cooking liquid.

Pork and Ham

This is so tender that it is unusual to braise any of the cuts of pork but fresh leg of pork is sometimes braised allowing 45 minutes for 1kg meat; it may be served with a purée of fresh or pulse vegetable, a pasta, etc. Although termed a braising joint, a cured leg of pork or ham, usually needs to be boiled before being finished by braising.

Jambon Braisé (Braised Ham)	Boil a gammon or a ham until nearly done, skin, trim then coat with brown sugar; cut a shallow trellis pattern and insert a clove at the point of each triangle; cook in the oven, basting with the melting fat and sugar until nicely caramelised. Serve with demi-glace. Suitable garnishes include broad beans, braised lettuces, noodles or other pasta, purée of spinach, pease pudding, gnocchi, etc., or it can be served as follows:
Jambon au Madère	Place the almost cooked and trimmed ham into a braising pan, add Madeira, cover with a close-fitting lid and braise for approximately 1 hour; serve with the cooking juices added to some demi-glace.
	If to be carved in the room the ham should be glazed by repeated basting under a salamander.
Jambon à la Bayonnaise	Serve the braised ham with a garnish of chipolatas, mushrooms, and risotto with diced tomato.
Bourguignonne	Braise in white wine and serve with sliced mushrooms in the reduced cooking liquid.
Chanoinesse	Braise in white wine and serve with buttered noodles finished with a little sauce soubise and julienne of truffle.

au Choucroute	Serve slices of braised ham with a garnish of plainly braised sauerkraut and boiled potatoes; coat with demi-glace finished with Alsace wine.
Comtesse	Stud with pieces of truffle, braise in Madeira and serve with braised lettuce and quenelles; coat with sauce madère made from the cooking liquid.
aux Epinards	Serve slices of braised ham coated with the reduced cooking liquid and garnish with buttered leaf or purée of spinach.
Fitz-James	Braise in Madeira and serve surrounded with stuffed mushrooms and moulds of risotto containing diced tomato; accompany with sauce Madère made with the cooking liquid and containing small cockscombs and kidneys.
Flamande	Serve with a garnish of small squares of boiled bacon, small balls of cabbage, turned carrots, slices of cooked garlic sausage, turned turnips and Madeira sauce.
Godard	Braise in Madeira and serve with a garnish of cockscombs, glazed sweetbreads, quenelles made of chicken with chopped mushroom and truffle in them, and truffles (This dish is also known as Jambon Financière).
Limousine	Serve with purée of chestnuts and the reduced cooking liquid added to demi-glace.
Milanaise	Serve with buttered spaghetti containing julienne of ham, mushroom and ox-tongue, mixed with cheese and tomato sauce.
Monselet	Braise in sherry and serve garnished with subrics of spinach containing diced tongue, and sauce madère made with the cooking liquid, and slices of truffle.
aux Pêches	Serve with glazed halves of peaches and sauce madère. Other fruits such as slices of pineapple, apricots, apple are also suitable as a garnish with braised ham.

Veal

Good quality veal is so tender that it does not really require to be braised; on the other hand, it can become dry by being roasted so the cushion, saddle and shoulder as well as the breast and small cuts such as grenadins and tendrons are best cooked by the white method of braising which is done by frequent moistening with white veal stock to cause a glaze, then the addition of more stock to come half-way up. It is then braised until tender.

Noix de Veau Braisé	Lightly colour the cushion and some sliced vegetables in hot butter, place the joint on the vegetables in a braising pan and add a little white stock; reduce it on top of the stove to a glaze, repeat this then moisten halfway with more stock, cover and braise; make the sauce from the cooking liquid. Among the large number of suitable garnishes are Bouquetière, Clamart, Financière, Jardinière, Milanaise, Piémontaise, Trianon and Viroflay.
Selle de Veau Braisée	Many of the following formulas are also suitable for other braised joints of veal. Some of these indicate a boned and tied saddle.
Agnes Sorel	Lard with tongue and truffle, braise and garnish with tartlets filled with duxelles and a round of ox tongue and of truffle on top; serve with the reduced cooking liquid.
Alsacienne	Braise a forcemeat-stuffed joint and also some sauerkraut and serve with the meat arranged overlapping on it and sauced with the reduced cooking liquid; slices of carrot, smoked sausage and squares of salt belly of pork, cooked with the sauerkraut, may be served as part of the garnish.
Bourgeoise	Stuff with pork forcemeat mixed with duxelles, braise and finish cooking with turned carrots, button onions and fried lardons of bacon; thicken the cooking liquid with espagnole.
Briarde	Lard with strips of speck, braise and garnish with braised stuffed lettuces and creamed carrots.

Chartreuse   Garnish the braised joint with moulds made by lining dariole moulds with a pattern of rings of carrot and turnip, beans and peas, kept in place with a coating of forcemeat, the centre filled with creamed macédoine then cooked au bain-marie.

Chatham   Lard, braise and serve with piles of buttered noodles each with a round of ox-tongue on top and serve with sauce soubise containing sliced mushrooms.

Citoyen   Braise until nearly done then add turned carrots, button onions and fried lardons and cook until tender; serve coated with the cooking liquid added to demi-glace and garnish with the vegetables.

Courlandaise   Stuff with soaked stoned prunes; braise and serve with the reduced cooking liquid, mashed potato and braised onions.

Dreux   Lard with strips of ham, ox-tongue and truffle, wrap in back fat and braise; serve with a garnish of cockscombs and kidneys, mushrooms, stoned olives and truffle and sauce madère finished with truffle essence.

Farcie   Stuff with chopped veal kidney and the surrounding fat mixed with breadcrumbs and eggs; braise and serve with slices of boiled ham and the thickened cooking liquid.

Gourmet   Lard with ox-tongue and truffle, braise with added Madeira and serve garnished with button onions, fried slices of potato, turned turnips and cooked tomatoes.

Lausannoise   Braise and garnish with tartlets of goose liver purée and with pommes macaire containing fines herbes.

Lison   Braise and serve garnished with glazed oval shapes of pommes duchesse containing chopped ox-tongue and darioles of chopped cooked lettuce mixed with béchamel and yolks and cooked au bain-marie.

Macédoine   Cut out the centre of a braised boned saddle to the shape of an empty box, fill with layers of buttered macédoine of vegetables and the slices of veal arranged overlapping, finishing with the meat.

Matignon Braise until half-cooked then cover with a thick layer of matignon (paysanne of carrot, celery, ham and onion stewed in butter and white wine); envelop in caul and continue to braise; serve as it is with the reduced cooking liquid.

Metternich Cut the two sides of a braised saddle into slices, spread the bones with paprika-flavoured béchamel and replace the slices in position spreading them with the same sauce and inserting slices of truffle; coat with the same sauce, glaze and serve with the reduced cooking liquid and pilaff of rice.

Milanaise Braise a larded joint and serve with spaghetti mixed with cheese and tomato sauce.

Nelson Cut the two sides of a braised saddle into slices and replace in position, spread with sauce soubise (béchamel with onion purée) inserting slices of ham; cover with cheese soufflé mixture held in place with a band of paper and cook. Serve with the reduced cooking liquid.

Nemours Lard and braise; serve with bouquets of carrots Vichy, peas and small balls of potato.

Nivernaise Serve with turned glazed carrots, glazed button onions and the reduced cooking liquid.

Orientale Cut the two central pieces of a braised saddle into slices and replace on the carcase, coated with curry-flavoured béchamel with some of it between the slices; coat the whole with tomato-flavoured béchamel, glaze and serve with the thickened cooking liquid and pilaff of rice.

Orloff Cut the two central pieces of a braised saddle into slices and replace in position with sauce soubise and slices of truffle; coat the whole with onion-flavoured sauce mornay, glaze and serve with the thickened cooking liquid and cucumbers cooked à la crème.

Piémontaise	Serve accompanied with risotto containing grated white truffle.
Renaissance	Serve the braised joint with bouquets of asparagus, beans, carrots, cauliflower, peas and turnips with sauce hollandaise on the cauliflower.
Romanoff	Cut the two central pieces of a braised saddle into slices and replace in position with finely sliced cèpes mixed with sauce crème; coat with béchamel finished with crayfish butter and garnish with braised fennel.
Soubise	Braise in white stock until two-thirds cooked, add sliced onions and rice and finish to cook; pass the cooking liquid through a sieve and serve as the accompanying sauce.
Surprise	Hollow out a braised boned joint to form a box with a lid; fill with a pasta or vegetable garnish, replace the lid, reheat and serve with the reduced cooking liquid and the slices of meat.
Talleyrand	Stud with truffle, braise and serve with buttered spaghetti mixed with cheese, diced foie gras and julienne of truffle.
Tosca	Cut the two central pieces of a braised saddle into slices and replace on a layer of creamed spaghetti and truffle, coating each slice with sauce soubise and inserting a slice of truffle; coat all over with sauce soubise and glaze.
Turque	Serve a braised joint with emptied cooked egg-plants filled with braised rice mixed with the flesh of the egg-plant; coat with sauce mornay and glaze.
Fricandeau	This is a large slice of veal, cut 4cm thick, larded, braised until well-cooked and served with any of the garnishes given for braised joints of veal.
Grenadin	This is a veal steak cut 4cm thick and weighing 150–180g. Flatten slightly, lard with strips of back fat and braise as for all cuts of veal, basting frequently. Grenadins may be garnished with any of the formulas given for braised joints of veal.

Tendron This is a portion piece cut from the breast of veal, parallel to the bones, free from skin and sinew. It is braised and served with any of the garnishes used for braised joints of veal.

Braised Poultry

Poultry includes chickens of all sizes, turkey, duck, goose, guinea-fowl and pigeons, most of which are tender by nature and therefore do not lend themselves to braising. Any of the garnishes given for poêléd meats are suitable for braised poultry.

To braise poultry, colour the bird all over in hot fat in a frying pan, place in a braising pan and cover half way up with equal quantities of brown stock and demi-glace; cover and braise at 175°C. When cooked, make the liquid into the accompanying sauce.

Braised Duckling and Goose

Chipolata Garnish a braised duckling with glazed turned carrots, grilled chipolata sausages, cooked chestnuts and fried lardons of bacon, allowing these to cook for a time with the duck.

Choucroute Serve a braised duckling surrounded with braised sauerkraut and triangles of bacon cooked with the sauerkraut; coat with the thickened cooking liquid.

Fermière Serve with sliced carrot, celeriac, onion and turnip, peas, and diamonds of beans added to the reduced cooking liquid.

Flamande Serve garnished with triangles of streaky bacon, braised small cabbages, glazed turned carrots and turnips and slices of garlic sausage.

Lyonnaise Serve garnished with glazed button onions and cooked chestnuts.

aux Navets Serve with turned pieces of turnip and glazed button onions cooked with the duck in half espagnole and half brown stock.

Nivernaise Serve with glazed turned carrots and button onions added to the cooking liquid to finish cooking; serve coated with the reduced cooking liquid.

aux Olives
When the duckling is almost cooked, add blanched stoned olives and serve surrounded with them and the reduced cooking liquid.

Orange
When the duckling is braised, add orange and lemon juice to the cooking liquid and reduce, add blanched julienne of orange and lemon rind and pour over the duckling; it may be garnished with orange segments.

aux Pêches
Stew skinned halves of peaches in brandy, water, lemon juice and sugar, add this liquid to caramelised sugar in vinegar and demi-glace to make the sauce; garnish the braised duck with the peaches and pour the sauce around. Pears, may also be used as a garnish with duck.

au Raifort
Serve the braised duck surrounded with buttered noodles or pilaff of rice accompanied by hot creamed horseradish sauce.

Turkey

Bourgeoise
Add turned carrots, button onions and fried lardons to the turkey when three-quarters done; finish to cook and serve with the thickened cooking liquid.

Financière
Serve a braised turkey with cockscombs and kidneys, mushrooms, olives, quenelles and truffle in the Madeira-flavoured reduced cooking liquid.

Godard
Serve with a garnish of cockscombs, mushrooms, decorated quenelles, braised lamb sweetbreads and truffle.

Pigeons and *guinea-fowl* may be cooked by braising, especially if they are old ones, and the formulas and garnishes are as for other braised meats.

Deep-fried Dishes

This method of cookery is carried out at a very high temperature which makes it necessary to add a protective coating of batter or breadcrumbs to most foods to prevent them from becoming dry. Drain fried foods on absorbent paper and serve uncovered with fried or picked parsley and the appropriate sauce. Garnishes are hardly necessary, indeed, the number of main dishes cooked by deep frying is very limited and most of them will be found in Sections on made-up dishes in this chapter.

Suprêmes of Chicken

A suprême is the whole breast of a chicken as cut from one side of a 1–1¼kg bird; each chicken yields 2 suprêmes. The fillet attached to the breast may be left in place or flattened and de-nerved and inserted inside a pocket cut into the thick part of the suprême. If the suprême has been cut from a larger chicken the fillet can be removed and used for other dishes; the optimum weight of a suprême is 120g. It is usual practice to leave a small piece of wingbone attached and to put a cutlet frill on it prior to serving but not if the suprême is to be covered with sauce.

Cumberland	Dip in frying batter and deep fry; serve accompanied with Cumberland sauce (cold sauce of redcurrant jelly, port, blanched chopped shallot, mustard and ginger with blanched shredded rind and juice of lemon and orange).
Jeanne d'Arc	Dip into frying batter, deep fry and serve with pommes noisettes and Madeira sauce.
Henriot	Sauté to seal, dip into sauce Villeroy and allow to set; pané à l'anglaise, deep fry and serve with creamed mushrooms.
Kiev	Flatten the suprême, cut a pocket in the thickest part and insert a baton of very cold butter; roll up to enclose, egg-and-crumb twice then deep fry for approximately 5 minutes. (May be served on a fried oval bread croûton).

Maryland	Coat with egg and crumbs, deep fry and serve with a grilled rasher of bacon, sweetcorn fritter, fried half of banana, a small grilled tomato and horseradish sauce (this dish is more usually shallow-fried).
Orly	Marinate the suprême in oil, lemon juice, chopped parsley and shallot for 30 minutes then dip into flour, then into yeast batter and deep fry; serve with tomato sauce.
Savoy	Garnish a deep-fried suprême with asparagus tips and serve with tomato sauce.
Southern Fried	Season pieces of chicken with herbs, various spices and salts; egg and crumb and deep fry preferably in a pressure fryer (this is often served 'in the basket' and eaten with the fingers).
Viennoise	Coat with flour, egg-wash and breadcrumbs, deep or shallow fry and garnish with lemon slices.
Villeroy	Parcook the suprême in a little butter and lemon juice, dip into hot sauce Villeroy and allow to cool; pass through flour, egg-wash and bread-crumbs and deep fry.
Chicken Drumsticks	Small ones may be coated with egg and crumb or with batter or flour only, and deep-fried for serving at a cocktail party or finger buffet.
Fritots	Marinate slices of raw or poached chicken, turkey, veal, etc., in lemon juice, olive oil and herbs for 30 minutes; dip in frying batter, deep fry and serve with tomato sauce.
Fritto Misto	Marinate small pieces of various meat, poultry, offal and parboiled small sprigs of vegetables; dip into batter and deep fry.

Grilled Meats

The correct way to grill is on the bars of an underfired charcoal or gas grill; the cooking of meats on a tray in an oven or directly on the surface of a solid top stove is not true grilling. A salamander has its source of heat at the top but is suitable for cooking grilled foods. The degrees of done-ness of grills are:

1 Very underdone (bleu) where the meat is well-seared on the outside but barely started to cook inside;
2 Underdone (saignant): the meat is soft to the touch because still fairly raw and pink at the centre;
3 Just cooked (à point): the meat is cooked all through but not so thoroughly cooked as to have lost all its soft nature;
4 Well done (bien cuit): the outside is well seared but not burnt and the meat inside has no trace of bloodiness left in it.

To grill, brush the meat with oil, season with salt and place onto the hot greased grill bars; cook to obtain the trellis pattern and the required degree of done-ness and colour. All grills are served with watercress, and cutlets with a paper cutlet frill (it is incorrect to use mustard and cress in place of watercress).

Some customers ask for their steak to be grilled without seasoning and oil. It is customary to serve a grilled piece of fat with beef steaks.

In some recipes, especially those for chicken, the meat is covered with breadcrumbs and grilled under a salamander; made mustard may be brushed on beforehand, to provide a devilled result. (It is advisable to finish to cook these items in an oven.)

The hot bars of a proper grill will cause a coloured pattern to form and it is necessary to change the position of the meat so as to create a trellis pattern on both sides. During the process it may be necessary to move the meats around and raise the bars to a higher position so as to achieve the desired degree of done-ness. A thin steak needs a short time on a very hot grill whereas a thick one required a less intense heat.

Because grilling is a fairly fierce method of cooking it means that only good-quality well-hung meat can be used if the result if to be tender. The following are the most suitable cuts in general use:

Beef	Chateaubriand, fillet steak, point steak, porterhouse steak; rump-steak, sirloin steak, (entrecôte), tournedos, minute steak.
Lamb and Mutton	Chop, chump chop, crown chop, cutlet, leg steak, noisette, roulade.
Pork	Chop, gammon.

Poultry	Leg of chicken, poussin, spatchcocked chicken.
Veal	Chop.

(See Checklist of Commodities for descriptions of these cuts.)

Others	Kebabs and brochettes of beef, lamb, bacon, etc; (grilled offals are dealt with in the Section on Offals in this chapter) marinated square pieces of meat, onion, bay-leaves, sometimes bacon and chipolatas, threaded on a skewer, grilled and served on a bed of pilaff of rice. Spiedino Romano is a kebab of bread and various cheeses.
Mixed Grill	Lamb cutlet and kidney, chipolata, bacon, tomato and open mushroom, grilled and garnished with straw potatoes, watercress and a slice of parsley butter.
Bones	Meaty rib bones left from a roast joint can be served grilled.

The garnishes for grilled foods are plain and simple ones that complement the straightforward method of cookery; many of the flavoured hard butters are suitable and the only appropriate sauces are béarnaise or diable.

Garnish name	Ingredients of garnish	Appropriate meats
Américaine	Grilled rasher of streaky bacon, open mushroom, straw potatoes and grilled tomato	Chicken
Anglaise	Grilled rasher of streaky bacon, pommes frites (chips) and parsley butter	Chicken, steak, etc.
Béarnaise	Pipe with sauce béarnaise, small pommes château	Entrecôte
Beaufremont	Serve on a bed of creamed spaghetti with tomato sauce handed separately	Filet Mignon
Bercy	Slices of beurre bercy (reduction of shallot and wine, diced bone marrow added to butter)	Entrecôte

Garnish name	Ingredients of garnish	Appropriate meats
continued		
Carpetbag Steak	Cut a pocket in a double thickness entrecôte, insert fresh oysters and sew up using strips of salt-pork fat; grill and serve with any of the appropriate garnishes in this list	Entrecôte
Charcutière	Sauce charcutière, mashed potato	Pork chop, gammon
Chartres	Decorate with blanched tarragon, small pommes château	Tournedos
Continentale	Grilled open mushroom and tomato, pommes soufflées	Lamb chop and cutlet
Danitcheff	Pipe with sauce béarnaise and add a line of caviar, peas and croquette potatoes	Entrecôte
Diablé	Spread with mustard and sprinkle with breadcrumbs; serve with sauce diable	Chicken
Foyot	Straw potatoes, watercress, sauceboat of sauce foyot (béarnaise with meat-glaze)	Entrecôte
Francillon	Serve on bread croûton, straw potatoes, anchovy-flavoured tomato sauce	Lamb chop and cutlet
Garni	Indefinite term used in place of any of those listed in this section	
Gourmet	Pommes Anna, sauce chateaubriand, gherkins	Poussin
Hauser	French-fried onion rings, straw potatoes, slices of beurre colbert (meat glaze and parsley mixed with butter)	Tournedos
Henri IV	Pommes pont-neuf, watercress	Chateaubriand fillet steak, tournedos, minute steak

Jetée-Prom-enade	Grilled half of tomato filled with sauce béarnaise, pommes soufflées	Steak, chicken
London House or Londo-nienne	Grilled rasher of bacon, lamb kidney, mushroom and tomato, pommes pailles	Porterhouse steak
Maître d'Hôtel	Slices of parsley butter, straw potatoes, watercress	All
Marseillaise	Slice of snail butter, cooked tomate concassée, black olive rolled in an anchovy fillet, pommes copeaux (deep fried potato ribbons)	All steaks
Mexicaine	Grilled mushroom and small pimento, cooked tomate concassée	All steaks
Mirabeau	Decorate with blanched tarragon, a black olive rolled in an anchovy fillet, ice-cold slice of anchovy butter	All steaks
Moelle	Poached slice of bone marrow, red wine sauce	All steaks
Montagné	Grilled mushroom, artichoke bottom filled with cooked tomate concassée	All steaks
Pergamon	Pipe with sauce béarnaise, pommes dauphine, tomato sauce	Tournedos
Planked	Place a grilled steak with mushrooms on the special wooden platter and garnish with an array of vegetables inside a piped border of duchesse potato. The customer uses the plank as his plate	All steaks
au Poivre	Coat with crushed peppercorns and allow to stand for 2–4 hours before grilling; jus lié finished with brandy and cream	Fillet steak, rumpsteak, entrecôte, cutlet
Prince Impériale	Pipe with sauce béarnaise, straw potatoes, green peas	Tournedos
Spatchcock (Cra-paudine)	Straw potatoes, watercress, sauce diable (Cut to the shape of a toad, par-grill then coat with breadcrumbs and finish under a salamander)	Poussin, chicken

Garnish name	Ingredients of garnish	Appropriate meats
continued		
Tivoli	Place on bread croûton, grilled open mushroom, noisette potatoes, asparagus tips	Tournedos
Tyrolienne	Sliced fried onion, cooked tomate concassée	Entrecôte
Vert-Pré	Slices of parsley butter, straw potatoes, watercress	Lamb chop and cutlet

Gammon rashers can also be garnished with several kinds of fruit including apple, banana, kiwi fruit, mango, orange, peach and pineapple; sweetcorn can also be served.

A *barbecue* is a form of grill for use outdoors and the foods cooked often pick up the scent from the burning charcoal or vine wood. It is usual to serve barbecue sauce with the meat.

Small items of meat and poultry may be dipped into melted butter then into breadcrumbs and grilled under a *salamander*, e.g. Suprême de Volaille St-Germain (served with moulded green pea purée and sauce béarnaise), Poussin Cendrillon (cut open, served with périgueux sauce), Laura (coat with tomato-flavoured spaghetti and wrap in caul; pass through butter and crumbs and grill).

Poêléd Meats

This method is used to cook good-quality joints of meat, poultry and game and is a sophisticated form of roasting. Poêlé-ing is sometimes translated as pot-roasting in English but the French word which means a frying pan, defies exact translation.

To poêlé – butter a braising-pan just large enough to hold the joint, add a layer of chopped carrot, celery, onion and bacon trimmings, a bay-leaf and sprig of thyme. Place the joint in the pan, baste with melted butter and cover with the lid. Cook in the oven at 200°C

(400°F) for approximately 1 hour then remove the lid, add a little good stock or wine and replace in the oven to cook and colour, basting frequently, until tender. Remove the joint, cover and keep it hot; heat the braising pan on the stove, add brown stock and jus lié and reduce to a sauce consistency, then skim off the fat, strain and pour over the carved meat. If to be served whole, the joint should be basted until it is covered with a glossy coating.

Dishes designated as *en cocotte* and *en casserole* are usually cooked by this method which can be carried out successfully in one of the various kinds of fireproof earthenware or enamel dishes, or merely placed in it for service after being poêléd in a braising pan.

The kinds of meat used include whole fillet and boned sirloin of beef, best end, loin and saddle of lamb, cushion of veal, poussin, spring chicken, duck, guinea-fowl and pheasant.

The most popular garnishes for poêlé meats are:

Agnes Sorel	Tartlets of duxelles with a round of tongue and truffle on top	Beef
Alsacienne	Tartlets filled with braised sauerkraut with a round of ham on top	Beef, veal
Andalouse	Shallow-fried thick slices of egg-plant with cooked tomate concassée in the centre, small braised pimentos filled with pilaff of rice, chipolata sausages	Beef
Arlequin	Florets of cauliflower coated with sauce hollandaise, small balls of carrot and turnip, pommes noisettes, tartlets filled with purée of spinach, cooked tomate concassée	Beef
Arlésienne	French-fried onion rings, deep-fried slices of egg-plant and courgette, halves of tomato	Beef
Banquière	Quenelles, slices of truffle	Chicken
Berichonne	Braised chestnuts, glazed button onions, braised small cabbages, squares of streaky bacon	Beef
Bigarade	Orange segments, julienne of orange zest	Duck

Bisontine	Braised stuffed lettuces and glazed duchesse potato nests filled with purée of cauliflower	Beef, veal
Boïeldieu	Foie gras, truffle and forcemeat, all cut into large dice	Chicken
Bonne Femme	Glazed button onions, lardons, pommes cocotte	Lamb, chicken
Bouquetière	bouquets of glazed carrots and turnips, French beans, cauliflower, peas and small pommes château	Beef
Brabant	Tartlets filled with button Brussels sprouts with Sauce Mornay and gratinated, small pommes croquettes	Beef
Brehan	Florets of cauliflower coated with sauce hollandaise, artichoke bottoms filled with purée of broad beans,	Beef, chicken
Bristol	Flageolet beans, croquettes of risotto, pommes parisienne	Beef, chicken
Cadmos	Carved, re-formed with mushroom-flavoured soubise and glazed with Parmesan; garnish of braised chestnuts and braised fennel	Lamb
Carême	Braised celery	Chicken, pheasant
aux Céleri	Braised celery	Chicken, pheasant
Champeaux	Glazed button onions, pommes olivettes	Lamb
Châtelaine	Braised chestnuts, artichoke bottoms filled with soubise, pommes noisettes	Beef, gammon
Chimay	Raw noodles sautéd in butter, dice of foie gras	Chicken
Clamart	Small round pommes macaire, tartlets filled with stewed peas	Beef
Demidoff	Crescent shapes of carrot, truffle and turnip, diced celery, sliced button onions	Chicken
Derby	Slice of foie gras and truffle, bread croûtons	Chicken
Diplomat	Calf's sweetbreads, mushrooms, cockscombs and kidneys	All

Dubarry	Moulded balls of cauliflower gratinated with sauce mornay, fondant potatoes	All
Duroc	Foie gras, ox tongue and truffle cut into julienne	Chicken
Favorite	Bouquets of asparagus tips, slices of foie gras and truffle	Beef, lamb
Fédora	A tartlet filled with asparagus tips, braised chestnuts, turned carrots and turnips, segments of orange	Beef, veal, chicken
Financière	Quenelles, mushrooms, cockscombs and kidneys, turned olives	All
Fin de Siècle	Small stuffed onions, fried slices of egg-plant, tomatoes, cèpes, cucumber, diced celeriac, pommes cocotte	Chicken
Flamande	Small braised cabbages, turned carrots and turnips, plain-boiled potatoes, pieces of salt belly of pork, sliced smoked sausage	All
Florida	Fried pieces of banana, glazed halves of peaches, tomatoes	Chicken, ham
Frascati	Turned mushrooms, bouquets of asparagus tips, glazed crescent shapes of duchesse potato, slices of foie gras, truffles	Beef, lamb, veal
Gastronome	Braised chestnuts, cockscombs, slices of truffle	Beef
Godard	Cockscombs, mushrooms, quenelles, lamb's sweetbreads, truffle	Beef, lamb
Gouffé	Darioles of risotto, mushrooms, quenelles, truffle	Beef
Grand'mère	Button mushrooms, baton-shaped fried bread croûtons	Chicken
Hongroise	Moulded balls of cauliflower gratinated with paprika-flavoured, sauce mornay, glazed button onions	Chicken
Hussarde	Open mushrooms filled with soubise, pommes duchesse	Chicken, veal

301

Jardinière	Bouquets of batons of carrot and turnip French beans and cauliflower florets coated with sauce hollandaise	All
Jockey Club	Stuffed tomatoes, croquette potatoes, quenelles, crayfish, truffle	Beef, chicken
Judic	Braised lettuces, slices of truffle, cocks' kidneys	Beef, chicken
Langue-docienne	Cèpes, fried slices of egg-plant, cooked tomate concassée	Beef, chicken
Limousine	Braised chestnuts, glazed button onions	Lamb
Livornaise	Mushrooms, glazed button onions, cèpes, lardons of bacon	Chicken, veal
London House	Stuff with foie gras and truffles; garnish with mushrooms and truffles	Beef
Lorette	Bouquets of asparagus tips, pommes lorette, croquettes of chicken	Chicken
Louisiane	Dariole moulds of pilaff of rice, tartlets of creamed sweetcorn, shallow-fried pieces of banana and sweet potato	Chicken, veal, lamb
Lucas	Braised stuffed lettuces and onions, croquette potatoes, turned olives, diced celeriac	Beef, chicken
Lucullus	Quenelles, truffle, cockscombs	Beef, chicken
Madeleine	Dariole moulds of purée of French beans, artichoke bottoms filled with soubise	All
Maintenon	Artichoke bottoms filled with diced creamed chicken and truffle and gratinated with sauce mornay, quenelles, mushrooms, braised rice	Chicken, veal
Marly	Cook with mange-tout peas	Lamb
Mascotte	Quarters of artichoke bottoms, pommes olivette, truffle	Lamb
Melba	Tartlets filled with purée of chestnut, braised stuffed lettuces, tomatoes	Chicken
Mexicaine	Open mushrooms filled with tomate concassée, braised small pimentos filled with rice	Beef, chicken

Mireille	Cook on a layer of pommes Anna containing sliced artichoke bottoms	Lamb
Moderne	Braised lettuces, quenelles, decorated darioles of mixed vegetables	Beef, veal
Mont-morency	Artichoke bottoms filled with macédoine of vegetables, bouquets of asparagus tips	Beef, chicken, veal
Niçoise	Bouquets of French beans, small tomatoes, small pommes château	Beef
Nivernaise	Bouquets of glazed carrots and glazed button onions	Beef
Normande	Sautéd quarters of dessert apples, cider, cream	Duck, pigeon, pheasant
Orientale	Darioles of rice pilaff turned out on to half tomatoes, croquettes of sweet potato	Chicken, veal
Orloff	Braised lettuces, truffle, Sauce Soubise	Chicken
Paramé	Glazed carrots and turnips, braised lettuces	Beef, chicken
Parisienne	Artichoke bottoms filled with mixed diced mushrooms, ox tongue and truffle, pommes Parisienne	Beef, lamb, veal
Paysanne	Thin round slices of carrot, celery, leek, onion, potato and turnip, diced salt belly of pork	Beef, lamb, veal
Petit-Duc	Artichoke bottoms with a slice of truffle in each, bouchées of asparagus tips	All
Portugaise	Stuffed tomatoes, pommes château	All
Provençale	Stuffed mushrooms, stuffed tomatoes	Beef
Renaissance	Bouquets of glazed carrots and turnips, cauliflower florets coated with sauce hollandaise, asparagus tips, French beans, peas, new potatoes	Beef
Richelieu	Stuffed mushrooms, stuffed tomatoes, braised lettuces, small pommes château	Beef, lamb, veal

Romanoff	Nests of duchesse potato filled with creamed celeriac and mushroom, glazed cucumber	Beef
Rossini	Slices of foie gras with a slice of truffle on top	Beef
Sainte-Alliance	Slices of foie gras, ortolans	Chicken
Saint-Germain	Glazed carrots, pommes fondantes, darioles of green pea purée	Beef, lamb, veal
Saint-Laud	Quartered small globe artichokes, chopped tomato	Lamb
Saint-Mandé	Bouquets of asparagus tips, French beans, peas, pommes macaire	Beef, lamb, veal
Sarah Bernhardt	Nests of duchesse potato filled with cauliflower covered and gratinated with mornay sauce, tomato halves filled with pommes Parisienne	Lamb
Saxon	Crayfish, florets of cauliflower gratinated with sauce mornay, crayfish sauce	Chicken
Souvaroff	Diced foie gras and truffle	Pheasant
Titania	Skinned and de-pipped grapes, orange segments, pomegranate juice	Chicken, pheasant
Tivoli	Bouquets of asparagus tips, open mushrooms filled with cockscombs and kidneys	Chicken
Tosca	Darioles of rice pilaff, braised fennel, diced foie gras	Chicken
Toscane	Poêlé between two layers of pommes Anna sprinkled with cheese	Lamb
Trianon	Quenelles of three different colours – plain, green and pink	Chicken
Valencienne	Darioles of risotto, slices of ham, tomato-flavoured sauce demi-glace	Chicken
Viroflay	Small balls of spinach subrics wrapped in spinach leaves and gratinated with sauce mornay, quarters of artichoke bottoms, small pommes château	Lamb, chicken
Windsor	Cockscombs and kidneys, mushrooms, truffle	Chicken

Roasted Meats

Roasting is the method of cooking food in dry heat in an oven with the meat resting on a trivet and given regular basting with fat. If a trivet is not available bones or sliced vegetables should be used to raise the meat from the fat in the bottom of the roasting pan in which it would otherwise fry; this is not necessary for poultry and game birds since they are turned regularly during the roasting. Roasts must be started to cook at a high temperature of 220°C then lowering it gradually to 180°C to prevent charring but keeping the meat moist so rendering it tender. Meat cannot be roasted successfully at a low temperature as although the cooking loss may be reduced from approximately 30 per cent to say, 20 per cent the resultant flavour is not that of a true roast. Cooking times and temperatures are given in the Checklist of Weights and Measures. Meat should be seasoned with salt just before putting it to roast.

The joints and birds suitable for roasting are:

Beef	Baron, ribs, sirloin, contrefilet, fillet, topside, thick flank
Lamb and mutton	Baron, best end, breast, crown, leg, loin, saddle, shoulder
Pork	Best end, cushion, loin, rolled shoulder
Poultry	Chicken, duck, goose, guinea-fowl, pigeon, poussin, turkey
Game	Goat, grouse, hare, partridge, pheasant, plover, quail, rabbit, snipe, venison, wild duck, woodcock

Barding is the covering with thin slices of salt-pork tied around joints and birds that do not possess a natural covering of fat; it is done to prevent excessive drying out during cooking.

Accompaniments for roasts are simple as shown below; it is usual to serve sprigs of watercress with each portion of all roasts.

Beef	Yorkshire pudding, grated horseradish or horseradish sauce, English mustard, thin gravy.
Lamb and mutton	Mint sauce, redcurrant jelly, thin gravy, (white onion sauce is usually served with roast mutton).

Pork	Sage and onion stuffing, apple sauce, thin gravy (it is usual to serve a piece of the crackling with each portion).
Veal	Lemon and thyme stuffing, thickened gravy (a slice of ham is traditional but optional).
Chicken	Bread sauce, game chips (thyme and parsley stuffing and grilled bacon are optional).
Duck and goose	Sage and onion stuffing, apple sauce.
Turkey	Bread sauce or cranberry sauce, sausage and/or chestnut stuffing, chipolatas.
Venison	Redcurrant jelly.
Game birds	Fried bread croûtons spread with chicken-liver farce, bread sauce, fried breadcrumbs, game chips.

Allow 6dl gravy and 1 bunch of watercress per 10 persons.

A simple or compound salad is normally served with plainly roasted meat, poultry and game except when it is being served with vegetables and potatoes as a main course. It is the exception to serve an elaborate garnish with any roast as the rule is to confine the use of garnishes to poêléd dishes.

—— STUFFINGS FOR ROASTS ——

Américaine	Chopped onion, fried lardons, thyme, parsley and breadcrumbs	Chicken
Anglaise	Chopped onion, thyme, parsley and breadcrumbs	Chicken
Apple	Sautéd sliced apple, sage and breadcrumbs made as a loose stuffing	Duck Goose Pork
Bonne Femme	Equal amounts of sausage-meat and duxelles	All
Californienne	Chopped onion, fried lardons, chopped chicken liver, thyme, parsley, breadcrumbs	Poussin

Chestnut	Parcooked chestnuts, pork sausage-meat, celery	Turkey
Game for croûtons	Sautéd shallot, pork fat, game liver, mushroom, blended to a purée	Game birds
Gratin	Bacon, onion, sautéd chicken liver, and butter, blended into a purée	Game birds
Oyster	Chopped onion, breadcrumbs, oysters, melted butter	Turkey
Parsley, thyme and lemon	Breadcrumbs, suet, grated lemon rind, thyme, parsley, eggs, milk	Veal
Polonaise	Soaked breadcrumbs, smooth purée of chicken liver and bacon, parsley	Poultry Game
Prune	Sautéd sliced apple, stoned cooked prunes, grated lemon rind, cinnamon, brown sugar, butter, breadcrumbs	Duck Goose Pork
Sage and onion	Chopped onion, breadcrumbs, sage and parsley, cooked in duck or pork fat	Duck Goose Pork
Sausage-meat	2 parts lean trimmings of meat to 1 part of fat, soaked rusks or breadcrumbs, herbs, spices	All
Thyme and parsley	Breadcrumbs, suet, thyme, parsley, eggs, milk	Lamb Veal Rabbit
Veal	Breadcrumbs, suet, grated lemon rind and mixed herbs, bound with egg	Veal
Walnut	Chopped turkey liver, chopped onion and celery, walnuts	Turkey

—— GARNISHES FOR ROASTS ——

Anglaise	Yorkshire pudding, horseradish sauce, thyme and parsley stuffing, bread sauce, game chips	Beef, Chicken
•	sage and onion stuffing, apple sauce	Duck

307

Boulangère	Joint cooked on top of a dish of pomme boulangère (sliced potato and sautéd sliced onion, mixed and baked with white stock and butter)	Lamb
Bretonne	Haricot beans, mixed with Sauce Bretonne (cooked chopped onion, reduction of white wine, demi-glace, tomato sauce and diced tomato)	Lamb
Bonne Femme	Glazed button onions, sautéd slices of potato.	Lamb
en Chevreuil	Marinate in red wine and aromates, roast and serve with venison sauce made from the marinade	Mutton
Connaught	Chestnut stuffing	Pheasant
Crown of Lamb – Couronne d'Agneau	Remove the backbone and sinew from a double best end without cutting through the outer skin, bare the cutlet bones and turn the joint inside out; sew at both ends to form a hollow crown and insert a mould or jar to keep in place. Roast and serve with a whole cauliflower in the centre, bouquets of various vegetables around, and a cutlet frill on each bone.	Pheasant
Farci	The appropriate stuffing cooked inside the joint or separately as a roll to cut into slices (see full list)	All
Persillée	Cooked chopped shallot, breadcrumbs and parsley coated on the parcooked joint and cooked until brown	Lamb
Saint-Fortunat	Stuff with the chopped liver, pearl barley, chestnuts and chipolata stuffing	Sucking pig
Sarlat	Joint cooked on top of a dish of sliced potato and truffle, baked with white stock and butter	Lamb
Tour d'Argent	Roast a duck underdone, cut into thin slices and coat with sauce made with	Duckling

	brandy, port, blood pressed from the carcase and the chopped raw liver	
Honey Roast Ham	Wrap in foil or greaseproof paper and cook in the oven at 180°C allowing 20 minutes per 500g; remove the foil, brush with honey and cook at 200°C basting regularly until nicely coloured	Ham, gammon
Truffée	Stuffing made of blended fresh pork fat and foie gras with diced truffle, cooked in the boned-out bird	Turkey
Yorkshire Pudding	Mix 110g plain flour with 5g salt, 1 egg and 1dl milk with a whisk until stringy but without lumps; gradually add another 1dl milk whisking well. Allow to stand for 1 hour then cook in hot dripping in a roasting tin at 220°C, until crisp and light	

Shallow-fried Meat Dishes

This is the most popular and widely used method of cookery particularly for small cuts of meat and poultry. Items must be placed to cook in hot shallow fat so as to sieze them, thus forming a coating which prevents loss of juices. Turn when sufficiently coloured and continue cooking until tender then place on a dish, drain off the fat and deglaze the pan with stock or wine as the basis of the accompanying sauce.

Items coated with breadcrumbs do not exude any sediment so it is not possible to make the sauce in the same pan.

Good quality oil gives the best results, a mixture of oil and butter is good as is clarified butter. By using a non-stick pan shallow frying can be carried out with little or no oil.

The French term for shallow frying is *sauté* or *à la poêle* and a *plat sauté* rather than a frying pan should be used. (It should be borne in mind that the word sauté is also used to describe a quickly made stew – see the Section on Stews.)

The list of suitable cuts of meat is wide and the choice of garnishes is extensive, details of cuts are given in the Checklist of Commodities.

Beef	Entrecôte, fillet steak, minute steak, mignon fillet, tournedos (the word rosette is sometimes used instead of tournedos)
Lamb	Cutlet, mignon fillet, noisette, rosette, roulade
Pork	Cutlet, escalope, mignon fillet
Veal	Chop, cutlet, escalope, grenadin, medallion, mignon fillet, scallopini (also called piccata and piccatine), schnitzel
Poultry	Escalope, suprême, fillet, magret

Combinations of any of these can be served, e.g. trois filets – a small escalope each of veal, duck and chicken, etc. Small items are usually served on a bread croûton.

Plain Fried Items

To cook, season, coat with flour and place into a pan of hot shallow fat and cook quickly to sear the outside then continue more slowly at the side of the stove or in the oven. In some formulas the meat need not be coloured.

The small cuts listed above are those in general use for plain and crumbed sautéing.

Adelaide	Tartlet filled with creamed sweetcorn, deep-fried egg-and-crumbed banana half; tomato sauce.
Agnes Sorel	Tartlet of chicken forcemeat, round piece of ox tongue and of truffle.
Aïda	Cover with creamed prawns, sprinkle with cheese and gratinate; Madeira sauce.
Aiglon	Galette of duchesse potato, slice of foie gras, Madeira sauce.
Alexandria	Tartlet filled with asparagus tips, slice of truffle.
Ambassadrice	Braised lamb sweetbread, bouquet of asparagus tips, Madeira sauce.
Amphytrion	Bed of duxelles; sauce périgueux
Andalouse	Fried round slice of egg-plant, small braised stuffed pimento, chipolatas, jus lié.

310

Antiboise	Cook tomate concassée in oil with garlic, reduce with white wine, add tomato sauce and pour over the sautéd item.
Arlésienne	French-fried onion rings, fried round slices of egg-plant, sautéd slices of tomato.
Armenonville	Small pommes Anna, bouquets of noodles à la crème and cockscombs and kidneys; Madeira sauce.
Baltimore	Tartlet filled with creamed sweetcorn, round of tomato with a round of green pimento on top; sauce chateaubriand.
Balzac	Stuffed olives, chicken quenelles, sauce chasseur.
Baron Brisse	Artichoke bottoms filled with small balls of truffle, pommes soufflées, tomate concassée, sauce périgueux.
Bayard	Julienne of artichoke bottom, mushroom, tongue and truffle mixed with Madeira sauce.
Beatrice	Quarters of artichoke bottoms, crescents of carrot, morels, new potatoes, demi-glace.
Beaucaire	Quarters of mushroom, squares of fried streaky bacon, glazed button onions, straw potatoes.
Beauharnais	Artichoke bottoms filled with tarragon-flavoured sauce béarnaise, blanched tarragon leaves as decoration, pommes frites.
Beaulieu	Artichoke bottom, tomato, black olives, pommes parisienne, jus lié.
Belle Alliance	Slice of foie gras and truffle, tomato-flavoured madeira sauce.
Belle-Hélène	Croquette of asparagus, slice of truffle, jus lié.
Belmont	Small balls of cucumber, button mushrooms, slice of truffle, Madeira sauce.
Benjamin	Small mushroom stuffed with duxelles, small round pommes dauphine made with the addition of chopped truffle, Madeira sauce.
Bergère	Fried lardons of bacon, glazed button onions, straw potatoes.
Berthier	Olives stuffed with anchovy, tomato filled with duxelles, tomato sauce.
Bignon	Tomato stuffed with risotto, sauce périgueux.
Billancourt	Chestnut purée, lima beans, Madeira sauce.

Bizontine	Duchesse potato nest filled with cauliflower, braised lettuce, jus lié.
Bonaparte	Artichoke bottom filled with diced creamed chicken, sauce périgueux.
Bonne Femme	Button onions, small rounds of potato, both cooked with the meat in a little stock.
Bordelaise	Poaches slice of bone marrow, red wine sauce.
Bouquetière	Bouquets of carrot, cauliflower, French beans, peas and small pommes château.
Bourguignonne	Lardons of bacon, mushrooms, glazed button onions, red wine sauce.
Bragance	Bouchée filled with asparagus tips, slice of foie gras and truffle, sauce périgueux.
Bréhan	Artichoke bottom filled with purée of broad beans, florets of cauliflower, small pommes persillées.
Brillat-Savarin	Artichoke bottom filled with asparagus tips, button mushrooms, slice of foie gras, sauce périgueux.
Bristol	Galette of savoury rice, flageolet beans, new potatoes coated with meat glaze.
Bruxelloise	Braised Belgian endive, button Brussels sprouts, small château potatoes.
Café de la Paix	Tomate concassée, chopped garlic, flame with brandy and make the sauce with cream. Dress on a fried bread croûton.
Café de Paris	Serve on a croûton and cover with a sauce made with brandy, diced tomato, garlic and cream.
Canova	Artichoke bottom filled with cockscombs, kidneys and truffle, slice of foie gras, Madeira sauce.
Carême	Olives stuffed with puree of ham, pommes croquettes, Madeira sauce.
Casino	Buttered spinach, mushroom, stoned olive, truffle; Madeira sauce.
Castillane	French fried onion rings, pommes marquise, tomato-flavoured jus lié.
Catalane	Sliced mushroom, diced tomato, chipolatas, glazed button onions.

312

Cavour	Small pommes anna, glazed button onions, tomato, poached slice of beef marrow, demi-glace.
Cecil	Bouquet of asparagus tips, button mushrooms, pommes soufflées, Madeira sauce.
Cecilia	Open mushroom filled with asparagus tips, pommes soufflées, jus lié.
Cendrillon	Artichoke bottom filled with soubise containing chopped truffle, jus lié.
Charollaise	Tartlet filled with purée of turnip, gratinated ball of cauliflower.
Chartres	Decorate with blanched leaves of tarragon, pommes château; tarragon-flavoured jus lié.
Chasseur	Coat with sauce chasseur, shallots, mushroom and tomate concassée, reduced in white wine, demi-glace.
Châtelaine	Artichoke bottom filled with onion purée, braised chestnuts, pommes noisette, Madeira sauce.
Chéron	Artichoke bottom filled with macédoine of vegetables, pommes parisienne, jus lié.
Chevreuse	Galette of savoury semolina containing chopped mushroom, slice of truffle, sauce bonnefoy.
Choiseul	Parcook, coat with forcemeat, decorate with tongue and truffle, cook and garnish with small artichoke bottoms, mushrooms and braised lamb's sweetbreads mixed with sauce allemande; sauce allemande
Choisy	Braised lettuce, small pommes château.
Clamart	Galette of macaire potato, petits pois à la française.
Clementine	Round of chicken forcemeat, creamed salsify, sauce suprême.
Colbert	Small chicken galette, fried small egg, slice of truffle; beurre colbert.
Coligny	Galette of sweet potato, chow-chow (chayote, an exotic member of the marrow family) stewed with tomato and garlic.
Comtesse	Croquette potatoes, artichoke bottom filled with asparagus tips, sauce périgueux.

Concorde   Slice of foie gras and truffle, artichoke bottom with a small tomato in it, pommes parisienne.

Crème et Champignons   Sliced button mushrooms, sherry, velouté and cream.

Cyrano   Artichoke bottom filled with foie gras purée and olive-shaped pieces of truffle; sauce chateaubriand (reduce white wine and brown veal stock, thicken with parsley butter and flavour with chopped tarragon).

d'Arenburg   A tartlet filled with buttered spinach and one with creamed carrots, slice of truffle; sauce béarnaise.

Dauphine   Small galettes of pommes dauphine, Madeira sauce.

Diane   This is usually cooked in the restaurant: shallow fry a flattened steak in hot butter, remove, add chopped onion and sliced mushroom, flame with brandy and make the sauce from the sediment with cream and Worcester sauce.

Dreux   Cockscombs, mushrooms, olives, quenelles and truffle mixed with Madeira sauce.

Dubarry   Gratinated small balls of cauliflower with mornay sauce, jus lié.

Duroc   Tomate concassée, pommes noisettes, sauce chasseur.

Elizabeth II   Stuff with mousseline forcemeat containing julienne of ham; garnish with asparagus.

Elysée Palace   Open mushroom, fried breadcrumbed slice of sweetbread, sauce béarnaise.

Epicurienne   Oval flat quenelle; sauce smitaine (sautéd onion reduced with white wine, cream sauce, sour cream and lemon juice.

Esplanade   Cover with julienne of ham, garnish with asparagus tips, artichoke bottom filled with tomate concassée, a piece of fried banana and a small ring of pineapple; sauce béarnaise.

Favorite   Slice of foie gras and truffle, asparagus tips, pommes noisettes.

Fermière   Paysanne of carrot, celery, onion and turnip cooked in butter.

Flamande	Small braised cabbage, turned carrots and turnips.
Fleury	Galette of duchesse potato filled with sautéd diced veal kidney, jus lié.
Forestière	Lardons of bacon, mushrooms, diced fried potato, jus lié.
Frascati	Asparagus tips, slice of foie gras, mushrooms, crescent-shaped potato croquette, truffle, jus lié.
Gabrielle	Galettes of duchesse potato containing diced chicken and truffle, braised lettuce, slice of bone marrow, Madeira sauce.
Gambetta	Green peas, fried squares of potato, fried egg, jus lié.
Gastronome	Cockscombs, braised chestnuts, truffle, Madeira sauce.
Gavarni	Braised lettuce, glazed button onions, decorate with tarragon leaves, sauce colbert (parsley butter mixed with meat glaze).
Glenfiddich	Flame with this single malt whisky and finish the sauce with cream.
Gourmet	Slice of foie gras and truffle, mushrooms, pommes château.
Grand-Duc	Asparagus tips, slice of bone marrow and truffle, Madeira sauce.
Helder	Pipe with béarnaise sauce and place tomate concassée in the centre; Madeira sauce.
Hôtelière	An artichoke bottom filled with sauce béarnaise, braised celery, pommes soufflées, demi-glace.
Hongroise	Small balls of cauliflower gratinated with mornay sauce containing paprika and chopped ham.
Hussarde	Open mushroom filled with soubise, pommes duchesse, sauce hussarde (reduced shallot and white wine, demi-glace and tomato sauce plus grated horseradish and garlic).
Imam Bayaldi	Deep-fried thick slice of egg-plant, fried half of tomato, dariole of rice pilaff, jus lié with tomato flavour.
Irma	Galette of duchesse potato, bouquet of asparagus tips sprinkled with julienne of truffle, jus lié.

Italienne	Galette of creamed macaroni, quarters of braised artichoke bottoms, sauce italienne.
Jacqueline	Deglaze the pan with port and make the sauce by adding cream; garnish with sliced sautéd apple and sprinkle with flaked almonds.
Jamaïque	Glazed half of banana, flamed with rum.
Japonaise	Galette of duchesse potato, bouchée filled with creamed stachys (Japanese artichokes), jus lié.
Judic	Braised lettuce, cockscombs, slice of truffle.
Jussieu	Braised lettuce, glazed button onions, Madeira sauce.
Kléber	Artichoke bottom filled with purée of foie gras, sauce périgueux.
Lakmé	Open mushroom, purée of broad beans.
Langtry	Artichoke bottom containing half tomato, stoned olive, decorated with blanched tarragon leaves; sauce périgueux.
Lavallière	Coat with sauce chasseur finished with julienne of truffle.
Léopold	Tartlet filled with creamed sliced cèpes, Madeira sauce flavoured with foie gras.
Lesdiguières	Hollowed-out onion filled with creamed spinach and gratinated with sauce mornay.
Lesseps	Galette of saffron-flavoured rice containing diced red pimento, tomato stuffed with purée of calf's brain, Madeira sauce.
Lili	Slice of foie gras, small pommes Anna made with sliced artichoke bottoms, slice of truffle, demi-glace.
Londonderry	Small dice of chicken, tongue and truffle mixed with sauce périgueux.
Lorette	Small croquettes of chicken, tartlet filled with asparagus tips, slice of truffle.
Louis XV	Stuffed with duxelles and a slice of truffle on top, small pommes Anna, sauce diable.
Louise	Stuffed tomato, stuffed mushroom, pommes noisette, demi-glace flavoured with lemon juice.
Lucullus	Cockscombs, quenelle, truffle, coat with meat glaze.

Madeleine   Artichoke bottom filled with soubise, dariole of broad bean purée; buttered meat-glaze.

Maintenon   Spread the par-cooked item with mixed béchamel soubise, sliced mushroom and yolks, sprinkle with breadcrumbs and butter and gratinate; sauce périgueux.

Maraîchère   Sautéd Brussels sprouts and salsify, pommes château, jus lié.

Marchand de Vin   Poached slice of bone marrow, red wine sauce.

Marguery   Creamed noodles mixed with julienne of truffle; brush with meat-glaze.

Marianne   Artichoke bottom filled with purée of green peas, jus lié.

Marie-Louise   Artichoke bottom filled with mixed duxelles and soubise, coat with meat glaze.

Marigny   Fondante potatoes, tartlet of buttered peas and beans.

Marly   Artichoke bottom filled with small balls of carrot, Madeira sauce.

Marquise   Small pommes marquise, tartlet filled with diced asparagus and julienne of truffle.

Marseillaise   Stoned olive in an anchovy fillet, deep-fried ribbon potatoes (pommes copeaux), tomato stuffed with onion, garlic and breadcrumbs, Sauce Provençale.

Mascotte   Quarters of artichoke bottom, pommes olivettes, pieces of truffle, jus lié.

Masséna   Artichoke bottom filled with sauce béarnaise poached slice of bone marrow, sauce périgueux.

Massenet   Artichoke bottom filled with diced French beans, small round of Anna potatoes, slice of beef marrow, Madeira sauce.

Matignon   Paysanne of carrot, celery, mushroom and truffle, straw potatoes.

Maxim   Galette of asparagus purée, nest of duchesse potato filled with peas, slice of tomato covered with sauce béarnaise and a slice of truffle, pommes frites.

Melba　Tomato filled with diced chicken, mushroom and truffle mixed with velouté, braised lettuce, port-flavoured demi-glace.

Ménagère　Haricot beans, sliced carrot, button onions and peas cooked together in butter.

Mercédès　Open mushroom, shallow-fried breadcrumbed slice of sweetbread, Madeira sauce.

Mexicaine　Open mushroom filled with stewed tomato, braised pimento, tomato-flavoured jus lié.

Mignon　Artichoke bottom filled with peas, flat round chicken quenelle decorated with truffle.

Mikado　Buttered stachys (Japanese artichokes), grilled half of tomato, sauce Provençale.

Mirecourt　Par-cook, coat one side with forcemeat and cook; purée of artichoke bottom; velouté with mushroom essence.

Mireille　Sliced artichoke bottom, new potatoes and truffle – all sautéd in butter with meat-glaze.

Mirette　Small moulded pommes mirette (sautéd small dice of potato and truffle) sprinkled with cheese and gratinated, sauce chateaubriand (reduced white wine and stock thickened with parsley butter and flavoured with tarragon).

Moderne　Braised lettuce, quenelle, dariole of mixed vegetables, jus lié.

Monégasque　Mushroom, fried breadcrumbed calf's brain, slice of ham, demi-glace with julienne of mushroom and truffle.

Monkey Gland　Spaghetti in tomato sauce.

Monte Carlo　One tartlet filled with French beans and one with peas, cucumber stuffed with duxelles, pommes croquettes, jus lié.

Montholon　Mushroom, slice of tongue and truffle, sauce suprême.

Montmorency　Bouquet of asparagus tips, artichoke bottom filled with macédoine of vegetables.

Montmort　Small emptied brioche filled with truffled purée of foie gras, slice of truffle, sauce chateaubriand (reduced white wine and stock thickened with parsley butter and flavoured with tarragon).

Montpensier Tartlet filled with asparagus tips and a slice of truffle.

Mozart Artichoke bottom filled with purée of celery, small potato basket filled with soufflé potatoes, sauce diable.

Narbonnaise Purée of haricot beans, round fried slice of egg-plant with tomate concassée on top.

Nelson Par-cook, coat with chicken and onion forcemeat and gratinate; serve with pommes croquettes, and Madeira sauce.

Niçoise Bouquets of French beans and small pommes château, tomate concassée flavoured with garlic.

Ninon Round of pommes ninon (baked potato flesh cooked in tartlet mould), bouchée of asparagus tips and julienne of truffle; Madeira sauce.

Nivernaise Turned carrots and turnips, glazed button onions, tomato-flavoured jus lié.

Normande Sautéd in butter, add cider, orange juice, garlic and French mustard, cover and cook in an oven; finish the sauce with sliced mushrooms and cream and garnish with glazed slices of apple.

Oliver Sauce of sautéd chopped onion, sliced mushrooms and olives, reduced with white wine and jus lié.

Opéra Nest of duchesse potato filled with asparagus tips, pastry tartlet of chicken liver flavoured with Madeira.

Orientale Galette of sweet potato, dariole of pilaff of rice containing peas, red pimento and sausage-meat, half of tomato, thin tomato sauce.

Orléanaise Creamed purée of frizzy endive, pommes maître d'hôtel, jus lié.

Orloff Spread with soubise, coat with mornay sauce, sprinkle with cheese and gratinate.

Orsay Julienne of ham, mushroom and tongue mixed with velouté.

Oscar A nest of duchesse potato filled with creamed small balls of carrot, and braised cabbage, jus lié.

Oscar of the Waldorf Garnish with crab-meat and buttered leaf spinach; sauce béarnaise.

319

Paco Pepper   Reduce crushed peppercorns in port, add demi-glace and finish with cream.

Palace Hotel   A small duchesse potato nest each of French beans and peas, tomato filled with purée of foie gras, demi-glace.

Palais Royal   Braised celery, braised sweetbreads, pommes berny, coat with soubise mixed with hollandaise sauce and glaze.

Palermitaine   Stuffed egg-plant, croquette of macaroni, half tomato, tomato sauce.

Parisienne   Artichoke bottom filled with mixed sautéd potato, artichoke, mushroom, tongue, truffle and velouté then gratinated; pommes parisienne, thin demi-glace.

Périgueux   Slice of truffle, sauce périgueux.

Persane   Sautéd sections of banana, braised pimento stuffed with rice, half of tomato, sauce chateaubriand (reduced white wine and stock thickened with parsley butter and flavoured with tarragon).

Petit-Duc   Bouchées of asparagus tips, tartlet filled with chicken purée.

Piémontaise   Dariole of risotto containing grated white truffle.

Pizzaiola   Brown sauce containing chopped garlic, onion, green and red pimento, tomato, oregano, anchovies, olives and tomato purée.

Planked   Serve on a specially made board with a garnish of several different vegetables, e.g. broccoli, carrot, celery, cauliflower, tomato, inside a piped border of duchesse potato (may be par-cooked on the plank).

au Poivre   Score, rub in freshly crushed peppercorns; when cooked, flame with brandy and make the sauce from the sediment.

Polignac   Sautéd egg-and-crumbed slice of sweetbread, coated with sauce chateaubriand; sauce au Marsala with julienne of truffle.

Pompadour   Artichoke bottom filled with small pommes noisettes, line of sauce choron, sauce périgueux.

Portugaise   Stuffed tomato with duxelles, small pommes château, sauce portugaise (tomato sauce with diced tomato, garlic and parsley).

Prince Charles   Stuff with a piece of Roquefort cheese, wrap in bacon and shallow fry, serve with pommes dauphinoise sprinkled with julienne of truffle and brushed with meat glaze; port wine sauce.

Provençale   Tomato stuffed with onion, garlic and bread-crumbs, stuffed mushroom, provençale sauce.

Queen Anne   Fill an artichoke bottom with duxelles, pipe the meat with sauce béarnaise and serve with sauce chateaubriand (reduced white wine with shallot and herbs, add stock and reduce, thicken with parsley butter and flavour with tarragon).

Rachel   Artichoke bottom filled with poached bone marrow; red wine sauce.

Raphaël   One artichoke bottom of sauce béarnaise and one of creamed small balls of carrot; straw potatoes.

Régence   Slice of foie gras, button mushrooms, cock-scomb, quenelle and truffle.

Richelieu   Stuffed mushroom and stuffed tomato, braised lettuce, pommes château, jus lié.

Richemont   Buttered noodles with truffle, Madeira sauce.

Rivoli   Small pommes Anna, sauce périgueux.

Rohan   Artichoke bottom with a slice of foie gras and a slice of truffle on top, tartlet of cockscombs and kidneys in sauce allemande; sherry-flavoured demi-glace.

Rostand   Quarters of artichoke bottoms, creamed mush-room quarters, sauce colbert (parsley butter with the addition of meat glaze).

Rossini   Slice of foie gras with a slice of truffle on top, Madeira sauce (buttered noodles may be served as part of the garnish).

Roumanille   Glaze with tomato-flavoured sauce Mornay; deep-fried slices of egg-plant, grilled half to-mato, stoned olive in an anchovy fillet.

Roxy   Tartlet filled with okras (ladies' fingers) and diced tomato, fried breadcrumbed banana, glazed slice of apple, sauce poivrade with julienne of green pimento.

Royale　　　　Croûton spread with purée of foie gras, soufflé potatoes, Madeira sauce.

Saint-Cloud　　Braised lettuce, tartlet filled with stewed peas, pommes château, demi-glace.

Saint-Florentin　Small cèpes sautéd with shallot, breadcrumbs and lemon juice, small pommes St Florentin (croquettes of duchesse potato and ham rolled in rushed vermicelli and deep-fried).

Saint-Germain　Small glazed carrots, tartlet filled with green pea purée, small fondante potatoes, sauce béarnaise.

Saint-James　　Stuffed mushroom, dariole of tomato-flavoured risotto, Madeira sauce with julienne of truffle.

Saint-Laurent　　Tomato filled with sauce béarnaise, pommes soufflées, demi-glace.

Saint-Mandé　　Bouquets of asparagus tips, peas, small galettes of macaire potato.

Saint-Ouen　　A small artichoke bottom each of peas, small sautéd balls of potato and tomate concassée; tarragon-flavoured demi-glace.

Samaritaine　　Braised lettuce, dauphine potatoes, dariole mould of braised rice.

Sarah Bernhardt　Braised lettuce, half of tomato, slice of bone marrow, port-flavoured demi-glace.

Sarde　　　　Cucumber stuffed with duxelles, stuffed tomato, croquette of saffron-flavoured rice pilaff, thin tomato sauce.

Savary　　　　Gratinated duchesse potato nests filled with chopped braised celery.

Senateur　　　Chestnut purée, Madeira sauce with julienne of mushroom and truffle.

Sévigné　　　Stuffed mushroom, stuffed lettuce, pommes château, Madeira sauce.

Sigurd　　　　Tomato stuffed with duxelles, pommes croquettes containing diced ham, sauce périgueux.

Sully　　　　　Cockscombs and kidneys, braised lettuce, pommes parisienne, Madeira sauce.

Suzanne Artichoke bottom, braised lettuce; decorate with tarragon leaves, tarragon-flavoured demi-glace.

Sylvestre Tartlet of foie gras and truffle purée; red wine sauce.

Talleyrand Creamed macaroni or spaghetti and truffle.

Tivoli Bouquet of asparagus tips, open mushroom filled with cockscombs, kidneys and sauce allemande, pommes noisetes, jus lié.

Tourangelle Diamonds of French beans and flageolets mixed with cream sauce.

Trianon A small tartlet each of carrot, chestnut and pea purées.

Valencay Fried galette of creamed noodles and ham; cockscombs, mushrooms, olives, quenelles and truffle – all mixed with Madeira sauce.

Vatel Round pommes anna, sautéd cèpes, braised endive, tomate concassée, border of purée of green peas, demi-glace.

Vendôme Tomato filled with sauce béarnaise, French-fried onion rings, pommes soufflées.

Ventadour Tartlet filled with purée of globe artichoke with a slice each of bone marrow and truffle on top, pommes noisettes, sauce chateaubriand (reduced white wine and stock thickened with parsley butter and flavoured with tarragon).

Verdi Duchesse potato nest filled with small balls of carrot, braised lettuce, slice of foie gras, white onion sauce.

Vichy Bouquet of carrots Vichy, jus lié.

Victoria Galette of purée of chicken, half of tomato, jus lié.

Victor Hugo Pipe with sauce béarnaise flavoured with horse-radish, tomate concassé, slice of truffle.

Villaret Tartlet filled with purée of flageolet beans, grilled mushroom, sauce chateaubriand (reduced white wine and stock thickened with parsley butter and flavoured with tarragon).

Visconti Mushroom filled with sauce chateaubriand, tartlet filled with purée of flageolet beans.

Voisin   One artichoke bottom filled with purée of peas and one of purée of spinach, pommes Anna, half tomato decorated with tarragon leaves, tarragon-flavoured jus lié.

Wladimir   Flat round of chicken forcemeat, slice of foie gras, sauce colbert (parsley butter mixed with meat glaze).

Xavier   Flat round of forcemeat mixed with spinach, tartlet with chicken purée topped with asparagus tips, an artichoke bottom filled with balls of beetroot and one of small balls of carrot; pommes noisettes; port-flavoured jus lié.

Zingara   Julienne of ham, mushroom, tongue and truffle mixed with tarragon and tomato-flavoured demi-glace.

SAUTED CRUMBED ITEMS
—— (SHALLOW-FRIED) ——

All items are coated with flour, egg-wash and breadcrumbs (pané) and shallow-fried unless otherwise stated. It is permissible to finish with a cordon of jus lié and mask with nut-brown butter.

Allemande   Pommes purée, demi-glace.

Argenteuil   Asparagus tips, jus lié.

Barberina   Coat with foie-gras-flavoured forcemeat, pané and serve with artichoke bottoms filled with duxelles.

Bardoux   Buttered peas and diced ham.

Bergère   Cut braised breast in diamond shapes and egg-and-crumb with the addition of chopped mushroom to the crumbs; sauce duxelles.

Berlinoise   Braised red cabbage, sliced apple, pommes purée.

Bonaparte   Coat with melted butter and crumbs mixed with powdered thyme and parsley; shallow fry and serve with sauce périgueux.

Buloz   Cook one side, coat the other with cheese-flavoured stiff béchamel; pané, fry and serve with truffled risotto.

Carignan	Egg and crumb with Parmesan added to the crumbs, garnish with cockscombs and kidneys dipped into batter and deep-fried; tomato sauce.
Charleroi	Cook one side, spread the other side in a dome-shape with soubise; sprinkle with cheese, pané, finish to cook and serve with jus lié.
Châtillon	Cook one side, spread the other side in a dome-shaped with duxelles mixed with béchamel, sprinkle with cheese, gratinate and serve with purée of French beans.
Colbert	Purée of globe artichoke, sauce colbert (parsley butter with meat-glaze).
Cordon Bleu	Sandwich two thin slices of veal, a slice of ham and gruyère cheese; pané and shallow fry.
Courland	Coat with melted butter and crumbs, shallow fry and serve with braised red cabbage and braised chestnuts; Madeira sauce.
Cussy	Serve on an artichoke bottom, slice of truffle, a cockscomb, jus lié.
Doria	Turned pieces of cucumber cooked in butter or deep fried, nut-brown butter and lemon juice.
Epigramme	A cutlet and a heart-shaped piece of breast cooled under pressure; pané, shallow fry and serve with asparagus tips, peas, mixed vegetables, purée of vegetables, etc.
Gendarme	Season with paprika, pané and sauté; tomato sauce.
Gismonde	Buttered leaf spinach, Madeira sauce with julienne of truffle.
Grand'Mère	Sautéd button mushrooms, 3cm × ½cm batons of fried bread, and lardons.
Gourmet	Sandwich with foie gras, pané and sauté; garnish with mushrooms and pommes château, Madeira sauce.
Henriot	Par-cook and dip into sauce Villeroy; pané, shallow fry and serve with creamed button mushrooms flavoured with lemon juice.
Holstein	Fried egg, trellis of anchovy fillets, sautéd potatoes.
Italienne	Pané with breadcrumbs and cheese; shallow fry and garnish with braised artichokes; sauce

325

	Italienne (tomato-flavoured demi-glace with duxelles and chopped ham).
Knickerbocker	Coat with melted butter and breadcrumbs; pommes frites, sauce colbert (parsley butter with meat-glaze).
Kurfürsten-dammer	Pané a sirloin steak, shallow fry and serve with sautéd potatoes.
Malmaison	A tartlet filled with lentil purée and one with purée of green peas; stuffed tomato, jus lié (the dish may be piped with duchesse potato).
Marchand	Cook one side and coat the other side with purée of globe artichoke, sprinkle with cheese and cook; garnish with bone marrow and pommes noisettes.
Maréchal	Bouquet of asparagus tips, slice of truffle.
Marie-Louise	Artichoke bottom filled with duxelles mixed with soubise, jus lié.
Marly	Artichoke bottom filled with small balls of carrot, Madeira sauce.
Maryland	Galette of sweetcorn, deep-fried piece of crumbed banana, tomato, rasher of bacon, horse-radish sauce.
Metropole	Fried egg, bouquets of carrot, cauliflower, French beans, peas and turnip.
Milanaise	Pané with mixed breadcrumbs and Parmesan cheese; shallow fry and serve with spaghetti mixed with tomato and julienne of ham, mush-room and tongue.
Montpensier	Bouquet of asparagus tips, slice of truffle.
Morland	Pané with chopped truffle in the crumbs; garnish with purée of mushroom, buttered meat glaze.
Morly	Par-cook, coat with forcemeat mixed with foie gras and pané; shallow fry and serve with chestnut purée.
Napolitaine	Shallow fry then coat with thick béchamel; pané and sauté, garnish with spaghetti mixed with tomato and cheese.
Navarraise	Cook one side, coat the other side with thick béchamel containing chopped ham, mushroom and red pimento, sprinkle with cheese and cook; serve with a cooked tomato and tomato sauce.

Nîmoise A chopped re-formed item coated with egg and crumbs, sautéd and served with garlic-flavoured tomato sauce.

Parmesan Pané with mixed breadcrumbs and Parmesan and serve on a flat shape of sautéd polenta (maize flour cooked in water to a stiff paste, spread to cool and cut to shape).

Pasteur Pané with chopped truffle and breadcrumbs; shallow fry and garnish with tartlets of duxelles; sauce périgueux.

Polonaise Shallow fry then sprinkle with fried breadcrumbs.

Réforme Pané with chopped ham and parsley added to the breadcrumbs; serve with sauce réforme (sauce poivrade with julienne of beetroot, gherkin, ham, mushroom, tongue, truffle and cooked white of egg).

Rhénane Trellis pattern of anchovy fillets and capers, sauté potatoes, anchovy sauce.

Riche Slice of foie gras and truffle, artichoke bottom filled with purée of peas, Madeira sauce.

Richelieu When cooked coat with nearly melted parsley butter; slices of truffle.

Sandringham Garnish with bouquets of asparagus tips, French beans and fondante potatoes; demi-glace.

Ségurd Chopped and re-formed meat; pané, sauté and decorate with a slice of truffle, sauce périgueux.

Seymour Pané with breadcrumbs and chopped truffle, serve on duxelles with a croquette of sweetbread; Madeira sauce.

Sévigné Cook on one side and coat the other with sauce allemande containing artichoke and mushroom; pané and shallow fry.

Sicilienne Pané with breadcrumbs and Parmesan; garnish with noodles mixed with purée of chicken liver and cream sauce.

Valdostana Sandwich with ham and Gruyère, spread with anchovy paste, coat with light batter of egg and flour and shallow fry. Serve with shallow fried slices of aubergine.

Valencay	Crescent-shaped bread croûtons coated with truffled forcemeat and cooked; purée of mushroom.
Valois	Cook one side and coat the other with forcemeat containing mushroom, tongue and truffle, pané and shallow fry; stoned green olives filled with forcemeat and poached, sauce valois (sauce béarnaise with the addition of meat glaze).
Vienna Schnitzel	This is another name for Escalope de Veau Viennoise using a thicker slice of meat.
Verneuil	Pané marinated items, shallow fry and serve with purée of globe artichoke and sauce colbert (parsley butter with the addition of meat glaze).
Viennoise	Lines of sieved hard-boiled yolk and white of egg and chopped parsley, a slice of lemon with a ring of anchovy and an olive in the middle; applies mainly to veal escalope.
Villeroy	Cook underdone, dip into villeroy sauce, pané and shallow fry; sauce périgueux.
Vittorio	Stuff with diced ham, grated mozzarella cheese and mustard, egg and crumb and shallow fry; serve with sour cream sauce.
Westmoreland	Pané with breadcrumbs and chopped truffle, shallow fry and serve with purée of mushroom; Madeira sauce.
Zingara	Bouquets of julienne of ham, mushroom and tongue mixed with a little sauce Zingara (tarragon and tomato-flavoured demi-glace).

Stewed Meat

There are many different kinds of stews, most of them being dark reddish in colour and very appetising; the eye appeal of the white stews is less marked but they are just as good nutritionally and deserve greater popularity; for cuts of butchers' meat suitable for stews see Checklist of Commodities.

To make a *brown stew*, colour the meat in hot dripping with a mirepoix of vegetables until browned, add flour and singe it brown in the oven before adding tomato purée, usually stock or water and a bouquet garni. Cooking time depends on the quality of the meat. When nearly tender remove the pieces of meat to a clean pan, strain the cooking liquid with slight pressure, correct for colour, consistency and taste and skim off any fat. Pour over the meat and any garnish and finish cooking together.

To make a *white stew*, seal the meat in fairly hot butter, or blanch it, cover with stock and cook until tender.

Quick Sautés can be made using tender cuts of beef, lamb and veal in thin strips or dice, following the method for Sauté of Chicken, as shown in these examples:

Sauté de Boeuf Strogonoff	Flavour with shallot, lemon juice and finish with cream; serve with braised rice.
Sauté de Boeuf Tolstoi	Flavour with paprika, chopped onion, tomate concassée and tomato purée; garnish with diamonds of gherkin.
Sauté d'Agneau Chasseur	Shallow fry quickly, deglaze the pan with white wine, add sauce chasseur, replace the meat and serve.
Sauté d'Agneau Forestière	Shallow fry with chopped shallot and morels, deglaze the pan with white wine, add jus lié and replace the meat; add lardons and sautéd diced potato.

Brown Stews

Name of dish	Cut of meat used	Moistening liquid	Additional flavouring ingredients	Thickening agent	Main garnish	Additions/variations (notes)
Alicot	Chicken winglets and giblets	Brown stock	Mirepoix of vegetables		Cèpes, chestnuts	Button mushrooms, button onions, lardons
Biryani	1½cm dice of lamb	Marinade of yoghurt and curry, stock	Onion, curry powder, lime juice	Rice	Raisins, flaked almonds	Sambals
Bourguignonne	2½cm dice of chuck or topside beef	Burgundy red wine	Garlic, tomato purée	Flour	Lardons, button onions, button mushrooms	Heart-shaped croûtons
Carbonnade	Thin slices of chuck of beef, or pork	Lager or other beer, Guinness	Sliced onion, brown sugar	Flour	Sliced onion	Non-alcoholic beer may be used
Capilotade	Boneless cooked chicken pieces	Sauce italienne		Sauce	Sliced mushrooms	Heart-shaped croûtons
Cassoulet	Squares of boned shoulder and breast of lamb	Haricot bean cooking liquid	Garlic, onion, garlic sausage, belly of pork		Haricot beans	Carcassone: add diced pork; Castelnaudry: add

Civet (Jugged Hare)	Hare, venison, rabbit	Red wine marinade	Garlic, tomato purée	Liver and blood, flour	Forcemeat Balls, heart-shaped croûtons, lardons glazed onions, mushrooms	Redcurrant jelly, braised chestnuts, Cèpes
Curry	$2\frac{1}{2}$cm dice of beef, lamb, pork, veal, chicken	Stock, yoghurt	Onion, tomato purée, curry powder, coconut, chutney	Flour	Boiled or braised rice, popadums, Bombay ducks	Dish of sambals
Daube	Cubes or thick slices of chuck or topside	Red wine from the marinade	Garlic, onion, belly of pork, thyme, bay-leaf	Long slow cooking		Daube Avignonnaise is made with diced lamb
Estouffade	100g cubes of chuck of beef	Red or white wine, brown stock	Garlic, onion, diced bacon, tomato purée	Reduction of cooking liquid	Button mushrooms and the lardons	Provençale: diced tomato and black olives
						Bourguignonne: button mushrooms and onions, heart-shaped croûtons

331

Brown Stews

Name of dish	Cut of meat used	Moistening liquid	Additional flavouring ingredients	Thickening agent	Main garnish	Additions/variations/(notes)
Gibelotte	Pieces of rabbit	White wine or beer and stock	Onion, garlic	Liver and blood, flour	Mushrooms, quarters of potato	Prunes
Goulash	2½cm cubes of stewing beef, lamb, pork or veal	White stock	Onion, paprika, tomato purée, garlic, caraway	Flour	Small turned potatoes	Chou pastry gnocchis, spaghetti, rice
Haricot	Boneless pieces of neck, breast and shoulder of mutton	Water or brown stock	Garlic, lardons of streaky bacon, tomato purée	Haricot beans	Haricot beans, the lardons, button onions	
Hot Pot	5cm pieces of middle neck of lamb	White stock	Sliced onion and potato	n.a.	None	
Meurette	2½cm cubes of beef	Red wine	Herbs	Beurre manié	Button onions	Garlic bread

Coq au Vin	Pieces of cockerel or other fresh chicken	Red wine	Fines herbes, sugar	Blood or beurre manié	Lardons, button onions, button mushrooms	Heart-shape croûtons (see also separate entry)
Navarin	5cm squares of middle neck and breast of lamb	Brown stock	Garlic, tomato purée	Flour	Button onions, small turned potatoes	Jardinière: 2cm batons of vegetable; Macédoine $\frac{3}{4}$cm dice of vegetables; Printanière: small turned carrot and turnip, beans, peas
Pilaff (Pilaw)	2cm cubes of lamb/chicken liver	White stock	Garlic, Tomato, saffron or ginger (optional)	Rice		Madeira Sauce, pieces of fish and shellfish
Ragoût	2½cm cubes topside or thick flank of beef	Brown stock	Tomato purée	Flour		Jardinière: 2cm batons of vegetables; Macédoine $\frac{3}{4}$cm dice of vegetables; Printanière: small turned carrots and turnip, beans, peas

Brown Stews

Name of dish	Cut of meat used	Moistening liquid	Additional flavouring ingredients	Thickening agent	Main garnish	Additions/ variations/ (notes)
Salmis	Pieces of game, pigeon, guinea fowl	Red wine, demi-glace	Brandy, shallot	Sauce	Button mushrooms, button onions	Heart-shaped croûtons spread with farce au gratin, slice of truffle
Sauté (rabbit)	Rabbit cut into pieces	Brown stock	Tomato purée, garlic	Flour		Same garnishes as for Navarin
Sauté (chicken)	Chicken cut into pieces	Wine, jus lié or demi-glace	Shallot or onion, garlic	Sauce		(see below for full list of garnishes – see also under white stews)
Sauté (veal, lamb)	2½cm cubes of shoulder of veal or fillet of lamb	Brown stock	Garlic, onion	Sauce	Button mushrooms	Tomato concassée

334

Stir-fry	Very small pieces of tender flesh	Stock, wine	Chopped or sliced vegetables, soya sauce, onion, garlic, monosodium glutunate	Cornflour	Bamboo shoots, mung beans, water chestnuts
Sweet-and-sour	Drumsticks, spare ribs		Soya sauce, sugar, vinegar, sherry, tomato purée, ginger		

White Stews

Name of dish	Cut of meat used	Moistening liquid	Additional flavouring ingredients	Thickening agent	Main garnish	Additions/ variations/ (notes)
Blanquette	2½cm cubes of lamb, veal, rabbit	White stock	Onion with clove, carrot, lemon juice	Roux, cream, liaison of yolks	Button mushrooms, button onions	Spring vegetables, new potatoes, bacon rolls
Coq au vin	Pieces of cockerel or other fresh chicken	Champagne, Reisling, or other white wine	Fines herbes, sugar	Blood or beurre manié	Lardons, button mushrooms, button onions	Heart-shaped croûtons
Fricassée	2½cm cubes of veal, pieces of chicken	White chicken stock		Flour, liaison of yolks and cream	Button mushrooms, button onions	Heart-shaped croûtons, crayfish, quenelles, spring vegetables
Irish	5cm pieces of middle neck and breast, or 2cm cubes of leg of mutton	Water	Celery, leek, potato, onion	The sieved vegetables and cooking liquid	Button onions, small, turned potatoes	Carrots
Meurette	Pieces of chicken, game, rabbit, etc.	White or red wine	Shallot	Beurre manié	Button mushrooms and onions	

Sauté	Chicken cut into pieces	White wine, velouté	Shallot or onion	Cream	(see below for full list of garnishes – see also under Brown Stews)
Waterzoi	Pieces of chicken or veal	White stock	Leek, celery	Cream (optional)	
OTHERS Osso Buco	3cm thick sections of knuckle of veal	White wine, white stock	Onion, diced tomato, garlic, lemon juice	The reduced cooking liquid	Buttered noodles, risotto, rice pilaff
Zrazy	Flattened rump or sirloin steak	red wine	Onion, lardons	Beurre manié	Thyme and parsley stuffing
Chilli con carne	Diced or minced beef or lamb	Stock or water	Onion, garlic, chilli powder, cumin, tomato, thyme	Reduction of liquid	Red kidney beans

Coq au vin can be made using any kind of red or white wine, including the name of the one used in the title, e.g. Coq au Vin de Chambertin (red), Coq au Vin de Riesling (white). The practice of using a freshly killed cockerel and thickening the sauce with its blood has largely died out.

337

Brown Sautés of Chicken – Poulet Sautés

Method: colour quickly in hot butter, cover and allow to cook slowly, remove and keep hot, deglaze the pan with stock or wine, reduce and add jus lié or demi-glace, add the garnish to the chicken and strain the sauce over or replace the chicken in the sauce. Any ingredients of the sauce can be cooked in the same pan but do not allow the chicken to boil in the sauce or it will become stringy. It is not necessary to cook the carcase.

Name	Sauce	Garnish
Algérienne	Garlic, tomate concassée, white wine	Olive-shaped pieces of chow-chow (brionne) and of potato.
Arlésienne	Garlic, white wine, tomato-flavoured demi-glace.	Deep-fried round slices of egg-plant, French fried onion rings.
Armenon-ville	Brandy, demi-glace	Quartered artichoke bottoms, French beans, pommes olivettes, tomate concassée.
Artois	Madeira, meat-glaze	Quarters of artichoke bottom, turned carrots, button onions.
Bayonnaise	Sherry, tomato-flavoured demi-glace	Chopped ham, braised rice.
Beaulieu	White wine, lemon juice, jus lié	Quarters of globe artichoke, black olives, small new potatoes.
Belle Mère	Madeira, demi-glace	Lardons, diced artichoke bottom, glazed button onions, peas, small balls of potato.
Biarritz	White wine, demi-glace	Diced sautéd egg-plant, glazed button onions, cèpes, pommes Parisienne.
Boivin	Meat-glaze, stock, lemon juice	Quarters of globe artichoke, button onions, small rounds of potato.

Name	*Sauce*	*Garnish*
Bonne Femme	White wine, jus lié	Lardons, button onions, pommes cocottes.
Bordelaise	White wine, jus lié	Quarters of globe artichoke, sliced potato, French-fried onion rings.
Bourgeoise	White wine, jus lié	Lardons, turned carrots, button onions.
Bourguig-nonne	Garlic, red wine, beurre manié	Lardons of streaky bacon, button onions, quartered mushrooms.
Catalane	White wine, espagnole	Braised chestnuts, chipolatas, quarters of mushrooms, button onions.
Cacciatore	White wine, brandy, tomato-flavoured demi-glace	Chopped shallot, sliced mushroom, diced tomato, tarragon and chervil.
Champeaux	White wine, meat-glaze, jus lié	Button onions, pommes noisette.
Chasseur	White wine, brandy, tomato-flavoured demi-glace or jus lié	Chopped shallot, sliced mushroom, diced tomato, tarragon and chervil in the sauce.
Côte d'Azur	Madeira, demi-glace	Diced artichoke bottoms, asparagus tips, French beans, peas, pommes olivettes.
Cynthia	Champagne, chicken glaze, lemon juice, curaçao	Peeled and depipped grapes, orange segments.
Danoise	Madeira, demi-glace	Glazed button onions, pommes noisettes, stuffed tomatoes.
Demidoff	Chicken stock	Crescent-shapes of carrot and turnip, sliced button onions, diced celery, slice of truffle

Name	Sauce	Garnish
Doria	Lemon juice, chicken stock	Olive-shaped pieces of cucumber.
Durand	Jus lié	Cornet of ham filled with tomato concassée, French-fried onion rings.
Duroc	White wine, brandy, tomato-flavoured demi-glace or jus lié	Chopped shallot, sliced mushroom, diced tomato, tarragon and chervil in the sauce, pommes olivettes.
Duse	Tomato sauce	Diced artichoke bottom; serve in a border of braised rice, sprinkle with julienne of truffle.
Ecossaise	Sherry, jus lié	Diced French beans, ox-tongue and truffle.
Egyptienne	Chicken stock	Diced ham, sliced mushroom, sliced tomato.
Escurial	White wine, demi-glace	Diced ham, quartered mushrooms, stuffed olives, diced truffle, in a border of boiled rice; French-fried eggs.
Espagnole	White wine, demi-glace	Braised rice containing diced red pimento, peas and slices of sausage; small tomatoes.
Estragon	White wine, demi-glace flavoured with tarragon	Blanched leaves of tarragon.
Fermière	Chicken stock	Paysanne of carrot, celery, onion and turnip, diced ham.
Forestière	White wine, jus lié	Chopped shallot, quartered morels, sautéd diced potato, square slices of streaky bacon.
Frou-frou	Madeira, demi-glace	Quartered artichoke bottoms, croquettes of spinach, pommes olivettes, slices of truffle.
Gounod	Brandy, tomato sauce	Sliced artichoke bottoms, carrots and mushrooms.

Name	Sauce	Garnish
Hermione	White wine, tomato-flavoured jus lié	Cornet of ham filled with asparagus tips, sliced mushrooms, French-fried onion rings, deep-fried ribbon potatoes.
Hôtel Cecil	Red wine, demi-glace	Artichoke bottoms, cèpes, stuffed tomatoes.
Hollywood	Season with curry and sage, orange juice, veal stock	Sautéd chicken livers, sliced mushrooms, fried slices of avocado.
Italienne	Sauce italienne	Braised small globe artichokes.
Japonaise	Jus lié	Crosnes (stachys).
Josephine	Brandy, mushroom cooking liquid, jus lié	Small dice of carrot, ham, mushroom and onion; cèpes.
Judic	White wine, demi-glace	Braised lettuces, slices of truffle.
Jurassienne	Thin demi-glace	Large lardons of bacon.
Madras	Curry powder, cream	Chopped onion, mushrooms, plain boiled rice.
Marengo	White wine, jus lié	Tomate concassée, button mushrooms, truffle, heart-shaped croûtons, French-fried eggs, whole crayfish.
Marigny	Jus lié	Diamonds of French beans, peas, fondante potatoes.
Marocaine	White wine, demi-glace	Garlic, tomate concassée, chopped onion; pommes noisettes, stuffed baby marrow, gombos (ladies' fingers).
Marseillaise	White wine, lemon juice	Garlic, sliced green pimento, quarters of tomatoes.
Mazarin	Madeira, demi-glace	Turned carrots and celeriac, glazed button onions, slice of truffle.

Main courses of meat, poultry & game

Name	Sauce	Garnish
Mexicaine	White wine, tomato-flavoured jus lié	Mushrooms filled with stewed tomato, braised pimentos.
Monselet	Sherry, jus lié	Sliced artichoke bottoms, slices of truffle.
Mont-morency	madeira, demi-glace	Asparagus tips, quartered artichoke bottoms.
Niçoise	White wine, jus lié	French beans, small tomatoes, pommes château.
Nemrod	White wine	Chopped shallot, diced tomato, mushrooms.
Orléans	Red wine, veal stock	Button mushrooms, glazed button onions.
Parmentier	White wine, veal stock	Pommes Olivettes.
Père Lathuile	Meat-glaze	Diced artichoke bottoms and potatoes and chopped garlic with the chicken to form a cake.
Périgord	Madeira, demi-glace	Truffle.
Piémontaise	White wine, meat-glaze	Sliced white truffle; serve in a border of risotto.
Portugaise	White wine	Chopped garlic and onion, tomate concassée, sliced mushroom, stuffed tomatoes.
Provençale	White wine	Tomate concassée, chopped anchovy, stoned black olives.
Ritz	White wine, demi-glace	Artichoke bottoms filled with tomate concassée, cèpes, pommes olivettes.
Rivoli	Sherry, jus lié	Pommes Anna containing julienne of truffle.
Romaine	Slivovitz, white wine, tomato sauce	Garlic, chopped onion, diced fried egg-plant, julienne of green pimento.

Name	Sauce	Garnish
Rostand	Brandy, tomato-flavoured jus lié	Crescents of carrot, celery, turnip and truffle, cèpes.
Saint-Mandé	Jus lié	Asparagus tips, peas; serve on a round of pommes macaire.
Saint-Lambert	White wine, mushroom cooking liquid	Purée of ham, carrot, celery, mushroom, onion and turnip added to the sauce; small balls of carrot, peas.
Stanley	Purée of onion cooked with the chicken, flavoured with curry powder	Button mushrooms, truffle.
Verdi	Asti wine, veal stock	Slices of foie gras and truffle; serve in a border of risotto sprinkled with cheese and grated white truffle.
Vichy	Veal stock	Sliced carrot.

White Sautés of Chicken

Method: Place the pieces in a shallow pan of hot butter and set quickly but without colour; cover with a lid and cook gently on the side of the stove. Remove the breast and wings first and give the leg portions a little longer. Make the accompanying sauce in the same pan by adding the alcohol, the cream and/or velouté and reducing it. Pour over the pieces of chicken, or replace them in the sauce to keep hot but not to boil.

Name	Sauce	Garnish
Alexandra	Brandy, velouté	Asparagus tips, slices of truffle.
Anversoise	Cream, sauce suprême	Hop shoots, julienne of tongue.

343

Main courses of meat, poultry & game

Name	Sauce	Garnish
Archiduc	Brandy, velouté, cream, lemon juice, Madeira	Sliced onion, slices of truffle.
Armagnac	Armagnac brandy, lemon juice, crayfish butter	Truffle.
Bagatelle	Madeira, cream	Asparagus tips, turned carrots.
Belle Otéro	Brandy, port, veal stock, cream	Cockscombs and kidneys, chicken croquettes, French-fried eggs, slices of truffle.
Bressane	White wine, cream	Chopped onion, cocks' kidneys, crayfish.
Bretonne	Cream, velouté	Sliced onion, sliced mushroom.
Delmonico	Velouté flavoured with paprika	Diced artichoke bottoms, cèpes and red pimento, slices of truffle.
Fédora	Cream, béchamel, lemon juice, crayfish butter	Asparagus tips.
Gabrielle	Mushroom cooking liquid, cream, béchamel	Julienne of truffle, leaves of puff pastry.
George Sand	Cream, meat glaze, crayfish butter	Crayfish, slices of truffle.
Georgina	Mushroom cooking liquid, hock, cream	Sliced button mushrooms, button onions, tarragon and chervil.
Hongroise	Sour cream	Chopped onion, paprika, tomate concassée, serve in a border of braised rice containing diced tomato.

Name	*Sauce*	*Garnish*
Laperouse	Brandy, cream, mushroom cooking liquid, thickened with egg yolks	Artichoke bottoms filled with duxelles and gratinated with sauce mornay.
Léopold	White wine, cream	Braised endives.
Mathilde	Brandy, sauce suprême	Turned pieces of cucumber.
Normande	Calvados	Sliced dessert apple.
d'Orsay	White wine, sauce allemande flavoured with paprika	Quarters of globe artichoke, quarters of mushroom.
Quatre Saisons	Brandy, cream, crayfish butter, chicken stock	Chopped shallot, sliced mushroom, crayfish, slices of truffle.
Van Dyck	Cream, sauce suprême	Hop shoots.
Vendéenne	White wine, velouté	Button onions.

– GARNISHES FOR FRICASSÉES –

Ancienne	Button mushrooms and glazed button onions.
Archiduc	Button mushrooms, slices of truffle.
Aurore	Flavour the sauce with tomato; tomato-flavoured and coloured quenelles.
Bretonne	Julienne of celeriac, leek and mushroom.
Chevalière	Cockscombs and kidneys, mushrooms and quenelles.
Chimay	Asparagus tips, morels.
Demidoff	Crescents of carrot, celeriac, truffle and turnip.
Duchesse	Asparagus tips.

345

Ecrevisses	Add crayfish butter to the sauce; crayfish tails, fleurons.
Française	Small balls of carrot and potato, peas.
Ivoire	Add meat-glaze to the sauce; quartered artichoke bottoms, button mushrooms.
Modern	Button onions and mushrooms, crayfish tails, truffle, fleurons; flavour the sauce with port.
Princesse	Asparagus tips, slices of truffle.
Printanière	Small turned carrots and turnips, French beans, peas, button onions.
Reine-Margot	Three kinds of small quenelles – crayfish, almond and pistachio.
Richemonde	Julienne of carrot and truffle.
Sultane	Flavour the sauce with pistachio butter; serve in a border of rice, sprinkle with diced red pimento.
Trianon	Add purée of foie gras to the sauce; three kind of small quenelles – with diced tongue, with fines herbes, and with truffle.
Victor Hugo	Flavour the sauce with paprika; quartered artichoke bottoms.

GARNISHES FOR —— BLANQUETTES ——

Ancienne	Button mushrooms, button onions; finish with a liaison.
au Céleri	Add 5cm par-cooked lengths of celery and cook with the meat.
aux Nouilles	Either cook the blanched noodles in the stew or cook separately and serve apart, finishing with a few sautéd raw noodles on top (other pastas may also be used).

Made-up Dishes using Raw Meat

This section contains all the entrées in which the meat has undergone a degree of processing but without necessarily losing its original identity or flavour. These are not rechauffé or reheated dishes made from leftovers but classical entrées that merit inclusion on luncheon menus of the most exclusive restaurants. Some of these can be made from more than one kind of meat so they are listed alphabetically instead of under types of meat.

Ailerons
Chicken and turkey winglets may be boned and stuffed with sausage-meat or cooked whole by stewing or grilling gently; any of the garnishes for other stews may be added and the usual garnishes for grilled meats apply (these are sometimes classified as an offal).

Attereaux
Thread small rounds or squares of ham, tongue, truffle, foie gras, sweetbreads onto small skewers and dip into reduced sauce duxelles or sauce Villeroy. When cool, trim, coat with egg-wash and breadcrumbs and deep fry. These are frequently served at receptions or as an hot hors-d'œuvre.

Ballotine
Bone out legs of chicken, stuff with forcemeat, sew up and braise in brown sauce; serve with a garnish of vegetables such as Jardinière, Macédoine or Renaissance, buttered noodles, risotto, etc.

Beef Olives –
Paupiettes
de Boeuf
Fold thin rectangles of topside into rolls with a filling of sausage-meat, tie and braise in brown sauce; serve with a garnish of vegetables such as Jardinière, Macédoine or Printanière, buttered noodles, risotto, etc.

Beef Tea
Cook lean minced beef in water au bain-marie; strain and remove any fat; this is usually served to invalids.

347

Bitkis	These are smaller versions of Bitocks; serve three or four per portion, usually with sauce smitaine.
Bitocks de Boeuf à la Russe	Mix finely minced or chopped beef with soaked breadcrumbs and butter, divide into 120g pieces and shape round with flour, or coat with egg and crumbs; shallow fry and serve accompanied with demi-glace, sauce piquante or sauce smitaine. This mixture may be used for mock escalopes by flattening it.
Bookmaker's Sandwich	This picnic-type meal consists of a Minute steak cooked rare and sandwiched under pressure between two butter-toasted slices of bread. It is also possible to make the sandwich with a raw slice of fillet of beef.
Bordure	Make a border by cooking forcemeat in a savarin mould; turn it out and fill the centre with a salpicon of chicken, ham, tongue, truffle, sweetbreads, etc., mixed with Madeira sauce, sauce suprême etc. If required, the mould can be decorated before being poached. A border may be made with duchesse potato, puff pastry or a pattern made from vegetables on a base of forcemeat.
Boudin	This is a large white sausage which is usually bought ready made but can be made with a fine mixture of chicken or pork with fat, egg, etc., filled into a prepared gut; it is poached and served cut into slices or further grilled and served with mashed potato.
Brasciole	Make small veal olives stuffed with forcemeat, impale on a skewer and sauté in butter.
Brochette	Thread round or square pieces of bacon, chicken liver, sweetbread, mushrooms, etc., onto skewers, coat with sauce duxelles then egg and crumb and grill gently; serve with a piquant sauce and braised rice.
Cambridge Steak	Mould pork sausage-meat into 120g oval galettes and shallow fry.
Chop Suey	Fry 1½cm dice of beef in hot fat to colour with chopped onion and celery, add stock and soya

sauce and cook for 1 hour; add grated carrot, shredded cabbage and 2½cm lengths of spring onions, cook for 10 minutes then thicken with cornflour. Garnish with cooked peas and serve with boiled rice.

Collops
Cook minced beef and onion in dripping until brown, add oatmeal and stock, season with Worcester sauce and cook for 30 minutes; garnish with triangles of toast.

Scotch collops – sauté thin escalopes of veal then cook in white wine and stock for 20 minutes; thicken the cooking liquid with a liaison of yolks and cream.

Confit
Dissect a fat duck or goose, rub with spiced salt and stand for 24 hours; render the fat and some pork fat and cook the duck in it for approximately 1 hour then place it in terrines or preserving jars. Evaporate the moisture from the fat, pour over the bird, seal and store at 5°C until required.

Cornish Pastie
Place a little filling of raw diced beef and kidney, chopped onion, carrot and diced swede in a 10–12cm round of short or puff pastry, fold over as a turnover or to the middle, crimp together, egg-wash and bake.

Crêpinette
Wrap a rectangular portion of minced meat in pigs' caul, dip into butter and breadcrumbs and shallow fry or cook in the oven; serve with mashed potato and a purée of vegetable. Raw minced lamb, pork, veal or chicken may be used and the mixture may be extended with soaked breadcrumbs, purée of foie gras, etc.

Epigramme
Boil or braise a breast of lamb, when tender remove the bones and press to 1½cm thick; cut into triangles or heart-shapes, coat with egg-wash and breadcrumbs and sauté golden brown. Serve with jus lié and a garnish of vegetables or pasta. If desired a best end may be boned out and braised as for the breast of lamb; serve a cutlet and piece of breast per portion.

Forfar Bridie   Fill rounds of puff or short pastry with a mixture of minced or shredded beef and chopped onion, fold over and make two small cuts; egg-wash and bake.

Fricadelle   Mix minced beef with soaked breadcrumbs and cooked chopped onion, mould into 100g flat rounds, dip in flour and shallow fry; serve with sauce piquante. A fricadelle can also be made with leftover cooked meat including beef and pork.

Galantine   As a galantine is always served cold, see the section on Cold Buffet.

Gayette   A gayette is made in the same way as a crêpinette but without a coating of breadcrumbs; pigs' liver may be used thus making it the French version of a faggot.

Hamburg Steak   Mix finely minced beef with chopped onion cooked in butter, and eggs; mould into 140g flat rounds using flour, and shallow fry. Serve with a piquant sauce and French-fried onion rings. A thin Hamburger may be served in a toasted bun, with melted cheese, a fried egg, rasher of bacon, baked beans, etc.

Involtini   Spread thin slices of veal, chicken, turkey, etc., with a stuffing made of liver, mushrooms, etc.; roll up, tie and braise in white wine and demi-glace with tomato.

Jambonneau   Bone out a chicken leg so as to form a pocket, fill with forcemeat and sew up in the shape of a small ham; braise and serve with a vegetable, pasta or rice garnish. This is the same as a ballotine.

Kebab   Marinate thin slices of lamb fillet in lemon juice and oil for 2 hours, then thread on a skewer with squares of raw onion and bayleaves; grill and serve on a bed of pilaff rice accompanied with demi-glace. Pieces of streaky bacon, chipolatas, chicken livers, etc., may be added. Kebab, shish kebab, brochette, and schaschlik are made in the same way.

Kebabs can also be made with small balls of minced meat mixed with onion, egg, breadcrumbs, etc.

Donar Kebab is a large spit made up of a number of slices of meat which rotates in front of a source of heat from which it is cut into pieces.

Keftede, or Keufte   Mix finely minced beef, pork or veal with a little chopped cooked onion and eggs, mould into flat round cakes and shallow fry. This is similar to a hamburger steak.

Knuckle of Veal – Jarret de Veau   Although used mainly for Osso Buco, thick slices of knuckle can be stewed and served in the ordinary way and served with a garnish of vegetables, pasta or rice pilaff.

Marrow Bone   Wrap a sawn-through marrow bone in a muslin and poach until cooked; untie and serve wrapped in a table napkin for eating with a special marrow scoop.

Meat Balls   Mould minced-meat mixture into small balls allowing five or six per portion and sauté in hot butter; serve with a piquant sauce. Any kind of meat may be used, and may be extended with soaked breadcrumbs and bound with eggs; chopped onion may be added.

Meat Loaf   Finely mince raw beef, ham or veal and mix with breadcrumbs and egg to a firm consistency; if desired minced cooked carrot, turnip or onion may be added; bake in a bread tin or steam as a rolled pudding and serve cut into slices, with demi-glace. The outside may be coated with browned breadcrumbs.

American meat loaf is made with a mixture of beef, pork and veal.

Mignonettes de Poulet   Form de-nerved mignon fillet from suprêmes of chicken into circles, poach and place an artichoke bottom filled with smooth purée of cooked chicken in the centre; serve with sauce suprême.

351

Mince Fry chopped onion in hot dripping, add raw minced meat and colour quickly; add brown sauce and allow to cook gently for 1 hour. Serve with braised rice or buttered pasta.

Mock Duck Spread a flattened slice of rump-steak with thyme and parsley stuffing, roll up to the shape of a duck, tie then braise for 40 minutes. (Another version is to bone out a shoulder of lamb leaving the shank in place and tie in the shape of a duck).

Mousse A hot mousse is made with the same forcemeat as mousselines, placing it in a buttered charlotte mould and poaching au bain-marie. Serve with a white sauce for chicken or a brown one such as Madeira for ham; garnish with macédoine of vegetables, etc.

Mousse of Ham Use a chopping machine to reduce a piece of lean raw gammon to a purée with egg-white and tomato purée; blend in double cream and fold in whisked whites; three parts fill buttered moulds and cook au bain-marie for 20 minutes. Serve with Madeira sauce.

Mousselines Mix finely minced raw ham, chicken, etc., with whites of egg and gradually add double cream to make a forcemeat; mould into egg-shapes with tablespoons and poach in chicken stock until firm. Drain and coat with a sauce such as mornay or suprême.

The following are examples of suitable garnishes for Mousselines:

Alexandra Coat with sauce mornay, sprinkle with cheese and gratinate; decorate with a slice of truffle and garnish with asparagus tips.
Florentine Place poached mousselines on a bed of buttered spinach, coat with sauce mornay, sprinkle with cheese and gratinate.
Hongroise Flavour the forcemeat with paprika, mould and poach as usual; coat with sauce

hongroise, glaze and garnish with small gratinated cauliflower florets.

Indienne   Place in a border of plain boiled rice
and coat with curry sauce.

Adelina Patti   Coat with sauce suprême flavoured
with crayfish butter; decorate with truffle and
garnish with asparagus tips.

Nonette   Place a par-cooked ortolan or other small bird
on a thin escalope of chicken or turkey, roll and
tie as a paupiette and cook in butter in an oven;
serve on a hollowed-out croûton filled with purée
of foie gras and brush with chicken glaze.

Oiseau-sans-   Line a thin slice of beef with a rasher of streaky
tête   bacon, spread with forcemeat or beef sausage-
meat, roll up and tie; braise in beer with sliced
onion.

Oxford Steak   Mould beef sausage meat into 120g oval galettes
and shallow fry.

Pain de   Mix finely minced veal with minced pork fat,
Veau – Veal   soaked breadcrumbs, and egg; fold in whisked
Loaf   egg-whites and whipped cream and cook au
bain-marie in a buttered charlotte mould. Serve
with sauce suprême.

Paella   Fry pieces of chicken in oil until brown, add
garlic and rice and fry together; moisten with
saffron-flavoured stock and add sliced squid, cook
then add sliced red pimento, olives, prawns,
cooked mussels in the half shell, pieces of
lobster, etc.

Pascalines   Combine equal amounts of chicken mousseline
forcemeat and cheese-flavoured chou paste and
pipe oval-shape in a buttered tray; poach in
chicken stock, drain, decorate with truffle and
gratinate with sauce mornay.

Paupiette   Flatten thin slices of beef or veal, spread with
forcemeat and roll up, wrap in a thin slice of salt
pork fat, tie and braise; if desired the stuffing
can be made of crab or other shellfish forcemeat.

The following are examples of suitable garnishes for paupiettes:

Algérienne Serve on a cooked half of tomato, surround with tomato sauce containing julienne of pimento and garnish with small croquettes of sweet potato.

Belle-Hélène Garnish with asparagus croquettes and surround with jus lié.

Brabançonne Serve each paupiette on a tartlet filled with button Brussels sprouts gratinated with sauce mornay, and garnish with small pommes croquettes.

Fontanges Place each paupiette on a galette of duchesse potato and garnish with purée of haricot beans.

Hussard Garnish with small pommes duchesse and tomatoes filled with a mixture of scrambled egg, sliced mushrooms and diced ham; sprinkle with fried breadcrumbs.

Madeleine Serve on an artichoke bottom and garnish with dariole moulds of haricot bean purée.

Marie-Louise Garnish with artichoke bottoms filled with thick purée of mushroom and onion.

Milanaise Decorate each paupiette with a round slice of ox tongue and a turned mushroom on it; fill the centre with spaghetti cooked with tomato mixed with julienne of ham, tongue and truffle; surround with tomato sauce.

Piémontaise Arrange the paupiettes in a border of risotto containing grated white truffle and Parmesan.

Portugaise Garnish with stuffed tomatoes and pommes château.

Savary Pipe a border of duchesse potato and fill it with chopped braised celery mixed with demi-glace, sprinkle with breadcrumbs and gratinate; arrange the paupiettes around.

Pilaff (Pilaw)   Sauté pieces of chicken or lamb in fat with onion until coloured then add long grain rice and stock in the proportions of 1 part rice to $1\frac{1}{2}$ parts good stock and cook together in the oven; or the meat can be cooked and placed on a pilaff of rice that has been cooked separately.

The following are examples of pilaffs:

Caissi   Sauté diced mutton, add soaked dried apricots and cook in a little stock until tender; serve in a border of rice pilaff cooked with tomato purée.

Egyptienne   Cook diced mutton with dice of egg-plant and tomato with rice in mutton stock.

Grecque   Colour pieces of meat in hot fat with chopped onion, moisten with stock and cook with currants, diced pimento, sultanas and diced tomato; serve with pilaff of rice.

Indienne   Cook the meat as for a curry and serve with rice pilaff instead of plain boiled rice.

Orientale   Colour the meat, sprinkle with ground ginger and cook in a little stock with currants, diced pimento and sultanas; serve on a bed of rice pilaff.

Parisienne   Sauté the meat, add rice and diced tomato and cook with white stock; serve surrounded with tomato sauce.

Persane   Cook diced mutton with rice and flavour and colour with saffron.

Turque   Sauté the meat until brown, add rice and diced tomato and cook in white stock, coloured and flavoured with saffron.

Pojarski   Mix finely chopped or minced chicken or veal with cream and breadcrumbs soaked in milk, mould into 150g cutlet shapes with flour and shallow fry in butter; serve with sauce smitaine. Pojarskis may be coated with breadcrumbs instead of flour and a small piece of blanched macaroni inserted to represent a cutlet bone.

355

Note: A pojarski may also be made of salmon, lobster, etc.

Polpettine Mix finely minced beef, pork and/or veal with eggs, mould croquette shape and brown in hot fat; cover with diced tomato and chopped garlic and simmer until tender.

Quenelles Mix finely minced chicken, ham or veal with white of egg and frangipane panada (melted butter, egg yolks and flour mixed to a firm paste with boiling milk, over heat); work on ice with double cream, mould-oval shape with dessert spoons and poach in stock. Serve with asparagus tips, rice pilaff, etc. Quenelles should be light and fluffy.

Quenelles and Mousselines are really one and the same thing. The use of Frangipane is optional.

Salisbury Steak Mix minced beef with cooked chopped onion, soaked and squeezed breadcrumbs and tomato purée; mould into oval galettes and shallow fry.

Sauerkraut – Braise sauerkraut with a piece of streaky bacon,
Choucroute whole carrots, garlic sausage and onions in white
Alsacienne wine with juniper berries; serve the sauerkraut with a thick slice each of carrot, bacon and sausage with poached Frankfurter sausages.

Saltimbocca Roll a leaf of sage and slice of ham or prosciutto
alla inside an escalopine of veal, fix with a cocktail
Romagna stick and sauté in butter, then cook in white wine; serve with saffron-flavoured risotto and a cordon of jus lié flavoured with the cooking sediment.

Sausages English sausages can be cooked by grilling, shallow frying or deep frying, they may also be dipped into batter or coated with egg and breadcrumbs before frying. Serve with braised red cabbage, mashed potato, fried onions, braised rice, bread croûtons, etc., and a piquant sauce, as a luncheon entrée.

Frankfurters, saveloys and many continental sausages are poached for a short time and served with braised sauerkraut, sautéd potatoes, etc.

Sausage Rolls Place a roll of sausage meat on a length of puff pastry, fold over and seal well; brush with egg-wash, mark with the back of a fork and bake at 220°C.

Scotch Egg Dust a hard-boiled egg with flour and envelop in sausage-meat; coat with egg-wash and bread-crumbs and deep fry in moderately hot fat. Serve with tomato sauce.

Schaschlik Marinate thin slices of lamb fillet in lemon juice and oil, thread on a skewer with squares of onion, bay-leaf, pimento, etc., and grill; serve on a bed of rice pilaff.

Shanks Marinate lamb shanks in oil, lemon juice, sugar and garlic; bake at 180°C for 45 minutes and serve with barbecue sauce or sauce créole.

Soufflé Make a mousseline forcemeat with finely minced raw chicken, ham or veal, egg whites and double cream and mix in stiffly beaten whites of egg; put into a buttered soufflé dish and bake at 200°C for 20 minutes until well risen and firm. The dish may be lined with white bread-crumbs or grated Parmesan. Cold béchamel may be added to the forcemeat in place of some of the cream.

Asparagus tips, fine julienne of pimento, sliced mushrooms, diced ham, tongue or truffle, diced tomato etc. may be layered in savoury soufflés.

Spaghetti Bolognaise Cook minced beef and onion in butter, add wine and reduce and cook with tomato purée and a little stock; pour over buttered spaghetti and serve with Parmesan cheese.

Spare Ribs The breast bones cut from a belly of pork are marinated with soya-bean curd, soya sauce, pea-nut butter, aniseed, garlic and ginger, and grilled.

Steak Diane Flatten the tail end of a fillet of beef and shallow fry quickly in butter; remove, add chopped onion and sliced mushroom, then flame with brandy and make the sauce with cream and a few drops of Worcester sauce. This dish is usually cooked in the restaurant.

Steak Tartare Finely chop 200g fillet of beef and mould into a round flat cake, make an indentation, place an egg yolk in it and garnish with finely chopped onion, chopped capers and chopped parsley. The various ingredients are mixed with tabasco, anchovy essence, etc., and eaten raw.

Sukiyaki Marinate slices of meat in soya sauce and sherry, cook by the stir-fry method and serve garnished with sliced raw spring onion and red pimento; garnish with boiled rice.

Swedish Meat Balls (Kotbullar) Mould minced beef bound with eggs and soaked breadcrumbs into small balls, allowing five or six per portion, sauté in butter then cook in demi-glace; serve with buttered pasta.

Swiss Steaks Season stewing steaks with mixed flour, mustard and seasoning; sauté to colour, then braise and serve with sliced cooked tomato.

Sylphide Place a poached mousseline of chicken on a barquette filled with sauce mornay, add a slice of breast of chicken and cover all over with cheese soufflé mixture, using a piping bag and tube; cook in a hot oven.

Tandoori Chicken Slash pieces of chicken, coat all over with lemon juice, vinegar, oil, yoghurt and spices, including garam masala, paprika, garlic, ginger, chilli-powder and turmeric; leave overnight then grill or barbecue.

Uccelli Scappati Roll up small escalopes of veal with a slice of ham and a sage-leaf inside, colour in butter and cook in the oven with a little white wine.

Ursulines Place a poached mousseline on a layer of purée of foie gras in a barquette, decorate with a slice of truffle, garnish with asparagus tips and coat with chicken glaze.

Veal birds These are made in the same way as paupiettes using veal and braising and garnishing as for Beef Olives.

358

Vienna Steak   Mix minced beef with soaked breadcrumbs and tomato sauce and cooked chopped onion; mould into 130g round pieces with flour, wrap in a rasher of bacon and shallow fry or bake in the oven. Serve with a piquant sauce.

Vitello Tonnolato   Stew chopped onion in butter, add a joint of cushion of veal and stiffen in the fat; moisten with white wine, veal stock and lemon juice, add anchovy fillets and tunny fish and cook in the oven for 1½ hours. Strain the cooking liquid with pressure and coat the meat.

This dish is often served cold, garnished with capers, gherkins and anchovy fillets.

Zampino   This is the lower part of a leg of pork, boned and stuffed with forcemeat, sewn-up and sold cooked. Wrap in a piece of muslin and poach until hot then serve cut into slices, with Madeira sauce and a purée of fresh or dried vegetable or pulse, sauerkraut, etc.

Made-up Dishes using Cooked Meat

This is *not* the left-overs section and the meat needed to prepare these dishes should be purchased specifically for the intended meal. When using left-over meat for rechauffé dishes the following rules must be observed:

1. Cool quickly.
2. Store cooked meat at 5°C, separately from raw meat.
3. Wrap or keep in closed containers.
4. Use up within 24 hours.
5. Recook thoroughly to boiling point.
6. Do not recycle for a second time.
7. Use as a lunch entrée.
8. Do not feature too many such dishes on one menu.

Andouillettes Bourguignonne	Cut the ready-cooked pork sausage into 1cm slices, sauté in butter and lard until brown then toss in snail butter (chopped garlic, parsley and shallot added to butter).
Andouillettes Lyonnaise	Add sautéd sliced onion to fried slices of andouillette and finish with a few drops of vinegar.
Barquettes	Fill barquettes with diced cooked chicken, ham, tongue and mushrooms mixed with Madeira sauce or sauce suprême.
Beignets Italienne	Mix diced chicken and ham with cooked calf's brain and finely grated Parmesan to a paste, mould into balls, dip in frying batter and deep fry.
Bobotie	Mix minced cooked lamb, soaked breadcrumbs, cooked onion, chutney, apricot jam, lemon juice and curry powder and bind with eggs; cook in a greased piedish at 180°C for approximately 35 minutes.
Bouchées	Fill small size vols-au-vent with various salpicons of cooked chicken, game, ham, tongue with mushroom, truffle, etc.; bouchées can be cut out square or diamond shape as well as round and the pastry lids can be put back on top of the filling, or a mushroom or slice of truffle may be used.
Bubble and Squeak	Coarsely chop left-over cabbage, potato and roast meat with cooked chopped onion and mix together; bake in a greased tin lined with brown crumbs or in a frying pan as a cake until well browned. This is also known as *Colcannon*.
Caisses	Use individual fireproof dishes or deep pastry cases and fill with salpicon of chicken, asparagus, foie gras, quenelles, sweetbread, etc., in either cream, or brown sauce.
Cannelons	Fill puff-pastry horns with salpicon or purée of chicken, game, etc., or roll up forcemeat spread on puff pastry and bake in the oven.
Capilotade	Reheat sliced cooked chicken, beef, etc. in sauce Italienne without over-boiling; arrange in a dish and surround with heart-shaped croûtons.

Cassolette Pipe individual fireproof dishes with duchesse potato, fill with sliced chicken, foie gras, tongue, truffle, etc. in sauce, cover with a lid of potato and bake; pastry may be used instead of potato.

Chartreuse Line a charlotte mould with a pattern of vegetables, spread with forcemeat and fill with a salpicon of cooked meat, etc.; seal with forcemeat and cook au bain-marie.

Chicken Chow Mein Stir-fry sliced water chestnuts, bamboo shoots, chinese leaves, French beans, mushrooms and spring onions and keep hot; fry grated root ginger, add stock and soya sauce, thicken with cornflour then add pieces of cooked chicken and the fried vegetables. Serve with shallow-fried noodles.

Chicken à la King Sauté diced green and red pimento in butter, add sliced button mushrooms and sliced cooked breast of chicken and toss over; add sherry and velouté and thicken with egg-yolks and cream but do not reboil or break up the chicken. Serve with hot toast, on a toasted crumpet, or garnished with pilaff of rice.

Chicken Tetrazzine Mix strips of cooked chicken, sliced mushroom and spaghetti with sauce suprême and sprinkle with cheese; bake for 30 minutes until brown. Cooked turkey may also be used.

Chop Suey Stir-fry chopped celery, onion, mushroom, water chestnuts, bamboo shoots and bean sprouts in oil, add a little stock and soya sauce then strips of cooked chicken; thicken with cornflour and serve on boiled rice.

Colombines Cook semolina in stock, flavour with cheese and thicken with yolks, and line tartlet moulds with it; fill with a salpicon of chicken, game, ham, etc.; cover with a second thin round of semolina mixture, demould, egg and crumb and deep fry.

Coquilles Pipe the rim of scallop shells with duchesse potato and dry under the salamander; fill with small slices of chicken, ham, tongue with mushrooms, asparagus tips, etc., mixed with sauce mornay or suprême; sprinkle with cheese and gratinate.

Corned Beef Fritters Dip small slices of corned beef in batter and deep fry; serve with tomato sauce.

Corned Beef Hash Mix finely diced corned beef and cooked potato, place into hot butter in an omelette pan and fry until brown underneath; fold over to the shape of an omelette and cook until crisp on the outside.

Cottage Pie Cook chopped onion in butter, add finely chopped or minced cooked beef and demi-glace and bring to a boil; simmer for 10 minutes until thick, pour into a pie-dish and pipe with duchesse potato. Brush with butter or egg-wash and brown in a hot oven.

Crêpes Spread finely chopped chicken, beef, etc., mixed with an appropriate sauce on savoury pancakes; roll up, place in a dish on a layer of sauce, cover with more sauce, sprinkle with cheese and gratinate. The sauce may be white or brown.

Cromesquis de Boeuf (or Kromeskis) Add finely diced cooked beef to demi-glace and cook until stiff; bind with egg yolks, spread on a tray and allow to cool; divide into 100g rectangles approximately 1½cm thick, dip into frying batter and deep fry. Serve with tomato or other piquant sauce.

Cromesquis de Volaille Add finely diced cooked chicken to velouté, cook until stiff and bind with egg yolks; spread on a tray and when cold, divide into 100g rectangles, dip into frying batter and deep fry.

Cromesquis may be wrapped in pig's caul, a rasher of streaky bacon or a thin pancake before coating with batter.

Croquettes Add finely chopped beef, game, lamb, etc., to demi-glace, reduce until stiff and bind with egg yolks; when cold, mould into cork-shapes, pass through egg-wash and breadcrumbs and deep fry.

For *Croquettes of Chicken* use velouté instead of demi-glace.

Croustade Line straight-sided individual patty moulds with short paste, bake blind, then fill with a salpicon of cooked beef, chicken, game, etc. with mushrooms, truffle, etc., mixed with an appropriate sauce. Instead of a pastry case, duchesse potato or cooked and thickened semolina may be moulded into flat round cakes, egg and crumbed, deep fried and hollowed-out for filling with the salpicon.

Croûtes Shallow fry rounds or squares of bread, 1½cm thick, hollow out the centre and fill with a salpicon of chicken, game, ham, tongue, truffle, etc., mixed with an appropriate sauce.

Cumberland Pie Mix cooked minced beef with minced carrot, celery, onion and leek, place in a pie-dish and pipe with mashed potato; sprinkle with cheese and bake.

Cutlets of Chicken Cook finely chopped cooked chicken in béchamel until thick, bind with egg yolks and when cold, mould cutlet shape; egg and crumb, deep fry and serve with tomato or other piquant sauce.

For beef, game or lamb cutlets use demi-glace instead of béchamel. A small piece of blanched macaroni may be inserted to represent the cutlet bone and a cutlet frill put on it.

Dolmas or Dolmades Stuff blanched large vine leaves with chopped cooked mutton mixed with rice; shape into small balls, wrap in a rasher of streaky bacon and braise in white stock. Serve with the reduced cooking liquid flavoured with lemon juice and thickened with yolk of egg.

Durham Cutlet Mix chopped cooked meat with flour panada or dry mashed potato; mould cutlet-shape, coat with egg and crumb and deep fry. Serve with brown or tomato sauce.

Emincé

This dish is made with thinly sliced cooked meat reheated with an appropriate sauce.

de Volaille Bonne-Femme Arrange overlapping slices of cooked potato on a buttered dish, cover the bottom with velouté, add sliced cooked mushrooms, then sliced cooked chicken; coat with sauce suprême and glaze in a hot oven.

de Boeuf Clermont Mix sautéd sliced onion with thick demi-glace, place in the centre of a dish and sprinkle with breadcrumbs; arrange sliced cooked beef around, coat with sauce duxelles and gratinate in the oven.

de Boeuf Ecarlate Arrange alternate slices of cooked beef and tongue on a dish and coat with demi-glace containing the finely diced tip of the tongue.

de Volaille Maintenon Arrange sliced cooked chicken on a dish, sprinkle with sliced cooked mushrooms, add slices of truffle and coat with sauce allemande flavoured with soubise; reheat and garnish with small deep-fried galettes of chicken.

de Boeuf Marianne Mix the flesh of baked potatoes with chopped chives, sauté in butter until coloured and pile dome-shape on a dish; surround with slices of cooked beef and coat with demi-glace flavoured with chopped chervil, parsley and tarragon.

de Volaille Valentino Arrange sliced cooked chicken and ox tongue on a dish, sprinkle with sliced cooked mushroom, add slices of truffle and coat with sauce suprême; pipe a border of duchesse potato containing finely chopped chicken, brush with egg-wash and glaze in the oven.

Favorites

Line dariole moulds with short pastry, fill with salpicon of cooked meat and truffle mixed with thick Madeira sauce, cover with a pastry top, bake then turn out and serve with sauce périgueux.

Flan Line a flan ring with short pastry, bake blind and fill with a salpicon of any kind of cooked meat with mushrooms, ham, tongue and truffle and an appropriate well-reduced sauce, or the filling can be put in a raw flan, covered with a plain or lattice top and baked.

Fondantes Mix together stiff purée of cooked chicken with foie-gras purée and chopped tongue, bound with well-reduced Sauce Allemande; mould to pear shapes, coat with egg-wash and breadcrumbs and deep fry.

These may be made with any kind of purée of cooked meat.

Friandines Place some salpicon of meat in 5cm rounds of puff pastry; cover with a lid of pastry, coat with egg-wash and broken vermicelli and deep fry.

Fricadelles Mix finely chopped cooked beef with chopped and cooked onion, dry mashed potato and eggs, mould into galettes with flour and shallow fry. Serve with a piquant sauce and a purée of vegetable.

Fritots Marinate slices of cooked chicken in lemon juice and oil, dip into frying batter and deep fry; serve with tomato sauce.

Hachis Add finely chopped cooked meat to demi-glace to form a stiff mixture, or add finely chopped chicken to velouté; it is usual to serve it gratinated in a border of duchesse potato.

The following are variations of Hachis:

Américaine Mix diced cooked beef in tomato-flavoured jus lié together with diced fried potato; sprinkle with more crisply fried diced potato.

en Coquille Pipe scallop shells with a border of duchesse potato, fill with hachis, sprinkle with breadcrumbs and gratinate.

Fermière Place some hachis mixture in a dome-shape in a dish, surround with sliced cooked potato, sprinkle with crumbs and gratinate; garnish with French-fried eggs.

du Grand'Mère Mix hachis beef mixture with dry mashed potato, place in a pie-dish, pipe with duchesse potato, sprinkle with cheese and breadcrumbs and gratinate.

Gratin Pour diced cooked beef mixed with demi-glace into a border of duchesse potato and cook in an oven until coloured.

Parmentier Chop the flesh of baked potatoes and fry it in hot butter; add the same amount of diced cooked meat and cooked chopped onion, flavour with vinegar and replace in the potato skins; coat with sieved onion sauce and reheat.

Portugaise Add cooked diced tomato to diced cooked meat, reheat and serve garnished with stuffed tomatoes.

Hashed Meat
Reheat sliced cooked meat in gravy and garnish with heart-shaped croûtons dipped in parsley.

Lobscouse
Mix mashed potato with chopped salt beef and evaporated milk and shallow fry.

Mazagran
Sandwich any kind of salpicon of meat between two layers of duchesse potato using a tartlet mould or flan ring; brush with egg-wash and bake in an oven.

Miroton
Arrange sliced cooked beef on a layer of Lyonnaise sauce, coat with more sauce, sprinkle with breadcrumbs and gratinate.

Moussaka
Cooked chopped onion and garlic in butter, add diced cooked lamb and demi-glace and continue to cook until fairly thick; pour into an earthenware dish, cover with sautéd slices of egg-plant and peeled tomato, sprinkle with breadcrumbs and butter and gratinate in an oven. Sliced cooked potato, sauce mornay, plain yoghurt may be added.

Pain de Jambon – Ham Loaf
Mix finely minced ham trimmings or boiled hocks of bacon with soaked breadcrumbs and eggs, pour into greased loaf-tins and bake at 180°C.

Pannequets Spread thin pancakes with a salpicon of any kind of meat mixed with reduced sauce; roll up, trim the ends and serve as they are, or coat with sauce mornay and gratinate.

Patties – Petits Pâtés Place a small amount of meat filling on small rounds or squares of puff pastry; cover with a pastry lid, egg-wash and bake at 210°C for approximately 15 minutes. The fillings can include finely chopped beef, chicken, duck, game, mutton, veal forcemeat, etc., with mushrooms, tongue and truffle.

Pâtés Mazarin Partly bake small fluted tartlets, fill with salpicon of veal, quenelles, mushroom, sweetbread, etc., then cover with a cooked pastry lid which has been egg-washed and baked.

Pâtés Nîmoise Fill puff pastry tartlets with salpicon of mutton, chicken liver and truffle; cover with a lid, egg-wash and bake.

Pellmènes Roll out noodle pastry, stuff with finely minced cooked meat, cover with a second layer of pastry and cut into rounds; poach and serve brushed with butter.

Piroguis Bind finely diced cooked beef or lamb with reduced demi-glace, spread 1½cm thick on a tray and when cold cut out crescent-shapes; coat with egg-wash and breadcrumbs and deep fry.

Quiche Lorraine Fill a lined flan ring with sautéd lardons of streaky bacon and grated Gruyère cheese; fill with savoury egg custard made with 3 eggs per 2½dl milk or cream and bake at 175°C.

Quichelettes Line deep tartlet moulds with short pastry, add thin slices of ham, chicken, etc., and fill with egg custard mix; bake at 175°C for 15 minutes.

Risotto Add sautéd items such as chicken winglets, lardons of bacon, sliced sausage, ham, chicken livers, to a risotto during the cooking process.

Rissoles Roll out short or puff pastry very thinly, cut out 7cm rounds, place minced cooked meat on one half, fold over and seal; coat with egg-wash and breadcrumbs or crushed vermicelli and deep fry.

367

The name of the meat used should be designated in the title.

Shepherd's Pie Cook finely chopped onion in butter, add chopped cooked lamb and demi-glace, boil and cook for 10 minutes; pour into a pie-dish, pipe with duchesse potato, brush with butter or egg-wash and bake until golden brown.

Stuffed Cabbage Separate the leaves of a cabbage, blanch until pliable, cool and drain; place a ball of meat stuffing in the centre of the leaves, roll up into a ball and braise at 175°C for approximately 1 hour. Serve coated with jus lié.

Any kind of finely minced cooked meat or sausage-meat may be used.

Stuffed Egg-plant Cut in half lengthways, deep fry then scoop out and cook the chopped pulp with onion and garlic; add minced beef or lamb, cook, add diced tomato and fill into the skins; sprinkle with cheese, breadcrumbs and butter and bake at 190°C.

Stuffed Marrow Peel, cut in half and remove the seeds, blanch in boiling water, drain well and fill with a cooked meat stuffing or sausage-meat; sprinkle with breadcrumbs and butter and gratinate in a hot oven. Baby marrows can be used.

Stuffed Pimentos Peel, cut off the tops and remove the seeds; fill with minced cooked meat and rice and braise in tomato sauce at 190°C for 1 hour.

Subrics Mix small dice of cooked meat with thick béchamel, bind with egg yolks and cream then take tablespoonfuls of the mixture and shallow fry in hot oil.

Tartlets Fill baked puff- or short-pastry tartlets with diced chicken, duck, game, etc., mixed with mushroom, truffle, etc., and an appropriate sauce. If desired the inside of the tartlet may be lined with forcemeat and rebaked before being filled.

Timbales Line buttered dariole moulds with forcemeat, fill with a purée of cooked chicken with ham, tongue, etc., and cook au bain-marie; serve with demi-glace. The moulds may be lined with a thin pancake before being spread with force-meat.

Vols-au-Vent Fill a large oval or round puff-pastry case with a mixture of meat with quenelles, mushrooms, tongue, etc., mixed with the appropriate sauce; replace the lid and serve. Vols-au-Vent may be made in individual sizes or for two to four persons.

The following are examples of vol-au-vent fillings:

Agnes Sorel Chicken, mushrooms, quenelles, ox-tongue.

Beaumarchais Game bird, foie gras, asparagus.

Cussy Chicken, artichoke bottom, mushroom, cockscombs, truffle.

Duchesse Chicken, mushroom, ox-tongue, truffle.

Epicurienne Beef, game bird, foie gras, truffle.

Financière Chicken, cockscombs, mushrooms, olives, quenelles, truffle.

Isabelle Chicken, ox-tongue, truffle.

Orsay Chicken, artichoke bottom, mushrooms, truffle.

Reine Chicken, mushrooms, truffle.

Toulousaine Chicken, cockscombs, mushrooms, quenelles, brain, truffle, crayfish.

de Volaille Chicken, quenelles, mushrooms.

Dishes made with Offals

Bone Marrow – Moelle

This is obtained from the leg of beef by splitting it open and extracting it whole; it is cut in slices and poached as a garnish with steaks, celery etc. or diced and added to brown sauce.

Brain – Cervelle

Calf or sheep's brain is used; soak well in cold water to remove all traces of blood, remove the membrane and poach in court-bouillon before proceeding for any of the following recipes.

Beaumont	Sandwich two thick slices of brain with gratin forcemeat containing foie gras, enclose in puff pastry and bake; serve with Madeira sauce.
au Beurre Noir	Dip slices of brain in flour, shallow fry in hot butter and sprinkle with capers; heat more butter until it turns brown, add a little vinegar and pour over.
Bourguignonne	Simmer thick slices of brain in red wine sauce with cooked button mushrooms and onions and serve garnished with heart shaped croûtons.
Florentine	Sauté in butter, place on buttered leaf spinach and gratinate with mornay sauce.
Gratin	Pipe scallop shells with duchesse potato, place some duxelles in the bottom, add sliced brain and button mushrooms and coat with duxelles sauce; sprinkle with breadcrumbs and gratinate.
Italienne	Shallow fry and serve with sauce italienne.
Maréchal	Coat slices with flour, egg-wash and breadcrumbs, shallow fry and serve with asparagus tips.
Parisienne	Pipe scallop shells with duchesse potato, fill with slices of brain, mushroom and truffle; coat with velouté, sprinkle with cheese and gratinate.

Poulette	Serve covered with sauce poulette (sauce allemande reduced with mushroom cooking liquid, stock, lemon juice and egg yolks).
Rambouillet	Coat with sauce allemande (velouté reduced with mushroom cooking liquid, stock, lemon juice and egg yolks).
Sainte-Menehould	Dip into sauce villeroy containing chopped mushroom; wrap in pig's caul, sprinkle with breadcrumbs and butter and grill.
Tosca	Mix slices of brain with crayfish and macaroni, add lobster sauce and serve in a puff pastry case.
Villeroy	Poach, dip into sauce Villeroy and allow to set; coat with egg-wash and breadcrumbs and shallow fry.
Zingara	Shallow fry in butter, garnish with an oval slice of ham and julienne of ham, mushroom and tongue mixed with tarragon and tomato-flavoured demi-glace.

Ears – Oreilles

Calf's or pig's ears may be used and should be thoroughly cleaned and blanched before being boiled or braised.

The following examples show how these may be used:

Diablée	Braise, cut in half then spread with made English mustard, coat with breadcrumbs and grill. Serve with devil's sauce (reduce white wine and vinegar with crushed peppercorns and chopped shallot and add demi-glace).
Frites	Braise, cut in half, dip in batter and deep fry; serve with tomato sauce.
Grillées	Spread with made mustard, coat with breadcrumbs, brush with butter and grill.
Italienne	Braise, cut into pieces and add to sauce italienne (tomato-flavoured demi-glace with duxelles, chopped ham and fines herbes).
Rouennaise	Stew boiled ears in Madeira sauce, stuff the flat part with sausage meat together with a piece of the thick end; envelop in pig's caul, sprinkle with

	breadcrumbs and butter and grill. Serve with Madeira sauce.
Sainte-Menehould	Cut boiled ears in half, spread with made English mustard, dip in melted butter and breadcrumbs and grill.
Tortue	Braise with Madeira, nick the edge and spread out like a fan; add a garnish of quenelles, mushrooms, gherkins and olives mixed with sauce tortue (turtle herbs, infused and added to tomato-flavoured demi-glace, flavoured with Madeira and truffle essence).

Feet – Pieds

Blanch calf's, lamb's or pig's trotters, cut in half and remove some of the bones then cook in a 'blanc' or tie each to a piece of wood and boil gently in stock for 3 hours, or braise. The following recipes illustrate the uses of these as luncheon entrées:

Custine	Braise, cut into small dice, add sliced cooked mushroom and bind with thick sauce duxelles (reduce white wine and mushroom cooking liquid with chopped shallot, add demi-glace, tomato purée and finely chopped mushroom), allow to cool then mould into squares, wrap in caul and cook in an oven. Serve with demi-glace.
Frits	Cut braised feet in half, spread with made English mustard, dip in melted butter and breadcrumbs then in egg-wash and breadcrumbs and deep fry. Serve with tomato sauce.
Grillés	Cut braised feet in half, spread with made English mustard, dip in melted butter and breadcrumbs and grill. Serve with devil's sauce.
Poulette	Cook in a blanc, cut into pieces and place in sauce poulette (allemande reduced with stock and egg yolks, and finished with cream and lemon juice).
Rouennaise	Sandwich two halves together with sausage-meat containing the well-reduced braising liquid

and brandy; wrap in caul, sprinkle with bread-crumbs and butter and grill.

Tyrolienne Place prepared trotters in a sauce made by adding chopped cooked onion, garlic and to-mato to sauce poivrade (cooked mirepoix reduced with red wine and vinegar, added to demi-glace with crushed peppercorns, strained and finished with butter).

Chicken Giblets – Abattis de Volaille

The cleaned gizzard, heart and liver of chicken and other kinds of poultry can be cooked as a stew or made into a pie. Various vegetable and other garnishes can be added to the stew or pie.

Head – Tête de Veau

Only calf's head is served as a classical luncheon entrée, as indicated in the following formulas. A pig's head can be cooked in the fashion of a boar's head but is usually made as a brawn.

Whiten a boned calf's head by soaking for 24 hours, blanch, rub with lemon and cut into square pieces; cook in a 'blanc' and continue as follows. (The brain and tongue may be cooked and served with the head or as separate entrées.)

Américaine Cook pieces of head in butter with chopped onion and fennel and diced tomato.

Anglaise Serve pieces of head with brain, tongue and a slice of boiled belly of pork and parsley sauce.

Destilière Serve coated with sauce espagnole and garnish with diced tongue and mushroom and sliced gherkins.

Financière Add cockscombs and kidneys, mushrooms, oli-ves, quenelles and slices of truffle to the head and coat with Madeira sauce.

Française Serve pieces of head with dishes of capers, chopped raw onion and parsley, and sauce vinaigrette (oil, vinegar, chopped capers, fines herbes and onion).

Godard	Add cockscombs, mushrooms, lamb's sweetbreads, quenelles and truffle to the pieces of head, together with demi-glace.
Gribiche	Serve pieces of head, brain and tongue with sauce gribiche (oil, vinegar, mustard, chopped capers, gherkins and fines herbes).
Poulette	Coat the pieces of head with sauce poulette.
Ravigote	Serve pieces of head, brain and tongue with sauce ravigote (oil, vinegar, chopped capers, onion and fines herbes).
Tarentaise	Cook pieces of head, slices of ox tongue and julienne of mushroom in Madeira sauce; sprinkle with julienne of lemon peel and garnish with halves of hard-boiled egg.
en Tortue	Garnish pieces of head, brain and tongue with gherkins, mushrooms, olives and quenelles; coat with sauce tortue and garnish with heart-shaped croûtons.
Vinaigrette	Serve pieces of head with a portion of brain and slice of tongue with sauce vinaigrette (oil and vinegar with chopped capers, onion and fines herbes).

Heart – Coeur

Lamb's and calf's hearts are usually braised and served with a vegetable garnish such as jardinière, printanière. The heart may be stuffed with thyme and parsley stuffing and braised, particularly ox hearts.

Kidney – Rognon

Calf's and lamb's kidneys are popular, pig's less so and ox kidney is for use in pies and puddings but can be cut into small thin slices and cooked quickly as a sauté. With care, the result with any kidney will be tender but if allowed to boil in the sauce it will be tough; do not overcook kidneys.

Bercy	Sauté slices or halves of kidney, remove and sauté chopped shallot; add white wine and reduce then make into a sauce with meat-glaze,

	jus lié and lemon juice, replace the kidney and serve.
Berrichonne	Sauté the kidney, remove and sauté lardons and sliced mushroom; deglaze with red wine, reduce and add red wine sauce; replace the kidney and serve.
Bordelaise	Add sautéd kidney to sauce bordelaise together with diced bone marrow and sliced cèpes.
Brochette	Impale slices or halves of kidney on a skewer together with squares of streaky bacon, par-cooked button mushrooms, etc., and grill gently. The brochette may be gratinated by coating with breadcrumbs.
Carvalho	Place sautéd half kidneys on croûtons, garnish with turned mushrooms and slices of truffle; deglaze the pan with Madeira, add demi-glace and pour over the kidneys.
Chasseur	Sauté the kidney and remove; sauté chopped shallot and sliced mushroom, reduce with white wine, add diced tomato, jus lié and fines herbes; replace the kidney but do not allow to boil.
Grillé	Skewer the kidney open, brush with oil and grill gently until just cooked; place a slice of parsley butter on each piece and garnish with straw potatoes and watercress.
Hussard	Gratinate a border of duchesse potato containing cooked chopped onion; sauté the kidney, deglaze with white wine, add demi-glace, tomato sauce and grated horseradish and pour in the centre.
Liègeoise	Flame the sautéd kidney with gin, sprinkle with crushed juniper berries and add jus lié.
Michel	Fill a flan case with braised sauerkraut containing diced foie gras and cover with sautéd kidneys rolled in meat-glaze.
Montpensier	Sauté the kidney and remove; deglaze with Madeira, add meat-glaze and lemon juice, coat the kidneys, and garnish with asparagus tips and a slice of truffle.

Moutarde	Sauté quickly, remove and sauté chopped onion; add cream and French mustard, mix the kidneys into the sauce but do not boil.
Sauté	Sauté the kidney in hot butter, keeping slightly underdone, place into hot demi-glace and serve. The pan may be deglazed with Madeira or other wine.
Turbigo	Sauté the kidney in hot butter, remove, add white wine and reduce then add demi-glace; place the kidney on oblong croûtons, coat with sauce and garnish with grilled chipolatas and sautéd button mushrooms.
Viéville	Sauté the kidney in hot butter, remove, add Madeira and demi-glace; place the kidney on crescent-shaped croûtons, coat with the sauce and garnish with chipolatas, button mushrooms and glazed button onions.

Lights – Mou

Lung may be cut into cubes and cooked as a brown or white stew allowing $1\frac{1}{2}$ hours; it is necessary to beat the air out before starting to cook.

Liver – Foie

The liver of calf, chicken, goose, lamb, ox and pig are all used, the best quality being that of the calf. The enlarged liver of a goose, known as foie gras is the most exclusive and expensive and although it is obtainable raw, is mostly seen ready cooked in a pâté or tin.

Fresh liver is usually served sautéd in $\frac{1}{2}$cm slices but can be cooked whole; it should not be too well done as it goes tough. It is advisable to dip in flour before shallow frying. The skin should be removed.

Américaine	Serve shallow-fried slices of liver with grilled rashers of streaky bacon and grilled tomatoes.
Anglaise	Grill or shallow fry slices of liver and serve with rashers of streaky bacon.
Bercy	Dip the slices in melted butter then into flour and grill gently; serve with Bercy butter (cooked

chopped shallot, poached diced bone marrow, parsley and lemon juice mixed with butter).

Bordelaise   Stiffen a whole liver in hot fat, wrap in caul and braise in tomato-flavoured demi-glace; serve cut in slices with a garnish of sautéd cèpes.

Bourgeoise   Stiffen a whole liver in hot fat, braise in wine and stock and serve coated with the reduced and thickened cooking liquid and turned carrots, glazed button onions and diced lardons.

en Croûte   Stiffen a whole liver in hot fat, coat with duxelles and thin slices of salt-pork fat, and wrap in hot water paste; bake for 2 hours, adding demi-glace through a hole in the top.

Espagnole   Garnish the sautéd liver with grilled tomatoes and French-fried onion rings.

Italienne   Arrange shallow fried slices of liver on a layer of sauce italienne (cook chopped shallot and mushroom in butter, add demi-glace, tomato sauce and chopped ham).

au Lard   Shallow fry, keeping slightly underdone; serve with grilled rashers of back bacon, surround with a little jus lié and coat with browned butter.

Lyonnaise   Shallow fry and coat with sauce Lyonnaise (sauté sliced onion, reduce with white wine and vinegar and add demi-glace).

Provençale   Arrange the sautéd liver on a layer of sauce provençale (chopped garlic cooked in oil, diced tomato, white wine and tomato sauce).

Turinoise   Arrange the shallow-fried slices of liver on a bed of risotto and coat with browned butter.

Veneziana   Sauté chopped onion in oil and butter, add the slices of liver and colour on both sides; serve with rounds of sautéd polenta.

Chicken Livers

Foies de Volaille can be used as a luncheon entrée by sautéing quickly and placing in a brown sauce with a garnish, or adding to pilaff of rice or risotto.

Sweetbreads – Ris de Veau

Lamb- and ox-breads are available but calf's are the best. Lamb's sweetbreads are small and although they make a good entrée they are more useful in a salpicon, vol-au-vent or as a garnish.

Oxbreads are very big whereas those from a calf are just right for braising and as shallow-fried escalopes. The round one is the pancreas and the long one is the thymus, both are used for brown and white braising but only the round one is suitable for an escalope of sweetbread.

To braise sweetbreads, blanch, trim off any fat and gristle then lay on sliced carrot, onion, celery and bacon trimmings in a buttered pan. Cover and cook in a hot oven for 20 minutes then add white stock to come one third the way up, cover and braise at 175°C for $1\frac{1}{4}$ hours, removing the lid and basting the breads for the last 15 minutes. Strain and reduce the cooking liquid for the accompanying sauce.

Braised Sweetbreads

Bonne Maman Sprinkle braised sweetbreads with julienne of carrot, celery and leek cooked in a little water and butter, and coat with the sauce.

Camargo Serve with small round pastry brioches hollowed-out and filled with peas and carrots cooked à la française.

Cévenole Garnish with braised chestnuts, glazed button onions and crescent-shaped brown-bread croûtons and coat with the reduced braising liquid.

Chambellane Place a slice of truffle at the bottom of fluted petits fours moulds, line with forcemeat, add chopped truffle in demi-glace and cover with more forcemeat; cook au bain-marie and serve as the garnish to braised sweetbreads together with purée of mushroom finished with julienne of truffle.

Clamart Serve with a tartlet filled with peas cooked à la française and a small round pommes macaire.

Comtesse Garnish with braised lettuces and decorated quenelles.

Cordon Bleu Garnish with an artichoke bottom filled with salpicon of kidney in Madeira sauce.

Crème Place the braised sweetbreads in a serving dish, strain and reduce the cooking liquid, add béchamel and cream and pour over.

Demidoff Garnish with crescents of carrot, turnip and truffle and coat with the reduced cooking liquid.

Egyptienne Garnish with a round flat rice croquette and a small stuffed and braised pimento; coat with the cooking liquid containing diced bone marrow.

Excelsior Add a garnish of three colours of quenelles – plain, green with spinach, and red with tomato; coat with white onion sauce containing julienne of tongue, mushrooms and truffle.

Financière Add a garnish of cockscombs and kidneys, mushroom, olives and quenelles, with demi-glace and decorate with truffle.

Florentine Place on buttered leaf spinach, coat with sauce mornay, sprinkle with cheese and glaze.

Gastronome Garnish with braised chestnuts, cockscombs, morels and truffle and flavour the sauce with truffle essence.

Gourmets Place braised breads in a cocotte with slices of truffle and some of the braising liquid; cover, seal with a band of pastry and bake for 10 minutes.

Guizot Garnish with a croquette potato and a small stuffed tomato; coat with mint-flavoured Madeira sauce.

Lausannoise Decorate with a slice of tongue, garnish with mushroom purée and coat with Madeira sauce.

Lavallière Garnish with button onions and peas and coat with velouté flavoured with soubise and containing diced ham.

Lucullus Garnish with cockscombs, quenelles and truffle in the reduced braising liquid.

379

Marigny Garnish each portion with one tartlet filled with peas and one with diced French beans.

Montauban Garnish with mushrooms, small round slices of truffled forcemeat and croquettes of rice pilaff mixed with diced ox tongue; serve with mushroom-flavoured velouté.

Montglas Garnish with a slice of foie gras and of truffle.

Nesselrode Serve with chestnut purée and coat with the braising liquid.

Parisienne Garnish with artichoke bottoms filled with salpicon of mushroom, tongue and truffle mixed with velouté and glazed, pommes parisienne and the reduced braising liquid.

Princesse Garnish with asparagus tips and slices of truffle and serve with mushroom-flavoured sauce allemande (velouté reduced with yolks, stock, mushroom cooking liquid and lemon juice).

aux Queues d'Ecrevisses Serve garnished with crayfish and the shells filled with crayfish-flavoured forcemeat and poached; coat with cream sauce.

Rachel Surround with artichoke bottoms filled with sauce Bordelaise and a poached slice of bone marrow on top.

Régence Garnish with cockscombs, slices of foie gras, mushrooms, quenelles and truffle and serve with truffle-flavoured sauce allemande (velouté reduced with stock, mushroom cooking liquid, yolks and lemon juice).

Reine Garnish with a dariole mould of purée of chicken cooked au bain-marie, and coat with sauce suprême.

Saint-Alban Place on a galette of chicken, decorate with a turned mushroom and serve with tomato sauce.

Sarah Bernhardt Garnish with small red pimentos stuffed with risotto and duxelles and braised; coat with Madeira sauce.

Sourcouf Garnish with quartered artichoke bottoms, asparagus tips, small turned carrots and turnips and coat with the reduced braising liquid.

Talleyrand	Serve with spaghetti mixed with butter, cheese, dice of foie gras and julienne of truffle; sauce périgueux.
Toulousaine	Garnish with cockscombs and kidneys, mushrooms, quenelles and truffle and coat with sauce allemande (velouté, stock, mushroom cooking liquid, yolks and lemon juice reduced together).
Verdi	Serve with a slice of foie gras, a few small semolina gnocchi and the reduced braising liquid.
Volnay	Coat with the reduced braising liquid and garnish one side with soubise and the other with purée of mushroom.

Shallow-fried Escalopes of Sweetbread

To prepare, press braised unglazed sweetbreads to flatten them and when cold cut in half horizontally; coat with flour or flour, egg-wash and breadcrumbs and shallow fry on both sides for a total of 5 minutes, to a golden colour. These are called escalopes or medallions of sweetbread and are finished with a little jus lié and nut-brown butter, in addition to the following garnishes:

Baden-Baden	Serve on small pommes Anna, garnish with asparagus tips and button mushrooms and coat with Madeira sauce.
Bristol	Place a poached egg on top, garnish with tomate concassée and pommes pailles and serve with sauce béarnaise.
Choiseuil	Sandwich the two slices with a filling of mirepoix plus truffle; egg and crumb and shallow fry and serve with sauce périgueux.
Favorite	Dip in flour and shallow fry and garnish with asparagus tips, a slice of foie gras and of truffle and surround with Madeira sauce.
Grand-Duc	Decorate with a slice of truffle, coat with sauce mornay and glaze; garnish with asparagus tips.
Judic	Garnish with a round slice of chicken forcemeat and a braised lettuce.

Maréchal	Garnish with asparagus tips and a slice of truffle.
Milanaise	Coat with egg-wash and breadcrumbs mixed with cheese; shallow fry and serve with spaghetti mixed with tomato, julienne of ham, mushroom and truffle.
Pompadour	Garnish with an artichoke bottom filled with lentil purée with a slice of truffle on top, and small pommes croquettes.
Rossini	Decorate with a slice of foie gras and of truffle, and serve with Madeira sauce.
Saint-Mandé	Serve on small pommes Anna and garnish with buttered peas and beans.
Viennoise	Serve with a quarter of lemon and fried parsley, with sauce hollandaise or melted butter.
Villeroy	Dip into sauce Villeroy, allow to cool then egg and crumb and fry; serve with sauce périgueux.
Waldorf	Garnish with an artichoke bottom filled with very small quenelles mixed with Madeira sauce.

Other Methods of using Sweetbreads

The following show the versatility of sweetbreads in providing interesting and nutritious entrées:

Attereaux	Thread small rounds of braised calf's sweetbreads or whole lamb's breads on skewers together with cooked mushrooms, squares of bacon, etc., dip into butter, then breadcrumbs and grill.
Attereau Villeroy	Dip a prepared attereau in sauce Villeroy and when cold, flour, egg and crumb, roll to shape and deep fry.
Chartreuse	Decorate a charlotte mould with small cooked rounds of different coloured vegetables, spread with forcemeat and cook au bain-marie; fill the mould with layers of sliced braised sweetbreads, sliced mushroom, sliced truffle and sauce allemande. Seal with forcemeat and cook in the

oven au bain-marie then turn out, garnish with turned mushrooms and serve with sauce allemande (reduced velouté, stock, mushroom cooking liquid, yolks and lemon juice).

Coquille Pipe a scallop shell with duchesse potato, fill with sliced braised sweetbread, mushroom, tongue and truffle in an appropriate sauce; coat with the sauce, sprinkle with breadcrumbs and/or cheese and gratinate.

Croustades Fill deep pastry tartlets, duchesse potato nests or hollowed-out deep-fried semolina galettes with slices of braised sweetbread, mushroom, etc., in an appropriate sauce.

en Croûte Enclose a cooked sweetbread with duxelles, tongue and mushrooms in a round of pastry; turn over, egg-wash and bake.

au Gratin Sandwich sliced braised sweetbreads with duxelles, surround with cooked button mushrooms, cover with sauce duxelles and sprinkle with breadcrumbs; gratinate in a hot oven and sprinkle with lemon juice.

Grillé Blanch, cool and press, cut into two slices, dip in melted butter and grill gently; serve with tomato or piquant sauce.

Grillé Châtelaine Place a grilled sweetbread on a layer of salpicon of foie gras, mushroom and truffle mixed with sauce allemande, in a hollowed-out brioche.

Grillé Gismonda Place the whole grilled sweetbread on a creamed layer of sliced artichoke bottom and mushroom in an oval flan just large enough to take it.

Grillé Jocelyne Shallow fry rounds of large potatoes 3cm thick in butter, cut a border around and hollow them out, fill with curry-flavoured soubise and place a grilled sweetbread on top; garnish with a grilled half of tomato and a grilled green pimento.

Grillé St-Germain Garnish with bouquets of glazed carrots and sautéd small rounds of potato, purée of peas and sauce béarnaise.

Timbale Fill a deep pastry case with pieces of braised sweetbread, sliced mushrooms, noodles, truffle, etc., mixed with an appropriate sauce.

Vol-au-Vent Fill a vol-au-vent with diced or sliced braised sweetbreads, cockscombs, mushrooms, quenelles, etc., mixed with sauce allemande; replace the lid.

Ox Tail – *Queue de Boeuf*

Cut into sections through the natural joints, reserving the tip ends for oxtail soup; fry in hot dripping and braise in brown stock.

Ancienne Coat braised pieces of oxtail with egg-wash and breadcrumbs, deep fry and serve with the thick-end braising liquid and a purée of vegetable.

Auvergnate Garnish with braised chestnuts, glazed button onions and lardons.

aux Carottes Garnish with turned glazed carrots.

Cavour Serve garnished with mushrooms and purée of chestnut piped around.

Charollaise Arrange in a glazed border of duchesse potato with turned carrots and turnips, quenelles and triangles of boiled salt belly of pork.

Chipolata Garnish with glazed carrots, braised chestnuts, grilled chipolata sausages and lardons of bacon.

Hochepot Poach the pieces with pig's trotters and ears, button onions, turned carrots and turnips and quarters of cabbage; serve with grilled chipolatas and boiled potatoes.

Jardinière Add a garnish of batons of carrot and turnip, peas and diamonds of French beans, tossed in butter.

Nohant Decorate the pieces of braised oxtail with braised lamb sweetbreads and slice of ox tongue; coat with sauce and garnish with 1cm dice of carrot and turnip with diamonds of French beans and peas.

aux Prunes Cook and serve with soaked and stoned prunes.

Pigs' tails can be cooked in a 'blanc' then shallow fried, or braised, grilled, or deep fried.

Tongue – Langue

Those of the calf, lamb and ox are used fresh but mainly cured in brine; they may be boiled or braised, usually a combination of both – boil then braise.

Alsacienne	Boil, skin, cut into 3mm thick slices and arrange on a bed of braised sauerkraut; serve jus lié separately.
Bigarade	Serve slices of braised tongue covered with sauce bigarade (add orange and lemon juice to the reduced braising liquid).
Bourgeoise	Braise until three parts done then add turned carrots and button onions and cook until tender.
aux Epinards	Serve 3mm thick slices of braised tongue on a bed of buttered leaf or purée spinach and surround with Madeira Sauce; garnish with triangular croûtons.
Flamande	Serve slices of braised tongue with turned carrots, turnips and potatoes, triangles of boiled salt belly of pork and small braised cabbages.
au Madère	Boil, skin and cut into slices 3mm thick; coat with Madeira sauce.
Nignon	Garnish with fried slices of eggplant, grilled tomatoes and sautéd cèpes.
Radewski	Serve slices of braised tongue coated with the braising liquid containing dice of carrot, onion and truffle, and garnish with fans of gherkin and pommes duchesse.

Tripe

This has been bleached and blanched ready for cooking but still requires an hour's steady stewing to render it digestible. It may be cut into 5cm squares or 6cm strips.

Anglaise (tripe and onions)	Boil 5cm squares of tripe and sliced onion in water for 1 hour; drain, place in cream sauce and reheat together.
Bourgeoise	Cook sliced onion and carrot in butter, add flour and white stock to make a sauce and cook 3cm squares of tripe in it for 1 hour; finish with chopped garlic and sliced mushroom.
à la Mode de Caen	Cook 5cm squares of tripe with a cow heel, studded onion, and carrot in cider and calvados in a sealed pan for 12 hours; serve pieces of tripe and cow-heel with the cooking liquid.
Créole	Cook strips of tripe, sliced onion and pimento, diced tomato and chopped garlic in the oven with very little stock and serve with boiled rice.
Espagnole	Add strips of cooked tripe and cow-heel and slices of garlic sausage to sautéd sliced onion and diced tomato in tomato and caraway-flavoured demi-glace.
Frit	Dip cooked squares of tripe in butter then in eggwash and breadcrumbs; deep fry and serve with a piquant sauce; or marinade the tripe in oil and lemon juice, dip in batter and deep fry; serve with tomato sauce.
Hongroise	Add strips of cooked tripe and julienne of red pimento to paprika-flavoured velouté.
Lyonnaise	Sauté large strips of cooked tripe in lard until brown, add sautéd sliced onion and toss over to mix; serve sprinkled with a little hot vinegar.
Poulette	Add strips of cooked tripe to sauce poulette (reduced velouté, mushroom cooking liquid, egg yolks and lemon juice).
Provençale	Fry 6cm strips of tripe in hot oil until brown, place in a braising pan with sautéd sliced onion, garlic, chopped tomato and sugar and cook in white wine for 4 hours at 125°C.
Troyenne	Spread cooked squares with made English mustard then flour, egg and crumb and deep fry; serve with sauce Gribiche (oil, vinegar, chopped capers, gherkins and fines herbes).

Vénitienne   Mix strips of cooked tripe and sliced mushroom with tomato sauce, sprinkle with Parmesan and butter and gratinate.

MISCELLANEOUS DISHES
—— USING RAW OFFALS ——

Bath Chap   This is the bottom part of a pig's cheek cured as for bacon and usually sold coated with yellow crumbs. It may be cut in slices and served cold or shallow-fried as part of breakfast.

Black Pudding   This is made in the form of a long sausage from pig's blood, suet, oatmeal, onion, etc.; it can be cut in round or long slices and shallow fried or grilled for breakfast.

Brawn   Salted pig's head and feet are boiled until the meat falls off the bones; it is then diced and moulded with some of the cooking liquid which should set naturally. Gherkins are sometimes included in it.

Cockscombs and kidneys   When preparing rough-plucked chickens for cooking, the combs may be cut off and put to use as a garnish. Soak in salt water then place in fresh cold water, bring almost to a boil and rub or scrape off the skin; place in a 'blanc' and cook gently. The aim is to change them from the natural red to pure white in colour.

The 'kidneys' are actually the cock's testicles and they need to be soaked well before cooking with the combs.

Faggots   These are made of minced pork, pig's liver and lights, onion, thyme and breadcrumbs or rusks; wrap in caul, bake in the oven and coat with brown sauce.

Foie gras   The average size whole specially enlarged liver of a goose weighs about 800g and is available in many forms, sometimes raw but mostly cooked in terrines or tins.

A whole raw foie gras can be stiffened by frying the outside in hot butter then cooking in an earthenware dish with a little veal stock for approximately 1 hour, or it can be baked in short pastry for approximately 45 minutes. Serve garnished with buttered noodles or other pasta accompanied by Madeira sauce, sauce suprême, paprika sauce, etc.

Foie gras Strasbourgeoise This is the whole liver baked in a tall pie mould lined with hot-water pastry or brioche pastry. It is served by the spoonful, either hot or cold – hot with pasta or rice and a sauce; cold with port wine jelly and a salad.

Goat The kid can be prepared in any of the ways as for lamb but mainly by roasting, stuck with sprigs of rosemary.

Haggis This is a sheep's stomach filled with a mixture of the boiled and minced heart, lights and liver with oatmeal, suet, onion and spices. To cook, prick with a needle, wrap in a cloth and place to boil for approximately $1\frac{1}{2}$ hours, according to size. Serve with whisky sauce (lightly whipped cream with whisky), and mashed swede and mashed potato.

Horsemeat When cooked by roasting, braising or stewing, horsemeat has a sweetish taste that distinguishes it from beef. The sirloin and fillet is cut into steaks for grilling. The fact that it is being served must be clearly stated on the menu.

Pluck This is the heart, liver and lungs of a sheep, attached to the windpipe and sold as a trade joint; it is used to make haggis.

Testicles The menu term for animal's testicles is animelles; to cook, blanch, soak then proceed as for a fricassée; coat with batter and deep fry; cut into slices and shallow fry; or grill and serve with a suitable sauce and garnish.

Whalemeat This can be cut into joints for roasting or braising, or into slices for shallow frying. It looks like beef and is sometimes called sea beef.

9 GAME

Game and Wild Birds – Gibier à Plume

The main game birds that add extra interest to the menu during the winter months are grouse, partridge and pheasant. The other wild birds that come into season from August onwards are snipe, wild duck and woodcock, but wood pigeons and quails also come into this category and are available throughout the year. To improve the flavour and tenderness they should be hung undrawn, in a cool place for a few days.

Game birds are best cooked by roasting, keeping just slightly underdone; the accompaniments are game chips, watercress, bread sauce, roast gravy and fried breadcrumbs; it is usual to place the bird on a croûton spread with a farce made from the liver. The slice of fat bacon used to protect the breast whilst roasting may be draped across the legs.

—PARTRIDGE AND PHEASANT—

The garnishes for use with partridge (perdreau) and pheasant (faisan) include the following in which the bird is cooked mainly by poêlé-ing:

Alcantara   Stuff a boned bird with a truffled foie gras and marinate in port; cook with butter in a casserole and serve with sauce made by reducing the port of the marinade; garnish with truffle.

Alexis   Poêlé the bird, garnish with raisins and coat with sauce made from the cooking liquid, curaçao and cream.

Ananas   Garnish with segments of pineapple and coat with sauce made with pineapple juice, the cooking liquid and brandy.

Angoulemoise Stuff with braised chestnuts and truffle and roast; serve with sauce Périgueux.

Bonne-Maman Garnish with $2\frac{1}{2}$cm × 4mm batons of carrot, celery, turnips, French beans and swede and coat with the reduced cooking liquid.

Bourguignonne Garnish the poêléd bird with lardons, button mushrooms and button onions and a sauce made by deglazing the pan with red wine and reducing it.

Carême Garnish the poêléd bird with sections of braised celery and coat with the pan juices finished with meat glaze and cream.

en Casserole Poêlé the bird in the usual way and add a little brandy and game stock to make the accompanying sauce.

Chartreuse Decorate a buttered charlotte mould with rounds of different coloured vegetables, line with braised cabbage and fill with the carved bird, slices of salt belly of pork and smoked sausage; cover with cabbage and cook au bain-marie for 30 minutes; serve with game-flavoured demiglace.

aux Choux Braise covered with blanched cabbage and a piece of salt belly of pork; carve and serve with the cabbage and sliced pork, with grilled chipolatas and slices of carrot cooked with the bird.

This dish may be served in portions by lining a soup plate with cabbage leaves, the breast of partridge or pheasant, a slice of sausage and pork, a little of the sauce and more cabbage; fold over and bake until very hot.

à la Crème Poêlé the bird then commence to baste with sour cream; serve coated with the strained cooking liquid.

Demidoff Poêlé with crescent-shaped pieces of carrot and turnip, dice of celery and rings of onion and finish with crescents of truffle.

Fermière Garnish with paysanne of carrot, celery, onion and turnip added to finish cooking with the bird.

Georgienne   Poêlé the bird with fresh walnuts, orange juice, grape juice and strong tea, colouring and basting towards the end; serve garnished with the nuts and sauced with the well-reduced cooking liquid added to a little game-flavoured espagnole.

Kotschoubey   Stuff with chopped pork fat and truffles and poêlé; serve with Brussels sprouts, lardons of bacon and coat with truffle-flavoured demi-glace.

Lucullus   Stuff with truffled forcemeat and serve garnished with cockscombs and truffle, coated with truffle-flavoured demi-glace.

Normande   Poêlé with a little calvados and cider and serve garnished with glazed slices of apple and the cooking liquid thickened with cream.

Périgueux   Stuff with pork fat and truffle and poêlé; garnish with truffled game quenelles and coat with sauce Périgueux.

Régence   Serve the poêléd bird on a bread croûton surrounded with cockscombs, slices of foie gras, mushrooms, quenelles and truffle.

Saint-Alliance   Stuff with woodcock and bone-marrow forcemeat and roast, adding a thick croûton spread with a purée of woodcock liver, anchovy, pork fat and chopped truffle; finish to cook and garnish with segments of Seville oranges.

Salmis   Cut a roast bird into portions and place into a cocotte; use the bones, shallot, crushed peppercorns and red wine to make the sauce, add to demi-glace and strain over the bird.

Souvaroff   Stuff with foie gras and truffle, poêlé and serve garnished with diced truffle heated in meat glaze and the cooking liquid made into the sauce.

Titania   Garnish with orange segments and peeled and depipped grapes and coat with the cooking liquid reduced and thickened with pomegranate juice.

Victoria   Stuff a boned bird with foie gras and truffle, poêlé and serve garnished with diced fried potato and the thickened cooking liquid.

Game birds may be cooked in the same way as for sauté of chicken and the same garnishes are applicable.

Wings of partridge and pheasant may be prepared as suprêmes and the recipes for suprême of chicken are suitable.

———— PIGEONS ————

There are many interesting recipes for using wood pigeons, either whole cooked by braising, or the breasts only, sautéd in the same way as for suprêmes of chicken.

Tender young pigeons can be grilled or cut into pieces for quick sautés. The ramier is a large and usually plump older bird. A young pigeon is sometimes referred to as a squab and can be roasted with a chestnut stuffing, wrapped in thin rashers of streaky bacon and served with game chips, watercress, gravy and browned crumbs.

Casserole	Colour in hot butter and poêlé adding white wine and demi-glace; add a suitable garnish such as bouquetière, bourgeoise, bourguignonne, forestière, jardinière, macédoine, niçoise, printanière, etc.
Chipolata	Poêlé, adding white wine and demi-glace and garnish with braised chestnuts, glazed carrots, chipolatas and lardons; coat with the reduced cooking liquid.
Compote	Poêlé, adding a little mushroom cooking liquid, demi-glace and white wine; garnish with button mushrooms and onions and lardons and coat with the reduced cooking liquid.
Grand'mère	Stuff with bacon, breadcrumb and liver stuffing; poêlé and garnish with button onions, lardons and small turned potatoes cooked in butter.
Lavallière	Garnish with peas cooked à la française with the addition of glazed button onions and diced ham; cover with Madeira sauce.
Nana	Poêlé, adding white wine and jus lié and garnish with glazed button onions, stoned olives, pommes noisettes and diced truffle.

aux Olives	Poêlé, add demi-glace and garnish with blanched black or green olives; coat with the reduced cooking liquid.
aux Petits Pois	Garnish with button onions, lardons and peas cooked with the bird; add demi-glace to make the sauce.
Printanière	Garnish with new season's carrots, button onions, turnips, peas and French beans and coat with the cooking liquid.
Saint-Charles	Garnish the braised bird with sautéd cèpes and coat with the cooking liquid finished with lemon juice.
Valencienne	Stuff with liver and mushroom stuffing, poêlé and serve around a pyramid of rice pilaff made with sliced artichoke bottoms, mushroom and red pimento; garnish with heart-shaped pieces of ham and surround with tomato sauce.

——— QUAILS – CAILLES ———

These small birds are now extensively reared in hatcheries so should really be classified as poultry rather than as game.

They are sold ready prepared all the year and unless they have been boned and given a good stuffing and an elaborate garnish, they should be served two plump ones per portion. The most popular ways of cooking is by poaching and poêlé and they can then be enclosed in pastry and baked.

If served roasted, the usual accompaniments are as for other game birds.

Ananas	Poêlé, garnish with triangles of fresh pineapple and flavour the accompanying sauce with pineapple juice.
Beaconsfield	Poêlé and place on a bed of purée of peas; garnish with button mushrooms and cover with the sauce made from the cooking liquid.
Bohémienne	Bone and stuff with foie gras and truffle, poêlé and coat with the cooking liquid added to jus lié.

Café de Paris	Place the poêléd quail in a scooped-out baked potato on a layer of purée of foie gras; cover with a sauce made from the cooking liquid.
aux Cerises	Garnish the poêléd quail with poached stoned morello cherries; add port and brandy to the pan, reduce and make the sauce with orange peel, redcurrant jelly and veal gravy.
Clermont	Stuff the boned quails with chopped chestnuts cooked with chopped onion; poêlé and serve covered with soubise sauce.
aux Coings	Marinate the quails with brandy and quince peelings for 48 hours; remove the peels, add butter and cook in the tightly sealed cocotte; serve with quince jelly.
Diane	Garnish the poêléd quails with chestnut purée and coat with creamed sauce poivrade garnished with diced hard-boiled egg and truffle.
Egyptienne	Garnish the poêléd quails with rice pilaff containing diced tomato and surround with tomato sauce.
Kléber	Serve on a shallow oval vol-au-vent filled with salpicon of foie gras and mushroom and coat with Madeira sauce flavoured with mushroom liquid.
Liégeoise	Poêlé the quails with juniper berries and flavour the sauce with gin.
Maintenon	Poêlé boned quails stuffed with truffled game forcemeat; garnish with cockscombs, mushrooms and truffle and coat with sauce périgueux.
Marianne	Poêlé with segments of apple and finish by gratinating with breadcrumbs and butter.
au Nid	Stuff boned quails with forcemeat and mould round; poach then place each on an artichoke bottom and coat with demi-glace; pipe with chestnut purée to represent a nest and garnish with small egg-shaped game quenelles.
Parmentier	Stuff the boned quails with foie gras and game forcemeat and poêlé; serve in a scooped out baked potato.
Périgourdine	Garnish with pieces of truffle and coat with Madeira sauce.

Piémontaise	Serve on a bed of risotto containing sautéd diced chicken livers and grated white truffle.
Princesse	Stuff the boned quails with foie gras and game forcemeat and poach; serve on a glazed nest of duchesse potato filled with asparagus tips and coat with sauce allemande flavoured with asparagus.
aux Raisins	Poêlé in butter, remove and garnish with peeled, depipped grapes; add white wine and jus lié to the cooking liquid and strain over the quails; finish with a squeeze of lemon. This dish is sometimes called Véronique.
Richelieu	Fill boned quails with a truffle, poach with julienne of carrot, celery and turnip and serve sprinkled with it and with julienne of truffle.
Urbain-Dubois	Stuff boned quails with game forcemeat, poêlé with Madeira and small dice of carrot, mushroom and onion.
Valenciennes	Serve on a bed of risotto containing peas and diced ham, artichoke bottoms and diced tomato.
Victoria	Bone and stuff with foie gras and truffle and poêlé with 1cm dice of potato; make the sauce with brandy and jus lié.
Vigneron	Wrap in a rasher of streaky bacon and a vine leaf then roast; garnish with peeled and depipped grapes and serve with Madeira sauce.

Quails may be boned and stuffed, parcooked then wrapped in puff pastry or brioche paste and baked.

SNIPE AND WOODCOCK – BÉCASSINE ET BÉCASSE

These small birds are never very plentiful in that they cannot be obtained in such large numbers as partridge and pheasant. The snipe has a long beak and legs which are used to truss it; only the gizzard is removed before trussing these two as the entrails are used to spread on the accompanying croûton.

Alcantara   Place a piece of foie gras and truffle inside the bird, marinate in port then poêlé until nearly cooked; garnish with truffle, add the reduced port flavoured with meat glaze, seal with pastry in a cocotte and finish in a hot oven.

Carême   Cut the breasts off a roast bird, coat with French mustard mixed with lemon juice and then with a sauce made of the carcase and intestine, brandy and game stock reduced to a cullis.

Favart   Cut the breasts off an underdone bird and fill the carcase with forcemeat containing the sieved intestine of the bird; replace the breasts together with sliced truffle and finish cooking in the oven; serve with woodcock-flavoured demi-glace.

au Fumet   Place the carved breasts on a hollow croûton spread with liver forcemeat mixed with the crushed intestine and coat with a sauce made with brandy, red wine, the juice from the crushed carcase and sieved raw liver.

This dish is sometimes prepared in front of the customer and the brain is extracted from the bird and used in making the sauce.

Riche   Place the breasts of a poêléd bird on a fried croûton spread with liver forcemeat and coat with a sauce made of brandy, the cooking liquid, lemon juice, foie gras purée and the intestine.

Souvaroff   Stuff with foie gras and truffle, poêlé and allow to colour until three parts done; deglaze with game stock, meat glaze and Madeira, garnish with diced truffle and seal in a cocotte with pastry; finish to cook in a moderate oven.

Victoria   Stuff the boned bird with foie gras and truffle and poêlé with 1cm dice of potato previously sauted in butter; finish with a little brandy.

WILD DUCK – CANARD
——— SAUVAGE ———

A small wild duck is only enough for one portion and the only other size available suffices for two persons. It is trussed by inverting the legs so that it is sitting up with the tail in the air.

To be tender it must be roasted very underdone at a high temperature – a small teal for 12 minutes, a mallard for not more than 20 minutes.

Bigarade	Serve with segments of orange and a sauce made of jus lié, orange and lemon juice, sugar and vinegar reduced to a caramel, and blanched julienne of orange and lemon peel.
au Porto	Serve with port wine sauce (demi-glace flavoured with port).
á la Presse	Carve a roast wild duck into thin slices (aiguillettes); crush the carcase, minus the legs, in the press and collect the juice. Fry a fine mirepoix in the same pan in which the duck was cooked, flame with brandy and add red wine and duck stock; strain, add the blood and juice but do not boil; thicken by stirring in the sieved duck liver mixed with a little butter and purée of foie gras. Serve with the legs which have been scored, spread with made English mustard and grilled.

Game Animals – Gibier à Poil

This section includes venison (venaison), hare (lièvre), leveret or young hare (levrault), rabbit (lapin), and wild rabbit (lapin de garenne).

VENISON

Venison is the general name given to all the different kinds of deer; it needs to be hung for a few days after killing in order to improve its flavour and tenderness. Any game that has been carefully hung is then ready for use and does not require to be marinated in wine, a process that is also meant to improve flavour and tenderness.

The large joints are the saddle (selle), and haunch or leg (cuissot or gigue), both suitable for roasting, keeping slightly underdone. There is very little fat on venison so it is necessary to lard or bard it with salt pork fat; the joint may be baked inside a fatless pastry to prevent drying out. Redcurrant jelly, cumberland sauce, braised chestnuts, and chestnut purée are the normal accompaniments; cranberry sauce is also suitable.

Cutlets, noisettes and steaks of venison are used for entrées by shallow frying or grilling. Poorer quality cuts are used for stewing in the form of a civet or salmis.

Saddle (and haunch) of Venison

Baden-Baden	Poêlé the joint, serve with pears poached without sugar and the cooking liquid made into the sauce; serve redcurrant jelly separately.
Berny	Garnish with pommes Berny and tartlets filled with lentil purée, decorated with a slice of truffle; serve with sauce poivrade.
Briande	Garnish with pears poached in red wine; make the gravy from the sediment in the roasting tray and serve with redcurrant jelly.
Cherville	Garnish with hollowed-out dessert apples filled with hot apple purée and serve with sauce groseille au raifort (port reduced with redcurrant jelly, flavoured with grated horseradish).
Créole	Garnish with sautéd bananas and serve with a sauce made by frying a mirepoix with venison trimmings, reducing with red wine and vinegar and cooking with crushed peppercorns; strain and finish with sugar and made mustard.
Cumberland	Serve with chestnut purée and Cumberland sauce (reduced port with orange and lemon juice,

redcurrant jelly, mustard and julienne of orange and lemon peel).

Genièvre Serve slices of roast venison with apple sauce and a sauce made by adding cream, gin, juniper berries and lemon juice to sauce poivrade.

Grand-Veneur Garnish with small round croquette potatoes, chestnut purée, French beans and venison sauce (sauce poivrade finished with cream and redcurrant jelly).

Livonienne Garnish with open mushrooms filled with creamed horseradish, tartlets filled with caviar, pickled cucumbers and the cooking liquid thickened with sour cream.

Poivrade Serve slices of roast venison coated with sauce poivrade (fry a mirepoix, reduce with vinegar and red wine, add demi-glace and crushed peppercorns).

Small Cuts of Venison

Beauval Serve the sautéd pieces of venison each on a deep-fried galette of duchesse potato mixed with chopped truffle; place an open mushroom piped with soubise on top and serve with cream sauce flavoured with juniper berries.

Caucasienne Serve the sautéd pieces of venison on an oval piece of buckwheat kache (mix soft dough from a buckwheat loaf with butter, spread 1cm thick, cut into 7cm ovals and shallow fry); coat with sauce poivrade flavoured with anchovy, fennel, garlic and coriander.

Conti Garnish with heart-shaped slices of ox tongue and purée of lentils and coat with sauce poivrade.

Diane Garnish with cooked triangular shapes of game forcemeat and purée of chestnut; coat with sauce Diane (add crescents of or diced hard-boiled egg and truffle to sauce poivrade and finish with cream).

Genièvre Place each venison steak on a heart-shaped croûton and coat with sauce poivrade flavoured with gin, juniper berry, lemon juice and cream; serve apple sauce separately.

Gourmet   Sauté on one side, spread with game and foie gras forcemeat and finish to cook in an oven; serve with Madeira sauce.

Josephine   Coat with egg-wash and chopped truffle, shallow fry and garnish with a tartlet filled with purée of game, a grilled mushroom and sauce périgueux.

Morland   Serve on an individual portion of pommes Anna and coat with sauce poivrade seasoned with mustard and finished with cream and blanched julienne of orange zest.

Nesselrode   Sauté on one side, coat dome-shaped with game forcemeat and decorate with a slice of truffle; finish to cook and serve garnished with chestnut purée and demi-glace.

Norvégienne   Garnish with one tartlet of chestnut purée and one of diced creamed salsify; serve with sauce grand-veneur (sauce poivrade with cream and redcurrant jelly).

aux Poires   Marinate in oil and lemon juice, sauté and serve with a hot spiced pear.

Romanoff   Serve on a hollowed-out oval piece of cucumber, cooked and filled with duxelles; garnish with creamed cèpes and serve with sauce poivrade (mirepoix reduced with vinegar and red wine, demi-glace and crushed peppercorns).

Saint-Hubert   Sauté on one side, spread with game and mushroom forcemeat flavoured with juniper, wrap in caul, sprinkle with breadcrumbs and butter and cook in the oven; serve with apple sauce and venison sauce (poivrade sauce with redcurrant jelly).

Saint-Marc   Braise the venison steak, garnish with small deep-fried balls of chestnut purée and serve with the reduced braising liquid and cranberry sauce.

Valencia   Serve on fried croûtons made from a brioche; garnish with orange segments and coat with bigarade sauce (demi-glace, orange and lemon

	juice, reduced vinegar and sugar, and blanched julienne of orange).
Villeneuve	Colour in hot butter, spread with game salpicon and wrap in caul, sprinkle with butter and finish to cook in an oven; serve with game sauce containing julienne of truffle.
Walkyrie	Serve on a galette of pommes berny with a mushroom filled with soubise, accompanied with juniper-flavoured cream sauce.

HARE – LIÈVRE (ALSO ——— RABBIT – LAPIN) ———

It is usual to hang a hare for a few says before skinning and paunching and before placing to marinate for 48 hours or more. Rabbit, especially wild rabbit (lapin de garenne), also benefits by being hung and marinated. The blood and liver, minus the gall bladder, is kept in a little vinegar and used as the liaison to thicken the cooking liquid by liquidising it in a blender and adding to the boiling liquid at the last moment; flour can be used instead.

To prepare for civet, cut off the shoulders and leave whole; cut each leg into two pieces, cut the saddle square and the forepart down the centre bone, discarding the belly; cover with red wine, using a heavy one for hare, a lighter one for rabbit; add a little oil, chopped carrot and onion, garlic, thyme and juniper berries, cover with a paper or lid and turn occasionally. Leave to marinate for several days.

The saddle can be used as an entrée in its own right, with the following garnishes; first, it is skinned, larded with strips of salt pork fat and kept in marinade if not being used at once. If plainly roasted, serve with redcurrant jelly or unsweetened apple sauce, or with a compote of cherries or soft fruit.

Râble de Lièvre

Allemande	Roast with butter on the vegetables from the marinade for 15–20 minutes in a hot oven, keeping underdone; drain the fat from the pan,

	add cream, reduce to a sauce and finish with lemon juice.
Diane	Roast and serve with chestnut purée and sauce Diane (sauce poivrade with whipped cream and crescents of hard-boiled white of egg and truffle).
Forestière	Garnish with lardons, morels and sautéd dice of potato; serve with sauce duxelles (demi-glace with duxelles and tomato purée).
Genièvre	Serve coated with sauce made of sauce poivrade, the marinade and crushed juniper berries.
Grand-Veneur	Garnish with chestnut purée and coat with sauce grand-veneur (sauce poivrade with some of the marinade and blood from the hare).
Morland	Serve with sauce poivrade containing julienne of truffle and blanched julienne of orange zest.
Navarraise	Garnish with open mushrooms filled with garlic and herb-flavoured thickened jus lié; coat with the deglazed pan juice.
Rôtisserie Périgourdine	Stuff with game liver, bacon and truffle stuffing, wrap in salt pork fat and braise in Madeira and brown stock; remove the fat, enclose in puff pastry, egg-wash and bake. Serve with the reduced braising liquid containing chestnut purée and julienne of truffle.
Russe	Braise in sour cream and serve coated with the cream reduced with some of the marinade and demi-glace, and finely diced beetroot.
Saint-Hubert	Roast with crushed juniper berries; garnish with button mushrooms or mousserons and galettes of game forcemeat; coat with the deglazed sediment added to sauce poivrade.
Viennoise	Roast, serve with small suet dumplings and demi-glace mixed with sour cream and capers.

Civet de Lièvre – Jugged Hare

Shallow fry the pieces of hare and the vegetables from the marinade, sprinkle with flour and singe in a hot oven; add tomato purée, brown stock, the marinade and garlic and braise for approximately 2 hours. Thicken the liquid with the liquidised blood and liver and with a little vinegar, but do not boil. Pour over the pieces of hare and garnish with deep-fried small balls of lemon and thyme stuffing, fleurons or heart-shaped croûtons and heated glacé cherries. Serve redcurrant jelly separately.

Small rolls of beef are sometimes cooked with the hare.

Rabbit may be prepared in this way and in those that follow.

Civet de Lièvre Bourguignonne	Add a garnish of glazed button onions, button mushrooms and lardons and decorate with heart-shaped croûtons with the points dipped in chopped parsley.
Civet de Lièvre Flamande	Cook in red wine and vinegar with sliced onion and sugar; garnish with heart-shaped croûtons spread with redcurrant jelly.
Civet de Lièvre Lyonnaise	Garnish with braised chestnuts and glazed button onions.
Civet de Lièvre Mère Jean	Cook with large dice of salt belly of pork and serve with sliced cèpes cooked in oil with onion, garlic and breadcrumbs mixed with diced fried bread croûtons.
Civet de Lièvre aux Pruneaux	Cook with soaked prunes and add redcurrant jelly to the sauce.
Lapin en Gibelotte	This is the same as civet de lièvre, cooking the pieces of rabbit in red wine and stock.
Sauté de Lapin	Fry pieces of rabbit and a mirepoix; singe with flour and cook in brown stock and tomato purée for approximately 1 hour.
Blanquette de Lapin	This is made in the same way as a blanquette of lamb and veal.

10 SAUCES

Sauces are dealt with under the following categories:

1. Basic sauces which can be used as made but are usually converted into minor sauces by further cooking with additional ingredients
2. Brown sauces based on demi-glace and jus lié
3. White sauces based on velouté and sauce suprême
4. Egg and butter sauces
5. Sauces used almost exclusively for fish dishes
6. Cold sauces
7. Butter sauces
8. Butters (hard sauces)

In addition there is a further category of purely à la carte sauces which are made for immediate use with the dish being prepared. They are made from a reduction of the cooking essence of the main ingredient after it has been cooked, with the addition of an appropriate wine or liqueur and stock, together with a thickening agent such as butter, cream, yolks, cornflour, cottage cheese, etc., and seasoning. There is no definite repertoire for this category of sauces. Many of the fish sauces are listed in the Fish section of this book.

Basic Sauces

Allemande   Whisk together 5 litres velouté, $2\frac{1}{2}$ litres white stock, 12 yolks, 1 litre mushroom liquid, lemon juice, nutmeg and pepper and reduce to 5 litres; finish with 500g butter.

Béchamel   Whisk 10 litres boiling milk into $1\frac{1}{4}$kg white roux, flavour with sautéd, sliced onion, bay-leaf and seasoning; cook for 2 hours and strain if necessary.

Demi-glace Cook equal quantities of espagnole and brown stock until reduced by half; finish with a little fortified wine, skim and strain.

Espagnole Mix 1¼kg brown roux into 20 litres brown stock, add a mirepoix and tomato purée then cook for 3–4 hours until reduced by three-quarters; strain and use.

Jus lié Reduce 20 litres brown stock by three-quarters and thicken with 150g diluted arrowroot; reboil, correct colour and flavour and strain.

Suprême Mix equal quantities of chicken velouté and chicken stock with a little mushroom liquid and cream and reduce by half; finish with butter and strain.

Tomato Fry a mirepoix with bacon, add flour, tomato purée, white stock and seasoning; cook for 1–1½ hours and strain.

Velouté Mix 11 litres veal, chicken or fish stock, as appropriate, into 1¼kg blond roux and cook for 1½ hours; skim off the fat and strain.

Brown Sauces

Algérienne Add cooked julienne of green and red pimento to tomato sauce (for general use).

Antin Add chopped mushrooms and truffle to sauce Madère (for small cuts of meat).

Barbecue Reduce red wine, vinegar, peppercorns, bay-leaf and sugar; add demi-glace, tomato ketchup, mustard and sweet pickle, cook and strain (for barbecue dishes).

Bigarade Use the sediment from a cooked duck with brown stock, orange and lemon juices, and caramelised sugar in vinegar; thicken with arrowroot and garnish with fine julienne of orange and lemon zest (for duck).

Bonnefoy	Reduce white wine and shallot; add espagnole and finish with meat glaze, lemon juice and diced bone marrow (for steaks).
Bordelaise	Reduce red wine, shallot and seasoning by three-quarters; add espagnole and finish with meat glaze, lemon juice and diced boned marrow (for steaks).
Bourguignonne	Reduce red wine, shallot and seasonings by half and thicken with beurre manié; finish with butter and cayenne (for steaks).
Bretonne	Sauté some chopped onion, add white wine and reduce then add equal quantities of espagnole and tomato sauce; flavour with garlic and finish with parsley (for joints).
Brown Onion	This is the English name for sauce lyonnaise.
Byron	Reduce some red wine with herb flavourings; thicken with diluted arrowroot and enrich with butter and garnish with short julienne of truffle (for grills).
Castellane	Add diced ham and cooked green pimento to sauce Madère (for pork).
aux Champignons	Add reduced mushroom liquid to demi-glace and garnish with very small mushrooms cooked in butter (for grills).
Charcutière	Add short thick julienne of gherkins to prepared sauce Robert (for pork dishes).
Chartres	Add an infusion of tarragon stalks to demi-glace and finish with chopped tarragon (for lamb and veal).
Chasseur	Sauté chopped shallots, sliced mushrooms and diced tomato; add white wine and reduce, then add equal quantities of demi-glace and tomato sauce; finish with butter and chopped tarragon and chervil (for many chicken and lamb dishes).
Chateaubriand	Add pieces of butter to some light meat glaze and finish with chopped parsley (for steaks).
Cherry	Reduce some port with mixed spice and grated orange zest; add orange juice, redcurrant jelly and cooked stoned morello cherries (for duck and venison).

Chevreuil	Finish sauce poivrade made with the appropriate stock by gradually adding red wine, a pinch of sugar and cayenne (for either game dishes or marinated steaks).
Colbert	This is a hard sauce being made of beurre maître d'hôtel with the addition of some meat glaze (for steaks).
Créole	Finish tomato sauce with a reduction of white wine and garlic and add julienne of red pimento (for barbecues).
Curry	Sauté chopped onions, add curry powder then flour and cook; moisten with stock, add tomato purée, chopped apple and chutney, coconut and garlic; it may be strained and finished with cream (for eggs, meats, and shellfish).
Diable	Make a reduction of vinegar, white wine, crushed peppercorns, shallots, thyme and bay-leaf; add demi-glace, strain and finish with butter and cayenne (for grilled poultry, meat and fish).
Diane	Add lightly whipped cream to sauce poivrade at the last moment and garnish with small crescents of truffle and hard-boiled white of egg (for small cuts of venison).
Duxelles	Reduce some white wine, mushroom liquid and shallots; add demi-glace, tomato purée and dry duxelles; finish with chopped parsley (for dishes made au gratin).
Esterhazy	Sauté chopped onion, add white wine and reduce; add demi-glace and sour cream and flavour with paprika; garnish with julienne of carrot and celeriac (for game).
Estragon	Infuse tarragon in reduced white wine, add to demi-glace and reduce by one-third; finish with chopped tarragon (for small cuts of veal and chicken).
Financière	Flavour some sauce Madère with truffle essence (for dishes done à la financière).
aux Fines Herbes	Infuse chervil, chives, parsley and tarragon stalks in boiling white wine, add to demi-glace

407

	and finish with chopped fines herbes and lemon juice (for steaks and chops).
Forestière	Add sautéd sliced mushrooms and diced tomato to jus lié (for small cuts of meat).
Garibaldi	Flavour demi-glace with diluted mustard, chopped garlic and cayenne; finish with some anchovy butter (for steaks).
Game	Finish sauce poivrade made with game trimmings, with redcurrant jelly and cream.
Gastronome	Reduce some champagne, add demi-glace and meat glaze and flavour with Madeira (for steaks).
Godard	Reduce white wine with a mirepoix containing raw ham; add demi-glace and mushroom liquid and strain (for dishes done à la Godard).
Grand-Veneur	Add some of the marinade and the blood from a hare to sauce poivrade made with venison stock; when cooked but not boiled, pass through a strainer (for roast and poêled venison).
Hachée	Sauté chopped onion and shallot, add vinegar and reduce, then espagnole and tomato sauce; finish with dry duxelles, small capers and chopped ham and parsley (for small cuts of lamb).
Hussarde	Sauté sliced onion and shallot, moisten with white wine and reduce; add demi-glace, tomato purée, crushed garlic and raw ham and when cooked, add grated horseradish and the ham cut in dice (for grilled steaks).
Italienne	Add duxelles and chopped ham to tomatoed demi-glace and finish with chopped fines herbes (for liver, cutlets and sautés).
La Vallière	Add reduction of game stock to demi-glace and finish with sour cream, julienne of truffle and chopped tarragon.
Livonienne	Add julienne of fennel and sour cream to demi-glace.
Lyonnaise	Sauté chopped onion, add vinegar and white wine and reduce; add demi-glace and use as it is, or strained (for liver, hamburg steaks, miroton of beef).

Madeira	Add Madeira to reduced demi-glace to give the correct consistency (for most small items and joints of meat and ham).
Malaga	Reduce white wine and chopped shallots, add demi-glace and flavour with Malaga wine, lemon juice and cayenne (for steaks).
Marchand de Vin	Chopped shallot reduced in red wine, add demi-glace and finish with butter (for steaks).
Moelle	Reduce red wine with shallots, bay-leaf and thyme, add espagnole and strain; finish with meat glaze, lemon juice and diced bone-marrow (for steaks, braised celery).
Milanaise	Add julienne of mushrooms to tomato flavoured demi-glace and flavour with garlic (for pastas).
Miroton	Add sautéd sliced onions and made mustard to tomatoed demi-glace. (for reheated sliced meats).
Moscovite	Add Malaga wine, infusion of junipers and toasted pine-seed kernels to sauce poivrade (for joints of venison).
Mousquetaire	Cook tomato flesh in oil with sugar and seasoning, garlic and parsley; cook until reduced then add chopped fines herbes (for dishes done à la provençale).
Napolitaine	Sauté a fine mirepoix with tomato, reduce with Marsala wine and add demi-glace (for pastas).
Parisienne	Reduction of shallots in white wine, then demi-glace, meat glaze and lemon juice (for tournedos, noisettes, etc.).
Périgueux	Add truffle essence to demi-glace and finish with finely chopped truffle (for noisettes, tournedos, etc.).
Périgourdine	Add truffle essence to demi-glace and finish with small balls of truffle (for noisettes, tournedos, etc.).
Piquante	Reduce white wine, vinegar and chopped shallots by half, add espagnole and finish with chopped gherkins and fines herbes (for pork dishes and émincés).

Poivrade   Sauté a mirepoix and reduce with vinegar and marinating liquid; add espagnole, crushed peppercorns and strain and finish with butter (for marinated meats).

For use with game, this sauce should be made from game trimmings and game stock (for all game dishes).

Port Wine   Add port to reduced demi-glace to give the right flavour and consistency (for wild duck, veal).

Portugaise   Cook chopped onion in oil, add diced tomato, garlic, seasoning and sugar, cook until well reduced then add meat glaze, tomato purée and bring to sauce consistency with thin tomato sauce; finish with chopped parsley. (for entrées).

Provençale   Cook chopped tomato in oil, add garlic, parsley, seasoning and sugar and cook until well reduced. (for dishes à la provençale).

Réforme   Cook a mirepoix, add peppercorns and vinegar and reduce, add demi-glace, brown stock and redcurrant jelly; pass and add a garnish of julienne of beetroot, gherkin, ham, mushrooms, ox-tongue, truffle and cooked egg white (for lamb cutlets à la réforme).

Richelieu   Add meat glaze and diced tomato to tomato sauce (for veal, pork and pastas).

Robert   Sauté chopped onion, add white wine and reduce; add demi-glace and finish with made English mustard and sugar (for use with pork dishes).

Romaine   Caramelise some sugar, add vinegar, espagnole and game stock; reduce and garnish with toasted pine-seed kernels, currants and sultanas (for venison).

Rouennaise   Reduce red wine with shallots, peppercorns and herbs; add espagnole, purée of raw duck liver and lemon juice (for roast duck).

Salmis   Sauté a mirepoix with game bones, add white wine and reduce then some demi-glace; flavour with mushroom liquid and truffle essence (for game stews).

Sicilienne	Flavour demi-glace with Marsala and garnish with fried onion rings (for game dishes).
Sultane	Dilute demi-glace with game stock, reduce until thick then correct with port.
Tortue	Add an infusion of turtle herbs to 2 parts demi-glace and 1 part tomato sauce; finish with madeira, truffle essence and cayenne (for calf's head).
Valeria	Flavour sauce bordelaise with mustard and horse-radish and finish with chopped chervil.
Venaison	Add redcurrant jelly and cream to sauce poivrade for game (for joints of venison).
au Vin Rouge	Cook a mirepoix in butter, add red wine and reduce; add garlic and espagnole and finish with butter and cayenne.
Yorkshire	Flavour demi-glace with port, add redcurrant jelly and garnish with julienne of orange zest.
Zingara	Reduce white wine and mushroom liquid by two-thirds, add demi-glace, tomato sauce and white stock; cook then garnish with julienne of ham, ox-tongue, mushrooms and truffle (for poultry and veal).
Xérès	Add dry sherry to demi-glace.

White Sauces

Albert	Add boiling water to beurre manié then add cooked grated horseradish, cream, butter and breadcrumbs; thicken with egg yolks and flavour with mustard and vinegar (for roast beef).
Albuféra	Add meat glaze and pimento butter to sauce suprême (for poultry).
Alexandra	Add truffle juice to sauce suprême (for poultry).
Ambassadrice	Add purée of chicken to sauce suprême and finish with slightly whipped cream (for poultry).
Apple	Cook sliced apple with sugar and lemon juice; sieve and finish with butter (for pork and duck).

Aromate   Place herbs, shallots, peppercorns and nutmeg to infuse in white stock; strain and thicken with roux and finish with lemon juice and fines herbes (for meat and fish).

Aurore   Add tomato purée to velouté and finish with butter (for eggs and poultry).

Berchoux   This is sauce allemande finished with chivry butter (for poultry).

au Beurre   Add boiling water to beurre manié whisking well; finish with a liaison of yolks, cream, lemon juice and butter (for asparagus, eggs and fish).

Bonnefoy   Reduce shallots, herbs and pepper in white wine; add velouté, meat glaze, lemon juice and chopped tarragon (for grilled lamb and veal).

Bread   Boil milk with onion and clove, add white breadcrumbs and sautéd chopped onion, and finish with cream (for roast poultry).

Caper   Add squeezed capers to mutton velouté (for boiled mutton).

Celery   Reduce mushroom liquid, add sauce allemande and garnish with chopped cooked celery (for poultry).

Cheese   Add grated Parmesan to béchamel and finish with butter and cream (for poached eggs, various vegetables, etc.).

Chivry   Make an infusion of herbs in white wine, add to velouté and finish with herb butter (for boiled chicken).

Crème   Finish béchamel with cream and butter (for fish, vegetables, etc.).

Ecossaise   Add stewed brunoise of carrot, celery, French beans and onion to sauce crème (for egg and poultry dishes).

Egg   Add diced hard-boiled egg to sauce crème (for croquettes, fish etc.).

Estragon   Add chopped tarragon to finished sauce suprême (for chicken).

Fennel   Add boiling water to beurre manié, when thick add diced cooked fennel, lemon juice and butter (for vegetables and mackerel).

Flamande	Add boiling water to beurre manié; when thick add made mustard, lemon juice and butter (for vegetables and fish).
Gascon	Add anchovy essence and infusion of herbs to veal velouté (for veal).
Hongroise	Sauté chopped onion with paprika, reduce with white wine then add chicken velouté and finish with cream and butter (for poultry and veal).
Horseradish	Add boiling water to beurre manié, add cooked grated horseradish, cream, butter and bread-crumbs; thicken with yolks and add mustard and vinegar (for roast beef).
Ivoire	Flavour and colour sauce suprême with meat glaze (for chicken).
Maintenon	Add onion purée, Parmesan and garlic to sauce crème (for dishes à la Maintenon).
Montigny	Colour velouté with tomato purée and flavour with meat glaze; garnish with fines herbes (for small cuts of veal, lamb).
Mornay	Flavour béchamel with cheese, finish with butter and cream and a liaison of egg-yolks in the form of a sabayon (for eggs, vegetables, etc.). Some of the cooking liquid may be added to give extra flavour.
Mustard	Add cream and butter to béchamel and some made English mustard (for croquettes, made-up dishes and herrings).
Onion	Stew sliced onion in butter and water, add béchamel and finish with cream (for roast lamb and mutton and egg dishes).
Paprika	Stew onion in butter, add paprika and cook; add velouté, strain and finish with cream (for fish, veal, poultry).
Parsley	Add butter and cream to béchamel and finish with chopped parsley (for calf's head, brains and boiled fish).
Poulette	Add reduced mushroom liquid to sauce allemande, flavour with lemon juice and chopped parsley (for vegetables, calf's head and sheep's trotters).

413

Princesse — Add mushroom liquid to chicken velouté and enrich with chicken glaze and cream (for chicken dishes).

Ravigote — Reduce white wine and vinegar, add velouté and finish with shallot butter and fines herbes (for poached chicken and calf's head).

Régence — Reduce white wine and mushroom liquid, add sauce allemande and finish with truffle essence (for poultry).

Reine — Add julienne of chicken to sauce suprême and finish with slightly whipped cream (for poultry dishes).

Russe — Add grated horseradish, sour cream and tarragon vinegar to velouté (for Russian dishes).

Solferino — Reduce tomato juice until syrupy, add lemon juice and meat glaze then whisk in parsley butter, shallot butter and chopped tarragon, to give a thick consistency (for grilled meats).

Ste-Menehould — Flavour sauce crème with meat glaze and garnish with diced mushrooms and chopped parsley (for pork, veal, offals).

Soubise — Sauté chopped onion in butter, add béchamel and cook slowly for 1 hour; pass through a strainer and finish with cream (for eggs and roast lamb).

Smitaine — Sauté chopped onion in butter, add white wine and reduce; add sour cream and sauce crème and finish with lemon juice (for Russian dishes and game).

Talleyrand — Flavour velouté with Madeira, add a garnish of cooked diced vegetables, ox-tongue and truffle and finish with cream (for dishes of lamb and pork).

Villageoise — Reduce jus lié, mushroom liquid and velouté by one-third, add some sauce soubise and egg yolks and when thick finish with butter (for lamb, pork and veal).

Villeroy — Add some ham and truffle essences to sauce allemande and reduce (for foods prepared à la Villeroy).

Egg and Butter Sauces

Alliance	Make in the same way as for sauce béarnaise, using white wine and tarragon vinegar for the reduction; finish with chopped chervil.
Arlésienne	Flavour and colour sauce béarnaise with reduced tomato pulp and anchovy essence; add diced cooked tomato.
Bavaroise	Add crayfish butter, diced crayfish and whipped cream to sauce hollandaise.
Béarnaise	Reduce white wine, tarragon vinegar, shallots, crushed peppercorns, chervil and tarragon, add yolks and cook then add softened or melted butter; strain and finish with chopped chervil and tarragon.
Beauharnais	Add tarragon purée instead of chopped tarragon and chervil to sauce béarnaise.
Caviar	Add some caviar to sauce hollandaise at the last moment.
Chantilly	Add stiffly beaten cream to sauce hollandaise.
Choron	Add well-reduced tomato to sauce béarnaise and omit the chopped chervil and tarragon.
Citron	Add grated lemon rind and juice to sauce hollandaise.
Daumont	Add oyster liquid to sauce hollandaise and garnish with diced cooked oysters, mushroom and truffle.
Divine	Add stiffly beaten cream to sauce hollandaise.
Dunant	Add crayfish butter and truffle essence to sauce hollandaise and finish with lightly whipped cream.
Foyot	Add melted meat glaze to sauce béarnaise.
Française	Add tomato puree and fish glaze to sauce béarnaise.
Girondin	Add French mustard to sauce hollandaise.
Henri IV	Add melted meat glaze to sauce béarnaise.
Hollandaise	Make a reduction of vinegar and peppercorns, add egg yolks and cook to a sabayon: add

415

	melted butter, strain and flavour with lemon juice.
Isigny	Add whipped double cream to sauce hollandaise.
Magenta	Add diced cooked tomato to sauce béarnaise.
Maltaise	Add grated rind and juice of blood oranges to sauce hollandaise.
Marguery	Add oysters and oyster juice to sauce hollandaise.
Marquise	Add caviar to sauce hollandaise.
Maximilien	Flavour sauce hollandaise with anchovy essence.
Médicis	Reduce some red wine and add to sauce béarnaise together with some reduced tomato pulp.
Montebello	Mix some sauce hollandaise into fairly thick tomato sauce.
Mousseline	Add whipped cream to sauce hollandaise.
Mousseuse	Whisk cold water into softened butter, add some whipped cream and lemon juice.
Noisette	Finish some sauce hollandaise with butter cooked to the nut-brown stage.
Nonpareil	Finish sauce hollandaise with crayfish butter and garnish with diced crayfish, mushroom, and truffle.
Paloise	Make sauce béarnaise using mint to flavour and garnish it, instead of tarragon and chervil.
Rachel	Flavour sauce béarnaise with some demi-glace and garnish it with diced cooked tomato.
Souvaroff	Add meat glaze and julienne of truffle to sauce béarnaise.
Sylvie	Make sauce hollandaise with tarragon in the reduction and chopped tarragon added when finished.
Tyrolienne	Add well-reduced tomato pulp when making sauce béarnaise.
Uzes	Flavour sauce hollandaise with Madeira and anchovy essence.
Valois	Add some meat glaze to sauce béarnaise.

Sauces for Fish

Alcide	Add grated horseradish and chopped sautéd shallots to sauce vin blanc.
Amiral	Add chopped sautéd shallots, grated lemon zest, anchovy essence and small capers to sauce vin blanc.
Anchovy	Flavour béchamel with anchovy essence and finish with butter and cream.
Américaine	Fry lobster shells with mirepoix, flame with brandy, add white wine, fish stock, diced tomato and tomato purée; allow to reduce, add demi-glace and pass through a sieve.
Archiduc	Add some reduced champagne to sauce suprême.
Aurore	Cook tomatoes to a smooth paste and add to velouté.
Bâtarde	Mix melted butter and flour together, add boiling water and when thick, a liaison of yolks, cream, butter and lemon juice.
Bavaroise	Mix some crayfish butter with sauce hollandaise and garnish with diced crayfish; finish with cream.
Bercy	Cook chopped shallot in butter, reduce with white wine and fish stock then add velouté and finish with butter and chopped parsley.
au Beurre	Mix melted butter and flour together, add boiling water and when thick, a liaison of yolks, cream, butter and lemon juice.
Bonne Femme	Sauté chopped shallot in butter, add fish stock and reduce; thicken with yolks and cream and flavour with lemon juice.
Bordelaise	Reduce white wine with chopped shallot and herbs, add velouté and finish with chopped tarragon.
Butter	Add boiling water to flour mixed into melted butter; season; flavour with lemon juice and finish with butter.

Bretonne Cook celery, leek, mushrooms and onion cut in julienne in butter; add velouté and finish with butter and cream.

Canotière Reduce the court-bouillon in which a freshwater fish has been cooked and thicken with beurre manié.

Cardinal Reduce fish stock and truffle essence, add béchamel and cream and finish with lobster butter.

Chambord Cook salmon bones and mirepoix in butter, add red wine and reduce; add demi-glace, strain and finish with anchovy essence and butter.

aux Crevettes Add fish stock and cream to béchamel and reduce; add shrimp butter and shrimps.

Diplomate Reduce velouté, mushroom and mussel cooking liquids, fish stock, yolks and cream; finish with butter and cream and garnish with diced lobster and truffle.

Ecossaise Reduce velouté, mushroom and mussel cooking liquids, fish stock, yolks and cream; finish with butter and cream and garnish with diced carrot, celery and truffle.

Egg and Butter Add seasoning, lemon juice, chopped parsley and diced hard-boiled egg to warm melted butter.

Fennel Make some Butter sauce and add chopped cooked fennel.

aux Fines Herbes Add chopped chervil, parsley and tarragon together with some shallot butter to sauce vin blanc.

Francois 1er Add diced tomato and mushroom to sauce vin blanc.

Genevoise Cook salmon bones and mirepoix in butter, add red wine and reduce then demi-glace and fish stock; strain and finish with anchovy essence and butter.

Gooseberry Cook unripe gooseberries with sugar and a little water, then make into a purée.

Gourmet Reduce shallots in red wine; add demi-glace and anchovy essence and garnish with diced lobster and truffle.

Gratin	Cook chopped shallots and mushrooms in butter and add demi-glace and chopped parsley.
Havraise	Add mussel cooking liquid to sauce vin blanc, reduce and finish with mussels and shrimps.
Homard	Add cream, lobster butter and red butter to velouté and garnish with diced lobster and finish with brandy.
Joinville	Reduce velouté, mussel and mushroom cooking liquids, fish stock, lemon juice and cream by one-third and finish with crayfish butter and shrimp butter.
Laguipierre	Add boiling water to flour mixed into melted butter and when thick add a liaison of yolks, cream, lemon juice and butter; finish with fish glaze.
Lapérouse	Reduce chopped shallots in white wine and vinegar with peppercorns and bay-leaf, strain and finish with meat glaze.
Lemon Butter	Add lemon juice, Worcester sauce and chopped parsley to beurre noisette.
Livonienne	Stew julienne of carrot, celery, mushroom and onion in butter, add velouté and finish with julienne of truffle and chopped parsley.
Lobster	Fry lobster shells and mirepoix in oil and butter, flame with brandy, add white wine, fish stock, diced tomato and tomato purée; allow to reduce then add velouté and strain.
Marigny	Reduce demi-glace with white wine, mushroom liquid and tomato purée; garnish with olives and sliced mushrooms.
Marinière	Add mussel cooking liquid to sauce bercy and thicken with egg-yolks.
Matelote	Reduce court-bouillon with mushroom peelings, add velouté, strain and finish with butter; garnish with cooked button onions and mushrooms.
Moutarde	Add some English mustard to sauce crème.
Nantua	Reduce béchamel with cream and finish with crayfish butter; garnish with small crayfish tails.
Newburg	Fry lobster shells in oil and butter, flame with brandy, add Madeira and reduce then add

419

	cream; strain and add the lobster tomalley or spawn; garnish with diced lobster.
Normande	Reduce fish velouté, mussel and mushroom cooking liquids, yolks, cream and lemon juice by one-third and finish with butter and cream.
Orientale	Flavour lobster sauce with curry and finish with cream.
Oyster	Add poached oysters to sauce normande.
Parsley	Add butter and cream to béchamel and garnish with blanched chopped parsley.
Polignac	Add julienne of mushrooms to sauce vin blanc.
Pompadour	Add crayfish butter to sauce vin blanc and garnish with diced crayfish and truffle and chopped chervil and tarragon.
Princière	Add crayfish butter to sauce vin blanc and garnish with diced crayfish and truffle.
Régence	Reduce white wine, fish stock and mushroom trimmings, strain and add to sauce normande and flavour with truffle essence.
Riche	Reduce velouté, mushroom and mussel cooking liquids, fish stock, yolks and cream; add diced truffle and truffle essence.
Rubens	Sauté mirepoix in butter, add white wine and fish stock; flavour with Madeira, thicken with yolks and enrichen with butter, red butter and anchovy essence.
St-Malo	Add chopped shallots cooked in wine, anchovy essence and mustard to sauce vin blanc.
Scotch Egg	Add the sieved yolks and sliced whites of hard-boiled eggs to béchamel sauce.
Shrimp	Mix flour with melted butter, add boiling water and a liaison of yolks, cream, butter and lemon juice; flavour with anchovy essence and add shrimps.
Souchet	Stew julienne of carrot and celery in butter and add to sauce vin blanc.
Vénitienne	Reduce tarragon vinegar, shallot and chervil; add to sauce vin blanc and finish with green butter and chopped tarragon and chervil.

Véron	Mix together two parts sauce normande and one part sauce tyrolienne and flavour with anchovy essence and meat glaze.
Victoria	Add diced lobster and truffle to lobster sauce.
au Vin Blanc	(a) Reduce fish stock, velouté and yolks by one-third and finish with butter.
	(b) Reduce fish stock, add yolks to make a sabayon and whisk in softened butter.
	(c) Whisk yolks to a sabayon then whisk in butter and fish stock.
au Vin Rouge	Reduce chopped shallots in red wine, add demi-glace and finish with anchovy essence and butter.

Cold Sauces

Aïoli	Emulsify garlic with egg-yolk and oil to sauce consistency and flavour with lemon juice.
aux Airelles	Cook cranberries with sugar and water until soft.
Antibes	Mix tomato purée with mayonnaise and flavour with anchovy essence and chopped tarragon.
Andalouse	Add tomato purée and diced red pimento to mayonnaise.
Bohémienne	Mix cold béchamel with yolks, seasoning and vinegar and whisk in oil as for mayonnaise; flavour slightly with mustard.
Cambridge	Emulsify hard-boiled egg-yolks, anchovies and fines herbes and add to mayonnaise; finish with chopped parsley.
Casanova	Add chopped truffle and shallot and sieved hard-boiled egg to mayonnaise.
Chantilly	Make mayonnaise with lemon juice and add stiffly beaten cream.
Chaudfroid	White – Reduce velouté and aspic jelly and finish with cream.
	Brown – Reduce demi-glace and aspic jelly and flavour with Madeira.

421

	Pink – Reduce velouté, tomato pulp, paprika and aspic jelly and finish with cream.
Colioure	Add anchovy essence to mayonnaise.
Cranberry	Cook cranberries with sugar and water; if desired it may be sieved.
Creamed Mustard	Mix mustard, salt, pepper and lemon juice and add double cream as when making mayonnaise.
Cumberland	Warm port and redcurrant jelly, add blanched chopped shallots, orange and lemon juices, made mustard, ground ginger and julienne of orange and lemon zest.
Genoise	Add pistachio, almond and mixed herbs blended to a pulp to mayonnaise and finish with lemon juice.
Gloucester	Flavour mayonnaise with sour cream, made mustard, Worcester sauce and chopped fennel.
Gooseberry	Cook gooseberries with sugar and water and make into a purée.
Gribiche	Mix cooked yolks of eggs with mustard, salt and pepper and gradually add oil and vinegar as for mayonnaise; garnish with chopped capers, gherkins and fines herbes and julienne of hard-boiled egg whites.
Horseradish	Add grated horseradish, breadcrumbs soaked in milk and vinegar to lightly whipped cream; variations include the addition of cranberries, walnuts, etc.
Italienne	Mayonnaise with the addition of purée of calf's brain and chopped parsley.
Livournaise	Mixed sieved hard-boiled egg, anchovy essence and chopped parsley and work in oil and vinegar.
Marseillaise	Add purée of sea urchins to mayonnaise.
Mayonnaise	Mix egg yolks, mustard, salt, pepper and vinegar and gradually add oil, thinning with more vinegar as necessary.
Mexicaine	Add diced red and green pimento to mayonnaise flavoured with anchovy essence.
Mint	Finely chopped mint leaves with sugar, a little boiling water and vinegar.

Mousquetaire	Reduce white wine with chopped shallots and add to vinaigrette or mayonnaise; finish with chopped chives and a little melted meat glaze.
Oxford	Warm port and redcurrant jelly; add blanched chopped shallot, orange and lemon juice, mustard, ginger and grated orange and lemon zest.
Ravigote	Mix together oil, vinegar, chopped onion and capers, fines herbes and seasoning.
Remick	Mayonnaise flavoured with celery salt, chili powder, paprika and tabasco.
Remoulade	Add mustard, chopped capers, gherkins and fines herbes and anchovy essence to mayonnaise.
Rouge	Mayonnaise coloured with raw beetroot juice.
Rougemont	Add mustard and chopped tarragon to mayonnaise.
Russe	Add purée of lobster tomalley and caviar to mayonnaise and flavour with bottled Derby sauce.
Suédoise	Mix purée of apple cooked in white wine with mayonnaise and finish with grated horseradish.
Tartare	Add chopped capers, gherkins and fines herbes to mayonnaise.
Trianon	Add tomato purée and purée of onion to mayonnaise and garnish with chopped red pimento and gherkin.
Verte	Make a purée of blanched chervil, chives, parsley, spinach, tarragon and watercress and add to mayonnaise to give a light green colour.
Vincent	Add sieved yolks of hard-boiled eggs and a few drops of Worcester sauce to mayonnaise.
Whisky	Add whisky and seasoning to whipped cream.

Butter Sauces

Beurre blanc	Cook 40g chopped shallot in a little water, gradually adding the juice of a lemon or lime as it evaporates; whisk in 400g butter a piece at a

time, keeping the pan in a bain-marie of water, until the sauce becomes white and frothy. Serve at once and do not allow to become too warm.

This sauce may also be made with white wine vinegar or white wine, instead of water.

Beurre fondu — Heat butter until warm but just melted, add a squeeze of lemon juice and serve immediately.

Beurre noir — Heat butter until it begins to colour brown, add a few drops of vinegar and pour over the food; capers and chopped parsley may be added at the last moment.

Beurre noisette — Heat butter until brown and pour over the food on the dish, if desired a little lemon juice may be added; this butter is frequently used in conjunction with jus lié by being added after it to shallow-fried foods.

Beurre rouge — Make as beurre blanc, but use red wine, not white.

Sauce au beurre — Add flour to melted butter then boiling salted water to make a smooth sauce; add a liaison of yolks, cream and lemon juice, allow to thicken and finish with plenty of butter added in pieces at the last moment.

Serve with poached fish, asparagus, etc.

Butter Sauce — Add flour to melted butter then boiling salted water to make a smooth sauce; add a squeeze of lemon juice and finish with plenty of butter at the last moment.

Egg and Butter Sauce — Heat butter, season, add lemon juice, chopped parsley and sieved hard-boiled egg.

Fennel Sauce — Add flour to melted butter then mix in boiling salted water to give a smooth consistency; add lemon and chopped cooked fennel and finish with plenty of butter at the last moment.

424

Butters – also known as Hard Sauces

Compound butters are used to accentuate the flavour of some sauces and forcemeats and to improve the colour of sauces. They are usually made cold to add to the finished dish at the last minute.

Some butters are made to serve as a hard sauce and are cut into pieces and placed on the food just as it is going to be served, or it may be placed in a sauceboat. It should be kept cold, but not frozen.

Almond	Pulverise freshly shelled almonds with water and add the butter.
Anchovy	Add anchovy paste or pounded anchovies to butter.
Artois	Add crayfish paste and meat glaze to maître d'hôtel butter.
Basil	Add a fine purée of fresh basil leaves and a little lemon juice to softened butter.
Bercy	Reduce chopped shallot in wine, add butter, bone marrow, chopped parsley and lemon juice.
Calvados	Flavour with Calvados spirit which is made from apples.
Caviar	Pound some caviar, pass through a sieve and add the butter.
Chivry	Pound blanched herbs and chopped shallot and add to the butter.
Colbert	Mix chopped tarragon and meat glaze into Maître d'hôtel butter.
Crayfish	Pulverise crayfish debris, add butter and pass through a sieve.
Curry	Add curry paste to softened butter.
Garlic	Blanch cloves of garlic, pulverise and add to the butter.
Green	Liquidise raw spinach, heat to coagulate and mix the substance with butter.
Hazelnut	Pound roasted hazelnuts and add to butter.
Horseradish	Pound grated horseradish with butter.

425

Lobster	Pound the tomalley and spawn, add butter and pass through a sieve.
Maître d'Hôtel	Add chopped parsley, seasoning and lemon juice to butter.
Marchand de Vins	Add shallot cooked in red wine, lemon juice and chopped parsley to softened butter.
Montpellier	Blanch chervil, chives, parsley, tarragon and watercress; pound with blanched shallots, capers, gherkins, garlic, anchovy, hard-boiled eggs, butter and oil, and pass through a sieve.
Mustard	Add French mustard to softened butter.
Nutty	Add finely chopped salted peanuts; the slices of butter may be dipped in chopped nuts.
Orange	Add grated rind and juice of an orange to the butter.
Paprika	Add chopped onion and paprika to butter and pass through a sieve.
Parisienne	This is another name for lobster butter.
Pimento	Pound braised red pimento with butter and pass through a sieve.
Pistachio	Pulverise freshly skinned pistachios with butter.
Printanière	Stew mixed vegetables in butter and liquidise with softened butter.
Ravigote	Pound blanched herbs and shallot, pass through a sieve and add to softened butter.
Red	Pulverise dried lobster shells, mix with butter and pass through a sieve.
Red Wine	Reduce shallots in red wine and add to butter with seasoning, lemon juice and chopped parsley.
Shallot	Pound blanched shallot with butter and pass through a sieve.
Shrimp	Pulverise boiled shrimps and add to butter.
Snail	Mix chopped shallots, crushed garlic, chopped parsley and seasoning with softened butter.
Smoked Salmon	Add purée of smoked salmon trimmings to softened butter.
Stilton	Add sieved debris of Stilton cheese to softened butter.
Tarragon	Pound blanched tarragon leaves, add butter and pass through a sieve.

Tomato	Mix reduced tomato pulp with butter; curry, orange, etc., may also be added.
Truffle	Pound truffle with béchamel and add butter.
Whipped	Beat softened butter until light and fluffy.

It is also possible to prepare these butters by coating butter pats with the flavouring media, e.g. toasted nuts, blanched mint leaves, chopped tarragon, etc.

Colouring butters are used to give a clean, authentic finish to certain sauces, soups, stews, etc., which might lack colour; they include green colouring butter made from fresh herbs and spinach, red colouring butter made from dried lobster shells, vegetable butters made by pounding one or several cooked vegetables, and shellfish butters made from the coral and tomalley of a particular kind of crustacean. The fluid of the seminal glands of the sea urchin can be used to flavour sauces, soufflés, etc., as orange-red colour.

11   COLD BUFFET

The word buffet indicates a display of dishes of food from which people help themselves to what they want, or are assisted by counterhands or carvers. According to whether chairs and tables are provided so the food should be appropriate: a finger buffet would mean that people eat standing up, therefore all items need to be cut into small pieces.

A buffet can comprise an entire meal of several courses or be the main course only, the others being served from the kitchen. A buffet can include both cold and hot foods. The kinds of functions where a buffet is appropriate include a wedding breakfast, gala supper, hunt ball, garden party, cocktail party, Christmas or Easter buffet meal.

The food must taste as good as it looks and all items must be of edible material even though they may be only for display. Centre-pieces for a buffet are made of ice, fat, pastillage, pulled or blown sugar, nougat and chocolate. Socles are made of rice, semolina or bread and are designed in the form of pedestals to raise items off the dish and give greater impact. No feathers or uncooked parts of birds or animals are allowed on buffet displays.

The chaudfroid sauce, aspic jelly and all decorations and garnishes must be nice to eat and must not be so thickly applied or so rich in flavour as to detract from the flavour of the main item.

Garnishes for cold buffet items

There are a number of classical garnishes that were created solely for use on cold buffet work but many of those normally associated with hot dishes are also suitable. The following list shows the best-known cold garnishes:

FISH

		Use for
Béatrice	Decorate with truffle, egg white and prawns, place on a layer of Russian salad and garnish with artichoke bottoms filled with mousse of pimento and halves of hard-boiled eggs filled with caviar.	Salmon-trout
en Belle-Vue	Decorate with egg-white, tarragon and truffle; glaze with fish jelly and place on a dish.	Salmon
Calypso	Cook as paupiettes leaving a hole in the centre to be filled with a tomato shell containing a crayfish and a slice of soft roe; glaze with jelly.	Fillets of sole
Cardinal	Chemise a mould and line with crayfish tails and slices of truffle, fill with mousse of crayfish and allow to set; turn out and garnish with crayfish carapaces filled with the same kind of mousse.	Crayfish
Escoffier	Make into paupiettes using half lobster and half truffle forcemeat; when cold cut into slices and use to line a mould, fill with crayfish mousse and allow to set before turning out.	Fillets of Sole
Isabelle	Coat with jellied sauce verte, decorate and glaze; garnish with cucumber barquettes filled with cooked purée of egg yolk, hearts of lettuce and small glazed tomatoes.	Salmon
Moderne	Cut the cooked fish into portions, coat with crayfish mousse, pipe with Montpellier butter and sprinkle with chopped coral and hard-boiled egg.	Salmon-trout
Moscovite	Decorate artistically, place in a chemised dish and garnish with cucumber barquettes filled with purée of smoked salmon, stuffed halves of	Salmon

	hard-boiled egg, small tomatoes and shrimps on leaves of lettuce.	
Néva	Cut fish into slices, coat with jellied mayonnaise, decorate and glaze with fish aspic jelly; fill the emptied carcase with jellied Russian salad and arrange the pieces of shellfish on top overlapping.	Crawfish and lobster
Norvégienne	Decorate with prawns and glaze; garnish with cucumber cases filled with purée of smoked salmon, barquette shapes of beetroot, small tomatoes and stuffed halves of hard-boiled egg.	Salmon and salmon-trout
Ondines	Line egg-shaped moulds with mousse of salmon-trout and fill with prawns; allow to set, demould, garnish with prawns and coat with fish aspic jelly.	Salmon-trout
Parisienne	Partially skin the salmon and coat the bared part with mayonnaise; pipe a border of Montpellier butter and sprinkle with chopped chervil and sieved hard-boiled egg. Garnish with artichoke bottoms filled with Russian salad.	Salmon
Riga	Decorate with shrimps and slices of hard-boiled egg; garnish with barquettes of cucumber filled with Russian salad and a crayfish head stuck in each, and halves of hard-boiled egg filled with caviar.	Salmon
Royale	Partially skin the salmon and coat the bared part with salmon mousse; decorate with cut-out crowns and fleur-de-lys from tomato or leek, and pipe a border of Montpellier butter.	Salmon
Russe	Cut fish into slices, coat with jellied mayonnaise, decorate and glaze; set the shell on a socle, fill it with Russian salad and arrange the sliced	Crawfish and lobster

shellfish overlapping. Garnish with
moulds of Russian salad and halves of
egg filled with caviar.

─────── MEAT ───────

en Belle-Vue	Decorate, set in a chemised cutlet mould and fill with jelly; turn out to serve and garnish with chopped jelly.	Veal cutlet
	Decorate and glaze, place on a chemised dish and garnish with bunches of asparagus tips, small tomatoes and chopped jelly.	Fillet of beef
Bon-Viveur	Open, stuff with foie gras and parcook; envelop with slices of Parma ham and enclose in puff paste; decorate and bake until cooked, cool then fill with aspic jelly.	Fillet of beef
Bouquetière	Garnish with bouquets of French beans, carrots, cauliflower, peas and turnips.	Any kind of meat
Caucasienne	Cut into thin slices and sandwich with anchovy butter; arrange around a mould of tomato mousse.	Cushion of veal
Chevet	Chemise and decorate a long mould, place the cooked fillet on top and completely fill with jelly; turn out when set.	Fillet of beef
Coquelin	Cut the cooked meat into slices and arrange overlapping on the dish; coat with the reduced cooking liquid containing a short julienne of vegetables and truffle.	Fillet of beef
Edouard VII	Bone out, fill with foie gras and cook, coat with jelly made from the cooking liquid.	Saddle of mutton
Jardinière	Serve garnished with artichoke bottoms filled with jardinière of vegetables, florets of cauliflower,	Any kind of meat

431

	bunches of asparagus tips, small tomatoes and grooved mushrooms.	
Mandragora	Glaze a slipper tongue with Madeira-flavoured jelly and garnish with tomatoes filled with pilaff of rice mixed with diced banana and mango and curry powder, and tartlets filled with purée of egg yolk and a star of truffle on top.	Ox-tongue
Milhaud	Stud with truffle, roast, carve and rearrange with interleaved slices of foie gras; glaze, garnish with tangerine skins filled with purée of foie gras and decorate with tangerine segments.	Fillet of beef
Mistral	Decorate and glaze, place on a chemised dish and garnish with tomatoes cooked à la Provençale.	Topside of beef
à la Mode	Arrange a piece of braised beef in a terrine with small turned carrots and turnips and button onions and small squares of calf's foot; fill with the jellied braising sauce and allow to set.	Topside of beef
Montlhéry	Decorate and glaze, place on a dish and garnish with moulds lined with strips of truffle and French beans and filled with Russian salad; also with artichoke bottoms filled with asparagus tips.	Fillet of beef
Riche	Cut into slices and re-form with interleaved slices of foie gras; garnish with fonds d'artichaut filled with asparagus tips and tomatoes filled with purée of foie gras.	Fillet of beef
Russe	Cut into slices and coat each with the reduced cooking liquid containing finely chopped truffle; arrange overlapping on a jellied dish.	Fillet of beef

Suédoise	Cut into slices, coat each with horseradish butter and cover with a slice of tongue; decorate with piped butter and arrange on a dish around a mould of Russian salad.	Cushion of veal

———POULTRY AND GAME———

Aspic	Chemise and decorate a mould then fill it with neat slices of fish, chicken or game, keeping them in place with the appropriately flavoured jelly.
Aurore	Coat suprêmes with tomato-flavoured chaud-froid, decorate and arrange on shapes of tomato mousse; glaze with jelly.
Buloz	Coat suprêmes of pheasant with brown chaud-froid and whole mushrooms with white chaud-froid; glaze and arrange on a chemised dish.
Café de Paris	Cover suprêmes with mousse of foie gras and coat half with white and half with pink chaud-froid; re-form the carcase, coat, decorate and glaze. Garnish with tomatoes filled with mousse of ham.
Carmelite	Coat suprêmes with white chaudfroid and replace on the carcase previously filled with mousse of crayfish; decorate with whole cray-fish.
Carmen	Cut a duck into slices, decorate with purée of foie gras, segments of tangerine and cherries; arrange on a dish and garnish with tangerines filled with almond-flavoured aspic jelly.
Cecilia	Chemise a charlotte mould, decorate with truffle and fill with breasts of quail coated with brown chaudfroid and slices of foie gras.
Châtelaine	Coat slices of pheasant, some with chicken mousse, and white chaudfroid, and some with mousse of pheasant and brown chaudfroid, decorate with truffle, arrange overlapping in a deep dish and glaze with aspic jelly.

Chaudfroid Chemise and decorate a charlotte mould and fill with neat slices of game, chicken etc. previously coated with the appropriately flavoured chaudfroid; fill with jelly and turn out when set.

Dampière Bone out and stuff with forcemeat before poaching, coat with almond milk chaudfroid and serve garnished with moulds filled with ox-tongue and foie gras.

Ecarlate Bone out and fill with forcemeat containing diced ox-tongue; poach, coat with white chaudfroid and decorate with shapes of ox-tongue; serve garnished with glazed halves of cured calves tongues.

Ecossaise Coat suprêmes with white chaudfroid containing very finely diced egg white, gherkin, ox-tongue and truffle; glaze and place each on a moulded salad of French beans with a crescent of ox-tongue at the side.

Estragon Coat suprêmes with white chaudfroid, decorate with blanched tarragon and glaze with tarragon-flavoured chicken jelly.

Eugene Lacroix Place small slices of chicken on barquette moulds filled with mousse of ham and glaze with Madeira-flavoured chicken jelly; re-form the carcase with mousse of foie gras containing sieved toasted hazelnuts, cover it with poached slices of apple and glaze with Madeira jelly. Surround the chicken with the barquettes and small truffles.

Gounod Place suprêmes on a rectangle of chicken mousse, coat with white chaudfroid and decorate with notes of music cut from truffle; glaze and arrange on a dish.

Gastronome Coat suprêmes of pheasant with brown chaudfroid, decorate and glaze; chemise and decorate a parfait mould and fill with mousse of game, turn out on a dish and surround with the suprêmes and small glazed truffles.

Jeannette Coat suprêmes with white chaudfroid, decorate and glaze, place each on a slice of foie gras and

434

arrange fan shape on a jellied dish (the practice of adding a garnish of asparagus tips and cornets of ham is not strictly correct).

Lambertye Coat elongated suprêmes with brown chaud-froid; decorate, glaze and replace on the carcase filled with mousse of foie gras.

Lucullus Pipe aiguillettes of duck with mousse of foie gras and decorate with sprigs of chervil and shapes of red pimento; glaze with sherry-flavoured duck jelly.

Mandarinette Fill emptied tangerines with mousse of quail and foie gras, place the chaudfroid breasts on top and garnish with segments of tangerine.

Montmorency Spread aiguillettes of duck with puree of foie gras, coat with brown chaudfroid and glaze; arrange on a dish with stoned morello cherries.

Néva Stuff the chicken with truffled forcemeat and poach, when cold, coat with white chaudfroid, decorate with truffle and serve garnished with moulds of Russian salad.

Normande Pipe aiguillettes of duck with puree of foie gras, coat with brown chaudfroid and glaze; serve garnished with poached quarters of apples sprinkled with blanched shredded orange and lemon zest.

Parisienne Stuff the chicken with forcemeat and poach; when cold, remove the suprêmes, coat with white chaudfroid, decorate and glaze. Fill the carcase with chicken mousse containing the diced forcemeat, decorate and glaze; place on a dish, and surround with the suprêmes and moulds of Russian salad.

aux Raisins Poach boned quails in veal stock then clarify the stock to form the jelly; garnish the quails with peeled depipped grapes and cover with jelly.

Rose de Mai Coat suprêmes with white chaudfroid, decorate and glaze; re-form the carcase with mousse of tomato, decorate it and glaze. Place the suprêmes on barquettes filled with tomato mousse and arrange around the chicken.

435

Rose-Marie   Coat suprêmes with white chaudfroid, decorate and glaze; re-form the carcase with mousse of ham, coat with pink chaudfroid, decorate and glaze. Place the suprêmes on barquettes filled with ham mousse and arrange around the chicken.

Rossini   Coat suprêmes with white chaudfroid, decorate with truffle and glaze; arrange each on a slice of foie gras.

Saint-Cyr   Coat chicken suprêmes with white chaudfroid and breasts of larks with brown chaudfroid; decorate, glaze and arrange alternately on a chemised dish.

Sévillane   Decorate breasts of duck with purée of foie gras and segments of orange, glaze and arrange around the carcase re-formed with mousse of foie gras; decorate with orange segments and glaze with aspic.

Cold Buffet Menus

In addition to the above, the complete list would include any of the following:

Hors-d'Oeuvre   Smoked mackerel, smoked salmon, smoked trout, cocktail canapés, melon, foie gras, avocado pears, seafood cocktails, Florida cocktail.

Soups   Jellied consommé, bisque soups, cream of chicken, gazpacho, vichyssoise, asparagus, green pea, mulligatawny, avocado.

Eggs   Hard-boiled, soft-boiled, moulded, poached – on an appropriate mousse and with a suitable garnish, in jelly.

Fish   Crab, crayfish, crawfish, lobster, frogs' legs, salmon, salmon-trout, fillets of sole, trout, turbot.

Meat   Beef   Baron, Derby round, fillet, pressed beef, salted tongue, sirloin, ribs.

        Veal   Cushion, cutlets, best end, saddle, grenadins.

Lamb	Best end, cutlets, leg, saddle, baron.
Pork	Sucking pig, boar's head, ham.
Poultry	Chicken, duck, goose, poussin, turkey.
Game	Partridge, pheasant, wild boar.
Pies	Chicken, foie gras, game, pigeon, pork, salmon, veal and ham.
Galantines	Chicken, duck, goose or pig's liver, hare, rabbit.
Mousses	Chicken, ham, foie gras, tomato, variegated vegetable.

Salads   Plain and composite salads.

Sweets	Fruit	Compotes, condés, fools, flans, fresh whole, macédoine, tartlets, summer pudding.
	Gâteaux	Croquenbouche, pâtisseries françaises, cheesecake, savarins.
		Bavarois, blancmange, caramel creams, charlottes, cold soufflés, jellies, trifle.

Drinks   Iced tea, iced coffee, claret cup.

12 SALADS, SALAD DRESSINGS AND DIPS

There are several different categories of salads – the very plain ones consisting of a few of the most common salad items neatly arranged in a salad bowl and the rather more involved ones made up of a number of different ingredients mixed together with a dressing, which can serve either as an accompanying salad or as an hors-d'œuvre course. Some salads are sufficiently substantial to act as main courses – these include such dishes as lobster salad and mayonnaise of chicken. The main place for salads in the menu is as the perfect accompaniment for cold fish and meat and with roasts and grilled meats.

The following list shows those salads in general use but in addition many establishments have their own speciality salads and some head waiters make their own particular kind of salad dressing with which to dress the salads they make.

Cold Salads

Adelina	Cooked lengths of salsify mixed with slices of cucumber and tomato; French dressing.
Aïda	Green pimento, raw artichoke bottoms and cooked egg-white cut into julienne, chicory, sliced tomatoes; mustard-flavoured French dressing.
Alice	Hollowed-out apple filled with small balls of apple, redcurrants and fresh walnuts mixed with acidulated cream; covered with the lids.
Américaine	Bouquets of sliced tomatoes, sliced potatoes, julienne of celery, sliced hard boiled eggs and onion rings; French dressing.

Andalouse	Rice flavoured with garlic, onion and parsley, quarters of tomato, julienne of pimento; French dressing.
Archiduc	Julienne of belgian endive, potato, beetroot and truffle; French dressing.
Asparagus	Arrange some cooked sprue on a leaf of lettuce; French dressing.
Astor	Lamb's lettuce, watercress, julienne of red pimento and sliced cucumber; acidulated cream dressing.
Aurore	Peeled and sliced apple and peeled fresh walnuts arranged on a leaf of lettuce; acidulated cream flavoured and coloured with tomato.
Avocado	Diced or sliced peeled avocado arranged on a leaf of lettuce; French dressing.
Bagatelle	Cooked sprue on top of mixed fine julienne of raw carrot and mushroom; French dressing.
Bagration	Julienne of cooked chicken, raw celery, artichoke bottoms, short lengths of spaghetti mixed with tomato-flavoured mayonnaise; decorate with a star made of truffle, and sieved yolk and white of egg.
Béatrice	Julienne of truffle, cooked chicken and potato with sprue; mustard-flavoured mayonnaise.
Beaucaire	Julienne of chicken, ham, apple, celery, celeriac and mushroom mixed with mayonnaise; surrounded with alternate rings of potato and beetroot.
Bean sprout	Bean sprouts, celery, green pimento, pineapple, water chestnuts and almonds, in vinaigrette.
Beetroot	Beetroot cut into dice or julienne with mustard-flavoured French dressing.
Belles de Nuit	Small crayfish tails and sliced truffle mixed with French dressing.
Biarritz	Diced celeriac and green pimento on a leaf of lettuce.
Bristol	Julienne of cooked chicken, gherkin, apple, celeriac, tomato flesh and truffle; mix with mayonnaise.
Caesar's	Garlic-flavour fried croûtons on cos lettuce with diced Parmesan and anchovies; raw egg, lemon

	and oil dressing; tossed well together and garnished with more croûtons.
Californienne	Orange segments, pineapple, French beans and florets of cauliflower on a leaf of lettuce; coated with mayonnaise.
Canaille	Rice, diced banana, diced celery and tomato with chopped onion; mixed with acidulated cream.
Caprice	Julienne of chicken, ham, ox-tongue, truffle and raw artichoke bottoms, mixed with mustard-flavoured French dressing.
Carmen	Diced chicken, diced red pimento, rice and peas; mustard-flavoured French dressing; chopped tarragon on top.
Caruso	Diced pineapple and diced tomato on a leaf of lettuce; acidulated cream.
Casanova	Julienne of celery and truffle mixed with mayonnaise; garnish with watercress and sliced hard-boiled egg.
Cendrillon	Julienne of apple, potato, celeriac, raw artichoke bottoms and truffle, with sprue; French dressing.
Châtelaine	Sliced hard-boiled egg, potato, artichoke bottoms and truffle; French dressing; sprinkle with chopped tarragon.
Chicago	Fine julienne of raw carrots and mushrooms, French beans, quarters of tomato, sprue, and a small slice of foie gras; mayonnaise.
Club	Macaroni, diced hard-boiled egg, celery, onion, pimento, olives; in mayonnaise.
Cole Slaw	Julienne of raw white cabbage and carrot mixed with mayonnaise; onion, celery, nuts, cucumber, apple, banana, orange, pear, pineapple, dried fruit and tomato may be added.
Comtoise	Crisp-fried small lardons with the fat, poured over hearts of lettuce; warmed vinegar.
Connaisseur	Julienne of celery, chicken and truffle mixed with mayonnaise, sprue and sliced tomato.
Cremona	Cooked Japanese artichokes, julienne of tomato flesh and of anchovies, mixed with mustard-

	flavoured French dressing containing fines herbes.
Créole	Diced melon and rice, flavoured with ground ginger and mixed with acidulated cream; may be served in small melon skins.
Cressonière	Watercress leaves and sliced potato; French dressing with chopped hard-boiled egg.
Capriccio	Orange segments, quarters of tomato and julienne of pimento; with sour cream dressing.
Cucumber	Salted and drained sliced cucumber; French dressing or vinegar.
Cobb	Diced avocado, cooked bacon, celery, chicken, chives, hard-boiled egg, tomato and watercress, with Roquefort dressing.
Dalila	Sliced apple and banana and julienne of celery, mixed with thin mayonnaise.
Danicheff	Bouquets of thin slices of cooked celeriac and potatoes, raw slices of artichoke bottoms and mushrooms, sprue; decorate with crayfish, truffle and sliced hard-boiled egg.
Delmonico	Diced celeriac and apple mixed with mayonnaise and cream; on a leaf of lettuce.
Demi-Deuil	Julienne of potato and truffle mixed with mustard dressing; surround with alternate rings of potato and truffle.
Demidoff	Cooked crescent shapes of celeriac, carrot and turnip and truffle, mixed with chopped onion and French dressing.
Diplomat	Pineapple pieces, diced celery and walnuts, mixed with mayonnaise.
Divine	Julienne of raw artichoke bottoms, celery and truffle mixed with acidulated cream; sprue and shrimps as the garnish.
Dumas	Diced beetroot, cucumber, potato and tomato-flesh mixed with mayonnaise and anchovy essence; garnished with lettuce, hard-boiled egg, gherkin and fines herbes.
Egyptienne	Rice, diced cooked chicken-livers, ham, mushrooms, artichoke bottoms, red pimento and peas, mixed with French dressing.

Elaine   Grapefruit segments and slices of pear on a leaf of lettuce, sprinkle with chopped red pimento; French dressing.

Eléonore   One artichoke bottom with a cold poached-egg and one with sprue, served with a heart of cos lettuce; mayonnaise.

Elizabeth   Lettuce heart served with acidulated cream dressing.

d'Endive   Quarters of Belgian endive; French dressing.

d'Estrées   Large julienne of celery and truffle mixed with mustard-flavoured mayonnaise.

Espagnole   Bouquets of quarters of tomato, French beans, sliced raw mushrooms and onions, sprinkle with chopped red pimento; French dressing.

Eve   Diced apple, banana, pineapple and fresh walnuts mixed with acidulated cream and used to fill a hollowed-out apple.

Excelsior   Julienne of celery, tomato-flesh and red pimento on a leaf of lettuce; covered with mayonnaise and sprinkled with chopped truffle.

Fanchette   Julienne of cooked chicken, raw mushroom, Belgian endive and truffle; French dressing.

Favorite   Bouquets of crayfish tails, sliced white truffle and sprue; oil and lemon dressing with chopped celery and fines herbes.

Fédora   Orange segments, slices of apple with julienne of celeriac mixed with mayonnaise; serve on a leaf of lettuce.

Figaro   Julienne of beetroot, celery and ox-tongue mixed with tomato-flavoured mayonnaise; garnished with trellis work of anchovy fillets.

Florida   Orange segments on a leaf of lettuce; acidulated cream dressing.

Francillon   Slices of potato and bearded mussels marinated with Chablis, served with sliced truffle; French dressing.

Française   Hearts of lettuce, sprinkled with fines herbes; French dressing.

Gambetta   Sliced raw artichoke bottom and truffle mixed with mayonnaise and chopped tarragon.

Garibaldi	Julienne of apple, celery and red pimento mixed with mayonnaise; served on a leaf of lettuce.
Gauloise	Slices of artichoke bottoms, mushrooms, potatoes and truffle; mayonnaise.
German Potato	Diced cooked potato, crisply fried lardons, chopped celery and onion; vinegar and bacon fat dressing.
des Gobelins	Bouquets of sliced cooked celeriac and potatoes, sliced raw artichoke bottoms and mushrooms, sprue; lemon-flavoured mayonnaise with chopped tarragon.
Gourmet	Julienne of celery, cockscombs and truffle mixed with mayonnaise; garnished with cooked chestnuts and morels; French dressing with fine herbes.
Grande Duchesse	Julienne of celery and potatoes, mixed with French beans; light mayonnaise.
Green Goddess	Leaves of frizzy endive, cos lettuce and ordinary lettuce with green goddess dressing and anchovy fillets as decoration.
Havanaise	Bouquets of shrimps and sprue on a leaf of lettuce; mayonnaise with cucumber purée.
Hélène	Bouquets of tangerine segments, sprue, sliced truffle and julienne of green pimento; French dressing with brandy.
Henrietta	Bouquets of turned carrots and turnips, cauliflower florets, haricot beans and slices of truffle; French dressing with chopped shallots and tarragon.
Henri IV	Diced artichoke bottoms and potatoes with chopped onion and French dressing.
Hermione	Julienne of chicken, celery, Belgian endive and potato, mixed with mayonnaise.
Hongroise	Julienne of white cabbage and potatoes with vinegar dressing and crisply fried lardons.
Impériale	Julienne of raw carrot, apple, truffle and cooked French beans; French dressing.
Irma	Diced cucumber, diamonds of French beans, cauliflower florets.

Isabelle	Slices of celery, mushrooms, truffle, cooked artichoke bottoms and potatoes; mixed with French dressing containing chopped chervil.
Italian	Sliced carrot, turnip, salami and anchovies with peas and diamonds of French beans; mixed with mayonnaise.
des Isles	Lettuce, grapefruit segments, diced avocado and pineapple; dressing flavoured with rum.
Japonaise	Pieces of pineapple, orange segments and tomato-flesh on a leaf of lettuce; acidulated cream.
Javanaise	Segments of orange on leaves of lettuce; covered with acidulated cream containing grated horseradish, and sprinkled with finely shredded orange skin.
Jeannette	Bouquets of cauliflower, French beans and watercress; French dressing with fines herbes.
Jockey Club	Bouquets of sprue and sliced truffle; marinated with French dressing and mixed with mayonnaise.
Lackmé	Diced tomato-flesh and red pimento, mixed with rice and curry-flavoured French dressing.
de Laitue	Quarters of lettuce with French dressing; may be sprinkled with fines herbes.
Laperouse	Diced ham, diamonds of French beans, sliced artichoke bottoms, quarters of tomato-flesh,; acidulated cream.
Lorette	Lamb's lettuce, julienne of beetroot and celery; mixed with French dressing.
Louis	Pieces of pineapple, diced celery and apple; mixed with sherry-flavoured mayonnaise containing cream.
Louise	Segments of grapefruit and depipped grapes on lettuce; covered with mayonnaise and sprinkled with chopped hazelnuts.
Louisette	Diced tomato-flesh and depipped grapes on cos lettuce; French dressing.
Majestic	Diced apple, celery and green pimento; mixed with light mayonnaise.

Mandragora	Slices of banana, green olives and tomato-flesh with cooked pieces of salsify; French dressing with mustard, Harvey's sauce and chilli vinegar.
Manon	Grapefruit segments on a leaf of lettuce; French dressing with sugar.
Maraîchère	Julienne of celeriac and rampion root with pieces of cooked salisfy, mix with mustard cream dressing and horseradish; decorate with rings of beetroot and potato.
Margaret	Diced cucumber, potato and tomato-flesh with shrimps, mixed with mayonnaise.
Marie-Louise	Slices of apple, banana, celery and truffle; mixed with mayonnaise.
Marie-Stuart	Julienne of celeriac, truffle and crisp lettuce, mixed with acidulated cream and chopped chervil; surrounded with sliced hard-boiled egg.
Mariette	Julienne of cooked carrot with orange segments; mixed with orange-flavoured French dressing and sprinkled with shredded orange skin.
Mascotte	Bouquets of sprue, crayfish tails, small cockscombs, quarters of gull's eggs, decorate neatly; mustard cream dressing.
Mercédès	Bouquets of julienne of Belgian endive, tomato flesh, red pimento and truffle; lemon-flavoured mayonnaise.
Miami	Segments of tangerine and slices of tomato on leaves of lettuce; French dressing with sugar and lemon juice.
Midinette	Julienne of apple, celeriac, chicken and gruyère cheese; mixed with light mayonnaise.
Mignon	Diced cooked artichoke bottoms and shrimps; mixed with creamed mayonnaise and decorated with slices of truffle.
Mignonne	Diced raw artichoke bottoms, celeriac, potato and truffle in French dressing; sprue on top; mayonnaise separate.
Mikado	Poached and bearded oysters, diced red and green pimento, and rice; mustard-flavoured French dressing.

445

Mimosa   Orange segments; depipped grapes and sliced banana on leaves of lettuce; acidulated cream and sieved yolk of egg sprinkled over.

Mirabeau   Diced potato and tomato with slices of cucumber, and trellis of anchovy; French dressing.

Mona Lisa   Julienne of apple and truffle, mixed with tomato mayonnaise on leaves of lettuce.

Monégasque   Quarters of artichoke bottoms, sliced potato, diced tomato, stoned black olives with French dressing made with anchovy essence and mustard.

Monte Carlo   Diced pineapple and orange, pomegranate grains; acidulated cream, served in hollowed-out tangerine skin.

Monte-Cristo   Diced potato, hard-boiled egg, truffle and lobster on leaves of lettuce; mustard-flavoured mayonnaise.

Montfermeuil   Small pieces of salsify, sliced artichoke bottoms and sliced potatoes and julienne of egg white, with French dressing; covered with sieved yolk of egg.

Montmorency   Stoned cherries with julienne of celery; acidulated cream with grated horseradish.

Moscovite   Macédoine of vegetables set with jellied mayonnaise in a chemised mould; turned out and garnished with tartlets, some filled with caviar, the others with sigui (a Scandinavian smoked fish).

Nantaise   Julienne of smoked salmon, shrimps and sprue arrange on leaves of lettuce, surrounded with sliced hard-boiled egg; French dressing.

Negresco   Slices of firm avocado, truffle and flaked almonds; coated with mayonnaise and served on leaves of lettuce.

Nelusko   Julienne of beetroot and potato, mixed with mayonnaise containing sauce Robert; a bunch of sprue on top.

Néva   Julienne of beetroot, Belgian endive and truffle; French dressing.

Niçoise   Quarters of tomato, sliced potato and French beans, mixed with mayonnaise; decorated with anchovy fillets, black olives and capers.

Ninon	Orange segments on leaves of lettuce; oil, orange and lemon juice dressing.
des Nonnes	Julienne of chicken with rice; mustard-flavoured French dressing, shredded truffle on top.
Olga	Julienne of beetroot, Belgian endive and celeriac; French dressing.
Opéra	Julienne of chicken, ox-tongue, celery and truffle, surrounded with slices of gherkin and cocks' kidneys and place sprue on top; light mayonnaise.
d'Orange	Thin segments of orange on leaves of lettuce; kirsch-flavoured French dressing.
Orientale	Rice, diced red and green pimento, diamonds of French beans, quarters of tomato all tossed in hot oil with chopped garlic; French dressing with chopped anchovy.
Orloff	Diced raw artichoke bottoms and melon; French dressing.
Otto	Diced apple, melon, orange and pineapple, depipped grapes; mixed with mayonnaise and arranged on leaves of lettuce.
Oxford	Diced chicken, tomato-flesh, gherkin and truffle on leaves of lettuce, garnished with sliced hard-boiled egg; French dressing with chopped tarragon.
Panachée	Leaves or quarters of lettuce, sliced beetroot, quarters of hard-boiled egg and tomatoes; French dressing.
Pascaline	Slices of avocado, segments of grapefruit and julienne of red pimento on cos lettuce; French dressing.
Paloise	Quarters of artichoke bottoms, and cooked salsify; French dressing, bunch of sprue on top.
Paulette	Julienne of celery, French beans, potatoes and truffle with mayonnaise.
Portuguese	Rice with julienne of tomato-flesh and red pimento; French dressing with anchovy essence.
Potato	Diced potato with chopped onion marinated in French dressing and mixed with mayonnaise; chopped parsley on top.

Rachel	Julienne of artichoke bottoms, celery, potato and truffle; thin mayonnaise.
Régence	Julienne of celery, truffle shavings and sliced cocks' kidneys with thin mayonnaise; sprue on top.
Réjane	Rice, slices of hard-boiled egg, truffle and grated horseradish with acidulated cream.
Riviera	Segments of orange and tangerine, pieces of pineapple, small strawberries and julienne of celeriac on lettuce; mayonnaise with chopped green pimento.
Rochelle	Diced apple, celeriac, pineapple and radishes; spiced French dressing.
Roosevelt	Diced asparagus, mushrooms, oranges and truffle with mayonnaise, filled into emptied halves of tomato.
Rosemonde	Diced asparagus and French beans with mayonnaise; bunch of sprue on top.
Rossini	Julienne of celery, frizzy endive, dandelion leaves and watercress on leaves of cos lettuce; French dressing.
Romaine	Quarters of cos lettuce; French dressing.
Russe	Macédoine of carrots and turnips with peas and diamonds of French beans with mayonnaise.
Saint-Jean	Artichoke bottoms and cucumber in slices, peas, diamonds of French beans and sprue; acidulated mayonnaise; decorate with sliced hard boiled egg and gherkin and chopped tarragon.
Saint-Pierre	Julienne of celery, sliced potato, grapefruit segments, pineapple pieces and asparagus tips on lettuce leaves; mint-flavoured French dressing.
Saint-Sylvestre	Julienne of celeriac, artichoke bottoms, mushroom, hard-boiled white of egg and truffle; decorate with a slice of potato with a smaller slice of truffle on top and pluches of chervil; thin mayonnaise with chopped walnut.
Salisbury	Julienne of beetroot, Belgian endive and celeriac; French dressing.
de Saison	Any kind of lettuce and other salad ingredients in season may be used; French dressing.

Sevillaise	Depipped grapes and orange segments on leaves of lettuce; French dressing.
Sicilienne	Diced apple, artichoke bottoms, celeriac and tomato flesh; mayonnaise.
Thérèse	Slices of apple, celeriac and potatoes; mayonnaise.
de Tomate	Sliced tomatoes, finely chopped onion; french dressing.
Tosca	Diced celery, chicken, white truffle and fresh Parmesan; mustard-flavoured mayonnaise mixed with French dressing.
Tourangelle	Diamonds of French beans, flageolets, julienne of potato; mayonnaise with cream and chopped tarragon.
Trédern	Poached and bearded oysters, halved crayfish tails, sprue and shavings of truffle; mayonnaise with crayfish cream.
Turquoise	Julienne of Belgian endive, celery, red pimento and tomato-flesh; mayonnaise.
Vénitienne	Julienne of celery and truffle with orange segments and stoned olives; green mayonnaise containing purée of cooked chicken liver.
Véronique	Julienne of beetroot, celery and crisp lettuce, crisp lardons, sliced hard-boiled egg; French dressing.
Vicaire	Lettuce, frizzy endive, radicchio and corn salad tossed in vinaigrette, covered with crisp-fried lardons finished with vinegar, toasted garlic croûtons and sieved hard-boiled egg.
Vicomte	Diced asparagus, celeriac, ox-tongue and green pimento; tomato, lemon, oil and sugar-dressing.
Victoria	Diced cucumber, crawfish and truffle with sprue; mayonnaise with crawfish flavour and colour.
Viennoise	Julienne of Belgian endive, gherkins, ox-tongue and truffle; French dressing, sprinkle with paprika.
Vigneronne	Skinned and depipped grapes on leaves of lettuce; acidulated cream.

Waldorf   Diced apple, celery and walnuts; mayonnaise or acidulated cream; may be served in a scooped-out apple.

Windsor   Julienne of celery, chicken, ox-tongue, raw mushrooms, truffle; mayonnaise flavoured with Derby sauce, garnish with rampion.

Yolande   Julienne of apple, beetroot, carrot and celery; mint-flavoured French dressing.

Warm Salads

These can be made by dressing any of the usual salad stuffs with items such as crisply fried lardons of bacon and the fat from this cooking, mixed into the main ingredients together with vinegar, lemon or lime juice, or by adding hot fried diced bread croûtons or pieces of garlic toast, etc. The selection of greens can include batavia lettuce, lamb's lettuce, chicory, escarole, feuille de chêne, frisé endive, purslane, quattro stagione, lollo rosso, and radicchio.

Salad Dressings

There are five basic types of salad dressings, all others being variations of these.

1. **French Dressing** 3 parts oil* to 1 part vinegar** with salt and pepper. This is also known as Vinaigrette Salad Dressing.
2. **Acidulated Cream Dressing** 4 parts single cream to 1 part lemon juice.
3. **Mayonnaise** 7 yolks to 1 litre oil, with vinegar, salt, pepper and mustard.
4. **Yogurt** Plain unsweetened set or runny yoghurt.
5. **Cream Cheese**, fromage frais or crème fraîche.

  * various oils may be used, e.g. corn, groundnut, hazelnut, olive, sesame, sunflower, walnut

** various vinegars including cider, malt, raspberry, red wine, sherry, tarragon, white wine

Variations on French dressing

Bar le Duc   Use lemon juice instead of vinegar and add melted redcurrant jelly.

Blue Cheese   Add sieved Roquefort, Danish blue or Gorgonzola cheese.

Breslin   Add chopped truffle and pistachios.

Caesar   Add a chopped soft-boiled egg, Parmesan cheese and cream to French dressing.

Californienne   Use grapefruit juice instead of vinegar.

Chiffonade   Add chopped hard-boiled egg, beetroot, celery, olives, gherkins, onions and parsley.

Cingalaise   Add hard-boiled egg, courgette, cucumber, pimento and tomato, all finely chopped, to curry-flavoured dressing.

Club   Flavour with cooking brandy.

Cressonière   Add sieved hard-boiled egg and picked watercress leaves.

Cucumber   Add finely grated cucumber and some made mustard.

Dijonnaise   Add sieved hard-boiled egg and French mustard.

Honey   Add honey, grated horseradish and chopped parsley and chives.

Lorenzo   Add chopped chives, parsley and watercress.

Mint   Add finely chopped mint.

Mustard   Mix made English mustard into the vinaigrette and add a little mayonnaise and cream.

Roquefort   Add vinaigrete gradually to mashed Roquefort cheese.

Sarladaise   Chopped hard-boiled egg and truffle; use lemon instead of vinegar and finish with cream.

Sweet and sour   Add chopped chives, onion and pimento, sugar, paprika and Worcester sauce.

Thousand Island   Add chopped red and green pimento, chives hard-boiled egg and parsley.

Verdurette   Add sieved hard-boiled egg and blanched chives.

Variations on acidulated cream dressing

Add paprika, sieved tomato pulp, shellfish purée, celery seeds, purée of avocado, chopped nuts, etc.

Variations on mayonnaise

Almond	Add almond milk and finely chopped toasted almonds.
Anchovy	Add anchovy essence and chopped anchovy.
Colioure	Add chopped anchovy and garlic.
Creamed	Add lightly whipped cream.
Chutney	Add chopped chutney.
Caper	Add washed capers.
Caviar	Add caviar or lumpfish roe and a little grated horseradish.
Créole	Add finely chopped olives, onion, pimento and sweet pickle with tomato ketchup and paprika.
Green Goddess	Add anchovy essence, chopped capers, chives, garlic, onion and parsley.
Horseradish	Add finely grated horseradish and vinegar.
Indian	Flavour with curry powder and chives.
La Varenne	Finely chopped raw mushrooms and chopped parsley.
Mousquetaire	Add chopped shallot and a little melted meat glaze.
Olga	Add chopped anchovy and chives.
Suédoise	Add chopped apple and grated horseradish; flavour with mustard.
Tomato	Mix with tomato pulp or tomato ketchup.
Verte	Colour with purée of spinach and green herbs.

Variations on yoghurt

Yoghurt can be combined with any of the following to make interesting dressings; celery salt, chutney, chopped cucumber, garlic salt, mustards, pine kernels, soy sauce, honey, tomato ketchup, fruit juice, etc.

Persian	Add chopped hard-boiled egg, gherkin and olives and some tomato ketchup.

Russian Add chopped onion, lemon juice, chilli sauce and Worcestershire sauce.

Variations on Cream Cheese and Fromage Frais

Lemon juice, honey, pineapple juice, cream, grated lemon rind, sugar, etc.

Dips

These are used at buffet receptions for guests to dip foodstuffs such as savoury biscuits, crisps, short pieces of raw carrot, celery, cucumber, pimento etc. They are slightly stiffer than a sauce but not so that the item dipped in breaks under pressure. They can be either cold or hot and may be blended in a liquidiser to a smooth consistency. Mayonnaise may be added to any of these.

Avocado Puréed avocado, cream cheese, cream, mayonnaise, chopped onion and parsley.

Celery Chopped celery, tomato ketchup, chopped onion, tabasco, lemon juice and grated horseradish.

Chili Tomato ketchup, chili sauce, chopped celery, pimento and horseradish, tabasco sauce.

Cucumber Grated cucumber squeezed out, chopped onion, lemon juice and cottage cheese.

Epicurienne Tomato ketchup, chopped gherkins and chopped onion, grated horseradish, Worcester sauce.

Piquante Tomato ketchup, onion juice, Worcester sauce, tabasco, cayenne.

Tapenade Anchovies, capers, stuffed olives, tuna fish with lemon juice, brandy, mustard, oil and a garnish of sliced stuffed olives.

Tomato Tomato ketchup, whipped cream, lemon juice.

Viveurs Cream cheese or crème fraîche, plain yoghurt, finely chopped cucumber, pesto.

Yoghurt　　　　Any of the following may be added to plain
yoghurt: grated cheese, cranberry purée,
chopped piccallili, diced salami, ground ginger,
flaked salmon, smoked salmon, muesli, tuna fish,
pickled walnuts, pesto, pastes, quark and
spreads.

13 VEGETABLES

Artichokes, globe – artichauts

These are mostly served as a separate vegetable course rather than as an accompanying vegetable.

Barigoule Blanch, remove the choke and fill with duxelles containing chopped ham; braise and serve with jus lié.

Boulangère Blanch, remove the choke and fill with sausage-meat; enclose in short pastry and bake for approximately 1 hour.

Cavour Boil until tender, remove the choke then dip in melted butter and coat with grated Parmesan.

Clamart Blanch small artichokes then cook in a covered cocotte in the oven with a few new carrots and peas, butter and stock. When cooked thicken the liquid with beurre manié.

Hollandaise Plain boil, remove the central leaves and scrape out the choke; replace the inverted centre leaves and serve with sauce hollandaise.

Nature Cut off the stalk and the top third, rub the base with lemon, tie with string and cook in boiling salted water until tender. Remove centre leaves, scrape out the choke, replace outer leaves and serve on a folded napkin with a suitable sauce such as hollandaise or beurre fondu. (It is usual to tie up large ones with a slice of lemon over the base.)

Provençale Cook small artichokes in a covered cocotte in the oven, in oil with a few new carrots, peas and shredded lettuce.

Artichoke bottoms – *fonds d'artichauts*

These are used mainly as part of some garnishes but can be served as a vegetable.

Beignets	Sandwich two cooked bottoms with duxelles, dip in frying batter and deep fry.
au Beurre	Cook in butter and lemon juice.
Cavour	Arrange cooked bottoms in a dish, sprinkle with cheese and chopped hard-boiled egg and coat with melted butter containing anchovy essence.
Cussy	Fill with truffled purée of foie gras and dip into hot sauce Villeroy; when set, pané à l'Anglaise, deep fry and serve with sauce Madère.
aux Fines Herbes	Simmer cooked bottoms in jus lié with mixed chopped chervil, parsley and tarragon.
Florentine	Fill cooked bottoms with buttered spinach containing chopped anchovy, coat with sauce mornay and glaze.
Lucullus	Simmer cooked bottoms in jus lié with chopped truffle.
Lyonnaise	Blanch then braise together with sautéd sliced onion.
Milanaise	Arrange cooked bottoms in a buttered dish, sprinkle with grated Parmesan and butter and gratinate.
Mornay	Coat cooked bottoms with sauce mornay, sprinkle with cheese and butter and glaze.
Niçoise	Cook in oil and white wine with chopped onion, tomato and anchovy.
Piémontaise	Fill cooked bottoms with risotto containing chopped white truffle.
Polonaise	Cover cooked bottoms with fried breadcrumbs, sieved white and yolk of hard-boiled egg and chopped parsley.
Sautés	Sauté slices of cooked bottoms in clarified butter.
Stanley	Cook bottoms with lardons of lean bacon and sliced onions in white wine, when reduced, finish to cook in white sauce; serve coated with

the strained sauce and sprinkled with the chopped bacon.

Villeroy	Coat cooked bottoms with sauce Villeroy, then with egg-wash and breadcrumbs and deep fry.

Artichokes, Jerusalem – Topinambours

à l'Anglaise	Cook in butter and finish by adding white sauce to coat them.
à la Crème	Add cooked artichokes to cream sauce and mix in gently.
Frit	Cut cooked artichokes into thick slices, dip into batter and deep fry.
Georgienne	Cut into slices together with some firm potatoes and cook in butter and stock with a pinch of sugar until coated with a glaze.
au Gratin	Cover cooked sliced artichokes with sauce mornay, sprinkle with cheese and butter and gratinate.
Hollandaise	Mix well-drained cooked artichokes into sauce hollandaise.
à la Orly	Dip cooked artichokes into orly batter, deep fry and serve with tomato sauce.
Polonaise	Cover cooked artichokes with fried breadcrumbs and sprinkle with sieved white and yolk of hard-boiled egg and chopped parsley.
Purée de	Purée cooked artichokes and mix with approximately a quarter of its volume of dry mashed potato.
Sauté au Beurre	Shallow fry cooked slices in clarified butter.

Asparagus – Asperges

This vegetable is nearly always served as a course in its own right, rather than as an accompanying vegetable. The thin sticks of asparagus known as sprue are mainly used as an hors-d'œuvre or garnish but may be served as a vegetable.

Argenteuil	Arrange tips on a fond d'artichaut.
en Branches	Plain boil and serve on an asparagus cradle or

	folded napkin, accompanied with a sauceboat of melted butter, or sauce hollandaise.
au Beurre	Toss cooked tips in melted butter.
à la Créme	Toss partly cooked tips in sufficient boiling cream to coat and cook until the cream is nearly reduced; finish with butter and lemon juice.
Flamande	Plain boil and serve with a sauce made of crushed yolk of hard-boiled egg mixed with a little hot melted butter.
Genevoise	Serve sprinkled with Gruyère cheese and beurre noisette.
Grand-Duc	Arrange tips on artichoke bottoms, coat with sauce mornay, glaze and decorate with a slice of truffle.
au Gratin	Coat the heads with sauce mornay, sprinkle with grated cheese and butter and gratinate, protecting the bottom part from drying.
Idéale	Serve plain boiled, accompanied with a sauceboat of sauce mousseline flavoured with tomato.
Italienne	Sprinkle the heads with grated Parmesan and melted butter and gratinate, protecting the ends from the heat.
Milanaise	Sprinkle the heads with grated Parmesan and beurre noisette and gratinate, protecting the ends from the heat.
Mornay	Coat the heads with sauce mornay, sprinkle with grated cheese and butter and glaze.
Polonaise	Sprinkle the heads with fried breadcrumbs, sieved white and yolk of hard-boiled egg and chopped parsley.
Princesse	Coat the heads with sauce crème or velouté.

Beans, broad – *fèves or fèves de marais*

Anglaise	Plain boil with a sprig of savory in the water and serve sprinkled with chopped savory.
au Beurre	Drain plain boiled beans and mix fresh butter into them.
à la Crème	Add double cream to the cooked beans and mix in.

| **Westphalienne** | Mix cooked beans and lardons of bacon with a little chicken velouté. |

Beans, french – *haricots verts*

Allemande	Cook finely chopped onion in butter, add veal velouté and the beans cut into short lengths; cook until tender.
Anglaise	Plain boil, drain well and serve plainly; do not overcook.
au Beurre	Plain boil, drain and toss in melted butter.
à la Crème	Parboil, drain and finish to cook in boiling cream; when slightly reduced finish with a little butter.
au Fromage	Sprinkle cooked beans with Parmesan and beurre noisette.
à l'Oseille	Mix with shredded sorrel previously stewed in butter.
Panachés	Mix together equal amounts of cooked French beans and flageolet beans.
Poulette	Mix cooked beans with sauce poulette.
Sautés	Toss cooked beans in hot butter until very slightly coloured.
Succotash	Equal quantities of 2cm lengths of French beans and sweetcorn kernels finished to cook in cream.
Tourangelle	Add freshly cooked beans to buttered cream sauce.

Beans, lima – *flageolets*

à la Crème	Cover drained canned beans with cream and cook until it is slightly reduced.
à la Française	Stew with a few button onions and shredded lettuce.
au Lard	Mix with fried lardons of bacon.
Purée Musard	Make cooked beans into a purée and finish with butter.
Succotash	Finish to cook equal amounts of lima beans or French beans and sweetcorn kernels in cream, fried lardons of bacon may be added.

459

Beans, runner (scarlet runner) – haricots d'espagne

These are usually shredded into slices, and plain boiled but may also be served in any of the ways as for French beans. Other beans include bobby beans from France and Kenya and garter beans from Holland.

Beetroot – betterave

Use only small new beetroots as a vegetable and plain boil or bake them before proceeding with any of the following.

au Beurre	Toss the cooked beetroots in melted butter.
à la Crème	Serve lightly mixed with cream sauce.
au Cumin	Serve covered with velouté that has been flavoured with caraway seeds.
au Moutarde	Serve lightly covered with mustard sauce.
à l'Orange	Make a sauce of orange and lemon juice, sherry, grated orange rind, butter and cornflour; add small cooked beetroot and simmer for a few minutes.
Orientale	Make a spicy sauce with chopped onion, vinegar, sugar and soy sauce, thicken with cornflour and coat the beetroot.
Polonaise	Toss the cooked beetroots in butter with a little vinegar and a pinch of powdered cloves.
Russe	Mix with beetroots with a little sour cream and chopped mint.

Belgian endive – endives belges

These are usually shallow braised in water, lemon juice and butter before being prepared in any of the following ways.

Ardennaise	Cook and serve with sautéd diced salt belly of pork and chopped ham.
à la Crème	When nearly braised, drain and finish to cook in cream; when reduced finish with butter and lemon juice.
Bourgeoise	Stew in butter with the lid on until cooked and coloured light brown.

Hollandaise	Serve coated with sauce hollandaise.
au Jus	Serve coated with jus lié.
Meunière	Fry braised endives in butter until light brown in colour and serve sprinkled with lemon juice, beurre noisette and chopped parsley.
Mornay	Arrange on a layer of sauce mornay, coat with more sauce, sprinkle with cheese and melted butter and glaze.
Milanaise	Sprinkle cooked endives with grated Parmesan and beurre noisette.
Polonaise	Cover cooked endives with fried breadcrumbs, sieved white and yolk of hard-boiled egg and chopped parsley.

Broccoli – brocolis. This is also known as calabrese

The methods for serving cauliflower can also be used for Broccoli.

au Beurre	Coat plain boiled broccoli with melted butter.
Hollandaise	Coat broccoli with sauce hollandaise, or serve the sauce separately in a sauceboat.
Italienne	Coat broccoli with sauce italienne, sprinkle with Parmesan, breadcrumbs and melted butter and gratinate in a hot oven.
Romaine	Dip cold cooked sprigs of broccoli into frying batter and deep fry.

Brussels sprouts – choux de bruxelles or *boutons de bruxelles*

à l'Anglaise	Plain boil for approximately 10 minutes, drain well and serve; do not overcook.
au Beurre	Toss freshly cooked sprouts in melted butter.
Bonne Femme	Parboil, drain and finish to cook by stewing in butter.
Bruxelloise	Arrange small buttered sprouts on artichoke bottoms.
à la Crème	Parboil, drain and finish to cook in boiling cream.

461

au Gratin   Place cooked sprouts in a buttered dish, coat with sauce mornay, sprinkle with cheese and gratinate.

Limousine   Mix two parts plain boiled sprouts with one part braised chestnuts.

Milanaise   Sprinkle with Parmesan and beurre noisette.

Polonaise   Cover sautéd sprouts with fried breadcrumbs, sieved white and yolk of hard-boiled egg and chopped parsley.

Sautés   Drain plain boiled sprouts and toss in hot butter until lightly browned.

Cabbage, green – chou vert

à l'Anglaise   Cook the leaves in plenty of boiling salted water, drain and press between a soup plate and dinner plate; cut into wedges.

Braisé   Blanch for 10 minutes, cool, squeeze into miniature cabbages inside large leaves and braise for 1 hour; serve coated with jus lié.

Farci   Blanch for 10 minutes, form into miniature cabbages with sausage meat, rice etc. then braise for 1 hour; serve coated with jus lié.

de Printemps   Keep the spring cabbages whole by tieing with string; plain boil, drain and fold into neat shapes; serve brushed with melted butter.

Cabbage, red – chou rouge

This is normally shredded and cooked by braising with the addition of lard, brown sugar and vinegar.

Alsacienne   Finely shred and braise in red wine with whole chestnuts.

Brésilienne   Cook finely shredded cabbage with chopped onion, lardons and belly of pork; serve with the pork cut into slices.

Flamande   Shred, braise with butter, brown sugar, diced apple and vinegar, preferably using a stainless steel or well-tinned copper pan.

Limousine	Braise in the usual manner then add braised chestnuts.
Pomeranienne	Braise with sliced apples, vinegar, brown sugar and caraway.
Russe	Mix shredded red cabbage with sliced onion, julienne of celeriac, vinegar, sugar and cloves, and braise.
Valencienne	Braise with lardons and sliced cooking apple and serve garnished with grilled chipolatas.
Westphalienne	Braise with sliced onions, red wine and vinegar.

Cabbage, white – chou blanc

Choucroute	Braise the sauerkraut in white wine with carrots, onions, a piece of streaky bacon and juniper berries; serve with slices of the bacon and carrot.
à la Crème	Finely shred, plain boil, drain and mix with sauce crème.
Espagnole	Shred, blanch, mix with julienne of carrot and braise in dry Madeira.
Farci	Blanch whole leaves, roll around sausage-meat to form miniature cabbages and braise; serve coated with jus lié.
au Fromage	Shred and braise in the usual manner; cover with thin slices of Gruyere cheese and melted butter and bake.
Lithuanienne	Braise with sliced apple, sauted onions and lardons.
aux Pommes	Shred equal amounts of white and red cabbage, mix and braise with an equal amount of sliced apple with sugar and vinegar.
Suisse	Shred finely, braise then place in a buttered dish, cover with a cheese-flavoured egg-custard mixture and bake.
Vin Blanc	Finely shred and braise in white wine with sliced apples.

Carrots – *carottes*

au Beurre	Turn to a barrel shape, plain boil, drain and toss in melted butter.
Bourgeoise	Cook in water with butter, salt and sugar then thicken with beurre manié.
à la Crème	Mix cream sauce with plain boiled pieces of carrots.
Flamande	Cook in water with butter then thicken with a liaison of cream and egg yolk.
Glacées	Turn to a barrel shape, cook in water with butter, salt and sugar until glazed.
Marianne	Cut into coarse julienne and cook with half the amount of button onions; finish with parsley butter and meat glaze.
Vichy	Cut into 2mm slices and cook in tap water with butter, salt and sugar until glazed.

Cardoons – *cardons*

This vegetable is not grown in Great Britain, it looks like a very long stick of celery but without that vegetable's distinctive taste and smell. Cardoons can be cooked in the same way as salsify and celery.

Cauliflower – *chou-fleur*

à l'Anglaise	Leave whole or cut into florets and plain boil; do not overcook.
au Beurre	Cover cooked cauliflower with melted butter.
à la Crème	Serve the cauliflower coated with cream sauce.
Dubarry	Squeeze the cauliflower into small balls, coat each with sauce mornay, sprinkle with Parmesan and gratinate.
Fritots	Dip cold florets into frying batter and deep fry.
Hollandaise	Coat the cooked cauliflower with sauce hollandaise, or serve with the sauce separately.
Mornay	Cut cooked cauliflower into portions, cover with sauce mornay, sprinkle with Parmesan and gratinate.

Milanaise	Coat cooked cauliflower with sauce italienne, sprinkle with cheese and butter and gratinate.
Persillé	Plain boil, brush with butter and sprinkle with chopped parsley.
Polonaise	Sauté cooked florets until brown, cover with fried breadcrumbs, sieved white and yolk of hard-boiled egg and chopped parsley.
Villeroy	Dip sprigs of cooked cauliflower into sauce Villeroy, allow to set, then egg and crumb and deep fry.

Celeriac – céleri-rave

Braisé	Cook sliced parboiled celeriac in sauce Madère.
à la Crème	Cut into 1½cm dice, parboil and finish by cooking in cream.
Espagnole	Trim to olive shape, blanch, then simmer in demi-glace with chopped onion and diced tomato.
Fritots	Plain boil, cut into rounds, dip into frying batter and deep fry.
Parmesan	Cover cooked slices with demi-glace, sprinkle with Parmesan and melted butter and bake.

Celery – céleri

Braisé	Blanch for 10 minutes then braise in white stock until tender; cut in half, fold over and serve with a little of the cooking liquid.
Italienne	Sprinkle cooked portions with Parmesan and beurre noisette.
au Jus	Blanch for 10 minutes, braise in white stock, cut into portions and coat with jus lié.
à la Moelle	Blanch for 10 minutes, braise in white stock until tender, cut into portions and coat with sauce moelle.
Mornay	Coat each portion with sauce mornay, sprinkle with Parmesan and gratinate.

Chow-chow – chayote or *brionne* (also known as Christophine)

This vegetable is a very small gourd of the same family as pumpkin and vegetable marrow. It is not necessary to peel or deseed them and they may be cut into slices and shallow fried, or stewed in butter, or cooked in any of the other ways as for cucumbers or courgettes.

Chard – blette

Chard is the midribs of the leaves of white sugar beet and can be cooked in the same ways as salsify and celery.

Chicory – endive frisée

Very often this is called 'endive' in English; it is really a salad vegetable, shaped like a lettuce but with thin spiky leaves that are pale to dark green in colour, having been covered while growing.

à la Crème	Braise blanched chopped chicory in velouté and finish with butter and cream.
Flamande	Braise blanched lengths in velouté and finish with butter and cream.
Pain de	Braise blanched chopped chicory in velouté, mix in 5 eggs per 1kg, fill into a mould and cook au bain-marie until set; serve with cream sauce.
Russe	Cook blanched chopped chicory in butter with chopped onion and fennel and finish with sour cream.
Soufflé de	Make a stiff purée of braised chicory, add grated Parmesan and egg yolks and fold in stiffly beaten whites; fill into small moulds and cook for 15–20 minutes.

Chinese leaves – feuilles chinoise

This vegetable can be prepared and served either like plain boiled cabbage or as braised lettuce; it is more commonly served as a salad.

Cucumber – concombre

Andalouse	Cook blanched pieces in tomato sauce then gratinate with Parmesan cheese.
à la Crème	Cooked blanched olive-shaped pieces in butter until nearly cooked and finish with cream and béchamel.
Etuvé	Cook turned pieces in butter and stock; when cooked thicken the liquid with either beurre manié or egg yolks and lemon juice.
Farci	Fill hollowed-out and blanched 5cm lengths with chicken forcemeat and cook in a little butter; they may be trimmed to a boat shape and sandwiched with chicken and duxelles stuffing before being cooked.
Glacé	Turn to a barrel shape; cook in water, sugar and butter until they are glazed.
Paysanne	Turn to a boat shape, hollow out and fill with sausagemeat; cook in butter in the oven.
Polonaise	Turn to a barrel shape, plain boil, drain and toss in butter; place in a dish and cover with fried breadcrumbs, sieved white and yolk of hard-boiled egg, and chopped parsley.
Provençale	Cut into 5mm slices and cook in butter; mix in one third its amount of cooked rice pilaff, a little béchamel then gratinate with breadcrumbs, Parmesan cheese and melted butter.

Egg-plant – aubergine (also called brinjal)

Andalouse	Cut in half lengthwise, score the flesh, brush with oil and bake until soft; scoop out the flesh, chop and mix with chopped ham, red peppers and tomato. Refill the skins, gratinate and surround with tomato-flavoured demi-glace.
Algérienne	Cut in half lengthwise, score the flesh, brush with oil and bake until soft; scoop out the flesh, chop and mix with chopped sautéd onion. Refill the skins, coat with tomato sauce, sprinkle with breadcrumbs and gratinate.

Beignets Peel, cut into 4mm slices, dip into frying batter and deep fry.

Bordelaise Peel, cut into 2½mm slices, dip in flour and shallow fry then add chopped shallot and breadcrumbs and toss over; finish with a little lemon juice.

Egyptienne Cut in half lengthways, score the flesh, brush with oil and bake until soft; scoop out the flesh, chop and mix with cooked onion and mutton; fill into the skins, cover with sliced tomato and reheat in the oven.

Farcie Cut in half lengthways, score the flesh, brush with oil and bake until soft; scoop out the flesh, chop and mix with chopped onion, mushroom and tomato; fill into the skins, sprinkle with breadcrumbs and oil and gratinate.

Frite Peel, cut into 4mm slices, dip in milk and flour and deep fry.

Génoise Peel, cut into slices and cook in butter with chopped onion; add diced tomato and when soft, stir in beaten eggs and allow to thicken.

au Gratin Cut in half lengthways, score the flesh, brush with oil and bake until soft; scoop out the flesh, chop and mix with duxelles; replace in the skins, sprinkle with Parmesan and butter and gratinate.

Imam Bayaldi Shallow fry sliced peeled aubergines, arrange in a dish with tomate concassée, sprinkle with breadcrumbs and oil and gratinate.

Lyonnaise Cut in half lengthways, score the flesh, brush with oil and bake until soft; scoop out the flesh, chop and mix with sautéd chopped onion; refill the skins, sprinkle with crumbs and gratinate.

Napolitaine Peel, cut into 5mm slices lengthways; flour and deep fry. Re-form by spreading with cooked tomato and Parmesan cheese, cover with tomato sauce, sprinkle with cheese and oil and gratinate.

Niçoise Cut in half lengthways, score the flesh, brush with oil and bake until soft; scoop out the flesh, chop and mix with diced anchovy and tomato and garlic; fill into the skins, sprinkle with cheese and oil and gratinate.

Nîmoise   Stuff the emptied skins with the chopped flesh, chopped red pimento and diced tomato flavoured with garlic; gratinate in a hot oven.

Orientale   Peel, cut into 5mm slices lengthways, flour and deep fry; sandwich two together with stuffing of aubergine flesh, tomato and breadcrumbs, brush with oil and bake for 30 minutes.

Provençale   Cut in half lengthways, score the flesh, brush with oil and bake until soft; scoop out the flesh, chop and mix with tomato flesh, garlic and breadcrumbs, fill into the skins, gratinate and serve surrounded with tomato sauce.

Serbe   Cut in half lengthways, score the flesh, brush with oil and bake until soft; scoop out the flesh, chop and mix with chopped cooked mutton, rice and tomato. Fill into the skins, sprinkle with breadcrumbs and gratinate; serve surrounded with tomato sauce.

Strasbourgeoise   Cut in half, deep fry then remove the centre, chop and mix it with liver sausage; replace in the skins, sprinkle with breadcrumbs and butter and gratinate in the oven.

Turque   Fill emptied skins with a mixture of the chopped flesh, chopped onion, tomato and cooked rice; sprinkle with oil and cook in the oven.

Aubergines can also be cut up like chips and deep fried.

Fennel – fenouil

Braisé   Blanch, braise in white stock, cut in half and serve with some of the cooking liquid; or they may be coated with jus lié.

à la Crème   Braise, cut in half and coat with cream sauce.

Etuvé   Blanch, cut into sections and cook gently in butter and lemon juice.

au Gratin   Braise, cut in half, coat with sauce mornay, sprinkle with cheese and gratinate.

Hop shoots – jets de houblon

The young shoots are available at certain times of the year when the bines are being trained. They are cooked in acidulated water and can be served tossed in butter or mixed with cream.

Kale – chou frisé

There are several different kinds of kale or Kail as it is sometimes spelt, the best known being the Scotch variety that has wrinkled purple-coloured leaves. Kale is usually boiled as for ordinary green cabbage but can be used in all the ways given for cabbage.

Kohlrabi – chou-rave

This vegetable resembles a turnip more than a cabbage and only the top leaves can be used in the same way as boiled cabbage. It should not be necessary to peel young kohlrabis and the tuber part can be prepared as follows:

Autrichienne	Slice, parboil and finish to cook with sautéd chopped onion in velouté; the chopped plain boiled leaves may be added.
au Beurre	Trim small pieces to a barrel shape; plain boil, drain and toss in melted butter.
à la Crème	Cut into slices, parboil then finish to cook in cream.
Farci	Parboil small whole ones, cut off the tops, hollow out and fill with a stuffing; sprinkle with breadcrumbs and butter and cook in the oven.
Frit	Cut into chips, blanch in boiling water until tender, drain well and deep fry as for pommes frites.
au Gratin	Cut into slices, plain boil, drain and place in a buttered dish; coat with sauce mornay, sprinkle with cheese and melted butter and gratinate.
Hongroise	Cut into dice, parboil and finish to cook in sauce paprika.
Russe	Cut into slices, parboil and finish to cook in sour cream.

Leek – poireau

au Beurre	Braise the leeks, fold in half and pour melted butter over.
Braisé	Wash, tie in bundles and braise in white stock for 1 hour, fold in half and serve with some of the cooking liquid; they may be served coated with jus liè.
au Gratin	Braise the leeks, fold in half, place in a buttered dish and coat with sauce mornay, sprinkle with cheese and melted butter and gratinate.
au Jambon	Wrap a slice of ham around each braised leek; coat with sauce mornay, sprinkle with cheese and butter and gratinate.
Milanaise	Arrange braised leeks in a dish, sprinkle with Parmesan and beurre noisette.
Nature	Plain boil, fold in half and serve with melted butter.
Polonaise	Arrange braised leeks in a dish and cover with fried breadcrumbs.
Vaudoise	Braise the leeks with a piece each of streaky bacon and garlic sausage; serve with slices of the bacon and sausage.

Lettuce – laitue

Braisée	Blanch, press and braise in white stock for 45 minutes; fold in half neatly and serve with jus lié.
au Croûton	Braise, coat with jus lié and garnish with a small heart shape croûton.
Farcie	Blanch, stuff with duxelles, chicken forcemeat or sausage-meat and braise as small balls; serve coated with jus lié.
Florentine	Blanch separate leaves, place 5–6 on top of one another, stuff with riz pilaff and Parmesan, mould into balls and braise; served garnished with a slice of poached bone marrow and tomato sauce.
Grecque	Blanch, stuff with riz pilaff and braise as small balls; serve coated with jus lié.

Moelle	Coat braised lettuce with sauce moelle and garnish with fried croûtons.
Nature	Plain boiled hearty lettuce can be served with a sauce such as crème, hollandaise, aux oeufs, etc.
Royale	Spread blanched leaves with chicken liver and ham farce, roll up and braise in tomato juice.
Serbe	Braise the lettuce, open and fill with riz pilaff and serve coated with tomato-flavoured jus lié.

Mangetout – snow peas

These are also called 'Sugar Peas'. They are topped and tailed and boiled whole and do not need much in the way of presentation, a little butter usually being sufficient to bring out the full flavour.

Baby marrow – courgette

à l'Anglaise	Peel if necessary, cut in half and remove the seeds, plain boil and serve as it is or with cream sauce or melted butter.
Beignets	Cut large marrows into 4mm slices, sprinkle with salt and allow to stand until limp; dip into frying batter and deep fry.
Espagnole	Cut into slices, toss in oil and arrange in a dish with layers of sautéd chopped onion and diced tomato; sprinkle with breadcrumbs and gratinate.
Farcie	Cut in half, remove the seeds and parboil; fill with duxelles, sprinkle with breadcrumbs and butter and gratinate.
Frites	Cut into 5mm slices, coat with milk then with flour and deep fry.
Milanaise	Arrange plain boiled courgettes in dishes, sprinkle with Parmesan and melted butter and gratinate.
Niçoise	Cut in half lengthways, scoop out the seeds, fill with risotto, sprinkle with breadcrumbs and oil and cook; serve surrounded with jus lié.
Provençale	Cut into slices, stew in butter, add a third of cooked riz pilaff and some béchamel; place in a

	dish, sprinkle with breadcrumbs, Parmesan and butter and gratinate.
Ratatouille	Stew courgettes, aubergine, tomato and onion in oil with bay-leaf, marjoram and thyme; it is often served tepid and with toast.
Sicilienne	Cut large ones into 3mm slices and sandwich two together with a cheese and egg filling; egg and crumb and deep fry.
Turque	Cut in half lengthways, scoop out the seeds and fill with a stuffing made of the chopped flesh, cooked mutton, hard-boiled eggs and rice.

Marrow – *courge*

Large marrows are cut into $4\frac{1}{2}$cm squares and plain boiled for serving with cream sauce or au gratin. Whole ones can be stuffed with sausage meat and braised.

Mooli or *white radishes*

Cut into sections and plain boil, or cook glacé.

Okra or *ladies fingers – gombos* or *gumbos*

Américaine	Blanch then stew in oil with tomate concassée and garlic; may be served lukewarm.
au Beurre	Plain boil for 10–15 minutes, drain and toss in melted butter.
à la Crème	Plain boil and finish to cook in cream.
Créole	Make a pilaff of rice adding sliced okras and julienne of pimento.
Etuvé	Blanch then cook slowly with sliced onions in jus lié.
Farci	Blanch, open, stuff with duxelles or forcemeat and braise.
Frite	Parboil, flour, egg and crumb and deep fry.
Janina	Blanch then sauté in mutton dripping with small dice of lean mutton and diced tomato and allow to cook slowly.
aux Tomates	Blanch and cook in butter with tomate concassée.

Onions – oignons

Braisés	Blanch for 10 minutes and braise in white stock for approximately 1 hour; serve coated with jus lié.
Farcis	Parboil, hollow out and fill with mixture of duxelles or sausagemeat with the chopped centre of the onions, braise until tender and coat with jus lié.
Frits à la Française	Cut into rings 3mm thick, separate, soak in milk, coat with flour and deep fry.
Glacés	Cook button onions in water and butter until it is reduced to a glaze that coats the onions; brown glazed onions are cooked in butter and sugar only.
Lyonnaise	Finely slice and cook gently in butter until golden brown and soft.

Palm shoots – coeurs de palmier

These are the terminal leaf-buds of several different species of the cabbage palm, a tree that grows in the West Indies, Australia and the southern United States. The canned hearts may be served as a garnish or a vegetable in the popular ways of au beurre, à la polonaise or with sauce hollandaise; fresh hearts need blanching before being cooked.

Parsnips – panais

Beignets	Cut into 5mm rounds, parboil then dip into frying batter and deep fry.
au Beurre	Turn to a barrel shape 5cm long and plain boil; drain and toss in melted butter.
à la Crème	Turn to a barrel shape, parboil, then finish to cook in cream.
Frits	Cut as for chips and deep fry until golden brown and cooked.
Persillé	Turn to an elongated barrel shape, plain boil, drain and toss in melted butter; sprinkle with chopped parsley.

Rissolé	Turn to an elongated barrel shape, parboil, drain and toss in melted butter or dripping until golden brown and tender.

Peas – petits pois

à l'Anglaise	Plain boil until almost tender, drain and serve as they are; do not overcook.
au Beurre	Plain boil, drain and toss in melted butter adding a pinch of sugar.
Bonne Femme	Stew the peas in white stock with lardons and button onions; thicken with beurre manié.
Fermière	Stew the peas in white stock with lardons and sliced carrot, onion and turnip; thicken with beurre manié.
Flamande	Mix together two parts plain-boiled peas and one part glazed carrots.
Française	Stew the peas in white stock with button onions, shredded lettuce, butter and sugar; thicken with beurre manié.
à la Marie	Stew the peas with small new carrots and potatoes and button onions and thicken the liquid with beurre manié.
à la Menthe	Plain boil the peas with a bunch of mint stalks in the water; drain, toss in butter with a pinch of sugar and serve decorated with blanched mint leaves.
Paysanne	Stew the peas in white stock with quartered onions and shredded lettuce; thicken with beurre manié.

Pimentos, capsicums, sweet peppers – piments doux, poivrons

These are available as black, green, red, white and yellow It is usually necessary to remove the skin by brief immersion in very hot fat, then to take out the seeds.

Créole	Blanch, fill with dry, plain rice boiled and braise in thin tomato sauce.

Farci	Fill with parcooked riz pilaff and braise until tender.
Orientale	Cut into squares and cook in oil with chopped onion; moisten with mutton stock and stew until tender.
Piémontaise	Parboil halves of pimento in stock, fill with risotto, sprinkle with Parmesan and melted butter and gratinate.

Pumpkin – *potiron*

Allemande	Cut into dice, blanch then stew in butter with lardons and chopped onion; finish with a little jus lié.
Braisé	Cut into dice, blanch and braise in jus lié.
Purée	Plain boil, mash and add a quarter its volume of dry mashed potato; finish with butter and cream.

Radicchio

This is used mainly as a salad vegetable and, because of its varigated colours, for garnishing many dishes. It can be cooked and served as for ordinary lettuce.

Samphire

This is a sea-plant that grows in mudflats and the grass alongside creeks of tidal water. Wash well, cook in cold salted water and serve plain, with vinegar or tossed in hot butter, usually as a vegetable in its own right.

Salsify – *salsifis*

This vegetable is also known as the Oyster Plant because of its taste. The kind that has a black skin is called scorzonera. Salsify can be peeled before or after cooking and it is usual to cook the peeled stalks in a 'blanc'.

au Beurre	Toss cooked salsify in hot butter to coat all over.
à la Crème	Place almost cooked salsify into thin béchamel and finish to cook, then add a little cream.

Frits	Cut cooked salsify into 8cm lengths, marinate with oil and lemon juice then dip into frying batter and deep fry.
au Gratin	Finish to cook sections of salsify in béchamel, then add cream and grated cheese; place in a dish; sprinkle with breadcrumbs, cheese and butter and gratinate.
Persillés	Toss cooked sections of salsify in hot butter and serve sprinkled with chopped parsley.
Polonaise	Cover cooked lengths of salsify with fried breadcrumbs, sieved white and yolk of hard-boiled egg and chopped parsley.
Royal	Finish to cook parboiled salsify in sauce Suprême.
Sautés	Toss cooked pieces of salsify in hot butter until golden brown.

Sea-kale – *chou marin* or *crambé*

à l'Anglaise	Tie the sea-kale in bundles and plain boil; serve on a folded table napkin accompanied with melted butter or sauce hollandaise.
à la Crème	Coat cooked sea-kale with cream sauce.
Hollandaise	Serve plain boiled sea-kale with sauce hollandaise.
Milanaise	Sprinkle cooked sea-kale with Parmesan and melted butter and gratinate.
Polonaise	Cover cooked sea-kale with fried breadcrumbs.

Spinach – *épinards*

à l'Ail	Fry chopped garlic in butter, add roughly chopped cooked spinach and toss over.
à l'Anglaise	Plain boil spinach leaves, drain well and serve.
au Beurre	Reheat drained and squeezed boiled spinach in hot butter, freeing the leaves with a fork.
en Branches	Plain boil, drain well then reheat in melted butter.
à la Crème	Pass well-drained cooked spinach through a mincer and reheat in melted butter; mix in

cream and serve surrounded with warmed cream.

aux Croûtons Garnish purée of spinach with a cordon of warmed cream and one triangular croûton per portion.

aux Fleurons Garnish purée of spinach with a cordon of warmed cream and fleurons of puff pastry.

au Gratin Reheat spinach in butter and mix in grated Parmesan and Gruyère; place in a dish, sprinkle with cheese and butter and gratinate.

Italienne Fry chopped garlic and anchovies in oil, add roughly chopped cooked spinach and mix.

Mère Louisette Cook roughly chopped raw spinach in butter and add diced ham and small fried croûtons.

Niçoise Reheat spinach in oil with garlic, mix with beaten raw eggs and cook au bain-marie in the oven until set.

Piémontaise Mix chopped cooked spinach with sautéd chopped garlic; add a little jus lié and finish with anchovy butter.

Purée Pass well-drained, cooked spinach through a fine mincer and reheat in melted butter.

Subrics Add 1kg roughly chopped cooked spinach to $\frac{1}{2}$ litre thick pancake mixture and shallow fry small spoonfuls until brown on both sides; serve with cream sauce.

Viroflay Wrap a subric made as above and containing some fried bread croûtons, in a large blanched leaf of spinach; coat with sauce mornay, sprinkle with cheese and melted butter and cook to gratinate in a hot oven.

Sorrel – oseille

This may be cooked and served as for Spinach but is usually shredded finely for flavouring soups.

Japanese artichokes – stachys

These are like miniature Jerusalem artichokes and are cooked in a 'blanc' in the same way. They are also known as Crosnes in

French, this being the name of the town where they were first grown locally. They are sometimes called Chinese Artichokes.

Beignets	Mix plain boiled artichokes with sauce allemande; spread to cool then mould oval shape, dip into batter and deep fry.
à la Crème	Cook blanched artichokes in butter then finish in cream; mix with a little thin béchamel and serve.
Milanaise	Stew blanched artichokes in butter then mix with grated Parmesan and Gruyère; place in a dish with a little jus lié and gratinate with cheese.
Sautés	Toss plain boiled artichokes in hot butter until coloured.
au Velouté	Mix plain boiled artichokes into mushroom-flavoured velouté.

Swede – *rutabaga* or *navet jaune*

au Beurre	Cut into dice, plain boil then toss in hot butter.
Glacé	Turn to a barrel shape, cook in water, butter and sugar until the liquid is reduced and coats the pieces with a glaze.

Sweetcorn – *maïs* or *épee de maïs*

Corn on the Cob	Simmer gently for approximately 20 minutes, drain, remove leaves and fibre and serve on a folded table napkin, with melted butter. They should be impaled on holders.
Galettes	Add sweetcorn kernels to a fairly stiff batter and shallow fry in the form of small thick pancakes.
à la Crème	Simmer the grains in cream with a pinch of sugar until slightly reduced.
Grillé	Remove leaves and fibre and grill gently, brushing frequently with butter.
Mexicaine	Add diced cooked red pimento, diamonds of French beans and sautéd chopped onions to buttered sweetcorn kernels.
O'Brien	Cook diced green and red pimento in butter, add cooked sweetcorn and mix together.

Succotash	Mix together equal amounts of sweetcorn kernels and lima beans, finishing to cook in cream.

Tomatoes – tomates

Stuffed tomatoes can be made using medium-size fruit and cutting off the top, or by cutting larger ones in half; the seeds are scooped out. It is not usual to skin them. They may be served surrounded with jus lié or tomato sauce.

Farcie Algérienne	Make the stuffing from chopped onion, tomato, breadcrumbs and garlic.
Farcie Américaine	Fill with creamed sweetcorn.
Farcie Ancienne	Fill with duxelles made with the addition of chopped garlic and ham.
Farcie Carmelite	Fill with a stuffing made of sieved hard-boiled egg mixed with béchamel, and sprinkle the top with cheese.
Farcie Carolina	Fill with riz pilaff.
Farcie Duxelles	Use duxelles stuffing thickened with breadcrumbs and brown sauce.
Farcie au Gratin	Fill with duxelles, sprinkle with breadcrumbs and oil and gratinate.
Farcie Hussarde	Fill with scrambled egg mixed with diced ham and mushroom.
Farcie Italienne	Fill with risotto flavoured with meat glaze and reduced tomato pulp.
Farcie Portugaise	Fill with riz pilaff containing diced tomato and red pimento.
Farcie Provençale	Make a stuffing with sautéd chopped garlic and onion, breadcrumbs and chopped parsley.
Farcie Turque	Fill with riz pilaff containing diced sautéd chicken liver.
Bressane	Cut in half, remove seeds and place in an oiled dish; sprinkle with parsley, garlic, breadcrumbs and oil, and cook in the oven; place a sautéd chicken liver in each.
Grillée	Remove the eyes of medium-sized tomatoes, cut a shallow cross on the round side, brush with

	buter and place under the salamander or in the oven.
Marseillaise	Cut in half, place in an oiled dish and sprinkle with breadcrumbs, chopped shallot and anchovy, sieved hard-boiled egg, fines herbes and oil; cook in the oven.
Provençale	Cut in half and remove seeds, place in an oiled dish; sprinkle with chopped parsley, crushed garlic, oil and breadcrumbs and cook in the oven.

Turnips – navets

au Beurre	Turn to a barrel shape, plain boil and toss gently in melted butter.
Farcis	Hollow-out small plain-boiled turnips and fill with duxelles or forcemeat; replace the top and cook in the oven.
Glacés	Turn to a barrel shape, cook in water with butter and sugar and remove when still slightly firm; reduce the cooking liquid to a syrup and replace the turnips in it.

Vine leaves – feuilles de vigne

Vine leaves can be served as a vegetable after being blanched, stuffed and braised. This dish is known as the 'Dolma' of near-East origin and the filling is usually parcooked rice and/or minced meat, flavoured with such items as pine nuts, sesame seeds, herbs, etc.

Yam – igname

This tuber with a yellow-orange colour can be served as a vegetable, baked, fried, mashed or roast.

Purées of Vegetables –
Purées de Legumes

The following are the names given to those purées that are served as a vegetable with a main dish. In the case of some of the soft vegetables such as turnip it is necessary to add dry mashed potato to counteract the slightly sloppy consistency.

Artichokes bottoms	**Rachel**
Artichokes, Jerusalem	**Palestine**
Asparagus	**Argenteuil**
Beans, French	**Favorite**
Beans, Lima	**Musard**
Brussels sprouts	**Bruxelloise**
Carrots	**Crécy**
Cauliflower	**Dubarry**
Onion	**Soubise**
Potato	**Parmentier**
Peas	**Clamart or St Germain**
Spinach	**Florentine**
Turnip	**Freneuse**

Mixtures of Vegetables

Mixed vegetables can be served as a vegetable dish, the following being the main ones. There are others that are served only as a garnish.

Bouquetière	Turned carrots and turnips, French beans, cauliflower florets and peas.
Brunoise	Carrot, celery, leek and turnip cut into 2mm dice.
Fleuriste	Peeled cooked tomato filled with buttered jardinière of vegetables.

Jardinière	Carrots and turnips cut into batons 2cm × 4mm × 4mm, diamonds of beans, peas.
Julienne	Carrot, leek, celery and turnip cut into strips 4cm × 1mm × 1mm.
Macédoine	Carrots and turnips cut into $\frac{3}{4}$cm dice, with diamonds of beans, peas.
Matignon	Carrot, celery, ham, leek and onion cut into 2mm dice used mainly for flavouring purposes, but may be served as a vegetable.
Mirepoix	Diced carrot, onion, celery and bacon, used for flavouring purposes. (This is also called Mirepoix Bordelaise).
Terrine de Légumes Covent Garden	Arrange layers of blanched vegetables including carrot, French beans, peas and asparagus points, in between layers of chicken forcemeat in an oblong dish to give a symetrical result; cook au bain-marie and serve cut into slices.
Croquettes and cutlets	Vegetarian dishes may be made with a mixture of puréed vegetables mixed with mashed potatoes, shaped, egg and crumbed and shallow fried.

COMBINATIONS OF VEGETABLES

Instead of serving just one vegetable as an adjunct to a main dish, it is good to cook several vegetables separately and combine them as suggested below. This is in addition to combinations listed as, e.g., bouquetière de légumes, méli-mélo de primeurs, etc., in which up to one dozen different vegetables are artistically arranged in a large serving dish.

Batons of carrots, strips of braised celery and lengths of French beans tossed together in butter.

Florets of cauliflower, strips of braised celery, diamonds of French beans and quartered mushrooms, tossed in butter.

Strips of braised celery, peas and quartered mushrooms; toss in butter or cream.

Lengths of French beans and braised celery with button onions.

Peas and diced turnip.

Button onions and peas.

Shredded cabbage and celery, blanched and sautéd in butter.

Buttered chopped leaf spinach and carrots.

Marrow and tomato – layers of slices baked in a buttered tray.

Tomato and onion pie – layers of sliced tomato and sautéd shredded onion in layers, sprinkled with crumbs and baked.

Sweetcorn with sautéd chopped green and red pimento and lardons.

French beans and sautéd shredded onion.

Lima beans with diced green pimento, chopped onion and dice of tomato.

Carrots cooked then tossed in melted butter, with sugar, English mustard and chopped mint and parsley.

Dried Pulses

These are the dried edible seeds of leguminous plants that usually need to be soaked overnight before being boiled. It is advisable to add salt towards the end of the cooking time rather than at the beginning as this may prevent them from becoming tender. Pulses are used extensively by vegetarians. Asian people refer to them as dhal.

Butter beans – haricots blancs

Bretonne	Mix sauce bretonne (made by sautéing chopped onions, adding wine and tomate concassée then demi-glace and tomato sauce) into almost cooked beans and continue to cook until tender.

au Gratin	Plain boil, drain and add a little dripping from roast lamb; place in a dish, sprinkle with breadcrumbs and melted butter and gratinate.
Lyonnaise	Sauté sliced onion in butter and mix with plain boiled beans.
Persillés	Toss cooked beans in butter and serve sprinkled with chopped parsley.
Provençale	Finish cooking the beans in oil with diced tomato, chopped anchovy and garlic.

Lentils – *lentilles*

These are boiled with a carrot, studded onion and bacon bone and made into a purée under the menu names of Purée Esaü or Purée Conti; they can be used as the main ingredient in a vegetarian stew or curry.

Lima Beans – Flageolets	These are small flat, pale green beans available in canned and dried form; they are good as an accompanying vegetable.
Navy Beans	This is the name given to small haricot beans of the kind sold as baked beans in tins, they can be boiled then finished to cook in an oven with brown sugar and molasses.
Peas – Green Split and Yellow Split	These are very good for making soups and vegetable purées.
Peas – Marrowfat	These are used as a vegetable, mainly in the cost sector of the industry where mushy peas and marrowfat pea croquettes are popular.

Other pulses include chick peas, black-eyed beans, red kidney beans, pinto and soya beans which have the highest biological value of all pulses and are available whole, powdered and as meat analogues.

Purées of dried pulses include:

Red Beans – Condé
Lima Beans – Musard
Haricot Beans – Soissonaise
Lentils – Conti and Esaü

Cereals

These are the edible grains of plants, usually husked and dried. They include corn or maize, oats and oatmeal, rice, semolina, sago and tapioca. Arrowroot and cornflour are processed cereals. Breakfast cereals are made from cereals that have been cooked to a mash then flaked or spun whilst being dried.

Maize meal – this is coarsely ground sweetcorn.

Gnocchi Piémontaise	Cook 250g cornmeal in 1 litre milk for 20 minutes, add 2 eggs then spread on a tray to cool,cut 5cm rounds, place in a dish and gratinate with cheese and butter.
Mamaliga	A porridge made of maize meal cooked in water and served with butter.
Polenta	Cook 250g maize meal in 1 litre water and flavour with cheese and butter; spread on a tray then cut into rounds or squares and shallow fry.
Tortillas	Thinly rolled maize dough cooked as a pancake on a griddle; when filled takes the names tacos, tamales, enchiladas, etc.

Millet

The flour ground from these seeds is preferred by some Indian sects for making chapatis and poppadums.

Rice – Riz

There are three main ways of cooking rice:

1. plain boiled
2. pilaff of rice
3. risotto

Ordinary *long grain rice* takes approximately 18 minutes to cook but the big *Italian rice* requires at least 20 minutes. The use of *pre-fluffed* rice ensures that the grains stay separate. *Carolina rice* is the short grain type which is used mainly for rice pudding but can be cooked as a pilaff.

The varieties in use are:

1. *Aborio*   Italian medium grain
2. *Avorio*   best quality Italian medium size grain.

These two are very good for risotto as they absorb plenty of stock but do not become mushy.

3. *Basmati*   the best quality long-grain rice with a distinctive smell and flavour; best if soaked before cooking
4. *Brown*   only the outer husk is removed; it has a strong, nutty flavour and chewy texture and needs long cooking
5. *Camargue* a medium-grain rice from France
6. *Carolina*   a short grain variety, best suited for sweet puddings; it increases fourfold in cooking and becomes very soft
7. *Patna*   the best all-round rice; it is grown in many countries
8. *Pre-fluffed* rice which has been steamed to remove some of the starch so making it easy to cook and serve; rather tasteless
9. *Spanish*   a medium-size grain rice
10. *Wild*   very expensive; nutty flavour and soft chewy texture; grows naturally

Wild rice is best boiled as follows:
Wash well, cover 450g with $1\frac{1}{4}$ litres boiling water, boil for 5 minutes, cover and remove from heat; allow to stand for 1 hour then drain, rewash and plain boil for 30 minutes.

Boiled rice

(i)   Bring 5 litres water and 60g salt to a boil, rain in 450g patna rice and simmer gently for 18 minutes, drain, refresh and dry out and reheat in a cool oven.

or

(ii)   Place 1 litre cold water, 15g salt and 450g patna rice in a pan, bring to a boil while stirring, cover and cook slowly for 10 minutes until water is evaporated and rice is soft and each grain separate.

Biriani   This is a curry in which the meat and rice are cooked together in yoghurt and water.

Créole   Boil 500g long-grain rice in 1 litre of water with 150g butter for 18 minutes, then add 150g butter.

Egyptienne   Add diced sautéd chicken liver, ham and mushroom to riz pilaff.

Espagnole   Add diced ham and cooked red pimento to a tomato-flavoured riz pilaff.

Fried   Stir-fry chopped onion, carrot, beans, pimento and mushroom, add peas, fennel seeds and spices; add cooked rice, reheat and finish with beaten egg that has been cooked in oil, as a broken-up omelette.

au Gras   Blanch the rice and cook in fatty stock until well done; this is used mainly as a stuffing.

Greque   Add sliced chipolata sausages, green peas and diced cooked red pimento to riz pilaff.

Matriciana   Make a risotto including diced sautéd pickled belly of pork and diced tomato.

Milanaise   Flavour risotto with saffron and garnish with julienne of ham, mushrooms and ox tongue; serve with grated cheese and tomato sauce.

Napolitaine   Make a risotto including lardons of salt belly of pork and diced tomato.

Parisienne   Add sliced mushrooms to a risotto and serve with tomato sauce.

Peverada   Sauté chicken livers, anchovy and green pimento in oil, cook in stock with lemon juice and mix with cooked rice.

Piémontaise   Garnish risotto with sliced cooked or raw white truffle, or diced ham.

Pilaff or Pilaw   Braise the rice in butter and stock in the ratio of $1\frac{1}{2}$ parts stock to 1 of rice, for approximately 19 minutes; fork in more butter to separate the grains. Finely chopped onion may be used.

Portugaise   Garnish riz pilaff with diced tomato and dice of cooked red pimento.

Pullao   Indian main dish of rice cooked with vegetables, spices, etc., similar to a pilaff. Also a sweet pudding of rice with fruit, spices, etc.

Risi Bisi	Mix cooked peas with riz au gras, forking them in lightly.
Risotto	Stew the rice in butter and stock in the ration of 3 parts stock to 1 of rice; when cooked add Parmesan cheese and serve with more cheese; may be garnished with mushrooms, squid, etc.
Soubise	Braise 500g sliced blanched onion with 125g short-grain rice; when cooked add Parmesan cheese and serve with more cheese.
Turque	Make a riz pilaff with saffron and garnish with diced tomato.
Valencienne	Add sliced chipolata sausages, diced ham, pimento and tomato, and green peas to riz pilaff.

Semolina – semoule

Semolina is coarsely ground wheat.

Gnocchi Romaine	Cook 250g semolina in 1 litre milk, thicken with 2 yolks, spread on a tray and when cold cut into 4cm rounds. Arrange overlapping in a dish and gratinate with cheese and butter.
Kache	Mix raw semolina with egg and dry it in the oven, pass through a sieve then cook in stock; spread on a tray and use for making coulibiac and rastegaî of salmon and in other dishes of Russian origin.
Subric	Rain 120g semolina into 6dl hot milk, cook for 5 minutes then add 2 yolks; spread on a tray to cool, cut out 5cm rounds and shallow fry.

Sago

This is purchased in the form of granules and is used mainly as a garnish in clear soups and for milk puddings. It is the starchy pith of a palm tree which is first roasted then milled.

Tapioca

This is made from the rhizomes of the cassava plant and is available as flakes or seeds, the latter being used to thicken clear soups such as consommés but its main use is for puddings. Perles du Japon which are used as a garnish in consommés and other soups, are made from tapioca.

Oatmeal

Oatmeal is available in several sizes from coarse to pinhead and its main use is for making porridge. Gruel is the very thin runny porridge that used to be served to invalids.

Buckwheat

This is a dark coarse type of flour that is used in Russian and Polish cookery mainly for pancakes such as blinis, and porridge.

Kasha   Make a loaf of buckwheat flour and water then mix the crumb part with butter to form a paste. Cool under pressure then cut into 3cm rounds and shallow fry.

Barley

Pearl barley is mainly used as a garnish in broth-type soups and for making barley water. When germinated it is made into malt flour and malt extract.

Rye

Rye flour is used for making rye bread, the rather solid, dark bread sometimes flavoured with caraway, used in Scandinavian countries.

Gnocchis and Pastas

Gnocchi   Pipe chou paste flavoured with Parmesan into
Parisienne   boiling salted water through a 1cm tube in 2cm lengths; poach, drain and serve gratinated with sauce mornay.

Noques au   Mix 250g soft butter with 2 yolks, 2 eggs,
Parmesan   seasoning, 150g flour and 1 whisked egg white.
Poach small balls in boiling water and gratinate
with cheese and brown butter.

Spätzle   Mix 250g flour, 2 eggs and 2dl milk, flavour with
nutmeg and salt and pour into a steamer held
over a pan of boiling water so that the batter
runs through in random pieces. Poach, drain and
toss in butter.

Pastas – Pâtes
Alimentaires

All the hundreds of different shapes of Italian flour products are
made from semolina produced from strong flour made of durum
wheat. After being shaped under hydraulic pressure it is dried and
packed. Some products contain egg and some are flavoured and
coloured with tomato or spinach.

It is possible to purchase freshly made pastas in most towns and
cities and kitchen machines that are capable of handling small
batches of dough are made that can produce up to two hundred
different forms of fresh pastasciutta (see the section entitled
Farinaceous).

Fruits served as a Vegetable or
Garnish

Certain fruits are suitable for serving with fish and meat dishes as
the accompanying vegetable and many more are appropriate as
garnishes. Some fruit sauces are served with meat dishes and
compotes of berries are much used in Scandinavian cookery.

Unripe bananas or cooking bananas known as Vudi can be
boiled or baked in the skin; blanched in the skin, peeled and

491

roasted in hot fat; or cut into chips and deep fried. The Plantain is similar to a banana and has similar uses as a vegetable.

Breadfruit can be cut and fried as chips and like egg-plant, can be stuffed and baked.

Egg-plants and tomatoes are of course fruits but are used only as vegetables.

——GARNISHES OF FRUIT——

The following are those fruits and nuts in general and specific use as garnishes with main dishes.

General	Kiwifruit (Chinese gooseberries), lemon, lime, avocado.
Pork and ham	Apple, banana, guava, melon, peach, pineapple, coconut, water chestnuts, mango, fig.
Lamb and mutton	Apricot, redcurrants.
Veal	lemon, mango.
Chicken and turkey	Cranberry, chestnut, pistachio, pine kernel, lychees, babaco.
Duck and Goose	Apple, orange, cherry, clementines.
Venison	Blackberry, cranberry, figs, cherry, guava.
Fish	Banana, grapes, almonds, orange, lemon.

Edible Fungi

Fungi, both cultivated and wild, are used as a vegetable, as a garnish and as a main dish, mushrooms being those most widely used.

Cep or *flap mushroom – cèpe*

Beignet	Sauté whole cèpes, cool, dip into frying batter and deep fry.
Bordelaise	Sauté thick slices in hot oil until fairly crisp; add the chopped stalks, shallot and breadcrumbs; toss over and finish with lemon juice.

au Gratin	Sauté thick slices in oil with chopped onion; sprinkle with breadcrumbs and butter and gratinate.
Grillée	Marinate in oil with chopped onion and garlic, brush with butter and grill under a salamander or in an oven; place a slice of beurre maître d'hôtel in each cèpe.
Moldave	Sauté thick slices in oil with chopped shallot, add cream and chopped fennel.
Piémontaise	Remove stalks, fill with duxelles, sprinkle with breadcrumbs and butter and gratinate.
Provençale	Sauté thick slices in hot oil until fairly crisp; add the chopped stalks, chopped onion, garlic and breadcrumbs; toss over and finish with lemon juice.
Rossini	Cook slices in butter with chopped onion, drain and finish to cook in cream together with slices of raw truffle; finish with a little meat glaze.
Russe	Sauté thick slices in butter with chopped onion, add chopped fennel and sour cream.

Mushrooms – *champignons*

Bordelaise	Cook in hot oil, add chopped shallot and breadcrumbs, toss to cook and finish with a squeeze of lemon juice.
Bourguignonne	Grill under the salamander or in an oven until soft; serve with a slice of snail butter in each one.
sous Cloche	Remove the stalks, place in a fireproof dish, add cream half way up and a squeeze of lemon juice; bring to a boil, cover with the glass dome and cook gently for approximately 10 minutes.
à la Crème	Cook mushrooms in butter with a little chopped onion; drain any moisture, cover with cream and cook gently until the cream is reduced.
au Cuisson	Place mushrooms in a pan with a little water, butter, lemon juice and salt, cover and bring to a boil quickly and cook until soft.

Farcis	Remove stalks, grill until half-cooked then fill with duxelles; sprinkle with breadcrumbs and butter and gratinate in an oven.
Forestière	Remove stalks, stuff with pork sausage-meat and cook in a little veal stock in an oven.
Grillés	Wash, remove stalks, place on a tray cup side up, season and sprinkle with butter; grill under a salamander or in an oven until soft. Serve with a thin slice of beurre maître d'hôtel in each mushroom.
Persillade	Sauté in butter, place in a dish and cover with fried lardons, chopped garlic and parsley and breadcrumbs; bake in the oven.
Piémontaise	Sauté in oil with chopped shallot, place in a dish, sprinkle with butter, breadcrumbs and Parmesan and gratinate.
Poulette	Cook in butter and lemon juice and mix with sauce poulette.
Sautés	May be left whole, cut into quarters or sliced; heat butter in a frying pan until just turning brown, add mushrooms and fry quickly, tossing frequently.
Toulousaine	Toss in butter with chopped garlic and shallot, add diced cooked ham and diced tomato and toss over to mix.

Chanterelles and morels

These may be cooked in the same way as cèpes and mushrooms.

Truffles – truffles

sous la Cendre	Wrap each one in a thin slice of salt pork fat then in several thicknesses of paper, place on a bed of cinders and cover with hot charcoal. Bake for approximately 45 minutes, unwrap and serve with butter.
au Champagne	Cook in champagne with a mirepoix bordelaise; reduce the cooking liquid, add jus lié and strain over the truffles.

Grammont	Cut into slices, sauté in butter then deglaze with port; add cream and a little glace de viande; may be served in a vol-au-vent case.
au Madère	Cook in Madeira wine with a mirepoix bordelaise; reduce the cooking liquid, add a little jus lié and strain over the truffles.
au Porto	Cook in port with a mirepoix bordelaise; reduce the cooking liquid, add some jus lié and strain over the truffles.
à la Serviette	Cook in Madeira wine with a mirepoix bordelaise, reduce the cooking liquid, add a little jus lié and strain over the truffles; serve in a silver timbale dish inside a folded table napkin.
Talleyrand	Cook sliced truffle in butter, deglaze with Madeira and add jus lié; serve in emptied brioches.

Edible flowers

Beignets	Pick acacia flowers when they are in full bloom, season, dip into a light batter and deep fry. Elder lily and the flowers of marrow may also be used.
Farcis	Fill the flowers of marrow with pilaff of rice or fish or meat forcemeat and fry briefly in hot oil. Only dry, fully-opened flowers should be used, ensuring there are no insects inside them. They can be filled with a cooked filling and served cold as they are.

Potatoes

The variety of potato used can have a bearing on the quality of the resultant dish and it is important to specify which variety is required when ordering potatoes from the supplier. The following list gives the names of the various varieties grown in this country and their most suitable uses.

Early potatoes are usually on sale from the end of May to the middle of August; the following are generally available:

Arran Comet	Good for baking, roasting, mashing, chips.
Epicure	Very good all-rounder.
Homeguard	Good for boiling.
Maris Peer	Very good for boiling, good for roasting, chips, sauté.
Pentland Javelin	Good all-rounder, but not good for boiling.
Ulster Sceptre	Good for boiling, sauté, chips.

Main crop potatoes are in season from September until they run out after about eight months time. The following are available:

Desiree	Very good for roasting, sauté, chips; good for boiling, mashing, baking.
King Edward	Very good for baking, boiling, mashing, chips, sauté.
Maris Piper	Very good for baking, sauté, chips; good for boiling, mashing.
Pentland Crown	Good for baking.
Pentland Hawk	Good for baking, boiling, mashing.
Wilja	Good for boiling and roasting.

New potatoes include Jersey Royals, Manna and Ukama. Genuine new potatoes come into season from about early May, the best being the Jersey Royals; other imported ones are small grades packed in sand, etc., to look like new.

It is sometimes possible to obtain from specialist wholesalers, potatoes that have been graded according to size; these cost more than those bagged as they are picked or taken from store. The size ranges are *Large* 65–90mm, *Mids.* 25–45mm; also available are 40–60mm and 60–80mm sizes, this last grade being suitable for baked jacket potatoes; kitchens that serve chips with everything find fewer irregular shapes and small pieces from using standard-size potatoes.

It is possible to classify potato dishes into categories according to the way they are cooked, e.g. deep fried or boiled, but since many of the following undergo two or more different methods, e.g. being first boiled, then mashed and then deep fried, it is felt they are best given in alphabetical order rather than repeating the formulas under several headings.

Allemande	Cut cold cooked potato into 5cm slices and shallow fry in fat; drain, add butter and serve sprinkled with chopped parsley.
Allumettes	Cut into batons 6cm × $\frac{1}{2}$cm × $\frac{1}{2}$cm, wash, drain well and deep fry.
Alphonse	Slice cooked potatoes, mix with fines herbes and butter; arrange in a dish, sprinkle with cheese and butter and gratinate.
Alsacienne	Cook small potatoes with lardons and chopped onion in stock and butter; sprinkle with parsley and serve.
Amandines	Mould duchesse potato mixture into approximately 5cm × $1\frac{1}{2}$cm rolls; coat with flour, egg-wash and nibbed almonds and deep fry at 185°C.
Ambassadeur	Arrange thinly sliced raw potato in Anna moulds with layers of grated cheese and cook in the oven at 220°C until brown.
à l'Anglaise	Trim potatoes to an even shape; plain boil in salted water, drain and serve as they are.
Anna	Slice raw potatoes 3cm × $1\frac{1}{2}$mm, arrange overlapping in Anna moulds or small frying pans and bake at 220°C until golden brown.
Annette	This is the same as pommes Anna adding some sautéd chopped onion and grated Parmesan.
Ardennaise	Scoop out the flesh of baked potatoes and mash it with chopped chicken, chives and ham; refill the skins, sprinkle with butter and cheese and gratinate.
Arlie	Scoop the pulp from baked potatoes, mash with chopped chives, refill the skins, sprinkle with butter and cheese and gratinate.
Bataille	Cut potatoes into 2cm cubes and deep fry until brown and crisp on the outside and soft inside.
Bernoise	Cut 1cm squares, blanch, drain and fry in clarified butter until brown.
Berny	Add diced truffle to duchesse mixture and mould into small balls; coat with flour, egg-wash and nibbed almonds and deep fry at 185°C.

Berrichonne   Shape potatoes into 5cm barrels, cook in the oven in stock and butter with chopped onion and lardons until brown; sprinkle with parsley.

Biarritz   Add diced ham and red pimento and chopped parsley to mashed potato and serve.

Bohémienne   Scoop out the pulp of baked potatoes and mash with raw sausage-meat; replace in the skins, sprinkle with butter and cook in the oven.

Bonne Femme   Turn the potatoes to a barrel shape and cook in butter with button onions.

Bordelaise   Cut potatoes into $1\frac{1}{2}$cm cubes and shallow fry in oil with chopped garlic until brown; drain off the fat and toss in butter; serve sprinkled with parsley.

Boulangère   Cut potatoes into slices $3\frac{1}{2}$cm × 2mm; mix with a third their weight of sliced sautéd onion; place in shallow dishes, add stock and butter and bake at 200°C; the top layer should be arranged overlapping.

Bourgeoise   Mash, sprinkle with grated cheese, butter and breadcrumbs and gratinate.

Brabançonne   Mix sliced cooked firm potatoes with chopped shallot and parsley, butter and grated cheese; fill into a charlotte mould and bake in the oven until set.

Brabant   Cut into 2cm cubes, deep fry and mix with diced cooked red pimento.

Bretonne   Cut into $1\frac{1}{2}$cm cubes and cook in stock with chopped garlic and onion and diced tomato.

Brioche   Mould duchesse potato mixture in the shape of small cottage loaves, brush with egg-wash and bake until golden brown.

Brown Derby   Slice raw potatoes thinly, layer with chopped cooked bacon and chives, moisten with milk, sprinkle with cheese and bake.

Bussy   Add chopped truffle and parsley and grated cheese to duchesse mixture; mould to a cigar-shape, egg and crumb and deep fry.

Byron   Make pommes macaire with an indentation on top, fill with cream, sprinkle with cheese and gratinate in the oven.

Carême	Add cream and grated cheese to mashed potato, fill into scallop shells, sprinkle with cheese and butter and gratinate.
Cendrillon	Trim the potatoes in the form of a small clog, coat with egg and crumbs, deep fry, then hollow out and fill with creamy mashed potato.
Chambéry	Fill shallow dishes with grated raw potato mixed with butter and cheese, sprinkle with butter and cheese and bake in the oven.
Chamonix	Mix 3 parts duchesse potato with 2 parts chou paste and flavour with cheese; mould into small balls on oiled paper and deep fry at 175°C.
Champignol	When pommes fondantes are cooked, sprinkle with cheese and butter and gratinate.
Chancelier	Plain boil 1½cm balls of potato and mix into sufficient sauce crème to bind; serve sprinkled with parsley.
Château	Turn potatoes to a barrel shape, seal in hot fat then cook in the oven at 200°C until brown; serve sprinkled with parsley.
Chateaubriand	Turn potatoes to an olive shape and shallow fry until golden brown; mix with melted meat glaze and chopped parsley.
Chatouillard	Cut slices of potato into spirals, wash, drain and deep fry.
Cheveux	Cut potato into very fine julienne; wash, dry and deep fry until crisp.
Chips	Slice potatoes approximately 4cm × 1mm and wash until crisp; drain, dry and deep fry until golden brown.
Cocottes	Turn potatoes to barrel shape 2½cm long, seal in hot fat and shallow fry until golden brown.
Colbert	Cut potatoes into 1½cm squares and shallow fry until brown, drain off the fat and toss in melted meat glaze; sprinkle with parsley.
Collerette	Trim potatoes to cylinder shape 2½cm diameter and groove the sides with a couteau à canneler; slice thinly on a mandolin, wash well and dry, then deep fry at 190°C until crisp and brown.

Colombine	Cut cooked potatoes into slices and shallow fry together with a julienne of green and red pimento.
Copeaux	Cut slices of potato into long ribbons; wash, drain and deep fry.
à la Crème	Cut almost cooked potatoes into ½cm slices, cook in milk and finish with cream.
Cretéan	Turn potatoes to a barrel shape and cook in the oven with stock, butter and crushed thyme until golden brown.
Croquette	Mould duchesse potato mixture into cylinders 5cm × 2cm and coat with flour, egg-wash and breadcrumbs; deep fry at 185°C and garnish with picked parsley.
Darphin, or Dauphin	As for pommes Anna but cutting the potatoes in julienne instead of slices.
Dauphine	Mix 3 parts duchesse mixture with 2 parts chou paste, mould as small balls onto oiled paper and deep fry at 175°C.
Dauphinoise	Mix thinly sliced potatoes with beaten egg, milk and grated Gruyére, place into a shallow dish previously rubbed with garlic, sprinkle with cheese and bake in an oven for 45 minutes.
Delmonico	Cut into 1½cm cubes and cook in milk; place in dishes, add cream, sprinkle with breadcrumbs and butter and gratinate.
Delysia	Cut medium-size potatoes into 3mm slices, wash, drain and shallow fry in hot fat with chopped garlic until cooked and brown.
Duchesse	Plain boil potatoes, drain and mash; mix with yolks and butter then pipe in rosettes 5cm × 3cm base; brush with egg-wash and glaze in the oven.
Duchesse Mixture	Plain boil 1kg potatoes; drain, mash and mix with 3 yolks and 50gm butter; use as required.
Elizabeth	Mix 3 parts duchesse potato with 2 parts chou paste; mould as small balls with a ball of leaf spinach in the centre and deep fry at 175°C.
Entiers Sautées à l'Ail	Wash but do not peel very small new potatoes, blanch for 2 minutes, drain and shallow fry in oil with garlic, crushed bay-leaf and thyme.

500

Faubonne	Cut into thick slices, add chopped onion and cook in thin espagnole.
Flamande	Cook barrel-shape potatoes in stock and butter with button onions and small turned carrots.
Florentine	Add chopped leaf spinach to duchesse mix; mould into small cakes, coat with flour, egg-wash and breadcrumbs and deep fry.
Fondantes	Turn potatoes to a barrel shape, cook in the oven in stock and butter until brown, brush with butter and sprinkle with parsley.
au Four	Wash large potatoes, dry, place on a tray and bake until soft; cut across the top and press open to insert a piece of butter inside.
Frites	Cut potatoes 6cm × 1cm × 1cm, wash and dry then blanch in deep fat at 170°C until soft; increase the temperature to 190°C and fry until brown and crisp.
Galette	Shape duchesse mixture into cakes 5cm × 1½cm in flour; shallow fry in clarified butter until golden brown.
Garfield	Cut potatoes into 1cm dice and shallow fry until golden brown.
Gastronome	Trim potatoes to cylinder shape, shallow fry, drain, then roll in melted meat-glaze and sprinkle with chopped truffle.
Gaufrettes	Slice potatoes thinly with a trellis pattern, wash and dry then deep fry until brown and crisp.
Godard	As for pommes dauphine; coat with egg and crumbs and deep fry.
Gratin aux Navets	Arrange layers of sliced raw potato, turnip and grated cheese in a shallow dish; season with nutmeg, add single cream and bake in the oven.
Gratinée	Cut baked potatoes in half, mash the pulp with butter and refill the skins; sprinkle with cheese and butter and gratinate.
Hashed Brown	Chop cooked potatoes, shallow fry in fat and mould to the shape of an omelette; fry until nicely coloured.
Hérisson	Roll duchesse potato mixture into small balls, coat with flour, egg-wash and broken vermicelli and deep fry.

Hollandaise	Cut into 2cm dice and cook in stock, butter and lemon juice in the oven; finish with chopped parsley.
Hongroise	Mix together sliced raw potato, sautéd shredded onion, diced tomato and paprika; place in shallow dishes, moisten with stock and cream and bake in the oven.
Idéale	Mix 3 parts duchesse mixture with 2 parts chou paste and short julienne of truffle; mould to cork shape, egg and crumb, then deep fry.
Impératrice	As for pommes noisette, then add and mix in sautéd sliced mushrooms and truffle.
Irlandaise	Add finely chopped raw chives and onion to mashed potato.
Italienne	Scoop out the pulp of baked potatoes and mash with risotto, grated cheese and tomato purée; refill the skins, sprinkle with butter and reheat in the oven.
Jetée Promenade	Cut potatoes, artichoke bottoms and truffle in julienne, arrange in layers in buttered Anna moulds or frying pans and bake at 220°C.
Joinville	Mould duchesse potato into 4cm flat squares, coat with egg and broken vermicelli and shallow fry on both sides.
Lafite	Mould duchesse potato mixture into small cigar shapes, coat with flour, egg-wash and breadcrumbs and deep fry.
au Lard	Cut potatoes into 1½cm cubes and cook with lardons and button onions in stock, covered with a lid, at 190°C for 1 hour; serve with chopped parsley.
en Liard	Use long potatoes to cut into spirals, keep in ice water then drain and deep fry at 190°C.
Lorette	Mix 3 parts duchesse mixture with 2 parts chou paste and grated Parmesan; mould into cigar shapes and deep fry at 175°C.
Lyonnaise	Add one part of sautéd sliced onion to two parts pommes sautées; mix together and sprinkle with parsley.

Macaire	Scoop the pulp from baked potatoes, mash with butter and fill into buttered frying pans; cook at 220°C.
Maire	Cook sliced parcooked potatoes in milk until it has been absorbed and reduced; sprinkle with parsley.
Maître d'Hôtel	Cut nearly cooked potatoes into $\frac{1}{2}$cm slices, cook in milk and finish with cream and serve sprinkled with chopped parsley.
Maria	Add grated cheese to duchesse mixture; mould to cork shapes, coat with flour, egg-wash and breadcrumbs and deep fry.
Marie	Pipe duchesse potato into rosettes 5cm × 3cm; brush with egg-wash, sprinkle with Parmesan and colour in the oven.
Marquise	Pipe duchesse mixture into 6cm base nests, colour in the oven then fill with cooked chopped tomato and sprinkle with parsley.
Mashed	Plain boil potatoes in salted water, drain, pass through a sieve and mix well with hot milk and butter to a creamy consistency.
à la Menthe	Plain boil new potatoes with mint in the water; drain, roll in melted butter and decorate with blanched mint leaves.
Menagère	Scoop the pulp from baked potatoes, mash with butter and add cooked chopped onion and ham; refill the skins, sprinkle with butter and cheese and gratinate.
Mignonette	Cut potatoes into batons 5cm × $\frac{3}{4}$cm × $\frac{3}{4}$cm; wash, dry and deep fry until crisp and brown.
Mireille	Arrange layers of sliced potato, artichoke bottom and truffle in buttered Anna moulds and bake in the oven until brown.
Mirette	Cut potatoes into $1\frac{1}{2}$cm cubes and shallow fry; drain off the fat, add melted meat glaze and julienne of truffle then gratinate with butter and grated cheese.
Misquette	Sauté diced potato in butter, add cream and finish with yolk of egg.

Monselet	Shallow fry thin slices of new potato, serve with sautéd sliced mushrooms and sprinkle with julienne of truffle.
Mont-Doré	Sprinkle mashed potato with cheese and butter and gratinate under the salamander.
Mongolienne	Mix equal quantities of pommes cocotte and stachys by tossing in butter.
Mousseline	Plain boil potatoes, pass through a sieve and mix with butter and whipped cream.
Nana	Cut potatoes in julienne, fill into buttered dariole-moulds and cook in the oven at 220°C until golden brown.
Navarraise	Cut potatoes into 1cm dice and deep fry until golden brown.
Nature	Plain boil even-sized potatoes in salted water, drain and serve.
Neige	Drain plain-boiled floury potatoes, press through a ricer into the serving dish, or pass through a sieve. Do not mix.
Ninette	This is the same as pommes darphin with the addition of grated Parmesan cheese.
Noisettes	Cut balls of raw potato with a spoon cutter and shallow fry in hot fat; serve sprinkled with chopped parsley.
Normande	Mix sliced raw potato with shredded leek and onion, place in shallow dishes, moisten with cream, sprinkle with butter and cheese and cook in an oven.
Nouvelles	Cook new potatoes by boiling in the skins, peel and replace in hot salted water.
O'Brien	Cut into 1½cm cubes, deep fry then mix with julienne of cooked red pimento.
Olivettes	Turn potatoes to the shape of large olives and shallow fry until golden brown.
Ortiz	Cut parcooked potatoes into ½cm dice and shallow fry until golden brown, then mix with diced red pimento.
Pailles	Cut potatoes into julienne 6cm long; wash, dry, and deep fry at 175°C; serve as garnish with grilled steaks.

504

Parisienne	Cut small balls of potato with a scoop, shallow fry then roll in melted meat-glaze.
Parmentier	Cut potatoes into 1½cm cubes and shallow fry until brown; drain, toss in butter and sprinkle with chopped parsley.
Paysanne	Cook sliced potato in stock with shredded sorrel and chopped garlic.
Persillées	Plain boil even-sized turned potatoes; drain and roll in melted butter and chopped parsley.
Polonaise	Plain boil potatoes, drain, place in a dish and cover with fried breadcrumbs, sieved hard-boiled egg and chopped parsley.
Pont-Neuf	Cut potatoes into 7cm × 2cm × 2cm bâtons; wash, dry and blanch until soft, then deep fry at 190°C until crisp and brown.
Portugaise	Cut potatoes in 1½cm dice and cook with chopped garlic and onion in thin tomato sauce.
Provençale	Fry chopped garlic in butter and add to pommes sautées; serve sprinkled with parsley.
en Purée	Plain boil potatoes; drain; mash and mix to a creamy consistency with hot milk and butter.
Quelin	Cut balls of potato 1½cm diameter; plain boil, drain and roll in melted butter and chopped parsley.
Riche	Trim potatoes to barrel shape, shallow fry then add sautéd chopped onion and chopped fines herbes.
Rissolées	Shallow fry small whole potatoes in hot fat until brown; drain off the fat and replace with butter.
Ritz	Cut potatoes in 1½cm dice, plain boil, drain and mix with sautéd diced onion and red pimento.
Robe de Chambre	These are small unpeeled new potatoes served plainly boiled.
Robert	Scoop the pulp from baked potatoes, mash with yolks, butter and chopped chives, then cook in the oven in buttered frying pans.
Rosette	Pipe duchesse potato with a fancy tube, brush with egg-wash and cook in the oven.
Rôties	Trim potatoes to an even size, place into hot shallow fat and cook in the oven at 220°C until brown.

Rosti (Baloise)   Parcook then grate finely, mix with cooked diced onion and small fried lardons then flatten into a frying pan coated with hot fat; cook in an oven until brown on both sides.

Roxelane   Fill emptied small brioches with duchesse potato mixture lightened with whisked whites of egg; bake until risen.

Royale   Add chopped ham to duchesse potato mix, mould to cork shape, dip in flour and egg-wash and coat with broken vermicelli; deep fry.

Sablées   Cut potatoes into 1cm dice and shallow fry until golden; mix with fried breadcrumbs.

San Remo   Mould duchesse mixture into small balls, dip in melted butter and roll in chopped parsley and grated parmesan; coat with egg and crumbs and deep fry.

Saratoga Chips   This is the American name for pommes copeaux but is usually deep-fried thin slices of large potatoes.

Sarladaise   Toss thin slices of raw potato in hot fat then finish with butter and sliced truffle.

Sautées   Plain boil potatoes until nearly done, cut 3mm slices and shallow fry in hot fat until brown; finish with butter and serve sprinkled with parsley.

Sautées à Cru   Shallow fry thin slices of raw potato in hot fat until brown and cooked.

Savoyarde   Cut into slices 3mm thick, sprinkle with salt, rub together and leave for 10 minutes in a pile; boil some milk and cream, add the potatoes, place in a shallow dish and bake at 130°C for 45 minutes.

Scalloped   Parboil potatoes, cut into thin slices and arrange in a buttered tray, cover with sauce béchamel and bake in the oven.

Scallops   Cut potatoes into 3mm slices, wash, drain and either deep or shallow fry.

Soufflées   Cut potatoes into oblongs 6cm × 4cm × 3mm; deep fry at 180°C until soft, then plunge into deep fat at 190°C until puffed up and crisp.

St-Florentin	Add diced ham to duchesse potato mixture; mould into oblongs of 30g each; flour, egg and coat with crushed vermicelli; deep fry at 185°C.
Subrics	Cut in small dice, blanch for 2 minutes then drain and bind with hot béchamel containing egg yolk; deep fry spoonfuls of the mixture.
Suédoise	Cut potatoes into slices and cook in jus lié with sautéd sliced onion.
Surprise	Remove insides of baked potato; mash with cream, butter and parsley, refill skins and replace the lids.
Tyrolienne	Cook small potatoes in white stock, then add cream, butter and cheese.
Vapeur	These are peeled potatoes cooked in a steamer and served plainly.
Vauban	Cut cubes $2\frac{1}{2}$cm, blanch, drain and shallow fry in clarified butter; sprinkle with parsley.
Vaudoise	Layers of sliced raw potato and Gruyère cheese; add cream, sprinkle with cheese and butter and bake.
Villageoise	Cut parcooked potatoes into dice and finish to cook in milk, cream and butter.
Voisin	Cut potatoes into thin slices and prepare as for pommes Anna adding grated cheese after each layer; cook as usual then serve whole or cut into wedges.
Vosgienne	Cook thinly sliced potatoes in cream flavoured with garlic; gratinate with breadcrumbs and butter.
Westphalien	Mix mashed potato with apple purée and serve sprinkled with browned crumbs.
Yvette	as for pommes Anna, made in dariole moulds.

Other potato dishes include:

Bubble and Squeak	Mix chopped cooked beef and cabbage with mashed potato, mould into individual rounds or ovals; dip in flour and shallow fry.
Colcannon	Mix chopped cooked onion, chopped cooked cabbage with mashed potato and shallow fry.

507

Pan Haggerty Arrange layers of sliced potato and onion and grated cheese in a dish, moisten with stock skimmings and bake in the oven.

Sweet Potatoes Can be served as a potato dish with a main course, the best methods being deep-fried in various sizes, sauté, or as fritters but as they soon go soft they must be fried and served quickly. They are also good when baked and served with butter or boiled and mashed.

14 SWEET DISHES
Basic Preparations

Apricot Glaze Boil four parts apricot jam with one part of water for 5 minutes and strain; use for glazing flans.

Baking Powder Sieve together one part bicarbonate of soda with two parts cream of tartar; the ratio of baking powder in self-raising flour is 9g to 400g of flour.

Bun Wash This is used to give a shiny appearance to yeast buns, cakes and fruit loaves and is applied when they come hot from the oven; it can be:

1. equal amounts of sugar and water boiled to a syrupy consistency;
2. two parts egg and one part each of sugar and water whisked together.

Butter-cream

1. Whisk 10 yolks, 350g sugar and a little water to the ribbon stage and add gradually to 500g creamed unsalted butter; colour and flavour as desired.
2. Boil 440g sugar and $1\frac{3}{4}$dl water to 115°C then pour onto 12 yolks and 100g sugar whisked to the ribbon stage; add 600g creamed butter.
3. Cream 400g unsalted butter with 1kg icing sugar and add 2dl evaporated milk.
4. Add 1kg softened unsalted butter to 400g warmed fondant then beat in 1dl evaporated milk.

Chocolate *Couverture* – this is available as plain or milk chocolate for making and moulding chocolates, Easter eggs, figures, and for carving as a buffet centrepiece; it has to be tempered for use to 45°C, then to 27°C and back to 32°C. Chocolate coating does not need to be tempered and can be grated and melted to up to 40°C for general use.

Chocolate shapes are made by spreading melted chocolate thinly onto greaseproof paper and when just set, cutting into the required shape and size for decoration purposes.

Chocolate decorations are made by piping an outline over a drawing on greaseproof paper and filling in as a silhouette; chocolate may be spread over a sheet of marzipan or cooked sweet pastry and cut out with fancy cutters.

Chocolate curls are made by shearing it just as it is setting, into long curls like cinnamon sticks. To pipe designs in chocolate add a little hot water to melted chocolate and place into a paper cornet.

Crystallised Fruit Place good quality pieces of fruit such as apricots, cherries, figs, peaches, pears, pineapple, prunes and also chestnuts and ginger, in stock syrup at 16° Baume (B) and cook gently until the syrup registers 20° B; cover, leave for 24 hours then repeat the process so increasing the density over several days until 34°B is reached. Drain and dry on a wire grill at 80°C. To use as petits fours dip the ends in melted chocolate or fondant.

Cream Information on the various kinds of real cream is given in the section entitled Checklist of Commodities. When whipping by hand or machine, double or whipping cream will increase in volume by 50 per cent.

Crème Chantilly is made by whisking cream until it reaches piping consistency, adding 60g caster sugar and a few drops of vanilla essence per 1 litre cream. It can be coloured pink with a few drops of cochineal.

Artificial creams are sold under various brand names but their whiteness shows they are synthetic.

Mock cream can be made by melting 125g butter in 1½dl of milk without boiling; dissolve 25g gelatine in cold water, place in a blender and gradually add the hot milk and butter.

Egg-wash Whisk 2 eggs with ½dl milk and a pinch of salt and use to brush over pastry to give a golden brown, glossy appearance when baked.

Fondant This form of icing is usually purchased ready-made but can be made by boiling 3dl water, 100g glucose and 1kg sugar to 115°C; pour onto an oiled slab, allow to cool slightly then work with a palette-knife until it turns opaque. Use fondant at 37°C making it smooth with hot stock syrup; colour and flavour to taste.

Frangipane Cream 250g each of butter and caster sugar, add 4 eggs one by one then 60g flour and 250g ground almonds; cake crumbs may be used in place of a third of the almond. This is used in bakewell tart.

French Pastries (Pâtisseries françaises) This term indicates a selection of small fancy cakes for serving at tea-time or supper, also for a buffet. It consists of a range of half a dozen chosen from the following – barquettes with fruit or baked fillings, cream buns, cream horns, éclairs, genoise fondant dips, japs, macaroons, marshmallow fancies, meringue chantilly, mirli-tons, slices of millefeuilles, strawberry tartlets, tartlets parisienne, viennese tartlets, etc.

Fudge Place 225g granulated sugar with 120g glucose powder and 1dl water in a pan and cook to 115°C; add 60g butter melted with 1¾dl sweet-ened condensed milk, stir over heat until it becomes fawn-brown then beat until it turns cloudy, add vanilla essence and pour into a tin lined with silicone paper. Allow to cool then score into pieces with a greased knife.

Ganache This is used as a filling instead of butter cream, as a centre for pastries, and as a coating icing; it can also be piped out for a decoration. Melt 500g chocolate to 40°C add 2½dl boiling double cream and mix well together; to facilitate coating, some stock syrup may be added.

Genoise This basic sponge cake for general use is made by whisking 8 eggs and 4 yolks with 200g caster sugar to a peak, folding in 250g soft flour and 100g melted butter. It is baked on a greased and lined tray at 195°C for approximately 25 minutes and is best used after keeping for a day. For a gateau, pour into a greased and lined 25cm cake tin and bake.

Glucose This is purchased in syrup form or as a powder to add to a sugar syrup for pulled sugar work, to prevent crystallisation; it is useful for keeping cakes from staling and gives extra gloss when added to fondant.

Glycerine Is added to royal icing to prevent it from setting hard when dry; it also keeps cakes moist when added to the mixture.

Icings There are many different kinds, the easiest to make and use being *Water Icing* made by adding 480g icing sugar to $\frac{3}{4}$dl hot stock syrup; *Royal Icing* is made by adding 500g icing sugar to 3 egg whites with a teaspoon of lemon juice; a little washing blue will enhance the whiteness. It is advisable to keep it overnight to make piping easier; it should not be aerated by excessive beating. Some cake decorators add honey to give a distinctive colour and to keep the icing soft to eat. *American Icing* – boil 450g sugar and 1dl water to 127°C; pour into $2\frac{1}{2}$ stiffly beaten egg whites and beat until stiff. *Fudge Icing* – warm 250g fondant with 125g of butter and a little evaporated milk and add $\frac{1}{3}$dl more evaporated milk. *Chocolate Icing* – melt 250g chocolate and add 1dl warm stock syrup a little at a time until thin enough to coat. *Ganache* and *fondant* may also be used to ice cakes. For a harder icing mix 50g warmed glucose with 1 egg-white, 450g icing sugar, glycerine and rosewater.

Marmelade de Pommes Cook 1kg cooking apples in $\frac{1}{2}$dl water, the juice of half a lemon and 125g sugar to a stiff purée; pass through a sieve and use as a filling for a flan or tartlet or as a coating on fancy cakes.

Marshmallow Soak 15g gelatine in 1dl warm water, heat until clear then dissolve 120g granulated sugar in it keeping the temperature at not more than 72°C. Add vanilla essence, stir in 175g glucose powder and whisk to a thick foam. Pour into a lined tin that has been oiled and dusted with cornflour and leave for 4 or 5 hours to set. It may be coloured and flavoured then dipped into chocolate couverture for a petit four.

Marzipan This may be purchased in prepared form, or made by boiling 1dl water with 500g sugar and 50g glucose to 115°C then adding 350g ground almonds and 2 yolks of egg. This kind is used for covering celebration cakes and for petits fours. For modelling use three parts sugar to one part of ground almonds and 25g melted leaf gelatine per 1kg of sugar and almond mix.

Meringue Mushrooms Pipe small dome-shaped rounds through a 6mm plain tube onto a greased tray already sprinkled with chocolate powder; also pipe small stems finished to a point approximately 1$\frac{1}{2}$cm high. Dry out at 93°C for 3–4 hours then make a small hole in the base of the round pieces and fix stems in place with a little melted chocolate.

Nougat There are two kinds – *montelimar* which is white and often used as part of a selection of petits fours, and the darker *caramel* kind which is the basis for praline and often used as an edible container for other sweet dishes.

For montelimar, cook 1kg sugar in 2$\frac{1}{2}$dl water, add 100g honey and 200g glucose and cook to 135°C; pour onto 6 stiffly beaten egg whites, beat then add 150g each of chopped glacé cherries and flaked almonds. Pour into a tin lined with silicone or rice paper, keep under light pressure for approximately 6 hours then cut with a hot knife.

Nougat Basket Caramel nougat is made by adding 250g hot roasted nib almonds to 550g caster sugar and the juice of 1 lemon. Using a sugar-boiling pan, cook the sugar and lemon juice and stir constantly over a low heat until it is melted and a pale amber colour. Add the hot almonds, turn out onto an oiled marble and roll out thinly, cut to shape and mould over an oiled receptacle of the desired shape and size; cut a handle and some diamonds or other shapes and stick together in the form of a basket by melting the ends where they join the body. This nougat can be re-softened for use by placing in the oven at 200°C for a short while.

Finely crushed nougat is known as praline.

Palmiers Roll out a piece of puff pastry 3mm thick, approximately 35cm wide and of any length; brush with white of egg, dredge with granulated sugar and fold the edges to the centre. Brush with egg-white, fold each side to the centre again and press together. Cut into 6mm strips, place on a damp baking sheet cut side down, allow to rest, then bake at 215°C until half-cooked, turn each one over and finish cooking. Palmiers may be served as a biscuit to accompany a cream sweet or sandwiched together with jam and whipped cream for a cake.

Paper cornets These are used for the fine piping of a decoration on finished sweets; cut a 30cm triangle of strong greaseproof paper, roll the lower right-hand corner to half way along the bottom and hold in place while wrapping the remaining paper around it.

Pastry Cream Pour 1 litre boiling milk onto 8 yolks, 250g sugar and 125g flour mixed together; return to the pan, bring to a boil and cook for 2 minutes. Flavour with vanilla, chocolate, coffee, etc., and use as a filling for éclairs, flans, tartlets, etc. The flour may be replaced with cornflour.

Pastillage or Gum Paste This is used for making presentation and decorative centrepieces for display purposes. It is made by sifting 1kg icing sugar and 100g cornflour then mixing to a paste with a few drops each of lemon juice and moistened laundry bag blue and 15g gum tragacanth soaked for 24 hours in $1\frac{1}{2}$dl cold water. If gum is unobtainable use the same amount of soaked then dissolved gelatine. Knead until smooth and plastic, cut out with templates, mould round if necessary and leave to dry, covered with greaseproof paper and a flat board. Turn over to dry out completely then assemble into shape using royal icing for the joints. Whilst still fresh and soft, pastel-coloured pastillage may be pressed into moulds or made into flowers, petals, etc.

Pastry See next section.

Praline Boil 500g sugar in 1dl water to a pale amber colour, add 500g toasted nib almonds and hazelnuts, pour on an oiled slab and when cold, crush into fine granules. Store in an airtight container.

Red Glaze Boil four parts red jam with one part water to a coating consistency; if necessary add a few drops of cochineal and use for glazing fruit flans, tartlets, etc., while still hot.

Rock Sugar This is used for decoration purposes on cold buffet displays; boil 1kg sugar in 1dl water to 150°C remove from the heat and mix in 50g finished royal icing; as it froths and begins to expand place it into an oiled basin, cover and allow to stand for 15 minutes until set. Turn out the bowl and break or cut into pieces.

Scones These can be made as individual scones or as larger rounds divided into 4 or 6 wedges. They are an essential part of a cream tea and plain ones can also be cooked on top of minced meat.

Rub 75g margarine into 400g plain flour sieved with 25g each of baking powder and dried milk; add 2 eggs beaten with 75g sugar and $2\frac{1}{2}$dl water or milk and mix to a paste. Roll out $1\frac{1}{2}$cm thick and cut out 6cm rounds, egg-wash and bake at 225°C for 15 minutes. 75g mixed fruit may be added to the recipe. If using self-raising flour, add $\frac{1}{2}$ teaspoon of bicarbonate of soda per 400g flour. Wholemeal scones are made from three parts wholemeal flour to one part plain flour, as for ordinary scones.

Sponge Cake The basic baked sponge cake is known as Genoise Sponge the recipe for which is given under that heading earlier in this section. A wide range of items can be made from this basic sponge including afternoon tea fancies, battenburg cake, etc.

Stock Syrup Bring 1 litre of water and 950g of sugar to a boil with the juice of half a lemon, a stick of cinnamon; a vanilla pod or cardamom seeds may be added. The syrup is then ready to use either hot or cold for softening fondant and chocolate, soaking cakes, for fruit salad, for water icing, etc.

Strawberry Shortcake This is an American version and is more similar to a Victoria Sponge cake than to a Scottish shortcake. It is served as a dessert but can be made in individual portions for afternoon tea. Cream 150g butter with 150g caster sugar, add 3 eggs then 300g self-raising flour and approximately $\frac{1}{4}$dl milk to make a smooth pastry; roll 1cm thick and cut out 20cm rounds, bake at 200°C for approximately 20 minutes then sandwich two rounds with whipped cream and strawberries. Dredge with icing sugar. The top layer should be divided into 8–12 wedges before placing in position.

Swiss Roll Whisk 4 eggs with 120g sugar over heat until light and creamy, fold in 120g soft flour, spread on a sheet of buttered paper in a Swiss roll tin and bake at 225°C for approximately 8 minutes.

Turn out on to a cloth sprinkled with caster sugar, remove the paper, spread with 200g warm jam and roll up by using the cloth. Trim the ends square. Swiss rolls can be made in individual sizes for use as an afternoon tea fancy, also for lining the mould for charlotte royale.

It is possible to make a chocolate Swiss roll without using flour – whisk 4 egg yolks with 120g sugar until thick, add 180g plain chocolate melted with 1 dspn water then fold in 4 stiffly beaten whites of egg; spread on a tray, bake at 177°C for 20 minutes and roll up with jam, butter cream, etc.

Victoria Sponge   Cream 160g margarine with 160g caster sugar, add 3 eggs one by one then mix in 170g self-raising flour (or 160g soft flour sieved with 10g baking powder); fill into 15cm greased and floured sponge tins and bake at 182°C for 25 minutes. When cold, sandwich together with jam, curd, cream, ganache, etc. and dredge with icing sugar.

This produces a light sponge cake but is more crumbly than a genoise so not so versatile.

Yeast goods   See separate section after 'Pastry'.

Pastry

Sift flour through a fine sieve before use and cut fat into small pieces before rubbing it in; use iced water to bind ordinary pastry. Place prepared pastry in the refrigerator for 30 minutes before rolling out, keeping it wrapped in greaseproof paper. For *flan pastry* a small amount of oil may be added to the water and milk may be used instead of water. Yolk of egg can be used to bind pastry used for fruit tartlets.

There are more than a dozen different kinds of pastry, each having its own particular use, so in order to achieve the right result it is necessary not only to know how to make the pastry correctly but to understand why it suits its particular purpose. It is as bad for pastry to be tough and hard to eat as it is to be too short and crumbly.

An establishment may stock only one kind of flour, usually general purpose, and one fat – margarine, therefore making only one kind of pastry possible. This denies customers the variety to which they are entitled.

All the different kinds of pastry are a mixture of fat and flour, in varying proportions, bound together with a liquid such as water, milk or egg. Amounts of ingredients and methods of making vary slightly but generally the recipes are as follows:

Cheese Pastry Make by adding 60g baker's cheese to the flour when making short pastry; it can be used for savoury flans, pasties and turnovers, and cheese straws.

Chou Paste Place 5dl cold water, 200g butter, 15g sugar and a pinch of salt to boil, remove from the heat, add 275g strong flour, mix well and stir over the heat until it leaves the sides clean. Allow to cool then work in 8–9 eggs. This is used for cream buns, éclairs, profiteroles and various cakes.

Flan Pastry Rub 250g mixed butter and margarine into 400g general purpose flour, add 25g caster sugar mixed with 2 eggs and a pinch of salt and mix; refrigerate before using. This amount of pastry will line 2 × 21cm rings. Sweet pastry can also be used to make fruit flans.

German Pastry Cream 300g butter with 90g caster sugar, add 1 egg and 450g soft flour; refrigerate before using then cook in paper-lined tins at 193°C. This pastry can be made in a chocolate flavour by adding 60g cocoa in place of 60g of the flour. German paste is used for tartlets, biscuits, etc.

Hot Water Pastry Bring 3dl water and 125g lard to a boil, pour into a bay in 450g soft flour and a pinch of salt and mix to a paste; knead well and use whilst still hot to line moulds for raised pies.

Noodle Paste Add 3 eggs, 5 yolks, ½dl water and ½dl oil mixed together, to 500g strong flour sieved with 10g salt; mix well then knead until smooth. Allow to rest then roll out very thinly for cutting into noodles, making ravioli or apfelstrudel. Milk may be used instead of water.

Pâte Brisée Grate or finely chop 200g butter, mix into 375g general purpose or plain flour with ½ teaspoon of salt and add and mix in 1½dl water without overworking. This flaky pastry can be used instead of puff pastry.

Potato Pastry This is a yeast pastry that can be used to make bread, rolls, pizza, croissants, etc.

Add 125g dry mashed potato to 450g strong flour and a pinch of sugar and salt; dilute 15g yeast in 3dl warm water and add to the flour to make a soft dough; knead well and allow to prove.

Puff Pastry Mix 250g strong flour sieved with 2g salt, with 1½dl cold water and a squeeze of lemon juice, knead well, rest it for 30 minutes then cut a cross; roll out as a star and insert a 250g piece of kneaded butter inside to enclose it completely. Roll out 60cm by 20cm, fold the two ends to the centre then fold in half again; allow to rest then repeat the rolling and folding operation twice more. Use for covering pies, making sausage rolls and vol-au-vent, millefeuilles, etc.

Rough Puff Is also known as Flaky Pastry and it has the same uses as puff pastry. Mix 400g strong flour, 5g salt, a pinch of cream of tartar, 300g butter cut into 2cm dice with 2½dl cold water; roll out 30cm by 15cm and fold in three; repeat then allow to rest for 30 minutes. Give a total of six turns.

Savarin Paste Mix 500g strong flour with 8 eggs and 20g each of yeast and sugar dissolved in 1dl warm water; add 250g butter, allow to prove and mix to an elastic paste. For Babas, add 60g currants.

Short Pastry   This is known as Pâte à Foncer and is the most versatile kind of pastry, being used for pies, tarts, tartlets, as well as flans. Rub 250g of mixed lard and butter into 500g general purpose flour, add 2g salt and mix quickly to a smooth paste with 1dl water.

Strudel Pastry   Mix 400g strong flour with a pinch of salt, 1 beaten egg, 50g melted butter and 1¾dl milk to a smooth paste, leave for 30 minutes then roll out very thinly in a cloth; proceed to stretch gently with the hands until transparent.

Noodle pastry and puff pastry are sometimes used to make apfelstrudel.

Suet Pastry   Add 300g shredded suet to 500g self-raising flour with a pinch of salt and mix to a dough with 2½dl water, or instead of using self-raising flour, sieve 15g baking powder into 500g plain flour. This is used for making steak pudding, dumplings, sea pie, etc; for jam roll and steamed fruit pudding add 50g sugar to the pastry recipe.

Sweet Pastry   Rub 300g butter into 500g flour and a pinch of salt; beat 2 eggs with 125g caster sugar, add to the flour and mix into a paste.

Wholemeal Pastry   Wholemeal flour can be used to replace all or a proportion of the flour in all the pastry recipes, except puff pastry. The idea behind wholemeal pastry is that it adds fibre to the diet.

Yeast goods

Most of these are bought fresh daily from a bakery though many restaurants have a good reputation for their home-made rolls and possibly for brioches and croissants. Apart from these and bridge rolls for cocktail parties, only yeast-dough sweets such as babas and savarins are made on the premises. The recipes for these are given earlier in this section.

Dinner Rolls   Sieve 3kg 175g strong flour with 60g each of milk powder and salt, rub in 120g white fat and add 100g yeast dissolved in 1.7 litres water at 37°C. Knead well, allow to prove for 1 hour then knock back, divide into 45g pieces, mould and prove. Bake at 230°C for 15 minutes with a tray of hot water in the oven.

Bridge Rolls   Sieve 3kg 100g strong flour, add and mix in 80g each of salt, sugar and white fat and 1.6 litre of water at 37°C in which 150g of yeast has been dissolved. Knead well, allow to prove then knock back; divide into 30g pieces, mould into ovals, egg-wash and allow to prove again. bake at 240°C for approximately 12 minutes.

Croissants   Roll out 1½kg bread dough to 90cm × 60cm, place 500g cold butter in pieces over half of it and fold to enclose; roll out, fold in three, allow to rest then give two more turns. Allow to rest overnight then roll out 3mm thick and divide into 12½cm triangles. Roll up tightly from the base, turn into a crescent and place on a warm greased baking sheet; brush with egg-wash, allow to prove until double the size and bake at 220°C for approximately 15 minutes. This makes approximately 35 croissants.

The list of buns include Bath, Chelsea, doughnuts, fruit, teacakes and Swiss; they are made with the addition of eggs and sugar to the Dinner Roll recipe.

Brioche   Dissolve 30g yeast in 2dl milk at 37°C and pour into 1kg strong flour sieved with 50g icing sugar and 10g salt; add 3 beaten eggs. Knead well, adding 2 more eggs and 90g butter in small pieces. Allow to prove until double in size; knock back and keep in the refrigerator overnight. Mould in 40g balls, press into fluted moulds shaping the top into a small knob; brush with milk, allow to prove, then bake at 230°C for approximately 12 minutes.

Brioche dough is used to make Beef Wellington and Coulibiac of Salmon but the butter and egg content of the recipe should be halved.

521

Bavarois

A bavarois is made with egg-custard sauce, set with gelatine and enriched and aerated with whipped cream. They can be made in many flavours including banana, chocolate, coffee, orange, praline and vanilla. Fruit bavarois is made with equal quantities of the basic egg custard and a purée of fruit such as apricot, peach, pear, raspberries, redcurrants and strawberries. Bavarois are usually moulded in an oiled charlotte mould and when set turned out and decorated with cream etc. Several flavours and colours of cream and fruit bavarois can be put into the same mould to produce a further range of sweets. A bavarois can also be named 'Crème' or 'Pouding'.

Aremberg	Arrange white and pink-tinted poached pears in the bottom of a mould, decorate with glacé fruits and line the sides with finger biscuits; fill with kirsch-flavoured bavarois.
Clermont	Add one part of chestnut purée to four parts rum-flavoured bavarois; add pieces of marrons glacés and pour into a mould; turn out and garnish with marrons glacés and whipped cream.
Diplomate	Decorate a deep border mould with crystallised fruits and fill with vanilla bavarois containing some macerated finger biscuits, currants and sultanas, and a little apricot jam.
Malakoff	Fill a mould with alternate layers of stiff apple and pear purée and vanilla bavarois containing diced macerated finger biscuits, currants, sultanas and candied orange peel; when set, turn out and coat with kirsch-flavoured sabayon.
My Queen	Line a mould with sweetened cream set with gelatine and fill with strawberry bavarois containing macerated small strawberries; when set turn out and garnish with strawberries.
Nesselrode (Pouding)	Mix together equal amounts of crème anglaise, chestnut purée and whipped cream, add chopped crystallised fruits and macerated sul-

	tanas and currants, fill into a mould and allow to set; turn out and garnish with marrons glacés.
Normande	Add diced cooked dessert apple to apple bavarois; turn out and garnish with poached quarters of apple.
Religieuse	Line a mould with vanilla bavarois and fill with chocolate bavarois.
Rizzio	Decorate a deep border mould with vanilla bavarois and fill with chocolate bavarois.
Rubanné	Arrange several layers of different colours and flavours of bavarois in a mould, allowing each layer to set before adding the next one; the bavarois usually used are chocolate, strawberry and vanilla.
Terrine de Fruits	Set one layer of fruit-flavoured bavarois in an oblong mould, cover neatly with squares or rounds of several fruits, cover with a layer of different fruit-flavoured bavarois and more fruit until the dish is full; when set, turn out and decorate and serve as slices, possibly on a coulis of fruit purée.

Biscuits

These home-made biscuits are for serving with ice cream and other cold sweets. They may also be used as part of a petits fours selection and as an accompaniment to drinks (such as champagne) in which it is customary to dip them. They may be dipped in chocolate or decorated.

Alexander	Cream 200g butter with 50g icing sugar, add 250g flour and vanilla and pipe out 6cm long; allow to rest for 30 minutes then bake at 230°C for 12 minutes. They may be sandwiched with butter-cream or dipped in melted chocolate.
Biscuits à la Cuillère	These are the same as ladies' finger biscuits and are also known as finger biscuits and sponge fingers.

Boudoir	This is another name for ladies' fingers.
Brandy Snaps	Melt 100g each of butter, sugar and syrup, add 100g flour, a little ginger and lemon juice. Put 3cm rounds on a tray, bake at 160°C for 8 minutes then curl around the buttered handle of a wooden spoon.
Champagne	This is another name for ladies' fingers.
Cigarettes Russes	Whisk 2 egg-whites until stiff and fold in 100g sugar, 45g flour, and lastly 50g melted butter. Pipe out oblong shape, bake in a hot oven for 5 minutes, then turn them over, and roll up around a pencil or wooden meat skewer.
Cornets	Pipe langue de chat mixture in $2\frac{1}{2}$cm rounds, bake at 220°C and whilst hot form around cream horn tins.
Croquants	Mix 60g caster sugar, 1 yolk and 150g butter, add 200g self-raising flour sieved with a pinch of salt then mix in 125g coarsely chopped hazel-nuts. Refrigerate then pat into $7\frac{1}{2}$cm × $3\frac{1}{2}$cm × $3\frac{1}{2}$cm, brush with egg-wash, score a crisscross pattern and bake. Cut into 5cm slices.
Finger Biscuit	This is another name for ladies' fingers or biscuits à la cuillère.
Flapjacks	Melt 120g margarine, 60g honey and 60g brown sugar, add 225g rolled oats, bake in a Swiss roll tin at 190°C for 20 minutes then cut into squares.
Florentine	Heat $1\frac{1}{2}$dl cream, 25g butter and 350g sugar, stir in 40g flour, 350g flaked almonds, 350g chopped mixed angelica, glacé cherries and sultanas; bake in rings on rice paper at 180°C. When cool dip one side in melted chocolate.
German Pastes	Cream 300g butter with 90g caster sugar, add 1 egg and 450g soft flour; refrigerate, roll and cut out and bake on a tray lined with rice paper. They may be coated with melted chocolate.
Ginger Nuts	Make a paste with 200g self-raising flour, 100g butter, 80g sugar, ground ginger, mixed spice,

treacle and milk; roll out, cut in 5cm rounds and bake at 180°C for 10 minutes.

Japonaise Make an ordinary meringue mixture with 10 egg-whites whisked with 50g sugar; add 200g ground almonds, 50g cornflour and 350g sugar, pipe in various shapes and bake at 175°C for approximately 15 minutes.

Ladies' Fingers Whisk 5 yolks with 120g sugar until creamy, fold in some of 4 stiffly beaten whites, then 120g flour; fold in remainder of whites and pipe 9cm × 1cm, sprinkle with sugar and bake at 220°C for 10 minutes.

Langues de Chat Cream 250g each of butter and sugar, add 6 whites one at a time then beat in 250g flour. Pipe 7cm lengths and bake at 220°C.

Leckerli Mix 300g ground almonds with 350g icing sugar and $1\frac{1}{2}$ egg whites; roll out, cut into $2\frac{1}{2}$cm × $3\frac{1}{4}$cm triangles and bake at 260°C for a few minutes. Glaze with gum arabic.

Macaroons Beat 8 whites until stiff, fold in 500g sugar and 250g ground almonds; pipe 5cm rounds on rice paper and bake at 160°C for 10 minutes.

Manqué Biscuits Whisk 250g sugar and 9 yolks to the ribbon stage; fold in 200g flour and a little rum, then 8 stiffly beaten egg-whites and 150g melted butter. Fill into sponge-cake moulds and bake in a moderate oven.

Marshmallows Place 3dl water, 120g glucose and 800g sugar to boil, add 30g soaked gelatine then beat on half speed until firm but not set; pipe out quickly.

Milanaise Mix 240g soft flour, 60g self-raising flour, 180g each of butter and icing sugar and 2 yolks to a smooth paste. Roll out, cut into various shapes, egg-wash and bake at 204°C.

Nougat Cook 220g nibbed nuts and 220g caster sugar with juice of half a lemon to a light caramel colour; pour on an oiled slab, roll and cut out.

Palets de Dames Cream 100g each of butter and sugar, add 2 eggs then fold in 125g soft flour and 20g currants.

525

	Pipe 2½cm rounds and bake at 204°C for 10–12 minutes.
Petits Fours Gommés	Pound 220g ground almonds with 3 whites, add 350g caster sugar and the grated rind of 1 lemon; pipe onto rice paper, leave to dry for 12 hours then bake at 240°C for 4 minutes. Brush with gum arabic.
Petits Gâteaux	Take 500g flour and 300g each of butter and sugar and mix to a paste with 1 egg, 4 yolks and 1 tbs orange-flower water; cut into various shapes and bake.
Punch Biscuits	Whisk 250g sugar with 6 yolks and 2 eggs; fold in 185g flour, a little rum and orange and lemon essences, then fold in 4 stiffly beaten whites and 150g melted butter and bake in sponge-cake moulds.
Ratafia	Mix together 4 egg whites, 250g each of sugar and ground almonds and 30g ground rice to a firm mixture; pipe 2cm rounds on rice paper, dredge with icing sugar and bake at 200°C for approximately 10 minutes.
Rout	Mix 300g ground almonds, 180g caster and 120g icing sugar with 3 yolks; cut in various shapes, leave to dry for 6 hours then bake at 250°C. *Parisian Rout Biscuits* are made with equal amounts of ground almonds and icing sugar, mixed with egg-white and piped into various shapes.
Savoy	Whisk 500g sugar with 14 yolks, add 185g soft flour with 185g cornflour and fold in 14 whisked whites; cook in buttered and floured finger shape moulds until dry.
Senoritas	Pound 90g almonds with 125g sugar and a little water, add to 3 stiffly beaten egg-whites then pipe into small paper cases, decorate with an almond and bake for 5 minutes in a moderate oven.
Shortbread	Cream 200g butter with 100g sugar, add 250g flour and 50g semolina; roll out, cut into fingers

	or triangles and bake at 160°C for 7–8 minutes. Allow to cool before removing from the tray.
Sponge Fingers	These are made with same mixture as ladies' fingers or may be made by whisking 3 whites until stiff then folding in 120g sugar, 3 yolks and 150g flour, piping them out in the usual way.
Tuiles	Mix 45g ground almonds and 50g flour into 2 egg-whites stiffly beaten with 100g sugar; add 50g melted butter then pipe out small balls and bake at 135°C for 4 minutes. Lay over a rolling pin so they take the shape of a curled tile.
Viennese	Cream 350g butter and 250g sugar, add 2 yolks and stir in 500g soft flour and 150g ground almonds; pipe into various shapes using a fancy tube, bake at 204°C, dust with icing sugar and pipe red jam in the centre.
Wafers	These are usually purchased ready-made; there are several different kinds and shapes including flat, oblong, rolled, fan shape, etc.

Blancmange

Blancmange is normally made with 100g cornflour per 1 litre of sweetened milk but can be made with gelatine and warmed milk. It can also be made with proprietary blancmange powder which is available in a variety of flavours and colours, including chocolate, coffee, lemon, orange, honey and strawberry. It can be made extra creamy by the use of half milk and half single cream.

Blancmange is usually set in fancy jelly moulds and when turned out may be served with a compote of fruit. It can be made in a rainbow effect by setting layers of several colours in the same mould.

If the mould is rinsed out with stock syrup before adding the mixture, it will turn out looking very shiny.

Charlottes, cold

These cold sweets are usually made with bavarois but in some cases, only whipped cream or ice cream. As the name implies they are set in charlotte moulds then turned out and decorated. They differ from bavarois by the inclusion of more ingredients such as biscuits, fruit, etc.

Arlequin	Line the mould with alternate strips of sponge glazed with chocolate, lemon, and pistachio fondant and fill with cubes of the same three flavours of bavarois, set in place with raspberry jelly.
Chateaubriand	Line the bottom of the mould with overlapping round pieces and the sides with strips of sponge, sticking them together with royal icing; allow to dry, then fill with maraschino-flavoured bavarois containing diced crystallised fruits.
Chantilly	Place a round base of baked short paste on a dish and stick wafer biscuits around the edge using cooked sugar; fill dome shape with vanilla bavarois made with extra cream, pouring it in almost at setting point; decorate with pink-coloured whipped cream. This may be made in a mould.
Colinette	Line the mould with very small meringues sticking them together with royal icing and fill with vanilla bavarois made with extra cream and containing crushed crystallised violets; when set turn out and decorate with crystallised violets.
Impériale	Chemise the mould with red jelly and line with ice wafers; fill with vanilla bavarois containing diced pears, turn out and garnish with poached halves of pear.
Metternich	Line the mould with finger biscuits and fill with chestnut bavarois made with extra cream.
Montreuil	Line the mould with lemon jelly, cover the base with sliced peaches and the side with slices of small Swiss roll; fill with vanilla bavarois.

Moscovite	Cover the bottom of the mould with red jelly, when set line the side with finger biscuits and fill with vanilla bavarois.
Napolitaine	Line the mould with finger biscuits and fill with whipped cream set with gelatine and flavoured with chestnut purée, containing diced pineapple, raisins and strips of candied citron peel.
Opéra	Line the mould with ice wafers and fill with chestnuts bavarois containing macerated diced crystallised fruit.
Orléans	Add pieces of finger biscuits and ratafia biscuits and diced crystallised fruit macerated in rum, to vanilla bavarois; mould and set as usual.
Parisienne	Glaze finger biscuits with pink fondant and line the mould with them; fill with vanilla bavarois.
Pompadour	Line the mould with finger biscuits and fill with pineapple bavarois; when set turn out and decorate with puff pastry fleurons which have been cut open and filled, some with plain and some with chocolate-flavoured whipped cream.
Profiteroles	Fill very small profiteroles with apricot jam, add to kirsch-flavoured bavarois and set in the mould in the usual way.
Renaissance	Line the side of the mould alternately with sponge fingers glazed with white and pink fondant and fill with vanilla bavarois containing diced crystallised fruit; when set turn out and place a ring of pineapple and some glacé cherries on top.
Royale	Line the mould with slices of small Swiss roll and fill with vanilla bavarois.
Russe	Line the mould with finger biscuits and fill with vanilla bavarois.
Sicilienne	Line the base with overlapping rounds and the sides with strips of sponge, sticking them together with royal icing; fill with chocolate bavarois containing coarsely chopped pistachios.

529

Charlottes, hot

Apple Line a mould with slices of bread dipped in melted butter and fill with cooked sliced apples, cover with a round slice of bread and bake at 230°C for 35–40 minutes; serve with apricot sauce. (These may also be made in individual size dariole moulds.) It is important to cook the apples to a stiff mixture.

au Madère Add some raisins to the apple mixture and serve with Madeira-flavoured apricot sauce.

Normande Flavour the apple mixture with calvados, proceed as for apple charlotte and serve with calvados-flavoured apricot sauce.

Pear This is made in the same way as apple charlotte using stiffly cooked pear filling.

Other fruits such as apricots, mangoes, peaches, plums may also be used for a hot charlotte but they must first be cooked to a stiff purée.

Chartreuses

This kind of sweet is very similar to a cold charlotte being made in the same kind of mould which has been previously lined with jelly or with fruit set in jelly.

aux Bananes Chemise the mould with lemon jelly, line with slices of banana and fill with vanilla or banana bavarois.

aux Fruits Line the mould alternately with strips of poached apple and pear cooked in pink syrup; cook the fruit trimmings to a stiff purée, add a mixture of cooked apricots, cherries and plums and fill the mould; when set turn out into a dish lined with lemon jelly and decorate all over with croûtons of red jelly.

Cheesecakes

There are two kinds, the traditional one which is baked and the more simple one that is made cold or with a proprietary brand of cheesecake mix.

Baked   For a cake 25cm × 6cm, line a loose-based tin with short pastry, spread with apricot jam and fill with a mixture of 500g cottage cheese, 150g caster sugar, 50g cornflour and 3 eggs, finished with 3dl whipped cream; bake at 200°C for 30 minutes, take out, and allow to sink, then bake for a further 30 minutes.

The addition of sultanas previously soaked in rum is traditional, as is lemon rind and juice. If desired, the whites of the eggs may be whisked and folded in.

Unbaked   Whisk 3 yolks and 50g caster sugar to the ribbon stage, add to 300g cream cheese together with 15g melted gelatine then blend in 1½dl whipped cream and the grated rind and juice of 1 lemon; fold in 3 stiffly beaten whites of egg with 25g caster sugar and pour into a loose-bottomed tin which has been covered with a mixture of 75g of melted butter and 150g crushed digestive or ginger biscuits. When set cover the top with any kind of fruit pie filling and pipe with cream or decorate with strawberries, sliced kiwi fruit, etc.

Variations to this includes the addition to the mixture of well-drained black cherries, chocolate, coconut, coffee, stewed apple, ginger wine and crystallised ginger, orange and any flavour of yoghurt.

Quark may be used instead of cream cheese.

A cheese-cake 25cm in diameter will give 12 average-size portions.

Sweets Made with Chou Paste

Profiteroles au Chocolat
Fill small chou buns with whipped cream or pastry cream, place in a bowl and either coat with cold chocolate sauce or dredge with icing sugar and serve the sauce separately.

Profiterole Pudding
Prepare a cooked custard using 9 yolks and 25g gelatine per 1 litre of cream, flavour with kirsch and pour in layers into a mould with small chou buns and raisins; when set, turn out.

Salambos à la Marquise
Fill grooved eclairs 4cm long, with rum pastry cream, dip in sugar at 160°C and arrange in bowls on a bed of cold chocolate sauce; decorate with whipped cream.

Strawberry Profiteroles
Fill baked profiteroles with strawberry bavarois and serve coated with Melba sauce (raspberry jam, redcurrant jelly and stock syrup boiled together).

Small Fancy Cakes Made with Chou Paste

Choux à la Crème
Pipe buns 3cm in diameter, sprinkle with nibbed almonds and bake at 220°C; fill with whipped cream or pastry cream and dredge with icing sugar. These buns may be iced with various colours of fondant.

Cygnes glacés
Pipe 6cm oval bodies and 75mm necks and bake; cut off the tops of the bodies, fill with drained fruit salad and replace tops with a layer of cream; attach the necks fixing currants for eyes and arrange on a bed of jelly.

Eclairs
Pipe 10cm lengths and bake until dry; fill with whipped or pastry cream and dip into coffee or chocolate fondant.

Madelons	Pipe S-shape, sprinkle with granulated sugar and bake; split in two and fill with whipped cream.
Choux de Noël	Fill with mincemeat and rum-flavoured whipped cream.
Pains de Mecque	Pipe in the shape of meringues, dredge with icing sugar and slit down the middle; when cooked fill with whipped cream, pastry cream or jam.
Rognons à la Crème	Pipe small kidney-shape buns, bake, then fill with whipped cream and glaze with chocolate or coffee fondant.
Religieuses	Fill tartlet cases level with pastry cream, cover with a medium-size cream-filled chou bun that has been glazed with chocolate fondant then with a smaller pastry cream-filled chou bun dipped in coffee fondant on top.

These buns and éclairs can also be filled with ganache (melted chocolate mixed with cream).

See also under Fritters and Gâteaux made with chou paste.

Sweets Made with Condé Rice Mixture

Basic condé rice mixture is used in many hot and cold sweets, the difference between them being that for cold sweets 2dl slightly whipped cream is added to the mixture which is made by cooking 180g rice in 1 litre of milk with 180g sugar and vanilla, in the oven. A liaison of 4 yolks and 60g butter is then added and cooked in.

Hot

Abricot Colbert	Sandwich two halves of cooked or canned apricots with condé rice, pass through egg-wash and breadcrumbs and deep fry; serve with apricot sauce.

533

Croquettes	Add diced glacé fruits to the rice mixture or leave plain; mould as croquettes, egg and crumb and deep fry; serve with apricot sauce. Other shapes such as diamonds and crescents may be made, and pears and other fruit such as pineapple added.
Infante	Fill a savarin mould with the rice, turn out and fill the centre with sliced peaches and stoned cherries mixed with apricot sauce.
Marquise	Fill a savarin mould with the rice, turn out and fill the centre with poached quarters of pears; coat with apricot sauce flavoured with Madeira.

Cold

Abricots Condé	Spread a layer of rice mixture in a dish, arrange halves of cooked apricots on top and coat with apricot glaze; decorate with whipped cream, glacé cherries and diamonds of angelica. Other fruits may be served in this way, including apples, bananas, mandarins, pears, peaches, pineapple, etc.
	Condés may also be made individually in glass dishes or coupes.
Ananas Créole	Mould the rice in a domed shape on a dish, cover with thin half slices of pineapple and brush with apricot glaze; decorate with currants and leaves of angelica to represent a pineapple.
	The rice may be moulded in a bombe mould then turned out and decorated.
Ananas Singapore	Flavour the rice mixture with maraschino and add some diced pineapple; fill in a savarin mould and when set, turn out and coat with apricot sauce.
Fraises Josephine	Spread a layer of rice mixture on a dish, arrange a circle of macerated strawberries on top and coat with strawberry purée; decorate with whipped cream.
Fraises Sarah Bernhardt	Line a savarin mould with red jelly and sprinkle with chopped pistachios; fill with rice mixture

and when set, turn out and fill the centre with wild strawberries and whipped cream.

Poires Marie-Rose Fill whole poached pears with praline pastry cream, coat with raspberry-flavoured cream and arrange on a bed of condé rice mixture; decorate with whipped cream and diamonds of angelica.

Other fruits may be presented in this manner.

See also under 'Sweets made with Impératrice Rice'.

Continental Specialities

Sachertorte Whisk 8 yolks of egg with 90g caster sugar and a pinch of salt to a thick sponge; melt 120g butter and 75g unsweetened chocolate and blend into the egg mixture. Whisk 7 egg whites with 120g caster sugar and the juice of 1 lemon to a firm but smooth meringue, add and mix in a third of it to the sponge together with 130g strong flour and 90g crushed hazelnuts. Fold in the remainder of the meringue, place into two torten tins and bake at 193°C.

German Paste for Torten bases Cream 300g butter with 90g caster sugar, add 1 egg and 450g strong flour; refrigerate then roll out and bake on greased and papered trays at 193°C. This can be made in a chocolate flavour by replacing 60g of the flour with cocoa powder.

Törten A törten is a rich and artistically decorated gateau made in a tin 25–30cm in diameter. It is composed of several layers of the rich sponge given below, sprinkled with a liqueur and spread with apricot jam and buttercream, laid on a base of German Paste. The sides are coated and decorated and the whole is cut into portions with a special cutter and each section individually decorated. A 30cm törten will yield 24 portions.

Dobos Sponge Whisk 400g warmed caster sugar with 6 yolks and 9 eggs to a thick, light sponge; fold in 200g each of plain flour and cornflour sieved together and 200g melted butter. Fill greased and floured torten tins with mixture and bake at 193°C for approximately 20 minutes.

Linzertorte   Cream 120g butter and 60g lard with 120g icing sugar, add 3 yolks of egg then add 225g soft flour, 120g ground almonds, 7g cinnamon and the grated rind and juice of 1 lemon. Mix to a ball and refrigerate for 30 minutes. Roll out to two 20cm rounds, place one on a greased tray, spread with raspberry jam and cover with the other; crimp the edge, egg-wash, sprinkle with flaked almonds and bake at 204°C for approximately 20 minutes.

Creams

Cream plays many useful roles in sweets; dairy cream is served with many hot and cold sweets in either liquid or whipped form, the latter usually being sweetened and flavoured, or coloured for piping as decoration. Cream is also the basis of many cold sweets and there are several which bear the name 'Cream' but are in fact made from egg custard.

Brise de Printemps   Whip double cream and sweeten and flavour with violet essence; serve very cold, decorated with crystallised violets and mimosa.

Crème Caprice   Mix broken meringues into sweetened whipped cream, fill a fancy mould and chill; turn out and decorate with raspberry or strawberry-flavoured whipped cream.

Crème Chantilly   This is the basic cream used for all decoration work on cakes and sweets; whip double cream until nearly stiff, sweeten with 60g caster sugar per 1 litre and flavour with vanilla essence and continue whipping to a peak.

Crème Chibouste   Prepare 1 litre of pastry cream, also prepare 14 stiffly beaten egg-whites with 100g caster sugar and add the boiling pastry cream; this must be carried out very quickly. Once it is mixed do not continue beating.

Crème Frangipane — Mix 250g each of flour and sugar with 4 eggs and 8 yolks, add 1 litre boiling milk and vanilla, boil for 2 minutes then add 50g crushed macaroons and 100g butter; use as a flan filling.

Crème Pâtissière — Mix 200g sugar, 75g flour, 50g cornflour and 12 yolks, add 1 litre boiling milk flavoured with vanilla and boil for 2 minutes; use as a filling for flans, eclairs, choux buns etc.

Crème Régence — Arrange layers of macerated finger biscuits and fruit purée in a deep dish, cover with a rich egg custard mix and cook au bain-marie until set.

Crème Saint-Honoré — Fold 15 stiffly beaten egg whites into the above quantity of pastry cream and use for filling Gâteau Saint-Honoré.

Lemon Cream — Add grated rind and juice of 1 lemon, 60g caster sugar, and ½dl sherry to 3dl double cream, whisk and fill into goblets. Serve decorated with blanched julienne of lemon peel.

Swiss Cream — Boil 6dl cream with 120g sugar, a pinch of cinnamon and the grated rind of 1 lemon; add 30g cornflour diluted with cream, reboil and pour over ratafia biscuits sprinkled with kirsch; decorate with julienne of candied orange peel.

Velvet Cream — Dissolve 15g gelatine in 1dl sweet sherry, allow to cool then whisk into 6dl double cream with 60g caster sugar; pour into goblets or into dariole moulds immediately.

White Cream — Stir 15g gelatine dissolved in 1dl milk into 6dl whipped cream, add 60g sugar and pour into a mould. Turn out and decorate.

Croûtes

These are made from savarin or brioche paste baked in a tall round mould and when stale cut into slices, sprinkled with sugar and glazed in the oven. There are many variations on this basic formula, most of them being served hot.

Lyonnaise   Spread the slices with chestnut purée, coat with reduced apricot sauce and sprinkle with toasted shredded almonds; arrange overlapping on a dish and fill the centre with cooked chestnuts mixed with Malaga-wine-flavoured apricot purée and soaked currants, sultanas and raisins.

au Madère   Arrange the slices overlapping and fill the centre with diced crystallised fruit, currants and sultanas mixed with Madeira-flavoured apricot purée.

Maréchal   Cut into triangles, coat with royal icing and dry in the oven, then arrange on a dish and fill the centre with pieces of pineapple, cherries, de-pipped grapes and orange segments mixed with apricot purée; surround with poached halves of pears, some coloured pink, the others white; surround with apricot glaze.

Montmorency   Arrange the slices overlapping and fill the centre with stoned cherries cooked in cherry sauce.

Montreuil   Arrange the slices overlapping, fill the centre with halves of peaches and coat with apricot sauce.

Normande   Arrange the slices overlapping and fill the centre with apple purée; arrange pink and white poached halves of apple in a pyramid on top and surround with apricot glaze.

Parisienne   Coat the slices with royal icing and dry in the oven; arrange overlapping with pineapple rings and fill the centre with fruit salad mixed with Madeira-flavoured apricot purée.

Victoria   Arrange the slices overlapping and fill the centre with marrons glacés and glacé cherries; serve with rum-flavoured apricot sauce.

Egg Custard Puddings

The basic mixture is 9 eggs and 180g sugar per 1 litre of milk, flavoured with vanilla and cooked au bain-marie at 165°C until set; if the internal temperature goes above 80°C the pudding will develop air holes and be spoilt; a folded newspaper or sheet of cardboard placed at the bottom of the bain-marie will help to prevent this from happening.

Hot

Baked Caramel Custard	Add some caramel to the basic raw mixture and cook in the oven in a bain-marie.
Baked Egg Custard	Pour the egg custard into pie-dishes, sprinkle with nutmeg and cook in the usual way.
Bread and Butter Pudding	Arrange small triangles of buttered bread in pie dishes with a few sultanas and cover with raw egg custard; allow to soak, then bake au bain-marie and sprinkle with caster sugar.
Cabinet Pudding	Fill greased dariole moulds with diced stale sponge cake together with dried mixed fruit and chopped glacé cherries; fill with custard mix and cook au bain-marie.
Chancellor's Pudding	This is another name for cabinet pudding.
Coconut Egg Custard	Add some dessicated coconut to the custard and cook as usual.
Crème Régence	Arrange layers of macerated finger biscuits and purée of fruit, such as pear, in a deep dish, cover with a rich egg-custard mixture and cook au bain-marie until set.
Crème Villageoise	Place layers of macerated finger biscuits and firm purée of fruit in a pie dish; cover with egg custard mix and cook as usual.
Créme Frite	Cook a custard made with 18 yolks per 1 litre milk in a tray 1½cm deep; when cold cut into 5cm squares, egg and crumb twice and deep fry quickly; serve with custard sauce.

Ibiza	Bake an egg custard flavoured with lemon juice and mixed spice and containing diced sponge cake, in a caramel-lined pie-dish.
Lemon Egg Custard	Flavour the egg custard with grated lemon rind and cook as usual.
Orange Egg Custard	Add grated orange rind to the egg mixture and cook as usual.
Queen of Puddings	Soak 200g fresh breadcrumbs in the basic mixture and cook in a pie-dish; decorate with trellis work of meringue and finish with red and yellow jams in the spaces.

Cold

Crème Beau Rivage (also known as Bordure Beau Rivage)	Coat a savarin mould with praline, fill with custard mix and cook au bain-marie; turn out and decorate with cornets filled with whipped cream.
Crème Brulée	Make the basic mixture with cream instead of milk and cook in shallow dishes; dredge with icing sugar and glaze under the salamander.
Crème Caramel	Line dariole moulds with caramel, fill with custard and cook au bain-marie; turn out when cold.
Crème Florentine	Flavour the custard with praline; when cooked turn out and decorate with kirsch-flavoured cream and chopped pistachios.
Crème Opéra	Flavour the custard mix with praline and cook in a fancy border mould; turn out, fill the centre with piped cream and decorate with crystallised violets; decorate with macerated strawberries and a veil of spun sugar.
Crème Praline	Add some crushed praline to the custard mix, cook as usual then turn out and decorate with whipped cream.
Crème Régence	Place some macerated finger biscuits in a tall charlotte mould, fill with basic custard and cook as usual; turn out, surround with halves of apricots and brush with apricot glaze.

Crème Sainte-Claire	Cook the basic custard in dariole moulds; turn out, coat with Melba sauce and decorate with whipped cream.
Crème Viennoise	Cook 200g sugar and 1dl water to the caramel stage, add to the basic custard and cook in moulds in the usual way.
Petits Pots de Crème	Make a basic custard with half cream and half milk and cook au bain-marie in special porcelain dishes. The mixture may be flavoured with chocolate or coffee.
Pouding Bohémienne	Add diced crystallised fruit and raisins to apple and pear purée, spread on small pancakes, fold in four and place in a savarin mould; cover with custard and cook as usual; serve coated with cold sauce sabayon.

Flans

Flans may be served either hot or cold and can be made with any of the following fruit fillings: apples, apricots, bananas, cherries, peaches, pears, pineapple, raspberries, rhubarb, strawberries. They can be made by arranging the fruit on a layer of pastry cream in the cooked flan case or on frangipane cream in a raw flan. The paste may be sweet paste or short paste. Other flans include:

Apple Meringue	Fill a baked flan with apple purée, cover with meringue and bake at 230°C for a few minutes to colour.
Alsatian Apple	Bake the flan filled with overlapping slices of eating apples for 30 minutes then fill with a mixture of 100g caster sugar, 2 eggs and 2dl of single cream and cook until set.
Bakewell Tart	Line the flan ring, spread with raspberry jam and fill with frangipane; cover with a lattice work of pastry and bake at 204°C.
Bourdaloue	Fill a baked flan with pastry cream, cover with halves of poached apricots or peaches then add

more pastry cream; sprinkle with flaked almonds and icing sugar and glaze under the salamander.

Chocolate

Mix chocolate-flavoured pastry cream with whisked egg-whites, put into a baked flan case and bake at 180°C for approximately 15 minutes.

Frangipane

This is another name for Bakewell tart.

Lemon

Mix 250g sugar with 3 egg yolks, and 50g cornflour and the grated rind and juice of 2 lemons; add 3dl boiling water, reboil and pour into a baked flan case and bake at 180°C for approximately 15 minutes.

Lemon Meringue

Fill a cooked flan with lemon-pie filling, cover with meringue, dredge with icing sugar and bake at 230°C for a few minutes to colour.

Normande

Line a flan ring with pastry, cover with quarters of apple, fill with raw egg custard and bake at 150°C until cooked and the custard is set.

Orange

Mix 120g caster sugar with 3 yolks and 20g cornflour, add $2\frac{1}{2}$dl hot milk or water and cook slightly; add a little rum and shredded orange zest. Fill into a baked flan ring and cover with poached slices of orange.

Pecan Pie

Mix 4 eggs with 300g brown sugar, 125g butter and 150g each chopped pecan nuts and flour; fill into a partly baked flan case and bake at 180°C for 35 minutes.

Pumpkin

Cook 1kg pumpkin until soft, pass through a sieve and add to 3 eggs mixed with 150g caster sugar, 80g flour, $1\frac{3}{4}$dl cream and the grated rind of 1 lemon; put into a flan case and bake at 200°C for 40 minutes.

Swiss Flan

Beat 3 eggs with 90g caster sugar, add 1dl white wine and place in a flan ring lined with savarin paste; bake at 220°C for 20 minutes, sprinkle with sugar and butter and bake for a further 15 minutes.

Thérèse

Fill the flan with frangipane cream and bake; pipe flowers with meringue, colour and decorate with redcurrant jelly.

Fritters – Beignets

There are six basic kinds of deep-fried fritters:

1. prepared fruit dipped into a batter;
2. yeast dough such as brioche, Viennese or bun dough;
3. chou paste in various shapes; these are known as soufflé fritters;
4. slices of stale savarin sandwiched with jam or fruit, dipped into batter;
5. sweet semolina or sieved condé rice, shaped, sandwiched and egg and crumbed;
6. egg custard set and cut into shapes then egg and crumbed.

Apple	Macerate round slices of apple with sugar, cinnamon, rum and lemon juice; dip into batter, deep fry then glaze with sugar under a salamander.
Apricot	Macerate halves of fruit with sugar and kirsch, dip into batter and deep fry; serve with apricot sauce.
Banana	Coat half or whole bananas with hot pastry cream; allow to cool and dip into batter, deep fry and glaze with sugar. Serve with custard or apricot sauce.
Brochettes de Fruits	Thread pieces of various kinds of fruit on a skewer, dip into batter and deep fry. If desired, the fruit may be dipped into hot pastry cream, sprinkled with butter and crumbs and gently grilled.
Bugnes	Mix 45g butter with 3 eggs, 35g sugar, 25ml rum and the grated rind of 1 lemon or orange, add 270g self-raising flour and mix vigorously, adding more flour if necessary to make a pastry. Allow to chill for 30 minutes then roll out and cut into 6cm strips then into 7cm diamonds. Cut a slit in the centre and pull the two corners through it, deep fry and roll in sugar.
Dauphine	Rounds of yeast dough sandwiched with a fruit purée or pastry cream filling, deep-fried.

Favorite Coat slices of pineapple with frangipane cream containing chopped pistachios; dip into batter, deep fry and glaze with icing sugar.

Grand-Mère Macerate slices of stale brioche in kirsch, spread with fruit purée then dip into batter and deep fry; glaze with icing sugar.

Parisienne Fill chou-paste fritters with rum-flavoured pastry cream and dredge with icing sugar.

Pets de Nonne Deep fry teaspoonsful of chou paste, increasing the heat as they swell up. Drain, sprinkle with sugar and serve with apricot or jam sauce flavoured with rum and lemon juice.

Pineapple Macerate slices of pineapple with kirsch, dip in batter and deep fry; glaze with icing sugar.

Porto Roso Fill chou-paste fritters with raspberry-flavoured cream, brush with jam and coat with grated chocolate.

Régine Sandwich two small thin rounds of stale sponge with apricot jam, sprinkle lightly with cream then dip into batter and deep fry; serve dredged with icing sugar.

Soufflé Deep fry spoonfuls of chou paste at 150°C for approximately 8 minutes, drain and dredge with a mixture of caster sugar and icing sugar; serve with apricot sauce.

Spritzkuchen Pipe spirals of chou paste onto oiled greaseproof paper, deep fry at 150°C for approximately 10 minutes, turning them over; drain, dust with cinnamon sugar and serve with sauce sabayon.

Strawberry Macerate large strawberries with kirsch and sugar, dip in batter and deep fry.

Surprise Fill chou-paste fritters with jam, fruit purée, diced fruit or Crème Saint-Honoré.

Sylvana Soak small emptied brioches with cream, fill with kirsch-flavoured macerated fruits and replace the tops; dip into batter and deep fry.

Suzon Coat round shapes of sieved condé rice with stiff gruit purée, dip into batter and deep fry; serve dredged with caster sugar.

Viennoise   Make yeast dough in the shape of doughnuts with jam or fruit purée fillings; allow to prove, then deep fry.

Fruit Salad – Macédoine de Fruits

This is made by cutting a variety of fruits into neat pieces and keeping them in a sugar syrup flavoured with cinnamon stick, lemon rind and coriander seeds. It may be made with all fresh fruit, all canned fruit or as a mixture of both. It should combine a good range of colours, flavours and textures, be well chilled, and served accompanied by liquid double cream or lightly whipped cream; finger biscuits may be served.

Suitable fruits include apples, apricots, bananas, cherries, guava, grapes, kiwi fruit, melon, mangoes, oranges, peaches, pears, pineapple, raspberries, starfruit and strawberries; the surface can be arranged in a neat pattern. Fruit salad can be flavoured with a liqueur such as curaçao, kirsch or maraschino, or with a few drops of Angostura bitters.

It is advisable to use the French name as given above as to put Salade de Fruits on the menu gives the connotation of it being some fruit on lettuce to serve as a side salad.

Fruit Fools

These are made by adding half its volume of whipped cream to a firm purée of raw or cooked fruit, adding colouring if necessary. Or cook 1kg fruit in an oven with 300g sugar, blend to a purée and mix with a cooked custard made with 6dl double cream thickened with 7 yolks of egg and 25g cornflour.

Suitable fruits include apple, apricot, gooseberry, raspberry, rhubarb and strawberry.

545

The fool is allowed to set in glass bowls then decorated with whipped cream and some of the fruit used as the base. Any kind of sweet dry biscuit may be served.

Stewed Fruits – Compotes

This wide range of sweets is made by cooking prepared fresh fruit or dried fruit in stock syrup without letting them boil so that they do not lose their shape. It is often necessary to cover the fruit with a piece of greaseproof paper or a lid to prevent it floating to the surface. It is usually allowed to become cold before serving and the most suitable accompaniment is liquid fresh cream.

Stock syrup is made by boiling 1 litre water with 750g sugar and the juice of 2 lemons. The rind of the lemons and some cinnamon stick or coriander seeds may be used to give additional flavour.

The following fruits are most suitable for stewing – apples, apricots, babaco, blackcurrants, cherries, gooseberries, guava, pears, kumquats, loquats, pears, plums, raspberries, redcurrants, rhubarb, strawberries. Dried fruits such as figs and prunes may also be served as compotes after being soaked and cooked. Mixed dried fruit that includes apple rings, halves of apricots, peaches and pears may be soaked, poached and served as fruit salad or compote.

Stewed fruits, in particular figs and prunes, are often featured on the full breakfast menu as a first course, but without cream.

In the case of soft fruit it is sufficient to place them into warm syrup and leave for a while without cooking them.

Fruit Crumbles

These are made by placing alternate layers of raw prepared fruit and sugar into pie-dishes and covering with a mixture of 2 parts flour to 1 part each of butter and sugar lightly rubbed together. The crumble is lightly pressed or smoothed with the blade of a knife to

level it, then baked. All the fruits used for making pies are suitable
for crumbles and canned or stewed fruits may also be used. Serve
hot with custard.

Fruit Pies

These are made with alternate layers of raw prepared fruit and
sugar in pie dishes, piled in a dome-shape, covered with short
pastry or puff pastry, brushed with water or milk and sprinkled with
caster sugar before baking at 215°C for approximately 15 minutes,
then at 190°C for a further 30 to 40 minutes. Individual or
multi-portion pie-dishes may be used.

It is generally accepted that fruit pies are made without decoration, to distinguish them from meat pies which are decorated with
leaves cut from pastry.

Serve with cream or custard.

Suitable fruits include apple, apricot, blackberry and apple,
blackcurrant and apple, cherries, damsons, gooseberries, plums
and rhubarb.

Sweets made with Fruit – Hot

This section includes the most popular hot sweets made with fruit
but only those that do not fit into the sections of Charlottes,
Croûtes, Flambés, Fritters, Meringued sweets, Pancakes, Pies and
the various rice sweets such as Condés, Créoles and Impératrices.

Apples – Pommes

Apple Amber Place cooked sliced apples in a pie-dish, cover
with meringue and colour in the oven.

Andalusia Poach, place on a bed of condé rice, cover and
decorate with meringue and bake.

Baked Remove core, fill with sugar and butter and bake
until soft but still retaining the original shape.

Bonne-Femme   This is the French name for baked apple, which is Pomme Bonne-Femme.

Bourdaloue   Poach whole, place in a dish and cover with pastry cream containing crushed macaroons; sprinkle with melted butter and glaze in the oven.

Brissac   Poach in sweet white wine, arrange in a flan case on a layer of frangipane containing crushed macaroons; cover with ordinary frangipane, sprinkle with macaroons and butter and glaze.

Brown Betty   Arrange layers of sliced apple and fried white breadcrumbs in a pie-dish, sprinkle with sugar, cinnamon and nutmeg and bake for 35–40 minutes.

Châtelaine   Bake the apples then fill the centre with diced glacé cherries mixed with apricot purée; cover with frangipane cream, sprinkle with macaroons and butter and glaze in a hot oven.

Chevreuse   Arrange poached quarters of apples on a layer of semolina pudding containing diced crystallised fruits and apricot purée; cover with another layer of semolina and pipe in a dome shape with meringue. Glaze then decorate with pink and white quarters of apple, a small whole pink apple and elongated diamonds of angelica.

Demidoff   Poach hollowed-out apples and fill with apple soufflé mixture; bake in the oven and serve with liquid cream.

Douillons Normande   This is the French name for baked apple dumplings.

Dumpling   Peel and remove the core, envelop in short paste, decorate, egg-wash and bake; serve with custard sauce.

Eve's Pudding   (a) Place cooked sliced apple in a pie-dish, cover with vanilla soufflé mixture and bake in a hot oven; *or*

(b) cover cooked sliced apple with sponge-cake mixture and bake; serve with custard sauce.

Gratinées   Arrange poached quarters of apple on a layer of stiff apple purée, cover with thin royal icing and

	bake until the icing is dry and lightly coloured.
Irene	Hollow out halves of poached apples, fill with a little apple purée and a ball of vanilla ice cream containing some plum purée; cover with kirsch-flavoured meringue and colour quickly in the oven.
Marie-Stuart	Hollow out poached apples, fill with pastry cream, envelop in puff pastry and bake; serve with custard.
Mariette	Arrange poached halves of apple on a layer of chestnut purée and coat with rum-flavoured apricot sauce.
Moscovite	Hollow out some apples, poach them, then fill one-third full with apple purée; cover with kummel-flavoured apple soufflé mixture and bake for 20 minutes.
Parisienne	Mould condé rice in a dome shape on a kirsch-sprinkled round of genoise; cover with poached halves of apple, decorate with meringue and colour in the oven. Coat the fruit with apricot glaze and decorate with glacé cherries.
Portugaise	Hollow out some apples, poach and fill with frangipane containing grated orange zest, crushed macaroons and macerated dried fruit; arrange on a layer of semolina pudding, reheat and cover with redcurrant jelly containing shredded orange zest.
Rabotte	This is another name for a baked apple dumpling (rabotte de pomme).

Apricots – Abricots

Bourdaloue	Fill a baked flan case with a layer each of frangipane containing crushed macaroons, poached halves of apricots and more frangipane; sprinkle with melted butter and crushed macaroons and glaze in a hot oven.
Colbert	Sandwich two halves of apricots with condé rice mixture; egg and crumb and deep fry; pierce with a stem of angelica and serve with kirsch-flavoured apricot sauce.

Cussy Spread macaroons with diced mixed fruit bound with apricot purée, place a poached half apricot on each and cover with meringue; dry in a moderate oven and serve with kirsch-flavoured apricot sauce.

Gratinés Arrange poached halves of apricots on a layer of either apple purée or semolina pudding; cover with icing made with egg whites, icing sugar and ground almonds, dredge with icing sugar and colour in a moderate oven.

Bananas – Bananes

Bourdaloue Poach whole, arrange on a layer of frangipane containing crushed macaroons and cover with more frangipane; sprinkle with melted butter and crushed macaroons and glaze in a hot oven.

Créole Poach in rum syrup and place on a layer of condé rice mixture; sprinkle with crushed macaroons and melted butter and glaze in a hot oven. Serve with rum-flavoured apricot sauce.

Norvégienne Fill half skins with banana ice cream, cover with rum-flavoured meringue and glaze quickly in a hot oven, placing them in a tray of crushed ice.

Russe Fill half skins with kummel-flavoured banana soufflé mixture and bake until risen.

Soufflé Fill half skins with banana soufflé mixture and bake in the oven for approximately 6 minutes.

Cherries – Cerises

Clafouti Placed stoned cherries in a greased dish, cover with batter made with 6 yolks, 6dl milk, 300g flour, sugar and kirsch, adding 4 stiffly beaten whites; bake for 45 minutes.

Jubilée Cover cooked stoned cherries with thickened cherry sauce or melted redcurrant jelly; pour in some warm kirsch, set it alight when about to serve and accompany with a dish of scoops of vanilla ice cream.

Valéria   Place balls of vanilla ice cream in tartlet cases and quickly cover with meringue italienne; insert a few stoned cherries cooked in red wine, place the dish in a tray of crushed ice and colour quickly in a hot oven. Coat the cherries with redcurrant jelly and sprinkle with chopped pistachios.

Grapefruit – Pamplemousse

Prepared halves of grapefruit can be served hot as a first course or as a sweet by sprinkling with sherry or a liqueur, some sugar and melted butter and browning under a salamander.

Oranges and tangerines – oranges et mandarines

Infante   Fill emptied fruit with strawberry ice cream, cover with soufflé mixture and cook quickly in a hot oven, standing them in a tray of ice.

Javanese   Fill emptied fruit with orange ice cream containing diced ginger; arrange orange segments on top, cover with meringue and colour quickly in the oven.

Norvégienne   Fill emptied fruit skins with orange ice cream containing diced pineapple; cover with rum-flavoured meringue and colour quickly in the oven.

Palikare   Fill emptied fruit with condé rice mixture, arrange on a pyramid of rice, Glaze with orange syrup and decorate with segments of orange skin filled with jelly.

Surprise   Fill emptied fruit with orange or mandarin soufflé mixture and cook in the usual way; serve immediately.

These fruits can also be peeled and poached in syrup flavoured with Grand Marnier and served hot or cold.

Peaches and nectarines – pêches et brugnons

Andalouse   Arrange poached halves on a layer of condé rice mixture; cover with meringue, brown in the oven and serve with apricot sauce.

Bourdaloue   Arrange poached halves of fruit in a cooked flan case, cover with pastry cream containing crushed macaroons, sprinkle with more macaroons and melted butter and glaze in the oven.

Colbert   Sandwich two poached halves with condé rice mixture, egg and crumb and deep fry; insert an angelica stalk and serve with kirsch-flavoured apricot sauce.

Cussy   Place a poached half of peach on a macaroon spread with diced fruit mixed with apricot purée, cover with meringue italienne and dry in the oven; serve with apricot sauce flavoured with kirsch.

Gratinées   Place poached halves of fruit on a bed of either stewed apple or semolina pudding, cover with almond-flavoured royal icing and colour in the oven.

Marie   Sandwich two halves of ripe fruit with rum-flavoured marzipan, enclose in puff pastry, egg-wash and bake. Serve with sauce anglaise.

Maintenon   Cut a sponge baked in a dome mould into thin slices, spread with frangipane containing diced crystallised fruit and chopped almonds and re-form it; cover with meringue italienne, colour in the oven and surround with poached halves of peaches.

Parisienne   Arrange poached halves of fruit on a slice of sponge cake coated with condé rice mixture; cover with meringue, decorate with glacé cherries and angelica and glaze in the oven. Serve with apricot sauce.

Vanille   Serve poached halves of peaches in thickened vanilla syrup garnished with slices of brioche cut in the shape of a cockscomb, spread with almond-flavoured icing and dried in the oven.

Pears – Poires

Bourdaloue   Arrange poached halves of pear in a baked flan case; cover with frangipane, sprinkle with crushed macaroons and melted butter and glaze in the oven.

Colbert   Sandwich two small halves of poached pear with condé rice mixture; egg and crumb, deep fry and serve with apricot sauce.

Gratinées   Cover poached halves of pears arranged on a layer of semolina pudding with almond-flavoured royal icing and colour in the oven.

Louise   Fill emptied poached pears with frangipane, dip into batter and deep fry; serve with apricot sauce.

Parisienne   Arrange poached halves of pear on a slice of sponge cake spread in a dome shape with condé rice mixture; pipe with meringue, decorate with glacé cherries and angelica and colour in the oven; finish by brushing the pears with apricot syrup.

Saint-George   Arrange poached halves of pear on slices of brioche, cover with meringue and colour in a hot oven.

Sultane   Place a border of sponge on a pastry base, cover it with meringue and colour in the oven; fill the centre in a dome shape with condé rice with added frangipane and chopped pistachios; cover with poached halves of pears and sprinkle with pistachios. Serve with thickened almond-flavoured syrup.

Valencienne   Fill a hollowed-out brioche baked in a charlotte mould with cooked sliced pears mixed with apricot purée and vanilla liqueur; cover with the lid, brush all over with apricot and decorate with crystallised fruit. Serve hot with kirsch-flavoured sauce.

Pineapple – ananas

Cussy   Spread macaroons with diced fruit mixed with apricot purée, cover with small pineapple rings then with meringue; dry in a moderate oven and serve with kirsch-flavoured apricot sauce.

Sweets made with Fruit – Cold

The sweets in this section are in addition to those in the sections of Bande, Compotes, Condés, Créoles, Flans, Fools, Impératrices and Suédoises. It includes some that are made using ice cream that do not come into the categories of bombes and coupes.

Apples – pommes

Carignan   Hollow out poached apples, fill with chocolate ice cream and place on a round piece of genoise which has been previously dipped in white fondant.

Cévenole   Hollow out poached apples and pipe with creamed chestnut purée mixed with whipped cream.

Dauphin   Arrange poached apples on condé rice and coat with kirsch-flavoured apricot glaze.

Félicia   Place poached halves of apple on a layer of crème viennoise, decorate with whipped cream and sprinkle with crushed praline.

Florentine   Fill the centre of whole poached apples with condé rice, mask with apricot glaze and arrange on a bed of chestnut purée; sprinkle with chopped pistachios.

Josephine   Hollow out poached apples and fill with pistachio-flavoured whipped cream; arrange on a layer of riz Impératrice and coat with raspberry purée.

Norvégienne Hollow out poached apples; fill with a fruit water-ice, cover with rum-flavoured meringue and colour quickly in the oven. Serve cold.

Petit-Duc Poach quarters of apple, coat with the thickened cooking liquid flavoured with redcurrant jelly and arrange on a layer of cold custard sauce flavoured with arrack and lightened with whipped cream.

Richelieu Arrange poached quarters of apple in a border of semolina pudding, coat with frangipane mixed with crushed macaroon and whipped cream, then decorate with whipped cream. Serve with cold kirsch-flavoured apricot sauce.

Royale Dry small poached apples and coat with redcurrant jelly; place each in a tartlet filled with plain blancmange.

Snow Mix stiffly beaten egg-whites with firm apple purée and fill into glass dishes.

Apricots – abricots

Aurora Arrange poached halves of apricot on a layer of strawberry mousse and decorate with whipped cream.

Carmen Arrange poached apricots in a dish, sprinkle with maraschino and decorate with whipped cream; sprinkle with crushed macaroons.

Dreux Fill hollowed small brioches with blancmange, place poached halves of apricot on top and cover with kirsch-flavoured apricot glaze.

Duchesse Place a poached half of apricot in a deep tartlet filled and cooked with egg-custard mix; coat with apricot glaze and decorate with whipped cream, glacé cherries and angelica.

Fémina Poach apricot halves in curaçao syrup; serve on a layer of orange ice and decorate with whipped cream.

Marquise Sandwich two halves of poached apricots with frangipane, place on a layer of condé rice and cover with Melba sauce; decorate with pink coloured whipped cream.

Mireille	Macerate halves of ripe apricots in kirsch and sugar; serve very cold decorated with whipped cream and crystallised violets and jasmine; the apricot kernels may be added.
Négus	Place poached halves of apricots on a layer of chocolate ice cream, coat with apricot sauce and decorate with whipped cream.
Parisienne	Sandwich two halves of poached apricots around a ball of vanilla ice cream, place on a round macaroon and decorate with a cone of whipped cream; sprinkle with crushed praline.
Royale	Set poached halves of apricots in a funnel mould with kirsch jelly and turn out onto a border of genoise which has been brushed with hot red-currant jelly and sprinkled with chopped pistachios; fill the centre with diced anisette-flavoured jelly coloured pink.
Sultane	Place halves of poached apricots on a border of genoise which has been glazed with meringue; fill the centre with condé rice mixture and sprinkle with chopped pistachios; serve with a sauceboat of thickened sweet almond milk.

Bananas – *bananes*

Copacabana	Poach small bananas in rum-flavoured syrup, place on a bed of vanilla ice cream and cover with chocolate sauce; sprinkle with flaked almonds.
Hôtelière	Macerate sliced bananas with kirsch, maraschino and sugar and serve very cold with double cream.
Orientale	Poach bananas in rosewater stock syrup; arrange on a layer of almond ice cream, cover with cold custard sauce, decorate with whipped cream and sprinkle with toasted almonds.
Split	Cut bananas in half lengthways, place on a long dish with vanilla ice cream and decorate with whipped cream.

Trédern	Brush poached or raw bananas with apricot glaze, decorate with crystallised fruit and place on the half skins filled with banana bavarois.

Cherries – cerises

au Claret	Poach the cherries in sweetened red wine flavoured with cinnamon; reduce and thicken the liquid with redcurrant jelly, pour over the cherries and serve very cold.
Dubarry	Cover a cooked cherry flan with whipped cream containing crushed macaroons and decorate with ordinary and pink whipped cream.
Flan Danoise	Make a cherry flan with frangipane; when cooked brush with redcurrant jelly and glaze with rum-flavoured water icing.
Frascati	Poach stoned cherries in kirsch syrup and serve decorated with whipped cream.

Figs – figues

Carlton	Cover peeled halves of fresh figs with a sauce made of one part strawberry purée to two parts whipped cream.
Crème	Macerate halves of fresh figs, with noyau liqueur and cover with vanilla-flavoured whipped cream.

Melon – melon

Créole	Fill an emptied melon with flesh scooped out with a spoon cutter and mixed with small strawberries, kirsch, maraschino and sugar.
Frappé	Fill an emptied melon with layers of melon granité and the macerated flesh.
Orientale	Fill an emptied melon with layers of the diced melon and wild strawberries.
Scheherazade	Balls of melon, raspberries, strawberries, diced pineapple, peach and banana all macerated in arrack and replaced in the melon skin.

en Surprise	Fill an emptied melon with fruit salad mixed with raspberry purée, flavoured with kirsch.
au Vin	Cut off the top, remove the seeds and then add sherry, port, Madeira or Marsala and sugar; serve by scooping out the flesh and adding some of the wine.

Oranges and tangerines – oranges et mandarines

Almina	Fill emptied skins with bavarois containing crushed crystallised violets and ladies fingers soaked in maraschino; when set replace the top.
Caramel	Peel and cook whole or in slices in caramel syrup and serve with thick cream.
Compote	Peel the fruit and cut into segments or slices, place into a lukewarm syrup at 36° Baume and allow to cool.
Crème	Fill the emptied skins with tangerine bavarois made with additional cream and cover with the tops.
Givrées	Fill the emptied skins with orange or tangerine ice cream, replace the tops, spray with water and place in the deep freeze until rimed with frost.
Ilona	Fill the emptied fruit with chocolate ice cream containing diced ginger, place segments of fruit on top and coat with rum-flavoured apricot glaze; decorate with whipped cream and sprinkle with crushed praline.
Madrilène	Fill the emptied fruit with apricot ice cream, decorate with whipped cream and arrange some macerated segments on top; serve with apricot sauce.
en Surprise	Fill the emptied skins with either jelly or ice cream of the appropriate flavour; cover with meringue, place on a bed of crushed ice and colour in a hot oven; decorate with a leaf made of pulled sugar.
Palikare	Fill emptied fruit in a dome-shape with saffron-coloured rice mixture; arrange the segments on a mound of conde ricé, coat with apricot glaze and surround with the filled fruit.

Peaches and nectarines – pêches et brugnons

Adrienne
Place a ball of wild-strawberry ice-cream in a dish, place a flat meringue on top and arrange a whole peeled peach on it; coat with curaçao mousse at setting point, cover with a veil of spun sugar and sprinkle with crystallised rose petals.

Aiglon
Arrange poached peaches on vanilla ice cream, sprinkle with crystallised violets and put a veil of spun sugar on top; serve on an eagle sculpted from a block of ice.

Alexandra
Arrange poached peaches on vanilla ice cream, coat with purée of strawberries and sprinkle with crystallised rose petals; veil with spun sugar.

Aurore
Arrange poached peaches on a layer of strawberry mousse and coat with curaçao-flavoured cold sabayon.

Cardinal
Arrange poached peaches on a layer of vanilla ice cream, coat with kirsch-flavoured raspberry purée and sprinkle with shredded almonds.

Dame-Blanche
Arrange thin slices of macerated pineapple on a layer of vanilla ice cream; place a poached peach on top and decorate with whipped cream.

Eugénie
Skin and stone the fruit and place in a dish with some wild strawberries, sprinkle with maraschino and kirsch and coat with cold champagne-flavoured sabayon.

Isabelle
Sprinkle halves of raw peaches or nectarines with sugar and red Rhône wine and allow to macerate; serve with vanilla ice cream.

Melba
Arrange a poached peach on a layer of vanilla ice cream and coat with raspberry purée or Melba sauce.

Marie-Louise
Fill a hollowed-out deep sponge with sliced peaches mixed with strawberry purée, cover with meringue and glaze; surround with half slices of pineapple, strawberries and crescents of sponge cake glazed with fondant.

Mistral
Sprinkle skinned and stoned fruit with sugar and coat with strawberry purée; decorate with whole skinned almonds and whipped cream.

Monte Carlo	Arrange poached halves of peaches or nectarines on peach ice cream and coat with purée of raspberries.
Montreuil	Arrange poached fruit on a layer of condé rice and coat with thickened peach syrup.
Nelusko	Arrange poached fruit on a layer of condé rice and coat with cold chocolate sauce.
Orientale	Arrange poached fruit on a layer of vanilla ice cream, cover with whipped cream and decorate by piping with redcurrant jelly; place a veil of spun sugar on top.
Petit-Duc	Arrange slices of macerated pineapple on a layer of vanilla ice cream; place poached halves of peaches on top and coat with redcurrant jelly.
Portugaise	Arrange halves of fruit on condé rice containing diced pineapple; coat with kirsch-flavoured apricot sauce and sprinkle with toasted shredded almonds.
Rose-Chéri	Arrange poached fruit on a layer of pineapple ice-cream, coat with creamed champagne-flavoured sabayon and sprinkle with crystallised rose petals.
Rose-Pompon	Remove the stones from poached fruit and remould with a ball of vanilla ice cream; place on a layer of raspberry ripple ice cream, decorate with praline-flavoured whipped cream and cover with a veil of spun sugar.
Sultane	Arrange poached fruit on a layer of pistachio ice cream, coat with rose-flavoured syrup and cover with a veil of spun sugar.
Trianon	Arrange peeled fruit on a border of vanilla mousse containing broken macaroons which have been sprinkled with noyau liqueur, and coat with purée of wild strawberries.
Vanderbilt	Line a border mould with champagne jelly, when set arrange sliced peaches inside and fill with jelly flavoured with goldwasser liqueur; turn out and fill the centre with whipped cream.
Wilhelmine	Place halves of poached fruit on tartlets filled with macerated wild strawberries, cover with

cold crème anglaise and sprinkle with chopped pistachios.

Pears – poires

Alma	Poach in port-flavoured syrup and serve in the syrup, sprinkle with praline and accompany with whipped cream.
Andalusia	Arrange poached halves on condé rice, cover with pink meringue and colour in a hot oven; serve with pineapple sauce.
Archiduc	Arrange poached halves on a layer of pineapple ice cream and cover with strawberry purée.
Aremburg	Place poached cored pears filled with redcurrant jelly on a layer of vanilla ice cream, cover with crème anglaise and sprinkle with chopped pistachios and crystallised violets.
Belle Hélène	Place a poached half of pear on a ball of vanilla ice cream, coat with hot chocolate sauce and decorate with whipped cream. The sauce may be served separately.
Cardinale	Arrange poached pears on a layer of vanilla ice cream, coat with kirsch-flavoured raspberry purée and sprinkle with shredded almonds.
Casanova	Place poached halves of pears on a layer of raspberry ice cream, decorate with whipped cream and sprinkle with grated chocolate.
Félicia	Arrange poached quarters inside a border mould of crème viennoise, cover in a pyramid shape with whipped cream and surround with half pears cooked pink; sprinkle with crystallised rose petals.
Florentine	Make a border mould of vanilla bavarois with the addition of semolina pudding; fill with poached halves of pear and coat with vanilla-flavoured apricot purée.
Mariette	Place poached pears on a layer of chestnut purée and coat with rum-flavoured apricot sauce.
Mary Garden	Arrange poached pears on Melba sauce containing some cooked stoned cherries.

Mireille Sprinkle peeled ripe pears with sugar, coat with purée of wild strawberries and decorate with almonds, crystallised violets and crystallised jasmine.

Montrose Arrange poached pears on a layer of chocolate ice cream, coat with apricot sauce and decorate with whipped cream.

Pralinées Cover poached pears with frangipane cream, garnish with spoonfuls of whipped cream and sprinkle with praline; serve with hot or cold chocolate sauce.

Religieuse Cover poached pears with the thickened cooking syrup, coloured pink and flavoured with rum.

Richelieu Build poached quarters inside a mould of semolina flamri, coat with creamed frangipane containing crushed macaroons, decorate with whipped cream and serve with kirsch-flavoured apricot sauce (see under Hot Milk Puddings for Flamri).

Trocadéro Place diced pear and finger biscuits in glasses, sprinkle with curaçao then pipe whipped cream on top; sprinkle with grated chocolate and praline.

Pineapple – ananas

Caroline Coat a border sponge with rum fondant, fill the centre with condé rice and garnish with slices of pineapple; mask with apricot sauce.

Georgette Fill an emptied pineapple with the diced flesh mixed into pineapple mousse and allow to set; replace the top with the leaves still attached.

Majestic Fill an emptied pineapple with the diced flesh added to vanilla bavarois and replace the top.

Ninon Line a soufflé dish with vanilla ice cream in the form of a cone; arrange thin slices of pineapple around it to come above the edge, fill with wild strawberries and cover with raspberry purée; serve sprinkled with chopped pistachios.

Orléans	Arrange macerated slices of pineapple on condé rice and decorate with whipped cream, glacé cherries and angelica; serve surrounded with kirsch-flavoured apricot sauce.
Princesse	Place a macerated slice of pineapple on a round of sponge cake, add a scoop of strawberry ice and decorate with whipped cream and small strawberries.
Royale	Fill an emptied pineapple with fruit salad made with some of the flesh and replace the top; surround with poached peaches and macerated strawberries.
Savoie	Place a half of peach on a slice of pineapple, arrange on a layer of condé rice, then coat with strawberry purée and decorate with whipped cream.
Virginie	Fill an emptied pineapple with the diced flesh and some wild strawberries mixed into strawberry bavarois; replace the top.

Raspberries – framboises

Anita	Sandwich the fruit between layers of vanilla and pineapple ice cream, cover with purée of raspberries and sprinkle with chopped pistachios.
Erika	Place raspberries macerated with apricot brandy on a layer of blancmange; cover with redcurrant jelly, sprinkle with almonds and serve with cream.
Ninette	Arrange on a layer of orange ice cream, cover with orange sabayon and sprinkle with chopped pistachios.
Summer Pudding	Line a mould with slices of stale bread, fill with soft fruit stewed in very little syrup; cover with more bread, weigh down and chill overnight. Serve with cream, ice cream or yoghurt. Black or redcurrants may be used.

In addition to the above most of the following dishes can be made using raspberries instead of strawberries.

Strawberries – *fraises*

Cardinal	Coat large cold strawberries with Melba sauce or raspberry purée and sprinkle with shredded almonds.
Cecil	Macerate the strawberries with orange and lemon juice and sugar and serve covered with whipped cream.
Créole	Arrange slices of macerated pineapple in a circle, fill the centre with macerated strawberries and diced pineapple and sprinkle with kirsch syrup.
au Champagne	Macerate in champagne and cover with champagne sorbet.
Chantilly	This is fresh strawberries served with whipped cream.
Eton Mess	Mash strawberries with a fork whilst mixing in some slightly whipped cream and sugar; decorate with small whole strawberries.
Fémina	Macerate strawberries with Grand Marniér then arrange on a layer of orange ice cream made with Grand Marnier.
Lerina	Fill an emptied melon with wild strawberries and pieces of melon macerated with Lerina liqueur.
Marguerite	Add wild strawberries to pomegranate sorbet and decorate with whipped cream flavoured with maraschino.
Marquise	Place a layer of wild strawberry sauce mixed with cream in a dish and cover with macerated strawberries rolled in sugar.
Melba	Arrange strawberries on top of a layer of vanilla ice cream and coat with fresh raspberry purée or Melba sauce.
Monte Carlo	Place meringue nests around a dome-shaped curaçao mousse, fill each with creamed strawberry purée and small strawberries; coat the mousse with the same purée, surmount it and each meringue with a veil of spun sugar and sprinkle with crystallised violets.

Nina	Mix equal amounts of wild strawberries and pineapple sorbet, place in a dish and decorate with whipped cream coloured with raspberry juice.
Ninon	Line the inside of a dish with vanilla ice cream and fill the centre with wild strawberries mixed with raspberry purée; surround with strawberries and slices of pineapple and sprinkle with chopped pistachios.
Parisienne	Cover strawberries, macerated in lemon juice and maraschino, with whipped cream mixed with raspberry juice.
Renaissance	Macerate with kümmel, place on a layer of pineapple mousse and cover with kirsch-flavoured custard; decorate with whipped cream.
Rêve de Bébé	Stick a square of genoise to a baked pastry base, coat with pink fondant and decorate with white royal icing and some strawberries; stand on it a pineapple which has been filled with layers of macerated pineapple, wild strawberries and whipped cream.
Ritz	Cover the fruit with wild strawberry purée mixed with whipped cream and coloured with Melba sauce.
Romanoff	Macerate with orange juice and curaçao and serve covered with whipped cream, piped with a fancy tube.
Sarah Bernhardt	Macerate with brandy and curaçao, place on a layer of pineapple ice cream and cover with curaçao mousse.
Shortcake	This can be either a shortbread base or a genoise sponge, garnished with cream and strawberries.
Victoria	Cover strawberries with curaçao syrup and when cold serve with whipped cream containing chopped pineapple.
Wilhelmina	Macerate the fruit with orange juice and kirsch and serve accompanied by whipped cream.
Zelma Kuntz	Cover strawberries with a mixture of cream and raspberry purée, decorate with the same cream and sprinkle with praline.

565

Gâteaux

The various kinds of gâteaux in the repertoire add great interest and variety to the sweet trolley which is often presented instead of the menu, for a customer to choose his sweet. The other main use is as one of the sweets at a buffet reception where their decorative appearance can make the table look very attractive. Slices of gâteaux are served for afternoon tea, to be eaten with a cake fork.

There are several categories of gâteaux, being made from genoise sponge, chou pastry, meringue, yeast or from a pastry base. The following are those most commonly used.

Gâteaux made with genoise and sponge

Whisk 8 eggs and 4 yolks with 200g caster sugar to the ribbon stage, fold in 250g soft flour then 100g cool melted butter; bake at 193°C, cover and leave for 24 hours before using. A liqueur may be sprinkled over it.

Alcazar Almond-flavoured genoise, pipe criss-cross with meringue and bake.

Aboukir Sandwich with chestnut butter-cream, coat with apricot glaze, cover with coffee fondant and decorate with pistachios.

Alexandra Almond and chocolate genoise, coat with chocolate fondant (no decoration).

Ambroisie Genoise made with diced crystallised fruit; coat with kirsch fondant and decorate with crystallised fruit.

Anniversaire Sandwich with jam and butter-cream, coat with red and white fondant and inscribe with the person's name and message, as appropriate.

Black Forest (Schwarzwalder Kirschtorte) Bake a sponge cake in a torten tin using 400g sugar, 5 yolks and 4 eggs then 200g cornflour, 150g soft flour and 50g cocoa sieved together and 200g cool melted butter. Bake at 194°C for approximately 25 minutes then split into three; layer with kirsch, black-cherry conserve and cream and coat the whole with cream; cover with chocolate shavings and decorate with cream.

Bourdaloue Sandwich with kirsch pastry cream, brush with apricot glaze and coat with chocolate fondant.

Bûche de Noël Cover a Swiss roll with coffee butter-cream and decorate as a yule log.

Champignons Stick langues de chat around the genoise to represent a basket and fill the centre with small mushrooms made with meringue.

Damier Sandwich a square genoise with praline butter-cream, mark the top into 36 squares as a chessboard and fill each with coffee or white fondant.

Faidherbe Sandwich and coat completely with rum butter-cream, and decorate with glacé fruits.

Lutetia Sandwich with hazelnut butter-cream, cover with chocolate fondant and decorate by piping with purée of chestnuts.

Marrons Bake a genoise in a savarin mould and sprinkle with rum syrup; cover with chestnut purée pressed through a 3mm plain tube; fill the centre with whipped cream containing broken meringue.

Mascotte Sandwich and coat completely with praline butter-cream and decorate with toasted nibbed almonds.

Mocha Sandwich and coat completely with coffee butter-cream and write the name 'Mocha' on top with coffee fondant.

Nougatine Sandwich and coat with coffee butter-cream, decorate with triangles of nougat and surround the side with crushed nougat.

Parisienne Sandwich with whipped cream, coat all over with more cream and cover with finely crushed macaroons; pipe with whipped cream and decorate with palets de dames. (See Petits Fours.)

Printanière Sandwich with plain butter-cream and cover the top completely with small stars of pink, natural, green and chocolate butter creams piped with a small fancy tube.

Sweet dishes

Orange	Sandwich an orange-flavoured genoise with curaçao-flavoured whipped cream; coat all over with orange-coloured fondant and decorate with orange segments dipped in sugar syrup cooked to 154°C.
Ratafia	Sandwich and coat completely with praline butter-cream and cover the top and sides with very small ratafia biscuits.
Regent	Sandwich with chestnut butter-cream, brush with apricot glaze and coat with rum fondant; decorate with piped chestnut purée.
Saint-Louis	Sandwich with chocolate butter-cream, brush with apricot glaze and cover with toasted coconut.
Triomphe	Sandwich an almond-flavoured genoise with almond butter-cream, cover the sides with toasted almonds and decorate with whole almonds.
Valencia	Sandwich an orange-flavoured genoise with apricot jam and cover with orange and lemon fondant in eight alternative sections.
Zuppa Inglese	Bake a genoise in a dome-shaped mould; when stale cut into slices, sprinkle with a liqueur, spread with jam and sandwich with frangipane. Coat the outside with frangipane then cover with meringue and glaze in a hot oven.

Gâteaux made with chou paste

Croquem-bouche	Arrange rows of cream buns filled with apricot jam, in order of ascending size around a cardboard cone, sticking them to each other with cooked sugar; remove the card, fill the centre with cream and fruit and invert onto a nougat base.
Paris-Brest	Pipe out a thick circle of chou paste and sprinkle with shredded almonds and sugar; when baked and dry cut open and fill with praline pastry cream; sprinkle with icing sugar.

Polka	Prepare a base of short pastry 22cm in diameter with a circle of chou paste around; when baked, fill the centre in a dome shape with pastry cream and sprinkle with sugar; brand criss-cross with a red-hot poker.
Religieuse	Fill a baked flan case with crème Saint-Honoré and cover with two triangular chocolate and two coffee éclairs and a chocolate-coated chou bun in the centre; decorate with whipped cream.
Saint-Honoré	Prepare a round of puff pastry 22cm in diameter and 20 small chou buns; when baked and dry fill the centre and the buns with St-Honoré cream, glaze the buns with cooked sugar and stick them around the edge of the gateau.

Gâteaux made with meringue

Daquoise	Add toasted hazelnuts and ground almonds with a little cornflour to the meringue; spread in two layers 25cm in diameter and bake at 177°C for 25 minutes; sandwich with butter-cream, dust with icing sugar and decorate with whipped cream.
Diane	Sandwich four thin meringue discs with chocolate butter-cream, cover with ganache and decorate with whipped cream.
Monte Carlo	Sandwich two baked discs of meringue 20cm in diameter, with whipped cream and grated chocolate, coat with chocolate butter-cream and decorate with crystallised violets.
Patricien	Sandwich two almond-flavoured meringue discs with vanilla butter-cream and dredge with icing sugar.
Progrès	Sandwich two almond-flavoured meringue discs with praline and chocolate butter-cream, coat the sides with toasted chopped almonds and pipe the name 'Progres' on top with chocolate fondant.

See also under 'Meringue Sweets'

Gâteaux made from puff pastry

d'Artois

Roll puff pastry to 25cm × 12cm, spread with jam and pastry cream then cover with a top layer of pastry; egg-wash, score with a knife and bake in a hot oven; serve cut into slices 4cm long.

Champigny

Spread a square piece of pastry with apricot jam, then with frangipane; cover with another piece of puff pastry, seal, egg-wash and mark in squares; bake in a hot oven and dredge with icing sugar.

Conversation

Spread a round of puff pastry with frangipane, cover with a top layer of pastry and spread this with royal icing; decorate with a trellis work of pastry and bake in a hot oven.

Jalousie aux Amandes

Spread a strip of puff pastry, 10cm wide, with redcurrant jam then with frangipane; cover with a top layer of pastry which has been slashed to 1cm from the edges at 4mm intervals, egg-wash and bake in a hot oven; brush the sides with apricot jam and coat with toasted almonds. A jalousie may be made with an apple, mincemeat or jam filling, giving the name to identify the filling.

Millefeuilles

Sandwich three rounds of cooked puff pastry, 25cm each in diameter, with jam and pastry cream pressing them together; brush the top with apricot glaze, spread with white fondant and feather it with lines of red and yellow jam, and coffee and chocolate fondant.

Pithivier

Spread a round of puff pastry, 25cm in diameter, with jam then with frangipane; cover with a top piece of pastry, egg-wash, score with a point of a knife and bake; dredge with icing sugar and return to the oven to glaze.

Saint-Honoré

See under Gâteaux made with chou paste.

Tom Pouce

Sandwich two lengths of cooked puff pastry, each 30cm × 15cm, with apricot jam then with a thick layer of bavarois; cover the top pastry

with white fondant and feather as for millefeuilles, then coat the sides with toasted nuts.
Serve cut into slices 6cm long.

Sweets made with Impératrice Rice

This mixture is made by adding an equal quantity of vanilla or
kirsch-flavoured bavarois to a basic condé rice mix, together with
diced crystallised fruits and a small amount of apricot jam. It is
obviously a cold sweet only.

Fédérale	Set a layer of red jelly in the bottom of a charlotte mould and cut the form of a red cross, discarding the surplus; fill with Impératrice rice and when set, turn onto a dish lined with red jelly.
Maltaise	Use orange-flavoured bavarois and add with grated orange rind to the rice mixture; pour into a mould lined with orange jelly and when set turn out and surround with orange segments.
Palermo	Line a savarin mould with red jelly and fill with Impératrice rice mixture; turn out and fill the centre with whipped cream and macerated orange segments.
Riz à l'Impératrice	Line a charlotte mould with red jelly, fill with Impératrice rice and when set, turn onto a dish and decorate with whipped cream.
Sicilienne	Pour the rice into a savarin mould and when set turn out and decorate with a variety of crystallised fruits.
à la Suisse	Line a mould with red jelly and fill with rice mixture, omitting the crystallised fruit; when set turn onto a dish lined with red jelly.
Tulips de Poires	Half-fill pastry tulip-shells with Impératrice rice, place poached halves of pears on top and cover with apricot glaze.

Jellies – Gelées

Jelly can be made quite easily using gelatine but most establishments now use a proprietary brand of jelly in powder or tablet form which needs the addition only of boiling water to give a crystal-clear, well flavoured jelly of the correct setting consistency.

To make *real lemon jelly* bring 1 litre water, 275g of loaf sugar and the zest and juice of 4 lemons plus cinnamon and coriander to a boil; add 50g soaked gelatine then stir in 3 slightly whisked whites of egg, bring back to a boil without stirring, when it should be crystal clear. Strain through a double sheet of muslin or jelly bag and use. To use powdered gelatine, sprinkle into cold water, leave for a few minutes then warm until it becomes a clear liquid.

Fruit jelly can be made with a purée of fruit, water and gelatine without clarifying it.

Milk jelly is made by adding evaporated milk to replace some of the water when making the jelly, or using hot milk. This can be flavoured with chocolate or coffee, or with the grated zest only of lemon or orange.

Harlequin jelly is made by adding diced set chocolate and strawberry jelly to a milk jelly.

Stiffly beaten egg whites can be folded into a jelly that is near to setting point.

Ordinary or whipped cream can be added to cold jelly then moulded until set.

Add 3 yolks to 6dl hot jelly, stir until it thickens but does not boil, cool and pour into an oiled mould.

Commercial jellies are made in most fruit flavours that may be set as made, in fancy moulds, or with pieces of fruit arranged in a neat pattern, or in a striped arrangement of several different colours and flavours.

Russian jelly is made by whisking any flavoured jelly when almost at setting point; this changes its colour and clarity and aerates it and it can then be moulded in the usual way.

Jelly is used in certain sweets such as charlotte royale to provide extra colour and taste; it may also be used as a garnish in the form of croûtons, or set in orange or tangerine skins and cut into sections.

A small quantity of liqueur may be added to a basic jelly provided the quantity of water is reduced so that the right degree of setting is maintained.

It is permissible to decorate a jelly with whipped cream after it is turned out.

A *Tivoli* is made by lining a fancy mould with jelly of the flavour as determined by the name, e.g. tivoli aux fraises, and filling with the appropriate flavour bavarois.

Junket

This cold sweet is made by heating sweetened milk to 36°C and adding rennet to coagulate and set it. As it is very soft-setting it is best made in individual dishes.

Junket tablets or powders which have flavour and colour incorporated may be used. Only pasteurised milk may be used, as UHT and sterilised milk will not set and homogenised milk gives a soft result. Allow the junket to set for 1 to 2 hours at ordinary room temperature, decorate with a rosette of whipped cream and serve with a dry biscuit such as langue de chat.

It should be remembered that rennet is an animal product which means that junket is not strictly vegetarian.

Meringue Sweets

There are three kinds of meringue mixture each having different uses. Basic meringue is made of whisked egg-whites or dried albumen, and caster sugar with a little acid such as salt, cream of tartar, lemon juice or vinegar to assist in developing the volume; this kind is used for dried meringue shells and bases. Italian meringue is sugar cooked with water to 140°C and poured into whisked egg-whites; this kind is used for soufflés surprise. Cooked meringue is made by whisking the whites until stiff then placing over a pan of warm water and whisking in the sugar gradually until it is thick and shiny. Swiss meringue is another name for ordinary meringue.

Abricots Meringués	Arrange half apricots on a bed of condé rice; cover with meringue, glaze in the oven and decorate with red and yellow jams. Other fruits may be prepared in this manner.
Baked Alaska	Cover a base of sponge with ice cream, place to freeze, then coat with meringue to give a ridge effect; bake in a very hot oven until brown.
Crème Meringuée	Cook a Crème Régence in a savarin mould, turn out, fill the centre with crystallised fruit mixed with meringue, then cover completely with meringue and colour in a hot oven.
Crème Monte Carlo	Mix crushed meringues and a little melted gelatine into whipped cream, set in a mould then turn out and decorate with dried meringues and whipped cream.
Lemon Meringue Pie	Fill a baked flan case with lemon filling, cover with meringue and bake at 225°C for 5 minutes. Other flavoured fillings may be used, e.g. banana, chocolate, butterscotch.
Meringue Chantilly	Sandwich two dried meringue shells with sweetened whipped cream and add a decoration such as grated chocolate or glacé cherries.
Meringue Glacée	Sandwich two dried meringue shells with any flavour of ice cream and decorate with whipped cream; the centre of the meringues may be scooped out.
Mousse d'Oeufs Réjane	Poach flat rounds of raw meringue in sweetened milk, arrange in a dish with a half apricot on each and coat with crème anglaise made from the milk.
Oeufs à la Neige	Poach spoonfuls of raw meringue in sweetened milk; arrange in a dish and coat with crème anglaise made from the milk; sprinkle with flaked almonds or pipe with cooked sugar at the soft ball stage.

Oeufs à la Neige Jour et Nuit	Proceeds as for ordinary Oeufs à la Neige, flavouring some of the custard with chocolate and coating the meringues alternately with this and the plain custard.
Oeufs à la Neige Moulés	Proceed as for ordinary Oeufs à la Neige, when cooked placing them into a savarin mould; fill with crème anglaise made with gelatine and when set, turn out.
Omelette Soufflé	Arrange lady finger biscuits on a bed of meringue, soak them with liqueur, cover with more meringue and bake at 217°C for 10 to 12 minutes and serve immediately. It is usual to add yolks cooked with sugar to the ribbon stage to colour the meringue mixture and to dredge well with icing sugar during the cooking.

Other omelettes covered with meringue but containing ice cream will be found in the section on ice cream. Omelettes Surprises will be found under that heading in this section.

Orange Surprise	Fill emptied orange skins with any flavour of ice cream or sorbet, cover with meringue and colour quickly in a hot oven.
Pavlova	Add cornflour and vinegar to ordinary meringue and fill into a flan ring; when dry, spread with whipped cream and decorate with fruit such as banana, pineapple, raspberries, kiwi fruit, or strawberries.
Pouding Reine des Fées	Add some quince jelly and diced macerated crystallised fruit to Italian meringue; poach round-shapes in sweetened water, drain and place in a charlotte mould on a layer of vanilla bavarois and cover with raspberry bavarois; turn out when set.
Ruche Edouard VII	Spread a layer of strawberry ice cream on a round sponge cake; add some peaches, sprinkle with orange-flower water and cover with meringue in the form of a hive; glaze quickly in a hot oven.
Ruche Georges V	Proceed as for ruche Edouard VII using vanilla ice cream instead of strawberry ice cream.

Snowballs	Poach rounds of meringue in sweetened water and serve in a glass dish on chocolate-flavoured crème anglaise.
Vacherin	Pipe meringue as a solid base and two or three rings and allow to dry; fit together with cream and fill with whipped cream, ice cream, fruits, marrons glacés etc. and decorate to choice.

The side may be spread with chestnut purée and coated with grated chocolate. These may be made as individual portions or as a whole 18cm in diameter.

Mousses

A sweet mousse is a combination of a flavouring base set with gelatine, agar agar or alginate and aerated with whipped cream or egg whites, or both. The flavouring base can be a whisked yolks and sugar mixture, a cooked cornflour or custard powder and milk mixture, a fruit-flavoured stock syrup, or a purée of fruit. It is set in moulds and turned out, or in bowls or coupes for serving and eating from, decorated with whipped cream and where possible identified by a garnish of the basic flavouring ingredient.

Chocolate	Melt some grated chocolate in milk, add melted gelatine and whipped cream; ordinary chocolate and/or white chocolate may be used.
	Another method for making chocolate mousse is to add 100g softened butter to 250g melted chocolate, add 4 yolks then fold in 6 egg whites whisked to a peak with 40g caster sugar.
Coffee	Flavour sweetened milk with coffee, add gelatine and whipped cream.
Honey	Add honey, rum and grated nutmeg to an egg-based mousse.
Lemon	Heat lemon rind and juice with sugar and water, set with gelatine and lighten with cream.
Orange	Heat orange rind and juice with sugar and water, set with gelatine and lighten with cream.

Raspberry	Use sweetened raspberry purée with lemon juice, gelatine and cream.
Strawberry	Make as for raspberry mousse using strawberry purée.
Vanilla	Make a vanilla-flavoured custard, add gelatine and whipped cream.

Omelettes

There are three kinds of hot sweet omelettes:

1. Soufflé omelette for which yolks and sugar are whisked until thick, then the stiffly beaten whites folded in. It is cooked in an omelette pan and finished in the oven; various fillings may be added.
2. An ordinary unseasoned omelette with a sweet filling, often flamed or branded with a red hot poker; a little caster sugar should be mixed into the eggs.
3. Surprise omelette made of meringue in the shape of an omelette. This is not a true omelette as it usually has a base of genoise or sponge.

Célestine	Place a small jam omelette inside a larger jam omelette before folding it over; dredge with icing sugar and brand with a red-hot poker.
Claremont	Fill an ordinary or soufflé omelette with stiff apple purée; fold over, dredge with icing sugar and brand with a red-hot poker.
Confiture	Fill an ordinary omelette with any kind of jam; it may be dredged with caster sugar and branded.
George Sand	Fill a soufflé omelette with dried crystallised fruit and pieces of marrons glacés mixed with apricot jam; when made sprinkle with crushed macaroons and sugar.
au Liqueur	Any kind of liqueur or spirit can be used to flame an ordinary or soufflé omelette and the menu name should be that of the liqueur used.
Martinique	Fill an ordinary sweet omelette with sautéd sliced of banana and flame with rum.

577

de Noël   Fill any kind of omelette with hot mincemeat and flame with rum.

au Rhum   Cook in the usual way, dredge with caster sugar, brand with a red-hot poker and flame with rum.

Soufflé Surprise   Suitable fillings for this kind of omelette include purée of stewed apple or apricot jam or lemon and orange flavour, or vanilla essence may be added to the eggs; the meringue should be dredged with caster sugar and placed in a very hot oven for a few minutes to colour.

Stephanie   Fill a soufflé omelette with sugared raspberries or strawberries.

Viennoise   Fill a soufflé omelette with raspberry jam.

See under Soufflés in the section on Ice Cream for Omelettes Surprise made with ice cream.

Pancakes – Crêpes

Pancakes are made with a batter consisting of 250g plain flour, 40g caster sugar, 2 eggs and 6dl milk with flavouring and seasoning to taste e.g. brandy, kirsch, rum, vanilla or melted butter; the whites of the eggs may be whisked and folded in to give a soufflé pancake. Wholemeal flour may be used. The batter should be allowed to rest for an hour before frying the pancakes in a pancake pan.

Apple   Spread the pancakes with apple purée, roll up and serve sprinkled with caster sugar.

Blintzes   Fill the pancake with cottage cheese mixed with sugar and sour cream and fold into triangles or parcels; they may also be filled with stoned black cherries or apple purée.

Carneval   Spread with banana purée, roll up and trim the ends and serve with sabayon or caramel sauce.

Cévenole   Spread with chestnut purée flavoured with rum, roll up, dredge with icing sugar and glaze under the salamander.

au Citron	Add grated lemon rind to the batter; when cooked sprinkle with sugar, fold into four and serve with quarters of lemon.
au Confiture	Spread with red jam and roll up; trim the ends and dredge with caster sugar.
du Convent	Add some diced pears when making the pancakes, cook as usual and serve sprinkled with sugar.
à la Crème	Spread the pancakes with frangipane mixed with crushed macaroons; roll up, trim the ends, dredge with sugar and glaze.
Créole	Spread with rum-flavoured pastry cream mixed with diced pineapple; roll up and sprinkle with caster sugar.
Déjazet	Spread with very cold coffee butter-cream, roll, cover with meringue and colour very quickly in a hot oven.
Georgette	Add some macerated diced pineapple when making the pancakes, cook as usual and serve sprinkled with caster sugar.
Gil-Blas	Spread the pancakes with hazelnut butter-cream flavoured with brandy; fold into four and sprinkle with sugar.
Impériale	Spread the pancakes with condé rice, sprinkle with diced cooked pear and fold over.
Normande	Add some calvados liqueur to the batter; when making the pancakes add some sautéed diced dessert apple flavoured with cinnamon, and serve them flat.
à l'Orange	Add grated orange rind to the batter; spread with very cold orange butter-cream, fold into four and serve garnished with orange segments.
Parisienne	Add some brandy and crushed macaroons to the batter; make the pancakes in the usual way and serve them flat.
Russe	Add some brandy, kümmel and cake- or biscuit-crumbs to the batter then make the pancakes in the usual way.
Suzette	Flavour the batter with curaçao, lemon juice and tangerine juice; when made, spread with curaçao butter-cream and fold in four.

Crêpes Suzette can also be made as a flambé dish (see the recipe in the section on Restaurant Service in Volume 2.)

Pancakes may be chilled for up to 4 days, keeping them stacked in a pile wrapped in foil; or interleaved with greaseproof and deep-frozen.

Other fillings for pancakes include lemon curd, mincemeat, jam and whipped cream and fruit yoghurt; syrup such as maple syrup may be poured over when serving.

Petits Fours

The following are the classical ones that should be in general use, the idea being to offer a dish containing at least half a dozen varieties that make a colourful and appetising display. Many of these are presented in foil or paper cases. For banquets and other special occasions petits fours should be presented in a basket or other kind of receptacle made of pulled sugar, pastillage, caramel nougat or marzipan.

Barquettes   Line small barquette moulds with sweet paste, add a little red jam and fill with frangipane; bake, then brush with hot apricot glaze and ice with fondant. Instead of using barquette moulds, small tartlet moulds may be used in which case they should be called 'tartelettes'.

Bon-bons   Mix equal amounts of ground almonds and icing sugar with a little whipped cream and a few drops of liqueur. Chill well, mould into oval shapes and dip in melted chocolate. Finish by rolling in icing sugar.

Cornets   Cream 250g each of butter and sugar, add 6 egg-whites one by one then beat in 250g flour; pipe out $2\frac{1}{2}$cm rounds and bake at 220°C. As soon as the edge starts to colour, remove and twist inside a cream horn mould while still hot. Fill with ganache, etc.

Conversations Line small tartlet moulds with puff pastry, fill with frangipane and cover with a trellis work of pastry; bake in a hot oven.

Crystallised Fruits This is fruit cooked gently in stock syrup over a number of stages, draining then replacing to cook in the ever more concentrated syrup, up to 34° Baume. Figs, apricots, pears, pineapple, cherries, etc., may be used.

Fondant Creams Warm fondant to 82°C, beat in colour and flavour as required then pour into fondant moulds and allow to set overnight. Instead of using moulds, drop small rounds onto waxed paper and allow to set. Peppermint fondant creams are usually dipped into melted chocolate, the fondant being flavoured with peppermint essence.

Fudge Boil 1kg granulated sugar in 3dl water, add 50g butter then 1dl condensed milk stirring until it reaches 118°C. At the same time boil 125g sugar, 25g glucose, 25g butter and ½dl water to 127°C, add to the first mixture and pour into a greased tin. Allow to set and cut into squares.

Ganache Truffles This is a mixture of melted chocolate and whipping cream which becomes light and aerated if beaten by machine; chill, roll into balls and dust all over with cocoa powder.

Glazed Fruits Dip very-well-dried sections of fruit into sugar cooked to 155°C (hard crack), place on an oiled tray to harden and use as soon as possible. Grapes, oranges, strawberries, cherries, cape gooseberries, figs, prunes and mandarines are all suitable.

Japonaise Whisk 10 egg whites, then add 400g caster sugar to make a firm meringue; fold in 200g each of caster sugar and ground almonds and 50g ground rice then pipe out with a 1cm tube and bake at 175°C for 18 minutes. These may be sandwiched with butter-cream.

Macaroons Mix 200g caster sugar, 100g ground almonds and 30g ground rice with 2–3 egg-whites for 3–4 minutes; pipe onto rice paper in 3cm

581

	rounds, add a split almond and bake at 175°C for approximately 20 minutes.
Marquis	Sandwich langues de chat with ganache containing crushed praline and dip the ends in chocolate.
Paganinis	Boil 2dl cream with ½oz strained strong tea, add 240g milk chocolate and 120g melted plain chocolate, bring to a boil and stir until it thickens. Refrigerate then work to a paste, spread on a tray, cut into oblongs and dip into chocolate.
Palets de Dame Truffés	Add 300g butter to 900g melted dark chocolate, add 300g each of icing sugar and ground almonds and when cool, mould into rounds and coat with chocolate vermicelli.
Physalis	Turn the leaves back and dip the round end of the fruit into any colour of fondant, or into sugar cooked to 155°C.
Rum Balls	Mix cake-crumbs with apricot jam and rum, roll into balls and dip in chocolate or fondant.
Schuberts	Line small foil cups with milk chocolate, add a maraschino cherry, fill with brandy-flavoured fondant and when set, cover with chocolate and pipe with a treble clef.
Strawberries in Fondant	Dip firm, ripe and dry strawberries into white or pale pink fondant.
Liqueur Chocolates	These are usually bought ready made but are expensive; they can be made by lining small foil cups with chocolate, filling with liqueur-flavoured fondant treated with invertase then covering with more chocolate. The fondant will liquify through the action of the invertase.
Marzipan Fruits	Glacé cherries, dates and prunes may be opened and filled with coloured marzipan; they may be served as they are but look better if dipped into sugar cooked to 155°C. Walnuts may also be done in this way.
Marzipan Fancies	Mix 450g marzipan with 60g fondant and 30g glycerine and sufficient icing sugar to bind;

582

divide in three and flavour and colour (1) yellow – lemon, (2) green – pistachio, and (3) pink – kirsch. Roll out square, layer together and cut into diamonds or other shapes. Dip the bottom into chocolate.

Marzipan may also be used to represent various fruits and vegetables, using angelica for the stalks and painting the blemishes with edible food colours. It may be coloured and made as for a Battenburg cake or in a roll of various colours then cut into slices.

Meringues	Pipe meringue mixture of varying colours into different shapes using a plain and a fancy tube; allow to dry then sandwich together with whipped cream and decorate with angelica and glacé cherry.
Nougat	Cook 1kg sugar, 200g glucose powder with 2½dl water and 100g honey to 135°C, pour slowly into stiffly beaten egg-whites; add chopped almonds, angelica, glacé cherries and pistachios, spread on rice paper in shallow trays, cover with rice paper and weigh down. Cut into small pieces when cold.
Orange Creams	Boil the grated rind and juice of 3 oranges and 450g sugar in 1½dl water to 119°C, pour onto a marble slab sprinkled with water, add a little curaçao and work as for fondant. Fill small foil cups, allow to set then cover with chocolate and decorate with a crystallised violet.
Othellos	Mix 5 yolks, 30g sugar and 90g flour and blend into 8 whites whisked to a meringue with 90g sugar, and 90g flour. Pipe 3cm rounds on a floured tray and bake at 240°C for approximately 6 minutes. Sandwich with cream.
Peppermint Truffles	Add 1dl whipping cream to 250g melted milk chocolate, flavour with peppermint oil and beat on a machine until fluffy. Refrigerate then mould into balls and roll in grated chocolate.
Pralines	Stir 550g sugar and the juice of 1 lemon over gentle heat until it turns a pale amber colour; add

	225g hot roasted nibbed almonds, turn onto an oiled slab, roll out and cut into pieces as it cools.
Sablées	Cream 180g butter with 120g sugar, add 3 yolks then 240g soft flour; place into a piping bag with a fancy tube and pipe rosettes, decorate with a piece of glacé cherry and bake at 195°C until golden brown around the outside.
	Sablées can also be made by filling small bouchées with frangipane and baking in a hot oven.
Toasted Marzipan	Roll out marzipan, mark with a pattern, egg-wash and allow to dry. cut into various shapes and sizes, dredge with icing sugar and grill under a salamander.
Truffles	Mix 200g melted chocolate, 2 yolks, 25g soft butter, 1dl cream, 100g ground almonds and a measure of brandy. Allow to stand until firm then roll into small balls and dip in cocoa powder or coat with chocolate vermicelli.
Tulips	Cream 250g butter and 500g icing sugar, gradually add 12 egg whites and 310g flour; allow it to rest then pipe 10–12cm rounds, bake quickly and mould around a cup whilst still warm.
Turkish Delight	Dilute 30g cornflour with a little water from 3dl, place the rest to boil with 175g granulated sugar; when dissolved add the cornflour then simmer gently until it hangs in strands from the spoon. Add flavour and colour, pour into a tin and press into shape with mixed cornflour and icing sugar. Cut into squares.

Many of the biscuits listed earlier in this section are suitable for serving as part of a petits fours selection but making them slightly smaller; small size palmiers, florentines and shortbread may also be included. It is usual to make them in bulk and to store in airtight containers, lined with absorbent paper, for up to a fortnight.

Hot Milk Puddings made with Cereals

A basic milk pudding made with a cereal or starch is an appetising and nutritious luncheon sweet providing it is made carefully with the correct proportion of ingredients. The cereals include cornflour, oatmeal, rice and semolina, and macaroni, noodles and other pastas come into this category; arrowroot, sago and tapioca are classed as starches. It is usual to flavour all these puddings with vanilla essence.

Barley	Make in the same way as sago pudding but using barley flour.
Brésilienne	Line dariole moulds with caramel and fill with prepared sago pudding; cook au bain-marie.
Fleur de Marie	Put semolina cooked with eggs into a caramel-lined funnel mould and cook au bain-marie. Serve with caramel-flavoured egg-custard sauce.
Flamri	Cook 150g semolina in 5dl milk, add 150g sugar and 12g melted gelatine, fold in 8 stiffly beaten whites; pour into dishes and allow to set. Serve lukewarm with hot redcurrant sauce.
Macaroni	Cook short-cut macaroni in water for 10 minutes, drain and finish cooking in hot milk; add a liaison of yolks and sugar and pour into pie-dishes. Gratinate under a salamander.
Noodles	Make in the same way as macaroni pudding.
Rice	Baked – place 100g washed short-grain rice and 100g sugar per 1 litre milk in a pie-dish and bake at 150°C for 2 hours.
	Boiled – using the same proportions as for baked rice, cook on the stove or in an oven then pour into pie-dishes, dot with butter and gratinate.
	French – add a liaison of 3 yolks and 50g butter to 1 litre of boiled rice pudding, pour into pie-dishes and gratinate.

	Ground – make in the same way as sago pudding.
Sago	Rain 80g sago into 1 litre boiling milk and cook for 15 minutes; add 100g sugar, 40g butter and 2 yolks; pour into pie-dishes and gratinate.
Semolina	Make in the same way as sago pudding using 80g semolina.
Tapioca	Make in the same way as sago pudding.

Milk puddings may also be flavoured with chocolate, orange or lemon zest, vanilla, etc., and dried fruit such as sultanas or seedless raisins may be added; sometimes jam is served with plain milk puddings. A little butter helps to enrich these puddings, adding it together with grated nutmeg before putting in the oven to bake.

Any of these puddings that are cooked on the stove may be finished with yolks of egg to thicken, but must not be allowed to boil. As an extension to this the stiffly beaten whites can also be folded in before the pudding is baked in the oven.

Any of these can be listed as e.g. Pouding au Riz Créole, by lining the pie-dish with caramel.

Steamed Puddings

There are two sorts of steamed puddings – sponge and suet; both may be made in any of the following flavours. These puddings are served with custard, jam or other sauce, depending on the filling.

Basic Sponge Pudding	Cream 250g each of butter and caster sugar, add 4 eggs gradually then carefully mix in 375g self-raising flour and $\frac{1}{2}$dl milk.
Basic Suet Pudding	Mix 250g finely chopped suet, 200g sugar, 250g white breadcrumbs and 300g self-raising flour; add 3 beaten eggs and approximately 1dl water, or $2\frac{1}{2}$dl water only. It may also be made in form of a roll, using ordinary suet pastry e.g. Roly-poly pudding is a steamed jam or syrup roll.

Américaine	Add mixed spice, diced crystallised fruit and rum or brandy to the basic mixture.
Black Cap	Cover the bottom of a basin with warmed syrup, add washed currants and fill with mixture.
Cherry	Add 100g chopped glacé cherries to the pudding mixture.
Chocolate	Reduce the amount of flour by a quarter and replace it with equal amounts of cocoa and cornflour.
Coconut	Add 120g desiccated coconut to the basic pudding mixture.
College	Use half white and half brown sugar, add mixed spice and mixed dried fruit.
Date and Walnut	Add 125g chopped dates and 75g finely chopped walnuts to the mixture.
Ginger	Add 15g ground ginger and 100g chopped preserved ginger to the basic pudding mixture.
Golden Syrup	Warm some syrup and pour in bottom of basins then fill with the basic mixture.
Jam	Place red jam in the bottom of pudding basins and fill with the basic pudding mixture.
Lemon	Add the grated rind of two lemons to the basic pudding mixture.
Marmalade	Place marmalade in the bottom of pudding basins and fill up with mixture.
Orange	Add the grated rind of two oranges to the basic mixture.
Spotted Dick	Add 180g currants and 60g sultanas to the suet pudding mixture; this may also be made in the form of a roll, being sprinkled with the dried fruit.
Treacle	Place warmed black treacle in the bottom of pudding basins and fill with the basic pudding mixture.
Vanilla	Flavour with vanilla essence and proceed as usual.

To prevent an aluminium pan in which the pudding is being steamed from turning dark, add some vinegar to the water. Some glass marbles placed in the pan will rattle should the pan boil dry.

Baked Sponge Puddings

The same sponge pudding mixture as used for steamed puddings can be made as a baked sponge pudding and most of the varieties as for steamed puddings are suitable for this type of pudding. They are cooked in pie-dishes at 180°C. In some cases they are made with alternate layers of sponge mixture and fruit or other ingredients.

Baked roll puddings are made with short pastry and any of the following fillings: diced apple and sultanas, jam, lemon curd, marmalade, mincemeat, syrup, etc.

Serve with custard, a jam or other sauce appropriate to the filling.

Upside-down puddings

These are a version of baked sponge pudding in which slices or halves of fruit such as apple, apricot, peach, pear or pineapple, or a combination of fruit, is arranged in a well-buttered pie-dish and covered with sponge mixture. When baked it is turned out so as to show the neat arrangement of the fruit.

Bread pudding

Mix soaked and squeezed stale bread with melted butter, sugar, dried fruit, eggs and mixed spice; spread in a greased dish, sprinkle with brown sugar and bake at 175°C. Serve hot or cold cut into squares, if as a hot sweet, with custard.

Soufflé Puddings

These are light delicate puddings that are cooked in the oven in dariole or charlotte moulds, turned out and served with either custard sauce, apricot sauce or sabayon.

The basic mixture is 100g each of butter, sugar and plain flour mixed to a paste to which 3dl boiling milk is added and cooked until it thickens then when cool 5 yolks are added, followed by 5 stiffly beaten whites. It is cooked au bain-marie, in buttered and sugared moulds at 200°C for approximately 20 minutes then kept hot at the entrance to the oven.

Albemarle	Add ground almonds to the basic mixture and serve with custard sauce.
Arlequin	Fill moulds half with vanilla and half with chocolate soufflé mixture; serve with sauce sabayon.
Beaulieu	Fill moulds half with vanilla and half with strawberry soufflé mixture; serve with sauce sabayon.
Cambacérès	Flavour with almond essence and add chopped angelica; serve with praline-flavoured custard sauce.
au Citron	Add grated lemon rind to the mixture and serve with lemon sauce.
Denise	Flavour with almond milk, kirsch and maraschino and serve with almond-flavoured apricot sauce.
Figaro	Fill moulds with layers of vanilla, chocolate and strawberry soufflé mixtures; serve with sauce sabayon.
Indienne	Add some ground ginger and diced preserved ginger to the mixture and serve with ginger-flavoured custard sauce.
Lyonnaise	Flavour with lemon essence and serve with sauce sabayon.
Normande	Add diced sautéd apple to the soufflé mixture and serve with apricot sauce flavoured with calvados.
à l'Orange	Add grated orange rind to the mixture and serve with orange sauce.
Régence	Cook in moulds lined with caramel and serve with caramel-flavoured custard sauce.
Reine	Sprinkle the mould with chopped pistachios and crushed macaroons, fill with the mixture containing chopped pistachios and crushed macaroons, cook, and serve with praline-flavoured custard sauce.

Rothschild   Add diced candied fruit and kirsch to the basic mixture.

Royale   Line the moulds with slices of very small Swiss Roll and fill with mixture; serve with apricot sauce flavoured with Marsala.

Sans-Souci   Sprinkle the moulds with currants and fill with mixture containing diced sautéed apple; serve with rum-flavoured apricot sauce.

Saxon   This is the basic mixture without any flavourings; serve with custard sauce or sauce sabayon.

Other flavours include chocolate, coffee, praline and vanilla.

Seasonal Specialities

Christmas Pudding   Mix 250g each of currants, mixed peel, raisins and sultanas with 175g brown sugar, 200g chopped apple, a little mixed spice, the grated rind and juice of 1 lemon and 1 orange, beer, brandy, rum and sherry; allow to mature for a few days then mix with 3 beaten eggs and sufficient breadcrumbs to give a stiff mixture. Fill greased basins with the mixture, cover and steam for 4 hours. Serve with brandy butter, custard, rum sauce, brandy-flavoured sabayon, etc. Flame by pouring warmed brandy over the pudding and setting it alight. The above amount will make 20 good-sized portions of 60g.

Mincemeat   Chop 250g each of apple, currants, raisins and sultanas; add 180g each of chopped dried apricots and suet, 75g each of mixed peel and chopped almonds, 250g brown sugar, a pinch of cinnamon, ginger and allspice, a few drops of almond essence and the rind and juice of 2 lemons. Mix well and leave to mature for 4 days before using. 500g of mincemeat and 800g of pastry will yield 20 mince pies of 7cm diameter.

Mince Pies Roll out 800g short or puff pastry 2mm thick and cut out 20 rounds of 8cm diameter and 20 rounds of 7cm diameter; place the small ones on a tray, pipe approximately 25g mincemeat on each, egg-wash the edge and cover with the larger rounds. Seal well, make an incision and bake at 215°C for approximately 15 minutes; dredge with icing sugar.

Christmas Cake Cream 200g each of butter and soft brown sugar, add 5 eggs one by one then fold in 250g soft flour, 25g ground almonds, 5g mixed spice, the grated rind and juice of 1 lemon, vanilla essence and 700g mixed dried fruit previously macerated in $\frac{1}{2}$dl rum overnight. When baked, cover with marzipan then with royal icing and decorate in traditional style. Bake in two cake tins of 15cm diameter at 182°C falling to 170°C over $1\frac{1}{2}$ hours.

Dundee Cake Fill baking tins with Christmas Cake mixture and cover the top completely with split almonds. When baked brush with syrup made with 200g sugar boiled in 5dl water with 50g gelatine.

Simnel Cake Cream 450g each of butter and sugar, add 10 eggs one by one then add 500g soft flour sieved with 4g baking powder; add 900g currants, 450g sultanas, 120g each of mixed peel and glacé cherries and place layers of this mixture with 2 rounds of almond paste in 15cm cake tins. Bake at 182°C falling to 170°C over $1\frac{3}{4}$ hours. Place a decoration of almond paste on top, crimp and egg-wash then glaze under a salamander. Decorate with fondant, small Easter eggs, chicks or bunnies, etc.

Hot Cross Buns Dissolve 40g yeast and 100g sugar in $3\frac{1}{2}$dl milk and water at 37°C and pour into 550g strong flour with 4g salt aded and 60g white fat rubbed in; add liquid spice and knead well. Allow to prove then knock back, mould into 35g rounds and pipe with a cross made by mixing 100g soft flour with 25g lard, a small pinch of baking powder and approximately 1dl water. Allow to prove until double in size, bake at 230°C for approximately 15 minutes then brush with bun-wash made by heating 1dl water with 125g sugar to boiling-point.

Hot Soufflés

These are baked in and served from a porcelain soufflé dish; they must be made to split-second timing so that there is no chance of them collapsing between the time they are cooked and when they are served to the customer.

For the basic recipe pour 2dl boiling milk onto a mixture of 80g butter, 120g sugar and 60g flour, cook this until stiff and when cool add 6 yolks followed by 8 stiffly beaten whites. Pour into 2 buttered and sugared 15cm soufflé dishes and bake at 210°C for 25 minutes, then dredge with icing sugar and replace in the oven briefly to glaze. A fruit soufflé can be made by cooking some sugar to 140°C, adding a purée of soft fruit then stiffly beaten whites.

A real soufflé is usually served entirely on its own without any sauce or garnish, but stewed fruit is sometimes served.

The usual flavours are almond, chocolate, coffee, lemon, praline and vanilla.

A spirit or liqueur may be added such as kirsch, rum, curaçao, Chartreuse, Mandarine, etc. In addition there are the following soufflés.

Arlequin	Fill the dish with a layer of vanilla soufflé mix then a layer of chocolate soufflé mix; bake in the usual way.
Camargo	Place layers of praline soufflé mixture, tangerine soufflé mixture and finger biscuits macerated with curaçao in the soufflé dish and bake.
Elizabeth	Arrange layers of soufflé mixture, small maca-roons macerated in kirsch, and crystallised vio-

lets in the soufflé dish; bake and place a veil of spun sugar on top before serving.

Hilda
Serve a lemon soufflé accompanied with a dish of fresh strawberries covered with raspberry purée.

Javanaise
Use brewed strong tea instead of milk to make the mixture and add some chopped pistachios; fill into the dish and bake.

Lucullus
Cover a savarin that has been soaked in kirsch syrup with any kind of fruit soufflé mixture, keeping it in place with a band of stiff paper; bake as usual.

Mercédès
Add diced crystallised fruit macerated in kirsch and maraschino to the mixture and bake as usual.

Montmorency
Flavour with cherry brandy and add some glacé cherries soaked in brandy.

d'Orléans
Add pieces of finger biscuit macerated with kirsch and with peach liqueur and add some diced glacé cherries and angelica to the mixture.

Palmyre
Fill the dish with layers of soufflé mixture and finger biscuits sprinkled with kirsch and anisette; bake in the usual way.

Paulette
Add small macaroons macerated in kirsch to the mixture and serve with a dish of fresh strawberries covered with raspberry purée.

Rachel
Fill the dish with a layer of vanilla soufflé mix and a layer of pistachio soufflé mix and bake in the usual way.

Rothschild
Add diced crystallised fruit macerated in Danziger Goldwasser to the mixture and garnish with strawberries when about to serve.

Royale
Place layers of soufflé mixture, finger biscuits sprinkled with kirsch, and diced macerated crystallised fruits in the dish and bake in the usual way.

Cold Soufflés

The basic recipe for a cold soufflé is often described as a Milanaise mixture; to make it, whisk 6 yolks and 200g caster sugar over heat until thick, add 30g melted gelatine, 5dl whipped cream and 6 stiffly beaten whites. Pour into a soufflé dish to come 5cm above the rim to give the impression of having risen, keeping in place by a band of stiff paper. This kind of soufflé is served cold but not frozen or chilled.

The name given would be that of the flavouring used which can be a liqueur such as Grand Marnier, Mandarine, Kirsch, Tia Maria, Drambuie, etc., an essence such as almond, coffee, lemon, vanilla, or a purée of fruit such as apricot, raspberry, strawberry.

The completed soufflé is decorated with whipped cream, almonds, glacé fruit etc., after removing the paper. (See also Soufflé Omelettes in the section on Ice cream.)

Strudels

These are of Austrian origin, made with various kinds of fruit and served as a hot sweet with custard or sauce sabayon, or with cream as a cold sweet. Roll out noodle, filo or puff pastry very thinly, brush with butter, cover with the filling and roll up; when baked dredge with icing sugar. The mixtures include:

Apfelstrudel   Sliced apple, fried white breadcrumbs, dried fruit and cinnamon.

Kirschstrudel   Stoned cherries, fried white breadcrumbs, grated lemon rind and sugar.

Nusstrudel   Ground hazelnuts, butter, sugar, eggs and vanilla.

Topfenstrudel   Cottage cheese, eggs, sugar, dried fruit and vanilla.

Subrics

This is a rich semolina mixture spread 2cm thick, cut into 6cm rounds then coloured in hot butter. To make the mixture rain 250g semolina into 1 litre of boiling milk, cook for 10 minutes, cool then add 12 yolks, 200g sugar and 100g butter. Serve with some redcurrant jelly in the centre of each piece or accompanied with a fruit sauce.

Sweet Sauces

Very often a sauce is an integral part of a sweet and its omission would detract from the resultant dish. Although sweet sauces are fairly straightforward to prepare, care should be taken to make them tasty and it is important to strain them before serving. Distinction is made between those sauces that are served with hot sweets and those served with cold sweets and ice cream; in addition a number of hard sauces are included.

Name	Formula	Cold	Hot
Apricot	5 parts apricot jam to 1 part water cooked for 5 minutes, strained and flavoured with kirsch.	√	√
Brandy	Sweetened milk thickened with cornflour, flavoured with brandy or brandy flavouring.		√
Brandy Cream	Add icing sugar, lemon juice, brandy and curaçao to whipped cream.	√	
Butterscotch	Brown sugar and butter added to cornflour sauce.		√
Cherry	Stoned cherries cooked in stock syrup with the addition of redcurrant jelly, flavoured with kirsch.	√	√
Chocolate	Grated plain chocolate, sugar and water cooked for 20 minutes and finished with cream.	√	√

Name	Formula	Cold	Hot
Chocolate	Sweetened milk thickened with cornflour and flavoured with cocoa.		✓
Custard	Can be made with eggs and milk as a basic cooked egg mixture or with custard powder. Other flavourings may be added.		✓
Fudge	Chocolate, butter, syrup and sugar melted in a little milk.		✓
Jam	Any kind of jam diluted with one fifth its amount of water and thickend with cornflour.		✓
Lemon	Rind and juice of lemon cooked with water and sugar and thickened with cornflour.		✓
Melba	2 parts raspberries cooked with one part sugar and $\frac{1}{2}$ part water until thick.	✓	
Mousseline	Whisked yolks and sugar mixed with half whipped cream.		✓
Orange	Rind and juice of orange cooked with water and sugar and thickened with cornflour.		✓
Raspberry	2 parts raspberries cooked with one part sugar and $\frac{1}{2}$ part water until thick.	✓	
Rum	Sweetened milk thickened with cornflour, flavoured with rum or rum flavouring.		✓
Sabayon	16 yolks whisked with 500g sugar and 4dl marsala or sweet wine until thick; often served in goblets as Zabaglione.	✓	✓
Strawberry	Strawberries cooked with one part sugar and one fifth its amount of water, thickened with cornflour.		✓
Tutti-Frutti	Cook crushed pineapple, ginger marmalade and a little water and garnish with chopped yellow, green and red glacé cherries.		✓

Name	Formula	Cold	Hot
Vanilla	Sweetened milk thickened with cornflour, flavoured with vanilla.		√

Hard Sauces

Brandy Butter	Softened butter mixed with an equal amount of sugar and flavoured with brandy.	√	
Cumberland Butter	This is another name for brandy butter.	√	
Rum Butter	The same as brandy butter, using dark rum.	√	

Cream can also be used as a sauce on hot and cold sweets, served as it is or lightly whipped and sweetened. It can be flavoured with honey, a liqueur or an essence.

Sweets using Savarin Paste

Savarin paste is a rich yeast dough with an open texture that enables it to absorb the syrup in which nearly all this type of sweet is soaked. In most cases a better result is obtained if the items are allowed to stale for 24 hours before being soaked.

Babas au Rhum	Add currants to the dough and bake in dariole moulds; soak in rum-flavoured syrup, sprinkle with rum and brush with apricot glaze; may be cut and filled with cream.
Croûtes	These are made from slices of savarin baked in a tall round mould; see under Croûtes in this section.
Marignans	Half-fill large barquette moulds with savarin paste, allow to prove then bake; soak in rum-flavoured stock syrup, sprinkle with rum and brush with apricot glaze; cut along one side and fill with cream.

Mazarins   Add currants to the dough and bake in dariole moulds; soak in rum-flavoured stock syrup, cool and coat with sauce sabayon.

Savarins

These are baked in a shallow ring mould.

Cardinale   Soak in maraschino syrup, glaze with apricot sauce, fill the centre with sliced peaches and coat with strawberry purée; sprinkle with shredded almonds.

Cédard   Soak in curaçao-flavoured syrup, glaze with orange fondant and fill the centre with orange segments macerated in curaçao.

Chantilly   Soak in rum-flavoured syrup, glaze with apricot and fill the centre with sweetened whipped cream.

Chibouste   Soak in rum-flavoured syrup, sprinkle with rum and glaze with apricot; fill the centre with tablespoonsful of Crème Saint-Honoré or Crème Chibouste.

Créole   Soak in rum-flavoured syrup, glaze with apricot and fill the centre with condé rice containing sliced bananas; cover with pineapple rings and brush with apricot glaze.

aux Fruits   Soak in rum-flavoured syrup, brush with apricot glaze and fill the centre with fruit salad, arranging the top neatly; decorate with whipped cream.

Médicis   Soak in maraschino-flavoured syrup, glaze with apricot and fill the centre with almond bavarois; decorate with whipped cream.

Montmorency   Soak in kirsch-flavoured syrup, glaze with apricot and fill the centre with stoned cherries cooked in cherry sauce; decorate with whipped cream.

Montreuil   Soak in maraschino-flavoured syrup, glaze with apricot and fill the centre with halves of peaches; decorate with whipped cream.

Normande	Soak in calvados-flavoured syrup, glaze with apricot sauce and fill the centre with poached apple sections coated with apricot sauce; decorate with whipped cream and place poached quarters of apple around the savarin.
à l'Orange	Soak in calvados-flavoured syrup, glaze with apricot and fill the centre with whipped cream flavoured with orange; decorate with segments of orange.
Soufflé Lucullus	Soak in kirsch-flavoured syrup, tie a band of stiff paper around and fill with fruit soufflé mixture; bake in a moderate oven and remove the paper before serving.
des Sylphes	Soak in rum-flavoured syrup and fill the centre with strawberry mousse; when set cover all over with meringue and glaze quickly in a hot oven.

Syllabub

A syllabus used to be a mixture of milk and wine, whisked until frothy, taking it off continuously as it formed and filling into glasses. It was rather like a milk punch to be drunk. A syllabub is best made with cream as shown below, various flavourings may be added and it may be decorated to choice.

1. Warm 3dl sweet sherry or port with the grated rind and juice of 2 lemons, 250g sugar and a little grated nutmeg; add to 5dl double cream, whisk well and remove the froth as it forms.
2. Whisk 3 whites of egg, add to 6dl whipping cream with the grated rind and juice of 1 lemon and 200g sugar; remove the froth as it rises and fill glasses with the mixture.

Tarts and Tartlets

These are open-faced round or square sweets made either in individual sizes or for cutting into portions, using short pastry or sweet pastry. They may be finished with a trellis work of pastry over the filling. In addition to the various kinds of fruit tarts which can include apple, apricot, blackberry, blackcurrant, cherry, gooseberry, peach, pear, pineapple, plum, raspberry, rhubarb and strawberry, there are these well-known ones.

Bakewell	Cover the base with red jam, then fill with frangipane, decorate with a trellis pattern of pastry and bake; when cooked and cool, cover the top with a thin coat of water icing or thin fondant, or dust with icing sugar.
Custard	Sprinkle the base with white breadcrumbs; fill with egg-custard mix, sprinkle with nutmeg and bake.
Frangipane	This is the same as Bakewell tart.
Jam	Fill with watered jam, cover with a trellis pattern of pastry and bake at 215°C.
Lemon	Fill with lemon curd, cover with a trellis pattern of pastry and bake at 215°C.
Manchester	Cover the cooked base with red jam, fill with made custard and sprinkle with toasted desiccated coconut.
Syrup	Sprinkle the base with white breadcrumbs, add grated lemon rind and juice to some warmed syrup and pour on top; cover with a trellis pattern of pastry and bake.

Note: It is advisable to dilute jam, etc., slightly with water when making these tarts.

Pies

Two crust tarts and tartlets are often called pies and they can be made with cooked fruit such as apple, apricot, blackberries, cherries, gooseberries, rhubarb, either alone, whole, or as a purée or pie filling, or as a mixture of several fruits, in short or sweet pastry. Different kinds of jam, mincemeat, etc., are also used. This kind of pie may be served with fresh or sour cream, yoghurt, custard or ice cream. When served with a scoop of vanilla ice cream it can be described as being 'à la mode', an American term which is fairly well-known in this country.

Timbales

These are hot sweets made by lining a charlotte mould with pastry or using a hollowed-out cooked brioche and filling it with fruit.

d'Aremburg	Line the mould with brioche paste, fill with layers of poached halves of pear and stiff apricot purée, allow to prove and bake; serve with maraschino-flavoured apricot sauce.
Bourdaloue	Line the mould with sweet pastry made with finely chopped almonds; fill with layers of stewed fruits and frangipane cream and bake; serve with vanilla-flavoured apricot sauce.
Favart	Fill a hollowed-out brioche with halves of cooked fruit and marrons glacés, mixed with kirsch-flavoured apricot sauce.
Marie-Louise	Hollow out a genoise and fill with sliced peaches mixed with strawberry purée and flavoured with kirsch; cover with meringue and colour in the oven.
Montmorency	Ornament the exterior of an emptied cooked brioche with baked diamonds and crescents of puff pastry; fill it with cooked stoned cherries mixed with redcurrant jelly.
Parisienne	Decorate the exterior of an emptied cooked brioche with crystallised fruits and fill it with quarters of apples, apricots, peaches, pears and pieces of pineapple, whole almonds, soaked raisins and sultanas, all mixed with kirsch-flavoured apricot glaze.

Trifle

Spread stale sponge cake or finger biscuits with red jam, cut into dice and place in a glass bowl or individual coupes; sprinkle with fruit juice, stock syrup, sweet sherry or a liqueur. Cover with hot custard and allow to get cold then pipe with whipped cream and decorate with angelica, almonds, glacé cherries, etc. The custard can be made using 12 egg yolks per 1 litre of hot milk and 200g sugar, cooking it until it thickens but does not boil. It can also be made with custard powder, thinning it with cream or evaporated milk. Fruit salad can be added or the sponge can be soaked with jelly which will then set; this is sometimes called *Scotch Trifle*.

Elizabeth	Soak the sponge with brandy and sherry, cover with chocolate mousse and decorate with whipped cream and grated chocolate.
Lemon Royal	Spread the sponge with lemon curd.
Swiss Trifle	Use Swiss roll instead of sponge cake.
Zuppa Inglese	This is sometimes made as a kind of trifle using Swiss roll spread with pastry cream and soaked with a syrup or liqueur; it is then covered with meringue and baked at 145°C until coloured; finish by piping with whipped cream and decorate with angelica and glacé cherries.

15 ICE-CREAM SWEETS

Many different kinds of ice-cream are available, or can be made on the premises, to provide light and interesting sweets. Ice-cream is the most versatile kind of sweet and there are several hundred ways of serving it.

Types of Ices

Traditional ice-cream	This is made from a cooked egg-custard mixture which is churned until frozen; its taste will depend on the richness of the mixture which can vary from 8 to 16 yolks and 250g to 500g of sugar per 1 litre of milk. It can also be made from a proprietary brand of ice-cream powder. This kind of ice-cream lends itself to any and every flavour.
Water ice	This is made with a cooked sugar syrup of 22°–32° on the saccharometer with the addition of a liqueur or purée or pieces of fruit; it is churned only until frozen.
Sorbet	This is made by adding a quarter of its volume of Italian meringue to a light water ice, whilst it is being churned. It is best served soon after it has been made. Flavours include wine, liqueur, fruit purée and any kind of essence.
Granité	This is a light water ice of any flavour churned only until it becomes grainy. It will lose the correct texture if over-churned.
Marquise	This is a type of sorbet made with the addition of a quarter its volume each of lightly whipped

cream and fruit purée, added at the frozen stage and being given only a few turns to incorporate them both.

Spoom

This is a type of sorbet containing wine, made by adding half its volume of Italian meringue to the water-ice mix when it is at the frozen stage. It should be very light and frothy.

Parfait

This is made by whisking a sabayon of yolks and sugar syrup with an equal amount of whipped cream. It is churned then moulded in flat oblong moulds in several colours and flavours and served frozen, cut into slices and is often called biscuit glacé.

Bombe

The mixture consists of whisked yolks and sugar syrup with an equal amount of whipped cream, flavoured and coloured, frozen then set in a bombshell-shape mould. Many additional fillings such as whipped cream or bavarois are used in making certain kinds of bombe.

Omelette Surprise

A block of ice-cream is placed on a base of genoise on a dish, masked and decorated with Italian meringue then coloured quickly in a very hot oven or under a salamander.

Baked Alaska

This is the American name given to Omelette Surprise and is mainly for domestic use.

Soufflé Vésuve

A block of ice-cream is set on a base of genoise sponge on a dish, garnished with some poached fruits; a silver timbale, nougat basket or dried meringue nest is set on top and the whole is surrounded with meringue. After glazing in a very hot oven, a compote of fruit and some warmed liqueur or spirit is placed in the central receptacle and set alight as it is taken into the room for serving.

Coupes

These take their name from the type of round glass or silver dish in which they are served. They consist of scoops of ice-cream of various flavours with a garnish of fruit, etc., and usually a final topping of whipped cream, sauce, nuts, etc.

Punch
This kind of ice is made from citrus fruit or wine-flavoured sugar syrup, with a quarter of its volume of Italian meringue.

Cassata
This is rich ice-cream of several flavours usually containing a good amount of diced crystallised fruits and chopped nuts, moulded in biscuit glacé moulds and served cut into slices.

Soufflé glacé
This is biscuit glacé mixture put into soufflé dishes to come above the brim. After freezing, the paper band is removed to give the impression of a risen soufflé. Not to be confused with soufflé froid or soufflé Viennois which are chilled, not frozen.

Ice Pudding
This is made by putting layers of various kinds of frozen ice-cream, or an outer coating of ice-cream and a contrasting filling, into a tall mould. After refreezing, it is turned out, decorated and served with a suitable cold sweet sauce.

Sundae
This consists of several scoops of various flavours of ice-cream, with fruit, chopped nuts, sauces, etc., and is similar to a coupe except that it is served in a long dish.

Knickerbocker Glory
Balls of different kinds of ice-cream are interspersed with fruit salad, sauce, nuts, cream etc., in a tall tapered glass; it needs a long spoon to eat it with and there are many versions as served in ice-cream parlours.

Accompaniments
Wafer biscuits of various shapes and colours, langues de chats, biscuits perlés, biscuits au champagne can be served with ice-cream sweets, also King Henry's Shoestrings (yolks and sugar whisked until thick, flour, whisked whites, grated lemon rind and juice and orange flower water spread thinly, baked then cut into thin strips and dredged with icing sugar), also any of the biscuits included in the Pastry Section.

605

Bombes

Name	Lining	Filling
Africaine	chocolate	rum and apricot
Aïda	strawberry	kirsch
Almeria	aniseed	grenadine
Andalouse	apricot and noyau	vanilla
Archiduc	strawberry	vanilla
Brésilienne	pineapple	rum with diced pineapple
Cardinale	redcurrant and raspberry	praline
Carmen	chocolate	vanilla
Ceylan	tea-flavoured	rum
Clarence	pineapple	violet
Cléopâtre	pistachio	rum
Colombia	kirsch	pear
Coppelia	coffee	praline
Cyrano	praline	cherry
Czarine	vanilla	kummel
Dame-Blanche	vanilla	almond
Danicheff	coffee	kirsch
Diplomate	vanilla	maraschino
Duchesse	pineapple	pear
Fanchon	praline	kirsch
Fauvette	pistachio	banana
Favorite	vanilla	strawberry**
Fédora	orange	praline
Florentine	raspberry	praline
Francillon	coffee	brandy
Frou-Frou	vanilla	rum
Georgette	praline	kirsch
Gismonda	praline	aniseed
Grand-Duc	orange	Benedictine
Grande-Duchesse	pear	Chartreuse
Havanaise	coffee	rum

Name	Lining	Filling
Hélène	hazelnut	Chartreuse
Hollandaise	vanilla	curaçao
Ida	strawberry	kirsch
Jamaïque	rum and pineapple	orange
Japonaise	rum and vanilla	tea-flavoured
Jeanne d'Arc	vanilla	praline and chocolate
Joinville	chocolate	maraschino
Josephine	coffee	pistachio
Léopold	vanilla	kirsch and strawberry
Madeleine	almond	vanilla and kirsch
Maltaise	blood orange	vanilla
Maréchale	strawberry	layers of pistachio, orange and vanilla
Marie-Louise	chocolate	vanilla
Marquise	apricot	vanilla
Mascotte	peach	kirsch
Mathilde	kirsch	apricot
Médicis	brandy	raspberry
Ménélik	tangerine	rum
Mercédes	apricot	Chartreuse
Mignon	apricot	hazelnut
Mogador	coffee	kirsch
Montmorency	kirsch	cherry
Moscovite	kummel	almond
Nelusko	praline	chocolate
Nesselrode	vanilla	chestnut***
Odette	vanilla	praline
Orientale	ginger	pistachio
Petit-Duc	strawberry	hazelnut
Pompadour	strawberry	curaçao**
Richelieu	rum	coffee
Royale	kirsch	praline and chocolate
Succès	apricot	kirsch***
Suzanne	rum (coloured pink)	vanilla
Tosca	apricot	maraschino
Trocadero	orange	layers of sponge and cream

Name	Lining	Filling
Vénitienne	half vanilla/half straw-berry	kirsch and maraschino
Victoria	strawberry	chestnut****

* indicates the use of ice-cream instead of bombe mixture
** indicates the use of mousse instead of bombe mixture
*** indicates the use of whipped cream instead of bombe mixture
**** indicates the use of plombière ice-cream instead of bombe mixture

Biscuits Glacés

Name	Layer 1	Layer 2	Layer 3	Layer 4	Finish
Arlequin	chocolate	vanilla	chocolate		
Bénédictine	praline	strawberry	vanilla	Bénédictine	
Comtesse	maraschino	strawberry	maraschino	strawberry	
Excelsior	vanilla	raspberry	pistachio		
Marquise	vanilla	strawberry	vanilla	strawberry	soaked finger biscuits added to 2
Mexicaine	pineapple	almond	banana		
Mont-Blanc	vanilla	chestnut	rum		
Napolitaine	pistachio	strawberry	vanilla		
Nicolas	chocolate	raspberry	praline		crystallised pineapple
Princesse	praline				coat with toasted shredded almonds
Reine	chocolate	tangerine	vanilla		
Sigurd	strawberry	pistachio			wafers
Tortoni	sherry	macaroon crumbs	sherry		crushed macaroons

Parfaits are similar to biscuits glacés but are usually made of one flavour only; the most popular ones are apricot, chocolate, coffee, kirsch, nougat, peach and vanilla.

Ice Gâteaux

Name	Layer 1	Layer 2	Liqueur	Finish
Brésilien	pineapple	chocolate	curaçao	crystallised pineapple
Cédard	orange		curaçao	
Japonaise	tea flavour	diced sponge biscuit	tangerine	
Reine	almond	strawberry	kirsch	crushed macaroons
Tortoni	praline		maraschino	toasted nuts

This kind of gâteau should not be confused with ordinary gateaux that have been deep frozen. The various flavours and colours of ice-cream may be sandwiched between thin layers of sponge cake and decorated with whipped cream or butter cream.

Omelettes Surprises

It is usual to lay the ice-cream on a bed of sponge cake, add the garnish and cover completely with Italian meringue. It is coloured quickly in a hot oven and served immediately.

Name	Ice	Garnish	Service
Aetna	maraschino	pineapple	flamed
Baked Alaska	vanilla	none	plain
Brésilien	coffee and rum	coffee meringue, almonds	plain or flamed
Elizabeth	vanilla	crystallised violets	plain
Macédoine	strawberry & vanilla	dice of mixed fruit	plain

Mandarinette	tangerine	segments of tangerine	plain
Milady	raspberry	peaches	plain
Milord	vanilla	pears	plain
Mont-morency	cherry	cerises jubilée	flamed
Napolitaine	vanilla & strawberry	marrons glacés, cerises jubilée	flamed
Néron	any flavour	rum	flamed
Norvégienne	vanilla	none	plain
Paquita	pineapple	diced pineapple, apricots & banana, strawberries, maraschino liqueur	plain
Vesuvius	(round shape) vanilla	rum	flamed
Vulcane	vanilla	cerises jubilée	flamed

When made in a round shape, these are usually called Ruches.

Ice Puddings

These may be served with an appropriate cold sauce.

Name	Type of mould	Lining	Filling	Decoration
Alhambra	shell	vanilla	whipped cream with strawberries macerated in Noyau liqueur	
Carmen	deep	none	vertical layers of vanilla, coffee and strawberry	
de Castries	bombe	vanilla	alternate layers of 1. vanilla bombe with finger biscuits saturated with anisette 2. tangerine ice	sprinkle with praline

Name	Type of mould	Lining	Filling	Decoration
			3. grated chocolate	
Comtesse-Marie	square	strawberry	vanilla	pipe with vanilla ice-cream
Dame-Jeanne	shell	vanilla	whipped cream with crystallised orange flowers	crème chantilly
Dora	shell	vanilla	kirsch-flavoured whipped cream with pineapple and redcurrants	crème chantilly
Etoile du Berger	star	raspberry	Bénédictine-flavoured mousse	
Fleurette	square	none	layers of strawberry and pineapple ice-cream	pipe with lemon ice
Françillon	square	crème coffee chantilly brandy		
des Gourmets	bombe	praline	layers of rum-flavoured chestnut ice-cream and of whipped cream	coat with pralined shredded almonds
des Iles	shell	vanilla	pineapple	
Lyrique	bombe	none	vanilla bombe with diced finger biscuits and crystallised pineapple	crystallised violets and gold leaf on chocolate trellis work
Madeleine	shell	none	vanilla ice-cream mixed with whipped cream and crystallised fruit	crème chantilly
Marie-Rose	charlotte	rolled wafers filled with strawberry ice	praline	pink and white whipped cream

611

Ice-cream sweets

Name	Type of mould	Lining	Filling	Decoration
Merveille	bombe	vanilla with chopped nuts and crystallised fruit	slices of Swiss roll	coat with cold chocolate sauce
Miramar	charlotte	pomeg-ranate with kirsch	sponge biscuits, strips of pineapple and tangerine segments	crème chantilly
Nancy	charlotte	sponge biscuits soaked in Grand Marnier	grated chocolate and crushed macaroons	
Plombière	bombe	vanilla	apricot purée and diced crystallised fruit	crème chantilly
Seymour	bombe	none	layers of sliced brioche soaked in cream and kirsch; sliced pears and peaches, redcurrants and pink coloured bombe mixture	crème chantilly flavoured with kirsch

Iced Charlottes

Name	Lining	Interior
Florentine	wafers	orange-flavoured ice-cream
Plombière	finger biscuits or wafers	layers of 1. vanilla ice-cream containing macerated crystallised fruit 2. Stiff apricot purée; decorate with whipped cream.
George Sand	thin chocolate éclairs	coffee ice-cream, decorate with whipped cream and trellis of redcurrant jelly

Iced Soufflés

The basic mixture is made by whisking 10 egg-whites until stiff, and then pouring in 500g sugar cooked in a little water to 115°C. When cool, fold in 5dl whipped cream and the appropriate flavourings or fruit purée. Fill into a soufflé dish to come above the rim.

Bénédictine — Flavour with Bénédictine liqueur, add diced finger biscuits soaked in Bénédictine.

Elite — Line dish with tangerine mixture, fill centre with diced crystallised orange and pineapple and sponge fingers macerated with brandy; fill with more tangerine mix and decorate with chocolate-work trellis.

Fédora — Alternate layers of praline and vanilla mixture.

Georgette — Layers of vanilla mixture containing diced finger biscuits and glacé cherries and thick purée of morello cherries.

Jamaïque   Rum-flavoured mixture containing diced finger biscuits soaked in rum.

Miracle   Tangerine-flavoured mixture containing diced macaroons and crystallised pineapple soaked in Grand Marnier; garnish with sugared wild strawberries.

Montmorency   Kirsch-flavoured mixture with chopped morello cherries soaked in kirsch.

Montrose   Vanilla mixture with diced pineapple macerated in maraschino, garnish with sugared wild strawberries.

Nesselrode   Vanilla mixture with diced candied chestnuts; decorate with small marrons glacés.

Paquita   Layers of (i) maraschino-soaked sponge, (ii) strawberry ice, (iii) dice of apricot, pineapple and banana, (iv) pineapple ice, (v) small strawberries, (vi) whipped cream.

Singhalese   Layers of (i) tea-flavoured mixture, (ii) banana mixture, (iii) diced finger biscuits and pineapple macerated in maraschino.

Sylvie   Vanilla mixture containing chopped walnuts, diced finger biscuits and crystallised apricots, both macerated in kirsch.

Tortoni   Praline-flavour vanilla mix; decorate with thin spirals of whipped cream and with praline.

Yolanda   Raspberry mixture with macerated diced pineapple.

Coupes

Name	Ice	Garnish	Finish
Adelina Patti	vanilla	cherries in brandy	whipped cream
Alexandra	strawberry	diced fruit salad	strawberry
d'Antigny	strawberry	peaches	veil of spun sugar

Name	Ice	Garnish	Finish
Bohémienne	vanilla with pieces of rum-flavoured candied chestnuts	marrons glacés	apricot sauce
Brésilienne	lemon	pineapple	whipped cream
Clo-Clo	vanilla with pieces of candied chestnuts	marrons glacés	raspberry-flavoured whipped cream
Créole	rum-flavoured lemon ice	diced banana and pineapple	whipped cream
Dame-Blanche	almond milk	half a white peach with whitecurrants inside it	pipe a border of lemon ice
Denise	coffee	small rum-flavoured sweets	
Divine	chocolate	diced peaches in Cointreau	cold crème anglaise, crushed meringues, crystallised violets
Edna May	vanilla	compote of cherries	raspberry-flavoured whipped cream
Eugénie	vanilla with pieces of candied chestnuts	crystallised violets	
Favorite	a small scoop each of vanilla, kirsch and maraschino		raspberry-flavoured whipped cream
Frou-Frou	vanilla	diced peaches	glacé cherry
Germaine	vanilla	macerated glacé cherries	candied chestnuts sieved into the coupe
Hélène	vanilla	half a pear	cold chocolate sauce

Ice-cream sweets

Name	Ice	Garnish	Finish
Jacques	a scoop each of lemon and strawberry	diced mixed fruits	
Jeannette	pistachio	strawberries	chocolate flakes
Jubilée	vanilla	compote of cherries	chopped pistachios
Louis	peach	apricot filled with marzipan	strawberry-flavoured whipped cream
Madeleine	vanilla with diced pineapple		liqueur-flavoured apricot sauce
Malmaison	vanilla	peeled de-pipped grapes	veil of spun sugar
Melba	vanilla	half a peach	Melba sauce
Midinette	vanilla	half a peach	small meringue
Mireille	a scoop each of vanilla and raspberry	half a nectarine filled with whitecurrant jam	veil of spun sugar
Monte Carlo	pistachio	diced mixed fresh fruits	whipped cream
Monte-Cristo	pistachio	diced mixed fresh fruits	whipped cream
Niçoise	orange	diced mixed fruits in curaçao	
Rêve de Bébé	layers of pineapple and strawberry	strawberries	crystallised violets
Petit-Duc	vanilla	half peach filled with redcurrants	pipe a border of lemon ice
Royale	vanilla	wild strawberries	whipped cream
Sans-Gène	vanilla	compote of redcurrants	whipped cream
Savoy	a scoop each of coffee and violet flavour	diced mixed fruits	
Singapore	lemon	slice of pineapple	macaroons soaked in anisette liqueur

616

Name	Ice	Garnish	Finish
Suédoise	vanilla mixed with apple purée	half a poached apple	redcurrant jelly and whipped cream
Sylvie	praline	diced banana	whipped cream
Suzette	vanilla with pieces of candied chestnut	marron glacé	whipped cream
Thaïs	vanilla	half a peach	chocolate flakes and whipped cream
Tutti-Frutti	layers of lemon, pineapple and strawberry	diced mixed fresh fruits	whipped cream
Venus	vanilla	half a peach	a very small strawberry at the centre of the peach
Victoria	a scoop each of strawberry and pistachio	diced mixed fresh fruits	

Miscellaneous Ice-cream Sweets

Ananas Edouard VII — Fill an emptied pineapple with scoops of vanilla ice-cream, diced pineapple and cherries previously macerated with kirsch.

Ananas Gastronome — Cover a layer of sponge with maraschino-flavoured banana ice-cream, lay thin slices of pineapple on top then vanilla soufflé mix; place the dish in a tray of crushed ice and bake in a hot oven.

Ananas Geisha — Fill a tartlet with a scoop of orange ice, cover with a thin slice of macerated pineapple and brush with pineapple glaze.

Ananas Ninon	Arrange scoops of vanilla ice in a dish, add thin slices of pineapple, wild strawberries and cover with raspberry purée; sprinkle with shredded pistachios.
Ananas Princesse	Place a thin pineapple ring on a round slice of genoise sponge, add a scoop of strawberry ice-cream and decorate with whipped cream and small strawberries.
Fraises Arlésienne	Fill tartlets with tutti-frutti ice cream, press macerated strawberries into it and glaze with kirsch-flavoured apricot glaze.
Fraises Cardinal	Arrange strawberries on a bed of vanilla ice-cream, coat with raspberry purée and sprinkle with shredded almonds.
Fraises Sarah Bernhardt	Macerate strawberries with brandy and curaçao then arrange on a bed of pineapple ice; coat with whipped cream well coloured with strawberry purée and flavoured with curaçao.
Glace Frite	Use small blocks of firm, well-frozen, lightly aerated ice-cream, egg and crumb twice, re-freeze, then deep fry in a very hot fat for only a few moments and serve immediately.
Mandarines Norvégienne	Fill emptied skins with tangerine ice, cover with rum-flavoured meringue, place in a tray of crushed ice and colour in a very hot oven.
Melon Frappé	Scoop out a melon, make some of the flesh into granité, cut the rest into dice and macerate in Midori liqueur. Refill the melon with layers of granité and the fruit.
Melon Marquise	Cut a lemon in half zig-zag fashion, scoop out the flesh with a spoon and macerate it; refill the melon with vanilla ice cream and the flesh.
Melon Moderne	Empty a melon and cut the flesh into dice, refill with layers of almond ice-cream, macerated wild strawberries and the diced flesh.
Oranges Bristol	Fill emptied orange halves with orange ice and cover with vanilla ice-cream containing chopped pineapple; coat with apricot glaze.
Oranges Infante	Fill emptied orange skins with orange ice, cover with meringue, place in a tray of crushed ice and colour in a very hot oven.

Oranges Javanaise	Fill emptied orange skins with orange ice containing macerated crystallised ginger; add a few segments of orange, cover with meringue and colour in a very hot oven.
Oranges Norvégienne	Fill emptied orange skins with orange ice containing diced pineapple, cover with rum-flavoured meringue and colour in a very hot oven.
Pêche Alexandra	Arrange a peach on a layer of vanilla ice-cream, cover with strawberry purée and decorate with red and white crystallised rose petals.
Pêche Melba	Arrange a whole poached peach on a layer of vanilla ice-cream and cover with raspberry purée or melba sauce.
Pêche Monte Carlo	Arrange on a layer of peach ice and cover with maraschino-flavoured pineapple glaze.
Plombière Ice-cream	Crush 350g almonds with 6 bitter almonds and add to $1\frac{3}{4}$ litre milk; cook as a custard with 10 yolks and 300g sugar then freeze, adding 8dl whipped cream. Arrange in a parfait mould with layers of stiff apricot purée and serve cut into slices.
Poire Belle Hélène	Place a pear on vanilla ice-cream, decorate with crystallised violets and serve accompanied with hot chocolate sauce.
Poire Ménélik	Place a pear on pistachio ice-cream and cover with raspberry purée.
Poire Montrose	Place a pear on a layer of chocolate ice-cream, cover with cold chocolate sauce and sprinkle with praline.

16 SAVOURIES AND SANDWICHES

Savouries

These are normally served as the last course of a formal meal, usually coming after the sweet at dinner. Many of them are also useful as part of a hot hors-d'œuvre selection. In some countries the savoury is served before the sweet. The portion size is fairly small and savouries must be neat which means they could dry out if prepared too far in advance; they must be served very hot.,

Anchovies on Toast	Arrange fillets of anchovy on a square of buttered toast and serve on a dish paper garnished with picked parsley.
Angels on Horseback	Roll raw oysters in thin rashers of streaky bacon and keep in place on a skewer; grill and serve 3 or 4 on a piece of toast.
Beignets Soufflés	Deep fry small balls of chou paste either plain or flavoured with cheese; fill with a savoury filling.
Buck Rarebit	Place a hot poached egg on a prepared Welsh Rarebit.
Canapé Baltimore	Mix diced smoked haddock into scrambled egg, pile on a round of toast, sprinkle with cheese and glaze.
Canapé Baron	Place a rasher of streaky bacon, a grilled mushroom and a poached slice of bone marrow on a round of toast.
Canapé Bengal	Mix grated cheese, chopped ham and tongue with béchamel and tomato ketchup and spread in dome shape on toast.

620

Canapé Cadogan	Cover a round of buttered toast with buttered leaf spinach; place 2 poached oysters on top, coat with sauce mornay and glaze.
Canapé Diane	Roll lightly sautéd pieces of chicken liver in thin rashers of streaky bacon, grill on a skewer and arrange 3 pieces on toast.
Canapé Ecossais	Spread creamed purée of smoked haddock on a round of buttered toast.
Canapé Epicurien	Mix finely grated Gruyère or Stilton with butter, brandy and chopped walnuts; pile in dome shape on a round of toast and glaze.
Canapé Fédora	Arrange grilled rashers of streaky bacon and mushrooms on toast and finish with a stoned olive.
Canapé des Gourmets	Flavour purée of ham with made mustard and spread in dome shape on a round of buttered toast.
Canapé Grosvenor	Mix sardine paste with cooked diced pimento and spread on toast; place a mushroom filled with sardine mixture on top and finish with a stoned olive.
Canapé Hollandais	Spread creamed purée of smoked haddock on a round of toast and decorate with a slice of hard-boiled egg.
Canapé Ivanhoe	Spread creamed purée of smoked haddock on a round of buttered toast and place a grilled mushroom on top.
Canapé Nina	Arrange sliced sautéd mushroom, sliced tomato and slices of pickled walnut on buttered toast.
Canapé Quo Vadis	Arrange sautéd soft roes and a grilled mushroom on toast.
Canapé Rabelais	Pile purée of ham and tongue flavoured with mustard on a round of toast and sprinkle with grated horseradish.
Canapé Rajah	Pile curry-flavoured purée of ham on a round of toast and cover with chopped chutney.
Canapé Ritchie	Spread creamed purée of smoked haddock on a round of buttered toast, sprinkle with cheese and glaze under a salamander.

Champignons sous cloche	Cook mushrooms in cream and lemon juice in an ovenproof dish under a close-fitting bell lid for 8 to 10 minutes.
Croque Epicurienne	Mash Stilton cheese with eggs and brandy; spread on toast and glaze.
Croque Madame	As for Croque Monsieur with the addition of a fried egg, or dip in beaten egg and shallow fry.
Croque Monsieur	Make a sandwich with 2 slices of buttered bread, 2 slices of gruyère cheese and a slice of ham, trim square or round and shallow fry in clarified butter.
Croûte Derby	Spread creamed purée of ham on toast and garnish with a half a pickled walnut.
Croûte John Bull	Spread a 7cm round of puff pastry with herb- and mustard-flavoured butter, place a piece of grilled herring fillet on top and cover trellis fashion with puff pastry; egg-wash, sprinkle with cheese and bake.
Croûte Windsor	Spread creamed purée of ham on a round of buttered toast and garnish with a grilled mushroom, black side uppermost.
Croûte Yorkaise	Spread creamed purée of ham in dome shape on a round of buttered toast and garnish with a large diamond-shape of ham.
Devils on Horseback	Fill stoned cooked prunes with chutney and roll in thin rashers of streaky bacon; grill on a skewer and serve 3 per portion on an oblong of toast.
Fried Camembert	Remove the skin from a Camembert and cut into shapes; sprinkle with cayenne, coat with egg and breadcrumbs and deep fry.
	Brie and other soft cream cheeses can be done in the same way, or may be wrapped in a rasher of bacon, dipped in batter and deep fried.
Marrowbone	Steam the length of marrowbone and serve as it is with a long thin spoon with which to eat it.
Mushrooms on Toast	Arrange grilled mushrooms on a square of toast serving them black side uppermost.
Oysters Lucifer	Spread poached bearded oysters with made mustard, enfold in puff pastry, egg and crumb and deep fry.

Oysters Queen Mary	Place a poached bearded oyster in a cooked mushroom; wrap in a very thin rasher of streaky bacon, dip into frying batter and deep fry.
Palebrouskis	Mix chopped almonds and diced Gruyère, ham and tongue into chou paste and deep fry in spoonfuls.
Profiteroles au Stilton	Fill small chou paste buns with creamed Stilton and reheat in the oven.
Ramequin au Fromage	Fill a pastry tartlet with diced Gruyère cheese and egg custard mixture made with cream, and bake at 175°C until set.
Sardines on Toast	Arrange sardines on an oblong piece of toast, if required they may be boned and skinned.
Scotch Woodcock	Pile scrambled egg in dome shape on a round of buttered toast and decorate trellis fashion with strips of anchovy; place a caper in each hole.
Soufflé Argenteuil	Make a soufflé mixture with asparagus purée, béchamel, yolks of egg and the stiffly beaten whites; bake in a soufflé dish.
Soufflé aux Champignons	Add a fine purée of raw mushroom to the soufflé mixture and bake in the usual way.
Soufflé de Crabe	Add equal amounts of flaked white and purée of dark crab meat to the béchamel and proceed as for ordinary soufflé.
Soufflé Florentine	Add purée of spinach to béchamel and flavour with nutmeg; make into a soufflé mixture and bake as usual.
Soufflé au Jambon	Add fine purée of ham to béchamel and proceed in the usual way for soufflés.
Soufflé au Parmesan	Flavour béchamel well with Parmesan, make into a soufflé mixture in the usual way and bake in a soufflé dish coated with grated Parmesan.
Tartelette Agnes	Fill a pastry tartlet with egg-custard mix made with cream, small lardons of bacon and grated Gruyère cheese and bake until set.
Tartelette Florentine	Fill a tartlet with cheese soufflé mixture containing diced crayfish and truffle and bake until risen.
Tartelette Gentleman	Place a poached slice of bone marrow in a cooked puff pastry tartlet, cover with duxelles

	then with ginger soufflé mixture and bake until risen.
Tartelette Kitchener	Fill a cooked tartlet with flaked smoked haddock mixed with curry-flavoured sauce Mornay and glaze under a salamander.
Tartelette Marquise	Pipe a circle of chou paste around an unbaked tartlet, fill the centre with sauce mornay, sprinkle with cheese and bake in the oven.
Tartelette Mephisto	Place a poached soft roe in a cooked tartlet, add a little sauce diable, sprinkle with fried breadcrumbs and heat in an oven.
Tartelette Raglan	Fill a tartlet with smoked herring roe purée, cover with smoked haddock soufflé mixture and bake until risen.
Tartelette Tosca	Fill a cooked tartlet with diced crayfish in sauce homard, cover with cheese soufflé mixture and bake until risen.
Tartelette Uncle Sam	Fill a cooked tartlet with diced lobster and mushroom in lobster sauce; place a cooked mushroom on top, pour warmed whisky all over and set alight as it is served.
Tartelette Vendôme	Mix a salpicon of cèpes, hard-boiled egg and bone marrow with melted meat glaze, fill a cooked tartlet and add a poached slice of bone marrow.
Toast Hawaii	Cover a round of toast with ham, Edam cheese and a ring of pineapple and grill under a salamander.
Toast Ménélik	This is another name for devils on horseback.
Toast Wellington	Flavour creamed purée of smoked haddock with cheese and sandwich between two slices of toasted or fried bread.
Toasted Cheese	Cover buttered toast with grated or sliced cheese, melt under a grill and trim.
Welsh Rarebit	Add grated Cheddar or Cheshire cheese, egg yolks, mustard, Worcester sauce and cayenne to hot béchamel, spread in dome shape on buttered toast and glaze under a salamander. Trim neatly and serve on a dish paper with picked parsley. A little reduced pale ale may be added to the mixture.

Sandwiches

Toasted Sandwiches

These can be made with either one layer of filling between two slices of toast or two or more layers with the requisite number of slices of toasted bread. They are usually served hot and it is necessary to cut them so as to make it easy for the customer to eat them; the crusts are cut off and the sandwich cut into four or more pieces, each held together by a cocktail stick. There are many versions but no strict rules for the sequence of placing the ingredients on the toast; they should be spread evenly.

Name	Bottom layer	Top layer
Club	mayonnaise, lettuce, streaky bacon	sliced chicken, egg and tomato, lettuce, mayonnaise
Diane	butter, bacon, chicken livers	sliced tomato, watercress, butter
Hans Andersen	bacon, horseradish	liver sausage, tomato, lettuce
Hawaii	mayonnaise, lettuce, pineapple	ham, cheese, lettuce
Maryland	mayonnaise, lettuce, streaky bacon	fried half banana, lettuce, mayonnaise
Monténégro	butter, anchovy fillets, hard-boiled egg	sliced chicken and tomato, lettuce
Moscovite	butter, caviar, shredded onion	sliced egg, grated horseradish, butter
Neptune	mayonnaise, crabmeat, tomato	sliced egg, smoked salmon, lettuce
Playboy	mayonnaise, lettuce, grilled gammon	Cheddar, tomato, lettuce, mayonnaise
St James	butter, ox-tongue, tomato	pickled walnut, watercress, butter
Super Club	mayonnaise, lettuce, sliced chicken	ham, chutney, tomato, lettuce

625

Afternoon Tea Sandwiches

These are different from those served as snack meals both as regards the fillings and the way they are cut. The bread should be sliced not more than 4mm thick and the fillings should be in the form of spreads rather than actual flesh. There should be at least six varieties for customers to choose from and the sandwiches should be cut, without crusts, into squares or triangles with sides not more than 5cm long. It is usual to trim the corners and to place them in piles on the dish, well-sprinkled with mustard and cress. Allow four or five pieces per person.

The appropriate fillings include:

Fish	Anchovy paste, shrimp paste, sardine paste, salmon mixed with white sauce or mayonnaise.
Meat	Chicken paste, ham spread, foie gras purée.
Miscellaneous	Sliced cucumber, sliced tomato, cream cheese and chutney, egg and cress, sandwich spread.

Ordinary Sandwiches

A substantial sandwich is often served as a main course for lunch or supper and the combination of bread and filling can be nutritionally significant. It should be moist, flavourful and nicely presented, as against one that looks dry and stale or where the bread has become soft because it has absorbed moisture from the filling and is served without any garnish. Ideally a sandwich should be made to order but as this is not always possible, prepared sandwiches must be kept between the cut-off crusts and wrapped in a moist cloth or sheet of paper.

There are hundreds of possible combinations of ingredients for use in the general run of sandwiches, the following being the most popular:

Fish	Caviar, crabmeat, shrimps, smoked salmon, tuna fish, tinned salmon.
Meat	Beef, chicken, corned beef, foie gras, ham, salami, tongue, turkey, luncheon meat.

Miscellaneous – Cheese, Egg, Dates, Pickles

Any kind of bread may be used and the sandwiches should be served overlapping on a dish paper, sprinkled with mustard and cress or garnished with lettuce, tomato, cucumber, watercress or pickled onions, etc.

Rolled sandwiches are made by rolling thinly sliced bread without the crust, around a filling such as asparagus, or with a spread in the form of a Swiss roll.

Sandwiches can be cut into halves, triangular or square quarters, and other shapes, using pastry cutters. They can be served in the hollowed-out crust of a loaf.

Fried Sandwiches

Fried sandwiches can be served as a savoury or for high tea or supper; a sandwich with a sweet filling such as jam or banana can be served as a pudding. The sandwich with any filling can be made square, triangular or rolled then either egg-and-breadcrumbed or dipped into batter and deep-fried, or they can be dipped into beaten egg and shallow fried, or simply fried without a coating.

A fried sandwich is called 'a hot rod' in America and various names are given, e.g. *Ranchero, Jockey Club, Denver*, according to the kind of filling used.

Ploughman's

A ploughman's lunch can be a large roll or hunk of crisp bread, with Cheddar cheese, pickled onion, apple and butter. Optional extras could include salad stuffs, chutney or other pickle, etc. A continental ploughman's lunch should be made with French bread and French or German cheese.

Smorrebrod

Smorrebrod are Scandinavian open sandwiches served as a meal, allowing three or four per person, offering a variety of fish, meat and cheese ones. They are meant to be eaten with a knife and fork and the bread should be the close-textured kind such as rye, wholemeal or French stick, firm enough to support the amount of topping added. When made they can be decorated to choice using apple, cress, cucumber, egg, gherkin, radish, mushrooms, olives, onion, prunes, mandarin segments and parsley, in order to make them as colourful as possible.

The main varieties include:

Beefeater	Beef, horseradish cream, sauce rémoulade, onion, lettuce, gherkin, tomato.
Carlsberg	Liver sausage, black grapes, scrambled egg.
Copenhagen	Russian salad with diced beetroot, ham, hard-boiled egg, beetroot.
Danish Delight	Smoked pork, pickled cabbage, prune, orange, lettuce.
Epicurean	Chicken, bacon, lettuce, tomato, cucumber, cress.
Guardsman	Salt beef, horseradish cream, onion, tomato, chopped parsley.
Hans Andersen	Pâté, bacon, mushroom, tomato, gherkin.
Harlequin	Potato salad, ham, cress, radish.
Kronberg	Ham, Russian salad, apple, onion, capers.
Maribo	Maribo cheese, salami, lettuce, gherkin.
Marmir	Rollmop, onion, asparagus, shrimps.
Roulette	Russian salad, sliced smoked cod roe, tomato, cucumber, gherkin.
Tivoli	Lumpfish caviar, hard-boiled egg, mayonnaise, tomato, lettuce.
Troubador	Ox-tongue, horseradish cream, pimento, anchovy, lettuce.
Zeeland	Russian salad, rollmop, tomato, chopped chives.

In addition to butter or low-fat spread it is permissible to use any of the flavoured or coloured butters for spreading on the bread or piping on top as part of the decoration. Peanut butter or cream cheese may be used in the same way. Thick mayonnaise can be piped with a star tube, and a thin line of Marmite or Bovril is a form of decoration.

Fillings include:

Fish	Anchovy fillets and paste, smoked cod roe, caviar, crabmeat, pickled and smoked herring, smoked oysters, pilchard, prawns, salmon – smoked or tinned; brisling, sardines, shrimps, tuna, smoked mackerel.
Meat	Bacon, roast beef, brisket, chicken, corned beef, frankfurters, garlic sausage, ham, liver pâté and sausage, luncheon meat, pâtés, spreads, salami, smoked sausages, smoked turkey, Parma ham.
Egg	Hard-boiled, scrambled; quail's; seagull's, guinea fowl.
Cheese	All varieties including cream cheese, grated Cheddar, etc.
Garnishes	Almonds, apple, asparagus, beetroot, Belgian endive, capers, grated carrot, celery, chutney, cucumber, dill, gherkin, grapes, horseradish, lemon, lettuce, kiwi fruit, mandarin oranges, mayonnaise, mushrooms, mustard and cress, olives, onion, parsley, pickles, pimento, pineapple, prunes, radishes, radicchio, red cabbage, sandwich spread, tomato, walnuts, watercress.

17 FONDUES

A fondue is a Swiss family meal or celebration party for family and friends on a special occasion. To make the event a successful and happy one it is necessary to have the right equipment and ingredients as otherwise guests may end up trying to eat something that looks and tastes like rubbery chewing gum.

Equipment: a caquelon which is the earthenware or enamelled pan; a spirit stove or gas burner as used for flambé work (a dishwarmer heated with nightlights is not hot enough); fondue forks or skewers of the right length. The following is the classic recipe:

Fondue Neuchâteloise
(*Ingredients for 10/12 persons*) (For a mild fondue, use all Emmenthal; for a medium one use 2 parts Gruyère to 1 part Emmenthal; for a strong flavour, use only Gruyère.)

400g Emmenthal
800g Gruyère
5dl dry white wine
1dl Kirsch or Schnapps
30g cornflour
Squeeze of lemon juice
Approximately 2kg French bread
Clove of garlic

Method
Rub the inside of the pot with garlic. Put the diced cheeses which have been coated with the cornflour or flour in the pot and mix on the stove; add the wine and lemon juice and stir until melted; when creamy and smooth, add the kirsch, a little nutmeg and cayenne pepper, then place the pot on the burner on the table, keeping it simmering, and stirring each time a person puts his piece of bread

630

in it. The bread should be cut so that each piece has some crust and is the size of a mouthful. If too runny, add more cornflour diluted with wine to bring it to a light coating consistency.

Variations

Bacon	Add diced fried bacon and some chopped parsley.
Caerphilly	Use beer instead of wine and replace the Emmenthal with Caerphilly cheese.
Cider	Replace the wine with dry still cider.
Curried	Flavour with curry powder or paste.
Devilled	Add Worcester sauce and horseradish sauce.
Farmhouse	Use milk instead of wine.
Niçoise	Add squeezed garlic, chopped anchovies and sliced stuffed olives.
Onion	Add finely chopped cooked onion.
Stilton	Use beer instead of wine and replace the Emmenthal with Stilton.
Tuna	Add flaked canned tuna and a few drops of Worcester sauce.

Fondue Bourguignon

This is not actually a real fondue and is a Japanese rather than a Swiss idea. Small pieces of very tender meat such as fillet steak are speared onto a long fork and held in a pan of heated fat placed on the dining table. When judged to be sufficiently cooked it is dipped into one of a number of cold or hot sauces or dips before eating. Safety precautions are important to ensure the pan of fat cannot be tipped over and that the fat does not heat beyond 180°C. The pieces of meat or offal may be marinated in advance so as to flavour and tenderise it. Suitable sauces include:

Barbecue
Bourguignonne

Cumberland
Sour Cream
Dips that can be flavoured with mayonnaise, yoghurt, horseradish, ketchup.

Sweet Fondue

The sauce is made and kept hot as for cheese fondue and customers are provided with small squares of dry sponge cake, langues de chat, small profiteroles, marshmallows, pieces of fruit, such as pineapple, banana or whole strawberries.

Banana	Liquidise bananas, heat with cream and sugar and flavour with brandy.
Cherry	Heat stoned cherries in wine and cherry sauce, add cream and flavour with kirsch.
Chocolate	Melt grated Toblerone chocolate and mix with cream, kirsch and brandy.
Mocha	Heat strong coffee with cream and grated chocolate; flavour with Tia Maria.
Orange and Chocolate	Melt grated chocolate with cream, flavour with Grand Marnier or curaçao and add grated orange rind.

18 PIZZAS AND
QUICHES

Pizzas are based on what used to be a primitive peasant-style snack meal made of bread dough with savoury ingredients sprinkled on top and baked in an oven fired with wood. From such humble Italian origins they now enjoy world-wide favour and have been made slightly more sophisticated and sufficiently substantial to constitute a main dish. They can be made in the form of a flan using pastry, or bread dough, and the depth of filling increased to merit the title of deep-dish pizza.

Pizzas can also be made in the form of a tart or slice with a top and bottom crust; small ones suitable for a buffet are called pizzettine and they can all be made on slices of French bread instead of the traditional base. Some ingredients such as mushroom, onion, pimento must be pre-cooked before being put on the dough but most pizzas can be cooked from raw.

A pizzeria is a restaurant or tavern that specialises in pizzas; a pizzaiolo is the person who makes them. Every major town and region of Italy is proud of its own version of what constitutes a pizza but there are also many fanciful names.

Pizza Dough   Dissolve 30g fresh yeast in $5\frac{1}{2}$dl warm water together with 20g dough improver powder; pour into the centre of 1kg strong flour sieved with 15g salt, and mix for 15 minutes. Divide into 75g pieces for individual pizzas and roll out 13cm diameter; prick well, brush with oil, sprinkle with the ingredients and bake at 220°C.

A mixture of strong and wholemeal flour may be used.

The most widely used cheese is mozzarella and the traditional herb is oregano, or wild marjoram.

Americano	Tomato, mozzarella, pimento, salami.
Bolognaise	Tomato, mozzarella, Parma ham, artichoke.
Brindisi	Tomato, oregano, mozzarella, capers and anchovies.
Calabrese	Tomato, mozzarella, anchovies, black olives.
Casalinga	Tomato, anchovies.
con Cozze	Cooked bearded mussels, anchovy, mozzarella, garlic, black olives.
Diavolo	Tomato, chilli powder, peperonata sausage, mozzarella.
Ferrarese	Tomato, mozzarella, parsley.
Fiorentino	Garlic, spinach, tomato, mozzarella, Parmesan.
Firenze	Tomato, mushroom, mozzarella, oregano.
Francescano	Ham, mushroom, Gruyère.
Genovese	Anchovies, garlic, pecorino cheese, tomato.
Giardiniera	Mixed vegetables such as egg-plant, onion, pimento, tomato, etc.
Gorgonzola	Slices of Gorgonzola cheese, ham.
Margherita	Mozzarella, tomato, basil, oregano.
Marinara	Anchovy, mushroom, mussels, prawns, tuna, Parmesan.
Marmora	Anchovy, black olives, tomato.
Napolitano	Anchovy, garlic, black olives, mozzarella, oregano, tomato.
O Sole Mio!	Tomato, mozzarella, basil, oregano.
Paesano	Tomato, sliced hard-boiled egg, mozzarella, oregano.
Palermitano	Tomato, mozzarella, capers, anchovies, tuna fish.
Quattro Stagione	Artichoke, capers, mushroom, olives, oregano, Parmesan, salami.
Religiosa	Sliced cèpes, anchovy, oregano.
Romana	Anchovy, artichoke, capers, ham, mushroom, olives, oregano, Parmesan, salami, tomato.
Rustica	Diced bel paese cheese, diced hard-boiled egg and ham, salami and sultanas all mixed into

	sauce mornay, cream cheese and whisked egg-whites.
Siciliana	Anchovy, ham, mozzarella, pecorino, tomato, garlic.
Tessin	Emmenthal, oregano, tomato, tarragon mustard.
Tonnaro	Peperonata, tuna fish, Gruyère cheese.
Torinese	Mushroom, tomato, Parmesan.
Umberto	Artichoke, bacon, mozzarella, tomato.
Veneziano	Tomato, mozzarella, oregano, rosemary, parsley, mussels.
Veronese	Peperonata, coppa, Gruyère, artichokes, praticelli (field mushrooms preserved in oil).
Vesuvio	Mushroom, pimento, ricotta, salami, tomato.

Pissaladière

This speciality originated in Alsace in France and is usually a deep tart or as a pizza. The base is spread with a cooked mixture of onion, garlic and herbs in oil, with a trellis work of anchovy and black olives, tomato, etc. arranged on top and baked.

Quiches

This speciality originated in Alsace in France and is usually a deep flan filled with savoury egg custard, together with other ingredients as listed below, and baked at 175°C for approximately 35 minutes until just set. Quiche is a snack or supper dish and small quiches, called quichelettes can be a part of an hot hors-d'œuvre selection, as a savoury, or a buffet item.

Quiche Lorraine is the best known. Line a flan ring with short pastry, add fried lardons, diced Gruyère cheese, fill with custard made with 7–8 eggs per 1 litre of cream or milk and cream and bake.

Camembert Slices of Camembert cheese.

Cheese and Onion Grated Emmenthal cheese, sautéd chopped onion.

Crab Add crabmeat to the custard mixture.

Ham and Peas Batons of ham, cooked peas.

Ile de France Fill with white sauce thickened with yolks and cream, sautéd mushroom.

Picardy Diced ham, cooked chopped leek.

Smoked Salmon Coarse julienne of smoked salmon, cooked chopped leek.

Snail Snails, cooked chopped leek and shallot.

Spinach Buttered chopped spinach, grated Gruyère cheese.

Tomato Diced tomato, grated emmenthal cheese.

Tuna Chopped cooked tuna fish, Gruyère cheese, thyme.

Wahen This is a Swiss version of a quiche that is filled with cheese, vegetables, fruit, etc., in the basic egg custard.

19 COOKING METHODS

1. **Baking** cooking in a previously heated oven, usually in dry heat but in some equipment steam or other form of moisture is introduced to give a better result; applicable mainly to bread and pastry work.

2. **Barbecue** grilling or roasting over an open hearth, usually outdoors; roasting is done on a rotary arm or spit and broiling is done on the bars over a wood or charcoal fire.

3. **Boiling** complete immersion of a food in a liquid which is brought to 100°C, boiling point, and kept at the same temperature until cooked.
   Parboil to parcook a food by boiling until it is partially done before continuing to cook it by another method.
   Blanching to whiten or set a food by immersing it in boiling water or by bringing it to a boil from cold; also used to reduce the acridity of certain foods.

4. **Braising** cooking food that is half-covered by a liquid, in a closely lidded container in the oven; it renders tough foods tender by the fairly long process and gives colour and flavour from the cooking liquid.

5. **Broiling** the old-fashioned term for grilling, still widely used on menus in the USA.

6. **Deep frying** complete immersion of a food in fat at a temperature of 160–195°C, according to the nature of the item being cooked and the kind of outer coating; the cooked result should have a crisp dry outside and moist but not fatty interior.

7. **Grilling** a fierce form of cooking that is done at a high temperature in close proximity to the heat source which can be charcoal, electricity or gas, directed from above or below.

Ceramic or metallic brickettes fired by gas also give radiant heat.

8. **Infra-red** this is a method of reheating dishes from frozen or chilled, of grilling small items of food, and keeping dishes hot on a buffet or carvery counter. The infra-red rays are produced from electric quartz elements which penetrate the food.

9. **Microwave** electro-magnetic waves produced by a magnetron penetrate the food in the closed oven, causing the molecules to agitate so creating friction which heats and cooks. It is not a distinct method of cookery but an item of equipment that raises the temperature of food very rapidly. A microwave oven cannot replace a conventional stove and there are certain limitations to its use, especially as regards pastry work. Metal containers can be used only in the Mealstream type of microwave oven. It is possible to have a programmed oven for automatic food service systems. The advantages claimed for cooking by microwaves are speed of operation, economy of fuel, retention of colour, flavour and nutritional values, safety of operation, and mobility. A microwave oven is very good for defrosting and for regenerating frozen foods. Special ovenware should be used and some items need to be stirred during the cooking cycle; seasoning should be done at the end.

10. **Poaching** there are two methods:
    1. deep poaching is total immersion in a depth of cooking liquid which is kept at approximately 95°C with barely discernable movement of the liquid;
    2. shallow poaching in a limited quantity of cooking liquid in a shallow vessel, usually in an oven; it is the practice to use the cooking liquid in the accompanying sauce.

11. **Pot roasting** there can be two meanings for this term: (a) cooking good-quality items in butter in a closed container in the oven, removing the lid towards the end of the cooking time so that the items may take colour – this is known as poêling; (b) cooking tough meat or poultry firstly by parboiling then in a closed container in an oven in the presence of fat so as to colour and render tender.

12. **Roasting**   cooking in a closed oven at a fairly high tempera-
    ture in an open vessel, with fat to lubricate by basting so giving
    colour and flavour; it should be done on a trivet rather than
    lying in the fat. Electronic programmed ovens, conveyor-belt
    ovens, forced-air-convection ovens, rotary ovens and other
    specialised ovens are available.

13. **Sautéing**   actually means the tossing over of food to cook and
    colour it in a small quantity of fat in a frying pan but applies
    equally to shallow frying by turning the food once only (see also
    Stewing).

14. **Shallow frying**   cooking in a plat sauté or other shallow pan
    in a small amount of heated fat to cook and colour items that do
    not require a great length of time; the French term is sauté or à
    la poêle.

15. **Simmering**   the same as poaching, in which food is cooked
    gently in a depth of water held at approximately 93°C at which
    there is barely perceptible movement in the liquid.

16. **Steaming**   cooking in the presence of steam in a pressurised
    vessel or steaming oven which can operate at anything from
    atmospheric pressure up to as high as 100kPa according to type.

17. **Stewing**   a slow, gentle method of rendering tougher pieces
    of meat tender and succulent by cooking in a closed vessel in
    the presence of a thick or thin liquid. A sauté is a stew made of
    better-quality meat cooked more quickly.

18. **Cooking by induction**   induction heating is done by produc-
    ing heat from electricity by creating an intense magnetic field
    and sending an alternating current through it so that when a
    pan is placed on it it undergoes rapid heating from inducted
    current. It only operates when a metal pan is placed in the stove
    and only that part under the pan is subjected to the current; the
    metal pan must be made of ferritic steel or have a special
    detachable bottom.

19. **Sous-vide**   this is an extension of the cook–chill method, but
    more sophisticated in its initial preparation stages, since it
    involves vaccum packaging and cooking 'en papillote'. Basically
    it requires that the food is placed in certain weights in sterilised

impermeable pouches, whence the air is removed by the vacuum process and the airless pouch is sealed to prevent any oxidation of the food materials through being further exposed to air. The food is then cooked in the pouch in a pressureless steamer for a specified period at a specific temperature, normally between 65 and 85°C. Once the cooking process has been completed the pouch must be rapidly chilled until it reaches practically 0°C and can be kept between 0–3±C for up to six days. If it is more rapidly frozen it will keep much longer. One of the main advantages of this process is that it appears capable of maintaining the natural colour of food products. The regeneration is best carried out in the original sealed pouch in a pressureless steamer.

20 CHECKLIST OF SMALL KITCHEN EQUIPMENT

This section shows all items of small utensils and equipment used in the traditional kitchen.

Personal Items

The complete set of chef's tools includes:

Small general purpose knife (couteau d'office)
Filleting knife, 15cm
Cook's knife, 20–22cm (for carving, chopping, slicing)
Chopping knife (for heavy cutting and chopping)
Boning knife 15cm
Carving knife 30–35cm (sometimes hollow ground)
Tranchelard or ham knife, up to 40cm
Palette knife
Sharpening steel
Kitchen fork
Vegetable peeler
Grooving knife
Trussing needle
Larding needle
Orange zester

Additional personal items

These may include:

Set of aspic cutters
Column cutters
Pastry cutters
Parisienne spoon cutters
Pastry wheel
Pastry nippers
Brush
Silver or stainless steel skewers
Ice pick
Can opener
Scissors
Serrated edge knife (cannelé)
Grapefruit knife
Piping bag and tubes (plain and fancy)
Corkscrew
Corer
Zester

Preparation Equipment

Metal:

chopper
cleaver
cutlet bat
marfor slicer
3 or 4 bladed rocker knife
meat saws
charlotte mould
dariole mould
scales
spoons

Wood:

spoons,
peppermill
spatulas
mushroom
mandolin
chopping board
salt box
pepper box
pot stand
rolling pin
Many wooden implements have been replaced by plastic as being
more hygienic.

China and glass:

basin
mixing bowl
oven-proof serving dishes
pie-dish
soufflé dish
raviers
thermometer
lemon squeezer

Tinned steel/stainless steel:

chinois
conical strainer
whisks
spoons
egg slicer
ladle
grater
salad drainer
frying basket
spider
flan ring
cake tin

barquette and tartlet moulds
sifter
pastry rack
ice cream scoop

Cooking Equipment

This is made of aluminium, copper or stainless steel.

Saucepans, general purpose	Frying pan
Sauté pan	Omelette pan
Sauteuse	Pancake pan
Stockpot	Oval fish-frying pan
Braising pan	Baking tray
Bain-marie pot	Sugar boiling pan
Roasting tray	Anna moulds
Grilling tray	Savarin mould
Fish kettle	Bombe mould
Salmon kettle	Mixing bowl

Stillroom Equipment

China:

cups (tea, coffee, demitasse), egg cups

Silver:

butter dish
coffee pot
milk and cream jug
hot water jug
tea strainer
teapot
toast rack

21 CHECKLIST OF COMMODITIES

This section gives brief details of staple commodities, in the form of hints on purchasing.

Meat

Beef

A large animal is divided into four sections – two forequarters and two hindquarters. A smaller beast such as an Aberdeen Angus is sometimes sold as two sides with each side consisting of a fore- and a hindquarter in one piece. The quarters are normally divided into the following joints.

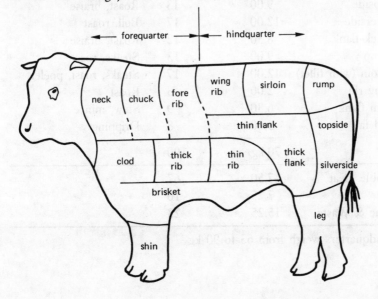

Checklist of commodities

Forequarter

Joint	Approximate weight kg.	%	Uses
Neck	5.50	8.5	Mince, stew
Clod	7.25	11	Mince, stew
Shin	3.20	6	Mince
Brisket	12.25	18.5	Boil (often pickled)
Thick rib	8.65	13	Stew, braise
Thin rib	3.00	4.5	Stew, braise
Fore rib	6.65	10	Roast
Chuck & blade	19.50	28.5	Stew, braise
	66 kg.	100	
Usable meat	46	70	
Fat	7	10	
Bone & Waste	13	20	

Forequarters weigh from 59 to 86 kg

Hindquarter

Joint	Approximate weight kg.	%	Uses
Leg	5.60	8	Mince
Topside	9.00	13	Roast, braise
Silverside	12.00	17	Boil, roast
Thick-flank	8.50	12	Roast, braise
Rump	9.00	13	Steaks, roast
Sirloin (with fillet)	12.00	17	Steaks, roast, poêler
Wing rib	2.00	3	Roast
Thin flank	6.30	9	Stew, mince
Cod fat	5.60	8	Dripping
	70 kg.	100	
Usable meat	47.50	67	
Fat	7.25	10	
Bone & Waste	15.25	23	

Hindquarters weigh from 63 to 90 kg

The following small cuts are obtained from the hindquarter. There are no small cuts from the forequarter excepting steaks suitable for braising and stewing.

Joint	Name of small cut	Average portion weight (g)	Description
Sirloin	Entrecôte	180	Slice of trimmed sirloin approximately 1cm thick
Sirloin	Double entrecôte	320	Slice of trimmed sirloin approximately 2cm thick
Sirloin	Minute steak	120	Flattened slice of sirloin approximately 4mm thick
Sirloin	Porterhouse steak	500	Cut on the bone with the fillet
Sirloin	T-bone steak	180	Has the T-shaped bone in place
Rump	Rump steak	150	2cm thick piece cut from a whole slice
Rump	Point steak	150	Triangular shape from the corner piece
Fillet	Chateaubriand	250	At least 2-portion piece cut from the head
Fillet	Fillet steak	150	slice approximately 3cm thick from the thick end
Fillet	Tournedos or medaillon	120	Round piece 3–3.5cm, from the centre

Beef is also available as baby beef with a hind- or forequarter weighing as little as 40kg. It is also sold as boneless primal cuts which are vacuum-packed in film.

Veal

Veal is the meat obtained from a calf that has been specially raised for the table. It is available in sides of approximately 35kg. The joints are as follows:

Joint	Approximate weight (kg)	General uses	Small cuts
Neck end	2	Stew	–
Neck	3	Stew	–
Best end	3	Roast	Cutlets
Shoulder	7	Roast, braise, poêler, stew	–
Loin	4	Roast, poêler, sauter	Cutlets
Breast	3	Roast, braise, stew	Paillards
Leg	10	Roast, braise, poêler	Escalopes, grenadins
Knuckle	2	Stew (osso buco)	–
Total	34		

In addition there is a large kidney surrounded with suet. The leg is usually divided into (i) cushion, (ii) under-cushion, (iii) thick flank, (iv) rump, each of which gives the small cuts. The approximate bone content of a side of veal is 20 per cent.

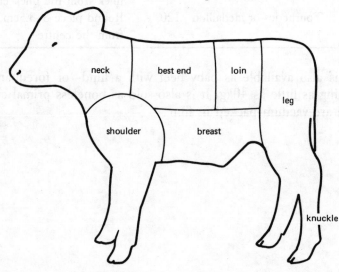

Lamb

Lamb is available as chilled and frozen New Zealand and fresh home-killed, in several weights, qualities and sizes. British lamb is generally heavy in size and weight as compared with New Zealand and the quality is excellent. Whole New Zealand lambs are graded as PL 9–12½kg, PM 13–16kg., PX 16½–20kg., PH 20½–25½kg. New Zealand mutton is labelled HX for those with a light fat content and HL for medium amount of fat. The joints cut from an average size carcase of lamb are as follows:

Joint	Approximate weight NZ	UK	Uses	Small cuts
Scrag end and neck	1.00	1.25	Stew	–
Best end	1.00	1.25	Roast, grill	7 cutlets or rosettes
Shoulder	1.00	1.50	Roast, stew	–
Breast	1.00	1.25	Stew	Epigrammes
Loin	1.50	2.25	Roast, grill	Chops, chump chops, rosettes, noisettes, filets mignons
Leg	1.50	2.00	Roast, boil	Leg steaks
Total	7.00	9.50 (×2 to give weight of whole carcase)		

The approximate percentage of bone in a carcase is 12½ per cent.

See overleaf for illustration.

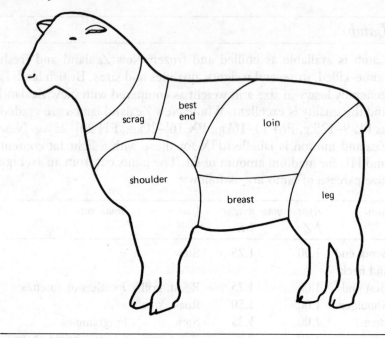

Pork

Pork is the meat from a pig and the joints from an average side of pork of 29kg are as follows:

Joint	Approximate weight (kg)	Uses	Small cuts
Head	1.25	Brawn	–
Blade	1.25	Roast	–
Hand	3.00	Roast	–
Spare rib	2.25	Roast, pie meat	Spare ribs
Long loin	10.50	Roast, grill	Chops
Belly	4.50	Boil	Streaky
Leg	6.25	Roast, boil	Escalopes
	29kg.		

The bones of a carcase of pork are small and the average bone content is approximately 10 per cent.

The range of weights for a side of pork is from 27 to 34kg.

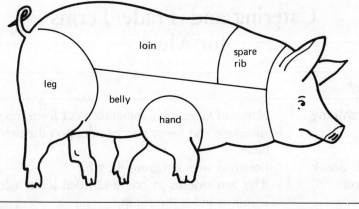

Bacon

Bacon is pork that has been cured by immersing the side in a brine or by dry salting, so as to preserve it. It is sometimes then subjected to smoking to develop further flavour and to keep it longer. The joints from a side of bacon are as follows:

Joint	Approximate weight (kg)	Uses	Small cuts
Hock	3.50	Boil	Rashers
Collar	3.00	Boil	Rashers
Back	7.50	Fry, grill	Back rashers, bacon chops
Streak	3.50	Fry, grill	Streaky bacon
Gammon	5.50	Boil, braise grill	Gammon rashers
	23.00		

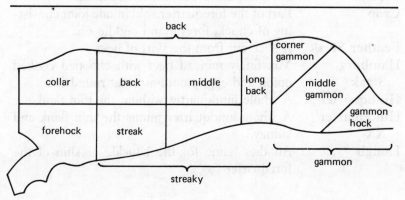

651

Catering and Trade Terms
—————— for Meat ——————

Beef

Aitchbone	Name of large joint sometimes cut from top of silverside and lower part of rump, on the pelvic bone.
Ball Steak	Boneless slice cut from the rib.
Baron	The two sirloins in one undivided joint; a full baron includes the rump.
Bola Steak	Looks like a piece cut from the fillet but is actually from the leg of mutton cut.
Carpet Bag Steak	Sirloin or rump steak with a pocket cut into it,filled with fresh or smoked oysters and sewn up before grilling.
Chateaubriand	As originally conceived, this was a double-thick slice of fillet sandwiched between two other steaks of the same size and grilled until the two outside pieces were burnt black. Serve the original double or treble size steak with sauce béarnaise.
Chuck	Joint of the forequarter lying between the clod and middle rib.
Club Steak	Slice cut from a wing rib.
Coast	The brisket and plate in one large joint.
Colchester Steak	Stuff a fillet steak with oysters, wrap in bacon and grill; serve with sauce béarnaise.
Crop	Part of the forequarter sold in one joint consisting of chuck, forerib and middle rib.
Feather Steak	A slice cut from the skirt of beef.
Hamburg Steak	Mix finely minced beef with chopped cooked onion and egg; mould as a flat round cake.
Hindquarter X	A whole hindquarter without the thin flank.
Hindquarter XX	A whole hindquarter minus the thin flank and kidney.
Hough	Another name for the knuckle or shin of the forequarter.

Leg of Mutton Cut	A forequarter cut consisting of part of the chuck and shoulder.
Médaillon	This can be another name for a tournedos or, in the plural, thin slices cut through the fillet, allowing 3–4 per portion.
Minute de Bœuf	Menu term for a minute steak.
Noix d'Entrecôte	The fully trimmed slice cut from a sirloin.
Paillard	A thin slice of beef or veal without bone or fat, for grilling or sautéing, cut from the breast part.
Pavé de Rumsteak	A square piece of rumpsteak.
Plank Steak	Any kind of steak cooked on a special piece of wood and garnished with vegetables as a complete meal.
Point End	The triangular shape part of the rump.
Pony	Section of a forequarter consisting of the chuck and middle rib.
Pope's Eye	A butcher's term for the top rump (Scotland).
Rib Eye Steak	Steak cut from a boned-out rib.
Shank	Bottom part of the foreleg.
Skink	Another name for the shin and leg (Scotland).
Skirt	Thin piece cut from the thin flank (goose skirt) or rump; quite tender. Classed as an offal.
Striploin	Boned and trimmed whole sirloin.
Tenderloin	Boned and trimmed whole sirloin.
Top Rump	Name given to the thick flank.
Undercut	The fillet from under the sirloin.

Veal

Grenadin	Oval shape 1½cm thick slice of approximately 60g, cut from the cushion or thick flank.
Osso Buco	Cut through the knuckle on the bone in 4cm thickness.
Paillard	Thin piece cut from the breast.
Piccata	Small escalopes of approximately 40g each; serve three per portion.

653

Piccatina	Very small escalopes, serve five or six per portion.
Rouelles de Jarret	A thick slice cut on the bone from the knuckle.

Lamb and Mutton

Barnsley chop	Double chop cut from across a whole loin.
Baron	The saddle and two legs in one joint.
Basses côtes	Uncovered cutlets from the front part of the best end and middle neck.
Béhague	A type of young milk-fed lamb.
Blade chop	Slice cut approximately 1½cm thick on the bone from the thick end of the shoulder.
Butterfly chop	Double chop cut approximately 1cm thick from across the saddle.
Canon d'agneau	The eye of the best end and loin rolled into a joint.
Chine	The best end and loin in one long joint on the bone.
Coeur de carré	The eye of the best end trimmed into a joint.
Crown chop	A cut through the whole loin approximately 2cm thick.
Double chop	Either a chop cut across a whole loin or a double thickness chop from the half loin.
Epigrammes	Braised and pressed breast cut into heart or diamond shapes; egg and crumbed and shallow fried.
Gigot	Scottish name for a leg.
Guard of Honour	Two best ends roasted and served with the cutlet bones interlocked and capped with cutlet frills.
Haggis	Boil the heart, liver and lungs, mince and mix with toasted oatmeal, suet, chopped onion, nutmeg and fill a sheep's stomach two thirds full; boil for 3 hours.
Leg Steak	Steak cut through a leg, on the bone.
Mock duck	Boned shoulder with the shank left on, rolled and tied to the shape of a duck.

Noisette	Pear- or heart-shaped piece cut from the loin or best end.
Pauillac	A young milk-fed lamb, originally from Bordeaux.
Pistola	Boned, rolled and tied loin and leg for roasting whole or cutting into steaks.
Pré-Salé	Lambs reared on salt marshes near the sea; these have a distinctive flavour.
Rack of Lamb	Prepared best end for roasting whole.
Rosette	Slice cut from a boned and rolled loin.
Rouelle d'Agneau	Round slice cut through a boned saddle.
Shank	The bottom part of the shoulder joint, cut off and cooked on the bone.
Short Fore	Two shoulders with the scrag and neck, in one piece.
Short Saddle	Pair of loins in one joint, without the chump end.
Shoulder Slice	Steak cut from the middle neck.
Topside Leg Steak	Thick slice cut on the bone from the top end of the leg.
Valentine Steak	A noisette cut almost through and opened out to give a pear or heart shape.

Pork

Hand	Lower part of the shoulder including the knuckle.
Petit salé	Lean salted belly; or piece of streaky bacon.
Spare Ribs	Upper part of a shoulder.
Speck	Salt cured thick fat from the loin, used for larding and barding.
Spring	Another name for the top part of a shoulder and spare rib.
Sucking Pig	Piglet of 5–7 weeks weighing from $4\frac{1}{2}$–9kg for roasting and serving whole.
Tenderloin	Fillet from under the loin.
Trotter	Hind or fore foot.

Poultry

This term covers all the usual domestic birds bred for the table but not usually the wild ones that have to be shot, although pigeons are included under this heading.

Bird	Average ready weight (kg)	Uses	Number of portions	Menu name
Milk fed chick	single 0.35 double 0.60	Roast, grill	1 2	Poussin
Spring Chicken	0.90–1.25	Roast, grill, sauter	2	Poulet de grain
Broiler	1.00–1.50	Roast, sauter, fry	4	Poulet reine
Fattened fowl	2.50	Poêler, poach	6	Poularde
Boiling fowl	3.00	Boil, braise	6	Poule
Capon-style	3.00	Roast	10	Chapon
Duckling	2.00	Roast poêler	2	Caneton
Duck	3.00	Roast, braise	4	Canard
Goose	6.00	Roast, (Season Oct.–Jan)	12	Oie
Turkey	5.00–14.00	Roast, poach (hens are the most succulent)	10–30	Dindonneau/ Dinde
Guinea fowl	1.00–1.50	Roast, poêler	4	Pintade
Pigeon	0.50	Roast, braise	1	Pigeon
Poulet noir (has a gamey flavour)	0.75–1.25	Roast, poêler	2	

Game

This term covers wild birds and animals which are suitable for eating; some are protected by law as to the season when they can be taken. They are sold by the unit and not by weight.

Name	Season	Uses	Average weight as purchased	Number of portions	Menu name
Grouse	12 August to 20 December	Roast, braise (old birds).	720g	1–2	Grouse
Partridge	1 September to 11 February	Roast, braise	380g	1	Perdreau, Perdrix (old one)
Pheasant	1 October to 11 February	Roast, poêler, braise	1.25kg	2–4	Faisan
Ptarmigan	12 August to 20 December	Roast, braise	700g	1	Lagopède
Quail	All year	Roast, poêler	60g	1	Caille
Snipe	12 August to 10 February	Roast	90g	1	Bécassine
Wild Duck	1 September to 10 February	Roast	700g	2	Canard sauvage
Woodcock	1 October to 10 February	Roast	300g	1	Bécasse

Name	Season	Uses	Average weight as purchased	Number of portions	Menu name
Hare	1 August to 28 February	Stew	3–4kg	6	Lièvre
Rabbit	All year	Stew	1–2kg	4	Lapin
Venison	Roebuck – all year	Roast, braise, stew –		20	Chevreuil
	Red Deer				
	b August–April				
	d November–February				
	Fallow Deer				
	b August to April	(in Scotland there is a slight difference in dates)			
	d November to February				
Wood Pigeon	All year	Braise, pie	500g	1	Ramier

b = buck   *d* = doe

(Roasted weight, on the bone is approximately 50% of as purchased rough plucked weight of poultry and game birds)

Fish and Shellfish

Sea fish – flat

Name	Best season	Best weight	Uses	Menu name
Brill	June–April	1–3½kg	Poach, braise, shallow fry	Barbue
Dab	February–April	150–600g	Grill, deep and shallow fry	Limande Commune
Flounder	Nay-February	400–900g	As for plaice	Limande
Halibut	June–April	1¼–13kg	Poach, braise, grill	Flétan
Plaice	April–September	200g–1½kg	Grill, shallow and deep fry	Plie

Name	Best season	Best weight	Uses	Menu name
Sole–Dover	September–March	whole 250–450g fillets ea. 40–75g	Poach, grill, deep and shallow fry	Sole de Douvres
Sole–Lemon	June–February	200–850g	Poach, grill, deep and shallow fry	Sole Limande
Skate, Wings	October–April	150g–1½kg	Poach, deep and shallow fry	Raie
Turbot	September–April	1–9kg	Poach, braise, grill, fry	Turbot

Sea fish – round

Name	Best season	Best weight	Uses	Menu name
Bass	April–November	450g–1½kg	Braise, poach, bake, shallow fry	Bar
Cod	September–April	2¼–5g	fry, boil, grill, shallow fry	Cabilland
Coley	November–March	2½–5½kg	Shallow or deep fry	Colin
Gurnard	February–September	350g–1¼kg	Boil, grill, bake	Grondin
Haddock	September–March	250g–2½kg	Bake, shallow and deep fry	Aiglefin
Hake	June–January	2½–6kg	Poach, braise, grill, fry	Merluche
Herring	May–June	120–500g	Grill, shallow fry	Hareng
John Dory	April–October	500g–2kg	Poach, braise, shallow fry	Saint-Pierre
Mackerel	March–October	150–750g	Bake, grill, shallow fry	Maquereu
Monkfish	February–August	350g–1¼kg	Deep fry	Baudroie
Rascasse	March–October	1–2½kg	Poach, fry	Rascasse du nord

Checklist of commodities

Name	Best season	Best weight	Uses	Menu name
Red Mullet	May–September	175–450g	Bake, grill, shallow fry	Rouget
Sardine	March–October	50–75g	Grill, deep fry	Sardine
Sea Bream	June–December	350g–3½kg	Bake, braise, grill, fry	Dorade
Sprat	November–February	40–75g	Grill, deep fry	Esprot
Whitebait	February–August	Small as possible	Deep fry	Blanchaille
Whiting	July–March	200–500g	Bake, deep and shallow fry	Merlan

Fresh water fish

Name	Best season	Best weight	Uses	Menu name
Carp	June to March	750g–3kg	Bake, braise, poach	Carp
Eel	May to October	250g–1.5kg	Bake, poach, deep fry	Anguille
Pike	June to March	1–10kg	Bake, poach, stew	Brochet
Salmon	February to August	1–9kg	Braise, poach, shallow fry	Saumon
Salmon Trout	May to July	450g–4kg	Braise, poach, shallow fry	Truite-saumonée
Smelt	April to October	100–150g	Bake, grill, shallow and deep fry	Eperlan
Trout, River	All year	150–450g	Poach, grill, shallow fry	Truite

Others such as barbel, bream, char, dace, perch, roach, shad are not available commercially

Shellfish

Name	Best season	Uses	Menu name
Crab	May to October	Dressed, pâté, mousse, vol-au-vent	Crabe
Crawfish	May to August	Decorated for buffet display	Langouste
Crayfish	October to March	Whole in cold or hot preparations	Ecrevisse
Dublin Bay Prawn	June to September	Hors-d'œuvre, garnish	Langoustine
Lobster	April to October	In halves for many cold and hot preparations	Homard
Prawns	All year	Whole, hot or cold, as fish course, garnish, etc.	Crevette rose
Scampi	All year	Mostly deep-fried or sauté	Langoustine
Shrimps	All year	Potted, salad, sauce, cocktail, bouchée	Crevette grise
Clam	All year	Available as long neck (soft shell) and round	Palourde
Cockle	All year	Usually sold cooked; as for mussels	Pétoncle
Cuttlefish	March to September	Fish course, garnish	Moule
Octopus	May to September	Kebab, deep and shallow fried	Poulpe
Oyster	September to April	Cold as an hors-d'œuvre; hot as a fish dish	Huître
Scallop	January to March	Shallow-fried as a breakfast or lunch dish	Saint-Jacques
Squid	All year	Fish course, kebab	Calmar
Whelk	All year	Cold in vinegar as an hors-d'œuvre seafood plate, vol-au-vent	Buccan

Smoked fish

Name	Uses	Menu name
Bloater	Grilled as a breakfast or lunch dish	Hareng saur
Cod Roe	For preparing as taramasalata for a first course	Laitance fumée
Eel	Cold as a first course	Anguille fumée
Haddock	Poached as a breakfast, lunch or supper dish	Merluche fumé
Kipper	Grilled as a breakfast or supper dish	–
Mackerel	Hot as a fish course Cold as an hors-d'œuvre	Maquereau fumé
Salmon	Cut into thin slices as an hors-d'œuvre, in cornets with caviar, shrimps, etc.	Saumon fumé
Sprats	Cold as an hors-d'œuvre	Esprot fumé
Trout	Cold as an hors-d'œuvre	Truite fumée
Tunny	As part of hors-d'œuvre variés, in a vol-au-vent.	Thon fumé

Other items

Name	Uses	Menu name
Frogs' Leg	Deep fried, meunière, au gratin	Cuisse de grenouille
Snail	à la Bourguignonne	Escargot
Sea Urchin	As an hors-d'œuvre	Oursin

Vegetables

Name	Best season	Menu name
Artichoke		
Globe	May to June	Artichaut
Jerusalem	December to February	Topinambour
Asparagus	May and June	Asperge

(*continued*)

Name	Best season	Menu name
Aubergine (Egg-plant)	June to October	Aubergine
Beans		
Bobby	Summer	–
Broad	June to August	Fèves de Marais
Fine	All year	Haricots fins
French	June to October	Haricots verts
Garter	July to September	–
Runner	August and September	Haricots d'Espagne
Sprout	All year	–
Beetroot	All year	Betterave
Breadfruit	All year	Fruit à pain
Broccoli (Calabrese)	June to November	Brocoli
Brussels Sprout	November to February	Choux de Bruxelles
Cabbage		
Green	September to February	Chou
Red	September to February	Chou rouge
Spring	January to March	Chou de printemps
White	October to April	Chou blanc
Carrots	July to March	Carottes
Cassava	–	Manioc
Cauliflower	August to March	Chou-fleur
Celeriac	October to March	Céleri – rave
Celery	June to November and April	Céleri
Chard	October to April	Blette
Chicory	All year except July and August	Endive
Chinese leaves	All year	Feuilles chinois
Christophine (Chow-chow, chayote)	Imported	Brïonne
Courgette	May to August	Courgette
Cucumber	All year	Concombre
Dasheen (Eddoe)	Seasonal	–
Endive	Autumn and winter	Chicorée
Fennel	April to December	Fenouil

Checklist of commodities

(*continued*)

Name	Best season	Menu name
Kale	January to March	Chou frisé
Kohlrabi	April to December	Chou-rave
Paksoi	All year	–
Leek	All year	Poireau
Mangetout (Snow peas)	July to October	Mangetout
Marrow	June to September	Courge
Mooli	All year	Rettiche
Okra (Ladies fingers)	Imported	Gombos
Onion	October to June	Oignon
Parsley	June to December	Persil
Parsnip	September to April	Panais
Peas	July to August	Petits pois
Pimento	August to December	Piment
Potato	All year	Pomme de terre
Potato, Sweet	Imported	Patate douce
Pumpkin	September to November	Potiron
Salsify	September to April	Salsifis
Scorzonera	Autumn and winter	Salsifis
Seakale	December to June	Chou de mer
Shallot	All year	Echalote
Spinach	August to November	Epinards
Sorrel	Spring	Oseille
Swede	September to May	Rutabaga
Sweetcorn	July to September	Maïs
Baby Sweetcorn	December to March	Epis de maïs
Sweet Potato	All year	Patate douce
Tannia (similar to potatoes)	Imported	
Taro (tuber of coco yam)	Imported	
Tindoori (similar to a courgette)	Imported	
Tomato	All year	Tomate
Turnip	May to February	Navet
Yam	Imported	Igname

Salads

Name	Best season	Menu name
Beansprouts	All year	–
Corn Salad	Spring	Mâche
Lettuce		
Cos	June to October	Romaine
Iceberg	June to September	Laitue de glaçon
Round	April to November	Laitue
Mustard and Cress	All year	Cresson alénois
Radish	April to October	Radis
Spring Onion	April to September	Ciboule
Watercress	April to October	Cresson
Radicchio	Summer	–

Fungi

Name	Best season	Menu name
Flap mushroom	September to November	Cèpe
Chantarelle	May to August	Chanterelle
Morel	September to November	Morille
Mushroom		
cultivated	All year	Champignon
Field	July to October	Champignon de Bois
Truffle	October to March	Truffe

Fruits in Season

January

Homegrown

Apples, cooking apples, pears, rhubarb

Imported

Apples, apricots, avocados, bananas, cherries, coconuts, cranberries, dates, figs, grapefruit, grapes, kiwi fruit, lemons, limes, lychees, mangoes, marmalade oranges, melons, nectarines, oranges, passion fruit, paw paws, peaches, pears, pineapples, plums, pomelos, persimmons or sharon fruit, strawberries.

Soft citrus: Clementines, minneolas, wilkings, orlandos, satsumas, temples, ugli fruit

---

February

Homegrown

Apples, cooking apples, pears, rhubarb

Imported

Apples, avocados, bananas, coconuts, dates, grapefruit, grapes, kiwi fruit, lemons, limes, lychees, mangoes, marmalade oranges, melons, nectarines, oranges, passion fruit, paw paws, pears, pineapples, plums, pomels, persimmons or sharon fruit, strawberries

Soft citrus: Clementines, minneolas, satsumas, kara, temples, wilkings, ugli fruit

March

Homegrown

Apples, cooking apples, pears, rhubarb

Imported

Apples, avocados, bananas, coconuts, dates, grapefruit, kiwi fruit, lemons, limes, lychees, mangoes, melons, nectarines, oranges, passion fruit, paw paws, pears, pineapples, plums, pomelos, strawberries

Soft citrus: Karas, minneolas, satsumas, temples, tango, topaz, ugli fruit, wilkings

April

Homegrown

Apples, cooking apples, pears, rhubarb

Imported

Apples, apricots, avocados, bananas, cherries, coconuts, dates, grapefruit, grapes, kiwi fruit, lemons, limes, lychees, mandarins, mangoes, melons, oranges, passion fruit, paw paws, pears, pineapples, pomelos, strawberries

Soft citrus: Temples, tangor, topaz, ugli fruit

May

Homegrown

Apples, cooking apples, rhubarb, strawberries

Checklist of commodities

Imported

Apples, apricots, avocados, bananas, cherries, coconuts, dates, grapefruit, grapes, kiwi fruit, lemons, limes, lychees, mangoes, melons, oranges, passion fruit, paw paws, peaches, pears, pineapple, strawberries, watermelons.

Soft citrus: Topaz, ugli fruit

June

Homegrown

Cooking apples, cherries, gooseberries, raspberries, strawberries

Imported

Apples, apricots, avocados, bananas, coconuts, grapes, gooseberries, kiwi fruit, lemons, limes, lychees, mangoes, melons, nectarines, oranges, passion fruit, paw paws, peaches, pears, pineapples, topaz, plums, strawberries, watermelons, fresh figs

---

July

Homegrown

Blackberries, blackcurrants, cherries, gooseberries, loganberries, raspberries, redcurrants, strawberries

Imported

Apples, apricots, avocados, bananas, coconuts, cherries, dates, figs, grapefruit, grapes, greengages, kiwi fruit, lemons, limes, mangoes, melons, nectarines, oranges, passion fruit, paw paws, peaches, pears, plums, pineapples, strawberries, watermelons

Soft citrus: Minneolas, tangerines

August

Homegrown

Apples, cooking apples, blackberries, blackcurrants, gooseberries, loganberries, plums, raspberries, strawberries, white currants

Imported

Apples, apricots, avocados, bananas, coconuts, cherries, dates, figs, grapefruit, grapes, greengages, kiwi fruit, lemons, limes, lychees, mangoes, melons, nectarines, oranges, passion fruit, paw paws, peaches, pears, plums, pineapples, strawberries, watermelon

Soft citrus: Minneolas, tangerines

Nuts: Cob nuts

September

Homegrown

Apples, cooking apples, blackberries, damsons, raspberries, pears, plums, strawberries

Imported

Apples, avocados, bananas, coconuts, figs, greengages, grapefruit, grapes, kiwi fruit, lemons, limes, mangoes, melons, nectarines, oranges, passion fruit, paw paws, peaches, pears, plums, pineapple, pomegranates, watermelon

Soft citrus: Minneolas, tangerines, tambors

Nuts: Cobnuts, walnuts

October

Homegrown

Apples, cooking apples, pears, plums, raspberries, strawberries

Imported

Apples, avocados, bananas, coconuts, dates, figs, grapefruit, grapes, kiwi fruit, lemons, limes, mangoes, melons, oranges, passion fruit, paw paws, pears, pineapples, plums, pomegranates, strawberries

Soft citrus: Tambors, clausellinas, satsumas

Nuts: Brazils, chestnuts, cob nuts, filberts, mixed nuts, pecans, walnuts

November

Homegrown

Apples, cooking apples, pears

Imported

Apples, apricots, avocados, bananas, coconuts, cherries, cranberries, dates, figs, grapes, grapefruit, kiwi fruit, lemons, limes, lychees, mangoes, melons, oranges, passion fruit, paw paws, pears, pineapples, plums, pomegranates, raspberries, strawberries, persimmons or sharon fruit

Soft citrus: Satsumas, clementines, michal

Nuts: Almonds, brazils, chestnuts, cob nuts, filberts, mixed nuts, pecans, walnuts

December

Homegrown

Apples, cooking apples, pears

Imported

Apples, apricots, avocados, bananas, coconuts, cherries, cranberries, dates, figs, grapefruit, grapes, kiwi fruit, lemons, limes, lychees, mangoes, melons, nectarines, oranges, passion fruit, paw paws, peaches, pears, persimmons, or sharon fruit, pineapples, pomegranates, strawberries

Soft citrus: Clementines, michals, satsumas

Nuts: Almonds, brazils, chestnuts, filberts, mixed nuts, pecans, walnuts

Popular Varieties of Apples and Pears

The following brief descriptions are of some of the varieties of dessert fruits available in this country nearly all the year round.

Apples

Alkmene	Cross between a Cox's Orange Pippin and a German apple to give a pale green apple with red streaks; crisp, sharp and juicy.
Beauty of Bath	Small, soft and juicy; the first to be harvested but has poor keeping quality.
Cox's Orange Pippin	Finest flavour of all apples, intense but delicate; fine texture.
Crispin	Large yellow-green apple of good flavour.

671

Discovery	Has a bright red skin with yellow streaks; firm, crisp and juicy.
Egremont	A russet apple, orange in colour and crisp, nutty texture.
Golden Delicious	Yellowy-green in colour, sweet, firm and tender.
Granny Smith	A round green apple that is crisp, juicy and sweet.
Idared	Large red apple with wine-like taste, crisp and succulent.
Jonag	New apple from Belgium with a firm, sweet sharp flesh and a red and yellow skin.
Laxton Superb	Similar to a Cox but matures later and is sweeter.
Tydemans	Similar to a Worcester but has a deeper red colour, juicy and sweet scented.
Spartan	Purple-red skin and very white crisp flesh, very good in fruit salad.
Worcester Permain	Red skin with pale green streaks; very juicy and sweet but does not keep, so available only in September and October.

Pears

Bartlett	Name given to the William's pear in USA.
Beurre Hardy	Short squat shape with dark green skin, with a juicy, sweet taste.
Comice	Very good flavour, sweet and juicy, has a tough skin that is greeny-yellow.
Conference	Long and thinly tapered in shape; very good for cooking as well as eating, apart from tough skin.
Passa Crassane	Grown only in France, a large, juicy, yellow coloured pear.
William's	Very popular; an early variety but will store only for up to three months; large and rounded, turns from green to yellow.

Citrus Fruits

This list gives the many varieties that are available from all over the world for use as dessert.

Bigarade	Bitter orange, used with duck	Early spring
Blood Orange	Very red streaky flesh; sweet and small in size	Early Spring
Clausellina	Easy to peel, fine skin and rich flavour; seedless	Occasional
Clementine	Hybrid of orange and tangerine, usually seedless	Christmas
Curaçao	Bitter orange from the island of its name	Occasional
Ellendale	Large clementine, from Uruguay	Occasional
Grapefruit	Smooth skin, bitter sweet, juicy, and usually seedless.	All year
	Also available with pink flesh	October to July
Honey Tangerine	Very sweet, medium size fruit with a distinctive flavour	Occasional
Lime	Pale yellow or green, round fruit, used for its juice and sliced as a garnish	All year
Kumquat	Smooth thin skin which can be eaten, tangy or bitter sweet; very small, a delicacy	December to March
Lemon	Shiny bubbly skin, very sour; used as a garnish and for its juice	All year
Mandarin	Type of orange, larger and sweeter than a tangerine	Christmas
Michal	Easy-to-peel clementine, smooth red skin; sweet and juicy; a lovely aroma	November to December
Mineola	Hybrid of tangerine and grapefruit; smooth thin easy-to-peel skin, tart and aromatic; has a knob on top	January to February

Navel	Smooth thick skin, very sweet and juicy, distinctive navel; usually seedless	November to January
Orange	Main suppliers: Israel, Spain, South Africa, Morocco, Cyprus	All year
Ortanique	Cross between orange and tangerine	Occasional
Pomelo	Large size thick goose-pimple skin, like a grapefruit, fairly juicy and can be eaten green; good for marmalade	December to April
Satsuma	Variety of tangerine	December to April
Seville Orange	Only used for making marmalade as they do not have sufficient taste for a dessert	January to March
Shamouti	Dimple-skinned orange; easy to peel and very sweet, juicy and seedless	December to March
Sunrise	Red grapefruit with a smooth skin, sweet, juicy, rich red flesh, seedless	November to May
Tambor	Easy to peel, soft-skin red orange	Occasional
Tangerine	Small loose skin mandarin	Christmas
Tangor	Large cross between orange and tangerine, sweet and juicy with pips	Autumn to Spring
Temple	Hybrid of mandarin and orange, very juicy, deep-coloured sweet flesh, medium size, and round	February to March
Topaz	Hybrid of orange and tangerine, easy-to-peel smooth skin, rich flavour and very juicy	March to May
Ugli	Hybrid of grapefruit and tangerine, with loose skin; sweet	Occasional
Valencia	Thin almost smooth skin, sweet, very juicy, and seedless	March to June

Exotic Fruits and Vegetables

Babaco	Elongated five-sided fruit from New Zealand, yellow in colour and tastes like pineapple; eaten raw cut into slices.

Breadfruit	Round or pear-shape fruit the size of a small melon, usually sliced and fried as a vegetable; tastes like sweet potato.
Carambola	Also called star fruit because it has five sharp ribs; yellow colour, sour-sweet taste; looks good cut in slices in fruit salad or as a garnish.
Christophine	Also called chow-chow and chayote, a fruit but served as a vegetable similar to marrow and cucumber; available white or green, spiny or smooth, and pear shaped.
Custard Apple	Also called annona fruit, heavy oval or heart-shaped fruit with reddish marks on yellow skin; served cut in half to eat with a spoon.
Dasheen	A tuber that is used as a potato, with a brown skin and white inside. Eddoe is the name of a smaller version.
Date	Fresh plump dates are served as dessert with other fruits; used in making petits fours or as a garnish.
Fig	Available as black-, green-, purple- or white-skinned; can be served as an hors-d'œuvre with other items, as a garnish, cooked as a compote, or as dessert.
Gourd	Also called Dudi, there are many kinds, this being the shape of a baseball bat with white flesh and many seeds; used stuffed and braised as a vegetable.
Guava	Looks like a plum with a thin green skin and strong smell, white to salmon-pink flesh; eaten raw with a spoon or cooked as a compote.
Jackfruit	Very large green fruit with yellow flesh and large seeds; has a jelly-like fruit flesh.
Karella	Dark green gourd with a bitter flavour.
Kumquat	Tiny citrus fruit with thin rind and aromatic scent, for eating whole and raw or used as a garnish.
Kiwi fruit	Used to be called the Chinese gooseberry; egg-shaped, furry brown skin and green interior with black seeds, tangy flavour; use raw in fruit salad and as a garnish with meat or can be eaten like a boiled egg.

Lime — Thin-skinned citrus fruit like a small green lemon, nice smell and strong taste; used as a flavouring and as a marinade.

Litchis or Lychee — Has a thin pinkish brittle skin and jelly-like flesh with seeds; can be eaten raw, in salads, with avocado or as a compote.

Loquat — Looks like a small plum with a yellow-orange downy skin, can be eaten raw or sliced in a salad; also known as Japanese medlar.

Mango — Comes in several sizes and shapes, yellow-orange in colour and has a clinging stone; advisable to cut off the top and bottom close to the stone and scoop out the flesh.

Mangosteen — Like a plum with a dark purple leathery skin and delicate scent; flesh is like an orange; serve in the skin to eat raw or in a salad.

Passion Fruit — Also called Granadilla; egg-shaped fruit with purple-brown, hard leathery skin; serve cut in half to eat with a spoon, including the seeds.

Papaw — Also called papaya – oval fruit up to 20cm in length with yellow skin and soft, juicy orange to salmon-pink flesh; serve as for melons.

Persimmon — Like a large orange-coloured tomato with a prominent calyx and soft purple colour; when fully ripe to eat scoop out with a spoon.

Plantain — Looks like a banana but is eaten cooked as a potato or for making soup; a staple in the West Indies.

Pomegranate — Round reddish-yellow fruit full of grains; serve cut in half with the inside membrane removed, as a drink or sorbet or in seeds as a decoration.

Pomelo — Citrus fruit that looks like a large pear-shaped grapefruit with thick pimply skin; cut or divided into segments, remove membrane and serve as hors-d'œuvre or in fruit or other salads.

Prickly Pear — A pear-shaped cactus with greeny-orange skin covered with prickles which can be brushed off; cut off top to peel back the skin and eat raw or as a compote or for a decoration.

Tientsin Pear — Yellow, juicy, thin-skin pear with crunchy texture, for dessert use.

Rambutan	Small dark reddish-brown covered with hair, with a brown oblong seed; eat like a boiled egg or peel and slice into fruit salad.
Sharon	A firm persimmon with a date-like texture, without seeds; looks like a beef tomato but sweeter; eaten whole or sliced in salads.
Tamarillo	Egg-shaped, tomato-like fruit with hard yellow or red skin, tastes like kiwi fruit; usually served skinned, baked or in a compote, also known as jambolan.

Flour

Brown	Strong white flour to which is added wheat-germ and bran; there are several proprietary brands used in making brown bread.
Buckwheat	Hard flour used only in some Continental countries.
General Purpose	Plain flour for all uses in kitchens where only one kind is kept.
Plain	White flour for general purpose use in making cakes, pastry, sauces, soups, etc.
Rye	Used only for making Continental-type bread and biscuits.
Self-raising	Plain flour to which is added raising agents; for use in making puddings.
Stoneground	Milled in the old fashioned way.
Soft	Weak flour with very little protein that is good for making biscuits, cakes and pastry.
Strong	Also called bread flour because it contains sufficient protein so that it can be kneaded strongly when making bread and rolls.
Wheatmeal	Made from 85–95 per cent extraction flour, thus high in fibre and colour.
Wholemeal	Made from the whole of the wheat including germ and bran.

677

Bread and Rolls

Allison Wholemeal	Proprietary brand of flour made into a loaf.
Bara brith	Welsh fruit loaf enriched and spiced.
Batch	Tall with pale sides and a rounded top.
Baguette	Crisp long French loaf shaped like a stick; stales quickly.
Bâton	Approximately 23cm long and up to 15cm girth tapered to a point, sometimes with a split.
Bermaline	Proprietary brand of flour used to make malt bread with a soft, sticky crumb.
Bloomer	Long crusty loaf up to 36cm in length with rounded ends and cuts across the top.
Cholla	Elongated oval with a plaited top, usually sprinkled with poppy seeds.
Jewish Cholla	Enriched sweet dough made as a plait and sprinkled with poppy seeds.
Cheese	Baker's cheese is mixed into the dough to give a distinctive taste.
Coburg	Sloping sides and large round top with four or more cuts from the centre.
Cottage	A small round is indented onto a larger round base; somewhat impractical for slicing.
Crown	Seven balls of dough baked together in a shallow round tin.
Danish	Light open-textured loaf usually dusted with flour.
Farmhouse	Oblong shape with rounded top, split down the centre; dusty with flour.
French Stick	Long and thin, up to 90cm, very crusty but stales quickly.
Fruit	Fairly rich dough containing dried fruit and with a glazed top crust.
Granary	Bread dough containing malted whole-wheat, wheatmeal and rye; sometimes baked in clean earthenware flower pots.
Gugelhopf	Continental fruit loaf made with butter, sugar and orange zest and baked in a fluted mould.

Harvest	Display loaf for harvest festivals shaped as a sheaf of wheat, windmill, horn of abundance or as a large plait.
Hovis	Proprietary brand brown loaf containing wheat germ and bran.
Malt	Soft and sticky texture achieved by the addition of malt and molasses to the dough.
Milk	Often baked in a long round, ridged tin; must be made from a milk dough.
Notched Cottage	Cottage loaf with markings around the top and lower edges.
Pitta	Flat oval Greek loaf for warming before splitting and filling the pocket with a variety of savoury fillings to eat as a sandwich; may also be filled with fruit, preserves, cream cheese or ice cream.
Pumpernickel	Black rye bread, steam-baked to give a sticky texture and sour taste.
Rustic	Made of whole wheat grains crushed into flakes which are then soaked before making into a smooth, moist loaf with a nutty taste.
Rye	Made from rye flour, black treacle and caraway seeds; has a sourish taste.
Sandwich	Baked in a lidded tin to give an oblong shape as quartern or half quartern (800g loaf).
Sliced	The national wrapped sliced loaf, sliced thin, medium or thick as brown and white.
Soda	Made with chemical aerating powder instead of yeast; was originally aerated with bicarbonate of soda.
Split Tin	Oblong with straight sides and rounded top, split along the centre.
Starch Reduced	Some of the starch is washed out so giving a light texture.
Tin	A sandwich loaf baked in a lidded tin.
Turog	Proprietary brown loaf as made to the manufacturers's formula.
Vienna	Long thin loaf made with milk and baked in steam to give a coloured crust and a high gloss; also made into rolls.

679

Vitbe	Proprietary brand loaf containing wheat germ and malt.
Youma	Malt loaf with a soft sticky crumb.

───── ROLLS ─────

Bakestone	Rough-cut pieces of dough cooked on a girdle or griddle.
Bannock	Also known as oatcakes; made with flour and oatmeal and usually cooked on a girdle.
Bap	Soft crust round or oval with a floury finish; served in Scotland for breakfast.
Bow	Length of dough tied up as a bow.
Burger Bun	Soft roll usually cut open and toasted to house a grilled hamburg steak.
Bridge	Small oval roll made with a slightly enriched dough, gilded and served filled for buffet meals; called in French Petits Pains de Windsor.
Brioche	Rich butter and egg dough made slightly sweet; baked in fluted tins in the shape of a cottage loaf.
Canon	Ordinary dough rolled flat then rolled up from each end, one roll twisted and placed over the other pointing upward.
Carcake	Spoonfuls of oatmeal batter, shallow-fried in bacon fat; usually served for breakfast.
Coil	Long thin piece of dough coiled from the centre.
Croissant	Fluffy crescent shape made from flaky yeast dough; also crescent-shaped rolls from ordinary dough.
Dinner	Name given to ordinary round rolls, although any shapes may be served.
Dorset Knob	Roughly-shaped small pieces of dough plainly baked.
Energen	Low-carbohydrate dough made into lightweight rolls for slimming diets.
Farl	Flat oblong variety made of potato and flour for toasting or frying for breakfast; no yeast is included.

Hoggie	Large wholemeal finger roll sprinkled with malted cracked wheat.
Italian	Flatten the two ends of the piece of dough, roll up each towards the centre and join them alongside each other.
Kaiser	Ordinary bread dough rolled to 6cm in diameter and folded five times to the centre as a rosette.
Knot	Length of dough tied into a single or double knot.
Plait	Made with one to seven strands, starting from the centre.
Potato	Known as Tattie cakes, made from a dough containing dry mashed potato.
Rocker	This is another name for a cannon.
Rope	Long thin piece twisted into the form of a coil of rope.
Shell	Mould round, almost divide in two, flatten one side and fold it over the other.
Soft	Baked without a crisp crust.
Scroll	Shape a length of dough into an S-shape.
Serpent	Long thin length of dough twisted into a ring with the end resting over it.
Sesame	Sprinkle the top of a round or oval shape with sesame seeds.
Twist	Thin length of dough with the two ends twisted inwards or outwards to the centre.

Dairy Produce

Milk

Buttermilk	Pasteurised skimmed milk with bacteria added to give a slightly sour taste.
Channel Island	Milk from Guernsey and Jersey breeds, having a higher fat content that other milk.
Condensed	Milk boiled with sugar to reduce the water content; sold in cans.

Dried	Powdered for reconstituting; available as skimmed or whole.
Evaporated	Milk boiled to reduce the water content; sold canned to add a creamy taste to soups, custards, etc.
Filled	Reconstituted skimmed milk with added vegetable fat or oil.
Homogenised	Does not have a cream layer because the fat globules have been broken up by high-pressure spraying; good for cooking but not in tea.
Light	Milk with some of the butterfat removed.
Longlife	Treated by Ultra Heat Treatment (UHT) to render it sterile for long storage.
Pasteurised	Milk heated to a high temperature for a very short time to destroy pathogenic organisms; most milk is sold in this form.
Skim	Milk without most of the cream.
Standardised	EEC regulations that govern the fat content at not less than 3.5 per cent give this name to ordinary milk.
Sterilised	Milk heated to 150°C to kill all micro-organisms so that it will keep without refrigeration for several months; has a cooked taste.
UHT	Milk heated to 132°C for 1 to 2 seconds so that when packed and sealed it will keep for several months without refrigeration.
Untreated	Milk as drawn directly from the cow.

Goats' milk and sheep's milk are also available in some areas.

Cream

Coffee	Name given to single cream for pouring purposes.
Clotted	Cream heated to make it clot by evaporation; has up to 60 per cent fat and spreads like butter; good for Devonshire Cream teas.
Double	Contains not less than 48 per cent butter fat; it is advisable to add a little milk when whipping.
Extended Life	Heat-treated and vacuum-packed; will whip slightly.

Heavy	Another name for whipping cream.
Single	Contains a minimum of 18 per cent butter fat so does not whip.
Soured	Flavoured by bacterial culture for use in dips, dressings, soups and in Polish and Russian cookery.
Whipping	Has approximately 40 per cent butter-fat content; has been pasteurised.

Cream is available in aerosol cans for decorating cakes and sweets.

Home-made cream can be made by putting butter and milk, melted to blood heat, through an emulsifying machine.

Boiling a tin of evaporated milk for 20 minutes then chilling it will render it suitable for whipping as a cream.

Butter

Concentrated	Butter without any salt or water content made especially for use in shallow frying, similar to clarified butter; can be used for pastry but is not good for sandwiches as it has added skimmed-milk powder.
Lactic	Butter as made in Denmark, France and Holland whereby the lactic acid is allowed to develop; it is paler in colour than dairy or sweet-cream butter.
Low Fat	Made from butter, vegetable oil and water and sold under proprietary brand names as being healthier than pure butter; unsuitable for cooking purposes.
Salt-free	Good quality butter for finishing sauces and soups but it does not keep as well as ordinary butter.
Sweet Cream	Made from pasteurised cream to give a sweet creamy taste and golden yellow colour.

Butter for use in making sandwiches can be extended by adding warmed milk, evaporated milk or water to softened butter; another way is to dissolve gelatine in warm water and whisk into softened

683

butter or to mix it with evaporated milk into softened creamed butter.

Yoghurt

This is made by adding special bacterial cultures to skimmed milk. It is available as fat-free, low-fat, set, fruit-flavoured, whole-fruit, drinking and frozen yoghurt.

Fat

Cake Margarine	A texturised blend of oils that creams easily and has a pleasant aroma and flavour.
Dripping	Edible tallow from meat fat used to baste roast joints.
Lard	Rendered fatty pig-tissues giving a firm yet plastic fat; not used very much in professional cookery.
Margarine	Blend of vegetable and fish oils with water, salt and vitamins A and D.
Puff-pastry fat	A plastic yet tough fat that will endure heavy rolling and give a better result than butter though it will not taste as good.
Shortening	Hydrogenated oils are aerated to make this fat cream easily.
Suet	Fat from around the beef kidney used for steamed puddings, dumplings, etc.
White Fat	Blend of oils without colour, flavour or liquid; very good for making pastry as it has been hydrogenated.

684

Oil

Corn	Very yellow and mild flavour, used for deep and shallow frying.
Groundnut	Good for cold sauces, deep and shallow frying.
Hazelnut	Has a concentrated aroma and flavour which makes it suitable for dressings and pouring over cooked food, especially grilled fish.
Olive	Very good for pouring over cooked food and for dressings; has a slight green tinge and is expensive.
Soya	An all-purpose oil with only a slight flavour.
Sunflower	A healthy oil as it contains polyunsaturates; good flavour for dressings.
Vegetable	A blend of oils for deep frying.
Walnut	Distinct but delicate flavour for use in dressings; does not keep for long.

Vinegar

Amongst the kinds available are:
cucumber, garlic, horseradish, mint, raspberry, shallot and wine.
Orleans vinegar is a wine vinegar.

Rice

Arborio	Italian bold grain rice, excellent for making risotto.
Basmati	Good quality Patna-style rice grown in India.
Brown	Unpolished rice with the germ still present; it requires twice the cooking-time of ordinary rice.
Carolina	Short-grain or pudding rice; can be used to make pilaff and risotto.

Cream of   Very finely milled rice useful for making short-bread and for making soups.

Cristallo   Parcooked Arborio rice.

Flaked   Rice processed into flakes for use as a thickening agent or as a pudding.

Frozen   Coated with sunflower oil before freezing so free-flowing; cooks in 3 minutes.

Ground   Rice milled to a fairly fine powder to thicken soups, sauce, etc.

Instant   Pre-cooked rice that has been dehydrated and can be quickly reconstitued by covering with boiling water.

Italian   Large plump grains that absorb plenty of moisture but do not distort in boiling.

Patna   The typical long grain kind of rice in general use for serving with curries; grown mainly in USA and Australia.

Processed   Has been steamed to remove some of the starch so does not stick when cooked.

Wild   Also known as Indian rice, very expensive.

Nuts

Name	Season	Menu Name
Almond	October–February	Amande
Brazil	October–February	Noix de Brésil
Cashew	All year	Acajou
Chestnut	October–January	Marron or Chataîgne
Hazelnut	October–January	Aveline
Macadamia	All year	Macadamie
Peanut	All year	Cacahouette
Pine Kernel	All year	Pignon
Pecan	All year	Pacane
Pistachio	All year	Pistache
Walnut	October–February	Noix

Herbs and their Uses

Basil – Basilic

Strong flavour that blends well with tomato dishes and in salads.

Bayleaf – Laurier

Widely used for stocks, sauces, stews, soups, etc.

Borage – Bourriche

Use fresh in drinks such as Pimms; has hairy leaves and blue flowers.

Chervil – Cerfeuil

Chopped as part of 'fines herbes' or whole in consommé; delicate fern-like spray.

Chive – Ciboulette

Succulent grass-like shoots that taste and smell of onion; use fresh in soups and salads.

Garlic – Ail

Used in most continental savoury dishes; is stronger when used raw than when cooked.

Marjoram – Marjolaine

Soft grey leaves that smell of mint; not widely used.

Mint – Menthe

For mint sauce with lamb, with peas, new potatoes and in drinks.

Oregano – Origan

Is wild majoram and more pungent; used in pizzas and in meat stuffings.

Parsley – Persil

Used whole more to decorate than eat, many dishes are served sprinkled with it for its appearance.

Rosemary – Romarin

Spiky leaves used to flavour roast lamb and goat and in many Italian dishes.

Sage – Sauge

Greyish-green hairy leaves used chopped in English stuffings and whole in Italian dishes.

Savory – Sariette

Looks like thyme but more peppery; used in stuffings and with broad beans.

Tarragon – Estragon

Long thin leaves used as a decoration or chopped in salads, sauces, stews, because of its subtle flavour.

Thyme – Thym

Has a very subtle effect on many foods including pork and veal and in stuffings.

Fines Herbes

Is a mixture of chopped chervil, chives, parsley and tarragon.

Spices and their Uses

Allspice – Piment Jamaïque

Also called pimento or Jamaica pepper; tastes like mixed cinnamon, cloves and nutmeg; used for pickling and ground, in sweet dishes.

Chilli – Chili

Very hot form of red pepper much used in Mexican cookery; used in meat stews.

Cinnamon – Canelle

Use whole for compotes or ground in buns and hot drinks; looks like a stick.

Clove – Clou de Giroffe

Nail-shaped dried flowers, use in apple pie, mincemeat and for studding baked ham and pork.

Ginger – Gingembre

Dried root available whole for pickling, chutney, etc; preserved in syrup; ground for cakes; is very hot and pungent and a constituent of curry powder.

Mace – Macis

Fragrant covering of a nutmeg; use in sausage-meat; and in cakes.

Nutmeg – Muscade

Use grated in sauces and in sweet dishes.

Paprika – Paprike

Mild pepper from red pimentos, also used for its colour; for stews, cheese dishes, sauces, etc.

Pepper – Poivre

Available in powder form and as black, white and green pepper-corns for grinding; the most widely used spice.

Saffron – Safran

Dried stigmas of a crocus used to give a yellow colour and fine flavour mainly to rice dishes.

Turmeric – Curcuma

Gives a brilliant yellow colour but not much flavour to dishes; of the ginger family.

Mixed Spice

Is a blend of ground allspice, cinnamon, cloves and nutmeg for general pastry use.

Curry Powder

Is available in packets as a mixture from cinnamon, coriander, cloves, ginger, nutmeg, mustard, pepper and turmeric.

Curry Paste

Is a blend of hot spices in a cooked oily base.

Aromatic Seeds

Aniseed – Anise

Liquorice flavour, good as digestive aid; main use is for cakes and sweets.

Caraway – Cumin

Taste and smell of aniseed, popular in Holland and Germany to flavour meat and vegetables; used here in seed cake and for pickling.

Cardamom – Cardamone

Use in cakes, in coffee, on melon, etc.

Celery – Céleri

Small brown seeds with strong flavour and smell of celery; use in soup, stock, etc.

Coriander – Coriandre

Use in sweet dishes, for pickling, biscuits and stuffings.

Cumin – Cumin

Looks like caraway seed; use in stews especially Mexican ones.

Dill – Aneth

Use in cheese spread, on rolls, in pickled cucumber, in sauerkraut, in salads, and gravelax.

Fennel – Fenouil

Smell of aniseed; used in fish dishes.

Juniper – Genièvre

Used for sauerkraut and with game; is the flavouring in gin.

Mustard – Moutarde

Used in salads, in making chutney and with cheese.

Poppy – Pavot

Slate-blue seeds, sprinkled on rolls, bread and biscuits; good in pasta.

Sesame – Sésame

Sprinkled on rolls, bread and biscuits to give a nutty taste; can be added to stews.

Charcuterie

The term denotes the products of the pork-butcher's trade comprising the manufacture of many kinds of cooked and raw foodstuffs, mainly made of pork but including other meats and poultry.

Each nation has its own special kinds of charcuterie products, usually made according to local preferences and available commodities. The specialities of several countries are widely available and are very popular because of their consistent quality, ease of use and storage.

There are three main sections:

1. Products that are already cooked, smoked, or air-dried so that they are ready for use.
2. Sausages and similar products that have been pre-cooked or smoked but are meant to be eaten hot or require further cooking.
3. Raw, perishable products that must be cooked and served as soon as possible, using the most appropriate method, mainly boiled, fried or grilled.

Pâté

There are hundreds of different kinds of pâtés ranging from very smooth ones made with genuine goose liver, to coarse cheap ones made of ox or pig's liver. They are available from factories in several different countries, cooked in earthenware dishes and attractively decorated, but many establishment prefer to make their own which allows them to entitle it 'Pâté maison' on the menu.

Although any kind of liver is the basis of most pâtés, other kinds of meat and offal can be used but it is the seasoning which really distinguishes one pâté from another. Brandy, sherry, or a liqueur can be added and cream, eggs or butter are the usual binding agents but it is spices and herbs that make the distinction.

The word *terrine* is interchangeable with pâté e.g. terrine maison, the name coming from the pottery dish used to cook it in and serve it from. Some pâtés are made with strips of meat, fat, nuts, etc., running the length of the mixture thus giving an attractive pattern when cut into slices.

Sausages

The following are the main kinds of sausage products which are widely available from local butchers, factories or importers and that can be used in several courses of the menu. The letter indicates the country origin:

Cz – Czechoslovakia
D – Denmark
F – France
G – Germany
H – Hungary
I – Italy
P – Poland
S – Spain
UK – United Kingdom

Andouilles (F) Usually white in colour, dried or smoked; a few are made in black skins and others have concentric rings of chitterling included. These are made of pork shoulder, tripe and chitterling

693

	minced together; the method of cooking is by boiling and they are bought ready cooked.
Andouillettes **(F)**	This is a small version of andouille, made using the small intestine; they are ready boiled, and are good when grilled and served with mustard.
Bierschinken **(G)**	A lightly smoked sausage that has been par-cooked; it is made of pork, chunks of fat and pistachios. It is often eaten cold.
Bierwurst (G)	A coarse-textured sausage made of beef and pork, garlic and spices; suitable for eating with a glass of beer.
Black pudding **(UK)**	Usually made of raw pig's blood, pieces of fat, groats, oatmeal, onion and rusk packed into a black skin and boiled. It is usually served cut into slices and fried.
Bockwurst (G)	Beef, pork and bacon saveloy, lightly smoked and scalded, for eating hot.
Boudin blanc **(F)**	Made from any white meat such as chicken, pork, rabbit or veal with fat, egg, cream, onion and crumbs in a white skin. It has been boiled and needs to be sliced and fried.
Bratwurst (G)	Made of pork or veal and spices then scalded; usually grilled whole.
Cacciatore (I)	Small-sized salami made of pork and beef.
Cervelat (F)	Similar to a saveloy, made of pork with garlic as the flavouring.
Chipolata (UK)	Thin sausages made of pork, beef or a mixture; available in skins or as skinless.
Chorizo (S)	A smoked sausage made of pork with red pimento. There are many varieties and sizes.
Coppa (I)	Slightly bigger than a salami and with a layer of fat; made of pork and often served as a substitute for prosciutto.
Cotechino (I)	Lightly-salted sausage made of pork with spices; usually served boiled and sliced.
Crépinette (F)	Similar to a faggot, individual portions of minced pork and herbs wrapped in a caul or salt pork fat; baked and served with a sauce.
Faggot	Made of minced pig's liver and pig's fry with fat and herbs, moulded into a small cake and

wrapped in caul; usually bought ready cooked for reheating. Also known as poor man's goose and savoury duck.

Frankfurter (G) Fairly long, thin red coloured sausage made of pork, beef, tripe and heart with mace and saltpetre. Sold boiled and dried or smoked for reheating in hot water.

Garlic Sausage (UK) Made of pork and beef with garlic; well-smoked ready for slicing and eating or for further boiling whole.

Haslet (UK) Made of pig's fry, fat and onion; cooked in a slab for cutting into slices to eat cold.

Kabons (P) Long thin smoked sausage made in many parts of the country of origin.

Knackwurst (G) A short stumpy sausage that is air-dried; cooked by boiling.

Leberwurst (G) (UK) The German name for liver sausage as made in many countries, predominantly from pig's liver with pork fat and offal; it is cooked ready for use and can be eaten cold.

Mortadella (I) A very large sausage usually made in a pig's bladder; it is made of pork and flavoured with garlic and contains whole peppercorns.

Pancetta (I) Rolled streaky bacon in the form of a sausage.

Parky (Cz) A Frankfurter sausage to cook by boiling.

Peperami (I) (also called Peperonata) Long thin spicy smoked salami for chewing raw.

Salami (I) (D) (F), (H) (G) (P) There are many versions of this popular sausage, each made according to its country of origin, only they are usually all the same size and differ only in flavour and colour. They are dried or smoked and made of pork and small particles of fat, usually garlic flavour and are eaten as they are, very thinly sliced.

Saucisson (F) Large size for boiling; there are many versions from all over France, all being made from pork, some being used fresh while others are smoked or air-dried.

Saveloy (UK)	A red-coloured sausage for boiling, made from cured pork offals; they are boiled before being sold, and are served hot.
Schinkenwurst (G)	A smoked sausage of flaked cured pork and large pieces of fat; it is sliced for use; also called ham sausage.
Teewurst (G)	A spicy sausage made of pork and beef that has a paste consistency.
Wienies	The name given in America to Vienna sausages which compete with Frankfurters for popularity. They are made of cured pork and beef, filled into thin skins and lightly smoked before being boiled. They are bought dry.
Zampino (I)	This is the lower part of the pig's leg without the trotter, the bone and flesh removed and replaced by pork forcemeat. It is boiled and dried and sold ready for reboiling as an entrée.

Ham

A ham is an item of charcuterie although those in general use are prepared in factories rather than in a butchery. Hams are first cured in a brine or with salt and the added flavourings distinguish the individual taste of the ham. The drying or smoked process and the kind of wood shavings used also have an effect upon the flavour and colour of the ham.

Ayrshire	Boned and rolled, brine-cured over peat.
Belfast	Dry salted, heavily smoked, has a white mould.
Bradenham	Salt cured ham then flavoured with molasses and spices; coal black exterior, brownish coloured fat (no longer available).
Cumberland	Dry salted with the addition of brown sugar, then air-dried.
Epican	Cured with treacle.
Mutton Ham (Herdwick)	A cured and smoked whole leg of mutton.
Suffolk	Also known as Seager ham; a short cut ham, brine, beer and sugar cured; has a blue mould; not widely available.

696

Wiltshire   Usually a gammon rather than a whole ham, cured with sugar and salt and smoked over oak chippings.

York   Dry cured over a long period of maturing; smoked over oak sawdust; green mould, pale colour and mild delicate flavour

France

Bayonne, Mayence, Morvan

Germany

Brandenburg, Black Forest, Holstein, Westphalia

Italy

Parma, San Leo, La Ghianda

USA

Maryland, New Jersey, Smithfield, Virginia

Others

Belgium – Ardennes; Spain – Serrano; Czechoslovakia – Prague.

22 DISH DECORATIONS

It is permissible to add further garnishes to help to decorate a dish over and above that garnish which is an integral part of the recipe. The use of real flowers or leaves, and feathers or head of birds is unacceptable; the flowers must be made from edible material as described below and leaves, feathers, and other adornments made from fat or gum paste. Vegetable decorations can be made as follows:

Flowers

Apple

Cut an unpeeled half of apple into very thin slices, soak in acidulated and salted water until pliable then form into a flower by rolling the first slice into a conical shape, and adding the remaining slices around the outside until the desired size is obtained.

Vegetable Rose

Trim a carrot, potato or turnip to the shape of a toy spinning-top then cut slits around the base as the outer leaves, cut a thin strip around the edge and cut slits in it to form petals. Blanch in boiling water for one minute then leave to soak in coloured cold water.

Tomato Rose

1. Remove the skin thinly in one long strand then wind it around to the shape of a rose.

2. Cut strips 2cm wide and as long as possible from the skin but not in one length; roll the longest strip to form the outer edge then roll shorter lengths and place inside one another until full. Add outer leaves cut from blanched green of leek.

Tomato

Cut the stem end of a tomato level and make several cuts through the skin only two-thirds of the way down the rounded part; cut back the skin only of each cut leaving it attached at the bottom, and fold these outwards. The centre can then be cut through with a column cutter and the inside emptied to fill as required.

Cut a firm tomato in half through the stem, lay flat on a board and cut a diagonal wedge from the centre; make four or five cuts diagonally at 5mm intervals on each side of the wedge, making them meet at both ends. Peel back the skin of the wedge making it form a petal and spread out the tiers of tomato.

Radish

Cut four small pieces from around a radish then cut slices from the stem end down towards the root but without cutting right through – these will form the petals when the radish is placed in iced water to open it up.

Raw apple, carrot, courgette, pimento can also be cut to form a flower.

Spring Onion

Make several cuts through the bulb then pull the central tubes separately to different lengths; place in ice water to make the petals open.

Cucumber Fan

Cut grooves around a cucumber then cut it in half through the length; remove some of the seeds and cut into lengths, each one sufficient for a fan. Lay on a board and cut from the square end gradually going thicker towards the rounded end so giving two pieces. Now cut through the skin into very fine slices leaving them attached at the thin end. Spread the cuts out flat to form a fan; if desired, place in ice water to crisp.

Baskets

Tomato

Cut the base level, then make two cuts 5mm apart from the top to half way down to represent the handle; cut around each half zig-zag fashion, remove the surplus then spoon out the bottom inside and fill as required. If desired, the outside can be scored and the resultant skin turned back to form an outer ring.

Orange

Make two cuts approximately 5mm apart from the top to half way down then cut zig-zag fashion around the circumference and remove the two surplus pieces; empty with a teaspoon.

Lemon

Cut in half then cut a thin strip of peel around the edge from a centre point thus leaving two strips attached to the fruit; tie each in a bow. A lemon can also be cut in half zig-zag fashion after cutting off each end so that the two halves stand upright.

Potato Nest

Slice a potato into fine julienne on a mandolin, soak in water for approximately 1 hour then drain, sprinkle with cornflour and line an oiled, round, frying-basket with them; place a smaller frying basket inside and deep fry in hot fat until golden brown. Use for serving potatoes. (Both sections of the basket must be dipped in very hot oil before moulding the basket in order to prevent it sticking.)

Spaghetti Basket

Boil whole lengths of spaghetti, refresh, drain and lightly coat the strands with oil; take about six strands, bend in half and drape the looped end over the edge of an oiled frying-basket. Arrange bundles of strands to cover all the basket, twining the loose ends together at the bottom. Place the other oiled basket inside and deep fry; if necessary use a ladle to keep the thing together.

Noodle Paste

Roll out very thinly, cut into various shapes, egg-wash and dry out in a slow oven; arrange them around the edge of the dish as decoration, sticking them to it if necessary.

23 BASIC CULINARY PREPARATIONS

Barder To cover an item that is lacking in natural fat with a thin slice of salt pork fat or streaky bacon so as to protect and lubricate whilst it is being cooked. The fat is tied on loosely then removed towards the end of the cooking time to allow the meat to colour; the fat may be served.

Beurre manié A raw roux made of two parts softened butter to one part of plain flour mixed to a smooth paste; it is added to a liquid towards the end of the cooking time and shaken in until it disperses and thickens but should not be boiled for too long.

Blanc Mix 100g flour with a little water then whisk into 5 litres of hot water containing salt and lemon juice; reboil until it thickens and add the item which needs to be kept white, e.g. calf's head, Jerusalem artichokes, or salsify. Cover with a cloth to exclude the air; sometimes a slice of suet is added.

Bouquet garni Flavouring ingredients including bay-leaf, celery, parsley stalks and thyme tied in a bundle and cooked in a liquid, e.g. stock, stew or boiled meat, to add a subtle flavour; to be made of a size in keeping with the amount of liquid.

Breadcrumbs Rub stale bread without crusts, through a sieve or crumble in a mixer.

Brown breadcrumbs (raspings or chapelure) are made from very dry crusts.

Brine Preserving liquid for meat e.g. brisket, silverside, belly of pork, ox-tongue; made by boiling 25 litres of water with 5kg freezing salt, 150g saltpetre, 250g brown sugar, peppercorns and bay-leaves. It gives a reddish colour to the meat.

Court-bouillon Fish cooking liquid used mainly for fatty fish and shellfish, made by boiling 10 parts water and 5 parts vinegar with sliced carrot and onion, peppercorns and bay-leaves, for 20 minutes. Whole fish go in before boiling; cuts into the cooked bouillon. For white fish the liquid is water, lemon juice and salt only. In some cases, wine is used.

Croûtons Cut a slice of bread of the appropriate thickness, trim to shape and size in keeping with the item and shallow fry in butter until crisp, or spread with butter and toast on both sides. A croûton serves the following purposes; to give colour to a pale-looking dish; to increase the size of a portion of food; to carry a soft mixture; to add crispness to a soft food, to soak up the juice from a piece of meat and for decoration purposes.

Croûtons are cut as follows:
for soups – $\frac{1}{2}$cm dice or diamonds (these are shallow-fried)
for stews – heart, pear, diamond or triangular shape
for vegetable purées – triangular, diamond or crescent shape
for game birds – oval, oblong or square, to sit the whole bird on
for tournedos, noisettes – round or pear shape the same size as the piece of meat.

Fried bread for breakfast is deep-fried and drained.

Cullis or Coulis Concentrated liquid made by cooking certain ingredients to a thick essence and using it to give extra flavour to a sauce, soup, stew, etc; can be made of a vegetable, shellfish, game, etc. A bisque soup can be enriched by using a cullis made of the shells, coral and creamy parts of lobsters or crawfish.

Diablotins	Toast ½cm thin slices of thin French bread, sprinkle with a mixture of grated Cheddar, Parmesan and cayenne, and toast until brown.
Duxelles	Sauté chopped onion in butter, add chopped mushroom and cook until dry; finish with chopped parsley.
Duxelles Stuffing	Add white wine, demi-glace and chopped garlic to Duxelles, allow to reduce and stiffen with breadcrumbs to a piping consistency (see also mushroom purée).
Egg-wash	For coating items for frying, whisk 5 eggs with ¼dl oil and ¼dl of water; for gilding, mix eggs or yolks only with milk.
Essences	Stock made in a more concentrated form than usual or by reducing it; not now widely used but very useful. Fish fumet (q.v.) is the main example.
Farce	This is the French word for a forcemeat; and refers to a raw mixture as against a stuffing which is cooked. It is made as a fine purée of fish, chicken, veal, etc., with panada, eggs and cream and is different from a quenelle mixture in that the latter uses egg-whites instead of whole eggs. A mousseline is similar to a quenelle but made without panada.
	Godiveau (q.v.) is also a farce.
	Farce: Add 250g of bread or flour panada (q.v.) to 500g finely minced flesh and pass through a sieve; add 3 eggs one at a time, then work in 3dl double cream. This is used for stuffing fish or meat.
Fines Herbes	Finely chop 3 parts parsley to 1 each of chervil, chives and tarragon; squeeze out and use in the food rather than for decoration on top.
Flamber	To sprinkle food with brandy or other spirit and set it alight so leaving the essence of the particular flavouring in the food. A Christmas pudding is flamed with brandy and most dishes that are cooked in the restaurant are set alight to add a dramatic touch.

704

Fleurons Roll out puff-pastry trimmings 2mm thick and cut out crescents using a plain or fancy 5cm-round cutter, or cut into diamonds, hearts, etc.; egg-wash and bake until golden brown and use to add colour and crispness to bland, soft dishes such as poached sole in white wine sauce.

Fonds de Cuisine Term used to denote basic methods or recipes that give rise to many extensions and variations.

Fonds Basic stocks, used in soups, stews, sauces, etc., made from bones, trimmings, vegetables and herbs as brown or white in these versions – beef, mutton, veal, chicken, game, fish.

Forcemeat A kind of stuffing made of raw fish, meat, etc. with panada, eggs and usually cream; see Farce.

Fumet Well-flavoured stock, mainly of fish used as a cooking liquid to give flavour to the item and the accompanying sauce.

Glaze Stock boiled to a concentrated jelly, used to enhance the flavour of fish, chicken, game and meat dishes, and on its own by melting and piping as a decoration on a food. It requires 10 litres of good stock to produce 2dl of a glaze.

Gnocchi Italian word for small dumplings which can be made of chou paste – parisienne; potato – italienne or piémontaise; semolina – romaine; maize – polenta.

Godiveau A fine forcemeat made of minced veal and beef suet with eggs and cream, usually moulded with spoons and poached.

Gratin Forcemeat A stuffing used mainly for game birds; made of sautéd onions, bacon and chicken or game livers, blended with butter to a paste.

Larding To insert strips of fat, etc. into chicken, meat, etc. to add succulence and to form a pattern in it. A large joint has ½cm square lengths inserted through the entire joint, a smaller portion is sewn with 3mm square pieces of the appropriate length, usually up to 8cm. Carrot and truffle are sometimes used to lard an item; it is advisable to chill small strips in iced water to facilitate threading, or they may be steeped in spice and brandy for a little while.

Lardons Small baton-shaped pieces of streaky bacon cut to a size in keeping with the item they will garnish; usually blanched and shallow-fried.

Liaisons These are thickening and binding mixtures that are added to a liquid to convert it into a sauce, soup, etc. There are several forms:

1. beurre manié, a mixture of 2 parts butter to 1 part of flour, added at the end of the cooking period
2. yolks of egg and cream using 8 yolks and 2dl cream per 1 litre of soup or sauce
3. a starch such as arrowroot or cornflour, diluted and mixed into boiling liquid
4. roux (q.v.) equal amount of butter and flour cooked to a sandy texture
5. eggs are used to thicken cold and hot sauces and hot mixtures of egg, fish, meat etc. in which they are cooked to bind

Marinate To keep beef, game, etc. in a liquid such as wine and oil to help tenderise, preserve and add flavour; it may be used cooked or raw. The time required to complete the process depends upon the size of the joint, etc., and the rate of penetration; it should be kept under refrigeration and the liquid utilised in cooking the meat. Vegetables, herbs and spices are added to the liquid.

Mise en place Advance preparation of all the items required to cook the dishes on the next day's menu.

Mousseline Forcemeat Fine purée of raw fish, chicken, veal, etc., made by blending with egg-whites and incorporating double cream; moulded into egg-shapes and poached.

Mushroom Purée Cook finely sieved mushroom in béchamel and finish with cream and butter.

Mushrooms – turned and decorated Cut grooves around button mushrooms using the head or the heel of a sharp knife, then use the point again to indent the centre in the form of a star, or outline a fish, etc. Cut off the stalk and cook in a cuisson.

Mushrooms, cooked

1. To cook them white, wash and leave small ones whole or cut larger ones into quarters on the slant, or into slices or julienne; cook in a small amount of water, lemon juice, butter and salt brought to a boil, then keep in the cooking liquid which is known as a cuisson.
2. To sauté, melt butter in a pan and add the prepared mushrooms just as butter is about to turn brown; season and toss over and over until soft.
3. To grill, wash open mushrooms and place dark side uppermost on a greased tray; season, sprinkle with melted butter and cook under a salamander until soft but not dried out.

Onion, studded

Attach a small bay-leaf to a peeled onion by means of a clove; use for giving an oniony flavour to a sauce or stock.

Panada

A panada is used to give strength and bulk to several mixtures including croquette mixtures, quenelles and mousselines. The main kinds in use are:

1. Bread panada – mix breadcrumbs with boiling milk and cook to a smooth and thick consistency.
2. Flour panada – add flour to boiling water and butter and mix on the fire until smooth and cooked.
3. Frangipane panada – mix egg yolks, flour and melted butter to a paste, add boiling milk and cook for 5 minutes.

Paner à l'Anglaise

This is the term used to describe the operation of coating items for shallow and deep frying with flour, then with egg-wash and breadcrumbs. The breadcrumbed item should then be flattened to make the coating adhere, the edges straightened and the best side marked trellis-fashion.

707

Parsley
To prepare, pick off short sprigs, wash and keep in ice-cold water or in a refrigerator, changing the water daily. To chop, remove all the stalk, chop with a three-bladed knife then wash in a chinois under the cold tap and squeeze out all moisture in the corner of a clean cloth. To fry parsley, dry the sprigs, place in a frying basket and deep fry until the noise ceases and the parsley is crisp but still green.

There are unwritten laws regarding the use of parsley for finishing foods and it is incorrect, for example, to sprinkle it over mashed potato or chips.

Pimentos
To skin for use, plunge into hot fat and cook until the skin blisters, then drain and remove the thin skin by rubbing or scraping with a knife. Cut off the top, remove the seeds and cook by stuffing and braising, or cut into julienne and cook gently in a little butter. It may be peeled by holding a pimento in a flame until the skin blisters.

Profiteroles
Small balls of chou paste used mainly as a sweet but also – when piped the size of a pea – used as a garnish in consommé, in some cases being filled with foie gras purée.

Quenelles
A fine mixture of raw fish, chicken, veal, etc., with egg-whites, panada and double cream moulded with spoons or piped out and poached. Made in several sizes from small pea-size pieces as a garnish for consommé, medium size as a garnish and large as a main course with a sauce.

Quenelles can be coloured and flavoured with additional ingredients, e.g. tomato or paprika for red, fresh herbs for green, or they may be stuffed.

Ravioli Filling
Sauté onion and garlic in butter, add lean meat and thin demi-glace and cook with herbs and spinach; pass through a fine mincer. The meat may be left-over cooked meat and cooked calf's

brain and cheese may be added. This filling is also suitable for other pastas, e.g. cannelloni.

Roux The classical way of thickening liquids made by cooking an equal amount of butter or other fat, and flour to a sandy texture; the three stages are: white roux for a pure white result such as for béchamel, blond roux for an off-white result such as velouté, brown roux for espagnole and all other brown sauces. It takes 800–900g of roux to make 5 litres of sauce, according to type and length of cooking time. A roux can be made in a soup or stew together with the other ingredients, using the fat in which they were coloured.

Royale A fairly firm savoury egg-custard mixture cooked au bain-marie and when cold, cut into various shapes as a garnish in consommés and other soups. In addition to the plain royale of 1 egg to $\frac{3}{4}$dl of milk, royales are made by adding a purée such as almond, asparagus, carrot, celery, chestnut, foie gras, game, etc.

Sabayon A cooked enriching and thickening agent made by whisking egg yolks and a little water over heat until fairly thick, adding it to a sauce such as mornay to give a better quality glazing than that given by adding raw yolks.

Sauerkraut Finely shredded white cabbage packed in salt and allowed to ferment for about three weeks; it is flavoured with cloves and juniper berries and cooked by braising.

Sausage-meat This can be made from any kind of meat with the amount of fat and seasoning as required, with soaked rusks or breadcrumbs to bind; it is used in pies and as a stuffing.

Socle A pedestal used for displaying food to greater effect than by placing it directly onto the dish; although not meant to be eaten it must be made of edible mateial. A socle must be fairly solid to bear the weight of food; of the appropriate size, shape and height and it may be carved, decorated and glazed.

The following are examples:

1. bread – cut from a sandwich loaf, decorate and trim and deep fry until crisp
2. semolina – cook in milk or stock and immediately place in dampened moulds
3. rice – cook blanched rice with alum and lard in a slow oven until thoroughly cooked then mix to a smooth consistency and immediately place in moulds
4. milk – boil 1 litre milk with 300g rendered mutton fat, add 75g soaked gelatine then mix in 175g potato powder; re-boil, whiten with cream and pour into an oiled mould.

Soubise

This is an onion purée or thick sauce made by cooking onion with béchamel or rice; it is passed and finished with cream and butter and served as a garnish or used as a stuffing, particularly with lamb.

Stocks

see under Fonds.

Stuffings

In addition to the forcemeats and English stuffings there are others such as braised rice, pearl barley, etc., which are used for stuffing chicken, meat, etc.

Pearl barley – braise with chopped onion in stock for approximately 2 hours and finish with butter.

Rice – braise with chopped onion in stock for 15 minutes then add butter, cream and velouté.

Tomatoes

To peel a tomato, remove the stem end with the point of a small knife, place in a drainable utensil and dip into boiling water for 10 to 15 seconds, according to firmness and ripeness; the skin can then be taken off by using the fingers or a knife. Use a colander or conical strainer when peeling several tomatoes but to do only one or two, hold in a gas flame on the end of a skewer or small knife and turn it until the skin blisters all over, when it will come away easily.

Diced Tomato – Tomate Concassée crue
Cut peeled tomatoes in half through the width remove the seeds and cut the flesh into approximately ½cm rough dice.

Diced Cooked Tomato – Tomate Concassée Cuite
Sauté finely chopped onion in butter, add diced tomato and a little chopped garlic and cook gently, adding a pinch of sugar if desired.

Tomato Essence
Liquidise ripe tomatoes and cook until reduced to a syrupy consistency; strain to remove the seeds.

Small Tomatoes
If cherry tomatoes are not available cut a peeled tomato in half or quarters and squeeze gently in a cloth to give a perfectly round shape.

Trussing
To truss poultry for roasting leave the legs whole, cut off all but the centre claw, remove the wishbone and wing tips and truss with two strings to give the best shape, the first through the centre of the legs and winglets tying it tightly, then through the carcase under the legs and back over the top of them, tying this tightly.

To truss poultry for braising, poaching and poêléing leave the legs whole and cut the tendon underneath at the joint so as to make it easy to bend back; make an incision under the breast and push the leg inside the bird, doing this on the other side as well. Tie as for roasting. It is also possible to break the leg nearly up to the end of the drumstick, to withdraw it and replace with the prepared claw end sticking out.

Watercress
Pick off long stalks and any blemished leaves, wash in cold water and keep in iced water during the service. Use for garnishing grilled and roasted meats.

Cuts of Vegetables etc. for use as Garnishes and Flavourings

Brunoise	Cut carrot, celery, leek and turnip or other vegetables into 2mm dice
Chiffonade	Finely shredded lettuce, sorrel, and/or spinach for use either raw or cooked, as a garnish in soup.
Jardinière	Cut carrots and turnips into bâtons 2cm long, and mix with diamond shapes of French beans, and small peas.
Julienne	Cut carrot, celery, leek, turnip, truffle, etc., into thin strips 4cm in length by 1mm thick.
Macédoine	Cut carrots and turnips into $\frac{1}{2}$cm dice and mix with peas and diamonds of French beans.
Matignon	Carrot, celery, onion and lean bacon cut into paysanne, stewed in butter with bay-leaf and thyme for use as a flavouring agent and as a garnish.
Mirepoix	Roughly cut up carrots, celery and onion, add bay-leaf, thyme and diced bacon trimmings and fry to give flavour to a sauce, stew, etc.
Paysanne	Cut cabbage, carrots, celery, leek, potato, swede, turnip, etc., into 1cm squares or 1$\frac{1}{2}$cm rounds.
Pluches	Pick small sprigs of chervil or parsley for use as a garnish in soups.
Printanière	Small balls of carrot and turnip, peas and diamonds of French beans in equal proportions.
Salpicon	Can be a single item but usually refers to several cooked foods cut into $\frac{1}{2}$cm dice and mixed with an appropriate sauce.
Turned	Cut carrots or turnips into 3cm long sections and turn into barrel-shape; potatoes are cut slightly larger into 5–6cm pieces and turned. Pommes cocottes are 2$\frac{1}{2}$cm barrel-shapes of potato.

Round and Oval Balls — Parisienne cutters are also known as spoon cutters and are made in many sizes in both round and oval shapes; they are numbered according to the size, e.g. No. 22 is 22mm round. Among the many items that can be cut with these tools are carrot, melon, potato, turnip.

Table Napkins for use in Dish Decoration

Gondola

Lay a square table napkin flat and line it with a sheet of paper, fold in half then bring in the two sides to a point at the centre top; continue to fold evenly from each side to the centre with the same number of folds on each side. Fold in half then wrap it in a clean cloth and hold a heavy object such as a small pan on the pointed end. Have the napkin near the corner of the table and whilst one person holds the pan on the end, another person tugs the cloth away bringing it around in a circular motion with a succession of sharp pulls. The more pulls and the more circular the cloth is tugged, the more rounded and pointed the end will be.

When judged to be sufficiently rounded, take the napkin out of the cloth and unfold it once only. It will appear as the end of a Venetian gondola turning round on itself and keeping its shape by means of the starch in the napkin and the lining of stiff paper. One is placed at each end of a dish being given special service treatment, a folded one is placed across the middle of the dish to cover the ends, and the dish of food is placed on top.

Use – mainly for cold preparations such as Canapés à la Russe

Lily

Open the table napkin flat and fold the four corners to the centre; do this twice more then turn it over onto the other side and again fold the four corners to the centre, pressing each turn well. Place the clenched hand in the centre and bring up each of the twelve corners from underneath, one at a time. It will be found that the lily will hold its own shape.

This shape can be used for presenting any small deep fried items, bread rolls, etc.

24 BASIC NUTRITION

Everyone connected with the supply of food and drink to the general public should possess a working knowledge of nutrition, which is the study of food values for nourishment of the body. This knowledge provides an understanding of the nutritive value of foods and their use in the body and should ensure that customers are being fed wisely and well.

Foods are composed of several different materials including protein, fat, carbohydrate, vitamins, mineral salts and water. Food is needed to build the body structure of bones, teeth and cartilege, to provide energy and warmth, to carry out bodily activities including walking, breathing and working, and for the repair of body tissue.

The unit of energy used to denote the value of a food is the kilocalorie or kilojoule, there being 4.2 kilojoules (kJ) in 1 kilocalorie (Kcal). Growth and replacement of the body tissues is going on all the time so it is necessary to eat a given amount of foodstuffs daily to ensure good health. Depending on their age, sex, kind of work being done, people need a certain number of kilocalories each day, comprised of a certain amount of each kind of food material.

The nutritional value of foods and dishes are listed in certain books and reference to these will assist a caterer in quantifying the nutritional value of his menus, written according to the kind of customers he has to serve. The entries list the protein, fat, carbohydrate, vitamin and mineral content of most of the everyday dishes, in the raw and in the cooked state, provided that good cooking practices have been followed.

Nutrients

Protein foods are essential to health as they are the ones that provide growth and repair. They are found in meat, poultry, game, fish, cereals and dairy products and are made up of a number of amino-acids, a number of which are essential to health, but not all protein-providing foods contain these and it is necessary to know which foods are of high biological value as against those that lack some of the essential amino-acids and are therefore of low biological value.

Fat, or lipid, is used by the body to provide warmth and it contributes more kilocalories per gramme than the other nutrients. Fat is found in many foods other than butter, margarine, dripping, etc., it is in the marbling of meat, in egg yolks, in fried fish and chips, cakes, pastry, cheese, chocolate and nuts. Excessive intake of fat should be avoided, especially animal fat.

Carbohydrate is the main source of energy in the diet and is contained in many foods, for example, sugar is 100 per cent carbohydrate. It is also present in such staple foods as flour, potatoes and cereals. Cellulose is the carbohydrate found in vegetables and fruit and is resistant to digestion. It does however furnish bulk or fibre which is required for the efficient elimination of waste from the body.

Water is an important material in nutrition because it acts as a solvent for amino-acids, carbohydrate and mineral salts, and carries substances in solution and allows chemical reactions to take place. Water may account for as much as 60 per cent of a person's body-weight.

Vitamins are vital elements that assist in the body process of coverting food we eat into energy and to build body tissues as well as to maintain body functions. The necessary reactions of the body that are vital to life cannot occur if vitamins are missing from the diet as the body is unable to make hardly any of them. Details of vitamins and minerals are given in the following table.

Name	Scientific name	Recommended daily intake	Function	Good sources of supply
Vitamin A	Retinol	40 000i.u.	Growth of children; growth and repair of eyes, teeth, hair, bones and skin	Butter, milk, margarine, liver, kidney, leafy vegetables, carrots, fish liver oils, eggs
Vitamin B1	Thiamine	2mg	For converting carbohydrate food into energy; keeps muscles, nervous system, heart and kidneys functioning. Aids digestion and absorbtion	Fish, pork, lamb, chicken, wholemeal bread, cereals, flour, milk, potatoes
Vitamin B2	Riboflavin	2mg	Assists in utilisation of carbohydrate, fat and protein; promotes healthy skin	Lean meat, liver, wholemeal bread, cereals, milk, eggs, green vegetables
Vitamin PP	Niacin	20mg	Necessary to convert food into energy; prevents loss of appetite and helps to maintain the nervous system	Lean meat, liver, eggs, bread
Vitamin B5	Pantothenic acid	10mg	For utilisation of carbohydrate, fat and protein	Liver, kidney, rice, wheat, bran, nuts, eggs, beans, peas.
Vitamin B6	Pyroxidine	2mg	For healthy skin and teeth; assists nervous system	Liver, beef, lamb, pork, herrings, salmon, walnuts, potatoes, wholemeal bread, eggs, cereals

Name	Scientific name	Recommended daily intake	Function	Good sources of supply
Vitamin B12	Cyanocobalamin	–	Makes healthy blood cells and the synthesis of haemoglobin – the colouring of red corpulscles – assists nervous system, and for steady growth of children	Lean meat, liver, kidney, shellfish, oily fish, eggs, milk, cheese
Folic Acid	–	300µg (mcg)	Similar to vitamin B12	Offal, wheat, bran, rye, spinach, beans, almonds, peanuts
Vitamin H	Biotin	300µg (mcg)	For putting together fatty acids, and breaking down carbohydrate; production of energy from glucose; has a vital role in many body systems	Liver, kidney, eggs, milk
Vitamin C	Ascorbic acid	30mg	For healthy bones, teeth, blood vessels and normal growth; as collagen, for tissue repair and healing of wounds	Citrus fruits, tomatoes, potatoes, cabbage, other green vegetables
Vitamin D	Calciferol	400i.u.	Assists absorption of calcium and phosphorus needed for making teeth and bones; important for growth of children	Fish, liver oil, liver, salmon, tunnyfish, milk

Name	Scientific name	Recommended daily intake	Function	Good sources of supply
Vitamin E	Tocopherol	40i.u.	Vital to the formation and function of red blood cells and muscle tissue; helps protect essential fatty acids	Nuts, oils, fruit, vegetables, lettuce, cereals

The fat-soluble vitamins are A, D, E and K; the water-soluble ones are B and C.

Minerals

There are many different mineral salts considered to be nutritionally essential for mental and physical well-being, for the formation of bones and teeth and as important constituents in tissues, muscles, blood cells and nerve cells.

The following table shows the most important minerals in the daily diet.

Name	Recommended daily intake	Function	Good sources of supply
Calcium	700mg	With phosphorus, builds and maintains bones and teeth; regulates clotting of blood and nerve behaviour	Milk, bread, cheese, pulses, root vegetables
Copper	2mg	For the storage of iron; needed for proper production of blood cells	Green vegetables
Iodine	250µg (mcg)	For the thyroid gland that regulates metabolism; affects growth	Salt, seafood

| **Iron** | 12mg | To produce haemoglobin and to combine with oxygen to take it through the blood system | Liver, lean meat, eggs, bread, green vegetables |
| **Potassium** | – | For healthy skin, normal growth and to stimulate nerves for muscle contraction | Milk, citrus fruit, nuts, breakfast cereals, vegetables, fish |

Others are sodium, phosphorus, magnesium, sulphur, fluorine, cobalt, copper, manganese and zinc.

Food Values

A knowledge of the nutritional values of foods should cover all the staple foods which include:

Meat, poultry and game	High-quality protein, iron, calcium and important amounts of B vitamins. Offals are similar to meat in nutritional value.
Fish and shellfish	High-quality protein. Fatty fish contains fat-soluble vitamins A and D. Small fish eaten whole, such as sardines and whitebait, are also a good source of calcium.
Dairy produce	Milk is a good source of high-quality protein, lipid, carbohydrate, calcium, a little iron, Vitamins A and D. Cheese contains high-quality protein, lipid and calcium. Butter is an energy food and contains 740 kilocalories per 100g; in common with margarine it contains Vitamins A and D. Eggs contain high-quality protein, lipid, calcium, iron, vitamin A and the B vitamins.
Vegetables and fruit	Leafy vegetables contain vitamins and mineral salts including iron and calcium. All vegetables

contain a small amount of the B vitamins and spinach is rich in the precursor of vitamin A. Others such as broccoli, peas and spinach contain vitamin C. Root vegetables are composed mainly of carbohydrate, that in potatoes being in the form of starch; potatoes play a large part in the British diet and are a good source of vitamin C. In general vegetables are low in calories but provide a sense of fulness and are a good source of fibre.

Fruit contains carbohydrate in the form of sugar, a very small amount of protein and a trace of liquid. Only oranges, grapefruit and figs contain calcium. Nuts are a good source of quality protein which is why nuts are used in vegetarian diets.

Pulses These contribute to the diet because of their protein content which is useful as a meat-substitute for vegetarians. Soya beans are used in making textured vegetable protein, which is cooked and can be made to taste like meat.

Cereals The usual cereals – wheat, maize, oats and rice – contain small amounts of protein, calcium, iron and the B vitamins. Flour for bread-making is fortified with calcium carbonate, iron, thiamine and nicotinic acid. Breakfast cereals are made from natural cereals as a mass which is then flaked and toasted, puffed or shredded; it is fortified with iron and vitamins. Sago, tapioca and arrowroot are not cereals but have a similarity and are almost pure starch.

Beverages Tea contains a good amount of tannin and a smaller amount of caffeine which is a mild stimulant.

Coffee contains a large amount of caffeine which could cause insomnia, which is why some people may ask to be served with decaffeinated coffee from which the stimulant has been removed. Decaffeinated coffee is also chosen by people with heart trouble.

Natural spring waters contain minerals and may be made sparkling by the addition of carbon dioxide, or are naturally effervescent.

Alcoholic drinks are mainly sources of energy. Beer provides nicotinic acid and riboflavin; wine can contain good amounts of iron, but spirits and liqueurs, many of which at 70° proof are 40 per cent alcohol, merely produce a large amount of energy.

Recommended Daily Intake of Nutrients

Nutrient	Female	Male
Kilocalories	2100	2900
Protein	63g	72g
Vitamin A	750μg	750μg
Vitamin C	30mg	30mg
Thiamine	0.9mg	1.2mg
Riboflavin	1.3mg	1.6mg
Nicotinic Acid	15mg	18mg
Folic Acid	300μg	300μg
Calcium	500mg	500mg
Iron	12mg	10mg

A typical traditional English main meal supplies 650 kcals, 26g protein, 82g carbohydrate, 27g fat and 12g fibre.

The nutritional value of a snack in a fast-food establishment is 1450 kcals, 39g protein, 190g carbohydrate, 66g fat and 7g fibre.

Diets

Diets are mainly prescribed by a physician though some people may decide they should follow a special diet for reasons of their own such as to lose weight. Apart from the special requirements of groups such as children, athletes, old people and expectant mothers, there is a wide range of diets, some of which are listed in the following table.

Name	Description	Uses
Light	Small, light, easily digestible meal	Post-operative
Soft	Minced or mashed; not insipid or watery	Persons without teeth
High Protein	Meat, fish, cheese or egg at each meal; eggnog or enriched milk drink	Damage to tissue, burns, kidney disease
Low Protein	Restricted amount of meat, fish, cheese, eggs, milk, flour, cereals, pulses	Diseases of liver or kidney
Low Calorie	No fat used in cooking	Obesity
Low Fat	White fish, lean meat, skimmed milk	Jaundice; inflammation in blood
Gastric	Small frequent meals; use of milk, eggs, fish; no fried or spicy foods	Gastric and duodenal ulcers
Low Animal Fat	Vegetable margarine, lean meat, no offal, skimmed milk	High level of cholesterol in blood
Low Sodium	Salt-free butter, saltless bread, no salt in cooking	Oedema, heart failure, cirrhosis of liver, kidney diseases
Coeliac	Gluten-free bread, cake, biscuits; no pastry made with ordinary flour	Coeliac disease; fatty diarrhoea
Diabetic	Controlled carbohydrate; no cakes, pastries, chocolates, preserves except sugar-free	Diabetus mellitus
Low fibre	Sieved foods, white bread	Intestinal complaints
High roughage	Wholemeal bread, cereals, salads, vegetables; addition of bran to meals	To stimulate bowel movement
Low Phenylalamine	Special foods as specified by physician	Treatment of phenylketanuria

──────── HEALTHY EATING ────────

Healthy food conjures up the idea of simple, plain cooking that takes away the joy of eating, but many people are concerned at the link between diet and health and want to eat food that reduces the risk of heart disease, high blood pressure and other ailments, as well as keeping the figure slim. Caterers must be prepared to cater for people who want to:

1. **Eat less fat** — Grill or shallow fry rather than to deep fry; develop the technique of sautéing in a non-stick pan; do not finish dishes with butter or cream.

2. *Eat less sugar* — It is quite easy to reduce the sugar content of most recipes without upsetting the balance nor detracting from the taste. Sugar-substitute can be used for cooking as well as putting into beverages but anything made with saccharin should not be boiled.

3. *Eat less salt* — It is thought that salt may contribute to high blood-pressure and it is advisable to reduce the amount ingested to as little as 5g per day except during very hot weather or for people doing heavy work. It must be remembered that many prepared foods are made with a large amount of salt and that cured meat and fish have been treated with it. Salt is needed in the diet and only people put on a special diet require a strict salt-free diet. It is possible to use low-sodium salt or demi-salt which is only 50 per cent pure salt.

4. *Eat more fibre* — Roughage as it used to be called performs many useful functions in the body – it stimulates the digestive system, reduces the risk of indigestion and gives a feeling of fullness in the stomach; can prevent constipation, and reduce the absorption of sugar and fat. Some fibre such as bran is completely insoluble but is still beneficial because it soaks up moisture and stimulates the digestive system by assisting the passage of food. Soluble fibre is provided by most fruits and vegetables, pulses and cereals. Many people

worry that the processing of foodstuffs removes much of the natural fibre and so they resort to sprinkling bran over everything they eat which is not a good solution as its use may reduce the ability to benefit from vitamins in the diet.

25 CALORIE VALUE OF FOODS

Food	Size of average portion	Calories
All-Bran	25g (without milk or sugar)	62
Anchovies	25g (without the oil)	45
Angel Delight	100g (made with water)	150
Apple, dessert	Small apple, weighing 120g	40
baked	Large Bramley	80
pie	Top & bottom crust 100+g	350
pie	with custard	420
Apricots, canned	100g	100
Artichoke – globe	Whole, plain boiled	40
Asparagus	10 spears, 250g	25
Aubergine	Half	20
Avocado	Half, plain	250
with prawns	Half avocado with 50g shellfish	300
Bacon	Fried back rasher, 60g	250
Banana	Whole, peeled	65
Beans, canned baked	100g	60
French	100g	20
Beef, braised	100g slices	180
roast	50g lean slices	200
steak	200g sauté entrecôte	410
stewed	200g including sauce	180
Bemax	25g	100
Biscuits, digestive	15g	70
water	25g	115
Black Pudding (as purchased)	75g	240
Brawn	75g	190

Food	Size of average portion	Calories
Bread, white or wholemeal	Per medium slice	60
Bread and butter	Per medium slice	130
Broccoli, frozen	75g frozen or fresh, boiled	30
Brussels Sprouts	75g, boiled	25
Bun, currant	(as purchased)	270
Butter	Per 5g portion pack	37
Cabbage	100g boiled	15
Cake, chocolate	100g slice	300
Carrots	100g boiled	20
Cauliflower	100g boiled	10
Caviar	25g	80
Celery	25g	2
Cheese, Cheddar	25g	100
cottage	100g	85
Parmesan	25g	120
Stilton	25g	95
Cheesecake	100g slice	400
Cheese straws	25g	170
Chestnuts	25g roasted	40
Chicken, boiled or roast	100g off bone	200
Chip potatoes	100g	300
Chocolate	50g plain or milk	250
Christmas pudding	75g (without sauce)	270
Cod, steamed	200g	170
deep-fried	200g	320
Corn Flakes	17g portion (without milk or sugar)	60
Cornflakes, Crunchy Nut	20g	90
Corned Beef	50g	130
Cornish Pasty	100g	350
Cottage Pie	250g	300
Crab, dressed	100g	100
Cream, double	1 tablespoon	125
single	1 tablespoon	55
Crisps, potato	Packet	140
Croissant	1 × 75g	260
Crumpet	1, toasted and buttered	420
Custard	Birds', made per 1dl	100

Calorie value of foods

Food	Size of average portion	Calories
Dates, dried	25g	60
Doughnut, plain	100g	400
Duck, roast	100g slices of boneless breast	320
Dumpling	1 × 50g boiled	120
Egg	1 large boiled	75
Egg, Scotch	1 × 120g fried	300
Energen Roll	1	25
Fishcake	75g fried	105
Fish fingers	5 × 28g fingers, deep fried	275
Flour	25g	85
Foie gras	50g, served plain	260
Fruit cake	100g slice	330
Gooseberries	150g compote	20
Grapefruit, fresh	Half	30
Grapenuts	25g portion (without milk)	100
Grapes	50g bunch	20
Grouse, roast breast	75g	150
Haddock, plain boiled	200g	260
deep-fried	200g	350
Ham	90g	230
Hamburg Steak, boiled	Quarter pound,	300
Herring, boneless, sautéd	200g	440
Honey	1 teaspoonful	15
Ice Cream	1 average scoop	60
Irish Stew	250g portion	400
Jam	1 teaspoonful	15
Jam Tart	100g	400
Kedgeree	150g	210
Kipper, boneless	1 × 300g	580
Lamb chop, grilled	1 × 200g	700
Lard	25g	260
Leeks, plain boiled	100g	25
Lentils, purée	75g	75
Liver, Ox, fried	100g	320
Luncheon Meat	80g	220
Macaroni, ungarnished, but cooked.	75g	90

Food	Size of average portion	Calories
Mackerel, shallow-fried	1 × 200g	380
Margarine, ordinary	25g	185
Outline	25g	93
Marmalade	25g	75
Mars Bar	1 × 68g bar	316
Mayonnaise	25g	110
Melon	1 × 200g slice	25
Milk, ordinary silver top	1 pint bottle	370
Muesli	30g	100
Mushrooms, fried	25g	60
Oil, frying	1dl	900
Orange	1 × 150g approximately	60
Ox-tongue	60g	180
Oysters	6 raw	90
Parsnips, plain boiled	100g	65
Peanut Butter	25g	175
Peanuts, roasted	1 × 50g packet	300
Pear, whole	1 × 150g	50
Peas, frozen, plain boiled	90g	50
Pineapple, fresh	1 × 100g slice	50
Plaice, deep-fried fillet	120g	280
Pork, chop, grilled	200g	400
leg, roast	60g	180
pie	100g	365
Porridge	1dl made with water	45
Potatoes, plain boiled	100g	80
Prawns, shelled	50g	50
Rice, plain boiled	25g	35
Rice pudding	2dl portion	240
Rissoles, deep-fried	120g	300
Ryvita	per crispbread	27
Salami	50g portion	260
Salmon, fresh, plain boiled	100g darne	185
Salmon, canned	100g	150
Sardines, canned	60g	170
Sausages, pork, fried	2 × 60g	190
Sausage roll	1 × 80g	300
Semolina pudding	2dl portion	175

Calorie value of foods

Food	Size of average portion	Calories
Shredded Wheat	1 portion (25g)	115
Spaghetti, plain boiled	75g	90
Spinach, leaf, boiled	100g	35
Sprats, deep-fried	90g	375
Strawberries, fresh	70g	15
Sugar	1 teaspoonful	25
Sweetbread, Ox, braised	180g	325
Sweetcorn	100g niblets	80
Syrup, golden	25g	95
Tea	2dl cup, with milk	23
Tomato, fresh	50g	10
Tripe, boiled	90g	90
Trout, sautéd	1 × 250g	310
Tunnyfish, canned in oil	50g	140
Turkey, roast	90g portion	135
Veal, Escalope, sauté	1 × 150g	300
Venison, roast	90g portion	165
Welsh rarebit	1 × 120g	450
Whitebait, deep-fried	60g	300
Yoghurt, plain	1 × 150g carton	75
fruit	1 × 150g carton	130
Yorkshire Pudding	1 × 50g	120

Beverages

Food	Size of average portion	Calories
Barley Water, Lemon	per fluid oz	30
Cocoa	2dl mug made with milk and sugar	180
Coffee, black	1¾dl, without sugar	4
made with half milk	1¾dl, with sugar	140
Coca-Cola	per 330ml can	172
Ginger Ale, American	per 500ml bottle	170
Lemonade, fizzy	per 500ml bottle	85
Lucozade	per 170ml glass	130
Milk, ordinary	1 × 568ml bottle	370
Orange, juice	per 1dl	30
squash	Diluted 2dl glass	60

Food	Size of average portion	Calories
Tea	170ml cup with milk and sugar	25

Alcoholic Drinks

Beer	per 1 pint	180
Brandy	per 20ml measure	65
Champagne	per 1dl glass	70
Cherry Brandy	per 35ml	70
Cider	per $\frac{1}{2}$pt	100
Crème de Menthe	per 35ml	130
Gin	per 20ml measure	50
Port	per 50ml	80
Sauternes	per 1$\frac{1}{2}$dl glass	125
Sherry, dry	per 50ml	50
sweet	per 50ml	60
Rum	per 20ml measure	50
Whisky	per 20ml measure	50
Wine, red	per 1$\frac{1}{2}$dl glass	80
dry white	per 1$\frac{1}{2}$dl glass	80

26 VEGETARIAN COOKING

There are many reasons why people are vegetarians, it can be because of humanitarian considerations, for ethnic or religious reasons, for philosophical or health cults or because they listen to pundits who say meat is bad and unnecessary. Caterers should not regard such customers as cranks or as a nuisance because they upset the kitchen routine, but should endeavour to satisfy their wants in the best possible way.

A vegetarian meal requires even more thought than an ordinary one because it is necessary to ensure that the customer receives the optimum amount of nutrients including the essential animo-acids.

Vegetarians do not eat fish, meat or poultry but do include eggs and dairy produce, especially yoghurt, in their diet; and the various forms of textured vegetable protein are acceptable. Most vegetarians are also whole-food addicts and dislike all over-refined foodstuffs. They may also have a tendency to high anxiety neurosis.

Veganism is the practice of living off plant-foods and it excludes the use of all commodities derived from animals, thus it is more difficult to cater for a vegan than for a vegetarian.

Vegetarian Dishes

Nuts

Nuts can be used in milled form to make meat substitute meals and instead of flour for pastry and puddings. Nuts contain protein, calcium, iron, potassium and phosphorus.

Hazelnut Roast	Mix ground hazelnuts, breadcrumbs and cooked chopped onion with egg and bake in the form of a loaf.
Steamed Nut Pudding	Mix self-raising flour, ground peanuts, bread-crumbs and chopped onion; bind with eggs and steam in a basin.
Walnut Rissoles	Mix ground walnuts with stiff béchamel, shape into croquettes, coat with breadcrumbs and deep or shallow fry.
Soyaburgers	Mix rehydrated tvp mince with sautéd chopped onion and eggs; form into hamburger shapes and shallow fry or griddle.
Soya Bean Soufflé	Mix soya beans purée with egg yolks, fold in the stiffly beaten whites and cook as a soufflé.

Cheese

Chese is an important protein food for vegetarians and contains good amounts of calcium, phosphorus, vitamins A and D, and is a rich source of protein and fat.

Cheese and Bread Pudding	Arrange triangular slices of buttered bread and slices of cheese overlapping in a pie-dish with chopped onion and parsley; cover with savoury egg-custard mix and cook au bain-marie.
Cheese and Nut Loaf	Make a mixture with ground cashews and walnuts, cottage cheese and cooked brown rice, bound with egg; bake in a bread tin.
Cheese and Vegetable Flan	Add cooked vegetables to cheese sauce, fill a baked flan case with the mixture and decorate with slices of the vegetables used.
Pizzas	Many varieties of these are vegetarian and cheese can be the main ingredient for the topping.
Welsh Rarebit and Buck Rarebit	These are good vegetarian meals.

733

Eggs

The calorie, fat and protein value of an egg is contained in the yolk, it also contains vitamins A, D, E and K; the white is composed mainly of water. The various ways of cooking and garnishing make eggs the most popular form of food for vegetarians, especially the uniquitous egg salad or plain omelette. The eggs used should if possible be free-range.

Egg and Cheese Pudding	Add breadcrumbs and grated cheese to a savoury egg-custard mix and cook au bain-marie.
Egg Fou Yong	Add sautéd chopped onion, celery, mushroom and water chestnut to beaten eggs; mix in some bean sprouts and soy sauce and cook as small pancakes.
Pancakes	Can be filled with various savoury fillings including fish, shellfish, cheese, sweetcorn, etc.
Savoury Soufflés	Can include fish, vegetables and cheese added to the basic soufflé mixture.

Cereals and Pastas

The most important cereals are wheat, barley, maize, oats, rice and rye; they are used in crushed or milled form and provide carbohydrate, protein, calcium, iron, vitamin B complex, flour has added calcium, iron, thiamine and nicotinic acid. Pastas are made from hard durum wheats processed to the form of semolina.

Sandwiches	All the various kinds of bread can be used in making interesting sandwiches of a vegetarian nature and when served with an attractive garnish can make a well-balanced meal; peanut butter can be used instead of ordinary butter.
Ploughman's Lunch	There are many interpretations of this meal which is basically bread or roll with butter, Cheddar cheese and a pickled onion; suitable additions include apple, hard-boiled egg, various kinds of pickles, potato crisps, radishes, tomato, tuna fish and watercress. Any kind of cheese may be used. A Continental ploughman's lunch

would include French bread and French, German, Dutch or Italian cheese.

Cornmeal Pancakes	These are the kinds used in Mexican cookery; many can be filled with vegetarian fillings.
Buckwheat Pancakes	Known as blinis and made of rye flour, these can be spread with vegetarian fillings and rolled up.
Pittas	These can be filled after reheating with any hot or cold spicy vegetarian mixture.
Rice	This is probably the most versatile commodity for making into strictly vegetarian dishes and many of the formulas given under rice in the section on Vegetables are suitable.
Pastas	Presented plainly with butter and grated cheese or with garnishes of fish, vegetables and eggs and neutral sauces, these are acceptable vegetarian dishes. They can also be made in layers as a pie. Macaroni cheese is a pleasant vegetarian dish.

Pulses

The many varieties can be incorporated into soups, stews and savouries; most need to be soaked before cooking then plain-boiled with sea-salt added towards the end of the cooking process. It is also possible to purchase pulses in ground form for use in breads, roasts, rissoles, etc. There are some rare kinds that help to make a vegetarian meal more interesting including aduki beans, garbanzo beans, millet, sesame seeds.

Bean Rissoles	Mix stiff purée of cooked haricot beans with cooked chopped onion and cheese and bind with raw egg; mould into cakes 5cm diameter, egg and crumb and deep fry.
Bean Savoury	Add tomato purée and brown breadcrumbs to stiff purée of haricot beans, bake, and serve cut into slices with a yeast-extract thick sauce.
Lentil Burgers	Mould lentil purée mixed with wheat germ into a hamburger shape and cook on a griddle.
Lentil Loaf	Make a mixture of puréed lentils, chopped nuts and brown rice and bake in a loaf tin; serve with rich brown sauce made from yeast extract.

Mung Beans or Bean Sprouts	Bean sprouts are cut fresh when sprouting and may be used raw in a salad or sprinkled over soup or stew. They can be cooked by the stir-fry method and added to most savoury dishes.

Vegetables

Vegetables, especially those grown organically (which means that no chemical fertilisers have been put in the ground) are the real basis of a vegetarian diet. They provide vitamins and minerals, mainly vitamins A and C, calcium and iron, and lend themselves to innumerable ways of presentation, as follows:

Artichoke Dietrich	Serve a plain-boiled globe artichoke in a bed of risotto cooked with yeast extract stock.
Artichoke, Stuffed	Remove the centre from a parboiled globe artichoke, fill with duxelles, sprinkle with breadcrumbs and finish to cook by braising.
Aubergine Steak	Peel large egg-plants, cut lengthways into $1\frac{1}{2}$cm slices, egg and crumb and shallow fry.
Avocado Burgers	Mix raw avocado flesh with cooked purée of soya bean and breadcrumbs; mould and shallow fry.
Leek and Egg Pie	Arrange layers of braised leeks, sliced hard-boiled egg and white sauce in a pie-dish; cover with short pastry and bake.
Stuffed Pimentos	Empty whole small pimentos, blanch, then fill with cooked rice or duxelles and braise.
Potatoes	These can be baked or steamed, cut open and covered with any vegetarian mixture.
Vegetable Curry	Cooked carrots, cauliflower, beans, potatoes or turnips, etc., can be dressed in a border of plain boiled rice and coated with curry sauce.
Vegetable Cutlets	Finely chop raw or cooked vegetables and bind with dry mashed potato and wheat-germ; mould into cutlet shapes, egg and crumb and shallow fry.
Seaweeds	Several varieties of seaweed are sold in dried form either in strips or as a powder, for use as a flavouring or as a vegetable. Some kinds of seaweed are used as colloidal substances by food manufacturers to render their products stable

and to increase the volume. Alginate is a processed seaweed.

Tofu

This is made of soya bean and is a high protein food, widely used throughout the Far East. Soymilk is mixed with a coagulant lactone to produce a smooth brown mass that is creamy, silky and naturally sweet, and can be served cold as it is, sliced for frying, puréed as a dressing or dip, spread in a sandwich, grilled or stewed. It is tetrapacked to keep for months without refrigeration and a 100g serving provides only 52kcals but 7gm of protein.

To shallow fry Tofu, cut it into 2cm slices, dry on a cloth, coat with flour and fry, or coat with egg-wash and breadcrumbs, shallow fry and serve with fried eggs, fried bread, etc.

Tofu may also be blended with strawberries and honey in the form of a chilled sweet dish.

27 PRINCIPLES OF NOUVELLE CUISINE

This style of cookery is not as new as the name implies as it has appeared and disappeared over the past two hundred years; Voltaire, Mercier and La Chapelle among others, have commented upon it during its several heydays, not always favourably, so it has come and gone in fashion. Today, its adherents are impressed by the artistry of chefs who produce wonderful picture-plates of food that demonstrate all the loving care that has gone into the presentation. Such works of art delight the eye though they may leave the appetite unsatiated.

The influence of nouvelle cuisine spread from France where it suddenly developed during the 1970s; it was conceived in the kitchens of such well-known chefs-proprietors as Paul Bocuse, Michel Guérard, Jean and Pierre Troisgros and Raymond Oliver and soon spread to this country, to the USA and even to Japan whence some of its inspiration derives. The founder was Fernand Point but he did not live long enough to see it achieve such widespread popularity.

The introduction of new technology at that time, especially the compact food processor, and improved transport facilities that made it possible to purchase hitherto unseen commodities in the markets of the West have been a spur; the machine helped to lighten the heavy duties of preparing meals and made the job of chef much easier. It could even be suggested that the job of head chef of a nouvelle cuisine establishment is suited to a woman who has done a Cordon Bleu course since she will have been trained more specifically in the art of embellishment with less emphasis on the need to make stockpots full of sauce.

The principles of nouvelle cuisine have not been codified and so far, nobody has attempted to write a book on its methods and formulas. Several books containing recipes have appeared and *Cuisine à la Carte* by Anton Mossiman, shows some of his formulas and outlines his approach to the subject. Some of its French instigators have written about it, notably Michel Guérard in *La Grande Cuisine Minceur*, Paul Bocuse in his *Cuisine du Marché*, and the Troisgros brothers in their book published in 1977 entitled *Cuisiniers à Roanne* and later one called *La Nouvelle Cuisine*. From these books the following rules appear to apply:

1. Make the operation as simple as possible both as regards the mise en place and the cooking methods employed; eliminate all complicated and unnecessary procedures so as to create a smooth and muddle-free atmosphere so that the facilities can be concentrated onto the preparation of only a few but extremely high-quality and costly dishes.

   It is unwise to endeavour to serve too many customers all at once as there is an uppermost limit to the number of covers that can be dealt with in a given period of time.

2. Tradition need not be abandoned entirely but staff should be made to feel free to experiment with new and exciting food combinations, however unlikely and apparently incompatible. Expression must be given to vivid contrasts of colour, taste and texture especially those that startle the eyes for colour appeal is one of the most important rules of nouvelle-cuisine menu-planning. The resultant dishes should be an astonishing and unorthodox combination of fish with meat, and fruit – especially exotic ones. There is no need to pay too much respect to the works of the founders of classical French cookery which were only good in the days when labour costs were cheap and the working-day long and arduous. The social status of chefs has changed from the times when they were mere artisans to being acclaimed as stars and constantly in public eye.

   To give two examples of the kind of changes brought about by the inventiveness of chefs it is permissible to discuss the vast increase in the use of purées and mousses and the changed attitude to simple salads. A criticism of nouvelle cuisine is the inclusion of a purée of one sort or another in every course of the menu, sometimes two on the same plate. It is not clear if these are served to add softness and blandness in contrast with the crispness of the main ingredients or if they are included to make a little go a long way.

Green salads by their nature should be self-effacing and play only a minor role in a meal yet they are now brought to greater prominence by the inclusion of the various flavours of oils and vinegars both hot and cold, and are arranged as works of art with the inclusion of prettily carved and crisped vegetables, the ubiquitous radicchio and the bacon and croûtons.

3. Everything must be cooked fairly underdone as this helps to make the portion look larger than if thoroughly cooked. The term used to describe the degree of cooking is pink or rosé, which is a grade under 'à point' and a grade above 'saignant'; perhaps the Italian term 'al dente' is the keynote to nouvelle cuisine. Undercooking helps to retain much of the original natural flavour and makes it worthwhile to devote the additional masticating process necessary to render it digestible. Crispness is very important and most vegetables require only to be blanched, not boiled. Any coarseness of texture of genuine foodstuffs will be tempered by the softness of the accompanying purées.

4. Produce must be bought and used at its peak of freshness and on the day of purchase. This may mean buying in the market or from the producer and it may be necessary to pay top price but no second-grade produce may be bought in the hope of rendering it tender by marinating or long slow cooking. Nor is it envisaged that meat or game be bought to hang to mature; commodities are purchased for that day and are cooked to order. Thus there is no need for a lot of refrigerated storage space since it is known that chilling reduces original flavours and detracts from the pristine taste of well-cultivated produce.

5. It is not necessary to keep a mise en place of traditional basic sauces as each item of protein food can provide its own sauce merely by swilling the pan with a wine or liqueur, or by reducing the cooking liquid and thickening it slightly with yoghurt, quark, cottage cheese, crème fraîche, etc. but not flour. The use of the various flavoured vinegars, lemon or lime juice is acceptable to connoisseurs of nouvelle cuisine, these may add to the cost of the dish in contrast to the use of demi-glace which refined itself in its own time at little cost yet resulted in a flour content of less than 5 per cent.

6. A return to the unsophisticated cooking methods of yesteryear is one of the tenets of nouvelle cuisine whereby simple

peasant-style dishes using purely local ingredients and formulas are in demand providing they are ornamented with twisted-tomato-skin roses and a few leaves of rare herbs. Old-fashioned simplicity of cookery is a way of selling nostalgia and a collection of old cookery books is invaluable for making new discoveries.

7. The new kitchen-machines have taken all the drudgery out of food preparation; whereas the recipe books said 'pound an item in a mortar' this is now done in seconds at the touch of a switch. The makers claim these machines are labour-saving but this is by doing a task quickly rather than employing a smaller number of staff. The warning is that a food-processing machine can easily destroy the texture of a preparation; as merely mixing it for a minute too long, the lightness can disappear and rubberiness set in.

8. One of the most important injunctions of nouvelle cuisine is that full use should be made of seasonal produce and that it should be purchased and used daily rather than being stored in a refrigerator for future use. The day's menu should not be composed until it is known what has been bought and how it is to be cooked and presented. Thought must also be given to the range of ancillary items that can be used to complement the main dish of fish or meat.

9. In the traditional kitchen where there is a long menu of à la carte dishes it is necessary to carry sufficient mise en place to carry out all orders but there is always a possibility of some dishes not being ordered very often with a consequence that the basic item and its mise en place will deteriorate. In contrast the nouvelle cuisine menu normally lists only a few dishes, these being produced from the day's purchases or of goods that are readily obtainable daily. No made-up or rechauffé dishes are offered and the system is not to cook until an order is given.

But even though the cooking process can be done quickly the customer must be informed that kitchen staff need time to cook and present the dish in perfect order. Nouvelle cuisine is quite time- and labour-consuming in its method of presentation as every plateful must meet the exacting standards as laid down by the chef. Decorative effects should be placed with precision and the marbling of sauces performed at exactly the right time so that the customer sees the vividness before it disappears. Instead of serving a dish of potatoes and vegetables the entremettier will devote care to each individual primeur he puts on the plate as the portion of vegetables (potatoes do not play much part in the menu).

Although this system is labour-intensive the number of covers that can be served is limited. It is possible to serve a banquet for several hundred people provided there is a length of hotplate counter sufficient to accommodate the number of plates laid out in readiness for filling, but it may be prudent to warn the organiser that there will be a lengthy pause between courses whilst each plate is being carefully filled – and then there is the problem of keeping it really hot.

A feature of nouvelle cuisine service is the 'menu-surpris' as used by Escoffier while he worked at the Savoy. Instead of showing the menu, a party of customers is invited to accept a meal at a stated price per person, leaving it entirely to the chef to decide what to serve.

10. The method of serving nouvelle cuisine dishes in the restaurant is not based on any of the best waiting traditions; rather it stems from the household or a budget restaurant. The plate of food as dressed by the chefs is covered with a hot dome-shaped silver lid and taken to the room by the waiter. It is placed in front of the customer and with a flourish the lid is removed by the waiter; to achieve any effect there must be one waiter per cover.

11. Adherents of nouvelle cuisine are supposed to be health-conscious and therefore do not indulge in lashings of cream and butter, but it is the chef who should have a knowledge of dietetics and ensure that his menus are nutritionally sound in that they supply metabolic needs and no more. Yet Michel Guérard could follow his book *Cuisine Minceur* by another entitled *Cuisine Gourmande*, a collection of dazzling recipes that epitomises all that is best in traditional high-class cookery.

The following illustration show a few examples of the way in which nouvelle cuisine dishes are written on a menu.

Hors-d'Oeuvre

Gelée de légumes au xérès, servie avec toasts au beurre basilic

Salade tiède de foie de canard aux artichauts et lardons

Coffret feuilleté d'asperges parfumé à l'orange

Flan de coquilles Saint-Jacques au foie gras et asperges vertes

Fish

Aile de raie à la tomate fraîche et estragon, beurre echiré aux câpres

Mousse de turbot étuvée aux épinards, pulpe d'oursins à l'éstragon

Escalope de bar au caviar de sterlet et ragoût fin de légumes

Rouelle de lotte poêlée à la basquaise aux huîtres gratinées à la mousse de laitue

Meats

Cervelle de veau aux écrevisses, spaghettis frais, jus de veau au porto

Rissoles de ris d'agneau arrosées au fin champagne, coulis de jambon

Viande du marché grillé à la fondu de fonds d'artichaut

Aile de pintadeau et sa cuisse en saucisse parfumé aux truffes

Sweets

Tartlettes sablées aux fruits rouges et kiwis à la crème legère

Poire meringuée farcie de glace plombière au coulis de fraises de bois

Glace aux pruneaux à l'armagnac au chocolat amer

Terrine de fruits éxotiques à la mousse parfumé au marasquin

28 TITLES OF MEMBERS OF THE FULL KITCHEN BRIGADE

Chef de Cuisine (Head Chef)
Sous Chefs (Second Head Chefs):

1. *Pâtissier* (Head Pastry Cook) who is responsible for
     Tourier (Pastrymaker)
     Confisseur (Confectioner)
     Glacier (Ice Cream Cook)
     Boulanger (Baker)
2. *Chef Garde-Manger* (Larder Cook) who is responsible for
     Chef de Froid (Cold Buffet Cook)
     Boucher (Butcher)
     Hors-d'Oeuvrier (Hors-d'œuvre Cook)
     Saladier (Salad Hand)
3. *Chef Saucier* (Sauce Cook) who is responsible for
     1st commis
     2nd commis
     3rd commis
     Apprentices
4. *Chef Poissonier* (Fish Cook)
5. *Chef de Nuit* (Night Cook)
6. *Chef Rôtisseur* (Roast Cook) who may be responsible for
     Grillardin (Grill Cook)
7. *Entremettier* (Vegetable Cook)
8. *Chef Tournant* (Relief Cook)
9. *Breakfast Cook* who may also act as
     Communard (Staff Cook)

Personnel (1) to (8) inclusive are called Chefs de Partie

Titles of members of the full kitchen brigade

There are also:
Secrétaire (Kitchen Clerk)
Aboyeur (Announcer)
Cafetiers (Stillroom Hands)
Econome (Storesmen)
Portiers (Kitchen Porters)
Plongeurs (Potwash men)
Argentiers (Silver room men)
who are all responsible to the Sous Chefs.

Each Chef de Partie will have an appropriate number of assistant cooks, known as commis or commise if female, to help carry out the work of the section.

29 SAFETY PRECAUTIONS

The smooth and efficient running of a kitchen is greatly assisted by staff who are safety conscious and do not therefore take risks during the hectic commotion that is often part of kitchen routine.

Personal

- Wear a double breasted jacket made of absorbent but fire-resistant material. Tuck apron string ends under the turned down apron top
- Do not use a wet kitchen cloth to hold hot dishes
- Wear a good pair of hard-wearing kitchen shoes
- Do not run and do not get up to any horseplay
- Carry knives point downwards; arrange them all facing one way on the workbench

General

- Turn saucepan handles away from the heat and from over the edge of the stove
- Sprinkle the handle of a pan that has come from the oven, with flour as a warning to others not to touch it
- Warn the plongeur about any very hot utensils you give him
- Do not store pans containing a liquid, above eye level
- Do not carry pans full of hot liquid with the lid on
- Know the uses of the different kinds of fire extinguishers
- Use tapers for lighting pilot lights on equipment
- Clean and dry any spillage on the floor
- Be careful when using the deep fryer; keep the fire blanket at hand
- Label containers of detergent and disinfectant

Safety precautions

- Keep hands away from moveable parts of machinery
- Ensure that all equipment is turned off before closing down at night
- Do not use a spoon to feed things into a mincer or mixing machine and never put the hand into it whilst it is operating.
- Use the leg muscles rather than the back muscles when lifting heavy objects

30 HYGIENE

Chefs have a responsibility to provide customers with food which possesses all the necessary quality characteristics that ensure entire satisfaction. This includes the fact that the food served should not present the risk of food poisoning, which can occur in either of two ways – chemical poisoning, or bacteriological poisoning.

Chemical poisoning can occur:
  (i) when food crops that have been sprayed with an insecticide are used without being properly washed or peeled;
  (ii) from verdigris which can form on copper pans that are used for cooking acidic foodstuffs; an undamaged inner lining of tin will prevent any adverse chemical reaction;
  (iii) when chemical poisons used to eliminate rodents and insects, come into contact with foods;
  (iv) when sterilising items of equipment with a chemical steriliser it is important to rinse thoroughly;
  (v) if a cook handles food after he has been handling any poisonous substances, it will be contaminated unless he washes his hands very thoroughly.

Bacterial food poisoning is usually caused by pathogenic bacteria which are minute unicellular micro-organisms which are essential for preventing the accumulation of waste and the speeding up of the process of decay. Some are beneficial, for example, many kinds of cheese are inoculated with various forms of bacteria to give the specific characteristic.

Under a microscope, bacteria can be recognised by the shape – *Cocci* are round, *Bacilli* are rod shape, and *Spirilla* are corkscrew shape. They combine into various forms, from which they acquire their names – *strepto*, a chain thus streptococci; *staphy* a cluster, therefore staphylococci, and *diplo*, a pair, therefore diplococci.

749

The three main types of pathogenic bacteria which are the causes of food poisoning are:

Salmonella

These are anaerobic bacilli that multiply rapidly in the intestine and can cause fatal illness.

Staphylococcus

These are found in the human skin on infected wounds and sores, and in the nose and throat. Food poisoning is caused through the toxins which develop in infected foods and cause extreme pain and nausea for several hours, the third kind is

Clostridium Perfringens

This is a bacterium that is transmitted into the soil by human beings and animals and is found in meat entrées such as stews, large-size joints and their gravies that are left to cool down in a warm atmosphere thus becoming possible sources of infection. The diagram shows the various temperatures that are critical to the subject of growth of bacteria.

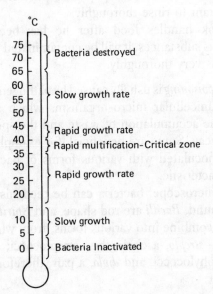

Safety Measures

Food should be cooked to an internal temperature of 75°C for a minimum time of 10 minutes and if not for immediate use, cooled quickly and held at not more than 5°C. Cooked and raw foods, especially meat, must be stored in separate refrigerators so as to avoid the possibility of cross-contamination. Working surfaces must be thoroughly washed and sterilised between preparing different items. Special care must be taken with foods which present a high risk of infection, these include cooked meat, poultry and game, stock, dairy products, shellfish and cooked rice.

Staff must be selected not only on the basis of their skills as craftsmen, but on their appearance which must be clean and tidy, and on their medical record which should be checked.

Means of prevention of infections

Infection	Mode of transmission	Prevention
Cold	Infected droplets from nose or throat transferred to food by touch, cough or sneeze	Clean personal habits; use of clean disposable handkerchiefs over mouth when coughing
Salmonellosis	Ingestion of incompletely cooked food which was previously contaminated either by diseased animal, faeces either human or rodent	Clean personal habits; following good cookery practices; control of rodents and infestation
Streptococcal	Ingestion of food contaminated from discharges from the nose, throat or absess of carrier, or by food handling by the infected person	Prohibit employment of those with respiratory disorders

Typhoid	Ingestion of food contaminated by an infected person or carrier, or by flies	Medical check and immunisation; prevention of infestation by flies
Trichinosis	Ingestion of active trichinae larvae from pork meat	Cook pork meats to well above 75°C for a minimum of 20 minutes.
Staphylococcus Aureus	Ingestion of food contaminated from a handler's boils, nose or throat droplets	Food handlers to be free from infections; thorough cooking of meat to 85°C for minimum of 15 minutes.

Refrigeration plays a big part in the prevention of food poisoning and the following table shows optimum storage temperatures and relative humidity.

Product	Temperature °C	Relative humidity
Dairy produce	3–5	70–80
Meat and poultry	3–6	80–85
Fish	1–+1	90–95
Vegetables	1–3	90–95
Cooked meat	3–7	75–80

A general purpose refrigerator should be maintained at 1–4°C. The temperature of the room in which meat is prepared must not exceed 10°C. Frozen food should be stored at −18° to −21°C, not for controlling the growth of pathogenic bacteria but to slow down enzymatic reaction which will adversely affect the food by discoloration and oxidisation.

The equipment used for cooking must be kept in perfect condition and kitchen porters and pot-washers must be encouraged to take pride in their jobs so that all items, whether fixed like stoves and ovens, mechanical such as mixing machines, or small utensils and cooking pots, are kept spotlessly clean. Detergents help to maintain a good standard of hygiene but must be used correctly. Their efficiency in terms of disinfection depends to an extent on the hardness of the water supply and on the nature of the soilage. All have highly specific functions rather than being all-purpose, for example, cationic products are good bactericides but poor detergents and anionics are good detergents but less efficient as bactericides, which means that a combination of the two may neutralise each other. Specialist advice will help to solve this problem.

It is the chef's responsibility to ensure that a cost-effective standard of hygiene is rigidly maintained so there is no possibility of an outbreak of food poisoning.

31 CHECKLIST OF WEIGHTS AND MEASURES

Small Amounts

1 teaspoonful (tsp)	$\frac{1}{5}$ fl oz or 5ml
1 dessertspoonful (dsp)	$\frac{2}{5}$ fl oz or 10ml
1 tablespoonful (tbsp)	$\frac{3}{5}$ fl oz or 15ml
3 tspns = 1 tbsp	
20 drops = 1 ml	

Liquid Measures

Official figures are always given in millilitres (ml) but for culinary purposes it is best to use the decilitre (dl) as this is shown on most measuring jugs whereas the millimetre is not.

1	gill ($\frac{1}{4}$ pint)	= $1\frac{1}{2}$dl
$\frac{1}{2}$	pint	= 3dl (approx.)
4	gills (1 pint)	= $\frac{4}{7}$ litre
1	pint (20 fl oz)	= 568ml (or 6dl)
2	pints (1 quart)	= $1\frac{1}{8}$ litres
1	gallon	= $4\frac{1}{2}$ litres (approx.)
1	pint	= 540cc
1	litre	= 845cc
3	dl	= $\frac{1}{2}$ pint
10	dl (1 litre)	= $1\frac{3}{4}$ pints
$4\frac{1}{2}$	litres	= 1 gallon
20	litres	= 4.4 gallons
25	litres	= $5\frac{1}{2}$ gallons (approx.)
100	litres	= 22 gallons (approx.)

Weights

1oz	=	28.4 grams	28g	=	1oz
¼lb	=	113 grams	100g	=	3½oz
½lb	=	227 grams	120g	=	4oz
1lb	=	454 grams	150g	=	5½oz
2lb	=	900 grams	200g	=	7oz
14lb	=	6.35 kilograms	250g	=	9oz (approx.)
(1 stone)			500g	=	17½oz
			1kg	=	2⅕lb
			3kg	=	6½lb
			5kg	=	11lb

Linear

1 inch = 25mm or 2½cm
2 inches = 5cm (50mm)
1 foot = 30cm
1 yard = 91cm
1 metre = 39¼in, 3.3ft or 1.1yd

Volume (e.g. refrigerator)

Cubic feet	Capacity in litres	Capacity in kg
2.0	55	17
2.2	62	20
3.5	100	31
5.3	150	45
6.0	170	50
7.1	200	64
8.3	235	75
10.8	307	98

USA

1 cup = 2½dl or 8fl. oz= 16fl. oz (4½dl)
1 pint = 32fl. oz (9 dl)
1 quart = 32fl oz (9dl)
1 gallon = 8½ US pints (6½ Imperial pints)

The cup is also used as a measure for solids, e.g. 1 cup = 125g (4½oz) flour; 1 cup = 225g (8oz) granulated sugar 1 cup = 150g (5½oz) flour

Temperatures

Baking Temperatures (using a traditional or convection oven)

Sufficient time should be allowed for the oven to pre-heat before cooking commences

Regulo or Gas No.	°F	°C	Definition	Uses
1	275	140	Very slow – cool	Meringues (120°C)
2	300	150	Slow	Milk pudding, egg custard
3	325	170	Moderate	Compote, rich fruit cake
4	350	180	Moderately hot	Braised meat, stew, shortbread
5	375	190		Shallow-poached fish
6	400	200	Hot	Roast meat, small cakes, baked potatoes
7	425	220	Quite hot	Flaky pastry, chou paste, pastry, scones, Yorkshire pudding
8	450	230	Very hot	Bread, puff pastry
9	475	240		Bread rolls
10	500	260	Extremely hot	To gratinate or glaze quickly

Stock Syrup using a saccharometer

°Baume	Amount of sugar (g)	Uses
12	150	Fruit salad
18	250	Compote, sorbet
22	325	Trifle, savarin
28	500	Ice cream
33	600	Candied fruit

Add the indicated amount of sugar to 5dl (18fl oz) water and boil until it reaches the required degree on the saccharometer.

Boiling point of water at different altitudes in °C	
Sea level	100.0
2000 ft	98.4
5000 ft	95.0
7500 ft	92.4

Sugar-boiling temperatures

It is advisable to use a sugar-boiling thermometer to check the temperatures as indicated.

°C	Definition	Uses
105	Short thread	Syrup for toffee, candied fruit, Turkish delight
110	Long thread	Sweets, crystallised fruit, marrons glacés
115	Soft ball	Soft centres, fondant, marzipan
121	Medium ball	Candy, fudge, nougat
125	Hard ball	Butterscotch, caramel toffees, Italian meringue, nougat for pièces montées
137	Soft crack	Blown-sugar fruits, moulded sugar, pulled sugar, boiled sweets, ribbons
155	Hard crack	Dipped and glazed fruit, spun sugar
182	Caramel	

Gravy browning: put 500g sugar in an old saucepan, allow to melt and turn black, then add 1½ litre water, mix well and keep in a bottle.

Proving temperature for bread = 24°C

Tempering temperature for chocolate: melt and heat to 45°C, cool to 27°C, reheat and use at 32°C.

Smoking point of fats

Fat	°C
Butter	148
Concentrated butter	190
Corn oil	221
Dripping	163
Lard	190
Margarine	155
Oil, vegetable	218
White fat	224

In determining the desirable temperature for deep frying any food it is essential to know:

1. the capacity of the fat to retain heat;
2. the rate of recovery of the fryer;
3. the volume of food to be fried within a given period.

Only a few foods such as browning chips require a temperature as high as 190°C and the ideal frying temperature is between 175 and 185°C, which helps to prolong the useful life of the frying medium.

Storage temperature for perishable foods °C

Item	°C	Item	°C
Bacon	5	Poultry: Cooked	5–7
Dairy produce	5–7	Fresh	4–5
Fish	2	Frozen	–18
Frozen foods	–18	Shellfish, raw and cooked	0
Meat: Cooked	4	Smoked fish and meat	4–5
Chilled, raw	–1	Cook–chill meals	3
Fresh, raw	1–2	Vegetables	6
Frozen joints	–18		
VacuumPacked	0		

Hotplate holding and serving temperatures in °C

Hot foods	80°
Cold foods	8°
Coffee	91°
Other beverages	95°

Defrosting time

Deep-frozen poultry must be thoroughly defrosted before being put to cook and it is advisable to let them thaw in the refrigerator at 7°C for at least the length of time indicated.

Up to   1kg – 12 hours
2kg – 22 hours
3kg – 30 hours
5kg – 2 days
8kg – 3 days
10kg up to 4 days

It is possible to speed up this time by defrosting in a microwave oven that has a defrost cycle or pulse power.

759

Roasting Temperatures

Type	Cut	Initial Temp°C	Time (mins)	Then Temp°C	Mins per 500g	Degree to which cooked	Internal Temp°C
Beef	Rib/	205	25	110	17	Underdone	60
	Sirloin	205	25	150	27	Medium	71
		205	25	150	32	Well done	79
Lamb	Leg	200	15	160	25	Pink	75
	(whole)	200	15	160	30	Well done	82
	Loin on bone	200	15	155	27	Pink	75
	Loin boned and rolled	200	15	155	37	Well done	82
	Shoulder	200	15	160	25	Pink	75
	(on bone)	200	15	160	30	Well done	85
Pork	Leg	230	15	160	40	Well done	85
	Loin	230	15	160	38	Well done	80
	Spare Rib	230	15	160	45	Well done	80
Veal	Leg Bone-in	220	15	160	37	Well done	82
Poultry		220	15	180	–	Well done	80
Game Birds		220	20	–	–	Rare (wild duck)	65
		220	15	–	–	Just cooked (grouse)	76
		200	15–18	–	–	Well done (partridge)	80

The use of a thermometer or a thermocouple attachment to an oven will show when the desirable degree of doneness is reached at the thickest part of the joint where the probe is and will give a scientific rather than an empirical or pragmatic decision, resulting in less wastage. Longer cooking can tenderise but the cooking temperature must always be maintained. Roasting temperature should be in terms of size of joint and required degree of doneness; large joints roasted on the bone are best. Size and shape of the joint and length of hanging time influence the cooking time needed.

The higher the oven temperature the greater the shrinkage and the loss of fat and flavour; the length of cooking time is another factor as meat with a large amount of surface-fat requires less time than lean meat since the melting fat acts as a conductor of heat thus cooking the meat more quickly.

Portion yields for poultry and game

Name	Weight range (oven range)	Number of portions
Poussin	300g – 400g	1
Double Poussin	450g – 800g	2
Spring Chicken	900g – 1¼kg	2– 4
Poularde	1¼kg – 3kg	4– 8
Duck	2kg – 3½kg	2– 6
Goose	5kg – 7kg	10–15
Guinea Fowl	1kg – 1½kg	2– 4
Turkey	4kg – 10g	16–36
	Rough-plucked/skinned Weight	
Grouse	300g–450g	1–2
Partridge	225g–350g	1–2
Pheasant	1¼kg–1½kg	2
Pigeon	250g–350g	1
Quail	225g–300g	½–1
Wild Duck	1kg–1¼kg	2
Woodcock	390g – 425g	1
Hare	3kg – 4kg	6
Leveret	1½kg – 2½kg	4
Rabbit	900g – 1-¼kg	4–6
Venison	(Haunch 5kg)	30 (allow 150g pp)

Note: Game birds are not normally sold by weight but by so much per bird or brace*: they may be purchased oven-ready but if to be hung, are best in rough-plucked form. The loss between rough-plucked and oven-ready is approximately 20 per cent. *1 hen and 1 cock bird

Gastronorme container sizes

Depth	Module	1/1	2/3	1/2	1/3	1/4	1/6	1/9
	Dimension (mm)	530 × 325	354 × 325	325 × 265	325 × 176	265 × 162	176 × 162	176 × 108
	Capacity (litre)							
40mm		5.5	3.5	2.5	1.5	–	–	–
65mm		9.5	6	4	2.5	1.75	1	0.6
(No. of portions of baked pie)		28	16	12	8	–	–	–
100mm		15	9	5.5	3.75	2.75	1.75	1
150mm		22	14	9.5	5.75	4.3	2.3	–
200mm		28	18	12.5	7.5	–	–	–
(No. of portions of soup)		100	70	50	30			

Note: Storage trays are made in full size (530 × 325mm) and double size (650 × 530mm), both 25mm in depth

Can sizes and contents

Size	Gross weight	Optimum drained weight	Uses
A10	3–3½kg	6–7lb	Solid-pack apples, fruit, baked beans, vegetables
A 6	2.7kg	6lb	Tomato purée, solid-pack apricots
A 5	1.0–1.3kg	1 quart	Fruit juices
A 2½	0.6–0.9kg	1½–2lb	Fruit
A 2	510–680g	1⅙–1½lb	Fruit, vegetables
A 1	400–450g	14–16oz	Baked beans, soups, fish
5 KC	5kg	11lb	Solid-pack apricots, tomato purée
3 KC	3kg	6¾lb	Fruit, meat, vegetables
1 KC	1kg		Fruit juice

Sizes of Cakes

Tin diameter (cm)	Weight of mixture (kg)	Baking temperature °C	Baking time
Round Tins Plain Genoese Sponge			
14	0.550		20 mins
15	0.725	190	20 mins
17½	1.100		25 mins
20	1.650		30 mins
Richly Fruited (in round tin)			
13	0.650		1½–1¾ hrs
15	1.050		1¾–2 hrs
18	1.350	140	2½–3 hrs
20	1.800		3½–4 hrs
25	3.000		4¼–4¾ hrs
30	4.300		5–5½ hrs
Square Tins			
13	0.900		
15	1.300		
18	1.750	Baking temperature and times as	
20	2.300	for richly fruited round tin	
25	3.750		
30	5.500		

Note: Baking loss is approximately 10 per cent.

Portion Sizes

Soup
1½dl for table d'hôte (6 portions per 1 litre)
2½dl for à la carte or canteen (4 or 5 portions per 1 litre)

Item	Subsidiary course	Main course
Eggs		
Boiled, poached	1	2
scrambled	2	3
Omelette	2	3

Checklist of weights & measures

Farinaceous (raw weight)

Pasta	45g	60g
Rice	30g (garnish)	50g
Gnocchi	150g	200g

Fish (raw weight)

Fillet	80g	120g
Darne	180g	200g
Small whole	200g	250–280g
Lobster	–	Half of 700g fish
Whitebait	120g	180g

	Raw	Cooked
Meat		
Beef boiled/braised/roast	90g boneless	65g
Lamb	120g bone in	65g
Pork	130g bone in	65g
Offal	100g	100g
Navarin	150g on bone	150g
Oxtail	220g on bone	200g
Pie	150g (including pastry)	200g (including pastry)
Poultry		
Chicken (oven ready)	175g on bone	80g boneless
Turkey (oven ready)	125g on bone	70g boneless
Vegetables (as purchased)	Fresh (g)	Frozen (9)
Carrots	110	90
Cabbage	200	90
Turnips/Swede	150	90
Runner beans	120	90
Marrow	200	–
Spinach	200	120
Butter beans, etc. 35g (raw)		
Potatoes		
Boiled, mashed, roast	150	–
Chips	200	90

Pastry 1×20cm flan $= 150$g pastry
1×23cm pie (top and bottom) 300g pastry
1kg puff paste $= 60 \times 5$cm bouchées

Sponge puddings 35g flour per portion
Custard $6\frac{1}{2}$ litres per 100

764

Ice cream

Scoop size	Approximate weight	Portion size
30	45g	50ml
24	50g	60ml
20	160g	70ml
16	90g	1dl
12	100g	$1\frac{1}{8}$dl

Amounts of fresh vegetables

The following amounts will yield a 60g cooked portion after allowing for average losses in preparation and cooking, assuming fresh produce.

Vegetable	Weight as purchased, (kg) per 100 portions
Asparagus	9
Broad beans	15
French beans	8
Runner beans	9
Beetroot	7
Broccoli	10
Brussels sprouts	9
Cabbage	10
Carrots	8
Cauliflower	12
Celery	9
Courgettes	7
Egg-plant	10
Fennel	7
Leeks	9
Marrows	12
Onions	8
Parsnips	9
Peas	14
Potatoes boiled*	9
chips*	15
mashed*	12
roast*	14

765

Checklist of weights & measures

Red cabbage	8
Salsify	8
Seakale	9
Spinach	15
Swede	9
Tomatoes	8
Turnips	8

e.p. – edible portion (less preparation waste)
a.p. – as purchased
*90g portions
The recommended amount of salt for plain boiling vegetables is $\frac{1}{2}$ teaspoonful per 1 litre water

Sandwiches

Number of slices per normal sandwich loaf (800g)*

Thin	*Medium*	*Thick*
29	25	19

*These include the end crusts

	Number of rounds			
	25	50	100	*Notes*
Butter (or low-fat spread)	250g	400g	800g	Softened and creamed for ease of spreading
Chicken	500g	1kg	2kg	Thinly sliced breast meat
Cheese, Cheddar, sliced	325g	650g	1¼kg	If using grated cheese diminish these amounts by 25 per cent
Corned beef	625g	1¼kg	2¼kg	Thinly sliced
Egg, sliced	18	36	70	If using sieved egg, diminish these numbers by 10 per cent, mix with mayonnaise
Fish or meat paste	650g	1¼kg	2¼kg	Made as a fine purée
Ham, ox-tongue	650g	1¼kg	2¼kg	Thinly sliced
Smoked salmon	500g	1kg	2kg	Thinly sliced
Tomato	750g	1¼kg	2¼kg	Peeled and sliced

Tea

Allow 40g tea-leaves per $4\frac{1}{2}$ litres freshly boiled water
plus $1\frac{1}{8}$ litres milk: this will yield approximately 28×2dl teacupsful

Coffee

Allow 220g average quality ground coffee per $4\frac{1}{2}$ litres water; for this quantity $1\frac{1}{2}$ litres hot milk will give a total of 6 litres, or approximately 28×2dl teacupsful.

Textured vegetable protein

Textured vegetable protein (tvp) and other similar plant foods may be used in meat dishes to reduce the quantity of real meat and thus, the cost. These products are sold in dehydrated form, flavoured or unflavoured, coloured or plain and are usually soaked to rehydrate giving a moisture content of 60–65 per cent by mixing 1 part tvp with 1.5 parts water. It is the wet weight that must be calculated in recipes. To determine the amount of tvp to replace part of the meat it has to be decided whether this is 10, 20, 25 or 30 per cent, using this table.

% tvp in final product	Raw meat (g)	tvp (g) dry weight	Water (for rehydrating)	Total product
30	700	120	1.8dl	1000g
25	750	100	1.5dl	1000g
20	800	80	1.2dl	1000g
10	900	40	0.5dl	1000g

By law, the presence of tvp in any dish sold to the general public must be stated.

32 GLOSSARY OF CATERING TERMS

Abalone	A bivalve shellfish found in the Pacific Ocean off California; also called an ormer as found around the Channel Islands.
Aceto dolce	Raw sweet pickled fruits and vegetables used as part of an hors-d'œuvre selection.
Achar	Hindu word for pickled fruit and vegetables that have been strongly spiced.
Agape	A religious banquet or feast held in connection with the Lord's Supper.
Agar-agar	Thickening agent derived from seaweed.
Agaric	Family of a fungus of which the oronge agaric is edible.
Agoursi	Pickled small cucumbers.
Aillade	A seasoning sauce made of basil, garlic, oil and tomato; served cold.
al Forno	Italian term for a dish cooked in the oven.
Aioli or aiolli	Pungent cold sauce made of pounded garlic and oil.
Alginate	Powdered form of a seaweed used as a commercial food thickener and stabiliser.
Alligator Pear	Another name for the avocado pear, usually the Hass variety.
Amaretti	Small macaroon biscuits usually served with espresso coffee.
Amourettes	Strips of the spinal marrow of beef.
Amphitryon	An hospitable person; menu term used to denote an elaborately garnished dish.
Amuse-gueules	Alternative name for cocktail canapés.
Animelles	Genitals of lamb, goat, etc. used as a dish of offal; sometimes referred to as lamb's fry.

768

Antipasto	The Italian equivalent of an hors-d'œuvre selection.
Apple bananas	Very small and sweet bananas from West Africa.
Arrowroot leaves	A green vegetable like large spinach leaves; nothing to do with the thickening agent.
Asafetida	Strong-smelling resin much used in Indian, especially Hindu, cookery.
Asparagus pea	Square pods cooked whole and eaten with the fingers as a vegetable; not related to the pea or asparagus.
Assiette Anglaise	Plateful of sliced cold meats including roast beef, York ham, ox-tongue, turkey, etc.
Avgolemeno	Greek egg and lemon sauce or soup.
Baba	Individual cake made from savarin paste, containing currants; usually featured as rum baba.
Baccala	The Italian name for dried salt cod.
Bagel	Shiny ring roll that has been boiled before being baked; can be served with various fillings.
Ballotine	Boned and stuffed leg, usually chicken but could be of lamb.
Baguette	Name given to the long French loaf.
Bamboo shoots	Leaf buds of the bamboo plant widely used in Chinese cookery and salad.
Bagna Cauda	Sauce or dip made of anchovy purée, garlic and olive oil.
Bannock	Type of shortcake containing almonds, oatmeal and mixed peel; usually cooked on a griddle.
Bap	Flat oval yeast roll, usually moulded oval in plenty of flour to give a floury finish.
Barbe-de-Capucine	Name given to a variety of endive.
Barquette	Boat-shaped pastry case made in several sizes to contain various fillings.
Basmati rice	Variety of long-grain rice as grown in India; it has an aroma of milk and nuts.
Batavia	Another name for the frizzy endive, a lettuce-like salad vegetable.
Bath chap	Cured lower jaw of a pig's head usually sold cooked and coated in breadcrumbs; can be sliced and fried.

769

Bath Oliver	Round dry biscuit for cheese, originally produced by a Dr Oliver in Bath.
Batterie de cuisine	Name given to all the small kitchen utensils such as saucepans, spatulas, frying baskets.
Bavette	Thin flank of beef cut from alongside the sirloin.
Baveuse	Word used to describe an omelette as being left soft inside.
Bay salt	Another name for freezing salt; coarse grains of salt for use in a salt mill obtained from sea water.
Bêche de mer	Sea slug or sea urchin of which only the ovary is eaten.
Beignet	Fritter, usually an item of sweet or savoury food dipped in batter and deep fried.
Belons	Flat kind of oysters from Brittany, regarded as being the best flavoured of all French oysters.
Bemax	Proprietary brand of food enrichener in the form of granules or powdered wheatgerm, bran and barley with vitamins and minerals.
Bengalines	Cold dish of slices of woodcock inside ovals of woodcock mousse, coated with brown chaud-froid.
Bergamot	(i) Pear-shaped orange; (ii) herb of the mint family.
Beuchelle	A ragoût of various kinds of offal, sometimes flavoured with lemon, capers and anchovy.
Beurre blanc	Warm creamy sauce made with shallots, vinegar and butter.
Beurre manié	Mixture of butter and flour used for thickening sauces and stews.
Biftek	The French way of writing 'a beef steak' on the menu.
Biltong	The South African name for pemmican or dried strips of beef as emergency rations.
Bird's nest	Swallows' nests used as a garnish for consommé, sweet, etc., imported from China.
Biriani	Indian method of making a mutton or chicken curry and saffron rice.
Bismarck	A pickled herring, similar to a rollmop; named after Baron Otto von Bismarck (1815–98).

Blackjack	Colloquial name for gravy browning, made by caramelising sugar to an advanced stage.
Black pudding	Sausage made from pig's blood and fat packed into a black skin.
Blanc de Volaille	Name given to a suprême of chicken.
Blinis	Small pancake made with buckwheat flour, for serving with caviar.
Blintzes	Potato pancake filled with savoury or sweet filling much favoured by Jewish people.
Bloater	Salted and lightly smoked herring, usually served grilled for breakfast.
Blue Point	Small-size oyster from Long Island in USA; much featured on recherché menus in that country.
Bolar Steak	Beef steak cut from the leg of mutton cut; unsuitable for grilling.
Bobotee	South African dish of minced meat, soaked bread, curry powder, lemon juice, chopped onion bound with egg and baked as a meat loaf.
Boletus	Another name for cèpe, a type of fleshy mushroom that has several varieties.
Bouquet garni	Flavouring agent for soup, stock, stew consisting of parsley stalks, leek, bay-leaf and thyme tied with string.
Boston lettuce	A tender Iceberg type of lettuce.
Bourride	Type of fish stew from the south of France, similar to bouillabaise.
Boutargue (Poutargue)	Pressed and preserved mullet or tuna-fish roe.
Brioche	Rich yeast bun made in the form of a small cottage loaf for breakfast or in a charlotte mould for use as a sweet dish.
Brissolette	A hollowed-out bread croûton filled with various salpicons.
Brochette	Skewer usually containing pieces of meat with onions, herbs, etc., served grilled.
Broil	Old English and American term meaning to cook by grilling.

771

Bubble and squeak	Dish of left-over cooked potatoes, cabbage and meat, mashed to a purée and shallow-fried in dripping as a round cake or in individual portions.
Buckling herring	Smoked herring, served as part of an hors-d'œuvre selection.
Buckwheat	Grain of Asian origin, unsuitable for making into bread on its own but used for making blinis.
Buisson	French term used to denote a piled-up portion of food, e.g. whitebait, goujons, scampi.
Bulima	Voracious appetite for food whereby eating becomes an obsession.
Bummalo	The correct name for the Bombay duck, the fish salted and dried in fillets for serving as an accompaniment with curry.
Burghul	Cracked wheat as used in Middle Eastern cookery (also written Bulghur).
Buttermilk	The liquid that remains after cream has been churned into butter; can be drunk or used in pastry.
Cadenas	Box containing the personal cutlery of a nobleman in medieval times.
Caffeine	Alkaloid substance found in tea and coffee; acts as a mild stimulant.
Caillete	(also spelt gayette and gaillette) A faggot made of liver, meat, herbs, etc.
Calabrese	Type of broccoli, bluish green with compact flowers.
Calipash	The fatty meat from the upper shell of the turtle, nowadays obtained in canned or dried form.
Calorie	Unit of energy used to denote nutritional values of food now called a kilocalorie, which is the amount of heat needed to raise the temperature of 1kg water by 1°C.
Canapés	Small savoury toasts, biscuits, etc., with various items on top served as appetisers before a meal.
Cantaloup	Large netted type of melon with orange-coloured flesh.

Capalin	Type of caviar obtained from a small member of the salmon family found in the Arctic Ocean.
Capercaillie	Large game-bird of the grouse family, now farm-reared in Scotland.
Capillaire	Variety of fern that used to be used to flavour stock syrup.
Capilotade	Stew made with cooked chicken and mushrooms; a rechauffé dish for using this commodity.
Capon	Chicken that has been fattened by being castrated which causes it to put on weight.
Caponata	Stew of onion, egg-plant, tomato, pimento, celery and olives, similar to ratatouille.
Capsicum	Another name for the pimento or pepper; available as green, yellow, red and white.
Caraque	Thinly spread melted chocolate, allowed to set and scraped into curls for cake decoration.
Carbonnade	Stew made of thin beef steaks cooked in beer with onions; a Belgian speciality.
Cardoon	Vegetable of the thistle family, similar to leek and celery.
Carpetbag steak	Double sirloin steak cut open to form a pocket into which raw oysters are placed before being grilled.
Carrageen	Purple-coloured seaweed used as a substitute for gelatine; also called Irish moss.
Carte du Jour	Daily menu of the table d'hôte type, priced by the meal, not by the dish.
Cashew nuts	Crescent-shaped nuts usually served as an appetiser.
Cassata	Cream ices of various flavours containing candied fruits macerated in maraschino and chopped nuts, set in layers in an oblong mould.
Cassava	Root of a tropical bush, ground and refined as a staple food of the West Indies and Africa; the residue is made into tapioca.
Casserole	Covered earthenware dish used for both cooking and serving.
Cassonade	Soft brown sugar as used for coffee to which it gives a slightly spicy flavour.

773

Cassoulet   Oven-cooked dish of goose, pork and haricot beans; a French regional stew.

Caul   Membrane that covers an animal's intestine, used for covering cromesquis, faggots, etc., before cooking.

Cayenne pepper   Very strong type of ground pepper, made from chillies.

Celsius   The Centigrade temperature scale invented by A. Celsius (1701–44)

Cèpe   Flap mushroom; thick, fleshy and moist.

Cerf   Venison, in particular stag or deer.

Cervelas   French smoked sausage similar to a saveloy, made of pork but also available made from fish such as pike.

Cerfeuil   Chervil, a delicate herb with fern-like leaves, used to garnish consommés and as an integral part of fines herbes.

Ceviche   Marinated raw fish in lemon and lime juices with onion rings; serve with julienne of pimento and hard-boiled egg.

Champ   Cold mashed potato with peas and sautéd onion, fried as a kind of bubble and squeak.

Chapelure   Breadcrumbs made from dried crusts, used for coating foods.

Charcuterie   Prepared products of pork butchery, iincluding offals and sausages.

Chard   Leaves and stalks of the seakale beet; the leaves are cooked as for spinach and the stalks as for asparagus.

Charollais   Breed of French cattle giving good quality beef; now crossed with British herds.

Châtrier   To remove the intestine from a crayfish; also called Décortiqué.

Chaudfroid   Sauce containing aspic jelly or gelatine for use in cold buffet work.

Chaufont   Saucepan of hot salted water used for reheating green vegetables as served in the professional manner in a large busy kitchen.

Chausson   A turnover such as an apple turnover, usually made with puff pastry.

774

Chemiser	To line a mould, usually with jelly before filling the centre with the main material.
Cherry tomato	Very small tomato produced mainly for decorative purposes.
Chichekebab	French way of spelling Shishkebab.
Chicory	Frizzy endive, flat lettuce-like salad vegetable also known as 'Batavia'.
Chiffonade	Finely shredded leaf vegetables or herbs for use as a garnish in soups.
Chili con carne	Well-known Mexican dish consisting of minced beef with chilli powder and a garnish of red kidney beans.
Chine	The spine or saddle and best ends of lamb in one joint.
Chipati (Chappati)	Kind of bread used throughout the East; flat, round, in shape to open up for filling with meat, vegetables, salad, etc.
Chipolata	Small thin sausage used in garnishes and for cocktail parties.
Chitterlings	The cooked and cleaned intestine, usually of pigs; used as an offal and for sausage skins.
Choesels	Name given to the beef pancreas or sweetbread in Belgium.
Chorizo	Spanish pork sausage that is highly spiced, dried then smoked; there are many varieties.
Chutney	Type of pickled condiment for serving with curry; usually contains dates, mangoes and spices.
Ciernikis	Hot hors-d'œuvre item made of cottage cheese, flour, butter and eggs in the shape of small dumplings; poached and buttered.
Cimier	Name given to a haunch of venison such as deer.
Citron	Citrus fruit grown mainly for its skin which is candied and for its juice as a cocktail ingredient.
Civet	Stew made from furred game, usually hare that is first marinated then thickened with the blood and raw liver.
Clafouti	Cherry flan, a speciality of Berry in France; it is made by pouring a rich batter over the fruit and baking.

Clam
Large bivalve shellfish like a mussel mainly found in the USA but cultivated around the coasts of France.

Clementine
Cross between an orange and a mandarine.

Cloche
Glass dome used when cooking chicken suprême, mushrooms, etc., in the sous-cloche style.

Cochineal
Red colouring made from a small insect but now usually an artificial colouring matter.

Cockscombs
The combs from chickens' heads, blanched, skinned and cooked as a garnish; nearly always associated with cock's kidneys which are the testicles.

Cocotte
Earthenware dish made for the dual purpose of cooking and serving.

Coeur de filet
The middle piece of a fillet of beef; a menu term for the fillet.

Coeur de palmier
Heart of palm, which are the terminal leaf-buds of the cabbage palm tree; available canned from Australia, West Indies, etc.

Coffre
The trunk of a bird or animal, e.g. the skinned breast of a chicken without the legs.

Coffret
Case made of bread, potato, etc., for holding salpicons as an entrée.

Cohoe
Small size of wild salmon from the North Pacific.

Colcannon
Irish dish made of left-over cabbage, onion and potatoes.

Collops
Small thickish slices of boneless raw meat, or a Scottish dish of minced beef with scones baked on top of it.

Comfits
Sugared caraway or anise seeds; or liquorice coated with cooked hard sugar.

Commis(e)
Assistant cook; there are several grades such as first, second or third commis. A commise is a female assistant cook.

Compote
Dish of stewed, fresh or dried fruit in syrup; the pieces should be intact.

Condiments
Seasonings, including salt, pepper and mustard.

Confit d'Oie	Preserved goose in its own fat (confit means preserved, therefore confiture is French for jam).
Conserve	Good quality jam containing unbroken fruit.
Consolante	Beer, lemonade or wine issued to kitchen staff to cool them down whilst working.
Contorni	Italian word for garnishes, accompaniments and vegetables served with meat.
Contrefilet	Boned and trimmed sirloin of beef; also known as faux-filet.
Cookie	Name used in the USA for a sweet biscuit.
Coquelet	Small size of chicken.
Coral	The ovary of the lobster that gives the intense red colour; also called tomalley.
Coralline pepper	Red pepper sometimes called oriental pepper, a milder form of cayenne.
Cordon bleu	Female cook who should have been trained at the cookery school of that name in Paris.
Coriander	Spicy seed used mainly in pastry work but in ground form is an ingredient of curry powder.
Cornstarch	Name given to cornflour in USA; very finely ground maize used mainly as a thickening agent.
Corn dog	Frankfurter dipped into batter and deep fried.
Cornet	Item of food, e.g. ham, pastry, etc., made into a small cone shape and filled with a suitable stuffing.
Corn pone	Bread made from maize flour and molasses, aerated with baking powder; usually eaten whilst hot.
Cos lettuce	Elongated type of lettuce that is crisp and dark green; French term is 'Romaine'.
Cotriade	Fish stew which includes potatoes and herbs.
Coulibiac	Layers of salmon, rice, hard-boiled egg and vésiga baked in the form of a pie, surrounded with brioche or puff pastry.
Courgette flowers	These blossoms can be eaten raw, cooked as a fritter, or used as a decoration around suitable foods.
Couscous	North African dish of stewed chicken or lamb with steamed semolina on top.

Crambé   French name for seakale, also called chou de mer.

Crapaudine   In English it is spatchcock, a method of cutting and cooking a poussin or chicken to resemble a leaping frog.

Crimp   To decorate the edge of a pie; also to cook fish by boiling immediately it is caught and after cutting incisions in it.

Croissant   Crescent-shaped roll made from yeast dough that has been further treated as for puff pastry.

Croustade   Base cut from bread or pastry, hollowed-out slightly and spread with farce; used for serving game-birds.

Croûte   Fairly thick slice of French flûte bread, fried or toasted to serve with soup.

Croûtons   Small cubes of bread, shallow fried for use as a garnish with soups or cut larger to garnish stews, vegetables, etc.

Crudités   Mixture of raw vegetables, e.g. celery, cucumber, fennel, pimento, radishes, served as a preliminary course with various dips.

Crullers   Ring doughnut sprinkled with sugar.

Crustacean   Class of shellfish which includes crab, crawfish, crayfish, lobster, prawns and shrimps.

Cuisine   (i) kitchen premises, (ii) cookery, (iii) the national or traditional style of cookery of a country or race.

Cuisine minceur   Type of classical French cookery in which the use of fattening ingredients such as butter, cream, flour and eggs is restricted.

Cuisine nouvelle   Style of cookery in which each dish is given individual artistic attention; usually written as Nouvelle Cuisine.

Cuissot   Large-size leg or haunch, e.g. of venison, pork, or veal.

Cullis   Concentrated purée used for soups and sauces; usually made of shellfish.

Cumquat   Smaller version of a mandarine for eating whole; grows in sub-tropical climates.

Daikon	Large white radish widely used in Japanese cookery for cooking. It may be carved and used as a decoration.
Daim	The fallow deer or buck.
Dariole	Small deep mould with sloping sides used for moulding eggs, pudding, etc.
Dariolette	Mould, which when dipped into batter and deep fried produces fluted pastry cases.
Darne	Whole slice cut through a large round fish such as cod or salmon.
Dartois	Two layers of puff paste with a filling in between, either savoury or sweet; served cut into slices $2\frac{1}{2}$cm thick.
Dasheen	West Indian vegetable similar to the Eddoe and Taro.
Daube	Type of meat stew given long slow cooking in a sealed pan.
Decorticate	To remove the gut from a crayfish by pulling it out from under the tail with a small knife.
Déglacage	To swill out and dissolve the sediment left after shallow frying by the use of stock, wine, etc., to make the accompanying sauce.
Delicatessen	Indicates Continental savoury items, usually eaten cold as a first course; could include sausages, preserved fish, compound salads, etc.
Demitasse	Small cup holding approximately 8cl, used for serving after-dinner coffee.
Demoiselles de Cherbourg	Small rock lobsters or crawfish as found in that part of the English Channel.
al dente	Term used to describe the degree to which all pastas should be cooked, i.e. still having a slight amount of firmness in it.
Dessert	The sweet course of the menu, but strictly only fresh fruit and nuts.
Devilled	Food that has been highly seasoned, mainly with pepper but also mustard and cayenne.
Dhal	General name for pulses used in Indian cookery, including chick peas, kidney beans, lentils, split peas, etc.

Digby Chick   Small fish named after the port in Nova Scotia where it is mainly landed; similar to a sprat.

Dill   Herb with an aniseed flavour, used in pickling and with salmon dishes; much flavoured by Jewish people.

Dindon   Turkey cock; Dindonneau is a young cock turkey.

Dobos   Continental sponge gateau made by incorporating stiffly whisked egg-whites; may be decorated to taste.

Dodin   Boned and stuffed whole duck, shoulder of lamb, etc., which is braised.

Dolmas or Dolmades   Near Eastern dish of braised stuffed fig leaves.

Donar kebab   Turkish spit-roasted meat, usually lamb, in the form of a large number of slices on a skewer rotating in front of an electric element; it is sliced and filled into pittas.

Dormers   Old English dish of left-over meat, rice and hard-boiled egg; moulded cutlet shape, crumbed and fried.

Double-cream   Thick cream with a minimum of 40 per cent butter fat; known as heavy cream in the USA.

Dragees   Sugared almonds, or any nut coated with hard cooked sugar.

Dripping   Fat and juices from roasting a joint; solid rendered beef fat.

Drumstick   Lower part of the leg of chicken.

Durian   Very large green tropical fruit that has a custard-like pulp and large seeds with an exceedingly strong smell.

Duxelles   Widely used form of stuffing made of mushroom stalks.

Eclanche   Name given to a shoulder of mutton.

Eddoe (Malanga)   West Indian vegetable with a nutty flavour and mealy texture; also called Dasheen.

Emincer   To slice food very thinly; or to shred it.

Encornet   Squid.

Engadine beef   Air-dried sirloin of beef from Switzerland and other central European countries; cut wafer-thin as an hors-d'œuvre.

Entrée	First and lightest of the main courses in an elaborate menu.
Entrements	Name given to the sweet course of a menu.
Entremettier	Chef de partie responsible for cooking all vegetables and often the soups, eggs and farinaceous dishes.
Epergne	Table centrepiece of crystal, gold, silver, etc., with several small bowls attached to hold sweetmeats and titbits.
Ephémères	Menu term denoting small, quickly eaten titbits.
Epicure	Person with a liking for, and understanding of, good food and drink.
Epigramme	Heart-shaped piece cut from braised breast of lamb, breadcrumbed and shallow fried.
Escabèche	Small fish fried then cooked in a marinade, allowed to cool for 24 hours then eaten cold.
Escarcoques	Oval puff pastry shells 4½cm – used to replace the real shells for serving snails.
Escarole	Plain as opposed to curly or frizzy endive; a salad vegetable also known as 'batavia'.
Espagnole	Basic brown sauce from which most brown sauces are derived.
Essence	Concentrated extract of fish, meat, etc., made by reducing an appropriate stock; not so solid as a glaze.
Estouffade	(i) Basic brown beef stock; (ii) a beef stew.
Etamine	Thick calico cloth used for passing thick soups and sauces.
Etuvé	Method of cookery by which food is cooked in its own steam at a fairly low level of heat.
Eugenia	Fruit similar to a cherry used in making a certain Italian liqueur which is used in cooking.
Falette	Braised breast of veal stuffed with pâté.
Faggot	(i) Bunch of celery, leek, parsley stalk, bay-leaf and thyme used as a flavouring in stock, soup, stew, etc., (ii) Small ball of minced pig's liver etc. with onion, sage, etc., covered with caul.
Faire revenir	To colour a food brown in hot shallow fat without actually cooking it.

Faisandé	Gamey as when a grouse or other bird is well-hung to become tender.
Farce	Forcemeat or stuffing made of raw fish or meat.
Farinaceous	Italian pastes such as macaroni and small dumplings such as gnocchi, polenta, etc.
Fatback	Term used in The USA for salted pork fat or speck.
Fécule	Thickening agent for soups and sauces; includes arrowroot, cornflour, chestnut flour and potato flour.
Felafel or **Falafel**	Small balls of a purée of chick peas, burghul and garlic; deep-fried and served as a titbit.
Fenugreek	Herb grown mainly in India and used as a component of curry powder.
Fetta	Goat's or ewe's milk cheese from Greece; crumbly and salty.
Filbert	Another name for a hazelnut; other names are Barcelona and cob.
Filo	Very thinly rolled out Greek variety of pastry (see also Phyllo).
Fine Champagne	Name used to denote brandy from Cognac in France, it being the name of one of the best areas in that district.
Filet mignon	Small fillet taken from the underpart of a loin or saddle of lamb.
Fines herbes	Mixture of chervil, chives, parsley and tarragon used in finely chopped form.
Flapjack	Name given to a pancake in the USA.
Flageolets	Pale green, kidney-shaped beans often served as a garnish with roast mutton.
Flamber	To set food alight with a spirit or liqueur to modify and concentrate the flavour of the alcohol.
Fleuron	Crescent shape of puff pastry, gilded and baked for a garnish, mainly with fish dishes; may also be cut in the shape of fish, hearts, etc.
Flummery	Moulded cold rice sweet flavoured with almond.
Flûte	Long thin French loaf used for making croustades.
Foccaccia	Type of pizza as traditionally served in Genoa.

782

Fogas	Fresh-water fish found in lakes in Austria and Hungary.
Foie gras	Fattened liver from an overfed goose cooked and served as a course or a garnish; also imported in the raw state.
Fonds blanc	Basic white stock used for making many soups and sauces.
Fonds de cuisine	Basic stocks and sauces from which all soups and sauces are derived.
Fondant	Soft icing made by cooking sugar in water to 115°C then mixing it to render it opaque.
Fondue	Dish of melted Gruyère or similar cheese with white wine and kirsch, into which guests dip pieces of bread.
Fool	Purée of soft fruit mixed with whipped cream, served as a sweet.
Force	Proprietary brand of breakfast cereal made of wholewheat-flakes.
Forcemeat	Stuffing made of raw fish or meat as used for making mousselines or quenelles.
Fourré	Filled by placing a garnish inside, e.g. an omelette.
Fraiser	To knead a paste to make it smooth and easy to roll out.
Fraize	Small fried lardons of bacon added to pancake batter and cooked as small savoury pancakes.
Frangipane	Filling for flans and gateaux; made of butter, eggs, sugar and ground almonds.
Frappé	Chilled and served on crushed ice, e.g. melon frappé.
French toast	Sliced bread dipped into raw egg-custard and shallow fried, often sprinkled with sugar and served to children; also known as gipsy toast or pain perdu.
Friandises	Fanciful menu term given to petits fours.
Fricadelle	Round flat cakes made of finely chopped raw or cooked beef and breadcrumbs or mashed potato; shallow fried.
Fricandeau	Joint of veal, larded, braised and glazed.

Fricassée	White stew of chicken, etc., made by first siezing, i.e. firming the pieces in hot butter.
Frill	Fancy-cut paper for placing on a bone, around a ham, or to surround a pie.
Fritto misto	Italian dish of small deep-fried mixed pieces of offal, meats and vegetables.
Fritot	Savoury fritter dipped in batter, and deep fried.
Fritter	Item of food dipped into flour then into batter and deep fried.
Friture	The fat or oil in a movable container for deep frying; also denotes a portion of deep-fried food, e.g. friture de blanchailles.
Fromage de tête	Brawn made from a pig's head.
Fruits de mer	Any edible fish from the sea but more particularly, items of shellfish.
Fuerte	Avocado with a smooth dark green skin; the Hass variety has a rough skin.
Fumet	Fairly concentrated stock made from good bones and a minimum of water.
Gadroon	Large silver serving dish with a raised decorated edge.
Gafelbitter	Scandinavian preserved herring fillets in spicy liquid.
Galantine	Elongated roll of chicken or veal forcemeat with an interior pattern of pistachios, tongue, truffle, etc.
Galette	Small round flat cake of maize, potato, etc.; or a small flat biscuit.
Gallimaufry	A light entrée made by using up a variety of left-over foods that can be combined.
Galuska	Small dumplings made like spaetzles; used in Hungarian cuisine.
Ganache	A mixture of melted chocolate and cream used for filling gâteaux, and making petits fours, etc.
Garde manger	Larder section of the kitchen where all raw and cold foods are prepared, also hors-d'œuvre, salads, sandwiches, etc.
Garni	Indefinite term meaning garnished, which does not convey any exact information as to its content.

784

Garnishing paste	Very black substance made of meat, fat and charcoal, for slicing as a substitute for truffle.
Garniture	Garnish; selection of appropriate items arranged around or added to a dish to add interest and attractiveness.
Gazpacho	Spanish soup made of raw vegetables, served cold with side dishes as accompaniments.
Gefiltefish	Jewish dish of stuffed carp cooked with vegetables; served cold or lukewarm.
Gendarme	Smoked herring fillet purchased in cans to serve as an hors-d'œuvre.
Genoise or Genoese	Basic sponge cake for general use in gâteaux and petits fours.
Ghee	Clarified buffalo-milk butter, widely used in Indian cookery.
Gibelotte	Stew made with tame or wild rabbit.
Gibier	Game, available as gibier à poil – furred animals – and gibier à plume – game birds.
Gigue	Large leg as of deer; also known as a haunch.
Girolle	Wild mushroom known as Chanterelle.
Givré	Well-chilled or iced.
Glace	(i) Ice cream or water ice; (ii) concentrated essence of fish or meat as glace de viande or meat glaze.
Glacer	(i) To glaze with sugar or icing; (ii) to chill or cool.
Glace de viande	Meat glaze, concentrated essence of a particular meat made by reducing stock.
Glacière	(i) Refrigerator or ice box; (ii) a chef glacièr is the chef who prepares all sweets made with ice cream.
Glutenin	Protein present in wheat flour, which when mixed with water forms Gluten.
Gnocchi	Small dumplings of chou paste, maize, potato, semolina, etc., served as a farinaceous dish.
Godiveau	Forcemeat made with raw veal, beef suet and cream or ice, used on its own or to stuff other items; also refers to pike forcemeat.
Gogues	Sausage made of stewed belly of pork, bacon, lettuce, onion, spinach and raw liver; poached then sliced and shallow fried.

785

Gougère Small cheese pasty made as for chou paste and cooked by deep frying.

Gougonnettes Small strips of fish, usually egg and crumbed and deep fried.

Gourd Vegetable similar to the marrow but round like a small pumpkin.

Gourmand Person who likes to eat heartily and drink deeply rather than discriminately.

Gourmandises Fanciful menu term for petits fours.

Gourmet Person with a profound knowledge of food and drink.

Graham Crackers Biscuits made with wholewheat flour and molasses, named after the nineteenth century food reformer, Sylvester Graham.

Granité Similar to a sorbet, iced confection made from sugar syrup and Italian meringue.

Granadilla or Grenadilla Passion fruit; vine fruit that looks like a wrinkled plum full of black seeds.

au Gras Cooked with fat, e.g. riz au gras is rice cooked in very fatty stock.

Gravlax Boned raw salmon pickled with sugar, salt, saltpetre, peppercorns and dill; to be eaten raw garnished with lemon and sprigs of dill.

Griddle Thick, round, cast-iron plate with a handle, used for cooking drop-scones, etc.

Grilse Small young salmon.

Grissini Long thin Italian breadsticks served with or instead of rolls.

Grosse pièce Large joint or whole poultry decorated for display as a centrepiece on a buffet.

Gruel Thin oatmeal or barley porridge.

Guava Tropical fruit with pink flesh and a strong musky smell.

Gudgeon Small river or lake fish of the carp family that grows only to about 12cm.

Gum arabic Acacia gum used for making gummy sweets.

Gum tragacanth Natural gum used in pastry work, particularly for making pastillage.

Gumbo Another name for okras or ladies' fingers; a vegetable.

Hachis   Finely diced cooked meat mixed with a sauce, and served as a rechauffé entrée.

Haggis   Sheep's paunch filled with finely minced offals, oatmeal and seasoning; sewn up and boiled as the Scottish national dish.

Halva   Sweetmeal of Middle East origin, made of honey, sesame, almonds, pistachios, etc., used as part of a selection of petits fours.

Hangi   Earthen oven as used by the Maoris in New Zealand; now the name given to the method and the food cooked on volcanic stones and leaves in this kind of oven.

Haslet   Commercially produced meat loaf made from pork offal; inexpensive.

Hass   Small, rough skinned avocado pear having the same flavour as the Fuerte variety.

Hâtelet   Ornamental silver skewer used for display purpose on decorated buffet items; also spelt as attelet.

Harvey's Sauce Commercial product used to flavour pâté and various fillings; made with anchovy, garlic, dried mushroom, shallot, vinegar, and pickled walnuts.

Haunch   Large leg and part of the saddle of venison, mutton, etc.

Haute cuisine Cookery of the highest possible standard.

High tea   Meal that combines tea and supper into a more substantial repast than either.

Hominy   Crushed maize, referred to as grits; used in the USA for making cakes, etc.

Hop shoots   Tender stems of the hop vine, used as a vegetable.

Horlicks   Proprietary brand of bedtime drink containing malted barley.

Hummus   Arabic dish of purée of chick peas with sesame seeds, oil and lemon juice; can be spread in pittas or served as a vegetable.

Hûre de Sanglier Wild boar's head as used as a centrepiece on a cold buffet display (usually a pig's head filled with brawn).

Iceberg lettuce	Tightly formed lettuce that keeps its crispness for a considerable time.
Igname	French for yam, grown in Africa and the Caribbean; not to be confused with the sweet potato.
Ikra	Pressed caviar garnished with black olives and lemon.
Ink fish	Squid or cuttlefish that contains black fluid useful in cooking, e.g. risotto.
Isinglass	Gelatinous substance made from the air-bladder of the sturgeon; used for clarifying purposes.
Jalousie	Double layer of puff pastry with almond filling, etc., the top being incised diagonally before baking.
Jambalaya	Greek or South American version of paella, made with pieces of fish, meat, poultry and vegetables in a pilaf of rice.
Jambonneau	Small-size ham, sometimes referred to as a picnic ham, approximately $3\frac{1}{2}$kg.
Jarret	Knuckle of veal as used for Osso bucco.
Jasy	Derogatory term for flour and water thickening used in soup, stew, gravy, etc.
Jelly roll	US term for Swiss roll.
Jerky	Sun-dried strips of beef for chewing whilst rounding up cattle or on safari.
Jugged	Name given to a stew made of hare or rabbit; originally made in an earthenware dish.
Juniper	Small dark blue berry used as a flavouring.
Junk food	Term given to packaged foodstuffs that have little nutritional value, e.g. bubble gum, crisps, cola, popcorn, pretzels, etc.
Junket	Easily digested sweet made of lukewarm milk, sugar, rennet and flavouring.
Jus lié	Thickened gravy; a basic sauce usually made fresh daily, more suitable for light dishes such as veal and chicken.
Kache	Russian-style dough made of buckwheat bread or semolina; can be served on its own or included in other dishes e.g., coulibiac of salmon.
Kataifa	Pastry made to look like a shredded wheat; filled with nuts, breadcrumbs and sugar and soaked in a stock syrup.

Kebab	Small pieces of meat, vegetables and herbs impaled on a skewer and grilled; also known as schaslick.
Kedgeree	Anglo-Indian dish of finnan haddock, rice and hard-boiled egg, served with curry sauce and often featured on breakfast menus.
Keftedes	Veal or beef meatballs, highly flavoured with herbs and deep fried.
Kephir	Fermented milk of ewes, goats, horses, etc., used in Middle Eastern cookery.
Keta	Name of the Pacific salmon.
Ketchup	Proprietary brands of spicy, vinegary sauces.
Kickshaws	Fanciful game given to edible titbits such as canapés and petits fours.
Kid	Young goat, often spit-roasted but can be dry to eat; not so strong-smelling as goat-flesh from a mature animal.
Kilkis	Small fish caught in Northern waters and sweet-cured for serving as an hors-d'œuvre.
Kirsch	Dry white liqueur made from a variety of cherry, used for flavouring fruit salad, ices, fondues, etc.
Kiwi fruit	Used to be known as the Chinese gooseberry; small oval fruit with rough skin and green centre with black pips.
Knob celery	Another name for celeriac.
Kohlrabi	Hard round turnip-like vegetable.
Kosher	Food prepared according to strict Jewish religious dietary laws, which has to be supervised by an authorised person.
Koumiss	Fermented milk of an ass or horse, made by adding yeast, honey and flour; mildly alcoholic.
Krona pepper	Red-coloured pepper that is stronger than ordinary ground pepper but milder than cayenne.
Kugelhopf	Rich chocolate and poppy-seed sponge cake, served with coffee in Austria.
Kulfi	Ice cream made with rose-water and pistachios.
Kumquat	Very small orange eaten whole; has a bitter – sweet taste.
Kvass	Liquid made by fermenting rye bread, malt, yeast and water; used as a drink and for cooking.

Lambs' lettuce   Small fragile green leaves without any heart, used as a salad vegetable; also known as corn salad and mâche.

Lamprey   Small fish like an eel, in season during April and May; needs to be decorticated before use.

Langue de chat   Dry sponge-finger biscuit served as an accompaniment with ice cream and other sweets.

Lardons   Small strips of streaky bacon, blanched and fried as a garnish with stews, omelettes, etc.

Latke   Savoury mixture of grated raw potato, eggs and matzos meal made in the form of small pancakes; served with jam, apple marmalade, cream, etc.

Laver   Edible red seaweed that can be used as a vegetable; also used to make small savoury cakes as served for breakfast in Wales.

Lax   Also known as lox and gravlax; fillets of salmon cured in the Swedish style with salt, sugar and dill.

Lecithin   Kind of fat contained in egg yolk, cocoa beans and brain.

Leckerli   Gingerbread biscuit containing almonds and peel; of Swiss origin.

Légume   Plant group that produces beans suitable for drying such as lentils, peas, soya.

Leveret   Young hare of from $1\frac{1}{2}$ to $2\frac{1}{2}$kg; the brown hare is the best quality.

Liaison   Thickening used for white soups and stews, usually of egg yolks, cream and butter.

Lié   Thickened, usually with a starch such as cornflour, ground rice or arrowroot, diluted in water and added to boiling liquid.

Lièvre   French for hare; civet de lièvre is jugged hare; with the skin on the fully grown one weighs 3 to 4kg.

Lights   Animal lungs used as food.

Lima Beans   Pale green or white flat beans available as dried, fresh or canned.

Litchi or Lychee   Small brown, sweet fruit of Chinese origin, can be eaten raw or poached in syrup; the flesh is white after being peeled.

Lobscouse (or Scouse) Originally a naval stew of hashed meat, vegetables and broken ship's biscuits; now a speciality of Cumbria and Merseyside.

Locust bean Fruit of the carob tree, the pods are dried then ground into flour for making cakes and biscuits.

Longe Loin of lamb or pork; half of the saddle cut through the chine bone.

Lontong Rice cooked so as to form a solid cake; used in Indonesian cookery as a form of bread.

Loquat Known as the Japanese medlar; has a downy skin and large stone and very sweet, scented flesh.

Lumpfish Roe The hard roe of the lumpfish made into cheap Danish caviar; very black in colour but not very much flavour.

Maatjes Whole or fillets of herring pickled in vinegar with sugar and spices.

Macadamia Small round nut similar to a cobnut, grown in Malawi; served roasted for a cocktail party.

Mace Outer covering of nutmegs; a mild spice available in blade or powdered form.

Macerate Add additional flavour and tenderness to food by steeping it in a wine or liqueur and flavourings.

Magret Breast of duck, equivalent to the suprême of chicken; usually from a bird bred for its foie gras.

au Maigre Food made without meat or meat products; Lenten dishes.

en Manchon This is a method of deep-frying gudgeons or similar small fish to give the impression that they are inside the end of a sleeve; egg and crumb the fish, then cut off the head and tail so that the fish will open out during the frying process.

Mango Large pear-shaped fruit with large stone and juicy, sweet, orange flesh.

Mangosteen Fruit with a thick rind and seeds, has a sweetish sour taste.

Maple syrup Thick syrup obtained from the sap of the maple tree; used with pancakes and waffles.

791

Marbling	To draw several different coloured foods through each other or icings on a cake; much used in cuisine nouvelle.
Marinade	Flavouring and tenderising mixture of vinegar, wine, oil and aromats, used for tough meats and for fish.
Marrons glacés	Candied whole chestnuts used as petits fours.
Marrowbone	The sawn-off femur bone of beef that provides bone marrow; used to be served boiled as a breakfast or savoury dish.
Maté	Herbal tea from Paraguay, known as Yerba de Maté.
Matefaim	Two light thick pancakes sandwiched with sautéd chopped onion.
Matzos	Flat biscuits made of unleavened dough, mainly for use by Jewish people during Passover.
Mazagran	Filling of fish or meat between two layers of duchesse potato, baked and served as a hot hors-d'œuvre.
Mechoui	Algerian speciality of a whole spit-roasted lamb.
Megrim	Type of sole, similar to Torbay sole and much inferior in taste to a Dover sole.
Melba toast	Very thin toast made by slicing through a slice of ordinary toast and regrilling to curl up and dry out.
Mendiants	Fanciful name given to dried figs, raisins, almonds and hazelnuts served as dessert (so called after the colours of the dress of mendicant monks).
Mesclan,or **Mesclum**	Cress, corn salad, dandelion leaves, chicory, fennel and frizzy endive grown together and cut whilst young to use as a garnish or as a salad.
Mignardises	Fanciful menu name for petits fours.
Mignonette pepper	Coarsely ground white peppercorns.
Milky Way	Well-known item of confectionary invented by Frank Mars, sometimes served melted as a sauce.
Millefeuilles	Small pastry or larger gâteau consisting of layers of puff pastry. jam and cream, finished with fondant and marbled.

Milt	Soft roes obtained from the male fish.
Milliard	Hot sweet made of black cherries, honey and batter; similar to clafouti.
Minestra	Generic term applied to a range of broth-type Italian soups.
Mirabelle	Small European plum.
Mirepoix	Flavouring of coarsely chopped carrot, celery, onion and herbs and bacon, used in making stock, soup, stew.
Miroton	Sliced cooked meat reheated in a piquant sauce, served as a luncheon entrée.
Mise en place	Advance preparation of the ingredients and utensils necessary to produce a dish or a meal.
Miso	Thick, sour, rice and soy-bean paste widely used in Japanese cookery; it can be used as a soup base, in a marinade, or diluted as a breakfast drink. Available in white or red colours depending on the variety of soy-bean used.
Mitan	Large middle cut of a whole fish, usually salmon.
Mocha or **Moka**	Arabic kind of coffee bean originally shipped from the port of Mocha in the Yemen.
à la Mode	Done in the style or fashion of a particular place; in USA denotes that ice cream is served.
Moelle	Bone marrow as removed from beef; used mainly with celery, steaks and savouries.
Molasses	Thick and dark syrup expressed from sugar cane.
Mole	Thick sauce made of chillies, onion, garlic, raisins, almonds, etc., enriched with chocolate and served with meat, poultry, especially turkey, in Mexico.
Monosodium glutamate (MSG)	Fine white flavouring powder derived from hydrolised wheat or beet; used to enhance any savoury flavours.
Monter au beurre	To add butter to a reduction or essence to enrich and thicken it, as when making a fish sauce.
Monkey-gland steak	Facetious name given to a steak tartare or a thin steak served with spaghetti in tomato sauce.
Mooli	Radish which looks like a white parsnip; can be eaten raw, in salads, or as a vegetable to sauté or boil.

793

Morels	Type of funghi with irregular pitted conical shape.
Mortadella	Large dried sausage the shape of a rugby ball; made of pork and beef.
Mostado	Dish of candied fruits in syrup flavoured with pepper and mustard powder; cherries, peas; pumpkin, apricot, etc., are used.
Mouclade	Mussels served in a saffron-flavoured cream sauce, a speciality of the district of Charentes.
Moule à manquer	Round baking-tin with sloping sides using for baking sponges.
Mousserons	Small white mushrooms; also known as St George's Agaric.
Moussette	Fanciful name given to a small quenelle of fish, chicken or veal.
Muesli	Swiss-style breakfast cereal; a mixture of oats, bran, vine fruit, nuts, dried apple, etc.
Muffin	Small, flat, yeast bun bought ready-made for toasting and buttering to serve at tea-time.
Mung beans or Bean sprouts	The most common item used in Chinese cookery; usually grown in the kitchen overnight.
Musette	Shoulder of lamb, boned and rolled into a round shape for braising.
Mushroom cooking liquor	Liquid left after cooking mushrooms in water, salt, butter and lemon juice; or made expressly by boiling mushrooms.
Muslin	Fine porous material used for straining consommé or jelly and to tie up herbs, etc., for flavouring stock, stew, etc.
à la Nage	Shellfish plainly cooked in court-bouillon, served hot or cold as it is.
Natives	Oysters cultivated in beds along the Essex and Kent coasts.
Navarin	Brown lamb or mutton stew garnished with vegetables.
Navy beans	Small dried bean, the sort using in making baked beans.
Neat's foot	Old name for cow heel; a neat's tongue is an ox-tongue.
Nectarine	Fruit which tastes the same as a peach but with a smooth skin.

Nockerln	Small rich dumpling similar to gnocchi.
Nonnat	Very small fish like whitebait, found in the Mediterranean.
Nonpareils	Sugar strands of different colours used to decorate cakes.
Noque	A small round chicken quenelle.
Norway lobster	This is another name for a Dublin Bay prawn.
Nougat	Toffee made with almonds that can be shaped into the form of presentation baskets for petits fours; Montpelier nougat is a sweet served as a petits four.
Nymphes	Fanciful name given to frogs' legs.
Offals	Internal organs of animals including heart, kidneys, liver, sweetbreads.
Oiseau sans tête	Another name for a paupiette of meat.
Okra	Also called gumbos or ladies' fingers; long, thin, pale green pods served as a vegetable.
Olla Podrida	Stew of pork, beef, chicken and game with vegetables.
Ondine	Name given to light quenelle or mousse stuffed with shellfish and set in aspic.
Onglées	Pieces of meat cut from inside the end of the rib bones of beef.
Oporto	French term for port wine as used on menus, e.g. Melon Oporto, sometimes written as au Porto.
Organ meats	Another name for offals; they are also called variety meats, glandular and utility meats.
Oregano	Wild marjoram; a delicate herb used widely in Italian cookery.
Orly	Method of cooking fish by deep-frying in batter.
Ormer	Large bivalve shellfish found mainly around the Channel Islands; needs to be well beaten to tenderise.
Ortolan	Bunting, a small bird used mainly in France after being netted and fattened.
Oslo meal	Nutritionally balanced meal for school children to include an orange and a sandwich but no crisps or chocolate bars.

Oursin   Sea urchin, a small spiny denizen of the sea, the interior of which is served as an hors-d'œuvre.

Paella   Pilaff of saffron rice with shellfish, beef, chicken, pork or rabbit and tomatoes, peas, beans and pimentos.

Paillard   Fairly thick slice of beef or veal, plainly grilled or sautéd.

Paillettes   Cheese straws or spangles, made with puff pastry; paillettes d'oignon are French-fried onion rings.

Pain bis   Brown bread.

Paklava (or Baklava)   Cake made of phyllo pastry filled with nuts, spices, etc., and soaked in stock syrup.

Pain perdu   French name for a slice of bread dipped into beaten egg and shallow-fried for the children's high tea; also called Gipsy toast.

Paksoi   Green leaf vegetable like spinach with thick white ribs; tastes like a peppery endive.

Palm hearts   Shoots of a palm tree, used as a vegetable or an hors-d'œuvre.

Pamelas   Strips of grapefruit rind cooked in syrup and dried; dipped into melted chocolate and served with after-dinner coffee.

Panada   Cooked mixture made of milk with breadcrumbs, flour, potato or rice, used to provide body to a forcemeat.

Pancetta   Smoked streaky bacon.

Pané à l'Anglaise   To coat foods with flour, egg and breadcrumbs prior to cooking.

Panettone   Large spiced yeast cake, speciality of Milan.

Pannequet   Another name for a pancake.

Pantler   Title of the officer in charge of the bread pantry in medieval times.

Papaya (Paw Paw)   Exotic fruit with smooth skin and pinkish flesh and lots of seeds, served as for melon; yields a powerful tenderising enzyme.

Papillote   Paper case in which partly cooked items of fish or meat are enveloped and baked.

Parfait   Light, frozen iced confection of sugar syrup, egg-yolks and cream, flavoured with a liqueur.

Parisienne cutter	Scoop made in various sizes for cutting out balls or other shapes from potatoes, melons and vegetables.
Passata	Concentrated sieved tomato-flesh.
Pastèque	Water melon, large dark green melon with pink flesh and black seeds.
Pastrami	Spiced and salted brisket of beef; sold cooked for serving sliced either hot or cold as a snack, sandwich or main meat dish.
Pâte	Pastry such as short paste, suet paste, etc.
Pâté Maison	Terrine made of various kinds of liver with spices, brandy, etc., according to the chef's own recipe.
Pâte à pâté	Pie pastry, another name for short paste.
Pâtisseries françaises	Selection of small fancy cakes and pastries as served for afternoon tea including éclairs, tartlets, millefeuilles.
Patum Peperium	Brand name of anchovy-flavoured spread; also called Gentleman's Relish.
Pauillac	Small milk-fed lamb named after the area of France where first reared.
Paupiette	Thin slices of fish, meat, or vegetable rolled up with a forcemeat inside.
Pecan	Nut served as an appetiser; crescent-shaped; reddish shell; grown in USA.
Pelmenes	Pieces of dough with a meat filling similar to raviolis but shallow or deep fried.
Pemmican	Dried buffalo or deer, powdered and mixed with fat and re-dried as for Jerky.
Peperami	Small, thin, highly-spiced cured sausage, used in making pizzas or for chewing as it is.
Peperonata	Tomatoes, red and green pimentoes, onion and garlic, stewed in the same way as ratatouille.
Perles du Japon	Small round dry pellets made of tapioca, used as a garnish in consommés.
Persillade	Mixture of chopped shallot, parsley and breadcrumbs for coating a joint of lamb, etc., for roasting.
Persimmon	Fruit similar to a tomato with orangy-yellow pulp; can be stewed as a compote.

Petit salé	Lean salted or smoked belly of pork.
Pesto	Cold sauce made of sweet basil, garlic, olive oil, sea salt, Parmesan and sometimes pine nuts.
Petticoat tails	Scottish shortbread made with caraway seeds in the shape of elongated triangles.
Phyllo	Type of pastry used in Middle Eastern countries to enclose various savoury and sweet items.
Physalis	The Cape gooseberry, a flower-like fruit used for petits fours usually by being dipped into fondant.
Piccalilli	Mixed vegetables pickled in mustard-flavoured sauce.
Pièce monté	Spectacular centrepiece of food on a cold buffet display made of meat, poultry, fish, sugar or chocolate work.
Pièce de résistance	The largest and most important dish on a special menu.
Pig in a blanket	Grilled rolls of bacon enclosing a slice of smoked salmon; or a small grilled sausage rolled in bacon.
Pignoli	Kernels of the pine cone, used in Italian dishes.
Pignons	The French name for Pignoli.
Pikelet	Name given to a crumpet or muffin as made in Yorkshire.
Piperade	Omelette made with onion, pimento, tomato and Bayonne ham.
Piroquis	Small crescent-shaped pieces of mixture made of fish, meat, game or cheese, either enveloped in puff pastry and baked, or egg and crumbed and deep-fried. Served as an hors-d'œuvre.
Pissaladière	Flan, similar to a pizza, as made in the south of France.
Pistachio	Small green nut covered with a purple skin.
Pistou	Basil, garlic, Parmesan and pine kernels pounded to a paste for serving with, e.g., grilled fish.
Pitta	Flat oval type of bread made with yeast and baked so as to form an air pocket which is then filled with meat, salad, curry, etc.
Pizzetine	Small pizza for serving as a snack or on a buffet; any kind of filling can be used.

Plaisirs des Dames	Alternative menu title for a dish of petits fours.
Plantain	Looks like a banana but is eaten cooked as a vegetable, either baked, boiled or in fritters.
Pleurot	Type of wild mushroom.
Pluche	Very small branches of leaves of chervil, parsley, etc., used as a garnish in soups, etc.
Pluck	The heart, liver and lungs with the connecting pipes of a lamb or pig.
Poêle	Frying pan or shallow saucepan for frying or sautéing.
Poêler	To cook good-quality joints with butter in a closed container in the oven; called pot-roasting in England.
Pomegranate	Fruit composed of tightly packed seeds in a pink jelly-like covering; used for making Grenadine, a flavouring syrup used in mixed drinks.
Popcorn	Grains of maize heated until they explode; coated with sugar and sold in a poke.
Poppedum	Thin dried rounds of lentil flour paste, deep fried and served as an accompaniment with Bombay duck (dried fillets of flying fish) for curry.
Porcini	Dried cèpes – very pungent.
Pot-roasting	Term used to denote poêlé-ing, a method of cooking good-quality meat, etc., in butter in a closed container.
Poubelle	Silver dish put on the dining table for putting food debris, shells, skins, etc., in.
Poularde	Large fattened chicken that has not started laying eggs.
Poulet de Bresse	Special French breed of chickens that are fed on corn and milk, then on rice.
Poussin	Baby chick, usually milk-fed; in America it is known as a squab.
Pralin	Sugar cooked with almonds or hazelnuts until brown and hard, then crushed to powder for use in ice-cream, sauces, etc.
Praline	Sugared almond, a whole almond encased in a hard sugar coating.
Pré-salé	Lambs fed on salt marsh lands near the coast.

Pretzels	Biscuit made in the shape of a knot, boiled then baked and glazed.
Prickly pear	Edible fruit of the cactus family eaten raw after peeling, or cooked as a compote.
Primeurs	New season or forced vegetables such as carrots and turnips of a very small size.
Profiteroles	Small balls of chou paste baked as a sweet, e.g. choux à la crème, or as a garnish with soup.
Puffball	Type of fungus with a ball-shape spore case, of varying sizes; they are edible.
Pullao	Similar to rice pilaff, served as a main dish flavoured with spices and made with vegetables; can be garnished with eggs, nuts, yoghurt, etc. Also made as a sweet dish with fruit, nuts, etc.
Pulled bread	The crumb from the inside of an ordinary loaf, pulled into irregular pieces whilst still warm and crisped in the oven.
Pumpernickel	Dark dry German bread made of rye flour.
Queen olive	Large-size green Spanish olive.
Quenelle	Light forcemeat dumpling made in various sizes from fish or meat with egg-whites and double cream.
Quiche	Savoury flan with egg-custard filling, plus cheese, bacon, mushrooms, etc.
Quince	Small round or pear-shaped fruit with a hard skin; used mainly for its high pectin content.
Râble	French name for a small saddle such as that of hare.
Rabotte	Baked apple dumpling.
Rack of lamb	American term for the best end of lamb.
Raclette	(i) Slices of Swiss cheese melted and served as a meal with potatoes boiled in their skin; (ii) a butter curler.
Radicchio	Crisp green or reddish coloured lettuce that is slightly bitter to the taste, usually served as a salad; it is a wild chicory.
Rafraîchi	Cooled but not chilled; refers to items served cold and very fresh.
Ragoût	Rich stew of meat with vegetables.

Rahat Lakoum	The Turkish name for Turkish Delight; a soft gelatinous sweetmeat.
Raidir	To stiffen an item in hot shallow fat.
Rambutans	Red oriental fruit with a soft pulp and spiny skin.
Ramekin	(i) Individual porcelain dish for baking soufflés; (ii) a cheese-flavoured chou bun served as a hot hors-d'œuvre or savoury.
Rastegaï	Small Russian pie containing salpicon of raw salmon, hard-boiled egg and vésiga; usually made with brioche paste.
Ratatouille	Vegetable dish of aubergine, onion, pimento and tomato, cooked in olive oil with garlic and other herbs.
Ravier	Oval or oblong dish used for serving hors-d'œuvre.
Ravioles	Russian dish similar to ravioli with a filling of ham and hazel hen.
Rechauffé	An entrée made of left-over cooked foods.
Refresh	To cool under running water so as to preserve the colour and flavour of a food.
Relevé	The main course of a formal meal consisting of a joint or whole bird, cooked other than by roasting.
Remove	English term for Relevé, the second of two main meat courses.
Rennet	Digestive juices of the calf, used to coagulate milk into junket.
Renverser	To turn out or demould.
Rettich	Very long white radish used as a vegetable; also known as mooli.
Revenir	To fry quickly in fat so as to colour but not to cook the item.
Rice paper	Edible sheet of paper made from the pith of a plant; used in pastry work, e.g. macaroons are baked on rice paper.
Rijstafel	Indonesian style of eating that is popular in Holland; it includes curries, rice, etc.
Rillette	Commercial product made in the form of potted meat.

Rillette d'Oie	Pieces of goose cooked in its fat, flaked and allowed to set.
Rissole	Salpicon of meat, game, etc., bound with demi-glace, enclosed in puff pastry and deep fried.
Rocambole	Mild onion that resembles a shallot, also called wild garlic.
Rock salmon	Name given to the pollack, a fish with a gelatinous backbone.
Rognon blanc	Polite culinary word for an animal's testicle.
Rognonnade	Refers to a cut through the saddle including part of the two kidneys.
Rollmop	Fillets of herring rolled up with sliced onion and marinated in vinegar.
Romaine	Elongated lettuce known as cos lettuce; has dark green leaves.
Rosette	Slice cut from a boned and rolled loin of lamb.
Rotis	Stiff dough baked as flat round pieces, filled with fish, meat, cheese and sauce then rolled up, as eaten in India.
Rouelle	Boned and rolled joint of meat, e.g. boned saddle of veal.
Rouille	Sauce made from soaked bread, fish stock, garlic, pimento and olive oil.
Roulade	Name given to a food made in the shape of a long roll, e.g. roulade de foie gras.
Royal honey	The rarest kind of honey as made by the queen bee.
Royale	Savoury egg-custard, plain or flavoured and coloured with vegetables, etc.; poached, cooled and cut into shapes as a garnish for several kinds of consommés.
Royan	Small fish the size of a sardine fished off the South of France.
Rubanné	Ribboned as when several different-coloured layers of food are set one on top of another.
Russet	Dessert apple with dull, rough skin but low moisture content, therefore very good for apple charlotte.
Rutabaga	Swede, large orange-yellow turnip-like root vegetable.

Sabayon
Light and fluffy sweet of whisked yolks, sugar and white wine; (ii) cooked whisked egg yolk added to a sauce.

Saccharometer
Thermometer for measuring the sugar density of a syrup in degrees Baume.

Saffron
Fine powder or stamens of crocus, used to colour and flavour food.

Saignant
Term used to indicate the degree to which a steak can be cooked underdone.

Saithe
Name given to the coley fish in Scotland.

Salaison
Any kind of salted preserved food served as part of hors-d'œuvre, e.g. anchovies, olives.

Salamander
Type of grilling equipment where the source of heat is at the top and used for toasting and gratinating.

Salep
Edible substance obtained from the orchis tuber that grows in the Near East.

Salmagundi
Mixture or hotchpotch of various small items in a sauce.

Salmagundy
Originally a supper dish of left-over meat but now a variegated salad of chicken, fish, hard-boiled egg, pickled items, even nasturtium flowers.

Salmis
Highly seasoned stew of part roasted game birds; garnished with mushrooms, button onions and croûtons.

Salpicon
Mixture of several compatible ingredients cut into small dice and bound with a sauce to form a filling, e.g. for vol-au-vent.

Salumeria
Italian for charcuterie or pork butchery items.

Sambals
Side dishes served as accompaniments to a curry, including coconut, cucumber, banana, preserved ginger, pineapple, peanuts, onion, pickled walnuts, chutney, etc.

Samosa
Deep-fried cone-shaped pasties with curried mince filling.

Samphire
Fleshy sea-plant like a miniature green tree 10cm high, that grows in mudflats around the coast and is in season during July; served like asparagus, or pickled.

Sanglier	Wild boar as still hunted in some parts of the world; a hûre de sanglier is the boar's head.
Saratoga chips	Name given in the USA to game chips; also known as potato crisps.
Sassafras	Dried leaves of a bush of the laurel family used to give a subtle aroma; also known as File which is widely used in Creole cookery, sassafras tea is brewed from the bark.
Satay	Kebab of meat or fish served with sour–sweet peanut sauce and cucumber; an Indonesian speciality.
Sausselis	Another name for a dartois, e.g. dartois aux anchois, served as part of a hot hors-d'œuvre or as a savoury.
Sauté	(i) To toss food over quickly in a frying pan to brown it; (ii) a quick kind of stew using small items of good quality meat or poultry.
Sauteuse	Shallow pan with sloping sides used mainly for making sauces or for tossing foods over to sauté them.
Saveloy	Red-coloured sausage sold ready cooked for reheating.
Savoy bag	Piping bag made of calico or plastic material used in decorative work.
Scallion	Another name for a spring onion.
Schnitzel	Flattened slice of veal which is egg and crumbed and deep fried.
Schwarzwalder Schinken	Air-dried loin of pork cut into tissue-paper-thin slices and served as an hors-d'œuvre.
Scorzonera	The black-skinned salsify, used as a vegetable in the same way as salsify.
Scratchings	Roasted pieces of pork rind served as titbits or a garnish.
Sear	To colour food quickly in very hot fat so as to seal the outside.
Sea Urchin	Spiny sea creature, the reddish-purple-coloured coral of which is eaten raw with soldiers of bread.
Sesame seeds	A much-used ingredient in Middle Eastern dishes both as a coating and as an oil.

804

Shaddock	Another name for a grapefruit.
Shaslik	Grilled pieces of meat, etc., on a skewer; also known as shishkebab and kebab; in France it is chiche kebab.
Shell steak	Entrecôte steak trimmed of all fat and sinew.
Shirred egg	US name for Oeuf sur le Plat; plainly baked in a fireproof dish.
Sigui	Smoked small silver trout from Northern Europe.
Sippets	Thin small triangles of dried or toasted bread-crust used as a garnish with broth and soups.
Smilax	Climbing shrub used for decorating a banqueting table.
Smorgasbord	Scandinavian buffet type of meal consisting of fish, meat, salads, etc. usually in the form of open sandwiches.
Snoek	Large fish from South African waters, imported canned and fresh during the rationing period after the Second World War.
Snow pea	A name given to the mange-tout pea.
Socle	Sculpted base or plinth made from cooked rice, fat or ice for use as a base on which to set items of cold buffet.
Sorbet	Liqueur-flavoured water ice made with sugar syrup at 18° Baume.
Sorghum	Long grass similar to sugar cane.
Soubise	Thick onion purée made with béchamel or rice for use as a sauce or a filling.
Sous Fassum	A whole cabbage stuffed with meat, rice, etc., and boiled.
Soy sauce	Thin brown liquid made from soya beans for use as a meat flavouring, particularly in Chinese cookery; sometimes spelt Soya Sauce.
Soya beans	Variety of légume having a high protein content; usually converted into a meat analogue known as textured vegetable protein (tvp).
Spatchcock	A chicken opened in a special way for grilling whole.
Spätzle	Thin batter poured through a colander into boiling salted water; served as a farinaceous dish or as a garnish.

805

Spoom	Sorbet of fruit, or of a sweet wine made with double the amount of Italian meringue used in ordinary sorbet.
Squab	Young pigeon or poussin.
Squid	A mollusc of the same family as cuttlefish or inkfish and octopus; the tentacles comprise approximately half its weight.
Stockfish	Salted dried cod as used for making Brandade; used particularly during Lent in Roman Catholic countries.
Subric	Savoury or sweet mixtures bound with eggs and cream and shallow-fried in butter in small pieces.
Succotash	Mixed buttered sweetcorn kernels and lima beans served as a vegetable.
Suédoise	Moulded jelly with layers of fruit arranged in an artistic pattern.
al Sugo	Dish served with a light sauce or gravy, e.g. ravioli al sugo.
Sundae	Several flavours of ice-cream with fruit, nuts, fruit sauces, cream, etc., served in a tall glass.
Suprême	Quality cut of meat or fish, e.g. surprême de volaille is the whole side of a breast of chicken.
Surf and Turf	Menu term that indicates a dish containing both fish and meat, e.g. a grilled steak garnished with scampi.
Syllabub	Frothy sweet made by whisking together cream, sugar and wine, removing the resultant froth as it arises.
Sylphide	Fanciful name given to a light dish of mousselines covered with soufflé mixture and baked.
T-bone steak	Steak cut from a sirloin on the bone.
Tabasco	Proprietary brand of seasoning liquid made of chilli peppers; often served with oysters.
Table d'hôte	Menu on which a price is given for the complete meal rather than each item being priced.
Taco	Tortilla filled with cooked meat or chicken and salad vegetables, eaten as it is or deep-fried.
Tahini	Paste made by crushing sesame seeds.

806

Talmouse
Hot hors-d'œuvre in the form of a tartlet filled with cheese-flavoured chou paste, when cooked filled with cream.

Tamale
Traditional Mexican dish of a maize bun filled with various mixtures of fish, meat, vegetables, etc.

Tamarilos
A sweet tomato.

Tamarind
Tropical fruit used in the making of curry and other Indian dishes.

Tammy cloth
Piece of unbleached calico used for passing thick sauces and soups.

Tandoori
Clay oven fired by charcoal; food marinated in yoghurt and ginger and spices are cooked crisp in this oven which sears the outside leaving the inside soft; chicken tandoori is an example.

Tansy
Herb with a bitter flavour.

Tapenade
Paste made from anchovy, capers, olives and tunny fish; a speciality of Provence in France.

Taramasalata
Hors-d'œuvre dish of smoked carp or cod roe pureed with oil, lemon, breadcrumbs etc.

Tarator
Sesame seed sauce made with the seeds, garlic and lemon juice.

Tavo
Tubers of coco yam, served as a vegetable or used as a thickening for soups.

Tartines
French name for sandwiches.

Tartufi
White truffles found mainly in Piedmont; served grated raw on top of all kinds of savoury dishes.

en Tasse
Served in a cup, e.g. Consommé en tasse.

Teflon
Non-stick coating applied to the inside of sauce-pans, mainly those for domestic use.

Tempura
Small items of fish and vegetables dipped into a light batter and deep-fried; served with sweet-and-sour sauce.

Tenderloin
Name given to a boned-out, trimmed sirloin of beef.

Tendron
Pieces of breast of veal, suitable for braising.

Terrapin
Small diamond-backed turtle usually cut into pieces for cooking and serving as a fish course.

Terrine
Earthenware dish in which a liver pâté would be cooked and served.

Thermopin   Needle which, when inserted into a joint, etc., conducts the heat to the centre so speeding up the cooking time.

Timbale   (i) Double container used for keeping food either cold or hot; (ii) a lidded pastry case for presenting a light entrée.

Tindoori   Indian method of cooking meats by marinating with red spices, yoghurt and lemon juice and grilling or cooking in a tandoori oven.

Tipsy cake   Sponge cake soaked in sherry.

Tisane   Herbal tea made without milk, usually to relieve a headache; various flavours such as camomile, jasmine are available as teabags.

Tomalley   Another name for the coral or ovary found in a lobster which provides the vivid red colour to lobster sauce.

Torten   Large continental gâteaux, richly finished with cream and liqueurs.

Tortilla   Flat omelette made with diced potato, garlic and onion. In Mexico it is unleavened corn bread made in the form of a pancake.

Tourte   Flan case with a lid; a closed tart.

Tracklements   Fanciful term given to the range of proprietary accompaniments and garnishes such as sauce, mustard, etc.

Trancheur   Carver; a member of the kitchen or restaurant staff responsible for carving cold and hot joints, etc.

Trevise   Red chicory used for salads.

Tronçon   Thick slice cut through a flat fish on the bone.

Turmeric   Yellow spice used to give colour to curry powder; also used in making piccalilli.

Turban   Savarin-mould lined with fillets of fish or chicken, filled with forcemeat and cooked.

Turkish Delight   Soft jelly-like sweetmeat made in several colours and flavours, served as a petits fours; called Lakoum in Turkey.

Turtle herbs   Mixture of basil, bay-leaf, marjoram, rosemary, sage and savoury, used to give an oriental or exotic flavour to dishes.

808

Twarogue or Tvorog	Cream cheese, butter and eggs mixed for use as a filling in several Russian hot hors-d'œuvre.
Uccelli Scappati	Humorous name given to an Italian dish of veal escalopes, sage and ham, rolled and braised.
Umbles	Old English name for offals obtained from the deer.
Ursulines	Name given to chicken or veal quenelles.
Vacherin	Sweet made with meringue in the form of a nest, filled with cream, fruit, etc.
Varenikis	Russian hot hors-d'œuvre similar to ravioli with various fillings such as Twarogue.
Vatrouski	Russian hot hors-d'œuvre made in the shape of a turnover of brioche paste filled with Twarogue.
Verbena	Herb with a pleasant fragrance used for making tea known as verveine which can help to cure a headache.
Verjuice	Sour juice expressed from unripe grapes, crab apples etc., for use mainly in salad dressings.
Vessie	Pig's bladder used for cooking a whole chicken in.
Visniski	Russian hot hors-d'œuvre made as a rissole of fish filling in brioche paste.
Vrille de vigne	Marinated vine tendrils prepared as part of an hors-d'œuvre selection.
Water chestnut	Seed of an aquatic plant grown in China, much used in Chinese cookery.
Wild rice	Long thin grass seed grown in America; it has a musky flavour and is very expensive.
Worcester sauce	A proprietary brand of thin sauce made from capsicum, garlic, mushroom ketchup, shallots, spices, soya sauce and vinegar.
Yam	Large tubers with white flesh that tastes like potato; can be boiled, baked, fried and roasted and served as a vegetable.
Yorkshire Relish	Proprietary brand of thin sauce similar to Worcester sauce.
Zabaglione	Italian sweet made with egg yolks, sugar and Marsala, beaten over heat until frothy and thick.
Zakouskis	Wide selection of cold Russian hors-d'œuvre served as appetisers before a meal.

Zampino   Lower part of a pig's leg boned and stuffed; served boiled as an entrée.

Zéphyr   Fanciful name given to a delicate cut of fish, poultry, etc.

Zucchini   The Italian word for baby marrows or courgettes.

Zuppa Inglese   Italian name for the British trifle as made from spongecake, jam, custard, cream, etc.